THE CHRISTMAS BOOK

NATIVITY: THE BIRTH OF CHRIST AND CHRISTMAS TRADITIONS

•

David Trigg

Christmas is one of the largest religious and cultural celebrations in the world, observed among believers and nonbelievers alike. At the heart of this Christian festival is the Nativity, one of the religion's best-known stories, memorialized by Christmas pageants, plays, and church services through the centuries. Its cast of characters—including Mary, Joseph, shepherds, angels, wise men, and the baby Jesus—is familiar to millions the world over. Less well known, however, is how many of our beloved Christmas traditions—from decorating trees and singing carols to the giving of gifts—evolved from the story of Christ's birth told in the Christian Gospels.

The word "Christmas" comes from the Middle English *Christemasse* (literally "Christ's Mass"), referring to a special service celebrated by Christians on the Feast of the Nativity in honor of Jesus's birth. Over time, Christianized pagan practices and ninteenth-century Victorian customs have codified the modern celebration of Christmas (see p.101), which today is a curious mix of sacred and secular traditions. Yet the earliest Christians had little interest in marking Christ's birth, focusing instead on his life, death, and resurrection, because they considered the celebrating of birthdays to be pagan.

No date is given in the Bible for Christ's birth, and the earliest mention of it being celebrated on December 25 is AD 336, in Rome. While scholars have competing theories on why this date was chosen—from the desire to usurp midwinter pagan revelries to the result of convoluted calculations—it was not until AD 350 that Pope Julius I officially added the new feast to the church calendar and it began spreading into Europe. Before this, Romans celebrated Saturnalia, a festival honoring Saturn, the God of agriculture, that was observed on the winter solstice, around December 25 under the Julian calendar. Feasting, drinking, and gift-giving were accompanied by the decorating of homes and the lighting of ritual fires to encourage the sun's return. In Scandinavia and northern Europe, the solstice was celebrated with Yule (see p.183); a special log was burned and rituals involving fir trees, holly, ivy, and mistletoe were performed to placate the Norse gods and ensure the return of spring. By coinciding Christmas with the solstice, the Roman Church linked Christ as "the light of the world" (John 9:5) with the darkest time of the year, and though it was hoped that pagan celebrations would be supplanted, some practices inevitably continued.

Today, anticipation and excitement are experienced during the Christmas countdown as cards are written, decorations hung, and presents wrapped. In Christianity, the season of preparation is called Advent, which begins on the Sunday closest to the feast of Saint Andrew on November 30. From the Latin *adventus*, meaning "coming," Advent originally focused not on Christ's birth but on the anticipation of his second coming—the belief that he will one day return to the earth.

The modern tradition of counting down twenty-four days to Christmas began in Germany, and the first Advent wreath appeared in 1839 when Christian pastor Johann Hinrich Wichern (1801–1881) decorated a cart-wheel with twenty small red candles (for weekdays) and four large white candles (for Sundays). Eventually, wreaths were made using evergreens, holly, and berries (see p.143), which, despite harking back to pagan traditions, were said to symbolize the everlasting life offered by Christ. It is still common to find Advent wreaths with candles in churches, usually erected on stands or placed on tables, although in domestic settings wreaths are primarily decorative and often hung on front doors to mitigate the fire hazard.

In the nineteenth century, German children counted the days to Christmas by drawing on doors twenty-four lines in chalk, rubbing one out each day until Christmas. This practice inspired the first Advent calendars, which were originally handmade from cardboard with small sweets or candies attached. They were not commercially produced until 1908, when Gerhard Lang (1881–1974) designed a cardboard calendar printed with Christmas imagery, onto which children pasted festive pictures (see p.170). Later, small doors or windows were introduced, which are still common today, sometimes with the reward of a chocolate behind them. Advent calendars vary enormously, from highly commercial imagery (see p.189) to traditional themes (see p.140) and explicitly religious designs drawing on the familiar Nativity story.

According to traditional telling, a harmonization of two accounts from the New Testament gospels of Matthew and Luke, a woman named Mary is visited by the angel Gabriel, who announces that she will become pregnant by a miracle of God, despite being an unmarried virgin. Having conceived, she later travels from Nazareth to Bethlehem with her betrothed husband, Joseph, to register for a census (see p.176). Because there is no room at the inn, they bed down in a stable, where Mary gives birth to a son, Jesus, the Son of God. She places him in a manger and his humble birth is celebrated by hosts of angels and shepherds. Meanwhile a wondrous star attracts wise men known as Magi from the East, who visit the Holy Child and present him with gold, frankincense, and myrrh.

The Nativity story became an important subject in Christian art from the fifth century, with many works varying the number of figures included and even the setting. In many early depictions, Mary was seen lying on a mattress (see p.14), while in medieval and Renaissance art, Nativity scenes often showed Mary seated or kneeling by the manger, as in Dutch artist Geertgen tot Sint Jans's painting, *The Nativity at Night* (see p.209).

The popular tradition of miniature Nativity scenes displayed in churches, homes, and public places can be traced back to Saint Francis of Assisi. In 1223, to counter the growing materialism of Christmas, the Italian friar devised the first live Nativity scene, setting up a wooden manger and two live animals—an ox and an ass—in a cave at Greccio. The townsfolk were invited to visit the scene while Saint Francis preached. Gradually, living Nativities were replaced by crèche (or *presepio*) scenes featuring handcrafted figurines.

The tradition reached its apex in eighteenth century Naples and an exquisite Neapolitan example, with many beautifully crafted characters, is displayed each year at the Metropolitan Museum of Art in New York (see pp.75, 162). Today, Nativity scenes come in all shapes and sizes, from Polish *szopki*—flamboyant displays incorporating Kraków's historical buildings, marionettes, and political satire (see p.169)—to the minimalist version created by Floris Hovers for Ikonic Toys (see p.87). In the 1980s, ornament manufacturer Department 56 released its Christmas village collections for America's homes, in which Nativity-themed porcelain models mingled with wintry Dickensian-inspired buildings and a North Pole series featuring Santa's workshop (see p.177).

Another common Christmas motif that takes inspiration from the Nativity story is the star. In Matthew's Gospel, the Star of Bethlehem led the Magi to the newborn Christ, and today stars appear on everything from cards, wrapping paper, and decorations to the centerpieces of colorful light displays illuminating city centers, shopping malls, suburban homes, and even airports (see pp.29, 44, 45). One of the most common places to see a star (see p.127) at Christmas is atop a Christmas tree decorated with baubles, tinsel, lights, and ornaments. The custom of decorating trees at Christmas likely originated with medieval Paradise Plays, which were staged in churches on December 24, the Feast of Adam and Eve. Popular across northern France and Germany, they vividly conveyed how the world was cursed when the first humans ate the forbidden fruit in the Garden of Eden (Genesis 3:1–6). A tree decorated with apples was integral to the performances, symbolizing humanity's downfall, and also alluding to the wooden cross on which Christ was crucified. Paradise Plays explained the theological rationale for Christ's birth: to save the world from the curse of sin.

Although Paradise Plays were prohibited during the Protestant Reformation, decorated Christmas trees continued to be publicly displayed in Germany. The earliest recorded example was in a hospital in Freiburg, Germany, in 1419; sponsored by a bakers' guild, it was decorated with apples, wafers, gingerbread, and sparkling tinsel. The tradition of trees in domestic spaces took hold in sixteenth-century Germany, where they joined other evergreens such as ivy, mistletoe, and holly, as symbols of everlasting life (see pp.31, 54, 218). The custom spread throughout Europe in the eighteenth and nineteenth centuries, first among royals (see p.130) and wealthy households, and later among the emerging middle class as Christmas became increasingly commercialized.

Domestic Christmas trees were likely introduced to the United States by eighteenth-century German immigrants, but in Great Britain, Queen Victoria and her German husband Prince Albert popularized them after an 1848 engraving showing the royal family decorating their tree, complete with candles and an angel, was published in the *Illustrated London News*. In sunny Australia, the hardy radiata pine is commonly seen in homes at Christmas, where it is decorated with summer-themed ornaments, such as seashells; in Africa, palm trees and mango trees are decorated in and outside of the home with items from nature.

In the twentieth century, artificial Christmas trees became a popular alternative to real evergreens, which are notorious for shedding their needles. Before plastic trees, German manufacturers sold tress made from dyed goose feathers attached to wire branches, and in Great Britain trees made with tinted pig hair enjoyed limited success. In the 1950s, metal trees were introduced to Americans and were an instant hit. Aluminum "Evergleam" trees briefly dominated the market until they were lampooned in 1965 by the animated television special *A Charlie Brown Christmas* (see p.135), in which they were presented as fake and soulless symbols of consumerism. Artificial Christmas trees are less popular in the public realm, where the most famous tend to be real, such as the mighty Norway spruce displayed each year at the Rockefeller Center in New York (see p.20). Norway donates an enormous spruce to Trafalgar Square in London, an annual tradition dating back to 1947 as an expression of gratitude for Great Britain's support during World War II.

In today's secular world, many religious symbols, such as the star, have somewhat lost their original meaning. Angels, another popular traditional tree topper that have roots in the Nativity story, representing the archangel Gabriel, has slowly been replaced atop the domestic Christmas tree by fairies (see pp.195, 222). Although there is no reference to angels in Luke's Gospel, the connection is made in art, including Everhard Rensig and Gerhard Remisch's stunning sixteenth-century stained-glass window, in which worshipful angels gather around the manger (see p.10).

Indeed, one of the best-loved Christmas carols (see p.193) is Charles Wesley's "Hark! The Herald Angels Sing," which encourages us to join with the angels in proclaiming Christ's birth. Christmas songs have been sung since at least the fourth century, the earliest example being "*Veni, Redemptor Gentium*" ("Come, Thou Redeemer of the Earth"), by Saint Ambrose of Milan. As Christmas spread across Europe, carols increased in popularity, with each country developing its own repertoire. In Britain, church carol services developed during the Victorian era and remain a popular Christmas activity, whether participating in person or listening on the radio.

Caroling is a popular activity in many countries across the world. In Greece and Cyprus, children go out singing carols on Christmas Eve, New Year's Eve, and Epiphany Eve, while in the Philippines—which boasts the world's longest Christmas season—it is common to hear carols sung as early as September (see p.37). In Malawi, children go door-to-door singing and play Christmas music on traditional instruments in return for money. In Mexico and other Latin American nations, carols are sung as part of *Las Posadas* (see p.229), a Nativity-themed festival that culminates with children smashing large star-shaped piñatas filled with candies.

One of our more modern Christmas traditions that perhaps surprisingly connects back to the story of the Nativity is gift giving, perhaps the element that seems to be the most commercialized. The first recorded Christmas gifts were those presented to baby Jesus by the Magi, each one of which was profoundly symbolic. Frankincense, a perfume used in Jewish worship, indicated that the baby would himself be worshipped; gold was associated with royalty and represented the belief that Jesus was the King of Kings; and myrrh was used as an embalming ointment, which pointed to Jesus's death. Although three gifts are mentioned, Matthew's Gospel does not record how many magi there were, nor their names, ethnic backgrounds, or social standing. This did not prevent legends from arising that embellished their story, promoting those that may have been Persian astrologers to kings—a notion that inspired many works of art, such as Gentile da Fabriano's stunning altarpiece (see p.80), and a magnificent tapestry by Morris & Co. (see p.107).

The tradition of gift giving is central to Christmas, yet there is little record of gifts being exchanged until the Early Modern era, when German markets sprang up selling seasonal products and the story of Saint Nicholas (see p.15) became popular. In England, gifts were once exchanged on January 6, the traditional date on which the feast of Epiphany—also known as the Feast of the Magi—is celebrated. Epiphany is, in fact, older than Christmas, arising in eastern Mediterranean churches during the second century as a commemoration of Christ's baptism. The feast day is still associated with gift giving in many Spanish and Latin American countries, where it is known as *Día de Los Reyes Magos* (Three Kings Day), on which children awake in the hope that Caspar, Melchior, and Balthasar, not Santa Claus, have brought them presents (see p.126).

The story of Saint Nicholas was introduced to the United States by nineteenth-century German immigrants, who also promoted the idea of Christmas as a child-centered holiday and a season for exchanging gifts. Manufacturers seized on the opportunity to sell their goods and shop-bought presents began to supersede homemade gifts. Ever since, the celebration of Christmas has been routinely criticized as being too commercial, even though its popularity owes much to the marketing professionals who standardized its modern image. Today, the festive season is big business, characterized by slick advertising campaigns and frenzied shopping for gifts, from must-have children's toys, such as Sylvanian Families (see p.185), the wildly popular Rubik's Cube (see p.188), and the Nintendo Switch, to that perfect Christmas jewelry piece from Tiffany & Co. (see p.116).

However, despite the encroaching tides of secularization and commercialization, Christmas remains for many a distinctly Christian celebration of the Incarnation—the belief that God became human and dwelt among us. It is this religious message that has inspired many of our modern-day Christmas traditions, which still bring hope and joy to millions of people across the world.

FOOD AT CHRISTMASTIME

•

Sam Bilton

Christmas feasting has been around for centuries. Britain has inspired many of the festive treats consumed around the holiday season in the English-speaking world, but it is now more than ever a global phenomenon, with countries across the world embracing, and exporting, their own traditions, even some that do not "officially" celebrate this festival. The United States, for example, has welcomed a diverse array of European eatables into its fold at this time of the year. It has also contributed possibly the most definitive Christmas component to our table in the form of the turkey. One thing is certain: wherever Christmas is celebrated, it is a joyous occasion and a time to indulge.

The propensity to gorge on rich food and drink in the last throes of the year is far from a new phenomenon, although it is undoubtedly more widespread in the twenty-first century than it was several hundred years ago. In the medieval era, Yuletide was a twelve-day affair with much feasting and merriment taking place between December 25 and January 5 across much of Europe. Some countries, such as Russia, still follow the Julian calendar and celebrate Christmas on January 7. Our forebears had good cause to celebrate, because Christmas was preceded by a forty-day fast where no meat or dairy could be consumed. The poor had little of these luxuries to begin with, but it was a relief to the wealthy to see them back on the menu again.

Our familiar Christmas treats have evolved over time, some significantly in even the past one hundred years. The mince pie (see p.132) is an icon of the British Christmas. Modern consumers wrinkle their noses when they learn the original mince pie also contained shredded meat, lending it an alternative title of shred pie. British cooking journalist and "domestic goddess" Isabella Beeton (1836–1865), author of the wildly popular guide to running a Victorian household *Mrs. Beeton's Book of Household Management*, included beef, as well as dried fruits and spices, in her nineteenth-century mincemeat recipe, although earlier food writers had suggested organ meats called "offal," such as tongue, as a component. These expensive ingredients denoted mince pies and similar dishes as celebratory fare that was eaten at feasts all year round. They were also rather large, with ornately decorated lids, making today's offerings seem dowdy by comparison.

That other festive favorite, the Christmas pudding (see p.90), began life as a thick, spiced porridgelike substance known as plum pottage. It also included meat or at least a meat-based stock, bread crumbs, and dried fruit, collectively known as plums (hence the name). The plum pudding we recognize today emerged in the seventeenth century. A more solid affair, the pudding contained similar ingredients to the pottage, but it was boiled in a cloth to produce the "speckled cannon-ball" dessert presented by Charles Dickens's Mrs. Cratchit to her family for Christmas dinner in *A Christmas Carol* (see pp.79, 133), published in 1843.

The pottage and pudding jogged along together for several generations before the latter won the day. By the mid-nineteenth century, plum pudding was indelibly linked with the festive period, with English food writers, such as Eliza Acton (1799–1859), referring to it as Christmas pudding rather than by its original title. The Victorians were also responsible for bigging up the mythology around the pudding. It was they who popularized the idea of "Stir Up Sunday" (the last Sunday before Advent begins, when people were encouraged to make their puddings) and suggested including charms (see p.91) to foretell the recipient's future for the coming year.

Plum pottage is now a relic of the past in Britain, however, in Scandinavia a creamy rice porridge or pudding is still served at Christmas time, often as the close to a smorgasbord. Sprinkled with cinnamon sugar, it is crucial to leave a bowl of the porridge out for the *jultomte*, or elves (see p.19), to thank them for taking care of the house and animals over the previous months. The Swedish appreciate the importance of pacing yourself when feasting at Christmas. Their festive *julbord*, or smorgasbord (see p.93), is designed to be enjoyed over several hours with small servings of each dish sampled by the guests, including pickled herrings washed down with a glass or two of aquavit; cured meats and liver pâté come next, followed by the hot meatballs and ham served with a variety of side dishes and breads.

There was a time when the British, like the Scandinavians, held pork, or more specifically wild boar, in high regard at Christmas—not the turkey or goose we now associate with the season. Our feathered friends have always had a place at the Christmas table, although the ubiquitous turkey is a relative newcomer. In the medieval era, the regal peacock was admired and was often presented with its spectacular plumage and head reattached post roasting. The turkey appeared in Britain in the early sixteenth century, many arriving from the Americas via Turkey (hence the name). It also had impressive feathers and soon replaced the peacock as the choice poultry for a grand feast. By 1573, turkey was listed alongside capon (a castrated chicken) and goose as ideal Christmas fare.

For centuries, the turkey remained something of an expensive Yuletide novelty. Goose was the more affordable option for much of the population (see p.133). The Victorian working classes could pay a little each month to a "goose club" to ensure they had a bird for their dinner on the big day. Turkey was seen as the aspirational option for the Victorian middle classes. In 1861, Mrs. Beeton declared that "Christmas dinner, with the middle classes of this empire, would scarcely be a Christmas dinner without its turkey."

Imports of turkeys after World War II saw the cost of this bird fall, making it more accessible to the masses and, by the mid-1970s, turkey was a staple of the British Christmas table. Other nations have resisted the turkey onslaught. In Germany, roast goose with apples remains popular. Although Japan does not officially celebrate Christmas, it has become the custom to eat Kentucky Fried Chicken on this day (see p.157). Those who fail to preorder their festive KFC bucket face long lines outside branches of the American fast-food chain on December 25.

In the United States turkey can be found on Christmas menus, but it may share the stage with other European imports like baked ham or even lasagna. The biggest fanfare in the country for this buxom bird occurs during Thanksgiving, on the fourth Thursday in November. American presidents have been gifted a Thanksgiving turkey since the 1870s, and some of these birds have been fortunate enough to receive a presidential pardon and escape the oven. It is not certain when this tradition started, however President John F. Kennedy did give a turkey a reprieve on November 19, 1963, stating "Let's keep him going," and the custom has been repeated by subsequent presidents. Thanksgiving also heralds the start of the countries Christmas shopping season, when Macy's the department store kicks off the proceedings with their famous Thanksgiving Day Parade, complete with giant inflatable cartoon characters (see p.203).

The festive fare barrage begins long before we sit down to our Christmas dinner. Shortly after Halloween the shops begin to fill with Christmas treats. In Great Britain, mountains of chocolate boxes jostle for attention with mince pies and fancy biscuits or cookies. Gingerbread gets a European makeover with German *lebkuchen*, Norwegian *pepperkaker*, and Dutch *speculaas*. These glamorous continental cousins have largely ousted regional Christmas specialties, such as Yorkshire pepper cake, traditionally eaten with Wensleydale cheese, from the British affections. The apogee of these spicy cookies is the gingerbread house. A spectacular specimen is produced by the White House chef each year for the incumbent president and his family (see p.214).

Many cakes associated with this season of merriment were originally destined to be eaten on Twelfth Night, which is celebrated on the evening of January 5. In France, they commemorate the visit of the three kings to the baby Jesus with a *galette de rois*, a buttery pastry dome filled with almond paste. New Orleans has its king cake decorated with green, purple, and gold sugar sprinkles. The Italians have their statuesque panettone laden with dried fruits (see p.108). It used to be traditional to keep a little of this cake until February 3, the Feast of San Biagio—the saint believed to cure sore throats and colds—when the leftover panettone was eaten for breakfast to ward off winter chills.

The British Christmas cake (see p.216) has evolved from its own version of a king cake. In the seventeenth century, the British twelfth cake was a spiced, briochelike dough with dried fruit that contained a single dried bean. If you found the bean, you were crowned king for the evening's festivities. As the years passed, the custom of using a cake to select a "bean king" waned and the mixture itself became the dense fruit cake covered in marzipan and icing now associated with Christmas. In the early nineteenth century, ostentatious twelfth cakes adorned many a professional baker's window at Christmastime. However, as Queen Victoria's reign progressed, it became customary to make your Christmas cake at home. The twelfth cake effectively morphed into the Christmas cake and it became another relic of Christmas past much like the plum pottage.

By Epiphany, on January 6, most of this Christmas fare has been consumed. With slightly expanded waistlines our minds turn to a more restrained form of eating. Most of us will have over indulged but, after all, it is Christmas, and it only comes once a year.

THE EVOLUTION OF SANTA CLAUS

•

Dolph Gotelli

"Yes, Virginia, there is a Santa Claus," wrote New York newspaper editor Francis Church in 1893 in a celebrated response to the query of an anxious young reader about whether the figure at the heart of Christmas really existed (see p.41). A more accurate answer might be, "Yes and no, Virginia."

Santa Claus was inspired in part by a real fourth-century archbishop, Saint Nicholas of Myra in Asia Minor (see p.15)—the name Santa Claus comes from the Dutch version of the Saint's name, Sinterklaas. Celebrated for his virtue and generosity, Saint Nicholas was later widely worshipped in the Christian world and became the patron saint of maidens, mariners, scholars, prisoners, travelers, bankers, and even thieves. He was also said to give gifts to children, a tradition that linked him with certain figures, such as Woden in Scandinavia, the three kings in Spain, and even the Christ Child (Christkind) himself (see p.134). Such gift bearers often left presents for deserving children and carried birch rods to punish those who had been disobedient (a frequent theme of European folktales).

In around the eighth century, when Christianity arrived in northern Europe, particularly the Netherlands, Scandanavia, other Germanic-speaking countries, and Russia, Saint Nicholas became associated with the pagan festival of Yule, when Odin was said to dispense presents from his flying horse. From northern and central Europe, local traditions spread to Catholic Mediterranean countries to mark the saint's annual visit— either on Saint Nicholas Day on December 6 (see p.220), or the Epiphany, January 6. The saint wore bishop's robes, a red or brown cape, or sheepskins, and traveled by foot, on a gray or white horse, on a wooden horse, or a donkey. He was accompanied on his travels throughout Europe by a varied cast of companions, including the fearsome Krampus of Bavaria (see p.69), who wore goatskins and wooden masks with jagged teeth; Knecht Ruprecht, who dressed in straw or animal skin adorned with bells; and Zwartepiet, his Moorish servant. He carried a bag or basket containing fruit, candies, and toys (see p.190), as well as a bundle of birch rods and his tally book, and he left presents in shoes, baskets, or stockings placed by the bed, by the hearth, or near the front door (see p.166). Why stockings? In one particular story, Saint Nicholas dropped some gold coins down a chimney, where they fell into stockings left to dry by the fire, to help an impoverished father pay a generous dowry for each of his three daughters.

Santa's arrival in North America is not particularly easy to document. European immigrants imported their own customs when they crossed the Atlantic Ocean, such as the Pennsylvania Dutch—a conservative German sect—who brought with them Kris Kringle, a kindly figure who left gifts at night on the branches of a Christmas tree, and the Dutch settlers of New Amsterdam who brought the tradition of Sinterklaas (see p.220). In the seventeenth century, the Dutch authorities banned people from handing out candies to children, the custom on Saint Nicholas' Eve, because it offended their strict Protestant views, but Sinterklaas was still central to Christmas celebrations when New Amsterdam was taken over by England in 1664 and renamed New York City.

Saint Nicholas's association with the Dutch made him popular in the decades following the American Revolution, when there was anti-British sentiment, and he became patron saint of New York City in the early 1800s. His popularity spread beyond Dutch communities, thanks to American writer and historian Washington Irving (1783–1859), who included the saint in his best-selling *Knickerbocker History of New York*, published in 1809. In places such as Buffalo, New York, where a heavy concentration of Germans had arrived around 1840, Saint Nicholas would come on Nicholas Eve, December 5, to take orders for presents to be delivered around Christmas.

In 1822, American scholar Clement Clarke Moore (1779–1863), professor in an Anglican seminary, wrote a poem for his children entitled "A Visit from St. Nicholas" (see p.84). The poem was published anonymously, because Moore was worried his academic reputation would suffer if it became known he had written a lighthearted story for children. He only admitted authorship in 1837. The poem is significant because it saw the first appearance of a different type of Santa: a corpulent "jolly old elf" who rides in a sleigh drawn by reindeer, and who no longer punishes children. Moore's vision inspired Thomas Nast (1840–1902), a German-born illustrator, who first drew Santa Claus in 1863 for the American newspaper *Harper's Weekly*. Throughout the years that followed, Nast's drawings for the magazine popularized many other associations people have with Santa, including his toy workshop at the North Pole, the letters children write to him every year asking for gifts (see p.130), and his lists of naughty and nice children.

Nast's work, in turn, was later echoed by the advertisements created by American artist Haddon Sundblom from the 1930s onward for Coca-Cola (see p.13). Inspired by his own Scandinavian background, Sundblom depicted Santa as a kindly grandfather with a twinkling smile and dressed in a red suit, crystallizing a modern icon far removed from the sterner European image of Saint Nicholas.

Meanwhile, a separate tradition had emerged in Great Britain in the figure of Father Christmas, an ancient personification of the season who briefly rose to prominence when England's Puritan government outlawed Christmas in the 1640s, at which time he became a symbol of "good old England." For another two centuries, he remained a minor folkloric figure of drinking and feasting (see p.24), until the rise in the popularity of Christmas among the Victorians in the mid-1800s. Like Saint Nicholas in Europe, Father Christmas became linked with secretly leaving presents for children on Christmas Eve. From the 1860s onward, as the figure of Santa Claus was reintroduced to Europe from the United States, the two characters became more closely identified with one another—and since early in the 1900s they have grown even more similar. However, the British imagining remains more inclined to be less a figure of universal good cheer and more a somewhat stoic old man faced with a challenging annual task. He is often portrayed in print with a holly wreath or sprigs around his head (see p.191).

Today, the Santa story has become universal around much of the world. Santa comes down the chimney to deliver presents—even in places where chimneys are rare—while children hang a stocking from the fireplace and leave snacks for him and for the reindeer (see p.83). They can even track his exact movements on Christmas Eve as he delivers all his presents, using online Santa trackers (see p.231). Children still write to Santa Claus and visit department stores every Christmas (see pp.155, 203), attracted by an idealized world view in which goodness is always rewarded and Santa is always jolly.

As time has passed, the legend of Santa Claus has expanded, with multiple portrayals in books and films (see p.40) influencing how he is perceived. There have been additions, such as Mrs. Claus, the elves that help in his workshop, and Rudolph the red-nosed reindeer, who first appeared in 1939 (see p.85). Santa has also diversified in the twentieth century. The first black Santas were reported in the early 1900s, and tap dancer Bill "Bojangles" Robinson made an iconic appearance at a 1936 Christmas party for underprivileged children in Harlem, New York, opening the way for department stores in New York City and Chicago to hire black Santas in the 1940s. Around the same time, in both the United States and Australia, a wartime shortage of men led to the appearance of the first female Santas. The figure at the heart of the story, however, remains so deeply ingrained in popular culture that Santa is instantly recognizable, regardless of race or gender.

Santa Claus has evolved over the centuries from thousands of legends, myths, and traditions, from Asia Minor to Europe and the United States, and back again. As every parent can attest, he has been admired and loved by children for centuries and ultimately, the enduring faith in a universal saint turned folk hero seems set to continue for years to come.

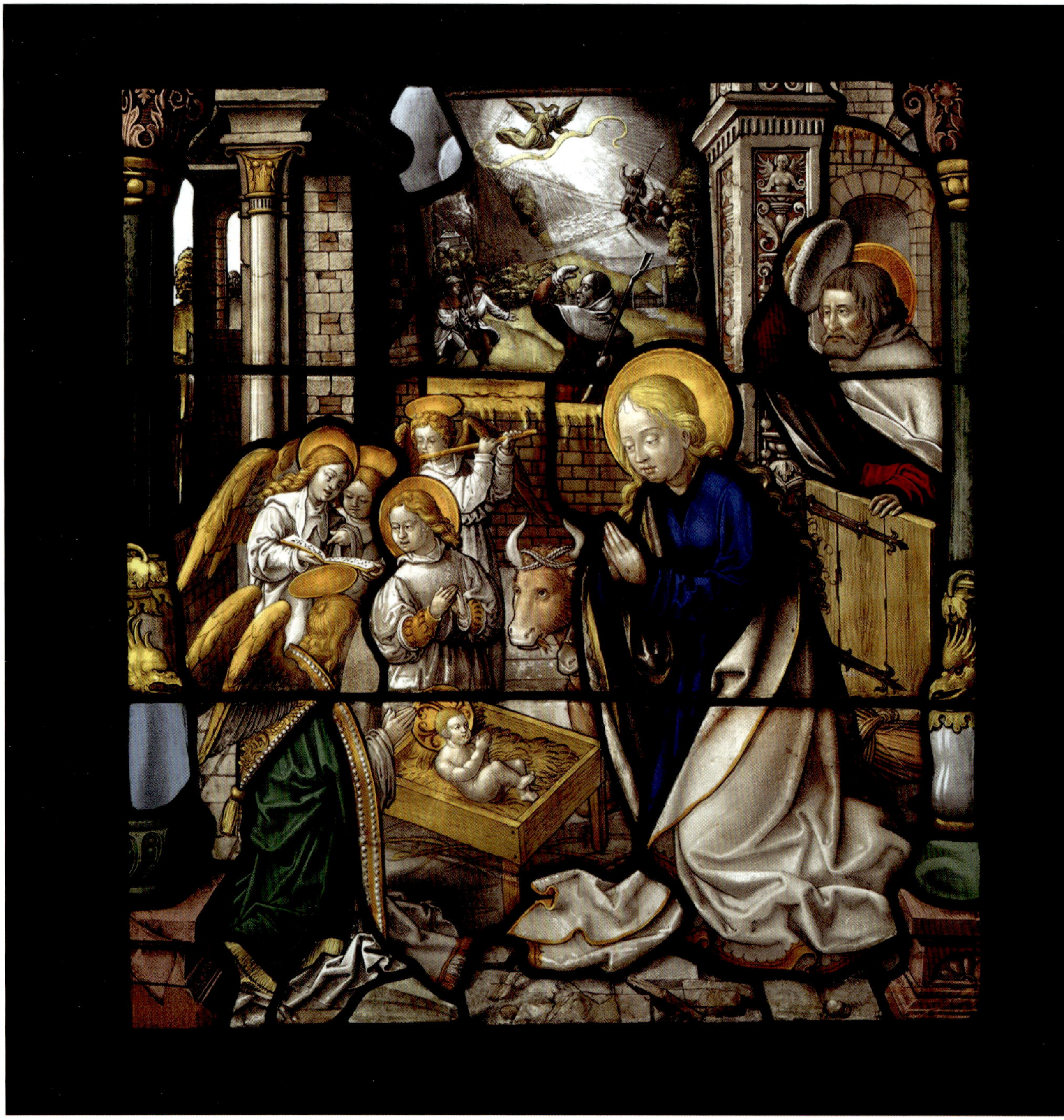

EVERHARD RENSIG AND GERHARD REMISCH

•

The Nativity, c.1522–26
Clear and colored glass with painted details, and yellow (silver) stain, 27 × 26 in / 69 × 65 cm
Victoria & Albert Museum, London

This exquisitely painted stained-glass window depicts the night of Jesus's birth as recorded in the Gospel of Luke. The baby, lying in the manger, is watched by his mother, Mary, who kneels in prayer. Beside her, an oblivious ox munches on hay, while on the right, Joseph hovers at the stable door, removing his hat in veneration of the savior. In the background, a herald angel unfurls a scroll, announcing the baby's birth to shepherds, who hurry toward the stone-built stable. This Nativity panel was produced in the workshop of master glaziers Everhard Rensig and Gerhard Remisch in Germany's Lower Rhine region for the cloister windows of the Cistercian abbey of Mariawald, which was dissolved in 1802 following the French Revolution. It was part of a larger design of panels across ten windows illustrating Old and New Testament stories and was originally positioned underneath Moses's famous encounter with God in a burning bush, a juxtaposition intended to reinforce the Catholic doctrine of the perpetual virginity of Mary; just as the bush was not consumed by fire, so Mary, it is said, remained a virgin her entire life. Compositionally, the design draws from Dutch painter Geertgen tot Sint Jans's earlier fifteenth-century oil painting *The Nativity at Night* (see p.209), but instead of engaging in silent prayer in a darkened stable, the five worshipful angels gather around the manger to sing and play music on a flute in a light-filled space.

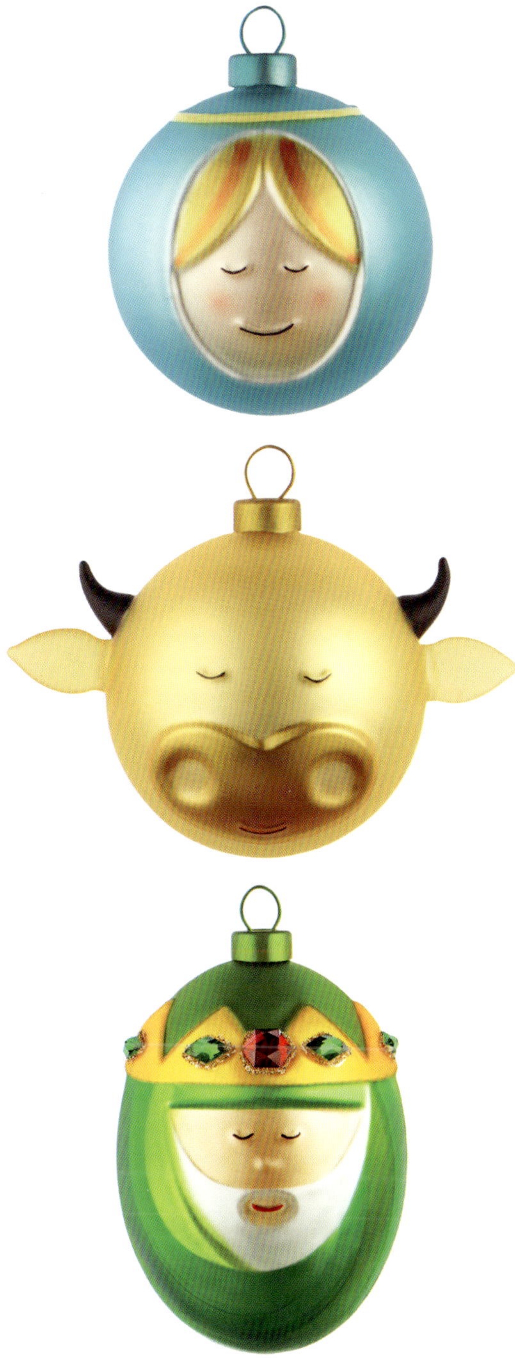

MARCELLO JORI

•

Le Palle Presepe, 2015
Hand-decorated blown glass,
H. 3½ in / 6 cm
For Alessi

These whimsical and witty Christmas baubles or ornaments are the work of the Italian designer Marcello Jori (1951–) for the groundbreaking Italian design company Alessi and its project *Palle Presepe* (literally "crib balls"). Taking two of Christmas's great traditions—the Nativity scene and Christmas tree decorations—Jori designed ten baubles, each representing a different character from the traditional Christmas Nativity scene, including the animals. Each glass bauble is blown by mouth and then hand decorated. The Mary bauble is blue while Joseph is easily recognized with his brown hair and beard, and the three kings are each suitably individual. For Jori, the baubles were the realization of a childhood dream, while his family put up a Christmas tree each year, what he really wanted in his home was a Nativity crib, complete with its figures.

The idea for the baubles came to him in a dream. He describes dreaming of an angel who hung baubles on the Christmas tree, which "spoke, sang, and prayed." The Christ bauble had to be the brightest of them all, so Jori designed it to resemble the sun, which also references the many representations of the baby Jesus with light emanating from him (see pp.81, 209). This combination of fantasy and irony is in keeping with the design principles of Alessi; founded in 1921 in Omegna in Northern Italy, the company has built its reputation on commissioning designers who reinterpret and reimagine everyday objects.

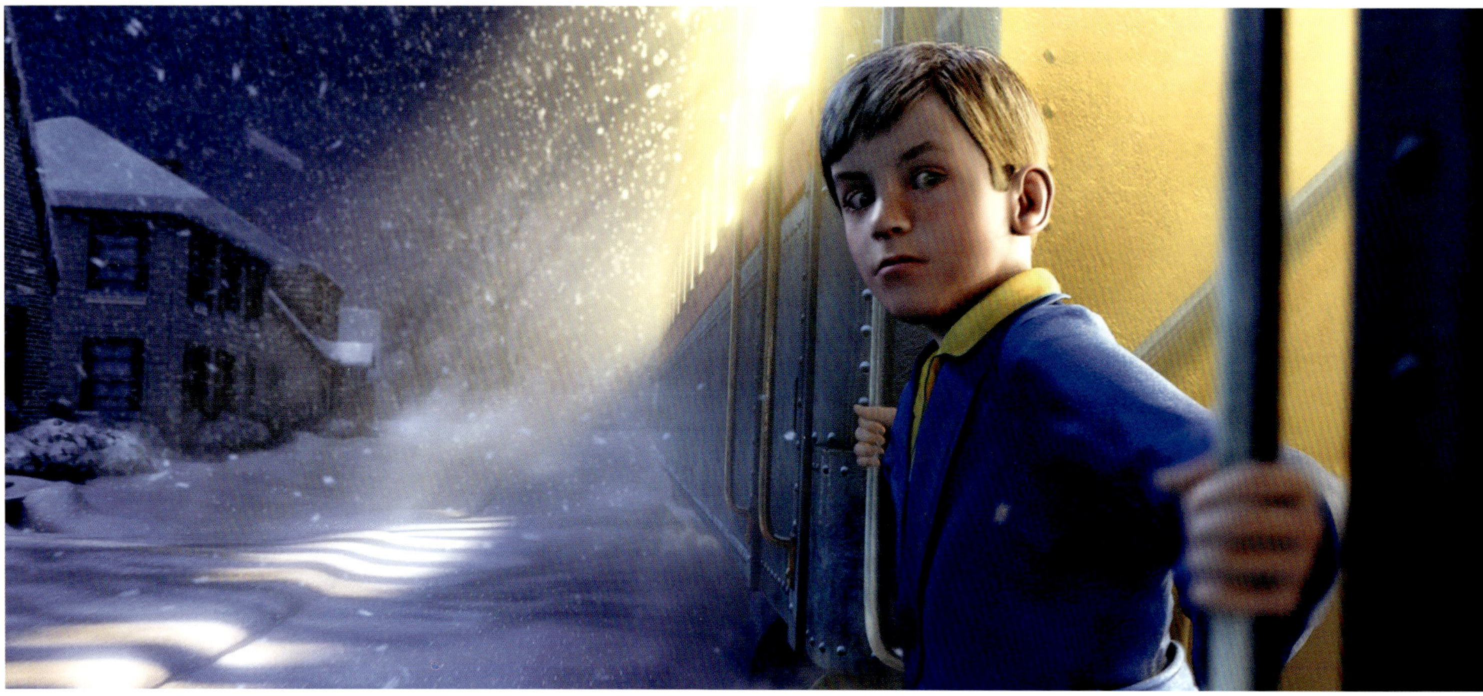

ROBERT ZEMECKIS

•

The Polar Express, 2004
Motion capture animation, dimensions variable
Warner Bros. Pictures

The classic film *The Polar Express* debuted quietly in 2004, but word-of-mouth gradually raised its profile to make it a Christmas staple in millions of homes. Directed and cowritten by Robert Zemeckis (1952–) and based on Chris Van Allsburg's eponymous 1985 book, this digitally animated movie tells the story of a young boy who, one night before Christmas, is invited by a conductor to travel with several other children on a mysterious train to the North Pole to meet Santa Claus. The story of the nameless boy's adventures is in many ways a study in faith. The boy no longer believes in Santa Claus, as symbolized by his inability to hear a bell that has flown loose from one of the reindeer's reigns. The boy retrieves the bell but loses it through a hole in his pocket before returning home on Christmas Eve. As he awakens on Christmas morning, he unwraps his gifts to discover the bell together with a note from Santa. He and his sister can both hear the bell ring, but their parents cannot: they have lost their belief. As the boy grows up, he remains able to hear the bell ringing—as can all those "who truly believe"— even after his sister loses the ability. *The Polar Express* was the first all-digital motion capture movie, created by filming actors wearing suits covered with sensors that provided the basis for the animation, and its appeal was enhanced by the popularity of its star, Tom Hanks (1956–), who voices multiple roles, including the conductor, the boy, and Santa Claus.

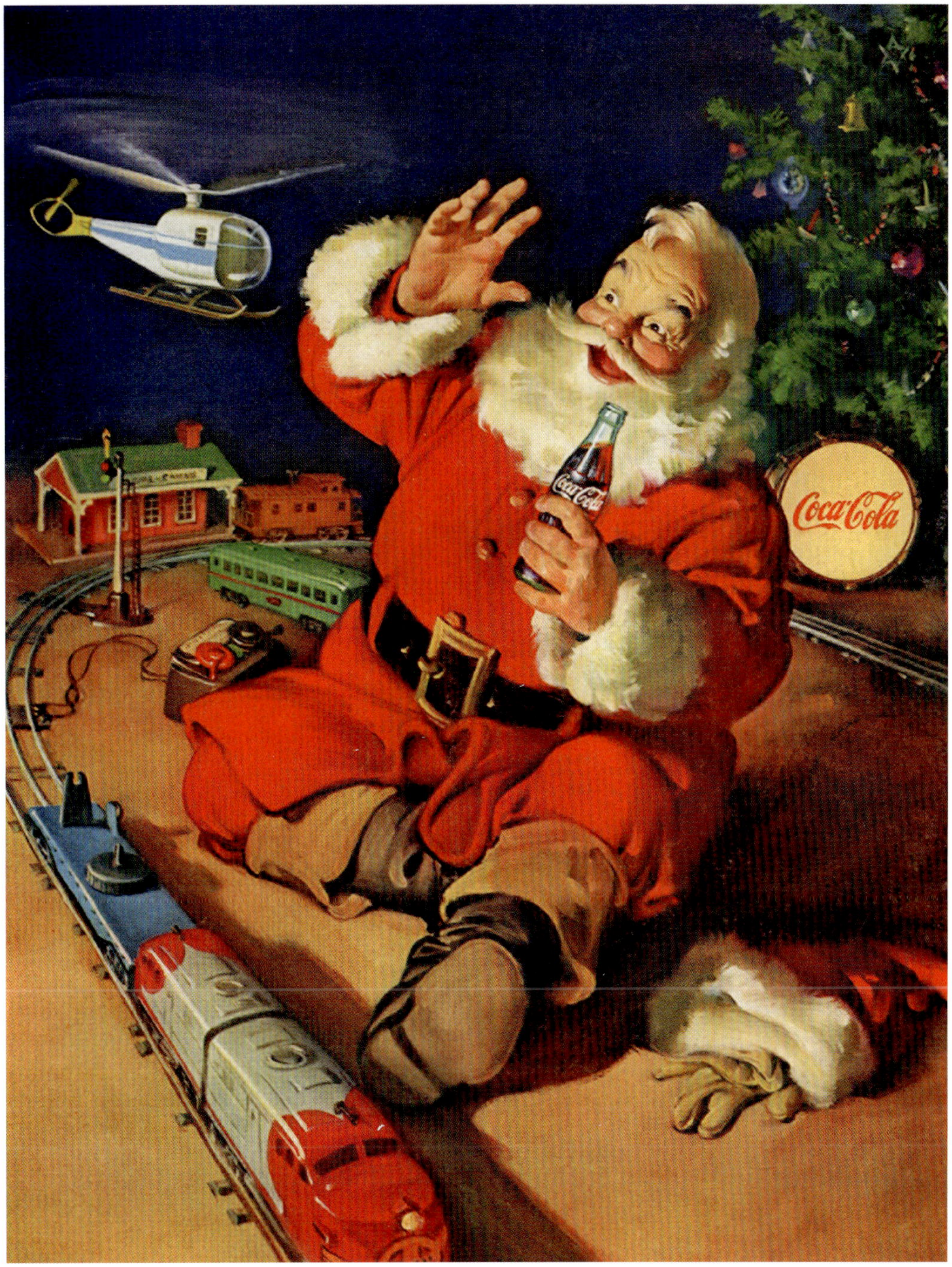

HADDON SUNDBLOM

•

Coca-Cola advertisement in *Life* magazine, 1962
Print, dimensions variable

The image that comes to mind for most people when they think of Santa Claus is the one created by American artist Haddon Sundblom (1899–1976) for Coca-Cola. In 1931, the beverage giant commissioned Sundblom to create an image of Santa for an advertisement. Inspired by Clement Clarke Moore's 1822 poem "A Visit From St. Nicholas" (see p.84), he imagined him as full-bodied and playful—a departure from his original European incarnations, Father Christmas and Saint Nicholas, who were represented as slender and thoughtful. Over the next thirty years of work for Coca-Cola, Sundblom refined his Santa, and in this 1962 depiction, as published in *Life* magazine, Santa sits on the ground in front of a decorated Christmas tree, a wooden train zooms by, and a helicopter whirls above his head—toys that he is delivering to good girls and boys. It seems to suggest that Santa really is a child at heart. Sundblom used oil on canvas to create his early works, initially using his friend as a model before taking to dressing himself up in the red regalia, standing in front of the mirror, and painting his reflection. While cartoonist Thomas Nast is generally credited with first showing Santa as round and jolly in the pages of *Harper's Weekly* in the late nineteenth century, it is Sundblom's take on the figure that became the quintessential image of the jolly old elf.

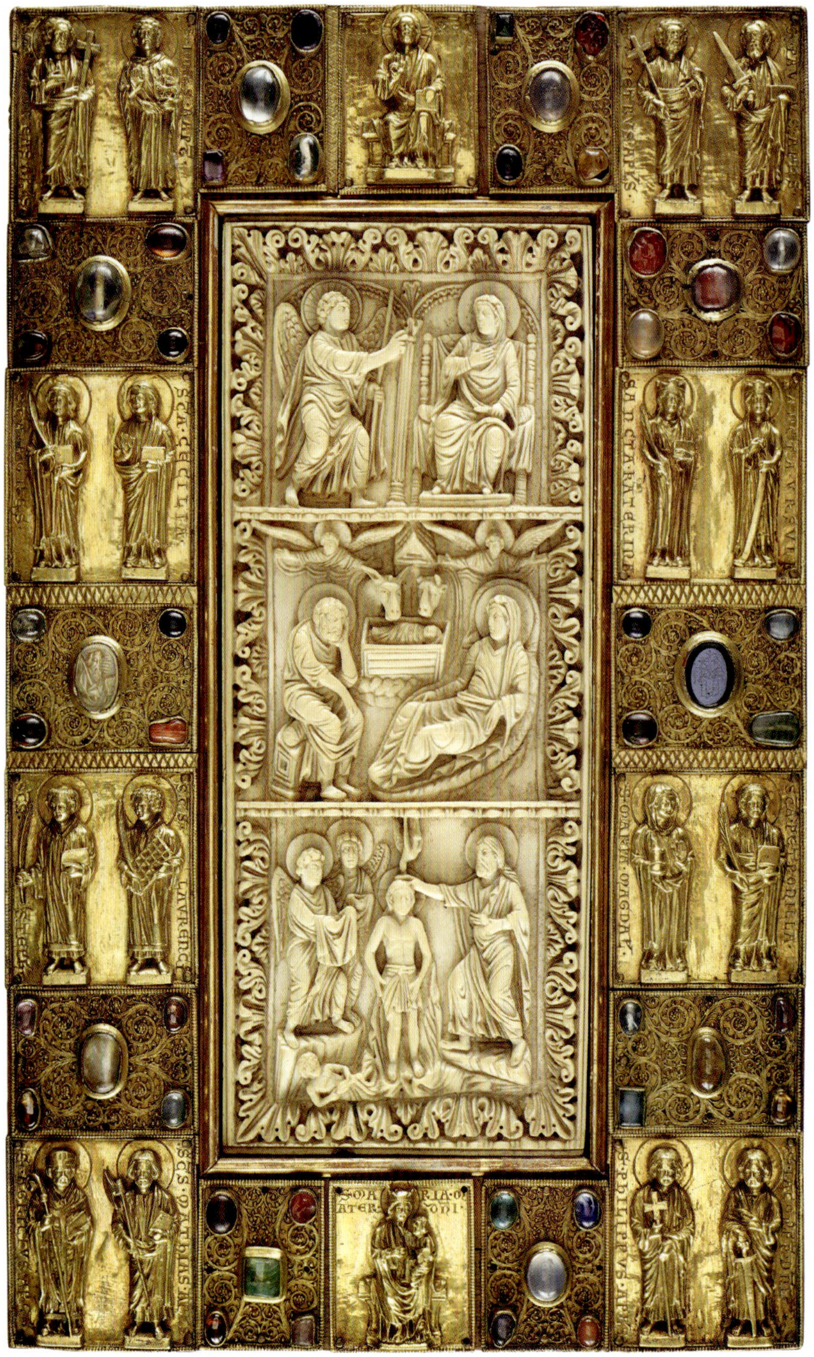

UNKNOWN

•

Trier bindings, c.10th–13th century
Ivory, silver gilt, and semiprecious stones,
16½ × 10¼ in / 42 × 25.8 cm
John Rylands Library, University of Manchester

This exquisite binding forms the front cover of a gospel book containing the four Gospels of the Evangelists. The ivory plaque in the center was made in Germany in the tenth century; the silver-gilt relief panels of saints surrounding it date to the twelfth or thirteenth century, as do the jeweled plates separating them. The plaque is carved with scenes, now central to the Christmas story, of the Annunciation to the Virgin by the angel Gabriel (top); the Nativity (middle); and the Baptism of Christ by John the Baptist. The story of the Nativity is narrated in the gospels of Luke (2:8–20) and Matthew (2:1–23), but the typical imagery, showing the Virgin Mary and Joseph with the baby Jesus in a manger, only appeared in the seventh century, with the circulation of an apocryphal gospel by "pseudo-Matthew." The image carved in this tenth-century ivory shows the Virgin reclining on a bed and Joseph seated opposite her, the swaddled Christ Child in the manger at center, overlooked by a donkey and an ox, and two angels on either side of a structure representing the stable. Medieval gospel books used for the Mass were believed to represent the physical embodiment of the Word of God, so they were protected by rich "treasure bindings," such as this one, decorated with precious metals and gemstones. Ivory panels were derived from Late Antique consular diptychs, commemorative plaques distributed as consular gifts.

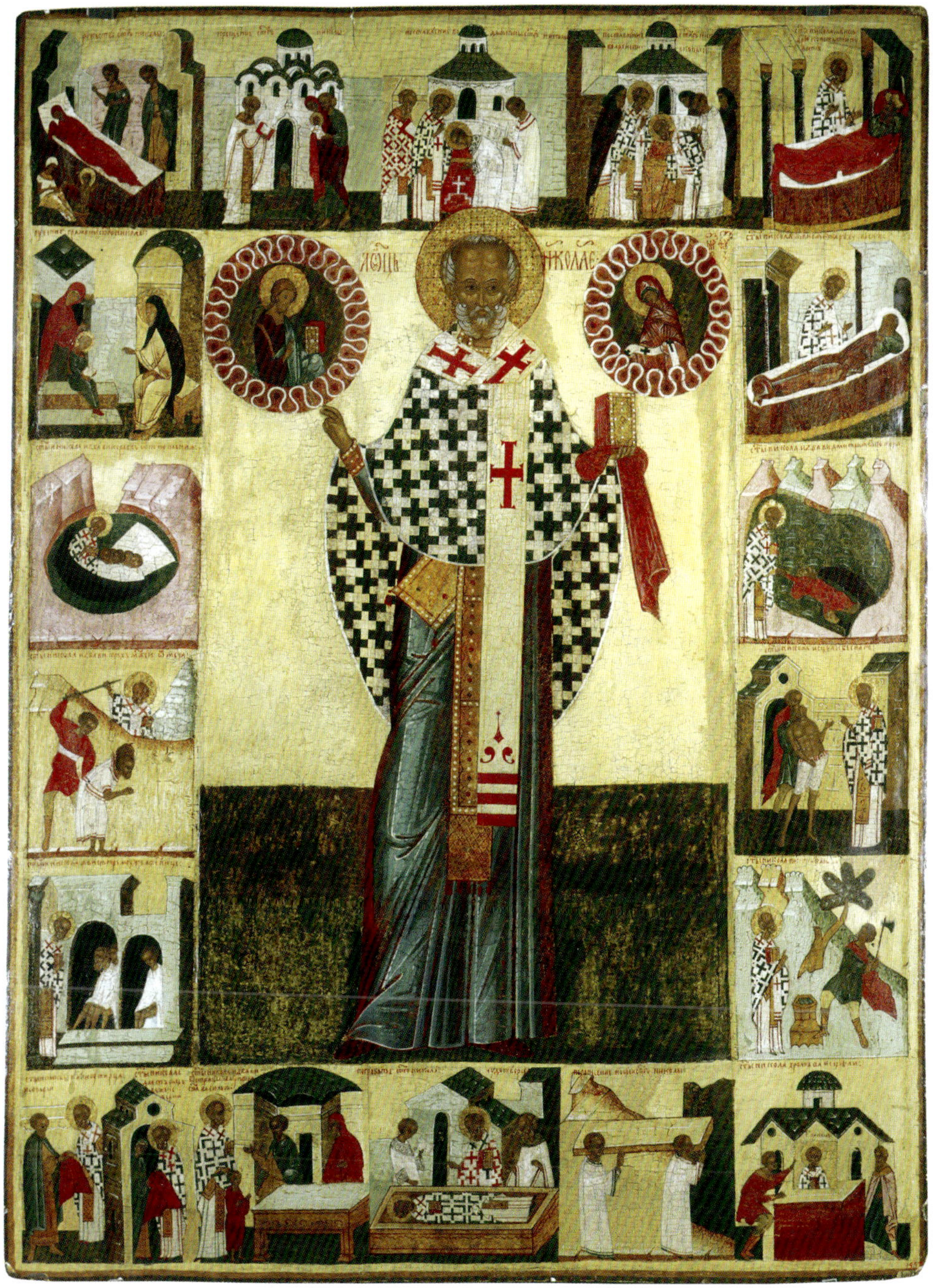

UNKNOWN

•

Icon of Saint Nicholas, c.1700
Paint on wood, dimensions unknown

An icon is a religious image, object, or event that usually manifests as a painting. This lavish example from Russia dates from the 1700s and depicts Saint Nicholas, Bishop of Myra (AD 300–399), in Asia Minor—the original inspiration for the figure of Santa Claus. Adorned with a gleaming halo, he holds a book of scripture in his left hand, while his right is raised in a sign of blessing. Around this figure are various scenes from his life, showing him performing the "miracles" he was most famous for. In one scene, Saint Nicholas is shown physically stopping an execution. In another, he is in dialogue with a king, illustrating his ease in engaging with the privileged and impoverished alike, his commitment to justice, and his generosity to those in need. He became renowned as a gift giver, a trait his namesakes would inherit, and was officially recognized as a saint around AD 800. From this symbol some recognizable traditions began to form. Dutch families called the winter gift giver Sinterklaas (see p.220) and developed the custom of leaving hay and carrots in shoes at Christmas in the hope that he would exchange them for gifts. Fast forward to North America in the 1900s and we see the amalgamation of Nordic folklore, Christian history, and myth collapse into a vision of red velvet, black boots, and fur trim. Paving the way for commercialization, the most contemporary expression and successor of the Saint Nicholas Christmas icon emerges: Santa Claus.

ON THE FIRST DAY OF CHRISTMAS MY TRUE LOVE SENT TO ME A PARTRIDGE IN A PEAR TREE.

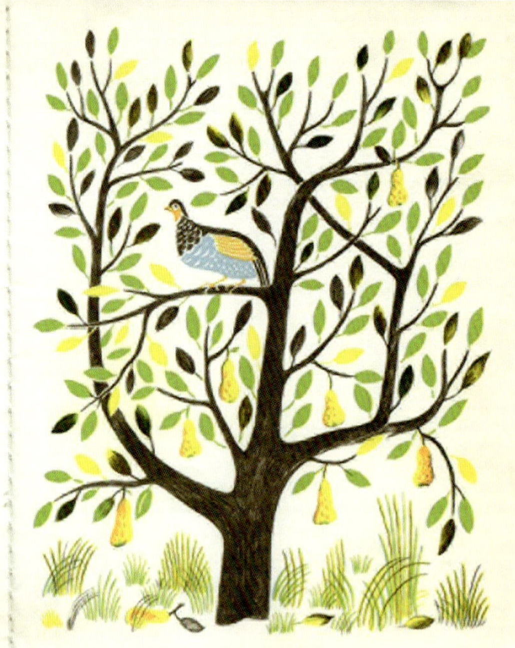

ON THE THIRD DAY OF CHRISTMAS MY TRUE LOVE SENT TO ME THREE FRENCH HENS, TWO TURTLE DOVES, AND A PARTRIDGE IN A PEAR TREE.

ON THE SEVENTH DAY OF CHRISTMAS MY TRUE LOVE SENT TO ME SEVEN SWANS ASWIMMING, SIX GEESE ALAYING, FIVE GOLD RINGS, FOUR CALLING BIRDS, THREE FRENCH HENS, TWO TURTLE DOVES, AND A PARTRIDGE IN A PEAR TREE.

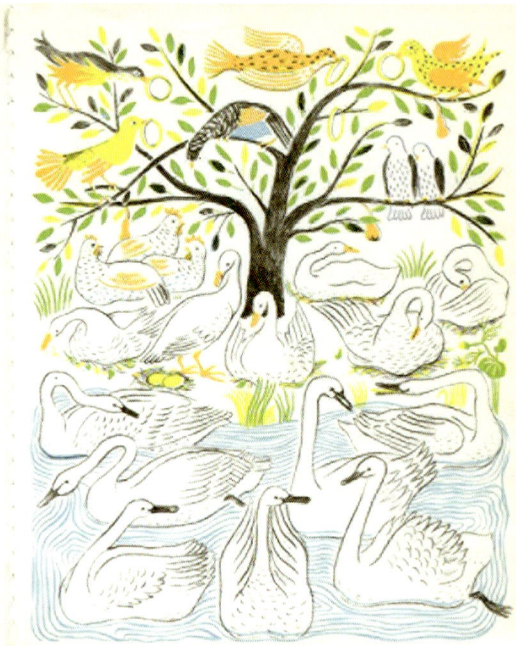

ON THE NINTH DAY OF CHRISTMAS MY TRUE LOVE SENT TO ME NINE LADIES DANCING, EIGHT MAIDS AMILKING, SEVEN SWANS ASWIMMING, SIX GEESE ALAYING, FIVE GOLD RINGS, FOUR CALLING BIRDS, THREE FRENCH HENS, TWO TURTLE DOVES, AND A PARTRIDGE IN A PEAR TREE.

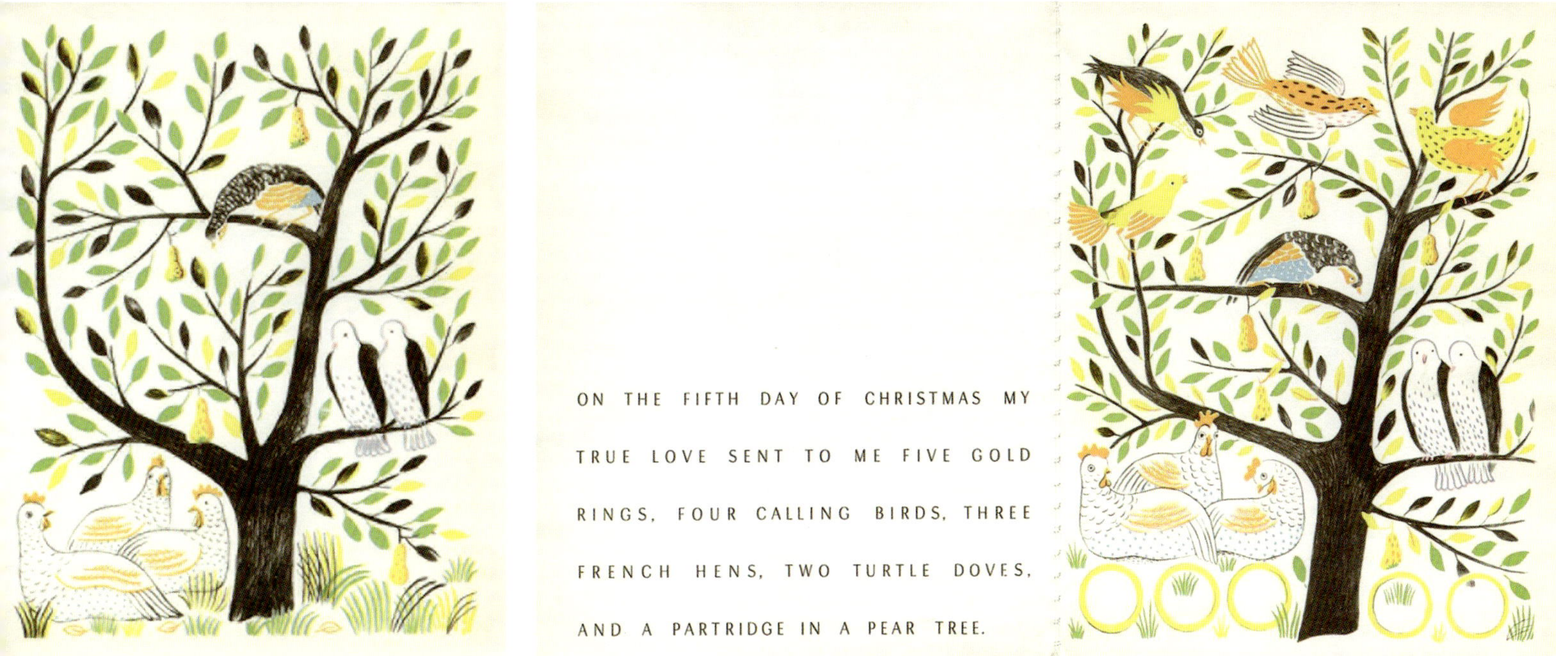

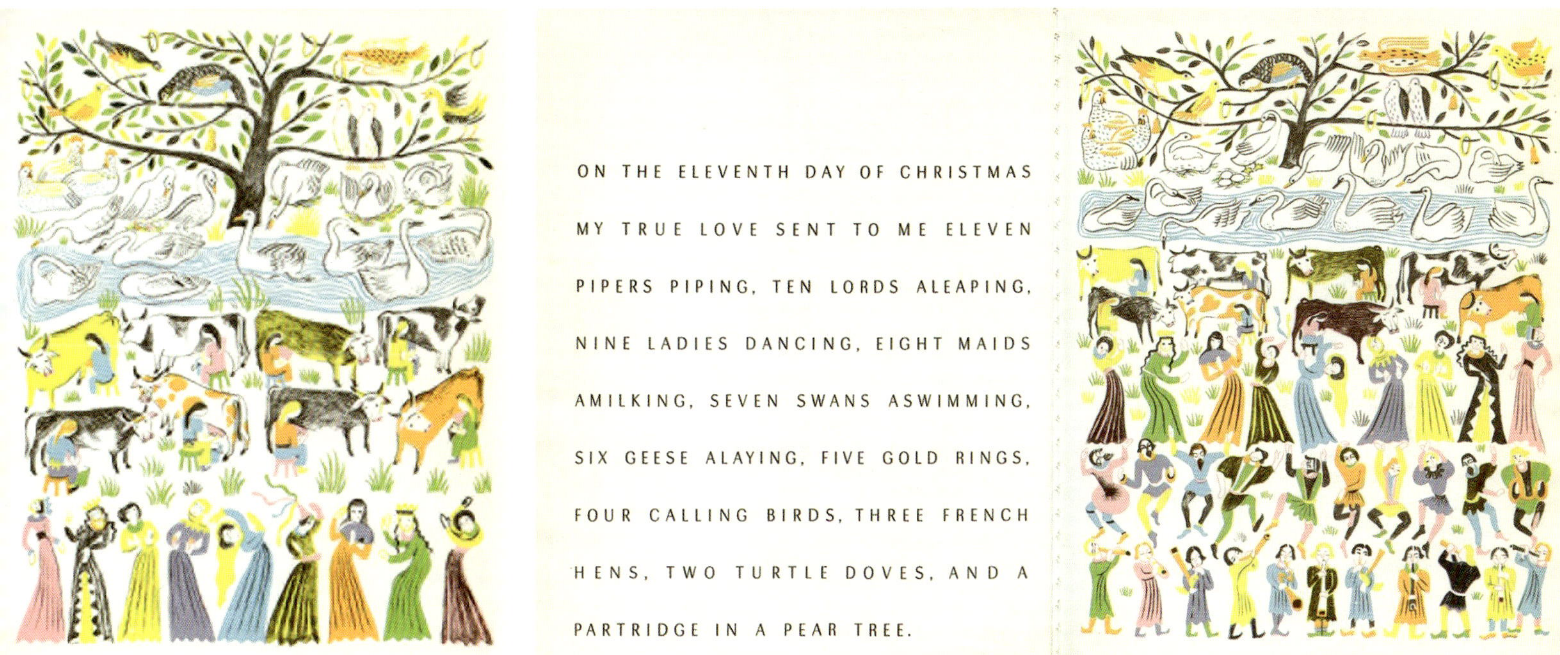

ILONKA KARASZ

•

Pages from *The Twelve Days of Christmas*, 1949
Printed book, dimensions unknown
Published by Harper and Brothers, New York

A beloved Yuletide staple for centuries, the festive season known as the Twelve Days of Christmas celebrates the Epiphany, the twelve days spanning from the birth of Jesus Christ to the arrival of the Magi, with the decidedly secular elements of music, dancing, and general merrymaking. This 1949 book by Hungarian-born designer and illustrator Ilonka Karasz (1896–1981) illustrates the well-known cumulative carol assiciated with "twelvetide," and was hailed as a "miracle of design and imagination" by the *New York Times* upon its publication. The illustrations begin with a single partridge in a pear tree and become increasingly overwhelmed with each new addition until the picture becomes one happy, crowded cacophony. The text that faces each illustration follows the same motif, filling the page as it goes. The carol most likely began as a "memory and forfeits" game, in which participants must remember each verse in sequence and then add their own until one player makes a mistake and must pay a penalty—a small trinket or candy, or even a kiss. The earliest known version was printed in the children's book *Mirth With-out Mischief* (1780) and has since been recorded by artists as diverse as Bing Crosby (see p.30), Frank Sinatra, and the Muppets and John Denver. Karasz experimented with many styles and artforms during her career, including furniture, silverware, and textile design, but she is best known for her covers of *The New Yorker*, commissions for which spanned almost fifty years.

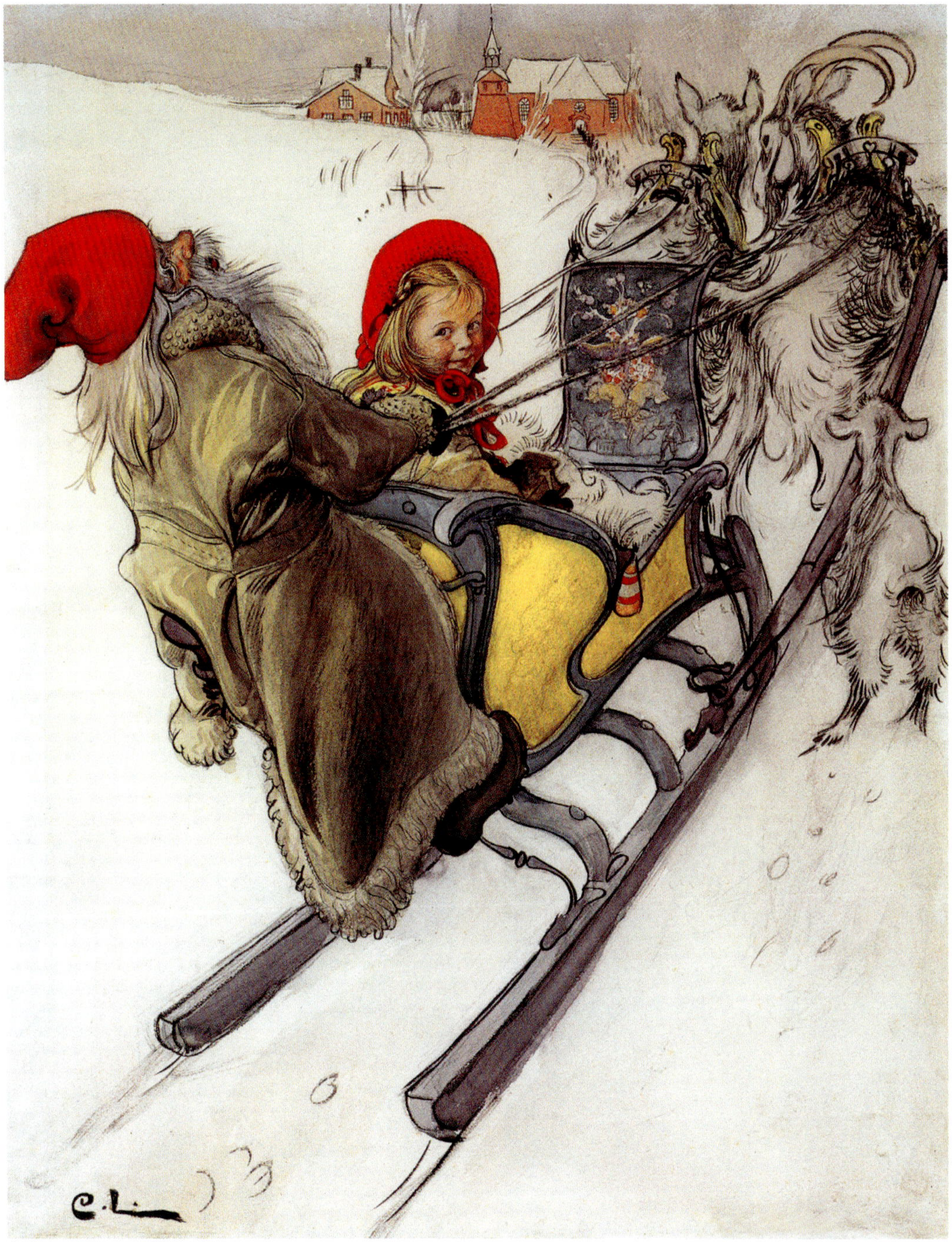

CARL LARSSON

•

Kersti Sledging, 1901
Watercolor, 24 × 19⅞ in / 61 × 48 cm
Private collection

The beloved Swedish painter, illustrator, and designer Carl Larsson (1853–1919) captured his five-year-old daughter in this charming Christmas-themed watercolor from 1901. Then in his late forties, Larsson was already well known in Sweden and abroad, and living in the cottage Lilla Hyttnäs in the quiet village of Sundaborn alongside his wife, Karin, and eight children. In this work, his seventh child, Kersti, sits gleefully in a sled piloted by a Father Christmas figure and being pulled by Yule goats, a traditional Christmas symbol in northern Europe and Scandinavia. Her gaze meets the viewer's as if bidding farewell before embarking on an exciting adventure. On the horizon, the snow-covered church of Sundaborn can be seen beneath a pale winter sky.

Born to a poor family in one of the roughest areas of Stockholm, Larsson earned a place to study at the Royal Swedish Academy of Arts. He became affiliated with the Arts and Crafts movement, a group focusing on domestic, interior scenes. Alongside Karin, a textile and interior designer, his home and family became the center of his life and the subjects of his paintings, particularly from the 1880s onward. In contrast to the artist's own upbringing, which was characterized by poverty and strife, Larsson's works capture the warmth and charm of an idealized domestic life, as well as the magical atmosphere of Christmas—a tradition he was deprived of as a child according to his autobiography *Jag*, published posthumously in 1931.

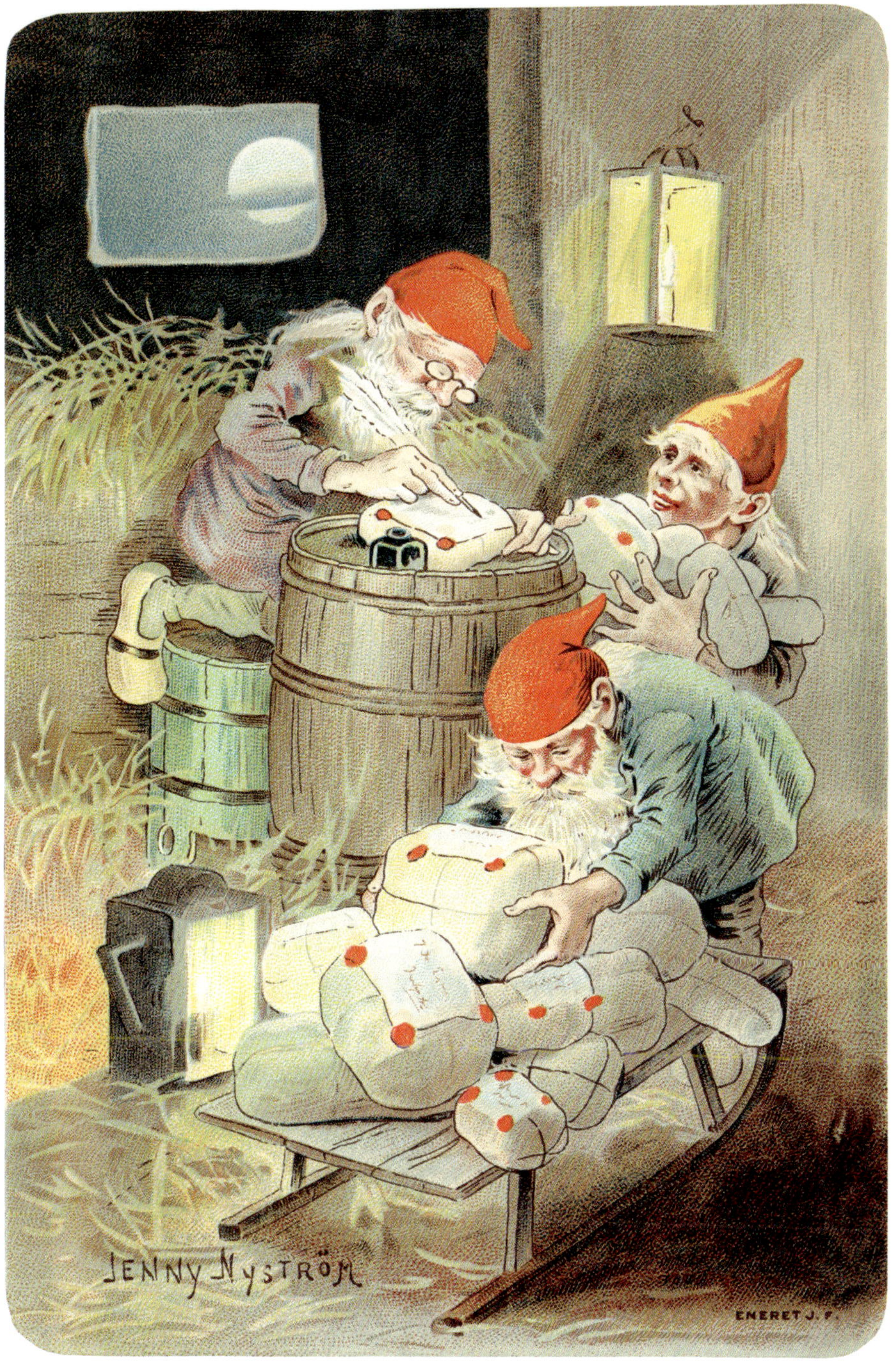

JENNY NYSTRÖM

•

Christmas motif, c.1899
Watercolor on cardstock, 5⅜ × 3¼ in / 13.8 × 8.2 cm
National Library of Norway, Oslo

At the heart of Christmas celebrations in Sweden is a small, goblinlike figure known as a *jultomte,* who appears everywhere from sitting in snowy gardens to the front of Christmas cards. The elevation of a little imp from traditional Swedish folklore to a central role in the Christmas story is almost entirely thanks to the prolific Swedish painter and illustrator Jenny Nyström (1854–1946), who created the phenomenon by first placing the goblins in scenes like this one, where they help load presents onto a sled. Unlike the jollier Santa Claus, the Swedish *jultomte* is an impish loner who is often portrayed with his pointed red cap pulled down over his eyes; while Santa Claus lives at the North Pole, the *jultomte* live year-round in Swedish homes and farms. According to Swedish folklore, if he is treated well, he will help ensure a good harvest; treated badly, he will cause havoc. At Christmastime, Swedes leave him a bowl of porridge with a pat of butter to ensure a happy festive period. Nyström started turning her watercolors into Christmas cards, such as this example from the late nineteenth century, helping to launch the tradition of sending cards in Sweden. The first woman to win the Swedish royal medal for her work, pieces like this remain popular today, long after her death.

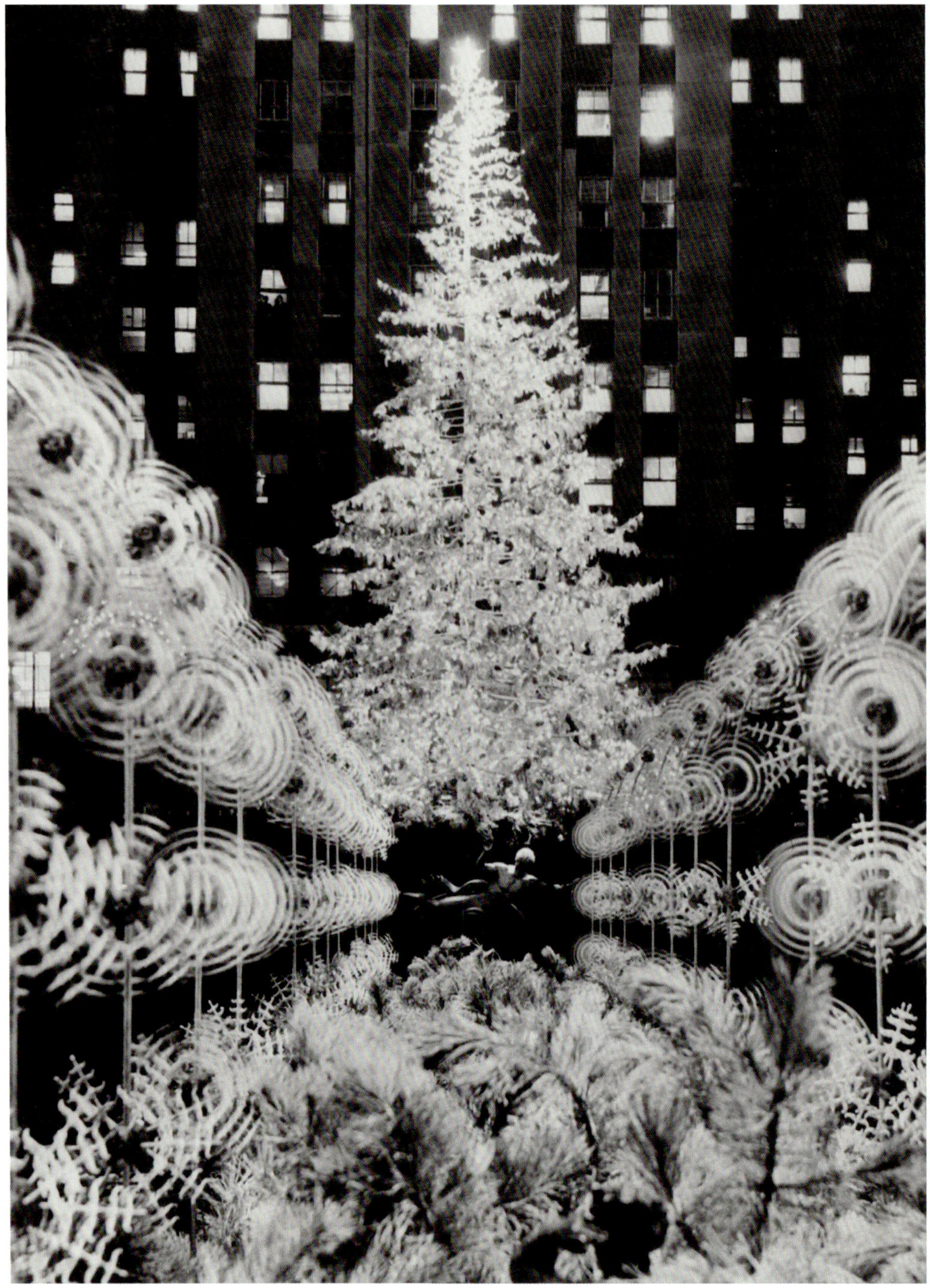

UNKNOWN

•

Rockefeller Center Christmas tree, New York, c.1954
Photograph, dimensions variable

Considered by many as an international icon of the Christmas season, the Rockefeller Center Christmas tree in New York is a spectacle enjoyed by millions. This black-and-white photograph shows the tree in the mid-1950s, its decorations mirrored in the skating rink beneath it. Even this spectacle differs greatly from its very humble beginnings in 1931, when the first tree was placed on this site. During America's Great Depression, the laborers at the construction site of the fourteen-building complex decided to contribute their own funds and resources to erect and decorate a tree with paper chains, cranberry garlands, and tin cans. It's reported that this spot was where they received their paychecks, and the twenty-foot (6 m) tall balsam fir served as a symbol of hope and optimism during the dire financial and economic times. By 1933, decorating a tree on this site had become an annual event, and this tradition has remained ever since. During World War II, the tree was decorated in patriotic colors and style, as was also done in 2001 following the September 11 attacks. NBC televised the tree illumination for the first time in 1951, and today it is a highly anticipated, star-studded TV special. Typically a Norway spruce, each year the tree stands up to one hundred feet (30 m) tall. The mighty evergreen is decorated with more than 50,000 lights—now energy-efficient LEDs—on the Wednesday evening following Thanksgiving and traditionally remains lit until January 6, the date of the Epiphany feast.

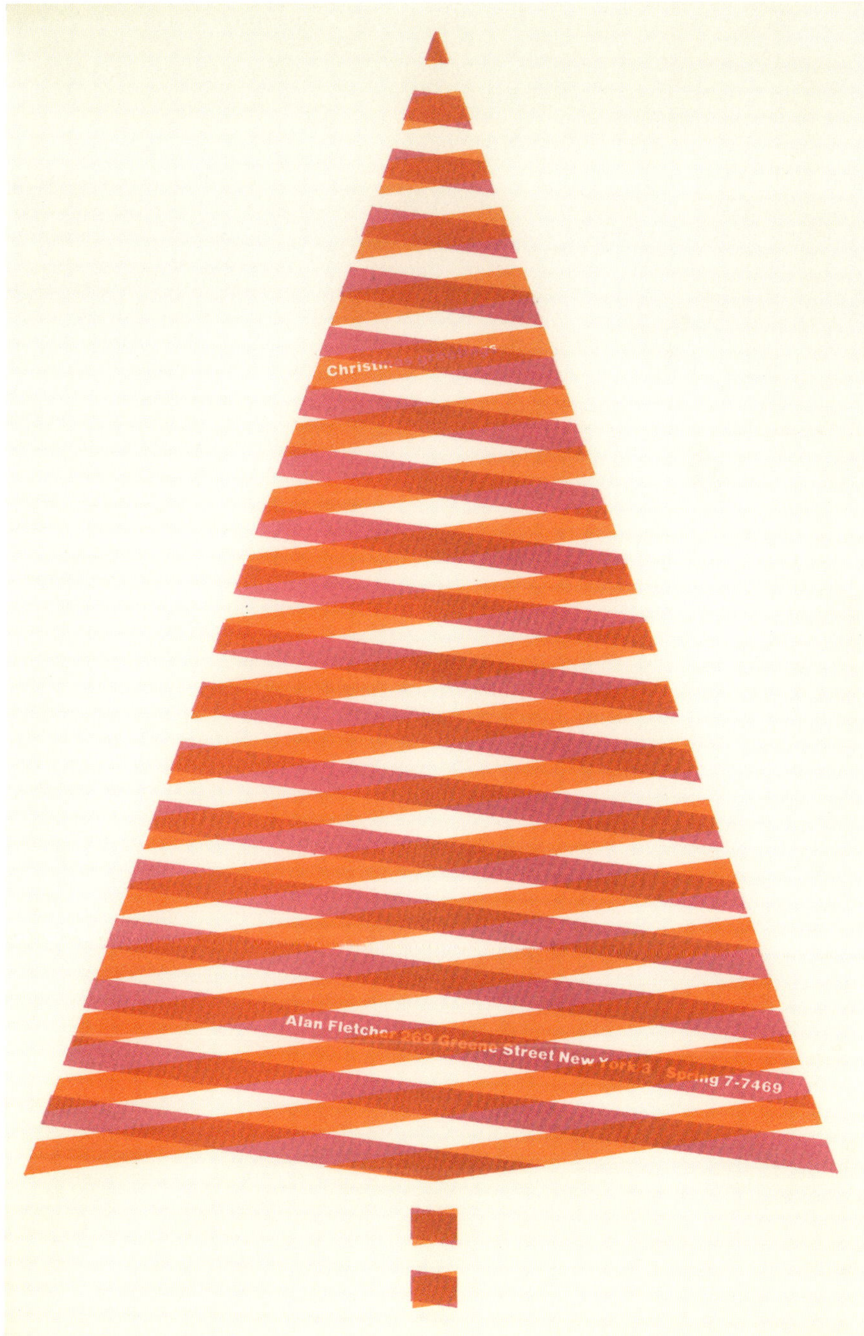

ALAN FLETCHER

•

Christmas Greetings, New York, 1958
Pen on cardstock, 8½ × 5½ in / 21.6 × 14 cm
Private collection

Bright lines of pink and orange form a lattice arranged in an elongated triangle instantly recognizable as a Christmas tree, despite the lack of the familiar dark green color or any decorations. Looking closer, this is in fact a Christmas card, with a greeting almost hidden six lines from the top of the tree. Toward the bottom the name of the artist is revealed as Alan Fletcher (1931–2006). He and his wife sent this card to their family and friends from New York in Christmas 1958. One of the most influential figures in British graphic design, Fletcher, a graduate of London's Central School of Art and Design and the prestigious Royal College of Art, was enrolled in an exchange program at Yale when, in 1957, he won a commission to design the cover of *Fortune* magazine, which helped him start to make his name in the world of graphic design. The exuberance and bounty of New York enthralled Fletcher, and his joyous image captured the color and glamour of the city, a stark contrast with the gray London of the 1950s. The card bears the influence of contemporaneous US pop culture, but in its wit and spirit are the characteristics of the work of the man who would cofound the world's largest independent design firm, Pentagram, in London in the 1970s and create the visual identity of numerous influential companies and institutions.

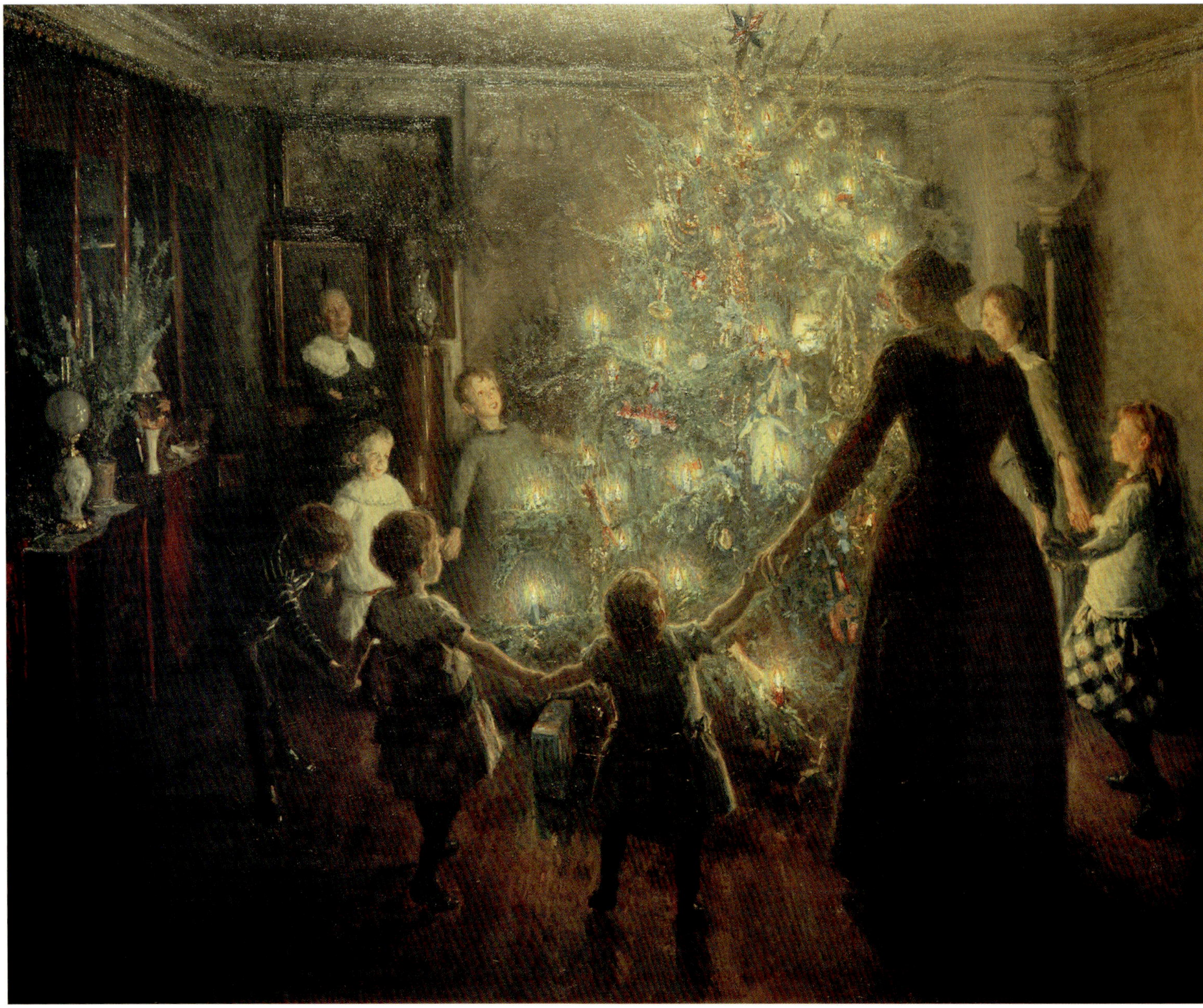

VIGGO JOHANSEN

•

Silent Night, 1891
Oil on canvas, 50 × 62⅜ in / 127.2 × 158.5 cm
Hirschsprung Collection, Copenhagen

Like so many enduring works of art, Danish painter Viggo Johansen's (1851–1935) depiction of his family surrounding a Christmas tree perfectly captures a moment in time. Titled simply, *Silent Night* but sometimes also referred to as *Happy Christmas*, the work itself appears to emit a glow, illuminated, as the subjects are, by the candles seen decorating the tree. The composition, showing the family joined hand in hand surrounding the large evergreen, so tall it appears to reach the ceiling, can be read as both celebratory and reverential. The tree, a physical representation of happiness and abundance with its plentiful decorations, contrasts with how few presents lie beneath it. Johansen used the parlor of his own home as the setting for this scene, and his own family as models. His wife, Martha, holds the hands of their daughters Ellen and Nanna as their son Fritz joins hands with other family friends. The artist was presumably stationed behind the easel, as he would have been for several months while he finished the painting, long after the tree had wilted and the festive season passed—although many choose to believe he is instead hidden from view behind the tree. The strong light radiating from the centerpiece of this image casts the rest of the room into shadow, giving a real sense of the shorter days and cold winter nights that the holiday season brings. The warmth and joy that can be found in an illuminated Christmas tree shines through this evocative painting.

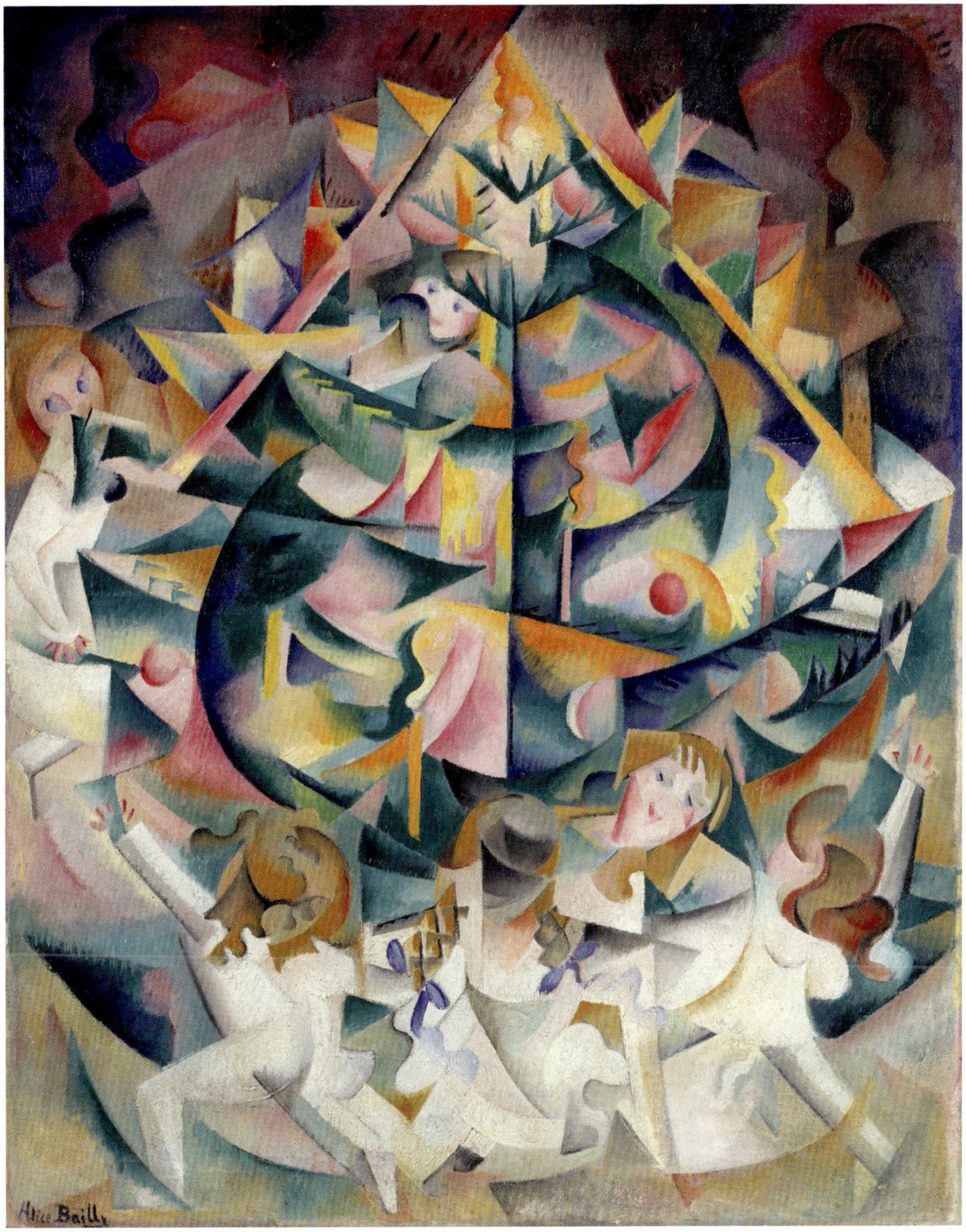

ALICE BAILLY

•

Joy Around the Tree, 1914
Oil on canvas, 39⅜ × 31⅞ in / 100 × 81 cm
SIK-ISEA, Zürich

In a kaleidoscope of color that contrasts with the archetypal green, red, and gold palette of many Christmas images, this exuberant painting captures the energy and excitement of a group gathered in a circle around a festive tree. Instead of being straightforwardly realistic, the image is splintered and fractured with spiked triangular forms and strong, curved lines. These echo the shape of pine tree branches but also inject a sense of overall movement into the scene, which is further emphasized by the figures' outstretched arms and active, leaping legs. The "joy" of the title is evident in the subjects' smiling faces. The work was painted by Alice Bailly (1872–1938), a Swiss-born artist who lived in Paris between 1904 and 1914. While Bailly was never wholly aligned to any of the city's burgeoning avant-garde art groups that came to define European art during the early twentieth century, her work has echoes of Fauvism, Cubism, and Futurism—three of the principal modernist art movements that bridged figurative painting and the pure abstraction of later, high modernism. Such artists sought a new style of art that better represented the speed and dynamism of modern life, and they often depicted urban life, machinery, transport, and warfare. Bailly, in contrast, demonstrated that such radical approaches to image making could also be applied to domestic life and even to a scene as commonplace, and potentially sentimental, as a family around a Christmas tree—elevating it to high art.

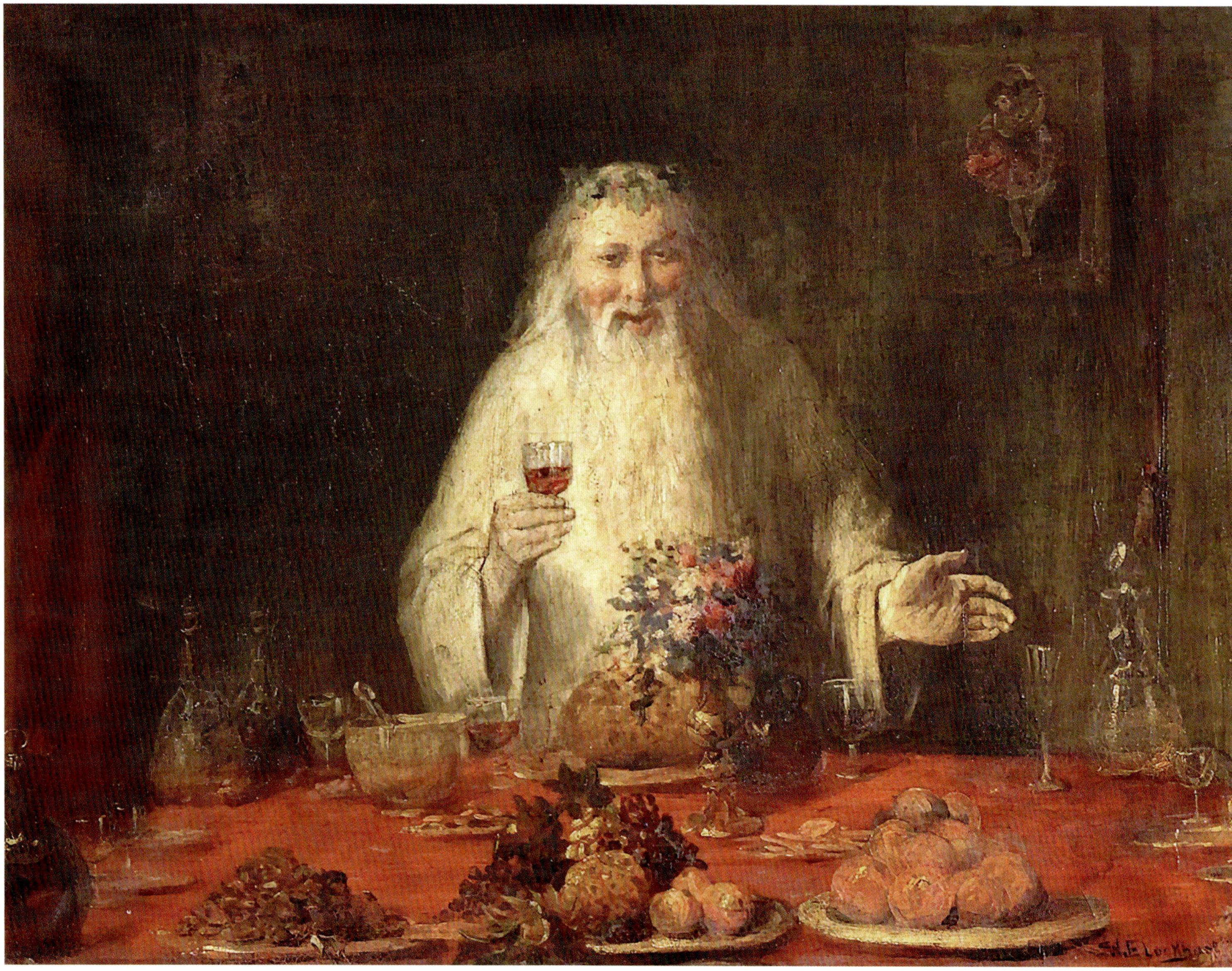

WILLIAM E. LOCKHART

•

Old Father Christmas, c.1895
Oil on canvas, 20¾ × 28⅝ in / 53 × 73 cm
The Hunterian Art Gallery, University of Glasgow

Painted during the Victorian era in Great Britain by Scottish artist William E. Lockhart (1846–1900), *Old Father Christmas* depicts a benevolent rosy-cheeked figure, wearing a white robe, sitting at a dining table in a dark but welcoming room. A feast of oranges and nuts is visible with carafes of wine, glasses, and colorful flowers in a scene that portrays a festive celebration. The Victorian period was a time of significant public reform, which saw Great Britain ramp up industrialization. The production of coal, steel, and iron became prolific, alongside advancements in art and science. Prior to the Victorian era, Christmas was not connected to family and children, but instead was a time for adults to host parties. In this context, Father Christmas was an allegorical figure who represented these festivities. If this is Saint Nicholas (see p.15), here his halo has transformed into a wreath, his book of scripture into a glass of wine, and the sign of the blessing into a welcoming open palm. It was not until the late nineteenth century, when America's Santa Claus, an evolution of the Dutch figure Sinterklaas (see p.220), reached Great Britain that Father Christmas would bring gifts for children. This painting then, by one of Scotland's most celebrated portrait painters, perhaps laments this transition of Father Christmas and recalls a time when Christmas was a respite from work and a nourishing of the soul in an increasingly chaotic, industrial world.

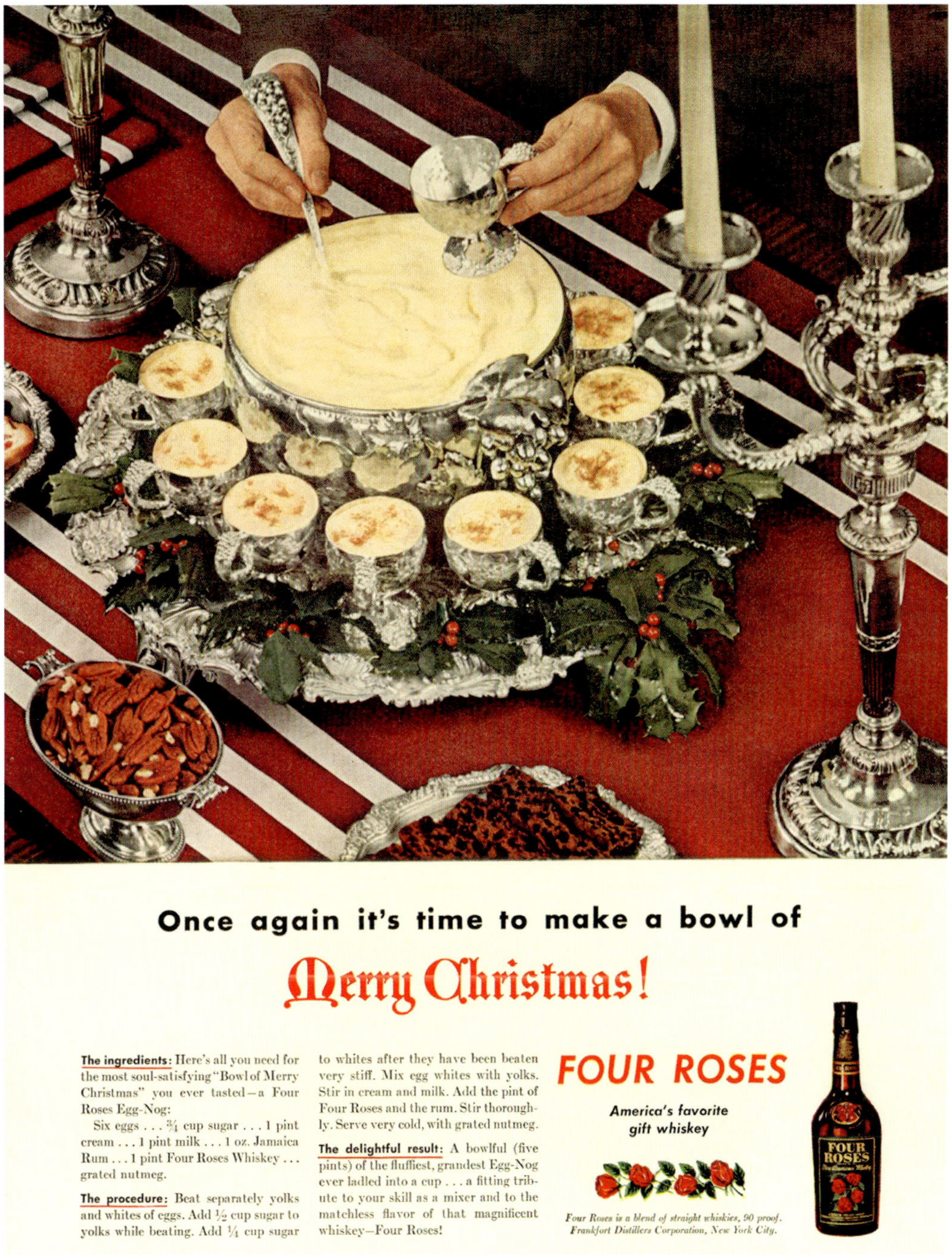

FOUR ROSES

•

"Merry Christmas!" advertisement, c.1960s
Chromolithograph, 14 × 10¼ in / 35.7 × 26 cm

Eggnog is a divisive drink. Whether loved or loathed, there is no denying that it is inextricably linked to the Christmas season. There are many recipes for eggnog, but the basic concoction is raw eggs beaten with sugar, milk, and cream, with the option to add a dash of something alcoholic, if desired. This advertisement for the Four Roses whiskey brand from the 1960s, featuring a well-dressed man dolloping out the eggnog mixture into individual silver cups delicately arranged on a silver serving tray, includes a recipe for five pints of the stuff that contains both rum and bourbon to give your Christmas that extra kick it needs. Various versions of eggnog exist around the world, such as *rompope* in Mexico and *eierlikör* in Germany. History suggests that in Europe as early as the thirteenth century, British monks drank posset, a warm egg-and-fig ale not to be confused with the modern sweet dessert. Over time this concoction evolved and, by the seventeenth century, it was made primarily with sherry and had become associated with aristocrats, likely because milk, eggs, and sherry were scarce and therefore expensive. Eggnog's association with Christmas began in the late 1700s, after the Revolutionary War, in what is now the United States, when the colonists began to include it as part of their holiday merrymaking. By the early 1960s, when the advertisement pictured here came out, eggnog was firmly entrenched as a drink served at dining tables around Christmastime.

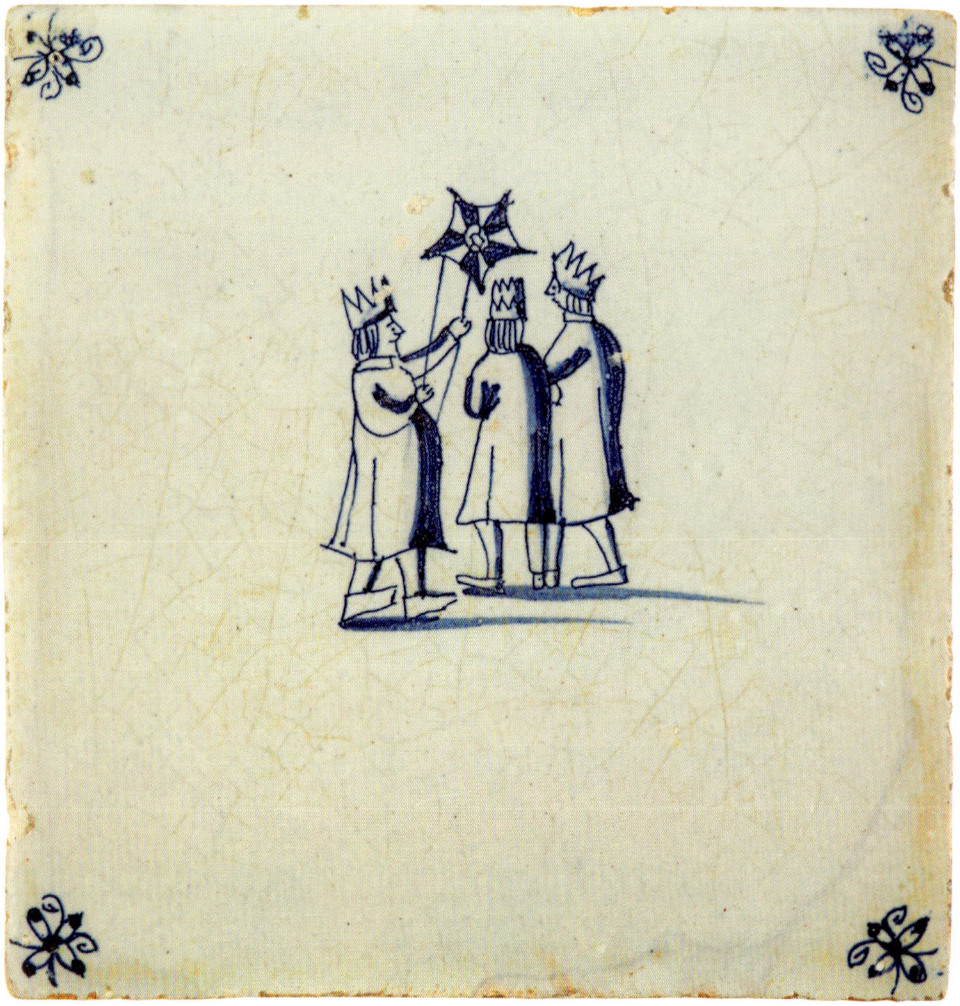

UNKNOWN

•

Three Kings, c.1670
Hand-painted tile, 5⅛ × 5⅛ in / 13 × 13 cm
Private collection

Delftware is an umbrella term that describes an array of tin-glazed earthenware—with tiles, plates, and jars being the most prevalent among them. Its distinctive blue-and-white motif was inspired by Chinese porcelain arts, and it became wildly popular in the Netherlands and England in the early 1600s. This tile, dating to the seventeenth century, depicts three children celebrating the Epiphany, or Three Kings Day, dressed as the Magi who followed the Star of Bethlehem to the baby Jesus (see p.126). In celebrating the holiday, children would traditionally parade around singing songs, going from door to door, carrying a symbolic star made of paper attached to a stick. This charming tile captures the celebratory spirit of the feast day, which marks the end of Christmas festivities for the season. The city of Delft in the Netherlands was the epicenter of the manufacturing of these tiles, drawing many artisans who intricately hand-painted the pottery. Unlike many decorative arts, there were no rules when it came to the subject matter on Delft tiles. The art was as individual as its maker, and scenes ranging from the pastoral to the sacred to the profane were all captured in this medium. Corner motifs were often employed and changed throughout the centuries, depending on what was in fashion. These are spider motifs, which were common around the mid-seventeenth century.

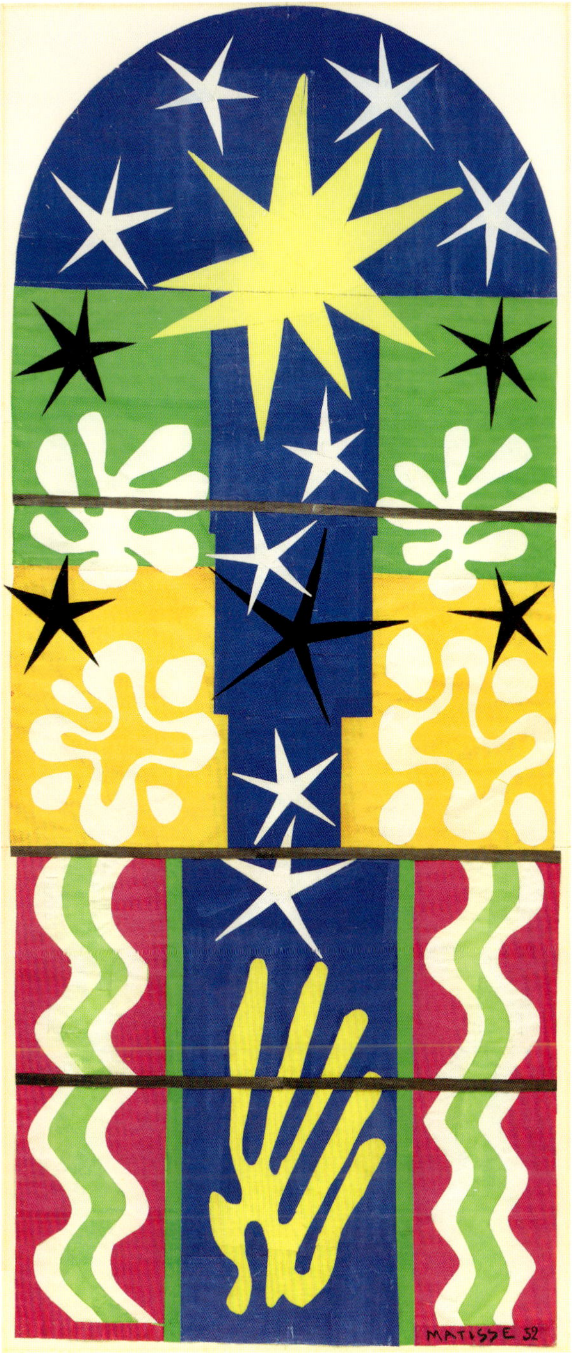

HENRI MATISSE

•

Maquette for *Nuit de Noël (Christmas Eve)*, 1952
Gouache on paper, 107 × 53½ in / 272 × 135.9 cm
Museum of Modern Art, New York

Henri Matisse (1869–1954) was commissioned by Time Inc. to produce *Nuit de Noël* (*Christmas Eve*), an eleven-foot (3.3 m) tall stained-glass panel that would be featured at the company's headquarters at the Rockefeller Center in New York during the 1952 Christmas season. This maquette (a sketch, or mock-up) was composed of gouache that was hand-painted on paper to Matisse's specifications and then hand cut by the artist himself. *Nuit de Noël* is dominated by a large star that hangs over a landscape filled with the types of organic shapes familiar in both his painting and cutout work. Like the Vence chapel windows, which Matisse completed a year earlier, this work conveys the spirit of Christmas without employing specific religious iconography, perhaps borne from Matisse's humanist beliefs. The four snowflakes hint toward the season, and the star is an overt reference to the guiding star followed by the Three Wise Men to the birth of Jesus. This maquette typifies the type of cutout work that Matisse was exploring near the end of his lifetime, when physical ailments precluded him from the grueling work of painting. Working beyond the confines of the canvas, he was able to create art on a much greater scale, with pieces functioning more like sculptures. The corresponding stained-glass panel was fabricated by Paul Bony in Paris, and both works were subsequently given to New York's Museum of Modern Art.

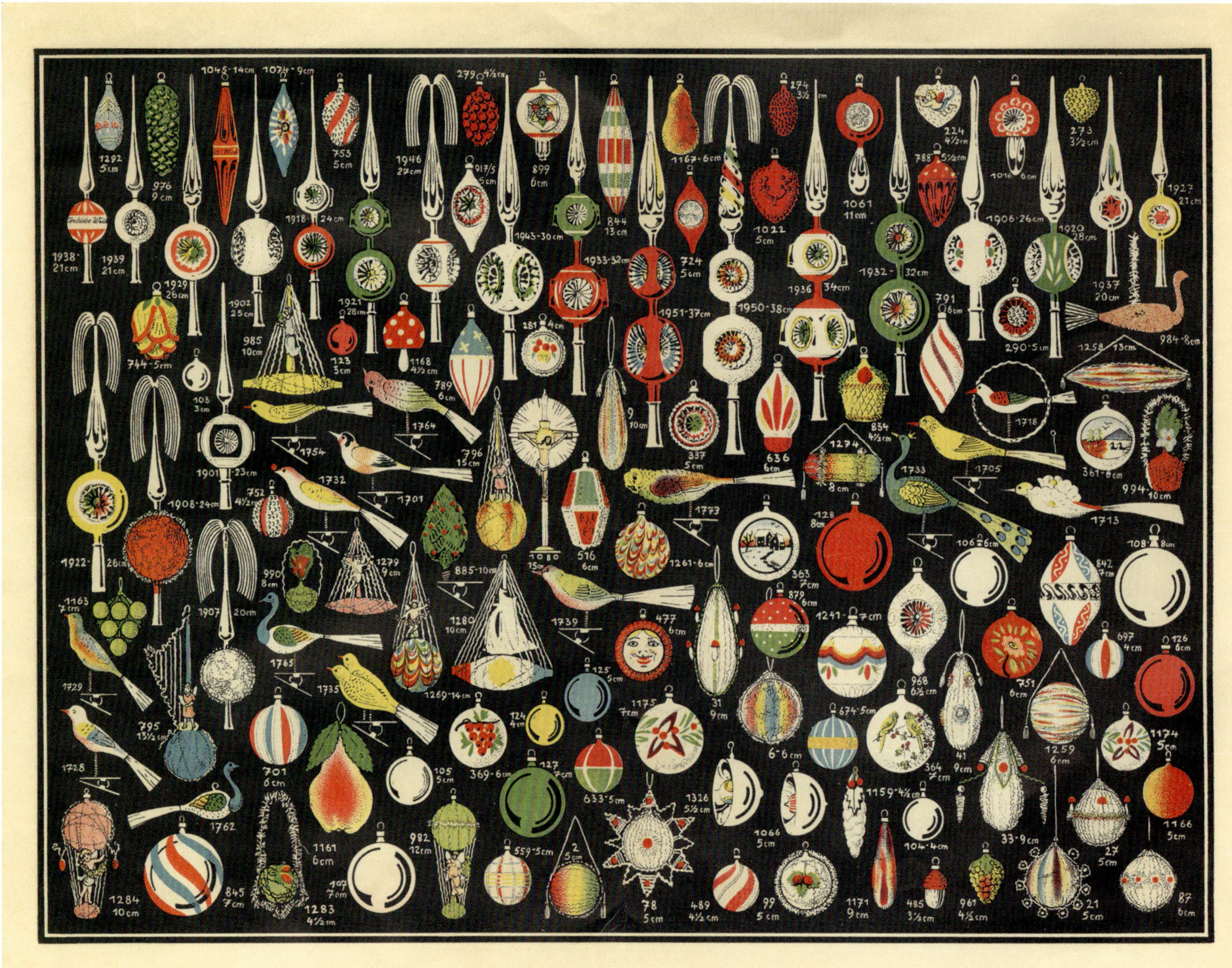

ERWIN GEYER

•

Page from trade catalog for glass decorations, 1936
Color illustration, 9½ × 13 in / 24 × 33 cm
Corning Museum of Glass, New York

It might not be clear how the variously shaped and colored Christmas ornaments in this trade catalog, some in the shape of birds, others classic finials, relate to glass eye prosthetics, but both were first produced around the same time by glass companies in the German region of Lauscha near the picturesque Thuringia Forest. Lamp glassblowing (the blowing and forming of shapes from glass tubes heated over an oil lamp) dates from the middle of the eighteenth century. In 1835, Lauscha's famous master craftsmen used the technique to manufacture the first glass eye and later its first mass-produced glass Christmas ornaments. In 1847, the process was commercialized when glassblowers at the Lauscha factories created molds from which ornaments could be mass produced, originally to be hung in windows. The molds allowed a much greater variety of glass baubles to be made, from miniature fruits, such as apples, pears, and cherries, to any number of spherical shapes. By the time this catalog appeared in 1936, the region had developed a sophisticated range of ornaments, demand for which had grown exponentially after Woolworth stores in the United States started selling them during the 1880s. Lauscha continued to dominate the glass-ornament market until the outbreak of World War II in 1939, when production ceased, allowing other countries, such as the former Czechoslovakia and Japan, to move into the lucrative market.

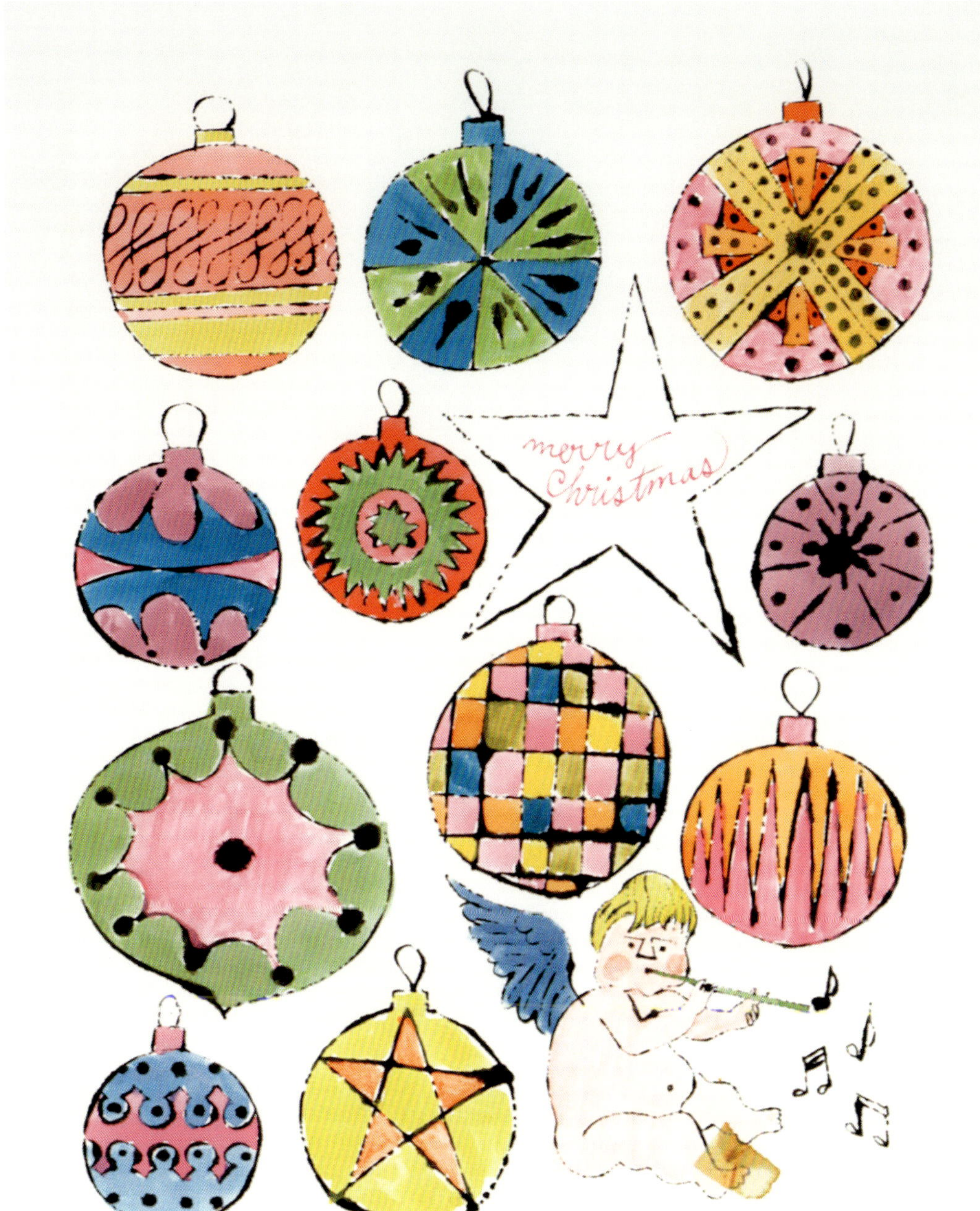

ANDY WARHOL

•

Fairy and Christmas Ornaments, c.1953–55
Graphite, ink, and Dr. Martin's Aniline Dye on Strathmore paper, 22½ × 14½ in / 57.2 × 36.8 cm
Andy Warhol Foundation

A chubby fairy pipes a festive tune amid an array of colorful baubles and a star inscribed with a Christmas greeting. While this whimsical line drawing is nothing like the silk-screened Pop art canvases featuring soup cans and Marilyn Monroe portraits that made Andy Warhol (1928–1987) world-famous in the 1960s, its style typifies the work he produced as a renowned illustrator in the preceding decade. The artist's hand-drawn images of shoes began appearing in publications, such as *Vogue*, *The New York Times*, and *Harper's Bazaar*, soon after he moved to Manhattan in 1949. When he began working at Tiffany & Co. in 1956, he created a range of annual Christmas cards for the luxury retailer, of which this image is a precursor. The design exemplifies the artist's blotted-line technique, whereby ink would be applied liberally and then blotted to produce splotchy lines of varying width. The colored-ink washes were likely applied during one of Warhol's coloring parties, hosted at the chic Serendipity 3 restaurant, where he encouraged friends to complete his black-and-white drawings—an approach that prefigured the collaborative methods he later employed at his legendary studio, the Factory. As a practicing Catholic with a penchant for consumerism and kitsch, it is no surprise that Warhol wholeheartedly embraced Christmas. Among the card designs he produced for Tiffany's are an exuberant band of musical angels, a silhouetted "star of wonder" formed from flying birds, and a Christmas tree made of fruit.

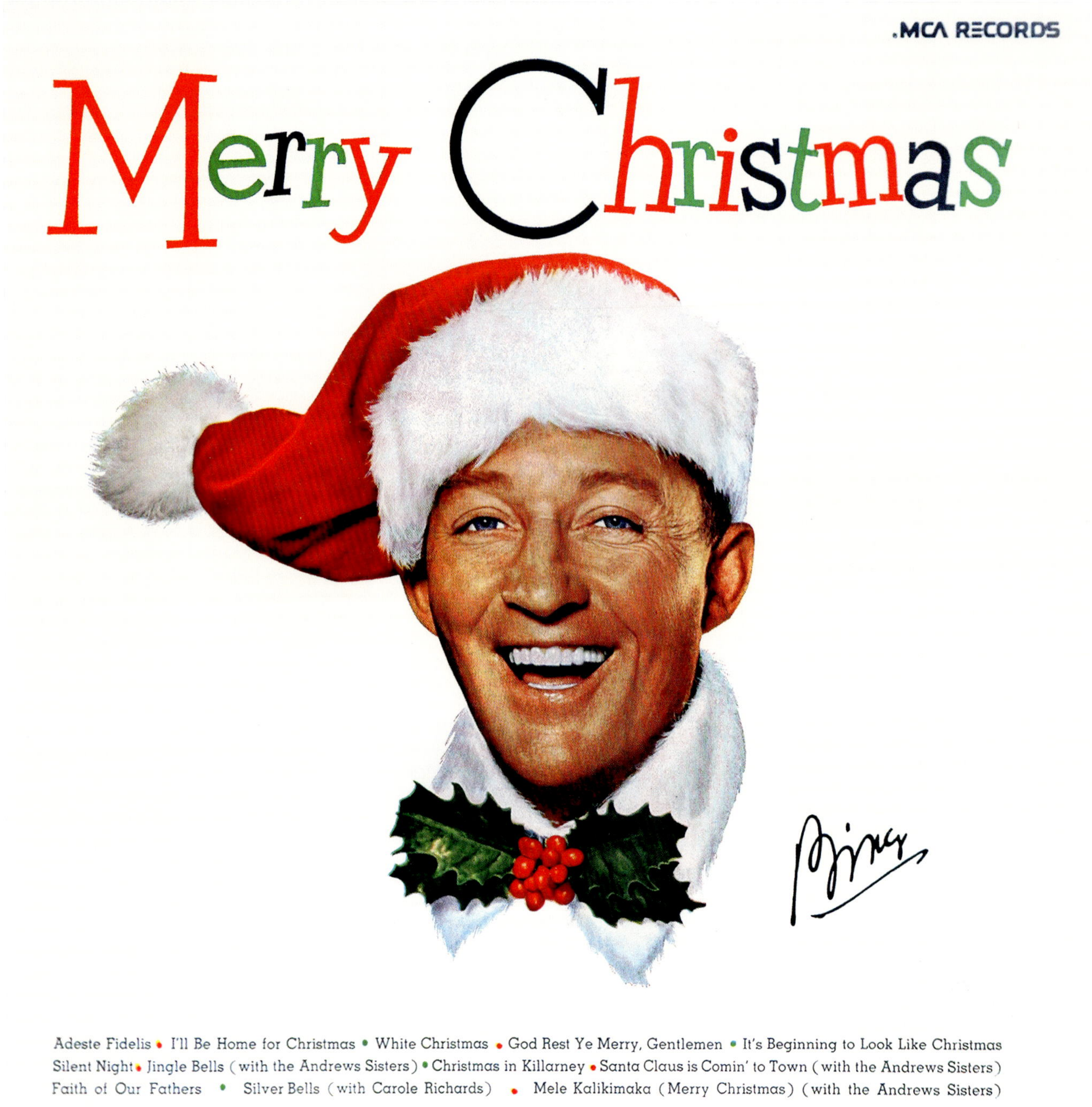

BING CROSBY

•

Merry Christmas LP cover, 1977
Printed card, 12⅜ × 12⅜ in / 31.4 × 31.4 cm
Originally released by Decca Records, London; reissued by MCA Records, Los Angeles (now Geffen Records)

Merry Christmas by Bing Crosby (1903–1977), originally released by Decca Records, is perhaps the best known Christmas album of all time. These songs are truly ubiquitous, and even now, almost eighty years after their release, they are still present at Christmastime. The first version of the album, from 1945, was a compilation of Crosby's previously released Christmas singles, including such classics as "White Christmas" and "Santa Claus Is Comin' to Town." In 1955, the cover was changed to the one that exists today—Crosby in a Santa hat with a holly bow tie against a white background—and four songs were added. On their surface, the songs on the album reflect the good tidings of Christmas, but upon closer listen they conjure a profound sadness, recorded as they were during the brutality of World War II (see p.199). The song "I'll Be Home for Christmas" perhaps most poignantly highlights this duality, capturing the cascading hope of a soldier's joyous return stateside for the holidays but negating it all with the closing qualifier "if only in my dreams." Even traditional songs, such as "Jingle Bells," couldn't avoid, by default, pointedly illuminating the disparity between the innocent Christmases of peaceful days and the dark cloud hanging over those of wartime. But the melancholy of this album is one of its greatest strengths, encouraging all of us to remember those we have lost, helping bring them back indoors to the warmth of the fire and our memories for yet another Christmas together.

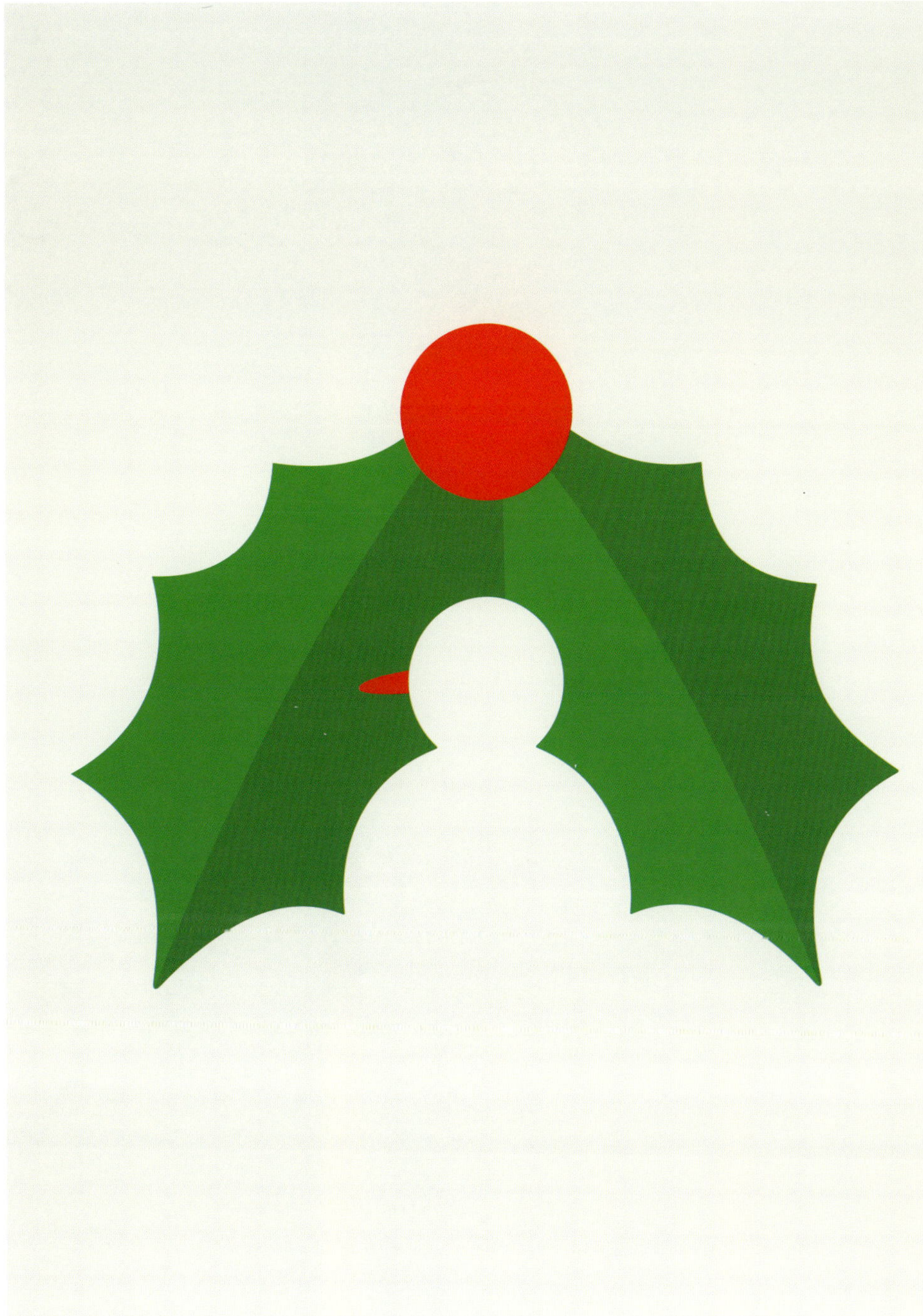

NOMA BAR

•

The Holly and the Snowman, 2015
Digital illustration, dimensions variable

The illustrations of Israeli-born, award-winning graphic designer and artist Noma Bar (1973–) have been featured on countless magazine covers and in books and advertisements. Yet it might be surprising to know that for all his digital wizardry, Bar's process is decidedly analog. Based in London since 2001, he spends each workday, rain or shine, cloistered in the Highgate Wood, tucked among the trees, sketchbook in hand, tapping into the power of nature. It was in the woods that the artist came by happenstance upon a sprig of fallen holly and noticed the space between the two leaves, which gave the impression of a tiny snowman nestled there. *The Holly and the Snowman* marries two jolly Christmas elements (see pp.57, 144, 174, 218) in one delightful, succinct package. The bright red and greens of the Christmas holly give way to the rounded snowman, with its little wink of a carrot nose. The interplay between positive and negative space, along with flat, simple color palettes, are hallmarks of Bar's style, as seen in his published works, such as *Guess Who?: The Many Faces of Noma Bar* (2008) and the *Bittersweet* (2017) volumes. He has said that his work strives for the maximum amount of communication with a minimum number of elements. And, indeed, the simplicity of this merry illustration speaks volumes.

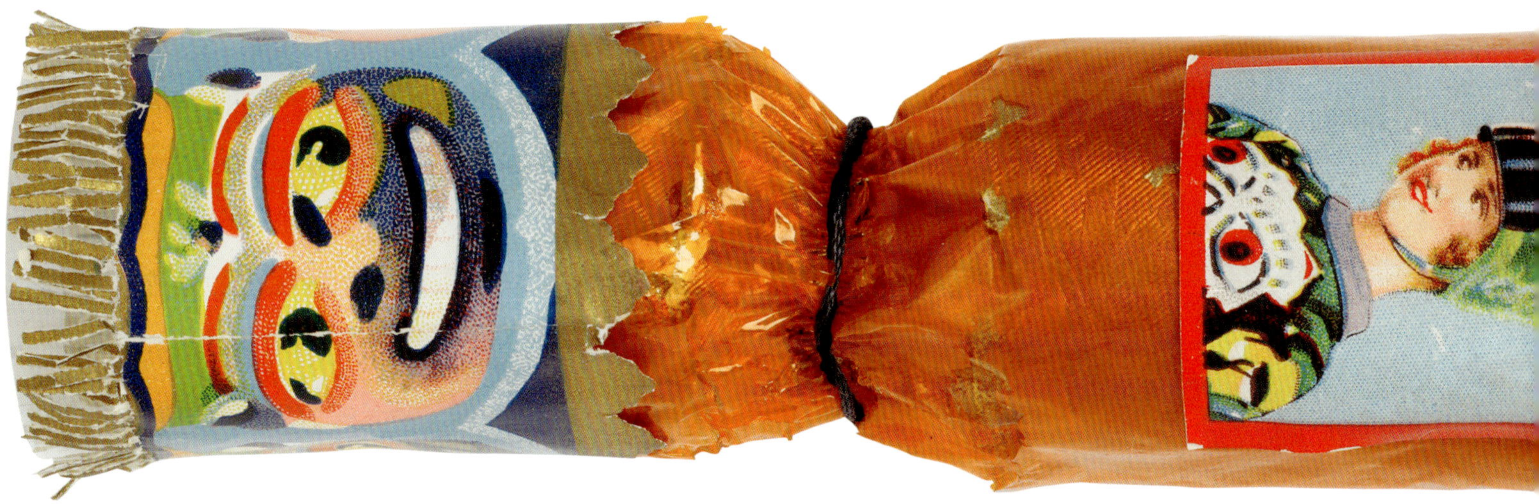

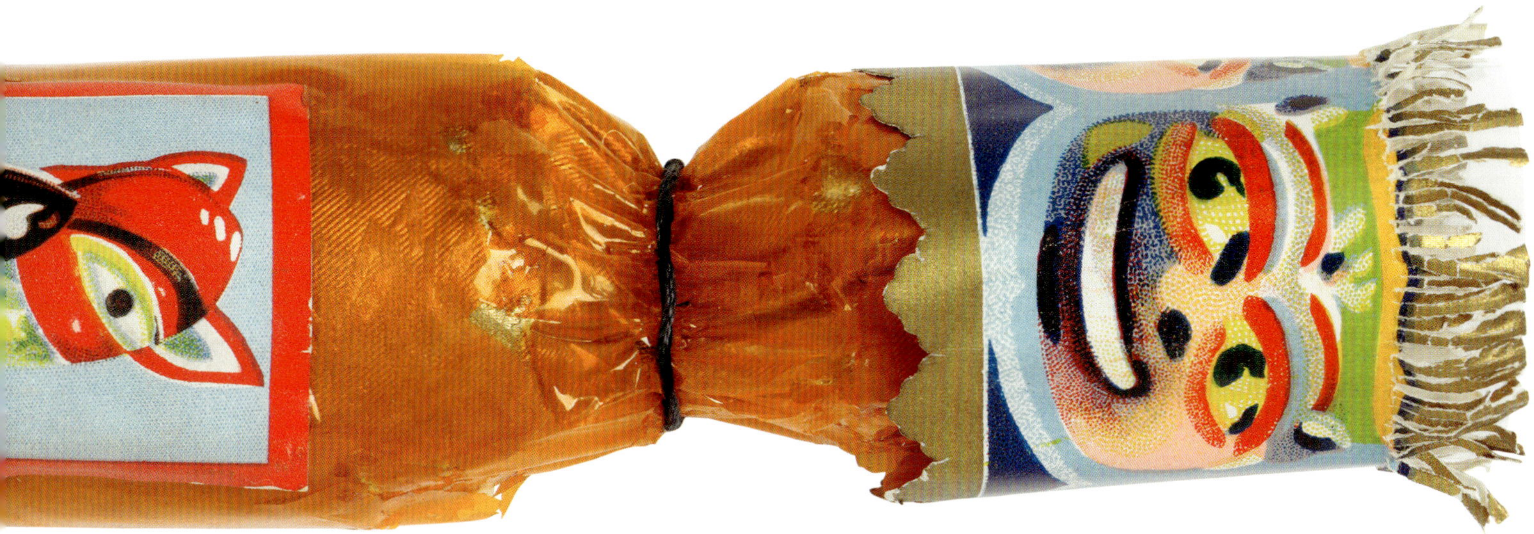

TOM SMITH

•

Cracker, 1927
Paper, foil, and cellophane, L. 9¾ in / 25 cm
Victoria & Albert Museum, London

This "totem cracker," with each end decorated as a smiling "native" idol, was created in 1927 by the self-declared kings of the Christmas cracker, Tom Smith & Company (see p.151). Founder Tom Smith (1823–69) had originally invented the cracker as a candy in twisted paper in 1847 to complement his confectionery business, and it had become a runaway success. In the 1860s, Smith added a small device that made the cracker bang when it was pulled. The popularity of this addition led to Smith's crackers being nicknamed *Cosaques,* a reference to the sound of a Cossack's horsewhip. The popularity of Smith's crackers continued to grow and, by the 1920s, they were advertised as "world renowned Christmas crackers. No party complete without them."

The totem crackers were created on the back of the popularity of musical *Rose-Marie*, which opened in March 1925 in London's Theatre Royal Drury Lane and ran for 851 performances, having earned rave reviews in New York in 1924. The scenery and costumes were so spectacular that Smith decided to create a set of crackers in homage. Set in the Canadian Rockies, it featured "totem pole" girls dancing in colorful costumes, as featured on the crackers. Each box of twelve crackers continued the theme, and each cracker contained paste jewelry, musical toys, a joke, or a wrapped chocolate resembling the cracker.

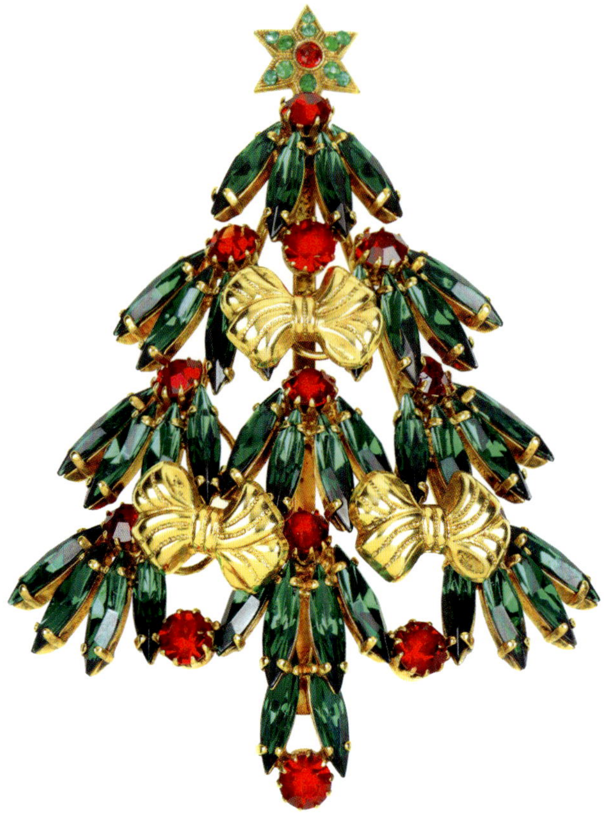

RUDOLF WEISS

•

Christmas Tree Brooch, c.1960
Tombac, gilt, colorless and colored cut Swarovski crystal glass stones, H. 3¾ in / 9.5 cm
Private collection

In the early twentieth century, especially in North America and Europe, women pinned sprigs of real holly or pine to their coats to show they were taken with the Christmas spirit. Later, during the lean years of World War II, this fashion evolved to include more ornate corsages of fresh greenery, ribbons, and ornaments the wearer had around the house. After the war ended and resources became more plentiful, these largely natural pieces of jewelry began to include synthetic holly and pine and more lavish decorations. Soon fine jewelers, such as Tiffany & Co. and Christian Dior, began manufacturing Christmas jewelry from precious metals and real gemstones for those who could afford it (see p.116). They were in the minority, because the United States was still recovering from the Great Depression and much of the world was trying to rebuild—literally and economically—after World War II. Numerous companies began making eye-catching, affordable Christmas costume jewelry for those who could not afford the offerings from fine jewelers. At first, this almost exclusively comprised Christmas tree brooches, such as the one shown here—a 1960s offering from Rudolf Weiss. But soon brooches depicting wreaths, Santa, candy canes, and other Christmas iconography came to the fore, followed soon after by earrings, necklaces, bracelets, and so on. Today, Christmas costume jewelry is available seasonally from retailers high and low and, because of the short window during which it can be worn, it has largely supplanted fine jewelry offerings.

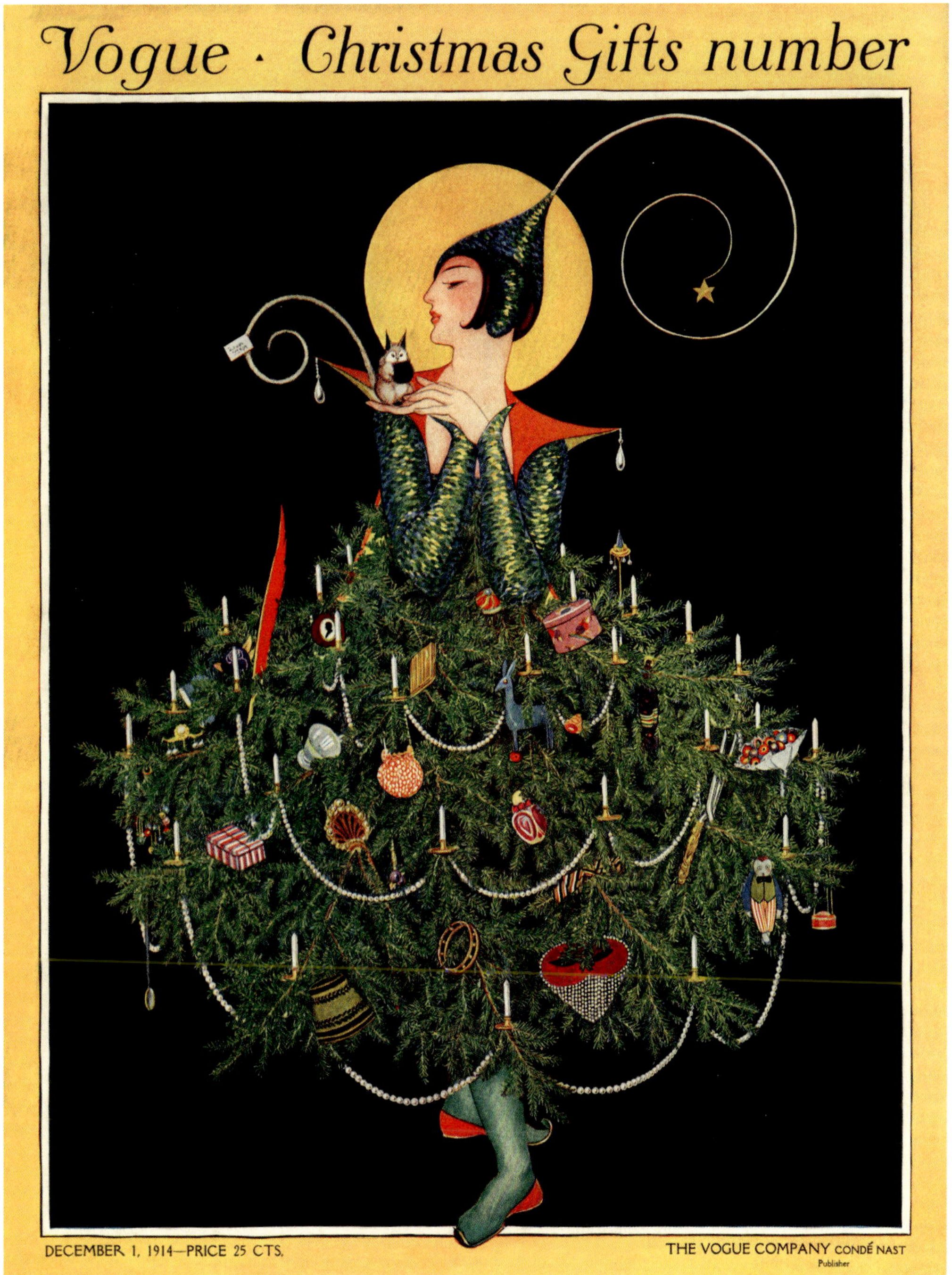

GEORGE WOLFE PLANK

•

Cover of *Vogue*, 1914
Hand-colored illustration, 10⅞ × 8 in / 28 × 2.3 cm
For Condé Nast

A century ago, *Vogue* was already established as a paragon of sophistication, trendsetting, and high style. This lavishly illustrated cover from December 1914 exemplifies the glamour of Art Deco style. It features a beautiful woman bedecked like a Christmas tree and holding a small rodent as if it were a piece of fine jewelry. A woman dressed as a Christmas tree could easily appear absurd or cartoonish, but this iteration comes off as extravagant fantasy. It exemplifies the aspirational aspects of Christmastime and the excitement of the shopping season, of which magazines have long been a primary driver. Indeed, this particular issue features pages upon pages of Christmas gift ideas for every woman—everyone from the “hostess” to the “amateur cook” to the “debutante.”

The illustration is likely the work of George Wolfe Plank (1883–1965), whose distinctive style was closely associated with the magazine at the time. *Vogue* began as a journal chronicling high society and transitioned to reportage on fashion, etiquette, arts, and culture after being acquired by Condé Montrose Nast in 1909. It was a highly influential title at a time when magazines were widely consumed by the masses and was known for its high-quality illustrative and editorial content. (Nast was adamant about hiring the best and brightest.) This cover suggests that the merriest Christmas would be one in which shiny baubles and ornaments might deck the halls—or better still, oneself.

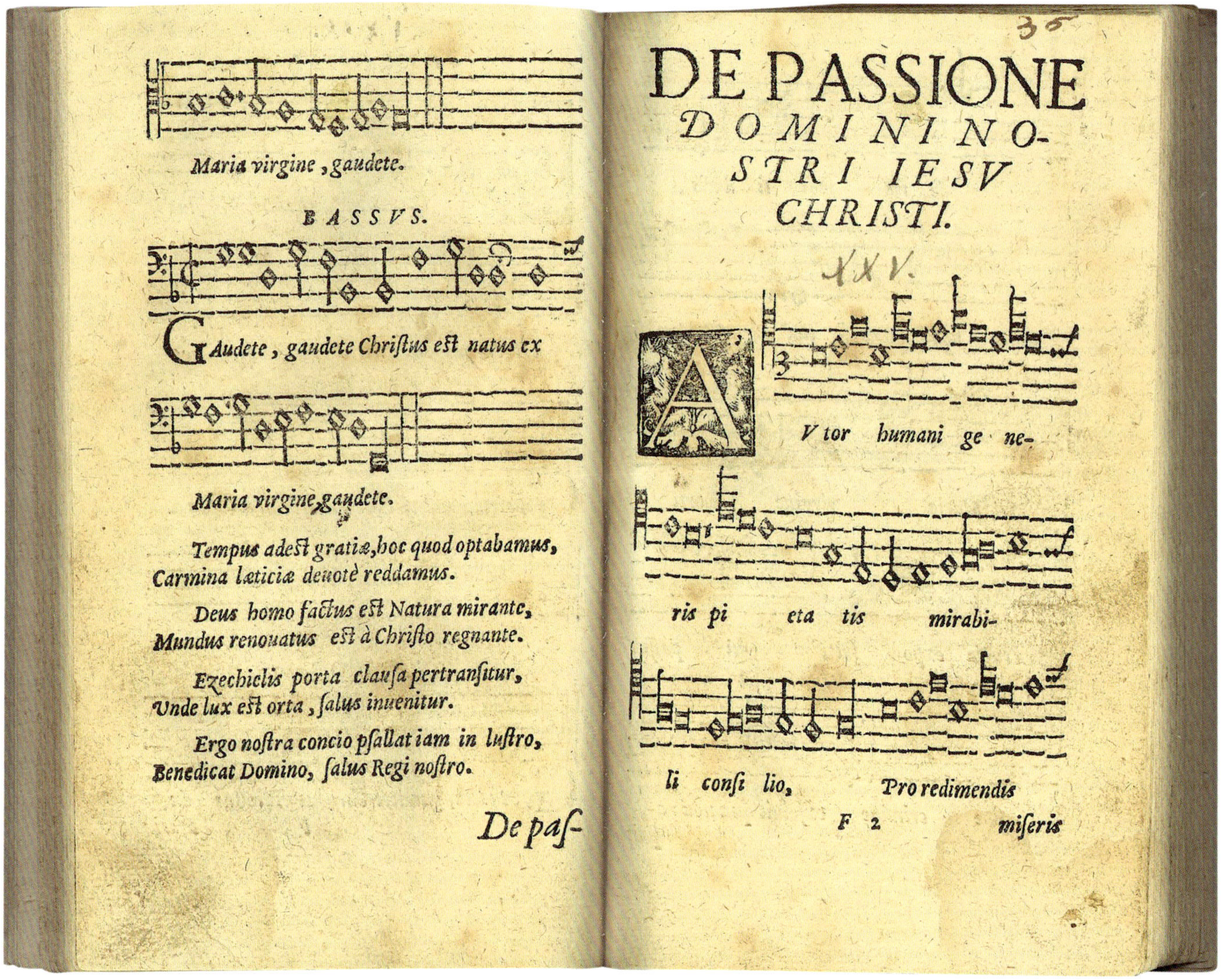

JAAKKO FINNO AND THEODORICUS PETRI

•

Piae Cantiones, 1582
Printed book, $7\frac{1}{8} \times 5\frac{1}{8}$ in / 18 × 13 cm
National Library of Finland, Helsinki

Gaudete, gaudete, Christus est natus ("Rejoice, rejoice, Christ is born") is one of the oldest Christmas carols, here preserved with its original music in the first edition of the *Piae Cantiones*, a collection of seventy-four medieval songs, both religious and secular, from Finland, Sweden, France, England, Germany, and Bohemia. The *Piae Cantiones* was compiled by Theodoricus Petri, a Finnish university student; Jaakko Finno, rector of the Turku Cathedral School, then edited the lyrics to accord with Lutheran orthodoxy before the collection was published. In the nineteenth century, a copy of the original 1582 edition was brought to England, where the Rev. John Neale translated twelve of the carols in his *Carols for Christmas-tide* (1853); later, the Rev. George Woodward would restore the songs to their original forms, prior to their editing by Jaakko Finno. Celebratory songs had long been sung by ancient Romans to mark the winter solstice, and Christmas-themed hymns are known from as early as the fourth century. Even when the Puritan Oliver Cromwell banned carols in Britain, they continued to be disseminated. They became particularly popular during the Victorian era in England (see p.193), and today they are ubiquitous at Christmas throughout the Western world to as far afield as the Philippines.

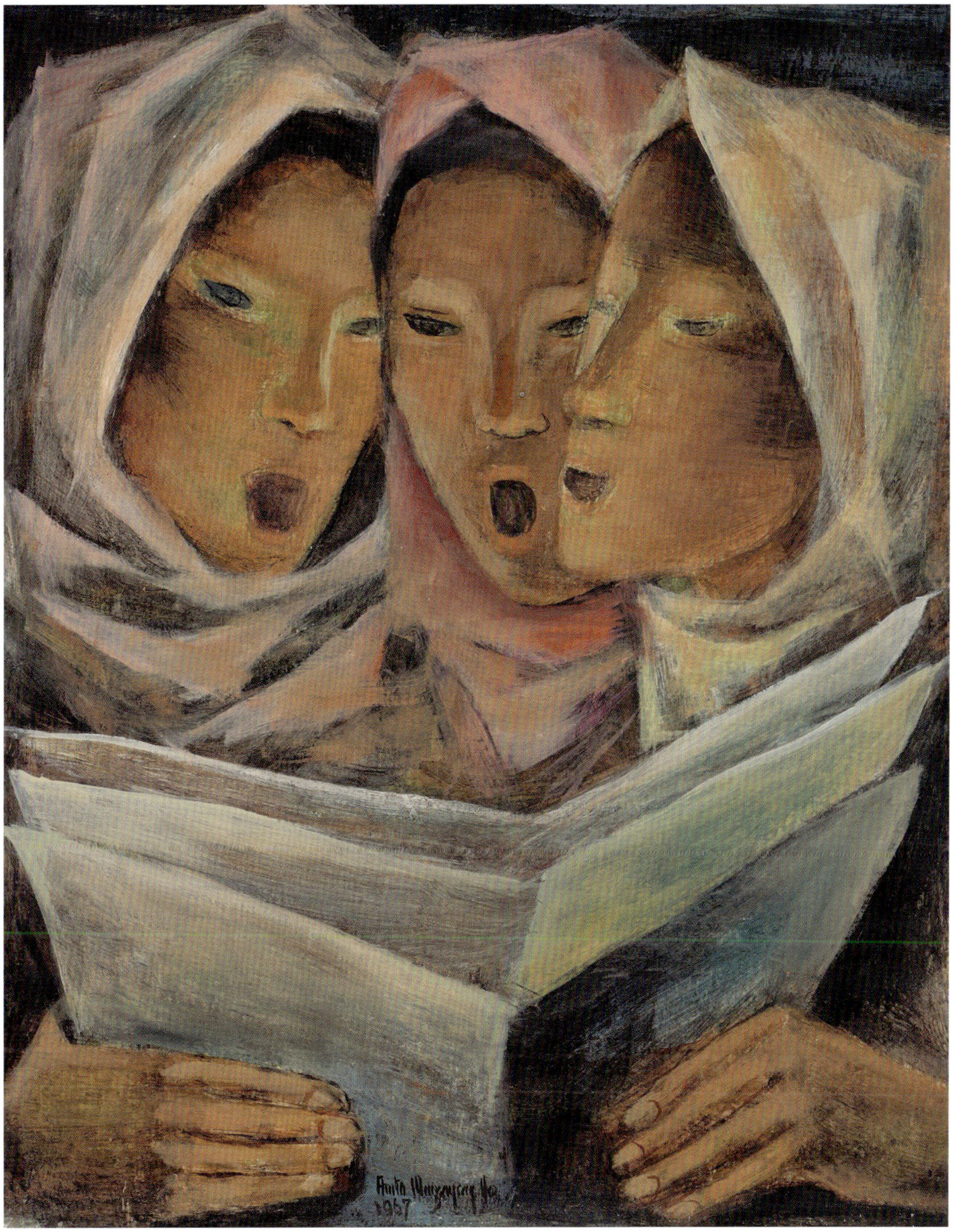

ANITA MAGSAYSAY-HO

•

Caroling, 1967
Oil on board, 13⅜ × 10⅝ in / 34 × 27 cm
Private collection

Three women huddled around a song sheet sing Christmas carols with gusto. Their overlapping faces, coupled with the composition's tight framing, emphasize their camaraderie, reflecting the warmth and communal strength of female relationships in Filipino society. Painted with bold and decisive brushstrokes, the stylized figures are typical of the hardy village women that Filipina artist Anita Magsaysay-Ho (1914–2012) loved to paint. Christmas is one of the biggest holidays in the Philippines, where the festive countdown begins as early as September 1. For a third of the year, decorations are hung in homes and carols are heard on the streets during the world's longest Christmas season. The popular tradition of caroling among Filipinos stems from the years of Spanish colonial rule between 1521 and 1898, which introduced Catholicism to the country. It is especially popular with children, who travel house-to-house performing with improvised instruments, such as tambourines made from bottle tops, hoping to be rewarded with coins for their efforts. Magsaysay-Ho was a pioneering artist and is regarded as one of the most significant painters in modern Filipino art. Embracing Western aesthetics from the 1950s, she painted in studios all around the world as she moved from city to city with her shipping-magnate husband. Her lively canvases, inspired by her childhood memories, depict Filipina women engaged in everyday tasks, such as harvesting fruit, catching fish, or meeting in the marketplace.

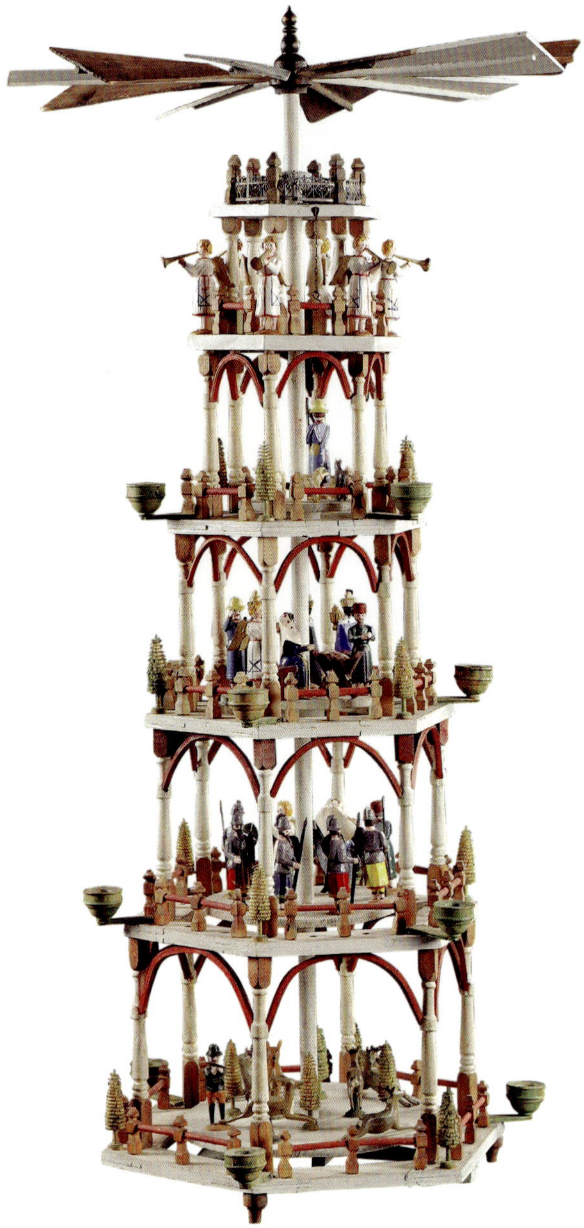

RUDOLF FLEMMING

•

Globenstein Christmas Pyramid, c.1910
Wood, metal, papier mâché, and paper,
41⅜ × 23⅝ × 23⅝ in / 105 × 60 × 60 cm
Staatliche Museen zu Berlin

The German Christmas pyramid (*Weihnachtspyramide*) is a traditional folk art form with origins dating back to sixteenth-century Saxony. The example pictured is named after Globenstein, the area in which it was produced, in the Saxon Ore Mountains in Germany. It was designed by Rudolf Flemming (1874–1962) in the early twentieth century and was offered in an assortment of varying sizes and with various decorative motifs. It has four rotating levels featuring different religious scenes (from top): shepherds watching their flock, a traditional Nativity scene, the flight to Egypt, and a hunt. There are turned and carved wooden figures as well as figures made of paper, all hand-painted, representing angels and trees typical of the mountains in the area. Most Christmas pyramids perform the same trick. The wooden structures are intricately carved and assembled to create a conical shape, usually in multiple levels. Candles are lit and placed in the holders on each level, and the platforms spin as heat rises from candles burning beneath, hitting the impeller, like the less intricate angel chimes that were so popular in northern Europe around the same time (see p.47). Some believe that these pyramids inspired the idea of the Christmas tree (see p.130)—Germany's most famous contribution to Christmas traditions. And, in turn, once trees became popular holiday decorations, these pyramids were subsequently marketed as low-cost substitutes for the German tannenbaum.

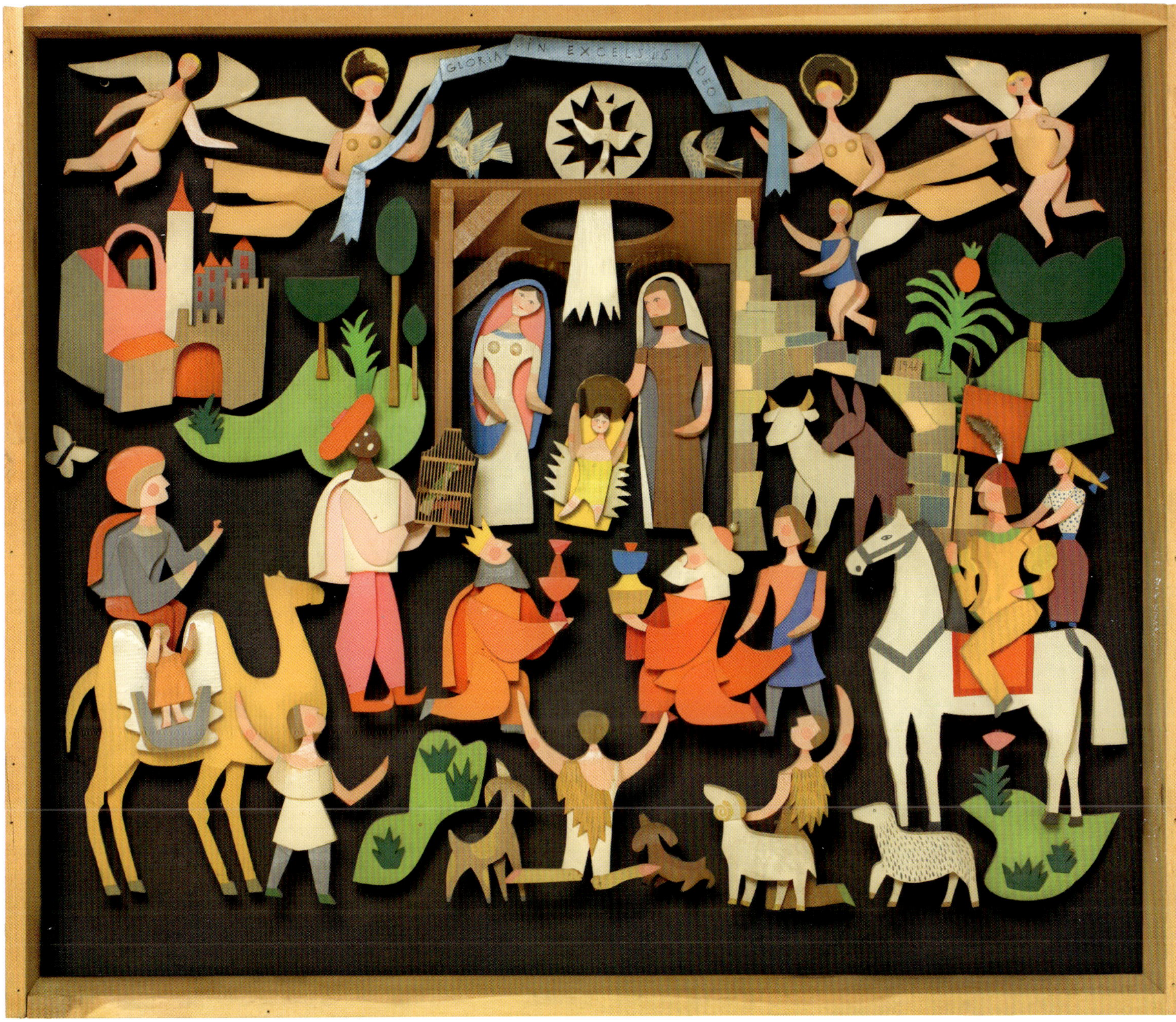

ALEXANDER GIRARD

•

The Nativity, c.1962
Painted wood, dimensions unknown
Vitra Design Museum, Weil am Rhein, Germany

This colorful Nativity-scene relief once occupied a prominent position in the Santa Fe, New Mexico, home of Italian-born, American-based designer Alexander Girard (1907–1993), reflecting the importance the Nativity occupied in his imagination. His almost childlike three-dimensional imaging of the scene is alive with a sense of joy and wonder. To the traditional figures, he added angels of differing sizes, men on horseback, and dogs, including a dachshund. This set was conceived for an exhibition of the same name that opened in 1962 at the Nelson Gallery of Art, Kansas City, which Girard curated. Over a lengthy career, the architect-trained polymath returned to the Nativity scene again and again, imagining the scene of Jesus's birth using different media, compositions, and scales in an attempt to understand the universality of the story of the birth of Christ. A childhood in Florence, Italy, had imbued Girard with a lifelong love of Christmas and its rituals—a time to celebrate family and friends. Over a long, distinguished design career that included working for the renowned Herman Miller Company, Girard became one of the world's leading collectors of folk art, amassing a vast collection of Nativities. This relief owes much to the folk aesthetic and its significance cannot be underestimated. Girard spent his final years curating his collection of Nativities, many of which are on display in the wing named for him at Santa Fe's Museum of International Folk Art.

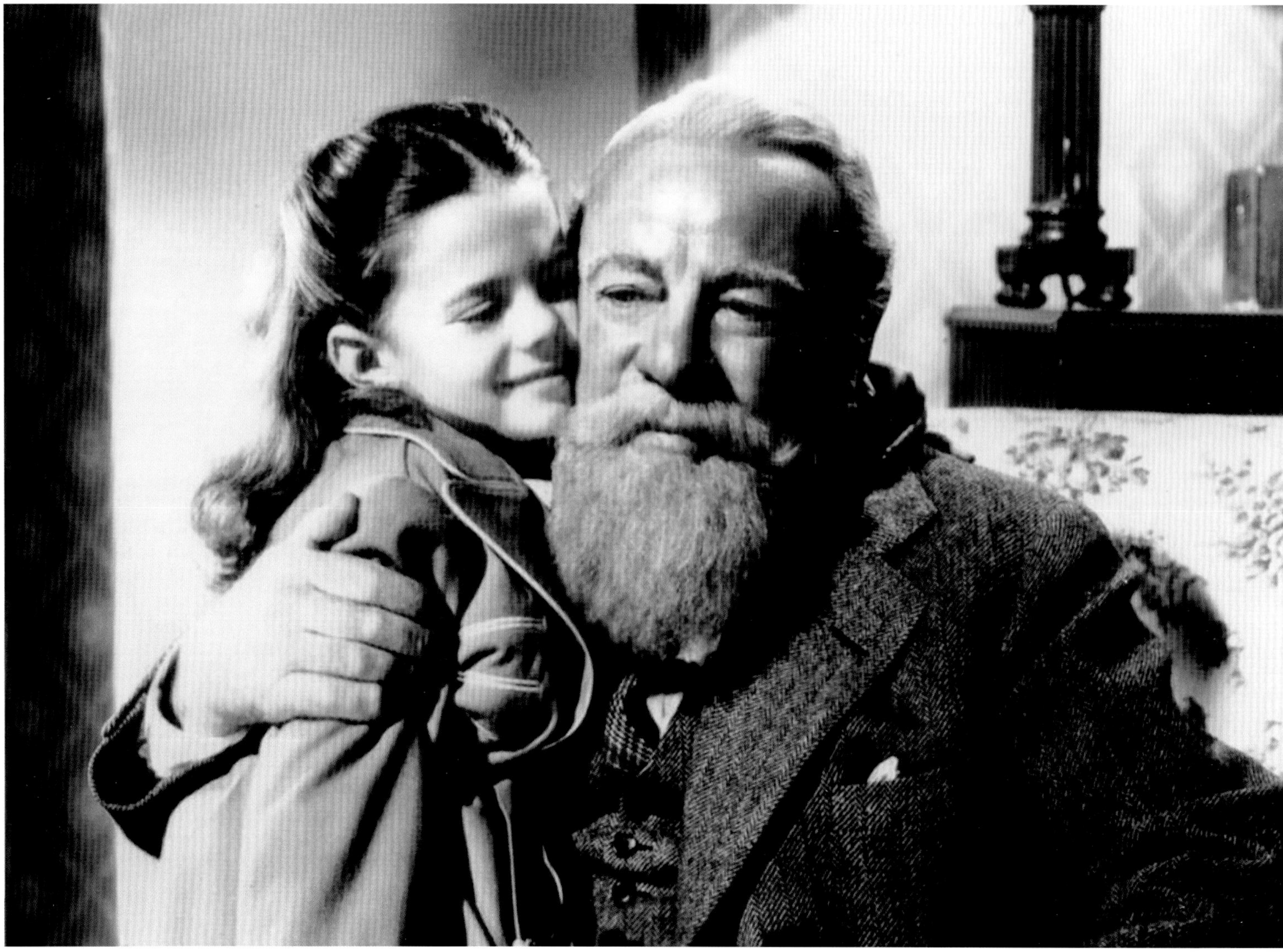

GEORGE SEATON

•

Still from *Miracle on 34th Street*, 1947
Film, dimensions variable
20th Century Fox

Released in 1947, only two years after the end of World War II, *Miracle on 34th Street* offered much-needed positivity and hope, championing the idea that the world—and people—were still good. It tells the story of a Macy's department store Santa (Edmund Gwenn) whose name is Kris Kringle and who claims to be the real Santa Claus. Divorcée Doris Walker (Maureen O'Hara), who hired Kringle at Macy's, is raising her young daughter, Susan (Natalie Wood), to be practical and not to believe in fairy tales. At Macy's, Kringle repeatedly sends customers to other stores for out-of-stock gifts instead of pushing his employer's overstocked items, making customers happy but angering store bosses. Believed to be delusional, Kringle is eventually committed to Bellevue mental hospital, and a court case ensues to determine whether his claims of being Santa are real or not. Ultimately both Doris and Susan learn to open their hearts and minds to the intangible, unexplainable magic the world sometimes delivers. The film was shot on location in New York, with scenes set during Macy's famous Thanksgiving Day Parade (see p. 203) filmed live, with great difficulty. A 1994 remake was set in the fictional Cole's shopping mall, after Macy's refused to lend its name to the movie. This movie about the true meaning of Christmas won three Academy Awards and still resonates as strongly today as it did eighty-five years ago.

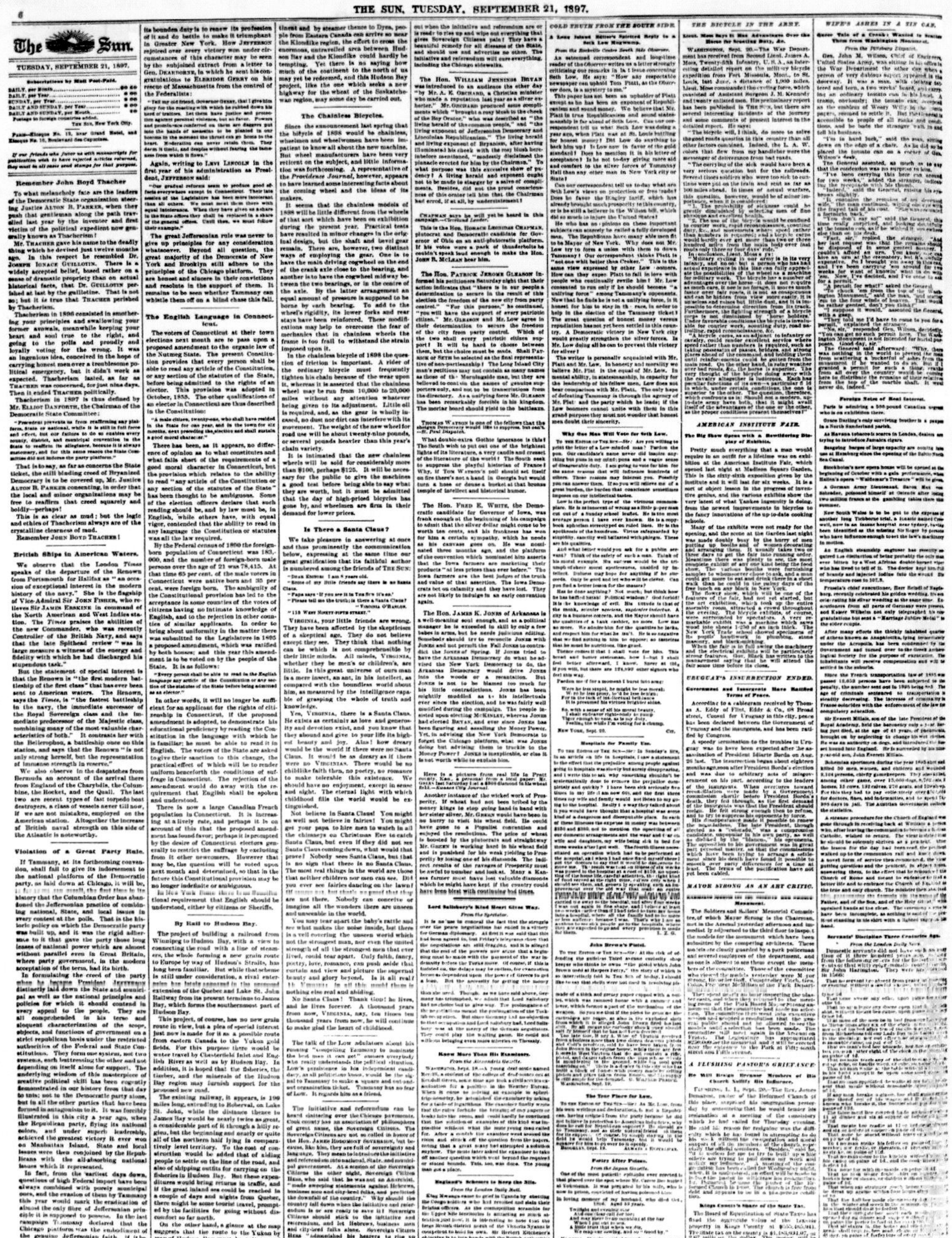
THE SUN, TUESDAY, SEPTEMBER 21, 1897.

FRANCIS P. CHURCH

•

Is There a Santa Claus?, 1897
Newspaper print, dimensions variable
Published in *The Sun*, New York

“Does Santa Claus really exist?” must be among the most inevitable and most dreaded questions any parent can face. The all-too-brief period when young children everywhere truly believe in Santa and his reindeer leads inexorably to that moment when, perhaps at the age of eight or nine, doubt creeps in and the existence of the chubby, red-suited man comes into question. An avalanche of queries follows as children begin to ponder the nature of Santa, his sleigh, the reindeer, and the plausibility of presents being delivered in the absence of a chimney. None of this is new: in 1897, eight-year-old Virginia O’Hanlon wrote to New York’s *The Sun* newspaper asking whether Santa Claus existed, because some of her friends had told her he did not. The reply, penned by newsman and former Civil War correspondent Francis Pharcellus Church (1839–1906), has since become the most reprinted newspaper editorial of all time. Church tells Virginia definitively that Santa Claus exists, because the most important things in life are precisely the things that cannot be seen, including among other examples love, faith, and charity. Church argues “Nobody can conceive or imagine all the wonders there are unseen and unseeable in the world.” His editorial, stressing the importance of faith as it does, has since become part of the fabric of the American way of life and the American idea of Christmas. It has been reprinted in the form of a children’s book and has served as the basis for musicals, television shows, and cartoons.

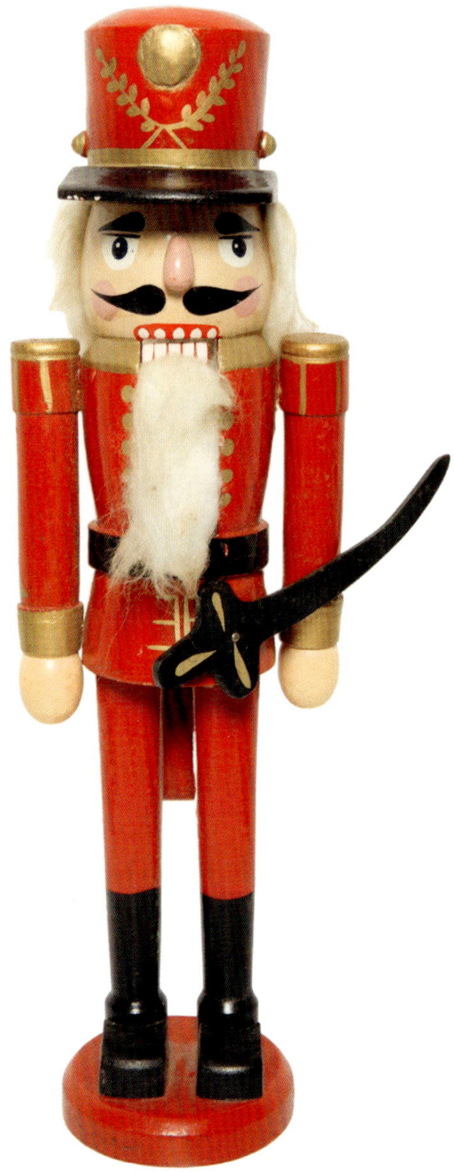

ERZGEBIRGE REGION

•

Christmas Big Red Nutcracker, 1970
Hand-painted wood,
14⅝ × 6⅜ × 3⅞ in / 37 × 16 × 10 cm
Private collection

Standing to attention, this hand-painted, bright red wooden German toy soldier, complete with sheathed knife, is actually a nutcracker, used to open the unshelled nuts that have long been a Christmas favorite in Germany. A nut is placed between the teeth of the soldier, and by operating a lever at his back, pressure is applied to the mouth, cracking the nut. According to German folklore, nutcrackers bring good luck, scare away bad spirits, and protect homes. The most popular themes for decorative Christmas nutcrackers are toy soldiers in a wide variety of designs. They date back to the fifteenth century, when craftspeople began to carve small figures from local wood, and have become more sophisticated over time, with some being made up of as many as sixty separate pieces. Since the seventeenth century, the most celebrated nutcrackers have come from the Erzgebirge region in the east of Germany, where they are intricately carved and hand-painted, with moving arms, accessories, and trimmings of real fur. As demand grew for nutcrackers, German woodworker Friedrich Wilhelm Füchtner (1844–1923) started the first mass commercial production in 1872 from his workshop in Seiffen, Erzgebirge. Originally given as gifts at any time of year, over time the nutcracker has become particularly associated with Christmas, thanks in part to the popularity of the 1892 ballet *The Nutcracker,* by the Russian composer Pyotr Tchaikovsky (1840–1893), which features dancing toy soldiers.

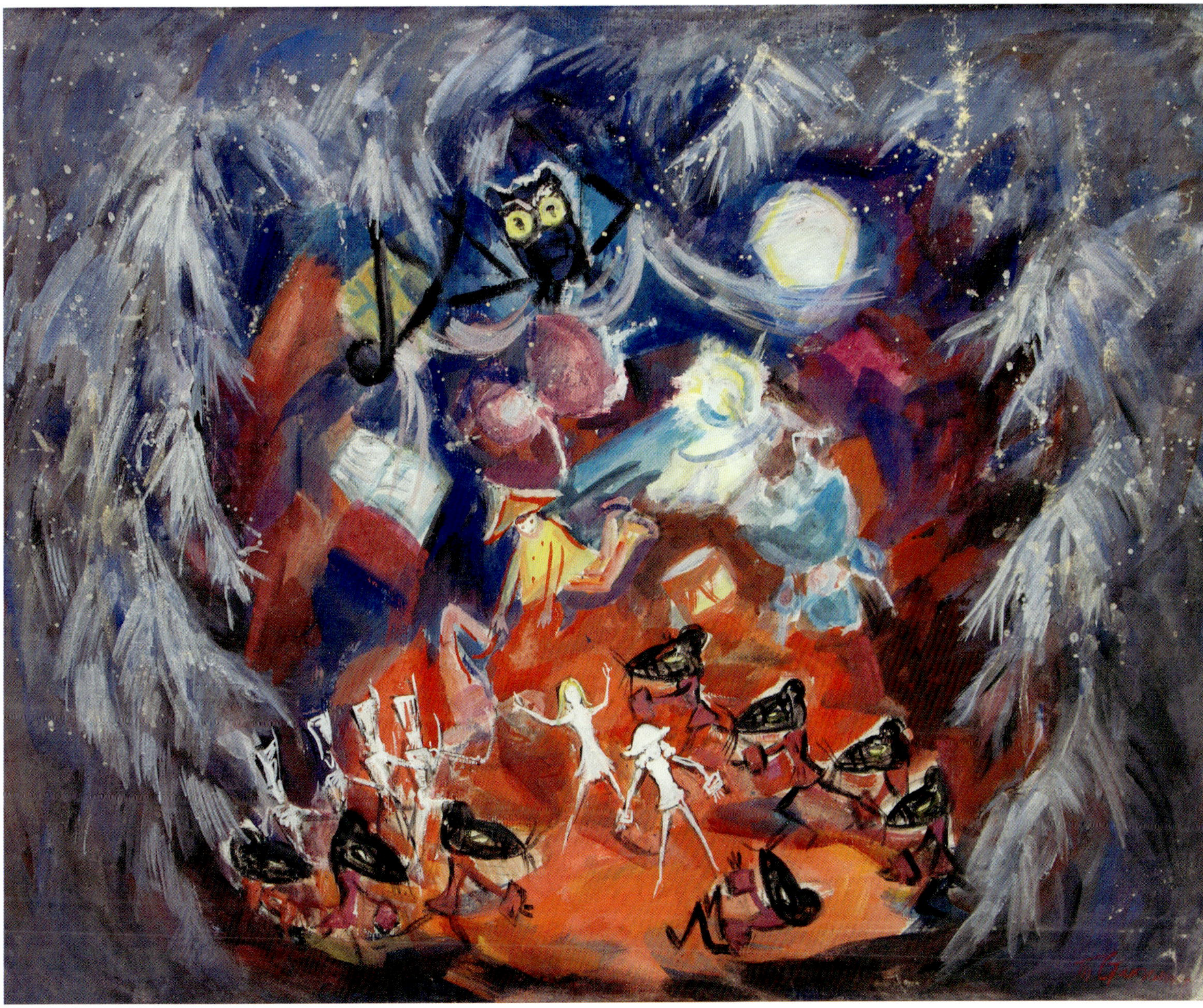

TAMARA GEORGIEVNA STARZHENETSKAYA

•

Stage design for the ballet
The Nutcracker, by Pyotr Tchaikovsky, 1978
Tempera on paper, 17⅝ × 14¼ in / 45 × 36 cm
Tchaikovsky Museum, Votkinsk, Russia

Fresh off the success of his ballet *The Sleeping Beauty*, which premiered in 1890, Russian composer Pyotr Tchaikovsky was looking for another hit. He sought it in Alexandre Dumas's 1844 adaptation of the earlier E. T. A. Hoffmann story *The Nutcracker and the Mouse King*, which shared much of the same fairy-tale DNA of his previous ballet. The whimsical tale, set on Christmas Eve, about a girl who receives the gift of a toy nutcracker that looks like a soldier, only to be transported in dreams to a magical fantasy world where her toy does battle with an army led by the evil Mouse King, seemed the perfect showcase for a spirited series of dances. Seen here is the stage design for a 1978 adaptation of the ballet by Soviet painter and production designer Tamara Georgievna Starzhenetskaya (1912–2002), showing the hectic, climactic battle with the Mouse King. The nutcracker soldiers, dressed in white, fend off the red-clad mouse army, all surrounded by the glittering branches of a Christmas tree. Tchaikovsky's original 1892 production was a flop, yet the ballet would long outlive its initial reviews, becoming a perennial Christmastime favorite—particularly after George Balanchine's staging of the New York City Ballet in 1954. Tchaikovsky also introduced a new instrument, the celesta, to audiences; it is the indelible harplike "voice" of the Sugar Plum Fairy.

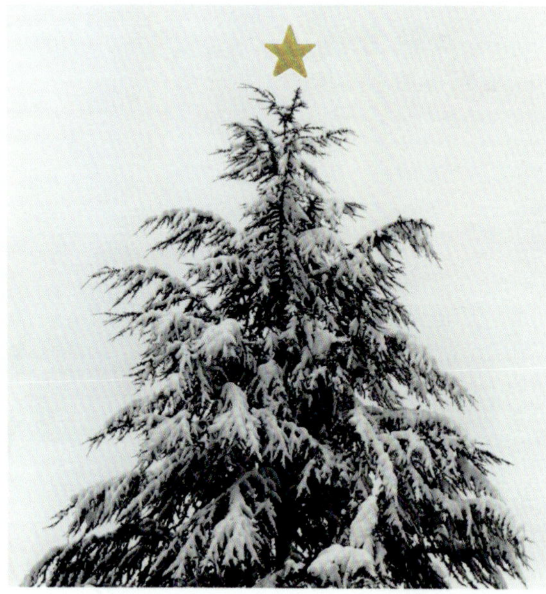

ROBERT MAPPLETHORPE

•

Christmas Tree, 1987
Gelatin silver print with die-cut gold star,
9⅞ × 7⅞ in / 25.1 × 20 cm

This quiet, black-and-white photograph of an undecorated snowy Christmas tree was taken by Robert Mapplethorpe (1946–1989) not long after he had been diagnosed with HIV, a disease which brought about his premature death at the age of forty-two. Mapplethorpe captured *Christmas Tree* in 1987 at the height of his fame and during the AIDS crisis. In the final years of his life, Mapplethorpe's work reflected a new existentialist outlook on life, and his portfolio shifted toward contemplations on beauty and mortality. He often chose subject matters that recalled the tradition of *memento mori*—symbols evoking the inevitability of death. References to religious iconography also feature prominently. In this work, a single gold star is hovering above the tree, unattached to the branches beneath. This motif became a recurring one in his work, with the symbol of the star representing a celestial force that alludes to his celebrity and the possibility of the afterlife. Born into a large, conservative Catholic family, Mapplethorpe would break free from his religious upbringing to become one of the most iconoclastic artists and LGBTQ+ figures of his era. Known for his elegantly composed, black-and-white nudes, portraits, self-portraits, and still-lifes, his photography was often provocative and challenged contemporary audiences.

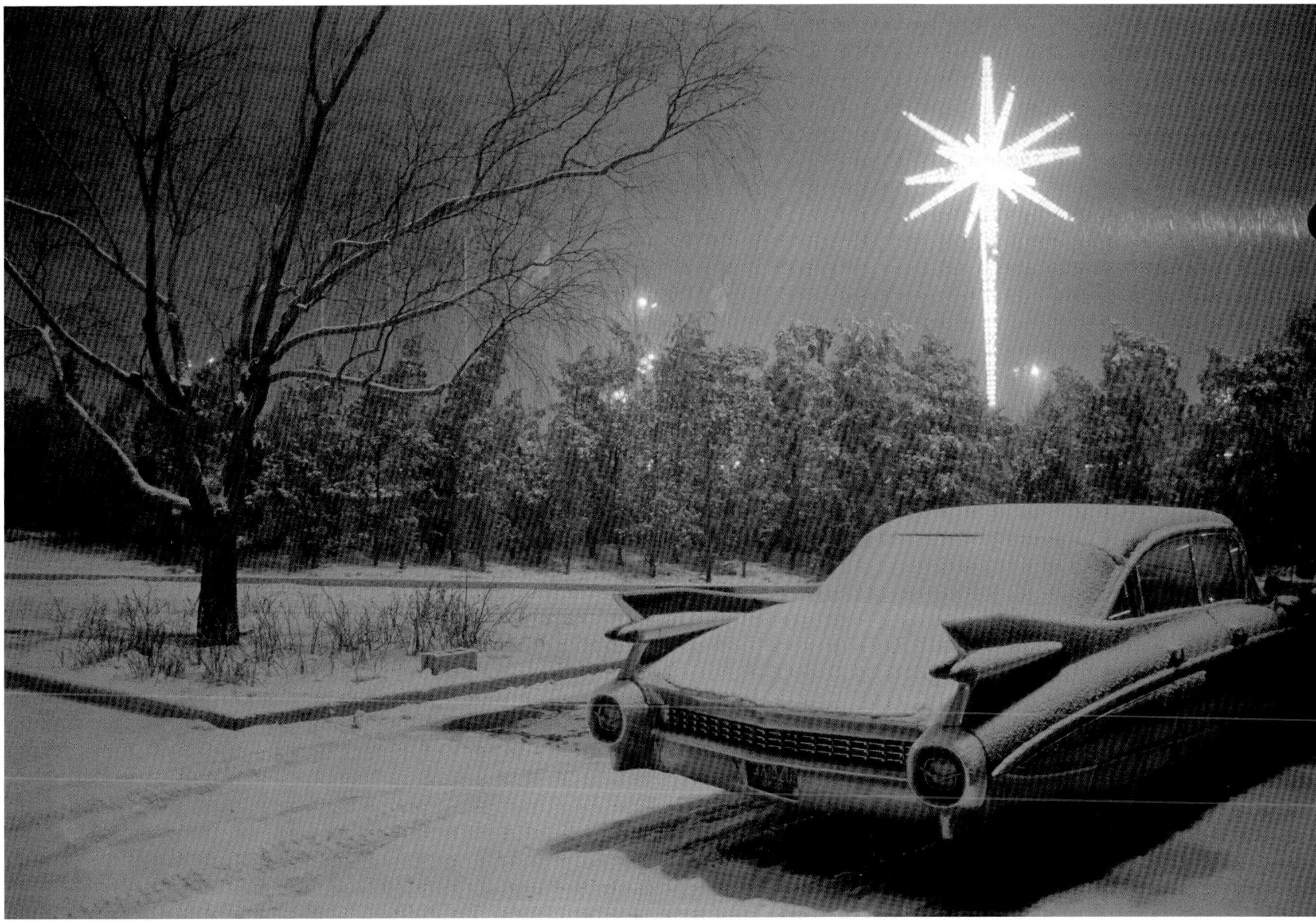

JOEL MEYEROWITZ

•

JFK Airport, New York City, 1968
Gelatin silver print, 8¾ × 13⅜ in / 22.2 × 34 cm

Airports and Christmas are closely linked, whether leaving from one to visit family and friends or picking up weary travelers as they descend upon us for the holidays. And while airports at Christmas are chaos, this gorgeous image, *JFK Airport, New York City, 1968*, by Joel Meyerowitz (1938–) offers a serenity and calm that is contrary to all of that. Meyerowitz stumbled upon this scene at a virtually deserted parking lot at Kennedy Airport, snow lightly dusting the ground and car, a huge, illuminated star decoration dominating the landscape in the distance. There is some irony to this image being black and white, because Meyerowitz is one of the photographers most associated with the transition from black and white photography to the vibrant world of color, as he felt that color photography could provide more narrative detail. In 1962, when he was an art director for a New York advertisement agency, he was assigned to work with noted documentary photographer and filmmaker Robert Frank (1924–2019). He soon quit his job and simply became a photographer. He refers to his specific style of street photography as "field photographs," and he strives for them to convey to the viewer the exact experience of being in a specific place at a precise moment in time. And this image does that: you can practically feel the cold in the air, accompanied by the smell of snow and a stillness that seems truly surreal for a busy airport at Christmastime.

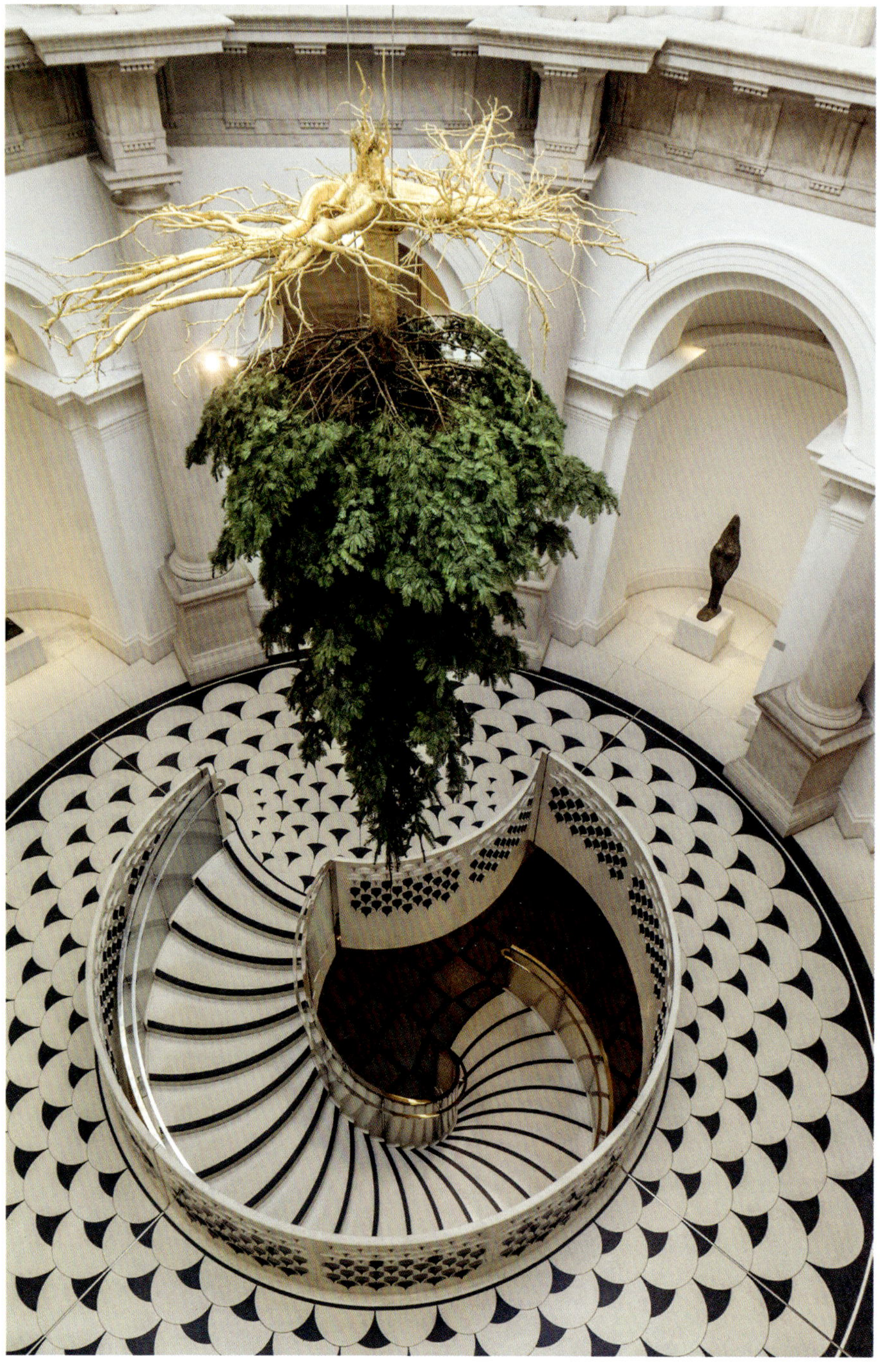

SHIRAZEH HOUSHIARY

•

Tate Britain Christmas tree, 2016
Tree and gold leaf, dimensions unknown

This Christmas tree, suspended upside down from the ceiling of the Rotunda in London's Tate Britain gallery, was first created in 1993 by Iranian-born artist and sculptor Shirazeh Houshiary (1955–). Since 1988, the Tate has commissioned a leading contemporary artist to create a seasonal installation each Christmas. Houshiary decided to move away from traditional ideas of decorating the annual tree, choosing instead to focus on the qualities of the tree itself: its texture, smell, shape, and color. Turning the tree upside down, she covered the roots in gold leaf, not only drawing attention to the intricacy and inherent beauty of a part of the tree that is usually hidden, but also paying homage to their essential role in nourishing the tree.

The gold leaf also serves to draw attention away from the tree's branches—which are devoid of the usual lights (see p.159)—to focus the viewer instead on its life force. The liminal spaces between shadow and light have long been a preoccupation of the London-based artist, who reimagined her tree for a second time in 2016. Hung in Tate Britain's new entrance above a spiral staircase, it greeted visitors when the gallery reopened following a three-year renovation. Houshiary's Christmas tree is in good company: Cornelia Parker (1956–) and Tracey Emin (1963–) are just two of the other contemporary artists to have worked on the Tate's festive commission.

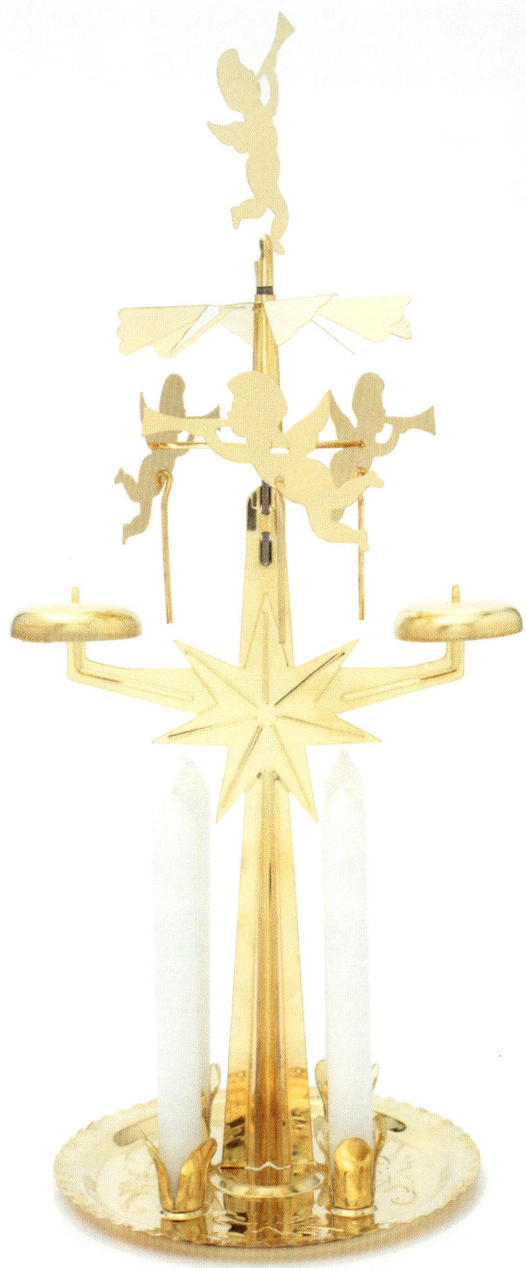

JINGLE ABRA

•

Angel Chimes, c.20th century
Nickel-plated steel, 11¾ × 4⅝ in / 30 × 12 cm

Candle chimes are a relatively low-tech way of combining light, sound, and motion in Christmas decorations. When the candles that sit on the engraved mount are lit, they create an updraft of warm air that causes the cherublike angel pieces to spin. As they move around the structure, the dangling rods strike the curved bell chimes below, creating a tinkling sound. This style of chimes came on the scene around the turn of the twentieth century and was largely manufactured in Germany, generally using embossed, lithographed tin. The impact of post–World War II resource scarcity and economic sanctions against Germany caused fewer of these objects to be made by the country and distributed outside of Europe. Makers in northern Europe, in places such as Sweden, rose to the occasion and began manufacturing these candle chimes in order to meet the export demand but instead used brass. This more modern "Jingle Abra," manufactured in Sweden in the latter half of the twentieth century, is made from nickel-plated steel. These chimes have mostly fallen out of fashion but were once extremely popular. Although most of these objects were created as stand-alone decorations, some were made to decorate trees when real candles were still the most affordable way to light them (see p.22).

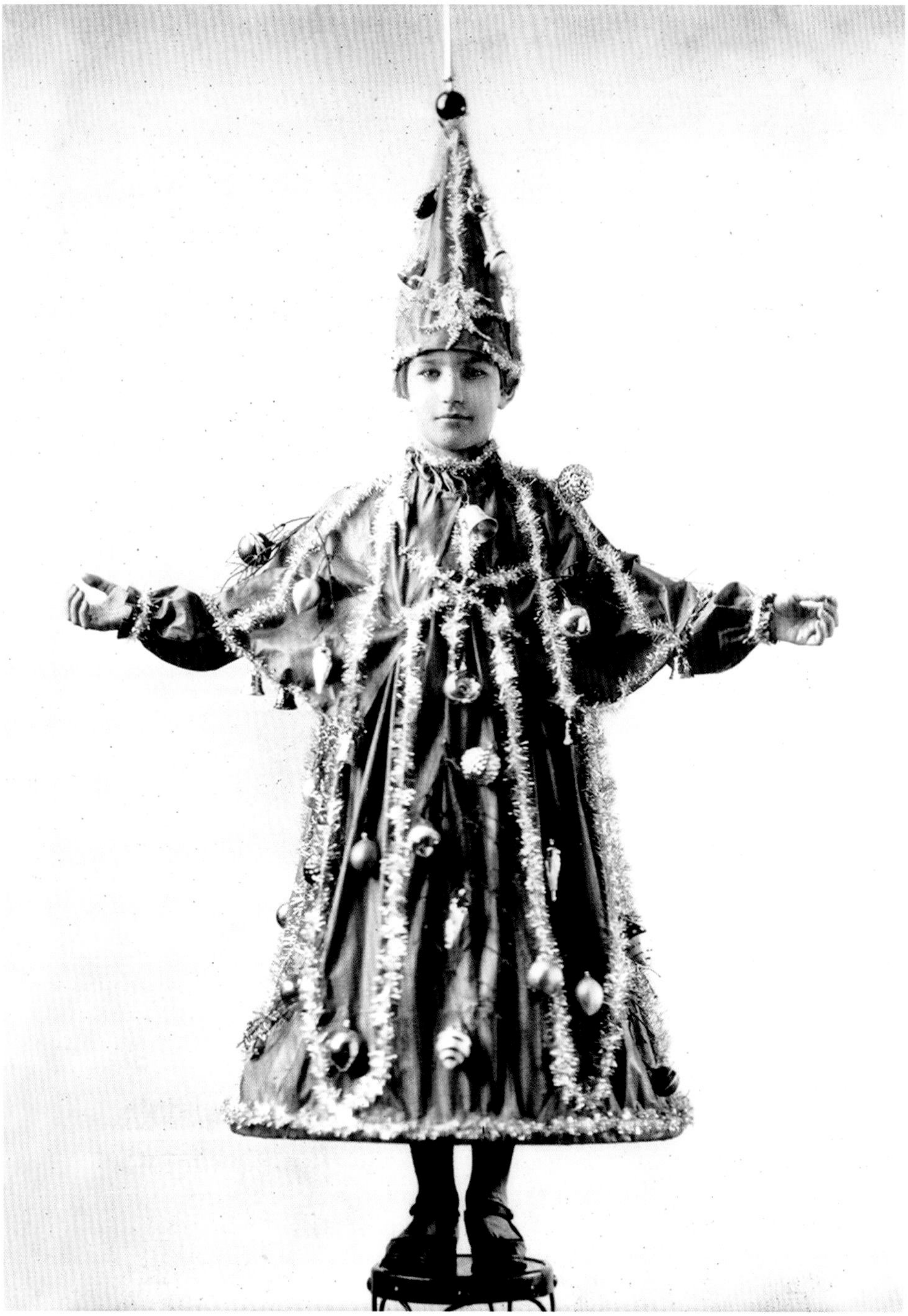

ANGUS B. MCVICAR

•

Girl Dressed as a Christmas Tree, 1927
Gelatin silver print, dimensions variable
Wisconsin Historical Society, Madison

A young girl stands on a stool, her dress adorned with ornaments, tinsel, and the odd twig to make her appear as if she is a living Christmas tree. The wire bottom of the dress helps give the outfit the traditional flat-bottom tree shape, as does the pointed hat with long topper. Taken in 1927, this photograph is in black and white, but one can imagine how striking and effective this costume would be in full color. This scene was captured by Angus B. McVicar, a trained commercial photographer who is noted as the first to use a flash for ancillary lighting in the Madison area. He started his own commercial photography business, McVicar Photo Service, in 1926 and worked for clients, including newspapers, car dealerships, insurance companies, the University of Wisconsin–Madison, sororities and fraternities, and a host of other local businesses. The removal of this photo from its original context leaves it to one's imagination as to why this girl was dressed as a Christmas tree. At the time this was taken, it was, as it is now, not uncommon for children to dress up around Christmastime as part of school and church holiday productions, and that is most likely what is going on here.

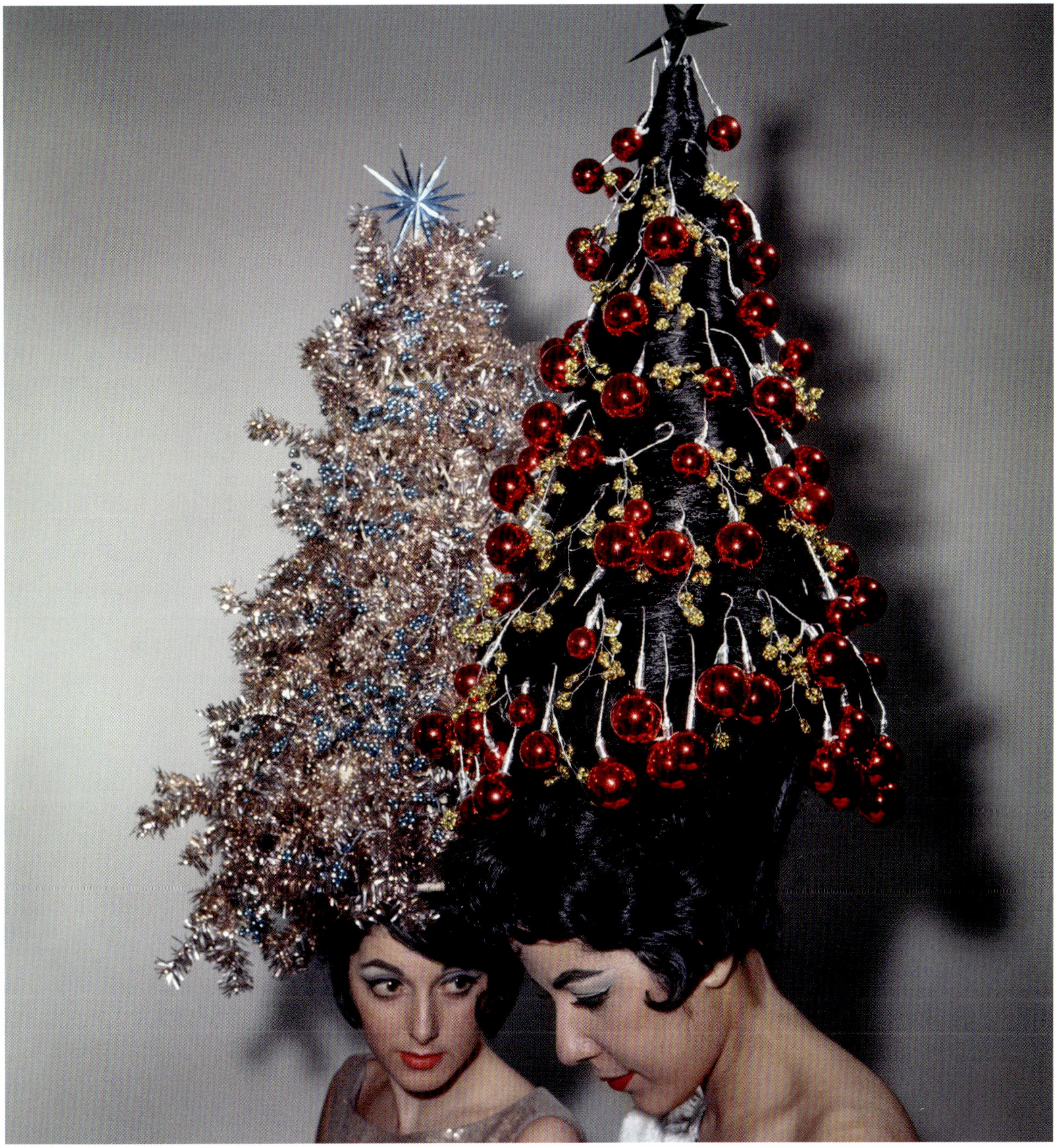

UNKNOWN

•

Women Modeling Festive Christmas Hairdos, c.1961
Photograph, dimensions variable

In this photograph by an unknown artist, two dark-haired young women support decorated Christmas trees on their heads in a perfect display of kitsch post-war fashion. The image features the models Claudette Ackrich and Gisella Roc, both sporting matching and quintessentially 1960s makeup: pale blue eye shadow, thick black eyeliner, and rouged lips. While Ackrich's tree is lined with glittering gold and silver tinsel, Roc's hairpiece is adorned with metallic red and gold ornaments (see p.52). A festive and experimental approach to hairstyling, each woman's real hair has been wound tightly around a florist's conical topiary tree, allowing their dark locks to stand at fourty-two inches (107 cm). The phenomenon of the Christmas tree hairstyle, or "holiday hair," developed in the 1950s, coinciding with the rise of the beehive and bouffant. This photograph, while capturing the joyous and playful spirit of Christmas, also speaks to the conflation of the women's beauty industry with consumer culture. In this instance, the women have become living Christmas ornaments. Nevertheless, the gimmick of holiday hair continues to inspire celebrities in contemporary culture who have appropriated the trend, exampled by Lady Gaga, who sported a tree on her head in 2013, and by Katy Perry in her 2019 music video for her festive single "Cozy Little Christmas."

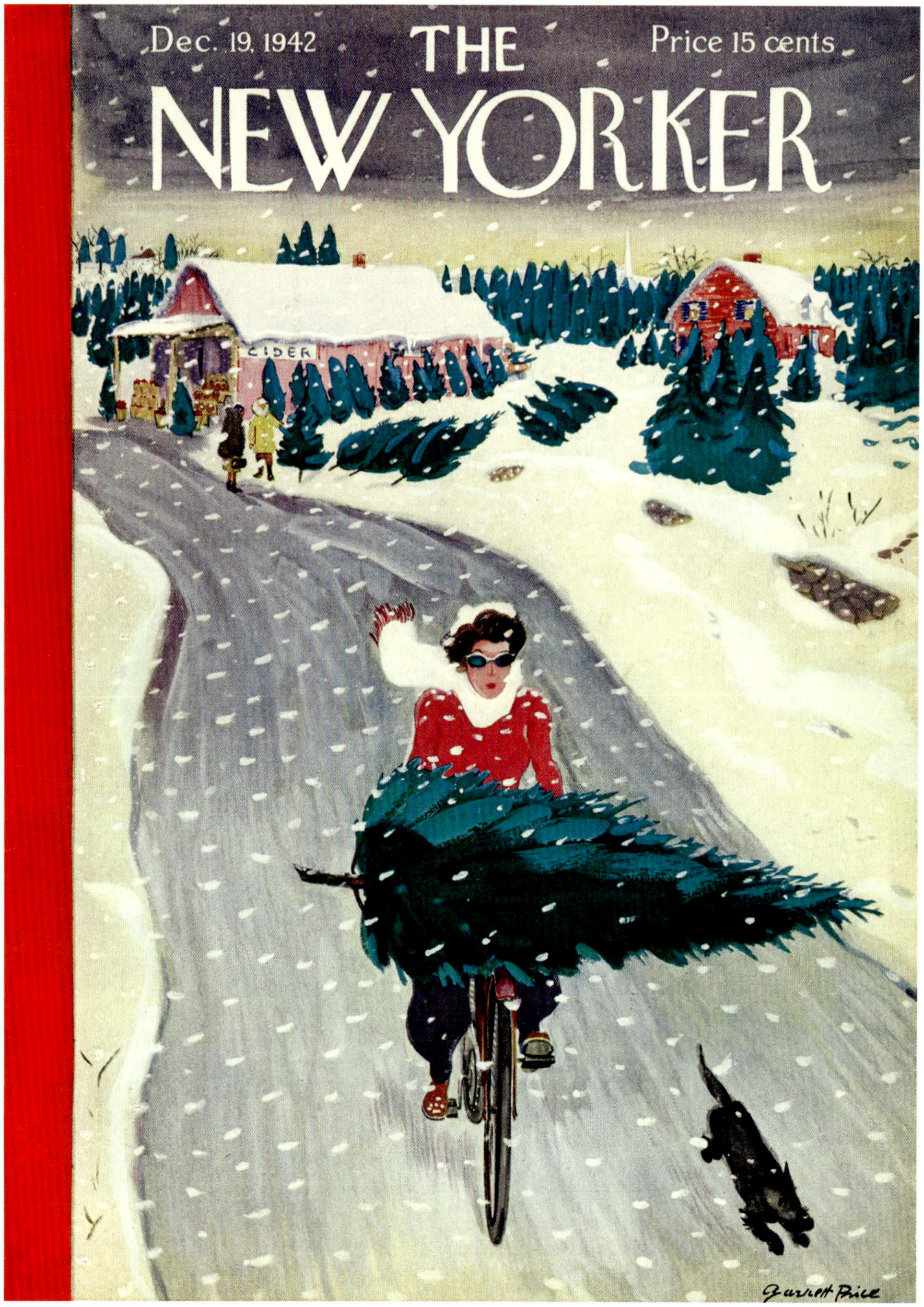

GARRETT PRICE

•

Cover of *The New Yorker*, 1942
Chromolithograph, 10¾ × 7¾ in / 27.3 × 19.7 cm
Condé Nast, New York

A glamorous woman, her dog by her side, cycles along a country lane, balancing her freshly cut Christmas tree on the front of her bicycle after a visit to the apple orchard—turned into a pop-up Christmas tree shop for the season—seen behind her. Snow swirls around her as she protects her eyes from the white glare with her cats-eye-shaped sunglasses. This was Christmas in the rural United States as imagined by the prolific illustrator Garrett Price (1896–1979) for the cover of *The New Yorker* magazine's Christmas edition of 19 December 1942. Visiting the countryside to get the Christmas tree remains one of the more romantic Christmas traditions in many countries, marking the start of decorating the home for the holidays. German settlers in the nineteenth century first introduced the practice of using a living fir tree to celebrate the holiday season, after which Americans generally simply helped themselves to fir trees from the nation's ample forests. As those natural supplies became depleted, however, the first commercial Christmas tree farm opened in 1901 in New Jersey, when farmer V. W. McGalliard planted twenty-five thousand Norway spruce trees on his land. That same year, President Theodore Roosevelt (1858–1919) was allegedly so concerned about the wide-spread destruction of the forests that he refused to have a Christmas tree in the White House (see p.221). Today, more than twenty-five million real trees are purchased annually in the United States, with most grown at dedicated farms.

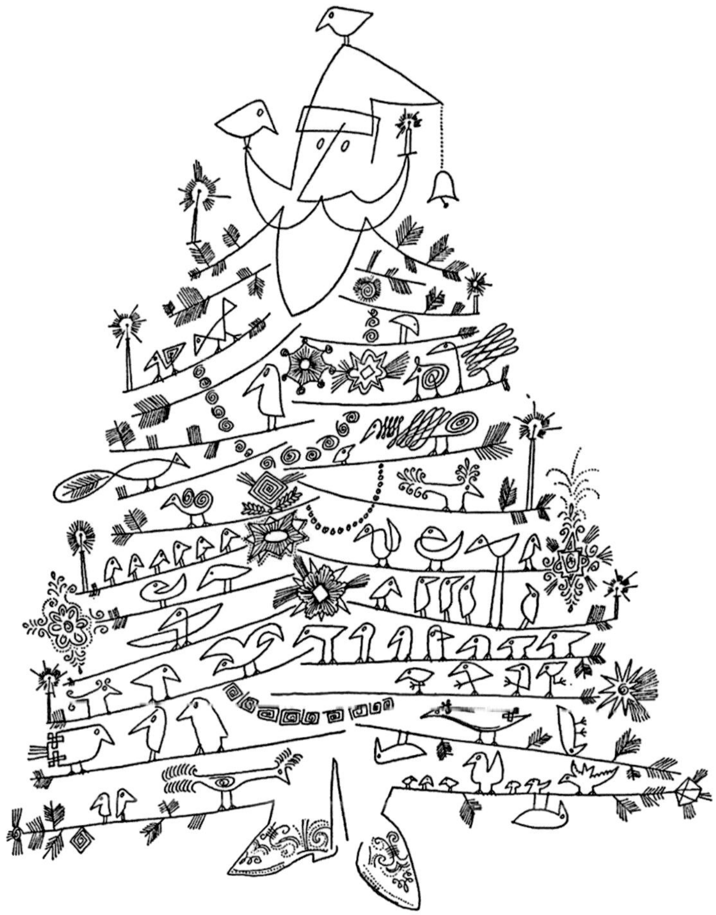

SAUL STEINBERG

•

Santa Claus as Christmas Tree, c.1949
Offset print, 7 × 5 in / 17.8 × 12.7 cm

Combining contemporary modernism with a cartoon-like Santa Claus—seen here with the body of a Christmas tree, its branches housing more than sixty varieties of bird, a bell hanging from his hat—this black line drawing on a white background is one of many works Romanian-born, New-York-resident Saul Steinberg (1914–1999) produced in partnership with the city's Museum of Modern Art, during which he brought his view of the festive season to the Museum's prestigious Christmas card each year from 1945–51. Steinberg, best known for a career almost six decades long producing drawings for *The New Yorker* magazine, created a unique idiom that set him apart. His work, widely exhibited in museums and galleries, defied categorization and became simply a "Steinberg." This work was perhaps a smaller version of a ten-foot (3.3 m) color drawing that adorned the entrance hall to the museum a year earlier. Eschewing the seasonal reds and glitter of the festive season, Steinberg's cards were black line drawings that were sold to the public to send to their discerning friends. Steinberg, who called drawing a "a way of reasoning on paper," smartly brought the traditional Christmas card into the modern age. Steinberg's distinctive drawings helped establish the MoMA card as a Christmas tradition and, in 1954, the museum began inviting other artists to submit their designs. Several were selected each year, giving a boost to the careers of selected artists, such as Bridget Riley (1931–).

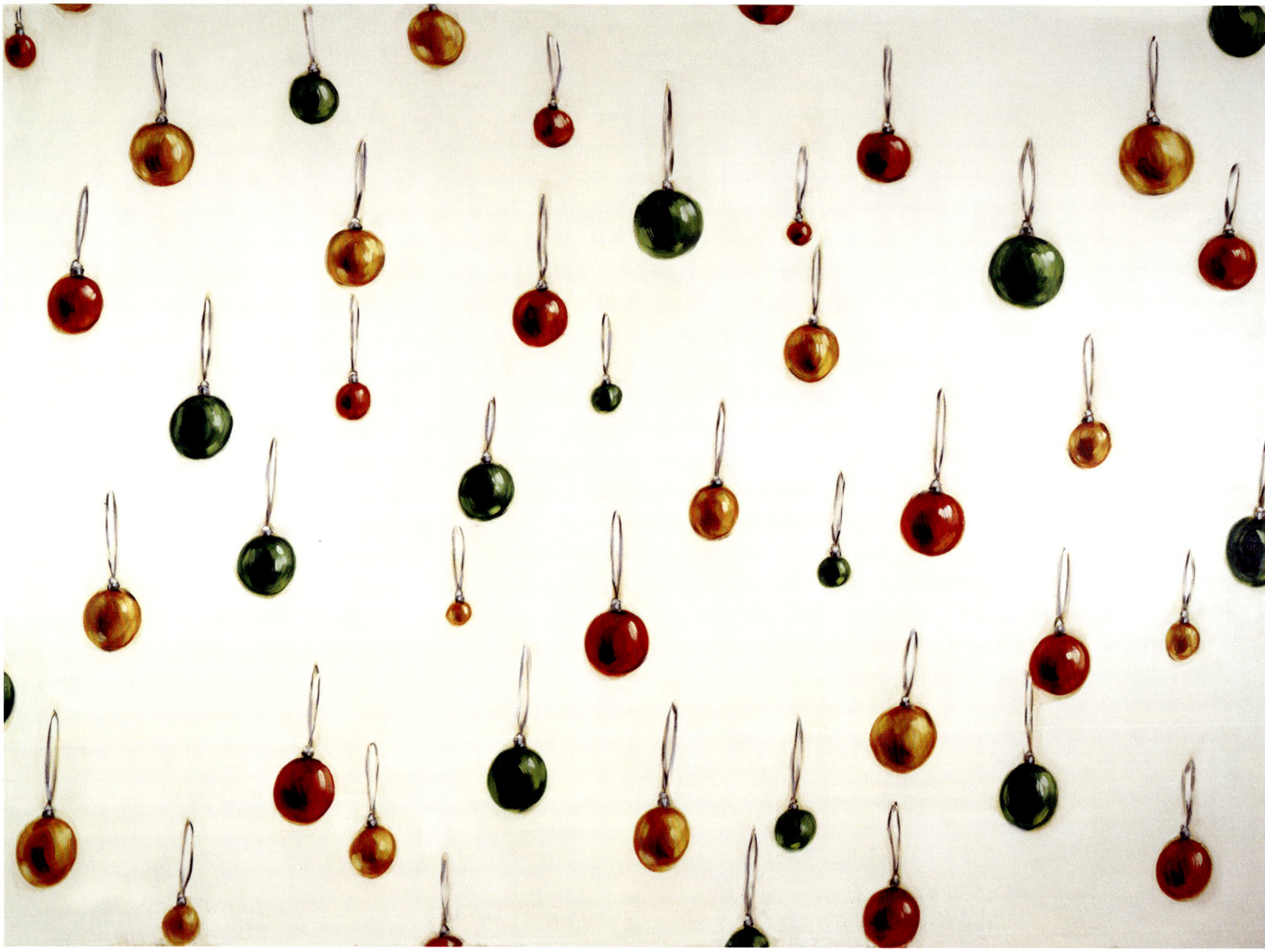

LISA MILROY

•

Baubles, 1987
Oil on canvas, 80 × 111¾ in / 203 × 284 cm

A series of painted glass baubles, varying in size and color, appear suspended in midair. The shapes of their loops of string and the patterns of light they reflect all differ, inviting the viewer to contemplate the interplay between "same and different." The Anglo-Canadian artist Lisa Milroy (1959–) is fascinated by the human relation to objects and the tradition of still-life painting is at the heart of her long-standing practice. *Baubles, 1987* is among the depictions of everyday objects that characterized her paintings in the 1980s. Here, Milroy takes a familiar item—a Christmas tree ornament—and repeats it many times across the canvas, as if to celebrate the object itself and amplify the enjoyment of describing it with paint. Glass decorations have been hung on Christmas trees since the 1840s (see p.28), when German glassblower Hans Greiner first created glass garlands to hang on fir trees. The highly anticipated ritual decorating of a Christmas tree—real or imitation (see p.135)—dates from sixteenth-century Germany, when evergreens were first adorned with nuts and berries as part of Christian celebration. Today, baubles can have great significance in the Christmas traditions of many families as they are put up and admired for a few weeks during the holiday season, then carefully repacked into boxes and stored in the attic, basement, or garage, hidden away for another eleven months.

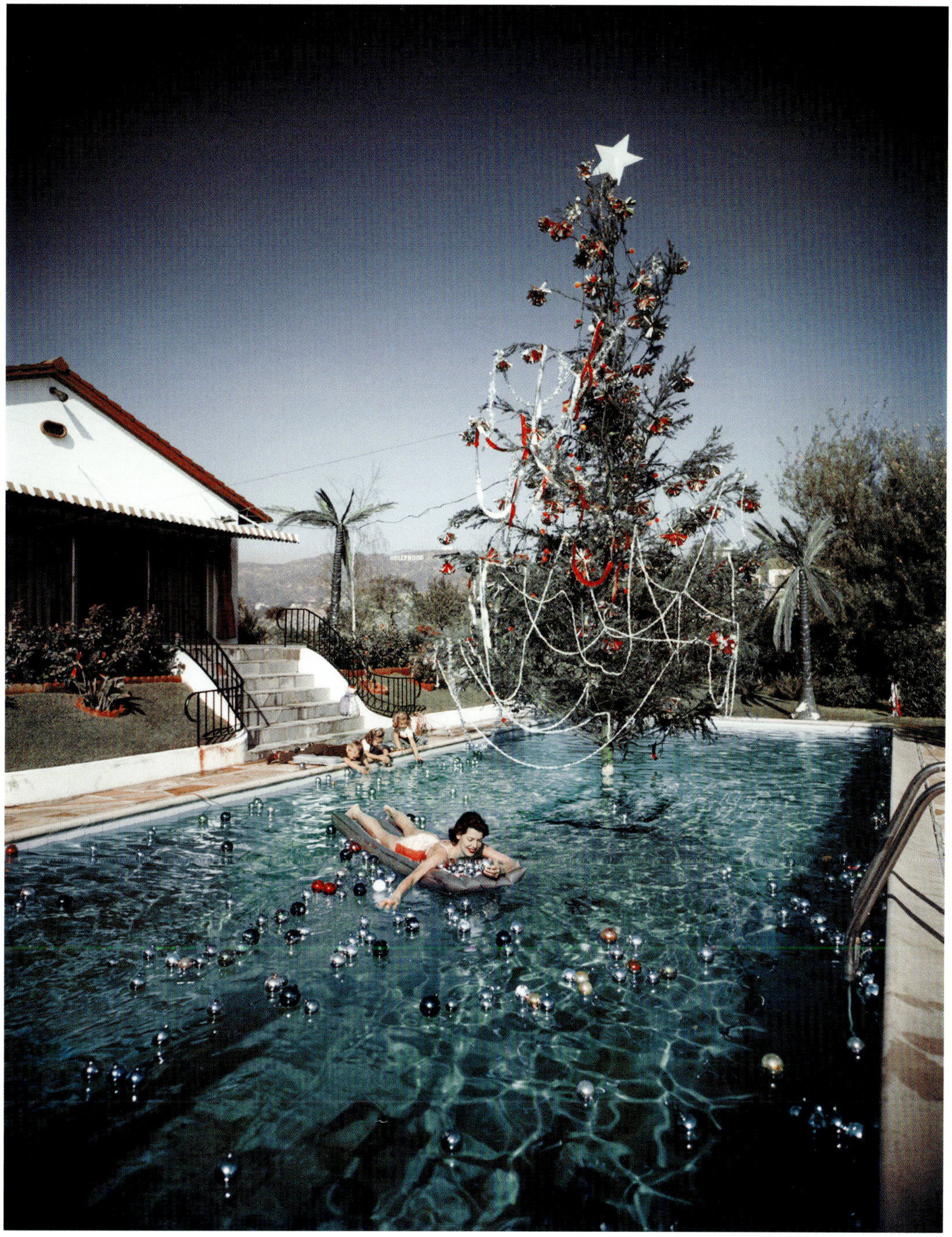

SLIM AARONS

•

Christmas Swim, 1954
Photograph, 51¼ × 41⅜ in / 130 × 105 cm

It comes as no surprise that the version of Christmas presented by Slim Aarons (1916–2006) in *Christmas Swim* does not foreground the Christian aspects of the holiday. He was Jewish, for one. But more importantly, by the winter of 1954—when he photographed his wife, Rita, floating among colored orbs while a trio of children lay poolside—Aarons was already committed to a decidedly secular photographic ideal that he later described as "attractive people doing attractive things in attractive places." This focus on "the good life" makes perfect sense, considering Aarons was steeped in the ugliness of World War II as a photographer for *Yank* magazine on the front lines. The scene portrayed in *Christmas Swim* is as fabricated as the decorations it features. The house, for instance, was rented for the shoot primarily because it had the perfect view of the Hollywood sign. The kids were rented too—cast for their all-American good looks. But this image was never meant to depict reality. Instead, it presents an absurdly idealized version of secular Christmas, in which the well-to-do housewife is literally immersed in the season—that immersion also manifests in the predominantly red-and-green color palette Aarons chose here, down to the unnaturally green hue of the water. *Christmas Swim* is one of Aarons's more famous photographs and, because of its striking Christmas imagery, it becomes a social media phenomenon throughout the holiday season each year.

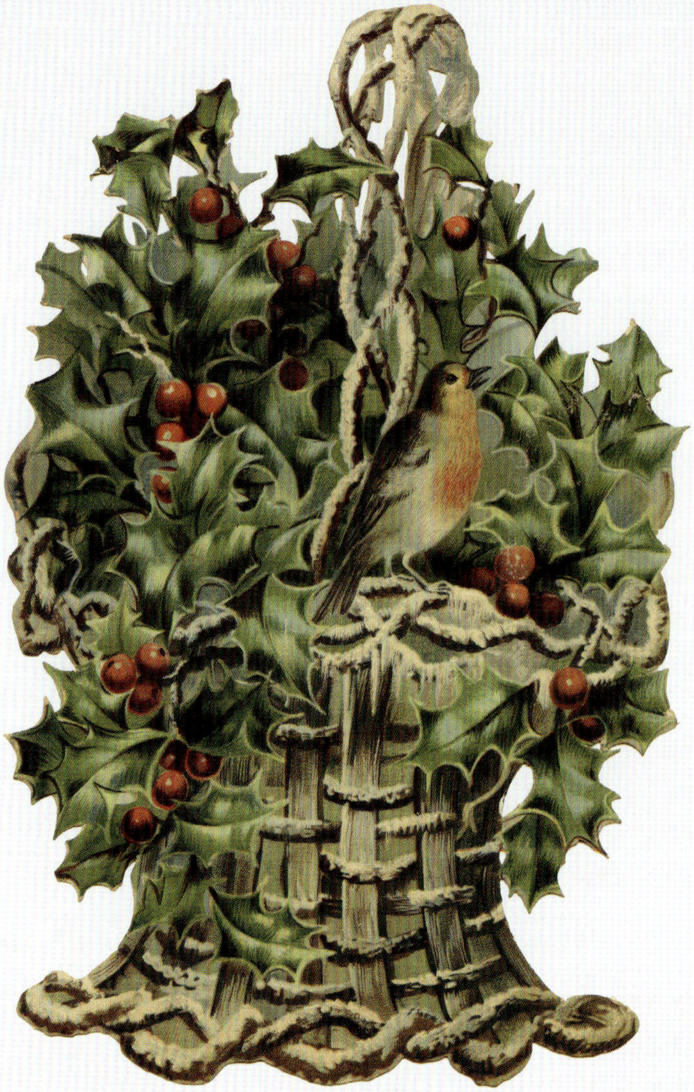

UNKNOWN

•

Wicker Basket Full of Holly, c.1837–1901
Paint on cardstock, dimensions unknown

This hand-painted Christmas craft, likely used as a small decoration to put up around the home or hang from a tree, is packed with Christmas symbolism. A wicker basket—its handle shown from a side angle to curve away from the viewer and give a sense of depth to the image—is filled to the brim with a bundle of holly (see p.218), with bright red berries gleaming from the tangle of spiny leaves. Perched deftly atop the rim of the basket, a red-breasted robin chirps happily. Holly has long been associated with varying religious festivals, including the pre-Christmas Saturnalia celebrated by the Romans, where it represented immortality and renewal, and was often given as a gift of good fortune. For Christians, the sharp leaves represent the crown of thorns Jesus wore on the cross, and the red berries his blood. Today, holly is a ubiquitous festive motif, appearing on everything from cards to wrapping paper and even festive jewelry (see p.144). The robin is similarly associated with Christmas, but for a more modern reason. In nineteenth-century Great Britain, when the sending of Christmas cards began (see p.198), Royal Mail postmen, with their signature bright red uniforms, were nicknamed "redbreasts," and it was their job to deliver the cards each year. Soon, artists began to illustrate cards with pictures relating to the delivery of letters, a common design being a robin perched atop a red postbox stuffed full of envelopes—a trend that continues to this day.

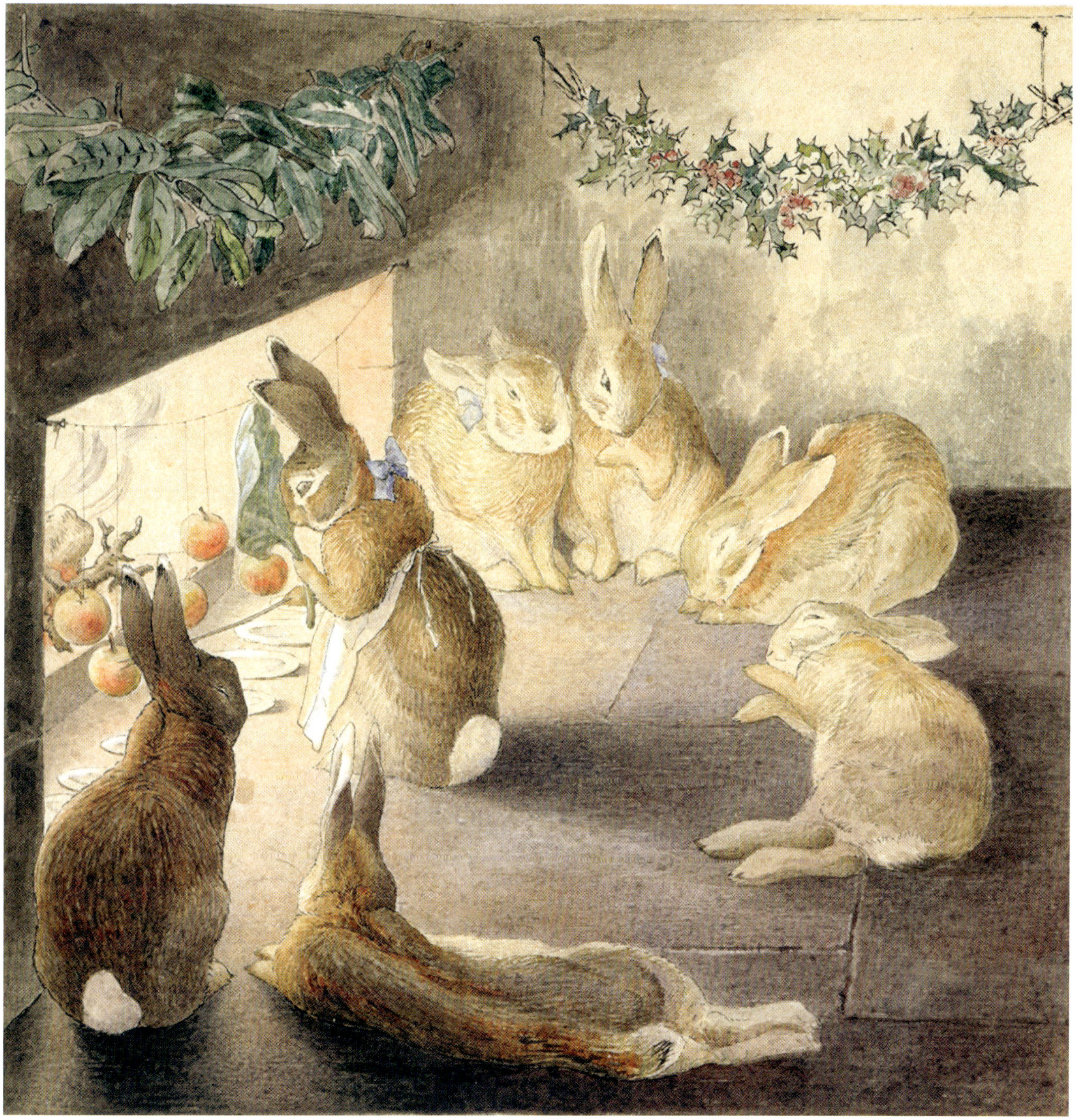

BEATRIX POTTER

•

The Rabbits' Christmas Party: Roasting Apples, c.1892
Watercolor and pen and ink over pencil on paper,
9¼ × 9⅜ in / 23.4 × 23.8 cm
Victorian & Albert Museum, London

Inspired by her pet rabbit Peter Piper, English author, illustrator, and natural scientist Beatrix Potter (1866–1943) would go on to create an artistic and literary franchise that would become beloved by children from around the world and lead to the creation of such works as *The Rabbits' Christmas Party: Roasting Apples,* from around 1892. Sitting before a fireplace in a room decked with holly and mistletoe (see p.95), the rabbits roast apples as part of their Christmas festivities. As a young girl growing up in the countryside outside central London, Potter sent illustrated letters to her governess, Annie Moore, embellishing each one with a drawing of Peter. These letters would later be transformed into *The Tale of Peter Rabbit,* first created for Noel Moore, Annie's five-year-old son. The story centers on a mischievous rabbit who disobeys his mother, Mrs. Rabbit, and regularly torments the farmer, Mr. McGregor, by rummaging around in his vegetable patch. First published in 1902 by Frederick Warne & Co., the whimsical tale captured the hearts of early twentieth-century society, who fell in love with the characters of Flopsy, Mopsy, Cotton-tail, and, of course, Peter, all of whom may even be depicted in this drawing. Potter would go on to become one of the world's best-loved children's authors and illustrators, having sold more than 250 million copies worldwide. Today, the charming, cozy, and quaint vision of pastoral English life presented through *The Tale of Peter Rabbit* conjures the spirit of Christmas.

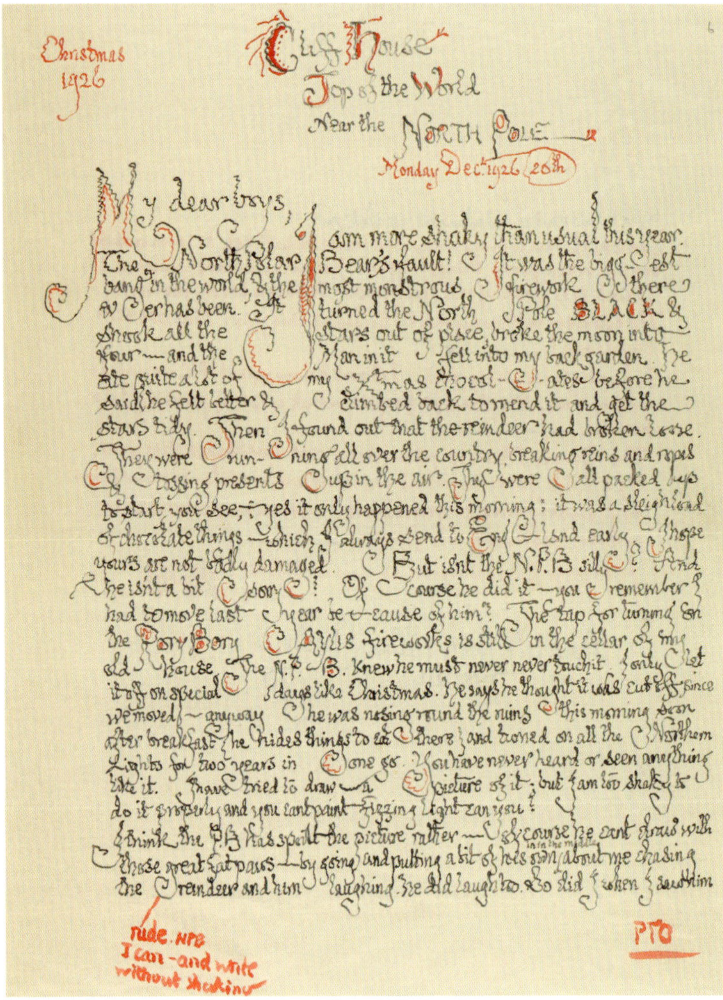

Christmas 1926

Cliff House
Top of the World
Near the NORTH POLE
Monday Dec 1926 20th

My dear boys,

I am more shaky than usual this year. The North Polar Bear's fault! It was the biggest bang in the world, & the most monstrous firework there ever has been. It turned the North Pole BLACK & shook all the stars out of place, broke the moon into four — and the Man in it fell into my back garden. He ate quite a lot of my Xmas chocolates before he said he felt better & climbed back to mend it and get the stars tidy. Then I found out that the reindeer had broken loose. They were running all over the country, breaking reins and ropes & tossing presents up in the air. They were all packed up to start, you see; yes it only happened this morning; it was a sleighload of chocolate things, which I always send to England early. I hope yours are not badly damaged. But isn't the N.P.B. silly? And he isn't a bit sorry! Of course he did it — you remember I had to move last year because of him? The tap for turning on the Rory Bory Aylis fireworks is still in the cellar of my old house. The N.P.B. knew he must never never touch it. I only let it off on special days like Christmas. He says he thought it was cut off since we moved — anyway he was nosing round the ruins this morning soon after breakfast (he hides things to eat there) and turned on all the Northern Lights for two years in one go. You have never heard or seen anything like it. I have tried to draw a picture of it; but I am too shaky to do it properly and you can't paint fizzing light can you? I think the PB has spoilt the picture rather — of course he can't draw with those great fat paws — by going and putting a bit of his own in the middle about me chasing the reindeer and him laughing. He did laugh too. So did I when I saw him

rude. NPB
I can — and write without shaking

PTO

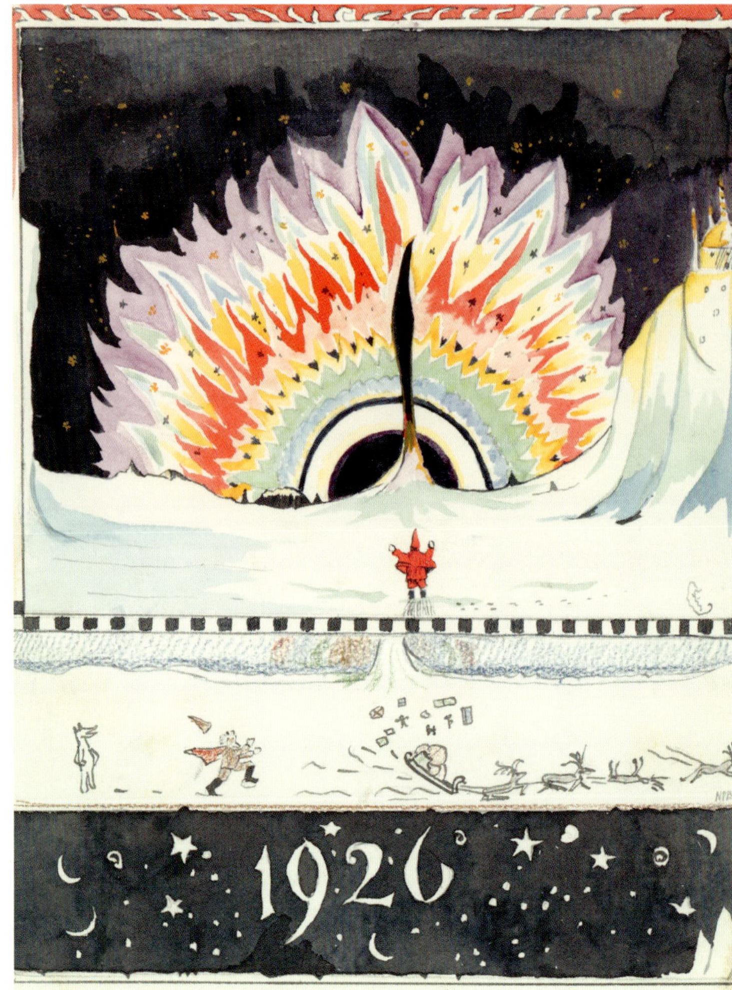

J. R. R. TOLKIEN

•

Pages from *The Father Christmas Letters*, 1976
Drawing in watercolor, ink, pencil, and colored pencil on paper; 9 × 7 in / 23.1 × 17.8 cm; Letter written in ink and watercolor on paper; 10⅝ × 8½ in / 27.2 × 21.5 cm
Published by George Allen & Unwin, London

This letter might not be from Father Christmas, as it purports, but it is from one of the most celebrated writers of the twentieth century: J. R. R. Tolkien (1892–1973), best known for *The Lord of the Rings*. Every December from 1920, when Tolkien's eldest son John was three years old, until 1943, the writer's four children received a card in their Oxford home in an envelope addressed in distinctive spidery handwriting and sometimes dusted with snow, bearing a stamp from the North Pole. The letter, accompanied by Tolkien's own illustrations, recounted the struggles Father Christmas had that year to prepare for the festive season. Each letter contained news from the North Pole, told either by Father Christmas himself or, later in the series, by his secretary, Ilbereth the Elf. The earlier stories featured the many escapades of Santa's chief helper, the accident-prone North Polar Bear, but the cast of characters grew to include snowmen, cave bears, red gnomes, and snow elves, as well as the troublesome bat-riding goblins who lived in caves below Father Christmas's home at the North Pole. Following Tolkien's death, the delightful stories were gathered into a posthumous collection published in 1976; they were later expanded to include several missing letters and illustrations and reprinted as *Letters from Father Christmas* in 1995. Devotees of *The Lord of the Rings* consider many of the Polar characters to be precursors of those that later appeared in Tolkien's most well-known work.

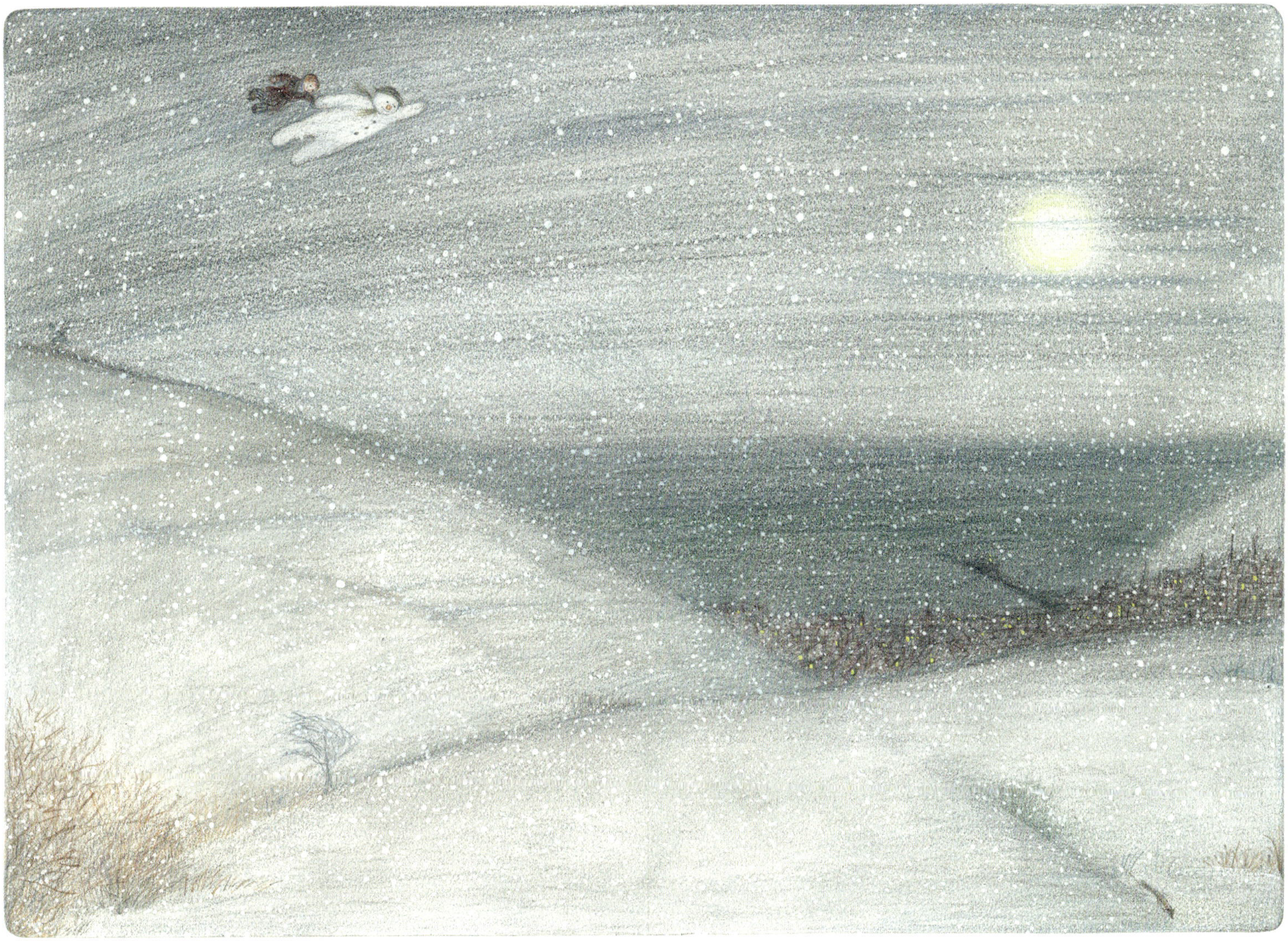

RAYMOND BRIGGS

•

Pages from *The Snowman*, 1978
Pencil illustration, 11⅞ × 17⅜ in / 30.2 × 44 cm
Published by Hamish Hamilton, London

Inspired by the heaviest snowfall he had ever seen, English writer and illustrator Raymond Briggs (1934–2022) sat down to write one of the best-loved of all children's books, telling the story of how a young boy flies with a magical snowman to the North Pole. In colored-pencil drawings, *The Snowman* describes how James builds a snowman—with coal eyes and buttons, a tangerine nose, and a green scarf and hat—that comes to life at midnight. After the amiable snowman explores the boy's home, and they indulge in a feast by candlelight, he takes James on a flight to Brighton, on the south coast of England. James and the snowman fly home before the sun rises. However, the next morning, Christmas Day, James finds the snowman has melted, leaving behind just his hat and scarf, the tangerine, and lumps of coal. Published in 1978, Briggs's wordless tale met with moderate success, because it could not be read like a traditional bedtime story. That all changed in 1982, when it was turned into a short, animated film based on Briggs's own illustrations. Expanded to include the song "Walking in the Air" during the flight sequence, it is now screened every year in Great Britain. Despite Briggs not intending this to be a Christmas story, *The Snowman* is now a beloved Christmas institution.

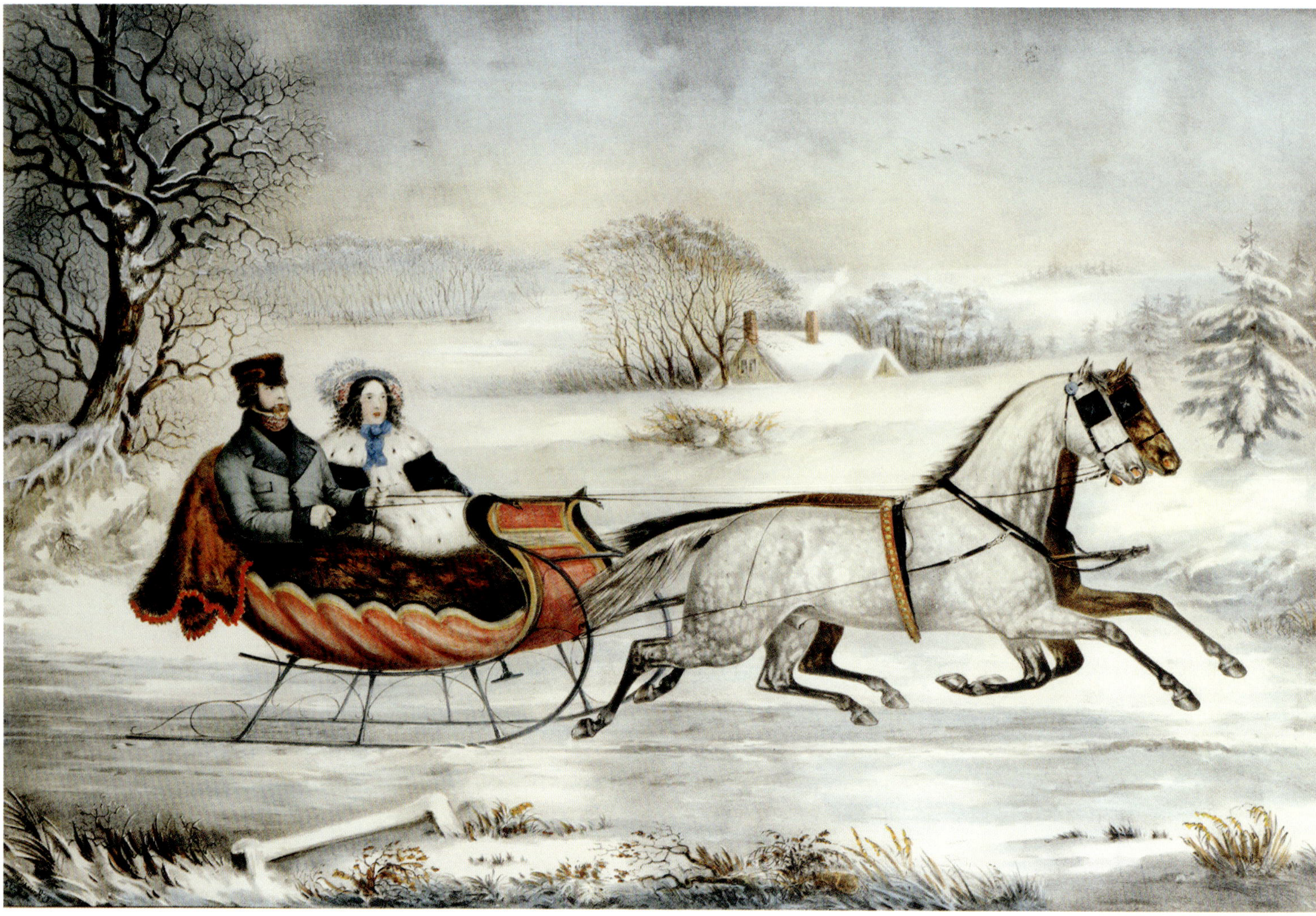

OTTO KNIRSCH

•

The Road,—Winter., 1853
Hand-colored lithograph,
17½ × 26¼ in / 44.5 × 66.7 cm
Private collection

Currier & Ives were the most prodigious and popular printmakers of the nineteenth century. By capitalizing on the relatively recent innovation of lithography, the company was able to offer images at a price point that almost everyone could afford, producing more than one million prints in their remarkable seven-decade run. This picture, *The Road,—Winter.*, was originally drawn on stone by German-born artist Otto Knirsch (1825–1895), who worked for the company, as a gift to Nathaniel Currier and his wife. It depicts the couple, wrapped up warm in furs, riding a horse-drawn sleigh through a tranquil snowy landscape. Currier liked it so much that he added it to the company's catalog. Nathaniel Currier (1813–1888) was born in Massachusetts and apprenticed with printmakers in both Boston and Philadelphia before hanging up his own shingle in New York in 1934. Currier & Ives not only led in decorative arts but was also a vital news source at a time before photojournalism. The firm produced numerous illustrations of historical and current events among its more than 7,500 images. The lyrics of "Sleigh Ride," written by Mitchell Parish (1900–1993) in 1950, will forever tie the printmakers to the Christmas holiday, but it was their prolifera tion of romantic wintry scenes, such as this one, that captured the hearts and imaginations of the American public and cemented Currier & Ives as household names.

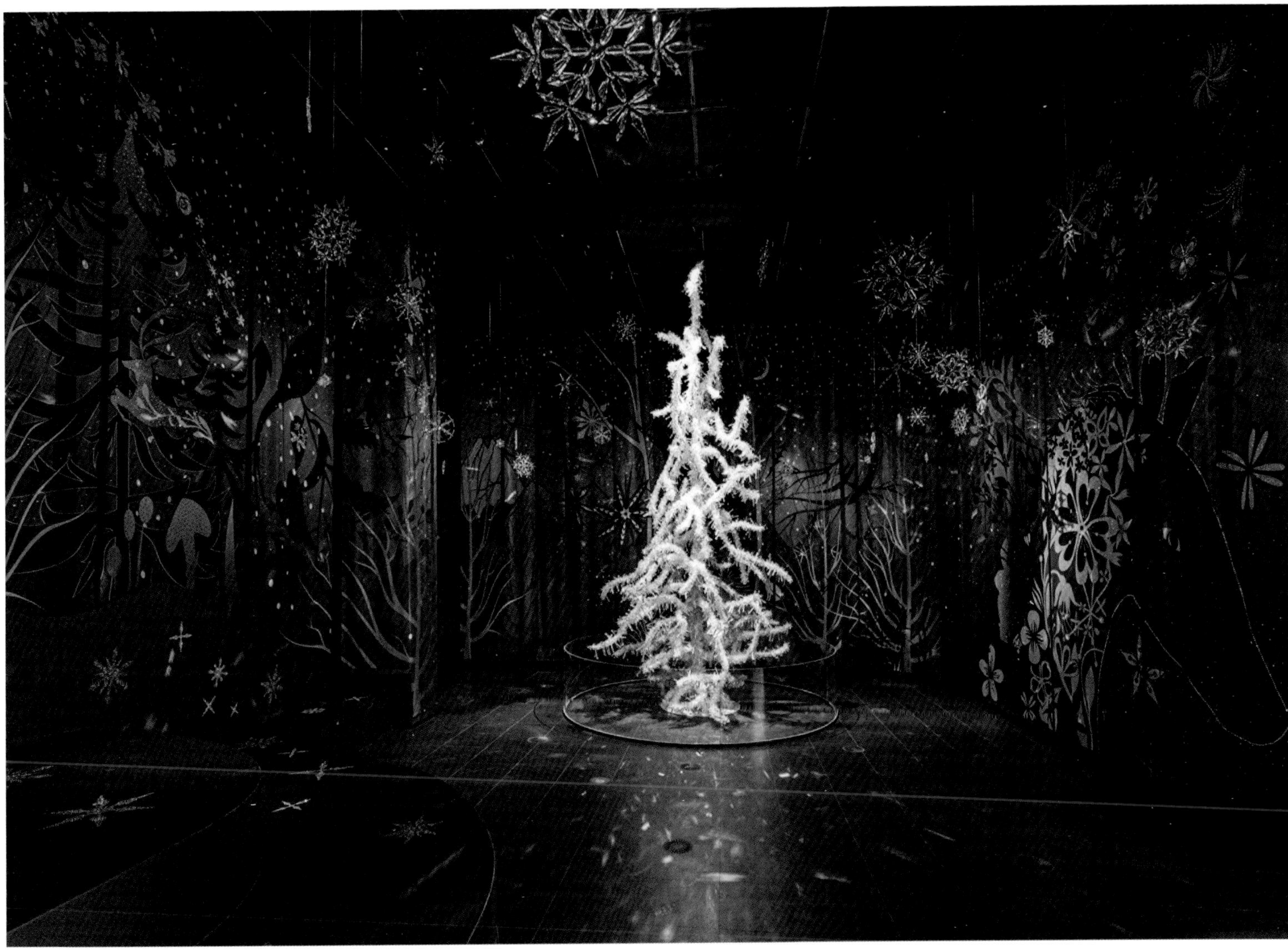

TORD BOONTJE AND ALEXANDER MCQUEEN

•

Silent Light, 2003
Steel and crystal, H. 20 ft / 6 m
Swarovski Crystal World, Wattens, Austria

Arriving at The Grand Entrance of London's venerable Victoria & Albert Museum during the 2003 Christmas period, a visitor would have been greeted by this glorious twenty-foot (six-meter) tall tree made from 150,000 sparkling Swarovski crystals attached to polished, stainless steel branches. Designed by Dutch-born designer Tord Boontje (1968–) and the British fashion designer Alexander McQueen (1969–2010), the *Silent Light* crystal tree was the first Christmas commission for the museum's main hall. Set on a shattered mirrored plinth surrounded by glass walls on two sides, the tree slowly rotated, scattering light around the walls to create a glorious, shimmering immersive space. The tree, said Boontje—who had previously collaborated with McQueen in 1998, when he designed eyewear and watches for the designer's eponymous label—was inspired by watching snow turn to ice as temperatures fell, creating something "magical, really pretty but very fragile." Following the 2003 festive season, the tree initially found a home in Swarovski's *Chamber of Wonders* exhibition in Austria, where it threw sparkling reflections from a slowly rotating turntable over a room transformed into a romantic winter forest scene, filled with crystal snowflakes and crystal-covered fabrics, as seen here. In 2020, it was moved again, this time to stand in a giant dome with 595 mirrors in a new exhibition, *Crystal World*.

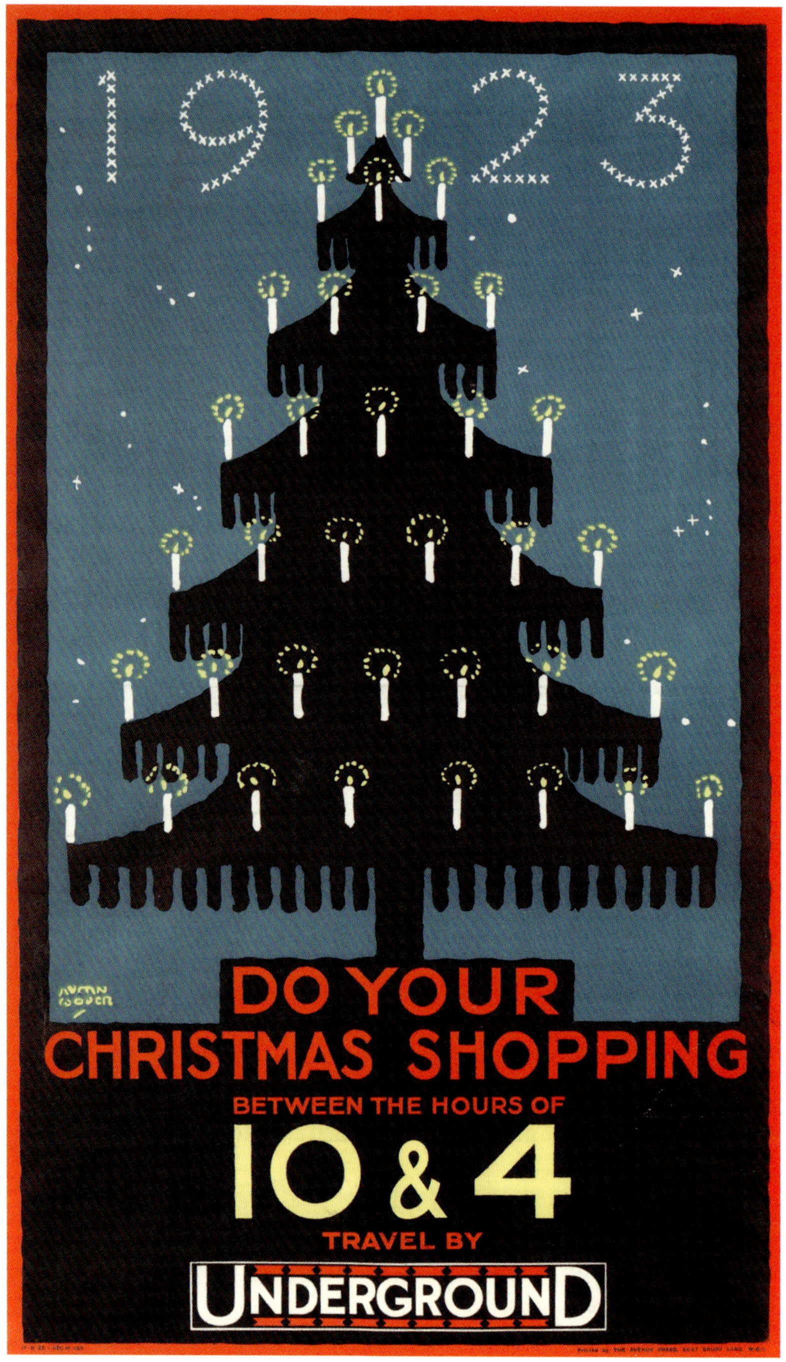

AUSTIN COOPER

•

Do Your Christmas Shopping, 1923
Color lithography on cream wove paper,
40 × 25 in / 101.6 × 63.5 cm
London Transport Museum

A minimalist tree, decorated with lit candles against a starry night, leaves the viewer in no doubt as to what time of year this poster referred to when it was printed in 1923. The work of the prolific graphic artist Austin Cooper (1890–1964), the poster urges Christmas shoppers to take the London Underground between the hours of 10 a.m. to 4 p.m., so they could avoid times when the trains were busy with commuters. A Canadian-born London resident, Cooper designed posters for a number of British railway companies as well as fifty-four posters for the London Underground. He was in good company: during the 1920s and 1930s, London Underground was a leading patron of the arts employing outstanding graphic designers, such as Cooper, as well as many of the leading artists of the day. Modern graphic posters had started to appear on the Underground in the 1890s as the network became more unified. As early as 1908, its chief executive, Frank Pick (1878–1941), realized the value of commissioning artists to convey not just the Underground's public messages but also its spirit of modernity. Pick was a perfect patron, who was happy to accept any artwork provided the subject was instantly clear. For this brief, Cooper had to remind leisure passengers that the Underground was the preserve of the commuter first thing in the morning and at the end of the afternoon, and they should travel during off-peak hours. Cooper was commissioned to provide another poster as a reminder in 1924, too.

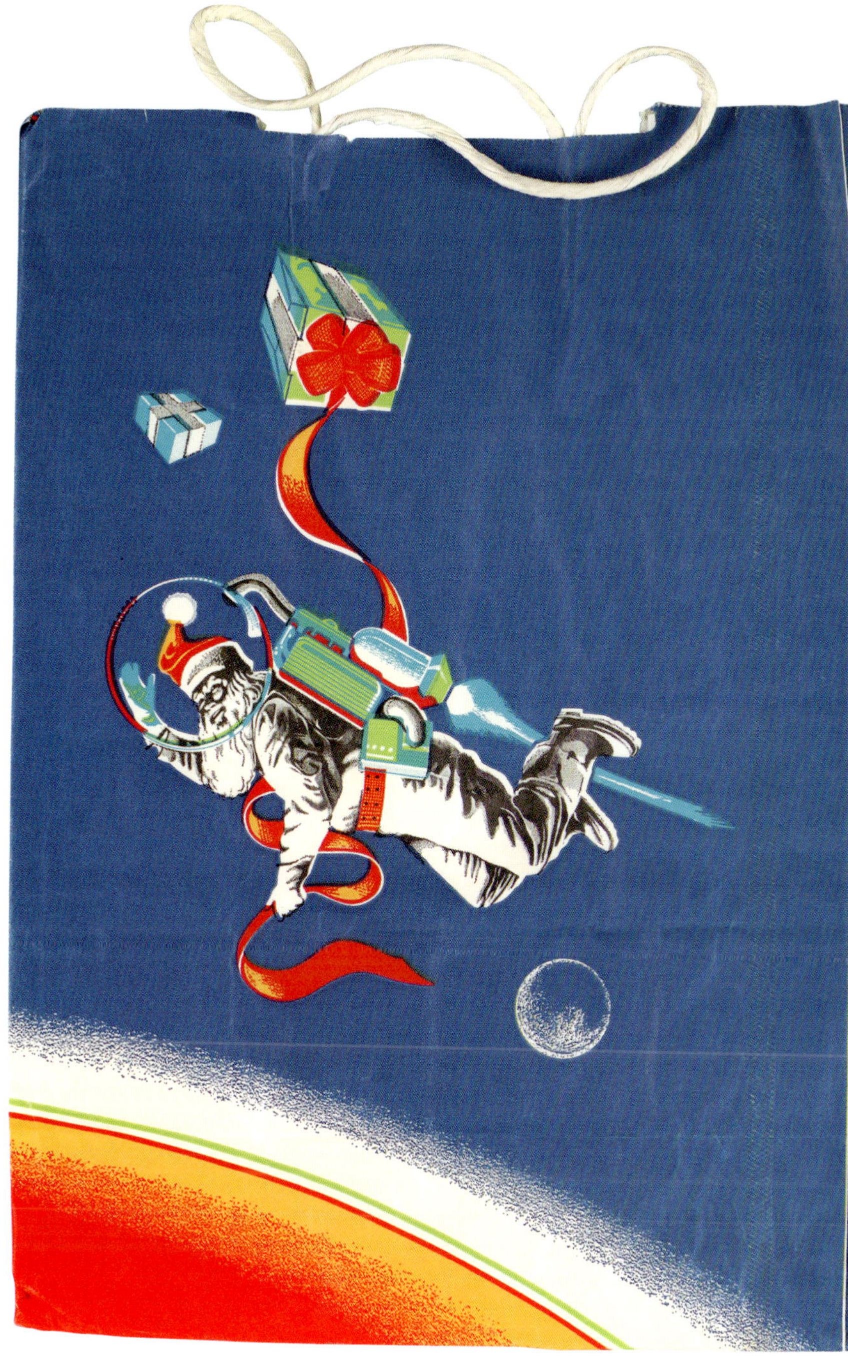

BOB ALCORN

•

Bloomingdale's shopping bag, 1979
Paper with raffia handles,
16½ × 12 in / 41.9 × 30.5 cm
Cooper Hewitt, Smithsonian
Design Museum, New York

As the Christmas season begins so does the holiday shopping, as stores become a grand pageant of glistening lights and aisles chockablock with gifts for one and all. The concept of retail as theater is imprinted in the DNA of Bloomingdale's, and the shopping bag, beyond being a simple conveyance, has been a centerpiece of that spectacle for nearly a century. When one thinks about iconic shopping bags, the Big Brown Bag—created for Bloomingdale's by Massimo Vignelli (1931–2014) in 1973—stands alone, an icon on the streets of New York for decades. Bloomingdale's has been one of the foremost pioneers in shopping bag design since the popularization of the modern-day handled paper bag in the 1930s. Continuing the retailer's long tradition of inventive bag concepts, in 1979 new creative director John Jay began commissioning limited-edition bag designs for store promotions, tapping creative minds across a number of different fields. Artists as varied as painter Karen Jakobsen, architect Michael Graves, and apparel designer Franco Moschino created designs for the store's bags in the ensuing years. Works of portable art, they became instant collectibles. This bag, designed by Bob Alcorn for the 1979 holiday season, is also emblazoned with the phrase "Christmas at the Dawn of a New Decade." It features Santa Claus as an astronaut, his signature hat firmly on his head, encapsulated in a futuristic bubblelike helmet, his jet pack propelling him toward the earth as wrapped presents float dreamily alongside him.

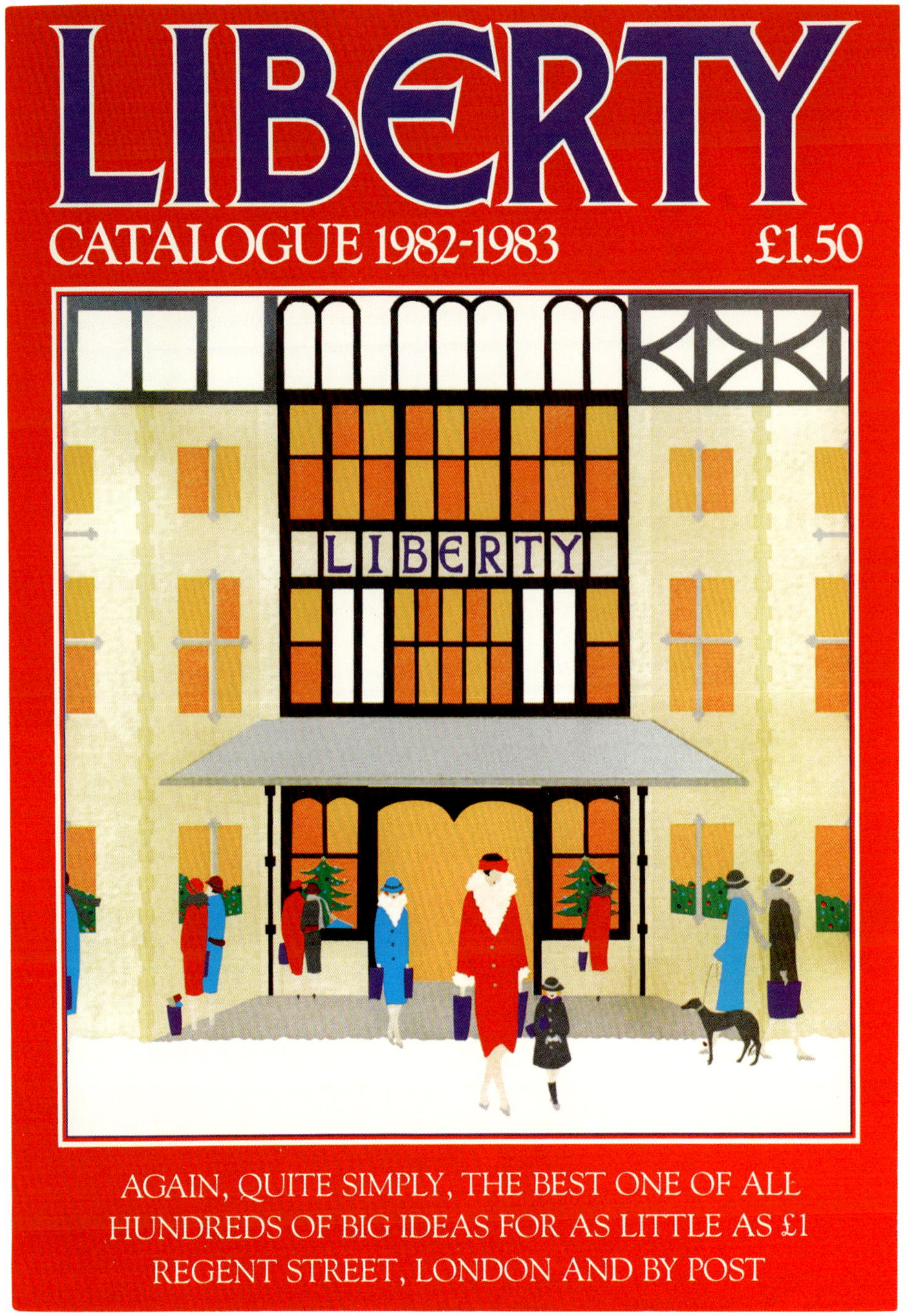

LINDA HILL

•

Christmas catalog, 1982–83
Printed magazine, 11¾ × 8¼ in / 30 × 21 cm
For Liberty, London

A colorful illustration by British artist Linda Hill (1961–) of the front of the iconic Liberty department store in London adorns the cover of the company's 1982 Christmas catalog. Christmas trees can be seen in the store windows, as well-dressed shoppers enter and exit. Long before online shopping took over the world and gift buying could be done without leaving home, shoppers set off to the store armed with a list of presents to buy. To make the task as easy as possible—and also to whet the appetite and get customers to buy something they had not previously considered—Liberty began releasing an annual Christmas catalog (see p.212) in the early part of the twentieth century. This edition featured many pages of its famous scarves and handkerchiefs, alongside glassware, soaps and scents, and leathers. The shop itself, with its unique black-and-white mock-Tudor facade just off Regent Street in London, is as famous for its building as for the goods it sells. The founder, Sir Arthur Lasenby Liberty (1843–1917), envisaged the store, which was completed in 1924, as looking like a ship that had docked on the city's streets and even included the timbers of two Tudor battleships in its construction. For those who could not make the trip to London to buy their Christmas presents, the Liberty catalog, which included a mail-order form in the back, provided a touch of cosmopolitan glamour and daydreaming.

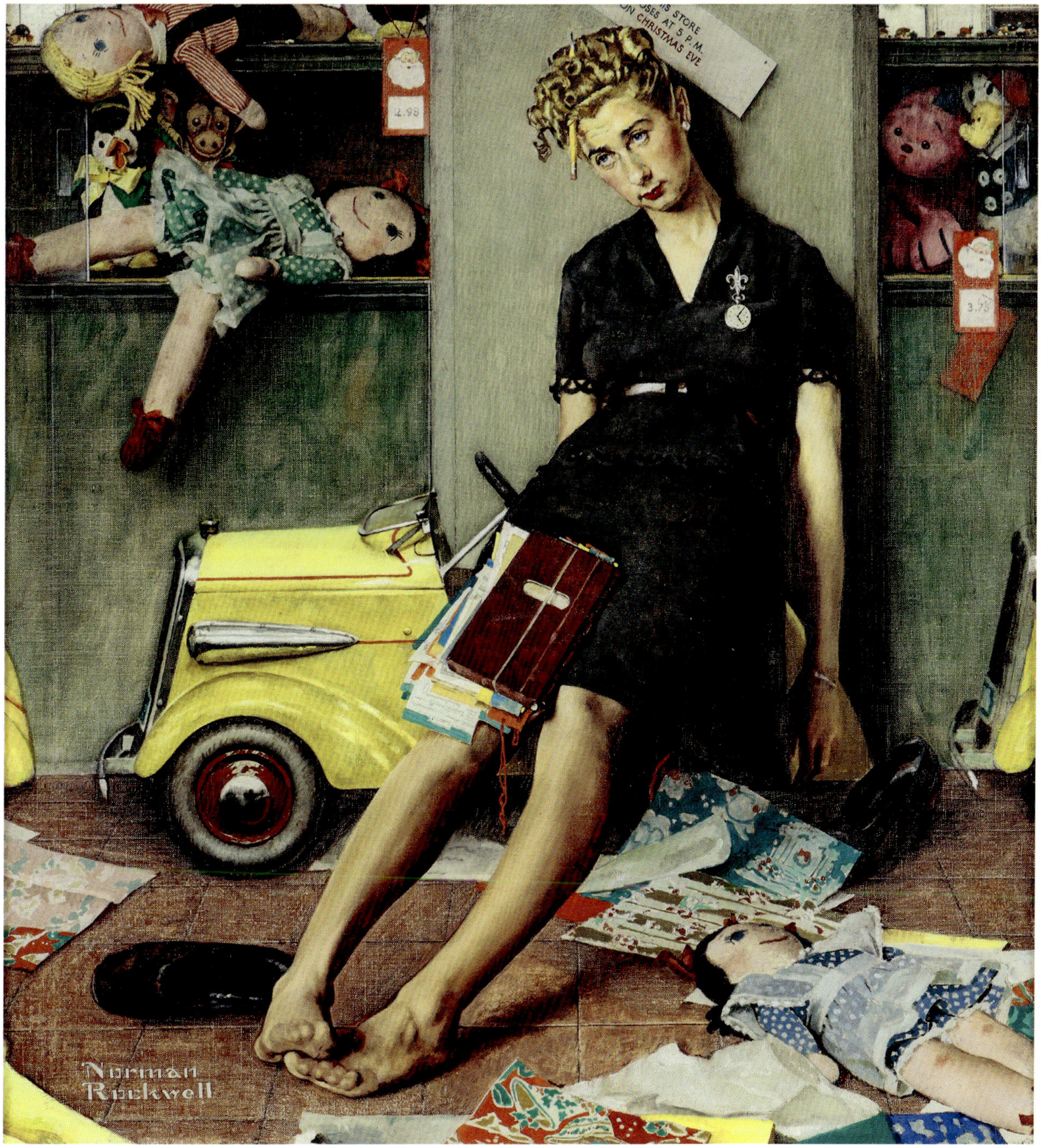

NORMAN ROCKWELL

•

Tired Salesgirl on Christmas Eve, 1947
Oil on canvas, 30¼ × 28¼ in / 77.2 × 71.8 cm
Private collection

As Christmas Eve, the busiest trading day of the year, ends, the salesgirl of the toy store in this painting by renowned US artist Norman Rockwell (1894–1978) has slumped down the wall to collapse in stupefied languor upon a shiny yellow toy car. The wrapping sheets strewn at her feet and her pocketbook, stuffed to the point of bursting with receipts for the orders she has processed, communicate the frenzied onslaught of eleventh-hour gift buying by parents desperate to please their children. Her pose, limp arms hanging from a crumpled torso on plank-stiff legs, offers a witty echo of the lifeless dolls, tossed aside unwanted, on the shelves and floor. As the principal illustrator for current affairs periodical the *Saturday Evening Post*, on whose cover this painting appeared, Rockwell documented the changing face of postwar America in his trademark style—a sort of exaggerated caricature realism. It could be said that Rockwell's images of rosy-cheeked nuclear families exchanging gifts or peering out from snow-lined windows came to define the American vision of the Christmas in the twentieth century. However, for all its humor and brightly colored trappings, this painting offers a somewhat oblique commentary on the excesses, pitfalls, and casualties of an increasingly commercialized festive season. In that sense, it anticipates Rockwell's eventual break with the *Saturday Evening Post* at the beginning of the 1960s, when, after painting 321 of its covers, he left to work on periodicals that allowed him the freedom to depict more politicized subjects.

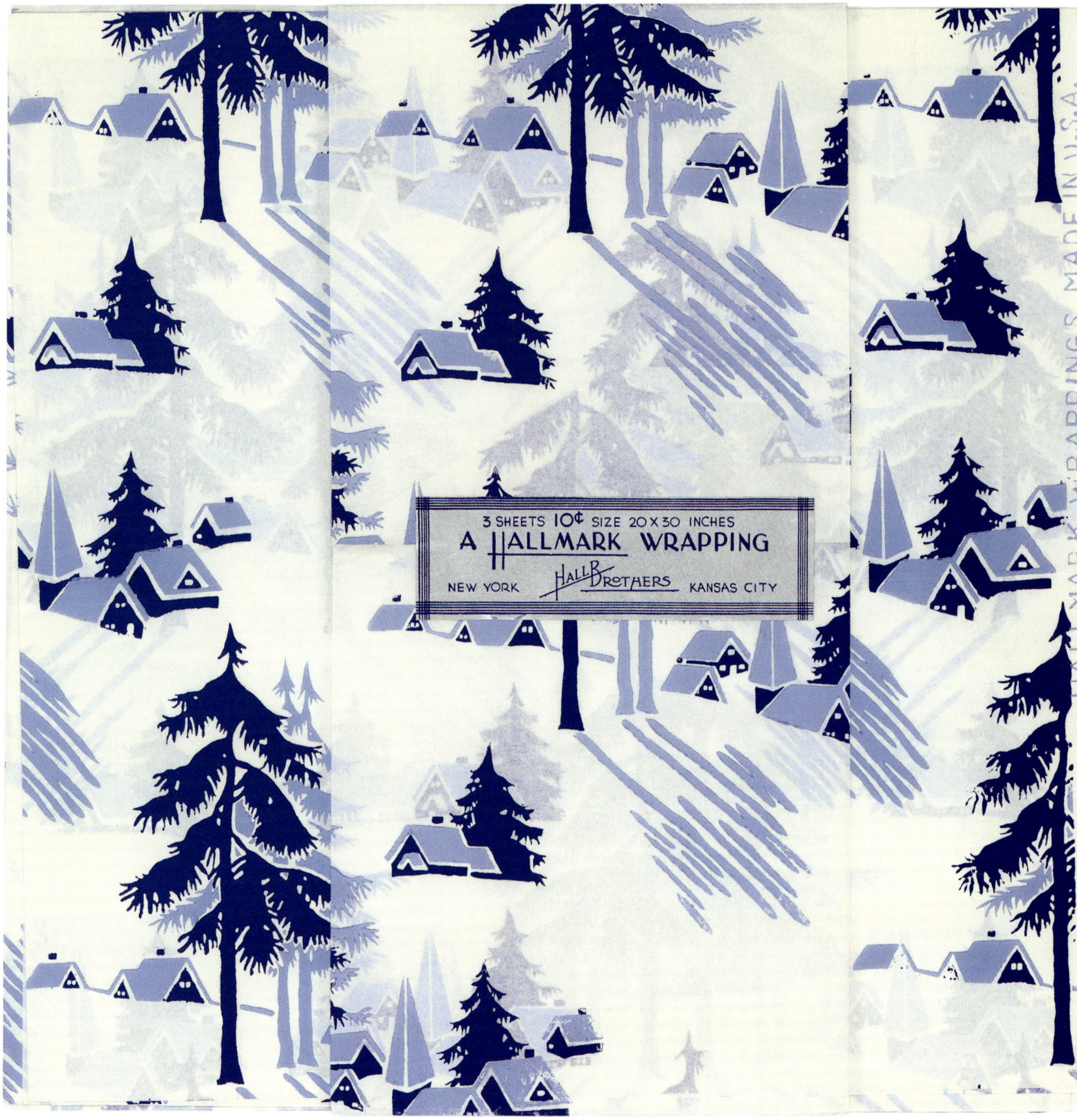

HALLMARK

•

Wrapping paper, c.1917
Printed paper, 30 × 20 in / 76.2 × 50.8 cm

Images of beautifully wrapped gifts under a decorated tree are the stuff of Christmas dreams. But until just over one hundred years ago, gift wrapping was typically basic, solid-colored tissue paper, newspaper, or brown packaging paper. It wasn't until the Christmas of 1917, when American company Hallmark, well known for being a giant in the greeting card sector even at that time, inadvertently founded the modern-day gift-wrapping industry. Having sold out of the traditional red, green, and white tissue paper at its store in Kansas City, Missouri, Rollie B. Hall (1882–1968), elder brother of company founder J. C. Hall (1891–1982), came across some colorful and elegantly illustrated French envelope liners. At ten cents per sheet, they quickly sold out, as they did again the following year. Hallmark soon began manufacturing its own designs and patterns. This example from around that time shows a tranquil village scene created in white and blue, hinting at snow-covered cottages upon a hillside. Throughout the following century, these evolved to keep up with fashion trends, including producing popular culture tie-ins. And so, a mega industry was born, now worth billions of dollars a year and including everything from bows and foil to bags and boxes. Wrapping now comes in every imaginable combination of colors and designs, and while bags may be easier and less messy (see p.61), nothing beats ripping open a beautifully wrapped gift on Christmas morning.

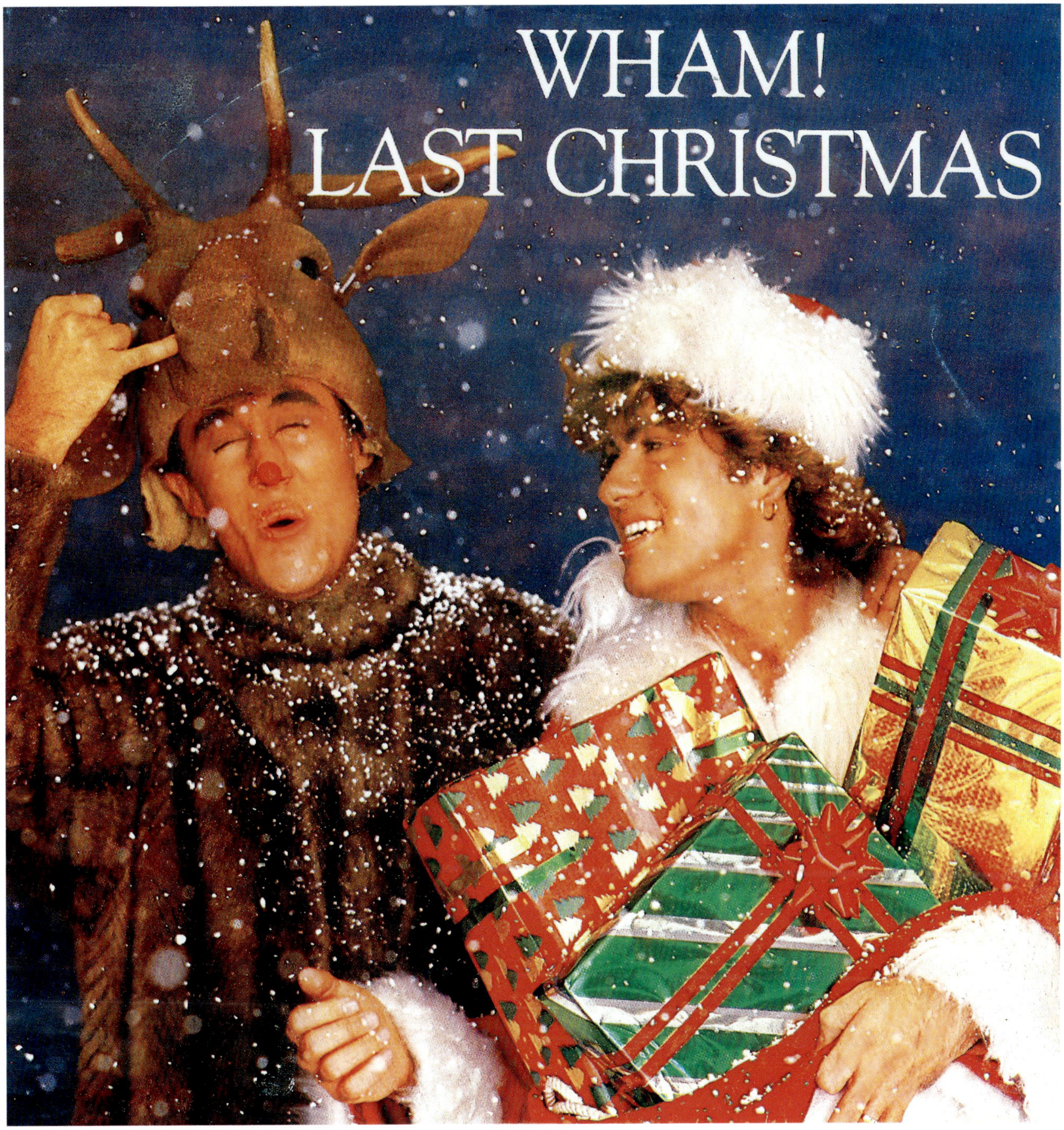

WHAM!

•

"Last Christmas" single cover, 1984
Printed cardstock, 7⅛ × 7⅛ / 18.1 × 18.1 cm
Released by CBS Records, New York

The improbably good-looking duo of George Michael (1963–2016) and Andrew Ridgley (1963–)—together forming the pop group Wham!—ham it up, dressed as Santa Claus and Rudolph respectively, under falling fake snow on the cover of their 1984 single "Last Christmas," an upbeat but ultimately bittersweet song about betrayal and lost love. Released to compete for the all-important number one spot on the Christmas charts, the single stalled in second position, where it remained for five consecutive weeks. The top spot that year belonged to the charity fund raiser "Do They Know it's Christmas?," by Band Aid (see p.97), on which Michael was also a lead vocalist. It was not until 2021 that Wham!'s rereleased single finally reached the top position in the UK Singles Chart on New Year's Day. Its enduring popularity, and its 1.9 million units sold, is testament to the chemistry between Michael and Ridgley, boyhood friends from Bushey, a commuter town outside London. Wham! not only caught the bubbly mood of the 1980s but also helped create it as their music—written and composed by the prodigiously talented Michael—defined a generation. In Great Britain, the Christmas number one remains the most prestigious chart-topper of the year. The charts themselves first appeared in 1952, when the music paper *New Musical Express* began listing records in order of their weekly sales, and hitting the top spot at Christmas was a virtual guarantee of achieving the highest sales of the year.

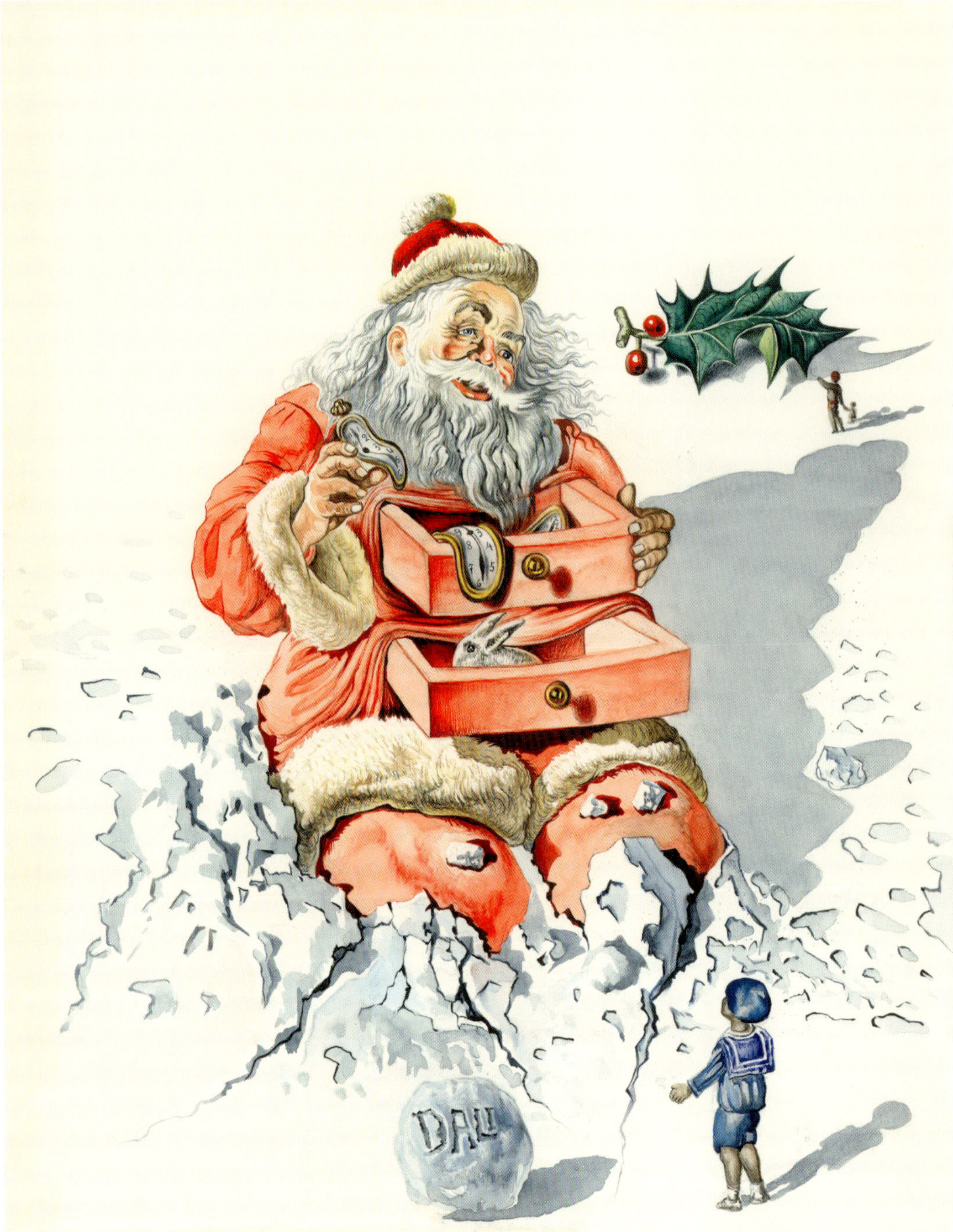

SALVADOR DALÍ

•

Santa with Drawers, 1948
Watercolor and graphite on paper,
13 × 10 in / 33 × 25.4 cm
Hallmark Art Collection, Missouri

Much of the artistic output of Salvador Dalí (1904–89) is very well-known today, but somewhat less celebrated are his forays into Christmas card design, often depicting his own Surrealist take on the season. Hallmark (see p.64) first commissioned Dalí in 1948 as one of fifty big-name artists to design a series of cards for its Gallery Artist Christmas Cards series, which implored customers to "let one of these fifty foremost Gallery Artists paint YOUR Personal Christmas Card." Dalí's three designs—a headless angel playing a lute at the Nativity among them—weren't popular with customers. Despite this, around ten years later in 1959, Hallmark asked him to produce ten more card designs, for which Dalí stipulated he receive $15,000 cash up front, no input from Hallmark as to the subject of the cards, and no deadline. The resulting designs—many of which he created in the bathroom of his New York hotel directly after the meeting and some he had created years earlier—were largely rejected by Hallmark. The image here, *Santa with Drawers*, is one such example, and shows a larger-than-life, weary-looking Santa pulling rabbits and melting clocks (a recurring theme in Dalí's works) out of drawers concealed within his coat as a child looks on in wonder. Three were eventually printed. Dalí later found success in Spain, designing Christmas cards for Barcelona company Hoechst Ibérica, many of which included Surrealist versions of the Christmas tree.

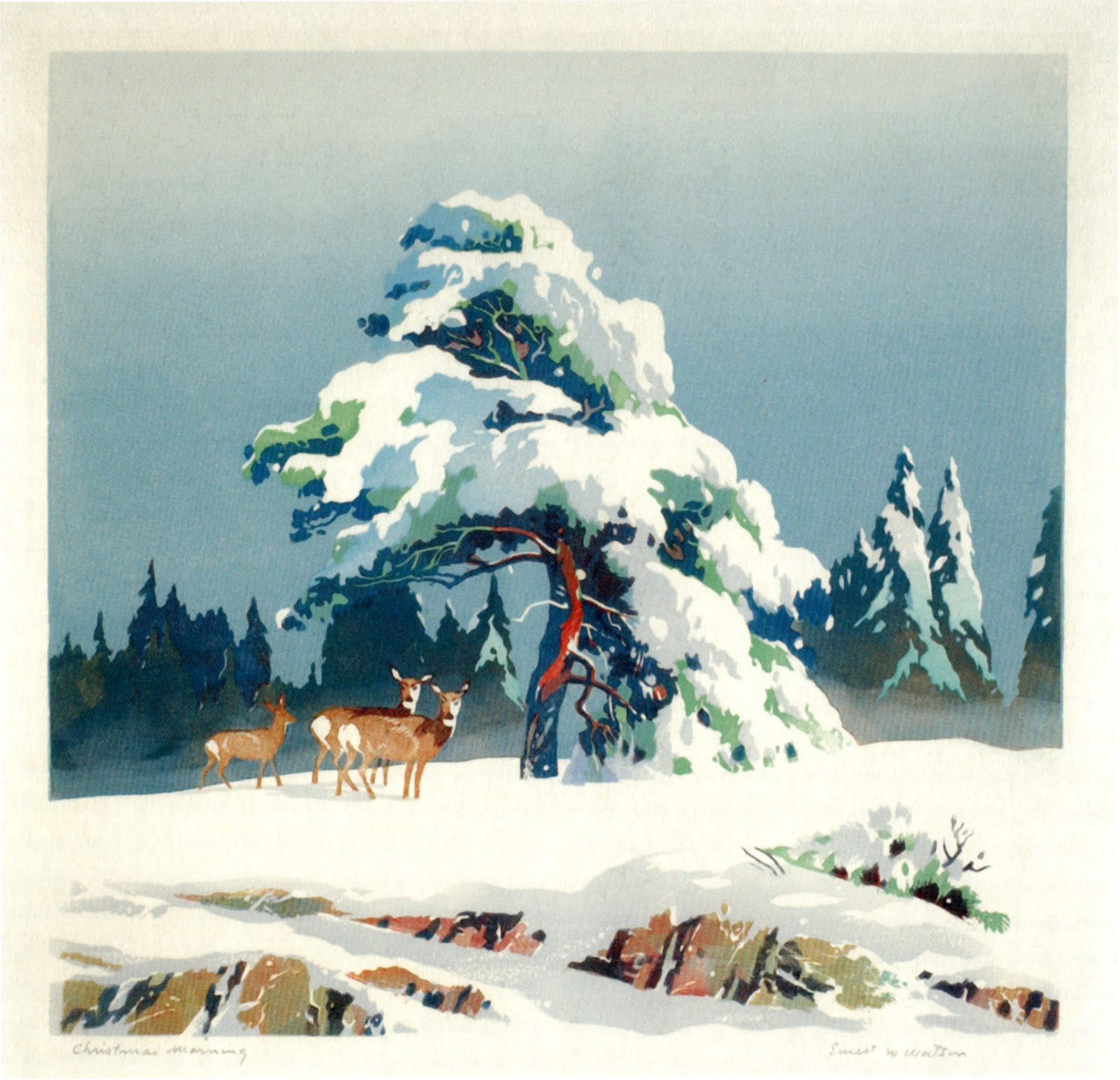

ERNEST W. WATSON

•

Christmas Morning, 1947
Color linoleum cut on paper,
10¾ × 12⅛ in / 27.3 × 30.8 cm
Smithsonian American Art Museum,
Washington, D.C.

Ernest W. Watson (1884–1969) was an accomplished author, educator, and artist best known for his linocuts and pencil drawings, as well as for his books on art technique. *Christmas Morning*, a late work created in 1947, exemplifies his linoleum block-printing techniques, featuring bold, saturated colors and depictions of pastoral scenes. This print reflects the unspoiled tranquility of an early Christmas morning, a trio of deer being the first to venture onto the crest of new-fallen snow. Two turn their heads, as if they have been made aware of the artist's presence. The other seems more concerned with a drooping, snow-covered tree. Watson was born in Massachusetts and educated at the Massachusetts Normal Art School and the prestigious Pratt Institute in Brooklyn. He cofounded the Berkshire Summer School of Art as well as Watson Guptill, a publisher that specialized in art and design books and offered the magazine *American Artist*. His writing for the magazine helped elevate the careers of many leading lights, most notably American visual artist Andrew Wyeth (1917–2009). He also enjoyed a longtime association with the pencil company Joseph Dixon Crucible Company (later Dixon Ticonderoga), for which he contributed regular advertising content, developing the Broadstroke pencil drawing technique for which he was famous.

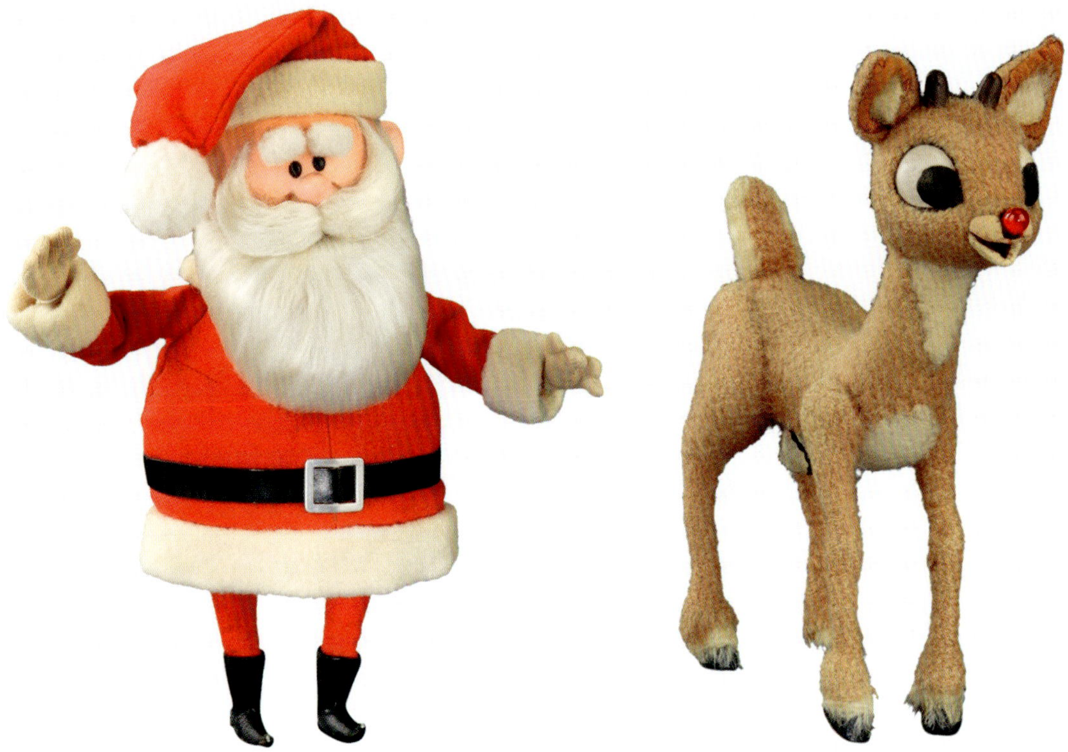

RANKIN/BASS PRODUCTIONS

•

Screen-used Santa and Rudolph puppets, 1964
Wood, wire, cloth, leather, and yak hair,
H. 11 in / 27.9 cm
Center for Puppetry Arts, Atlanta

Before streaming services brought on-demand entertainment to the masses, people had to be in front of their TV at an appointed time to bask in the warm cathode-ray glow of their favorite programs. And never was this truer than at Christmas, when annual specials were can't-miss events in many households, especially those created by Arthur Rankin Jr. (1924–2014) and Jules Bass (1935–2022). In 1964, *Rudolph the Red-Nosed Reindeer* (see p.85), their first holiday-themed animated special, aired on NBC. Rudolph, seen here with Santa, was the star—the fifty-five-minute-long show tells the unconventional tale of his discovery of the Island of Misfit Toys and his battle with the Abominable Snowman. It was a huge success and has become one of the longest-running Christmas specials of all time. Rankin and Bass first met at the American Broadcasting Company (ABC) in 1955, where Rankin was an art director and Bass a copywriter. In 1960, they formed a company later to be known as Rankin/Bass Productions, which was a pioneer of Animagic, a stop-motion animation process. Rankin/Bass produced many other specials that continue to be shown on TV around Christmastime, including a production of *Frosty the Snowman* (see p.174) in 1969 that spawned many sequels. These puppets are one of the only surviving pairs from the original special and were sold at auction in 2020, netting $300,000. They are now in the collection of the Center for Puppetry Arts in Atlanta, Georgia.

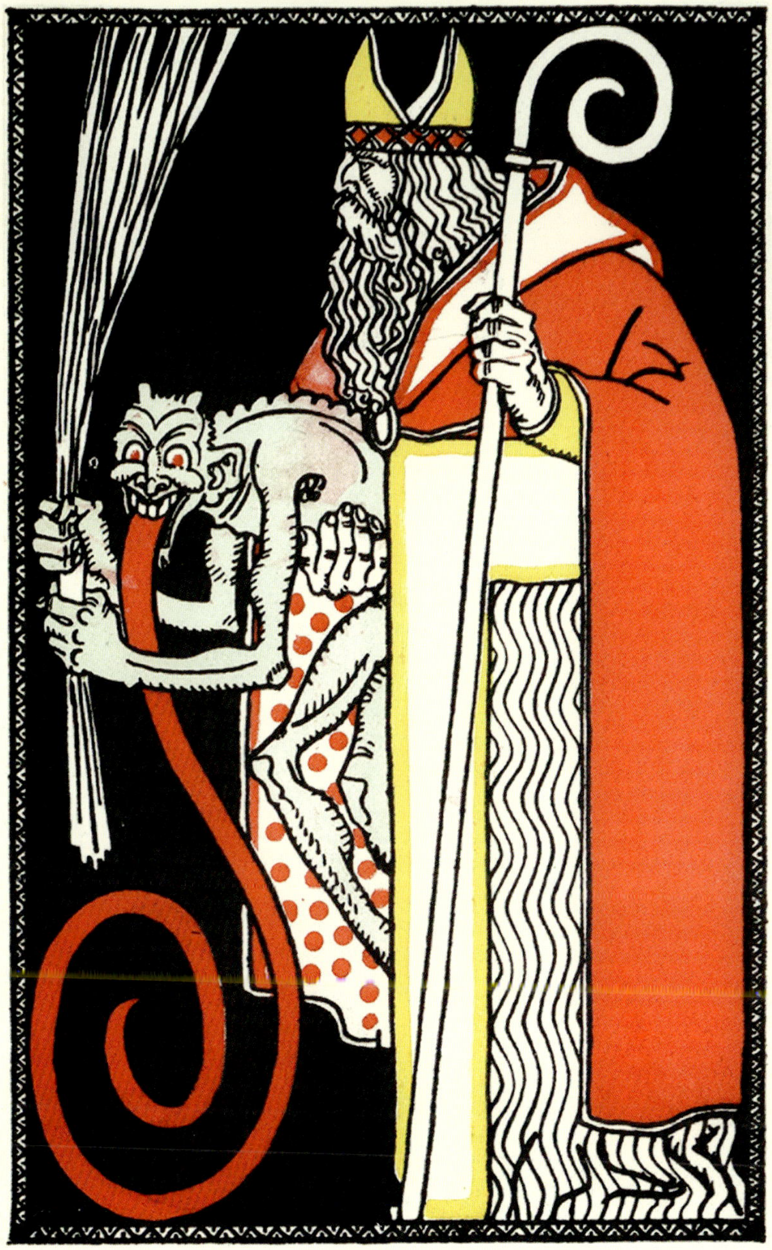

WIENER WERKSTÄTTE

•

St. Nicholas and Krampus card, 1911
Color lithograph, 5½ × 3½ in / 14 × 9 cm
Metropolitan Museum of Art, New York

The signature red cape and bishop's miter worn by the central character on this greeting card—created by an Austrian collective of architects, artists, designers, and artisans working in ceramics, fashion, silver, furniture, and the graphic arts—identify him as Saint Nicholas (see p.191). But instead of bearing presents, he carries a demonic-looking creature with a long, curling red tongue. Known as Krampus in Alpine folklore, this frightening beast is said to accompany Saint Nicholas on the night of December 5 (known as *Krampusnacht*) to scold naughty children. According to German and Austrian tradition, those who are good can expect oranges, dried fruit, walnuts, and chocolate, whereas those who have failed to behave receive a beating from Krampus. In some versions of the story, he carries a chain and bells along with a bundle of birch sticks, which he uses to whip youngsters before dragging them off to the underworld. Krampus's notoriety spread in the 1890s, when his image began appearing on alternative Christmas cards known as *Krampuskarten*, which feature the bestial character punishing children with his sticks and carrying them off in a bag, or, as here, accompanying the patron saint of Christmas himself on his rounds. Folklorists have suggested that the Krampus legend and its associated festivities predates Christmas, finding its roots in the pagan celebration of the winter solstice. *Krampusnacht* festivals have taken place across Germany and Austria for centuries and are still popular today.

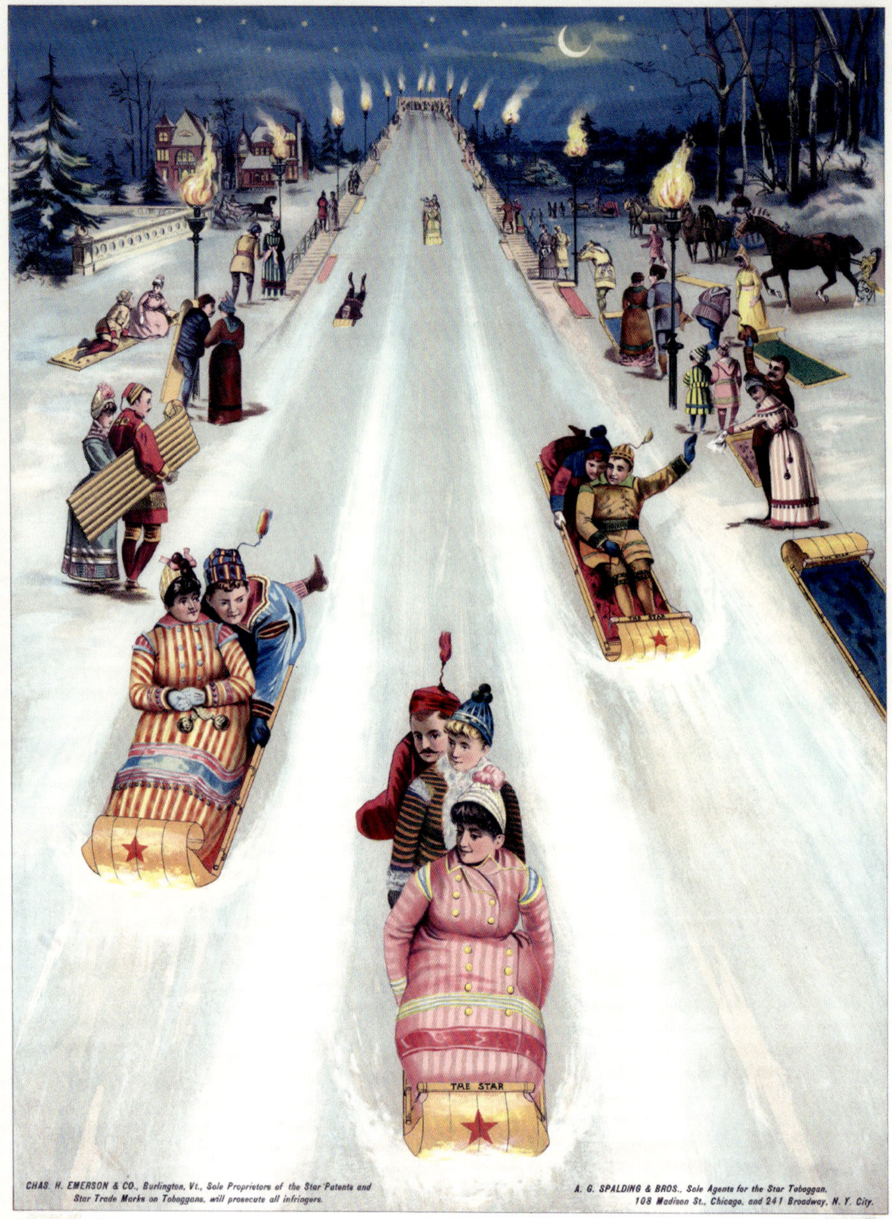

UNKNOWN

•

Star toboggans advertisement, c.1887
Chromolithograph, dimensions unknown
Phoenix Lithographic Company of Chicago

This vintage advertisement for Star toboggans depicts the thrill of sledding on a winter's evening, illuminated by torchlight. Sledding parties, often accompanied by mulled wine and hot cocoa, have been a long-standing winter tradition since the late nineteenth century, when recreational tobogganing was introduced to most of Europe, Canada, and the United States. It saw its peak as a leisure activity in the late nineteenth and early twentieth centuries and was perhaps most memorably featured as a central conceit in Edith Wharton's book *Ethan Frome* (1911). A good old-fashioned sled ride has been central to Christmas movies from old classics, including *It's a Wonderful Life* (1946) and *A Charlie Brown Christmas* (1965), to new classics, such as *National Lampoon's Christmas Vacation* (1989) and *Home Alone* (1990); (see pp.135, 182, 187). But the toboggan itself dates to the sixteenth century. The Algonquin North American Indians designed the flat-bottom wooden sled with a curved front end as a conveyance for transporting supplies and game across snow and ice (and, in fact, the word "toboggan" comes from the Algonquin *odabaggan*, meaning "sled")—and occasionally rode it, too. Ultimately, tobogganing metamorphosed into a number of modern competitive sports, including the Olympic events of luge, bobsled, and skeleton. Nowadays, you can still find children and adults alike sledding down snowy hills in local parks on cold, crisp winter mornings—not too dissimilar from the scene shown here.

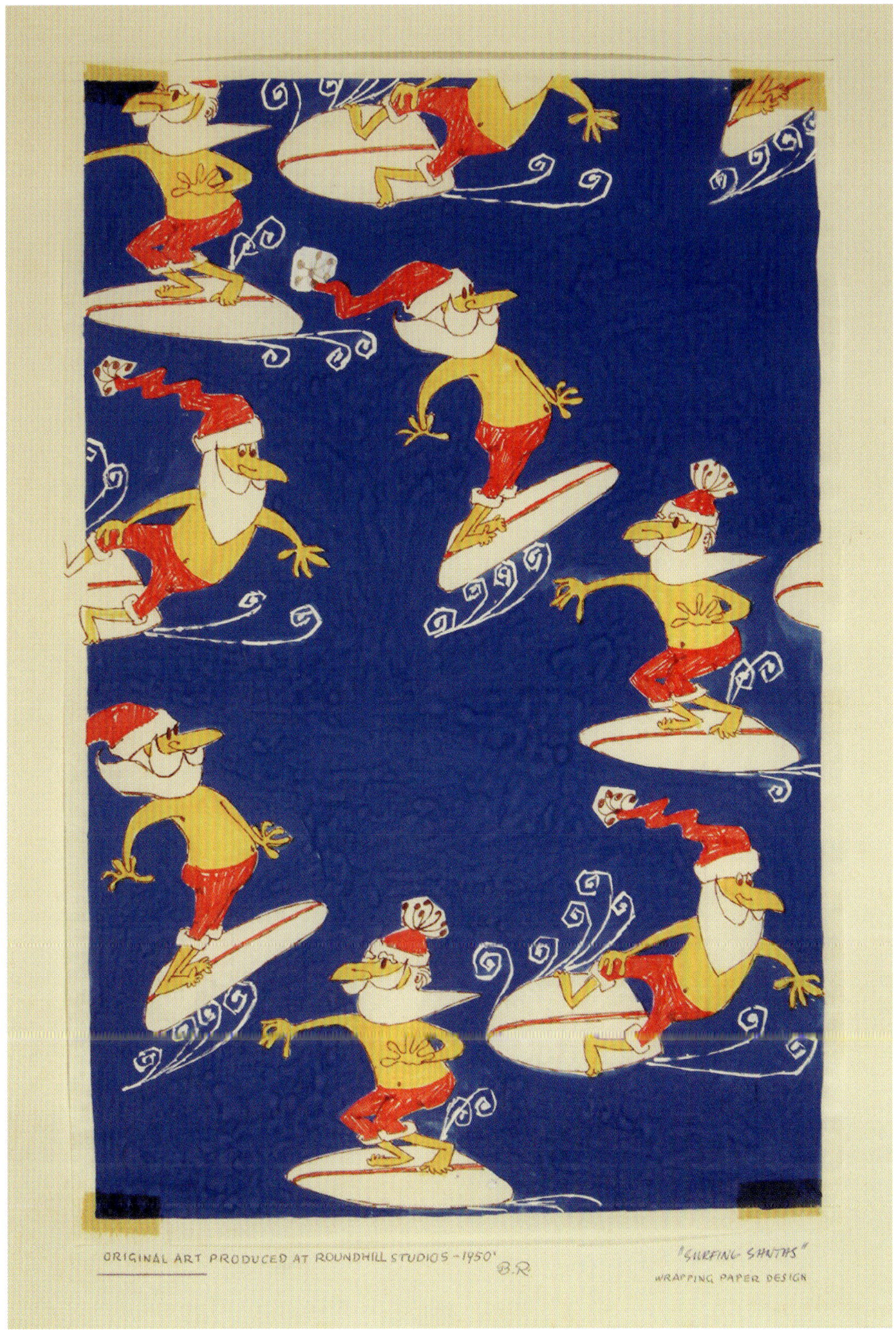

ROUNDHILL STUDIO

•

Surfing Santas wrapping paper, 1950
Pen and gouache on paper, dimensions unknown
Te Papa, Museum of New Zealand, Wellington

Surfboards piloted by a series of topless Santas throw out wakes of sharp white spirals that capture the giddy excitement of their riders in this Christmas wrapping paper design by New Zealand-based Roundhill Studio. Arms out and fingers splayed, with ankles and feet cocked for purchase, the Santas' red, fur-lined hats are a zigzag, whipped by the rush of forward momentum. Here, a character most often portrayed engaged in the labor of making or delivering gifts around the world appears instead focused solely on enjoying some well-earned downtime. Roundhill Studio took its name from its Dunedin-based founder Bernard Roundhill (1911–2005), who, from the 1930s onward, designed packaging and advertisements for a wide array of commercial goods in New Zealand, including soft drinks, canned foods, and children's toys. Much of the Studio's output is recognizable for Roundhill's own smooth, airbrushed style, whose enticingly plump forms encasing soft gradients of shining color had forged his reputation. The draftsmanship here is noticeably different—displaying a jagged energy reminiscent of Charles M. Schulz's *Peanuts* cartoons and an economy of line close to Saul Steinberg (see pp.51, 135)—suggesting it was undertaken by another artist at the studio. It is a design that shows the breadth of talent working under the Roundhill banner during its heyday and offers a humorous vision of what you might spot off the coast of New Zealand on Christmas Day.

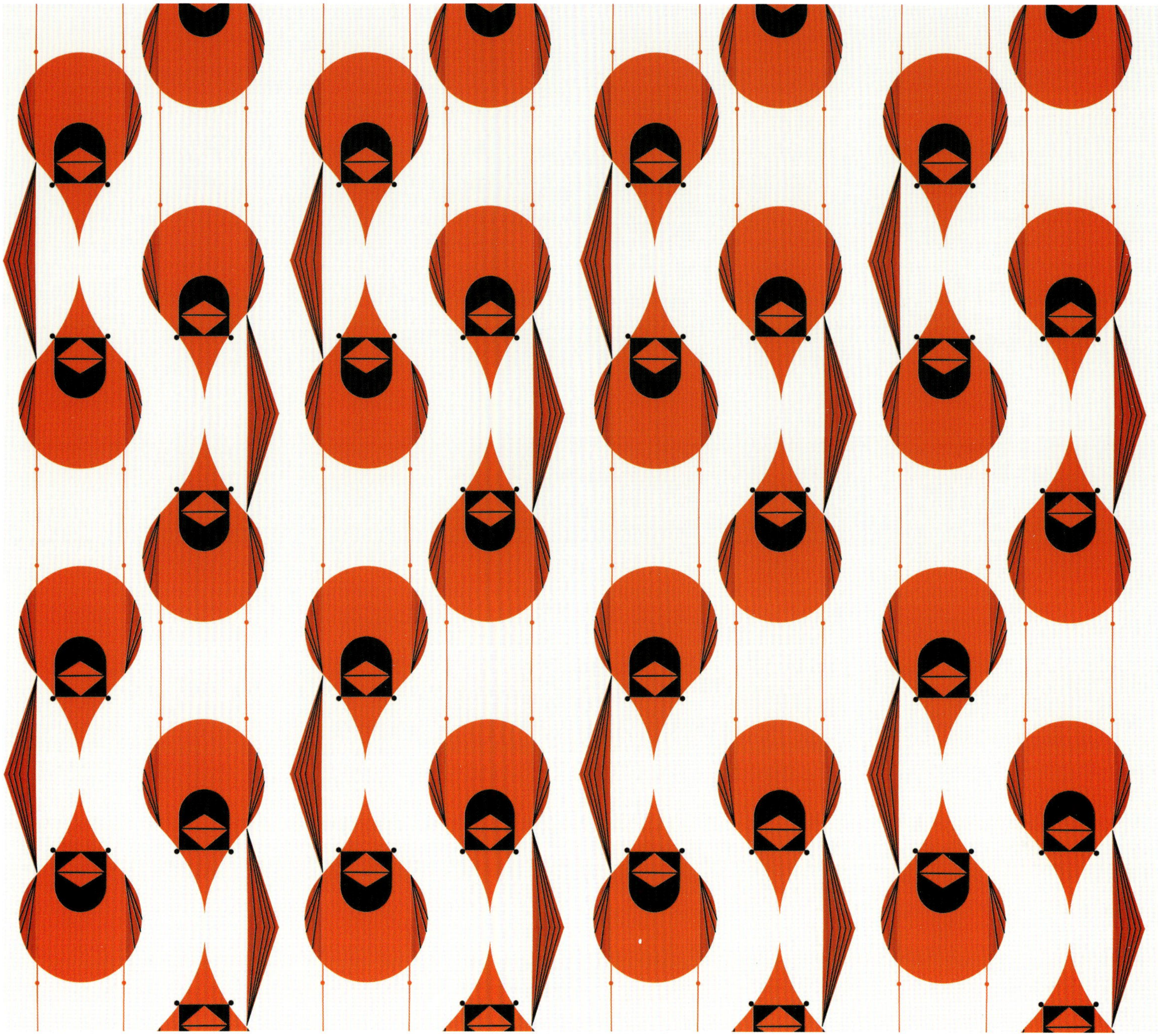

CHARLEY HARPER

•

Cardinal Stagger, 1960
Organic woven cotton, W. 44 in / 111.8 cm
For Birch Organic Fabrics, California

Red cardinals have long been associated with Christmas. Their distinctive red plumage has been read to mean many different things, including representing the blood of Christ. They were once considered symbols of faith, joy, and hope by early Christians, and were named for the distinctive red hats and robes of the cardinals who are senior officials of the Roman Catholic Church. This repeating pattern, titled *Cardinal Stagger* and printed on organic woven cotton by Birch Organic Fabrics, based in California, is an archetypical example of the bold, colorful designs created by American artist Charley Harper (1922–2007). Specializing in drawing birds and wildlife, his minimalist realism style allowed him to reduce his subjects to key features, best exploited in his illustrations for *The Giant Golden Book of Biology: An Introduction to the Science of Life*, published by Golden Press in New York in 1961, and studied by many young children throughout the latter half of the twentieth century. Here, the cardinal, common in North America, is imagined as a red teardrop-shaped bird, reminiscent of a Christmas ornament (see p.28), with distinctive black accents. This particular bird would become emblematic of Harper's work and is forever connected with Christmastime.

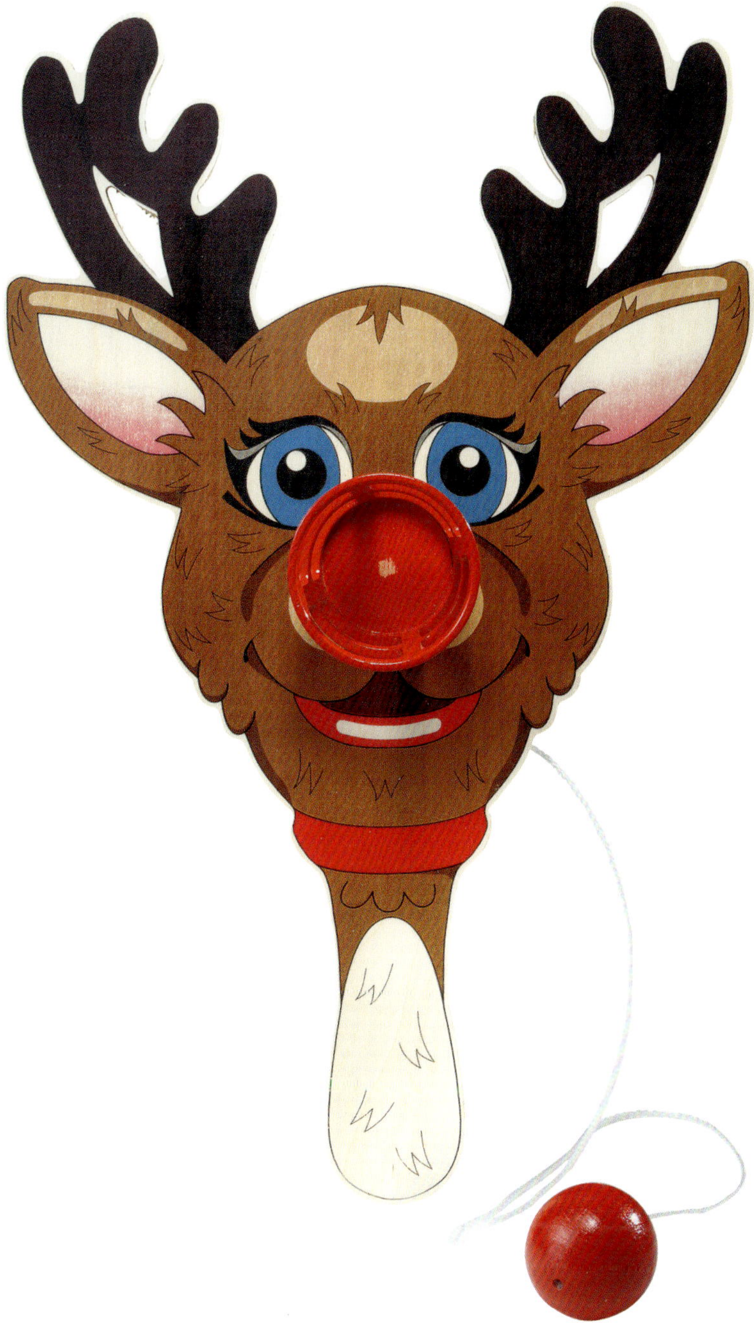

JEFF KOONS

•

Reindeer Paddle, 2000
Thermoprint on birchwood with painted metal and string, 12¼ × 8 × 2¼ in / 31.1 × 20.3 × 5.7 cm

Reindeer Paddle by American artist Jeff Koons (1955–) centers around Rudolph the Red-Nosed Reindeer, a long-standing feature of American Christmas festivities and the protagonist of a tale of acceptance and redemption. Originally created by Robert L. May in 1939 (see p.85) as a children's book character, Rudolph skyrocketed to fame in 1948, thanks to a musical adaptation of his story. Rudolph's ascendance into the mainstream in the 1950s coincided also with Koons's early years on the planet—a time he spent in his father's interior decoration store developing an interest in art and artifacts while absorbing generous doses of mass culture through television. Made in 2000 as a limited edition for the Deutsche Guggenheim in Berlin, *Reindeer Paddle* reprises some of the trademark themes Koons has explored through most of his career since his pivotal Banality series (1988). Rudolph's head is reproduced as a wooden paddle with a red ball in place of his iconic nose. On top of reinstating Koons's interest in Conceptual and Pop art, *Reindeer Paddle* is an indicator of the artist's predilection for representing animals and anthropomorphic figures, as exemplified by his appropriation of other fictional or real-life creatures, from Michael Jackson's chimpanzee Bubbles to the Pink Panther or the majestic floral sculpture *Puppy*.

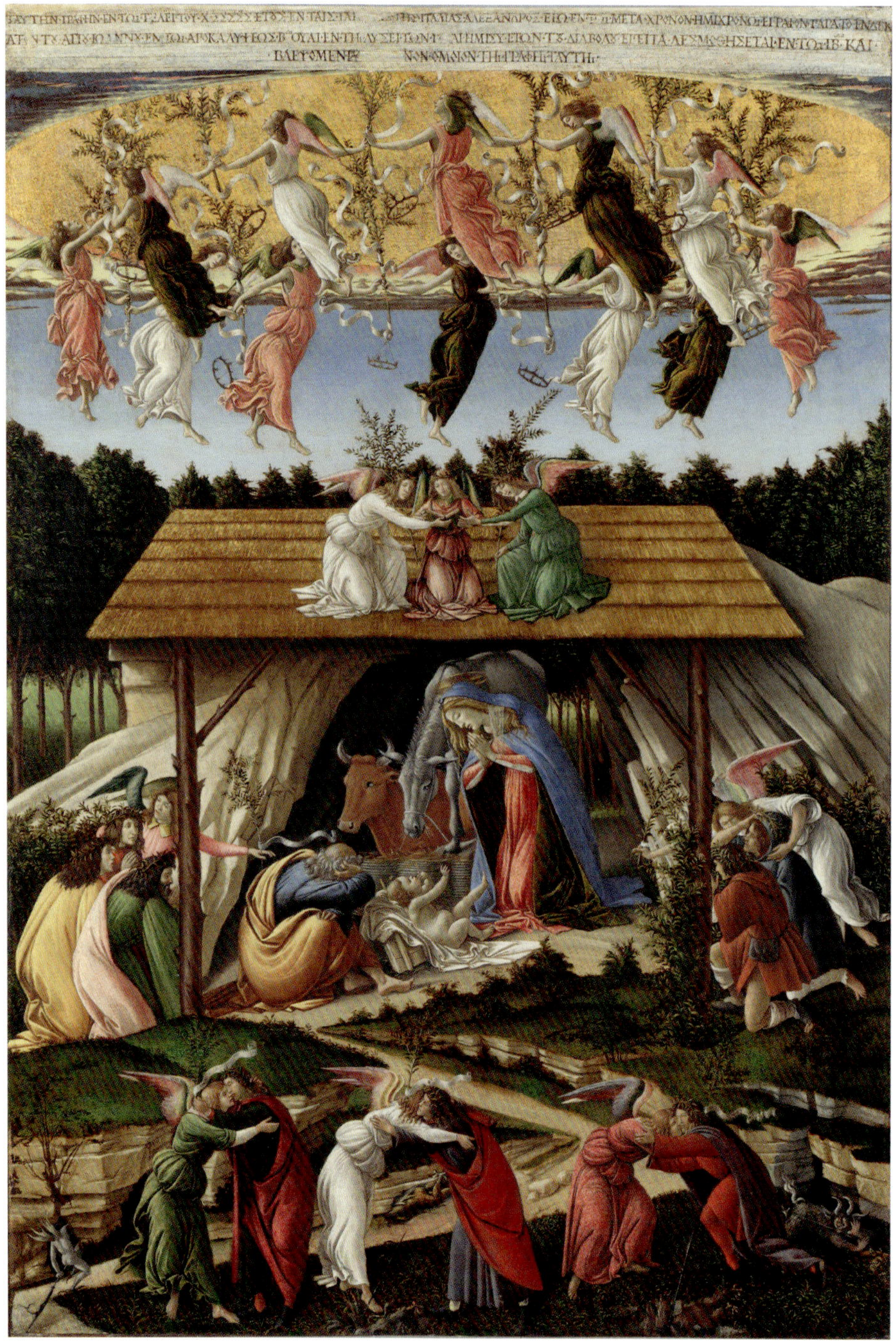

SANDRO BOTTICELLI

•

Mystic Nativity, 1500
Oil on canvas, 42¾ × 29½ in / 108.6 × 74.9 cm
National Gallery, London

Although this Renaissance painting includes all the elements of a traditional Nativity scene—the infant Jesus with Mary and Joseph, farm animals, the visiting shepherds, and Three Wise Men (see p.10)—*Mystic Nativity* by Florentine artist Sandro Botticelli (*c.*1445–1510) is not as straightforward as it might seem. In one reading, it is a conventional celebration of the Adoration of Christ; in another, it contains a premonition of the Apocalypse. The broken phrases of Latin and Greek above the painting refer to the recent invasion of Italy by France, and to the civil strife caused in Florence by the fanatical preacher Savonarola, whose attacks on worldly vanity had inspired Botticelli to destroy many of his own paintings. For Botticelli, these events recalled the turmoil predicted in the Book of Revelation as heralding the return of Christ. *Mystic Nativity* has at its heart an overscale Virgin Mary and baby Jesus, signifying their importance, while angels carrying olive branches circle the golden dome of Heaven, and angels and men hug on Earth. Demons rush to hide as the devil is buried. Unusually for the time, Botticelli chose to paint on canvas rather than wood, and it is the only one of his paintings he signed; he may have painted the Nativity for his own use. After Botticelli's death, the painting disappeared for three hundred years, until it was brought to England and its "mystical" elements were first noted by critics.

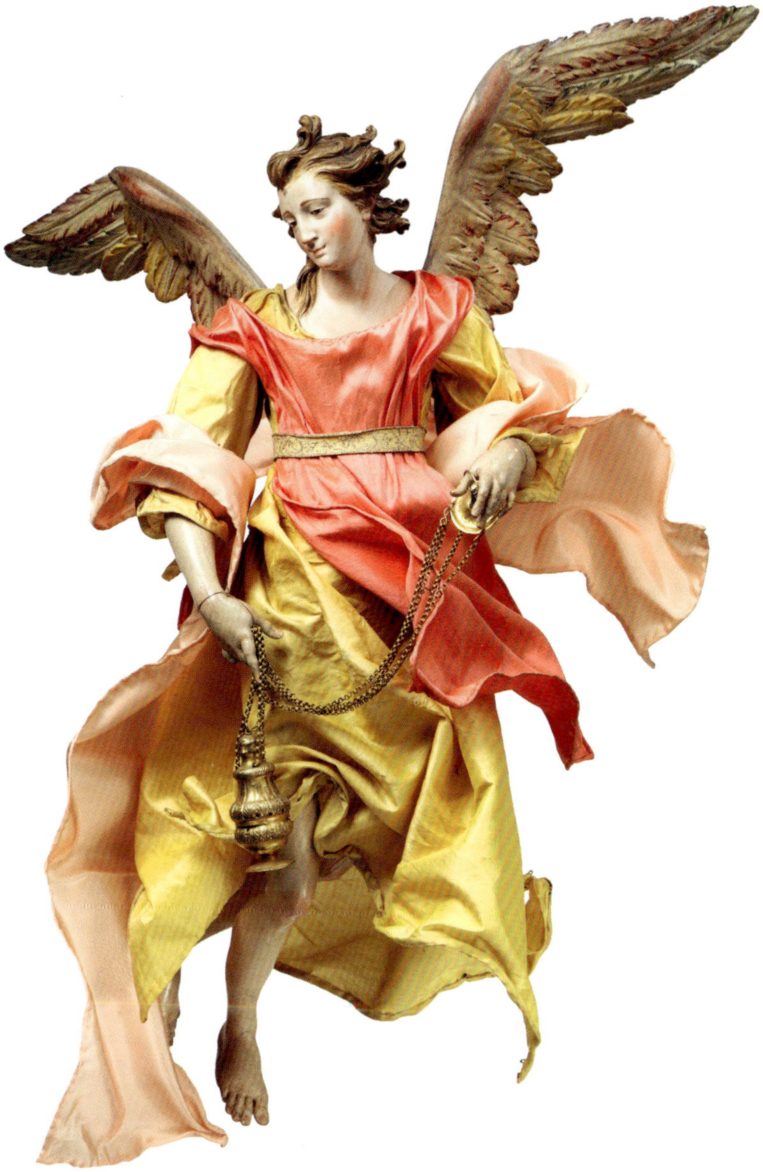

GIUSEPPE SANMARTINO

•

Angel, c.1775
Polychromed terra-cotta, wood, wire wrapped in tow, and various fabrics, H. 17¼ in / 43.8 cm
Metropolitan Museum of Art, New York

An angel, whose heavily lidded eyes and gentle smile express a beatific contentment, lifts herself into the air with short wings that reflect subtly the pink, rose, and embroidered gold colors of her flowing tunic. Her hair flows backward—matching the fabric's animated character—in rolling curls formed by the onrushing wind of her flight, and she gracefully lifts a gold incense censer burner, the finely crafted links of which convey a great weight. The work, crafted by the Italian Rococo sculptor Giuseppe Sanmartino (1720–1793), is one element of a grand traditional Neapolitan *presepio,* or sculpted Nativity scene, which included several other angels, shepherds, and wise men in the collection of the Metropolitan Museum of Art in New York (see p.162). Sculpted Nativities are displayed in almost all churches at Christmas, but the history of their creation is particularly rich and intertwined with the practice of leading fine artists in Naples. The eighteenth century marks the creative pinnacle of *presepio* construction. Sanmartino's most famous work is the prostrate *Veiled Christ* in the Cappella Sansevero, Naples. The crafting of fabric out of marble that Sanmartino finessed there as an astonishing, seemingly alchemical trompe l'oeil is displayed here as actual fabrics, with hems shaped by contorted stiffened wire. Lifted at the knee to reveal bare feet floating above the ground, the whole effect is designed to give the impression of weightlessness and a divine flight.

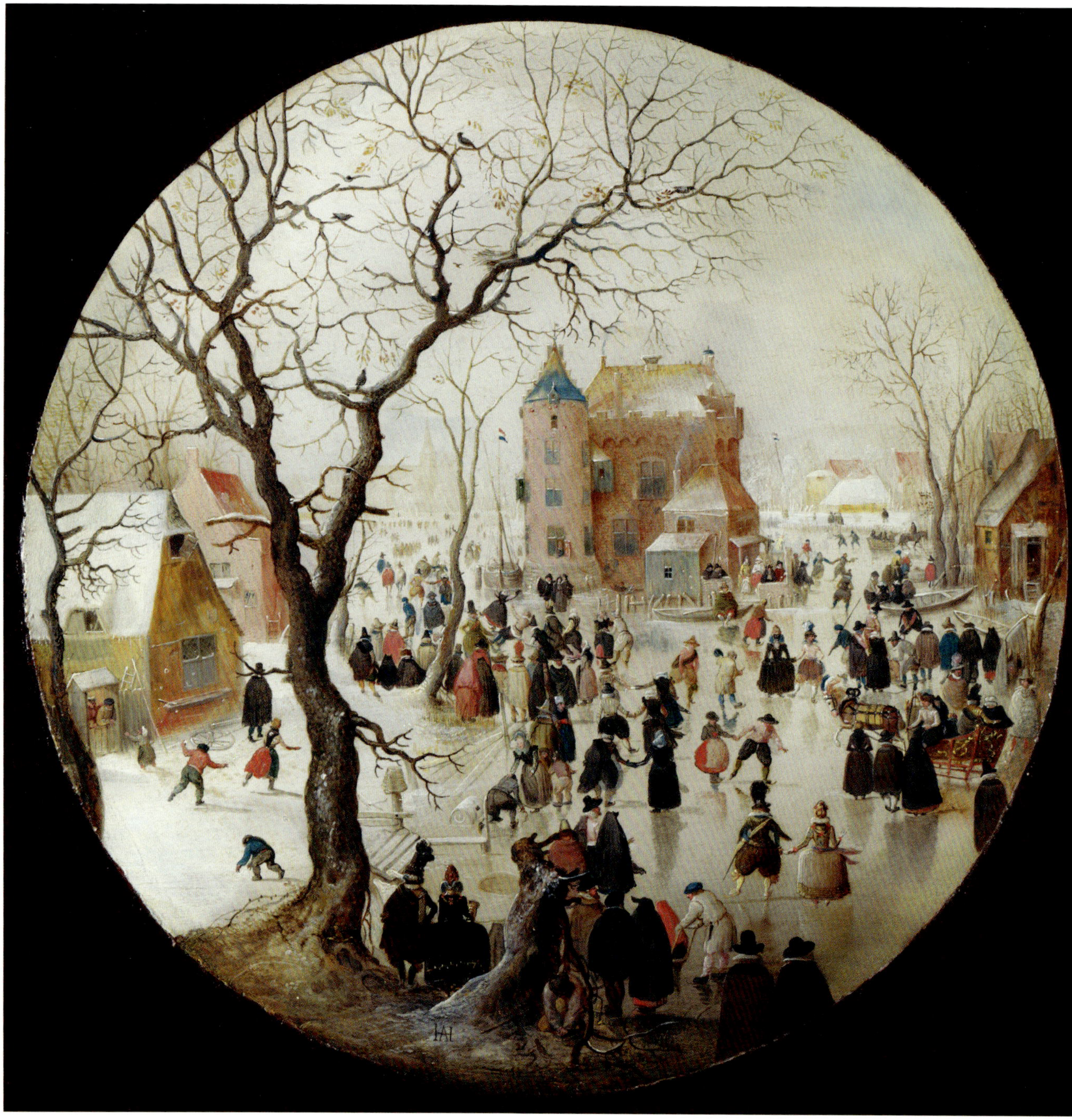

HENDRICK AVERCAMP

•

A Winter Scene with Skaters near a Castle, c.1608
Oil on oak, 16 × 16 in / 40.7 × 40.7 cm
National Gallery, London

The winter conditions have not dampened the spirits of this Dutch community, who are going about their daily business and enjoying themselves on the frozen canal. Secular works like this were a response to the rise of Calvinism during the Protestant Reformation, which forbade religious painting in churches and forced artists to seek new themes. This scene is therefore not overtly of Christmastime, but it is vividly reminiscent of activities one might do when the cold of the holiday season draws in (see p.179). People from all walks of life—rich and poor, young and old—mingle together on the ice; couples skate hand in hand, horses pull sleighs, and children throw snowballs, all surveyed from above by birds perching in a large, leafless tree. At the bottom left, a wealthy husband and wife have dressed for show, while near the center, another pair take an unceremonious tumble. In front of the castle, someone has fallen through the ice, seemingly unnoticed by the throng of skaters. This small, circular painting is typical of the richly detailed winter scenes that Duthc artist Hendrick Avercamp (1585–1634) specialized in, and although he spent most of his life in the small town of Kampen, the composition is entirely imagined. It started life as a series of drawings before being meticulously transferred to panel. Painted with a delicate hand, each tiny figure is rendered with just a few masterly brushstrokes, from the skaters in the foreground to those in the hazy distance.

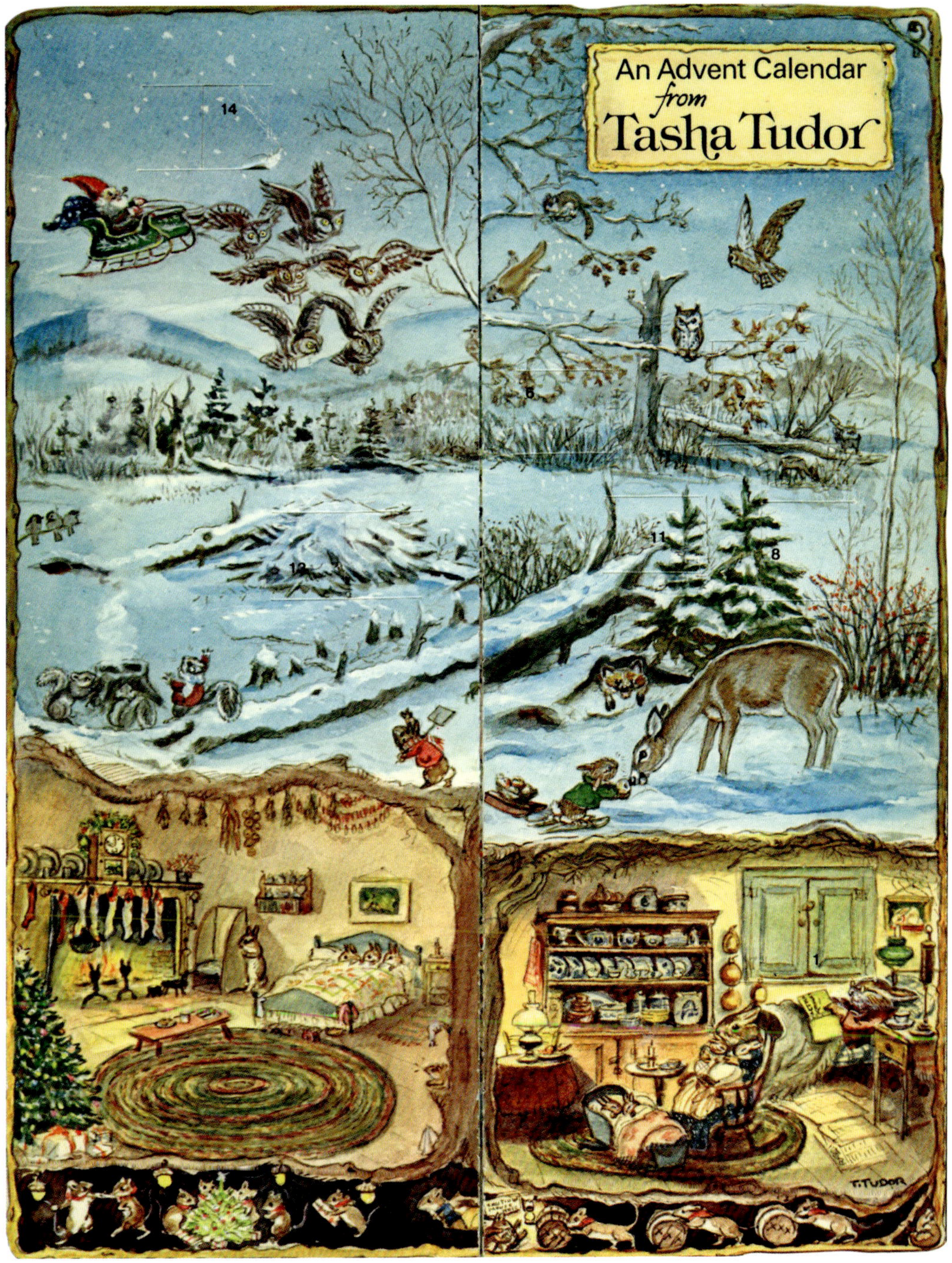

TASHA TUDOR

•

Lapin and Lapin, Afternoon Teas, 1978
Folded cardstock, 25½ × 11 in / 64.7 × 28 cm
Private collection

The outer wings of this advent calendar, created for the Rand McNally map company by the US artist and illustrator Tasha Tudor (1915–2008), show delicate winter scenes. Deer feed in a snow-covered landscape and anthropomorphized rabbits lie tucked up in bed in front of a roaring fire, with a mantelpiece lined with Christmas stockings. However, in the sky at the top left, the sleigh, pulled by a team of owls, hints at hidden wonders to be discovered when the trifold wings are pulled apart to reveal the calendar's interior. Not only is the expanded canvas where the traditional advent doors, numbered from one to twenty-four, can be found, it also reveals the rabbits' rooms to be only part of an underground dwelling, in which a raucous festive gathering is taking place.

Tudor's captivating children's book illustrations drew on her love of nature and firm commitment to living a traditional agrarian life in the New England countryside. Her animals might appear similar to Beatrix Potter's woodland creatures, such as Peter Rabbit (see p.55), or even forerunners of the wholesome Sylvanian Families (see p.185), but there is a more mischievous energy at play, epitomized by some carousing racoons who jig to the sound of a fiddle and whose brash legend boasts "No trash can has ever foiled us." In fact, the work is redolent with art historical reference, including in form and overall thronging effect, to Dutch artist Hieronymus Bosch's (1450–1516) celebrated oil painting *The Garden of Earthly Delights* (*c*.1490).

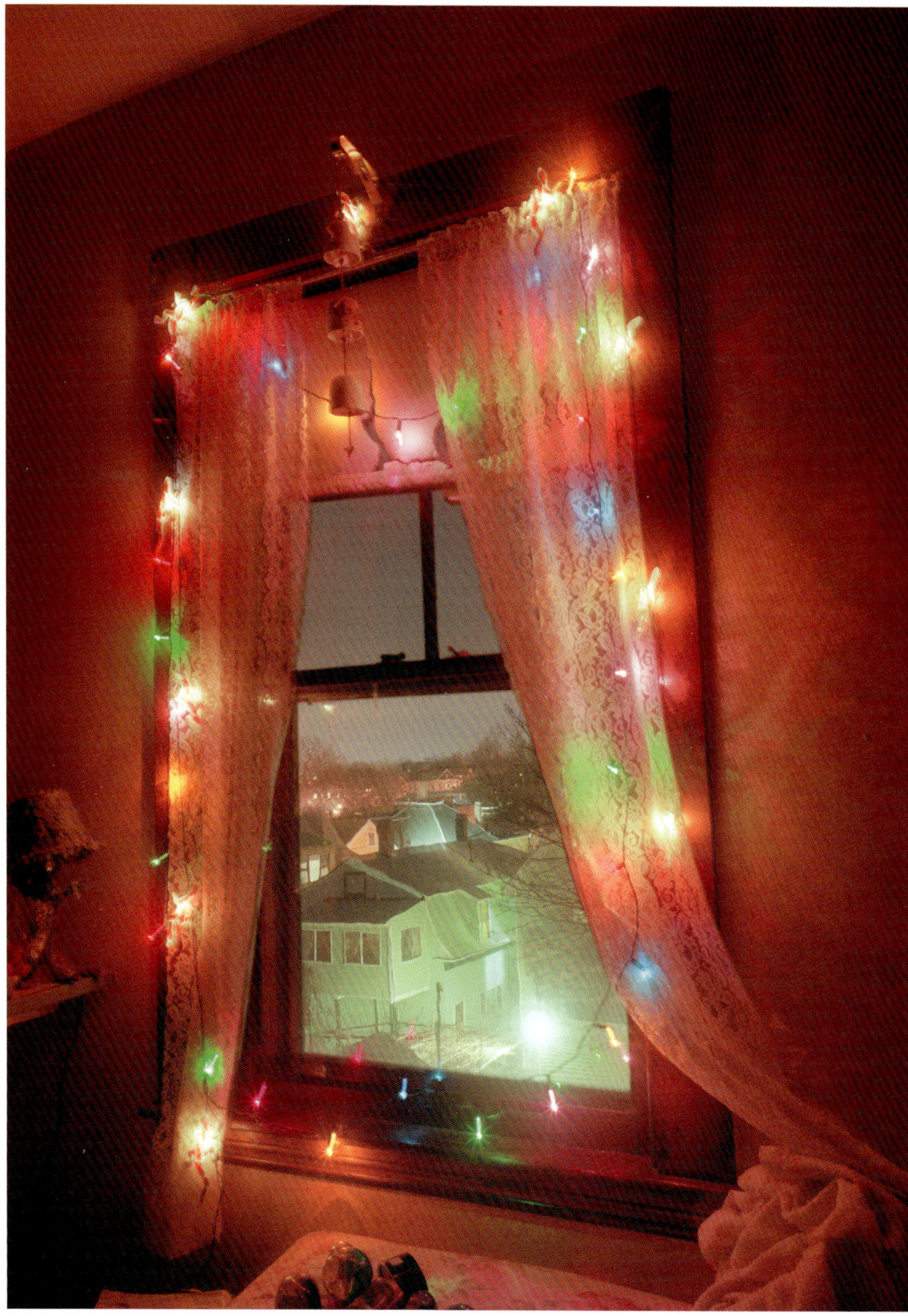

MARY KOCOL

•

Christmas Window, Somerville, Massachusetts, 1989
Chromogenic print,
36½ × 25¼ in / 92.5 × 64.1 cm
Museum of Modern Art, New York

Photographer Mary Kocol (1962–), in contrast to her day job digitizing Harvard University Art Museum's collection, works almost exclusively in analog photography. Each shot is unique, and she enjoys the element of surprise film photography offers, each frame a mystery until she develops it. *Christmas Window, Somerville, Massachusetts* (1989) exemplifies her work perfectly. Although taken in Somerville, it could be anywhere, conjuring the soft-edged, warm feelings of Christmas, tinged with the glow of multicolored lights, the cold held at bay outside while indoors it is snug and warm. The unique perspective offered by looking out of a window, as opposed to looking in on a cozy Christmas scene, seems to offer more comfort to the viewer.

After earning her MFA in photography from Rhode Island School of Design in 1987, she came to public attention in 1991, when the Museum of Modern Art (MoMA) in New York hosted her first exhibition. She later received a Guggenheim Fellowship, and her work is now included in the collections of many of the world's most lauded museums. Her work often concerns itself with the power of memory (itself unreliable, imperfect, and imprecise) and the ability of a photograph to evoke familiar feelings in the viewer that have perhaps been forgotten or lost to time. Fittingly, her inspiration often comes from memories of her own childhood growing up in Hartford, Connecticut.

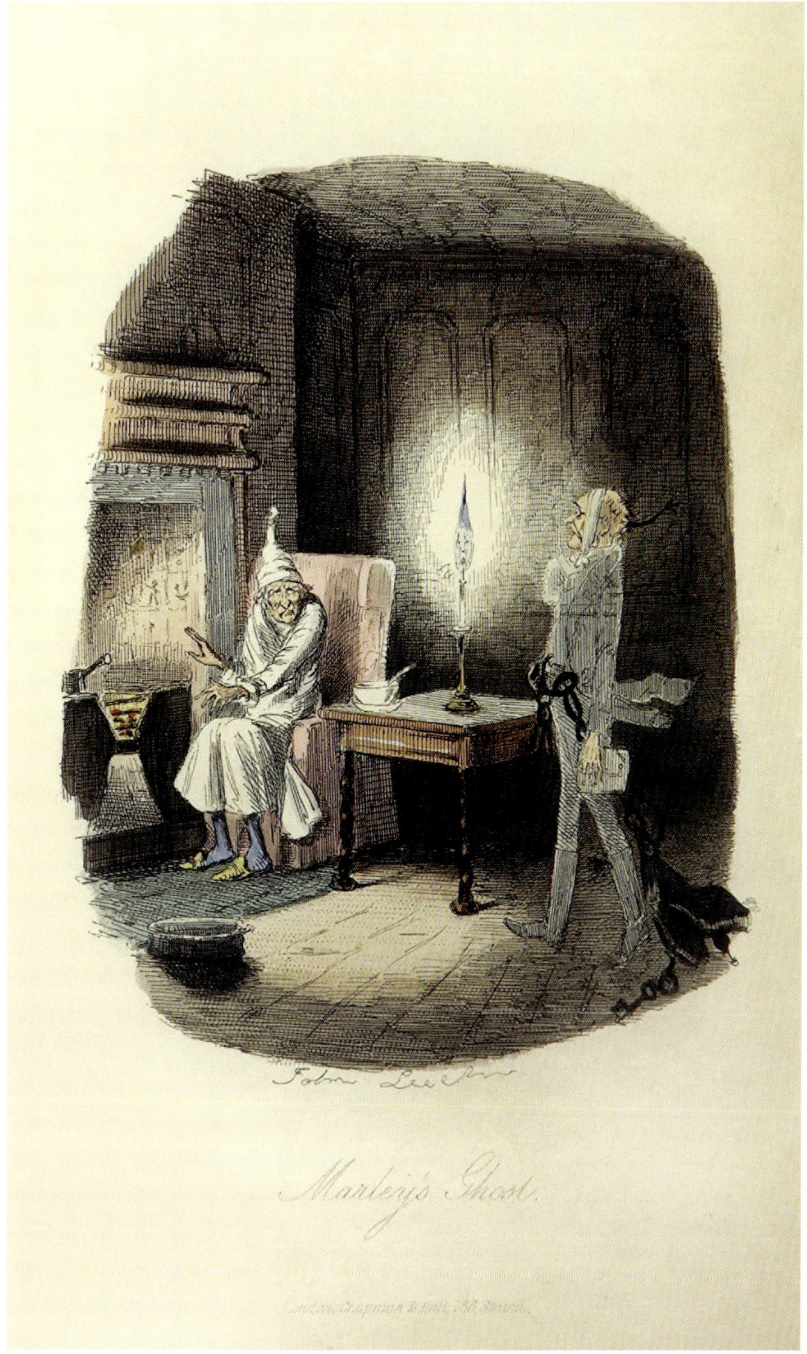

JOHN LEECH

•

Marley's ghost, from *A Christmas Carol*
by Charles Dickens, 1843
Hand-colored etching, 4½ × 3 in / 11.8 × 8.5 cm
Published by Chapman & Hall, London

Ebenezer Scrooge—the character whose observation "Bah! humbug!" became shorthand for the rejection of the Christmas spirit—shivers beside a meager fire on Christmas Eve as the ghost of his former business partner, Jacob Marley, appears before him wearing the manacles he explains he forged during his lifetime by putting money above people. This illustration by John Leech (1817–1864) comes from the first edition of *A Christmas Carol* (1843), by Charles Dickens (1812–1870), a writer whom many people credit for creating Christmas as it is now celebrated in the United Kingdom and North America—but it may be more accurate to say he helped reinvent Christmas alongside Queen Victoria (1819–1901) and Prince Albert (1819–1861). Dickens's story (see p.133) explains how Marley's ghost introduces three more ghosts—those of Christmas Past, Present, and Yet to Come—who together convince Scrooge to embrace the spirit of giving lauded in both the earlier Georgian era and the Victorian world. Scrooge realizes that while he may be rich, his life is spiritually and emotionally poorer than that of the impoverished family of his employee, Bob Cratchit, and is reborn on Christmas morning as a loving and generous man. *A Christmas Carol* was an immediate success upon publication, the story of Scrooge's redemption striking a chord with Victorian Britain, and its initial print run of six thousand copies sold out in just a few days. Leech, a friend of Dickens, was best known as an illustrator for the satirical magazine *Punch*.

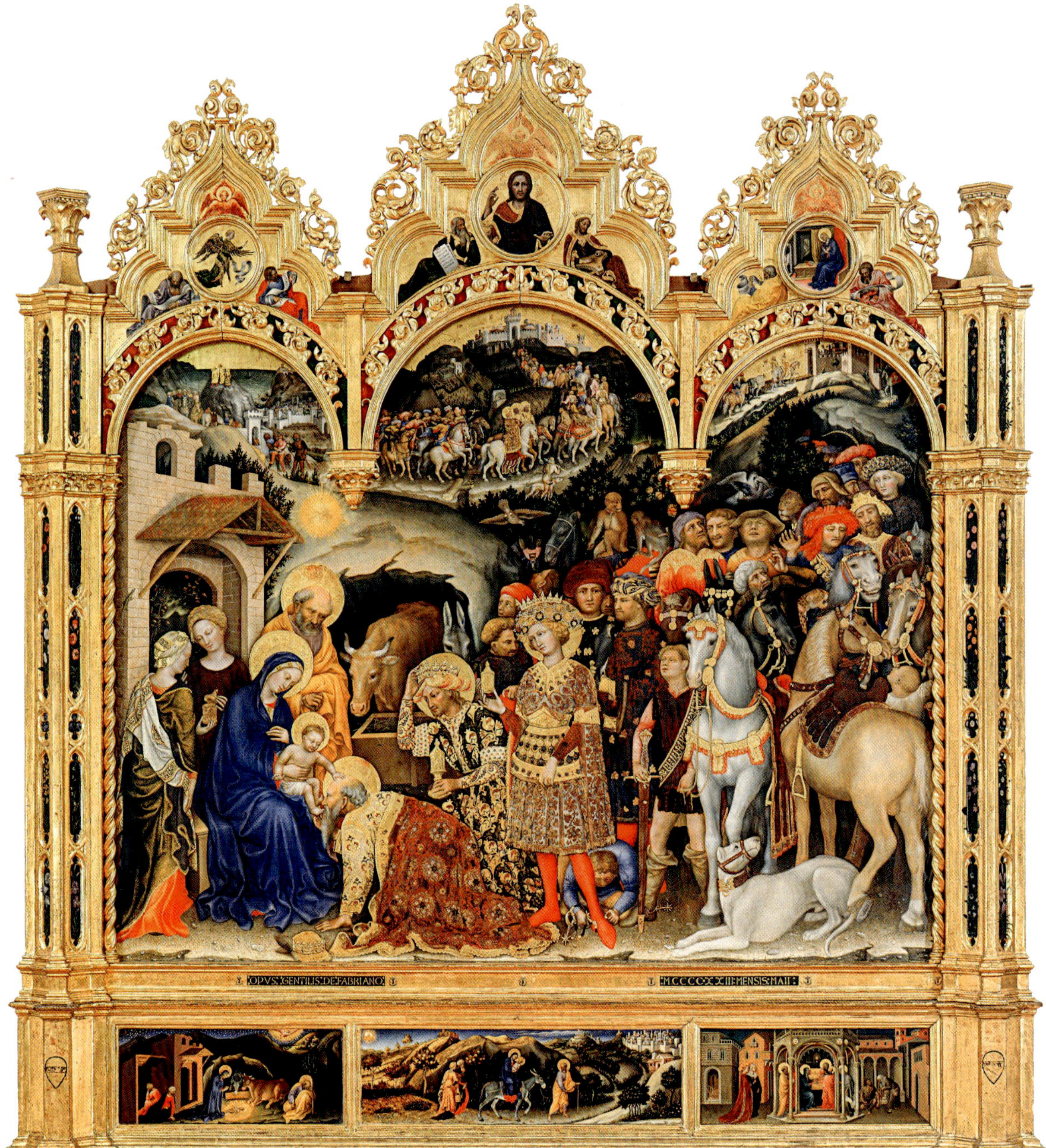

GENTILE DA FABRIANO

•

Adoration of the Magi, 1423
Tempera on wood, 118⅛ × 111 in / 300 × 282 cm
Galleria degli Uffizi, Florence

An ornate altarpiece by the early Renaissance painter Gentile da Fabriano (1370–1427), the *Adoration of the Magi* shows the Magi—the Three Wise Men—as they arrive in Bethlehem to honor the newborn baby Jesus and bestow him with gifts. The Italian painter creates a visual narrative to illustrate the journey described in the Gospel of Matthew, from the Magi sighting the star that announces the birth of Christ to their arrival in Bethlehem (see p.176). Into the narrative, da Fabriano weaves many references and allusions to the city of Florence and his patron Palla Strozzi (1372–1462), a wealthy banker. Encasing the painting is a remarkable gold frame decorated at the sides with painted flowers, while the predella (the front of the step beneath the altarpiece) shows a scene from Christ's childhood. The prodigious use of both gold and ultramarine, made from expensive lapis lazuli, used for Mary's gown highlights Strozzi's deep pockets. To maximize the effect of the gold in the chapel's candlelight, da Fabriano uses a raised gilt ornament—*pastiglia*—for the halos, swords, clothing, and spurs, giving the golden objects a three-dimensional quality. His inclusion of exotic birds and animals, such as falcons, monkeys, and a lion, hint at not just Strozzi's wealth—the rich sometimes collected animals—but also at the origins of the Christmas story in the Holy Lands of the East. The Magis' dress, their turbans, and exotic textiles further reflect the exotic East and its trading relationship with the mercantile city of Florence.

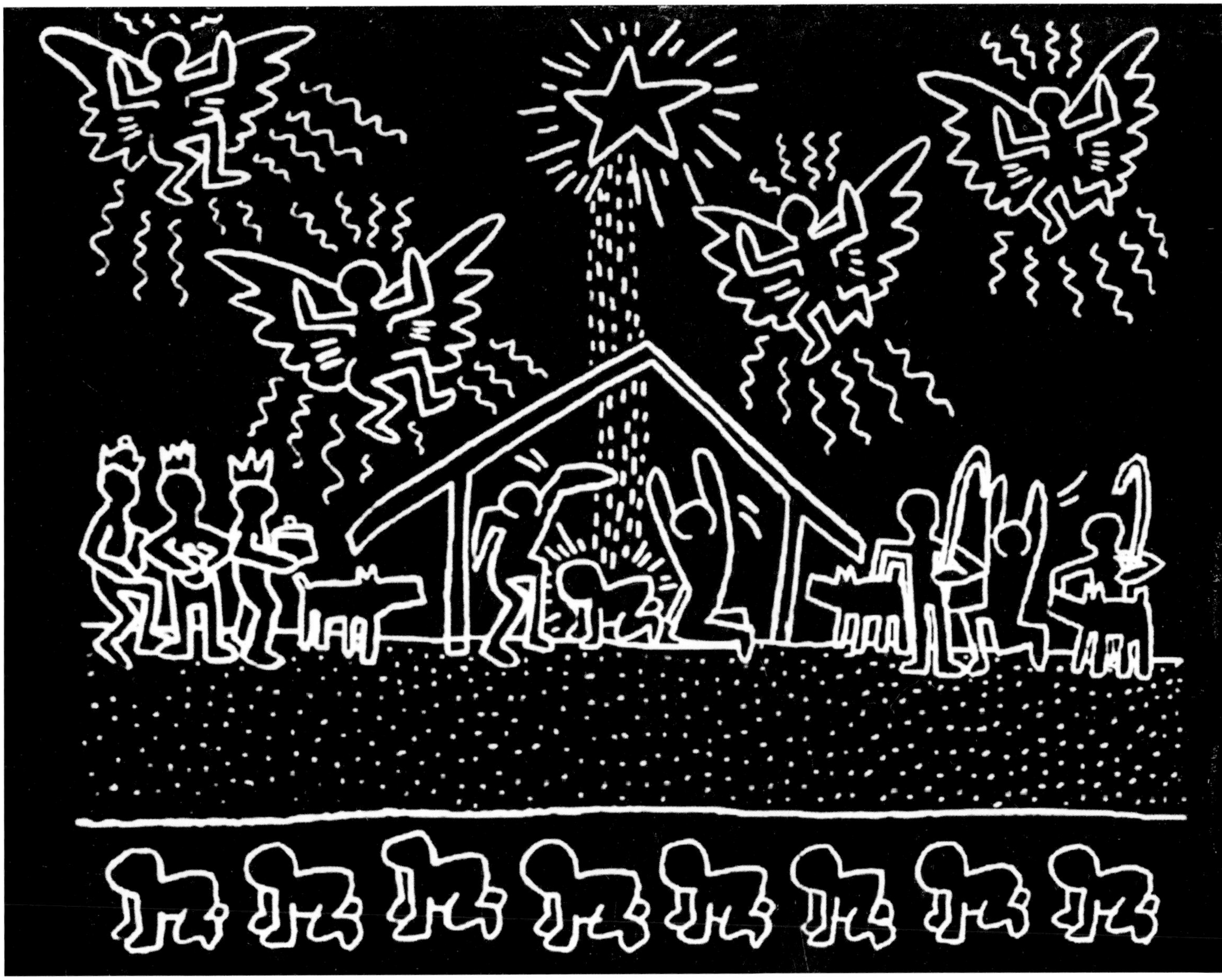

KEITH HARING

•

Untitled (Nativity), 1983
Chalk on paper, dimensions unknown
Keith Haring Foundation

Drawn with cartoonlike simplicity and pulsating with energy, this lively Nativity scene is a joyous celebration of Christ's birth. The black-and-white chalk drawing shows exultant angels, elated shepherds, and excited kings. A radiant star shining in the sky illuminates the stable below, where a jubilant Mary and Joseph dance around their newborn baby, whose body emits rays of light (see p.11). Keith Haring (1958–1990) was a prolific member of New York's graffiti subculture in the early 1980s. He drew this image on an empty advertising panel in the city's subway, where his cryptic line drawings of human figures, babies, and dogs were a ubiquitous sight. Although he is best known for his subsequent murals and colorful paintings conveying political and social themes—from antidrug and anti-apartheid messages to campaigns raising awareness of AIDS—he had an enduring interest in religion. His teenage encounters with the countercultural Jesus movement led to a brief but intense evangelical fixation. Around this time, he made religious images, including traditional Nativity scenes in which Christ appears with lines radiating from his body, a convention in Renaissance religious painting influenced by the visions of Saint Bridget of Sweden (1303–1373). Haring's radiant baby motif became a signature, or "tag," and appeared frequently in his work. Here, the image is elevated to a symbol of hope, reflecting the artist's enduring interest in the notion of Jesus Christ as divine savior.

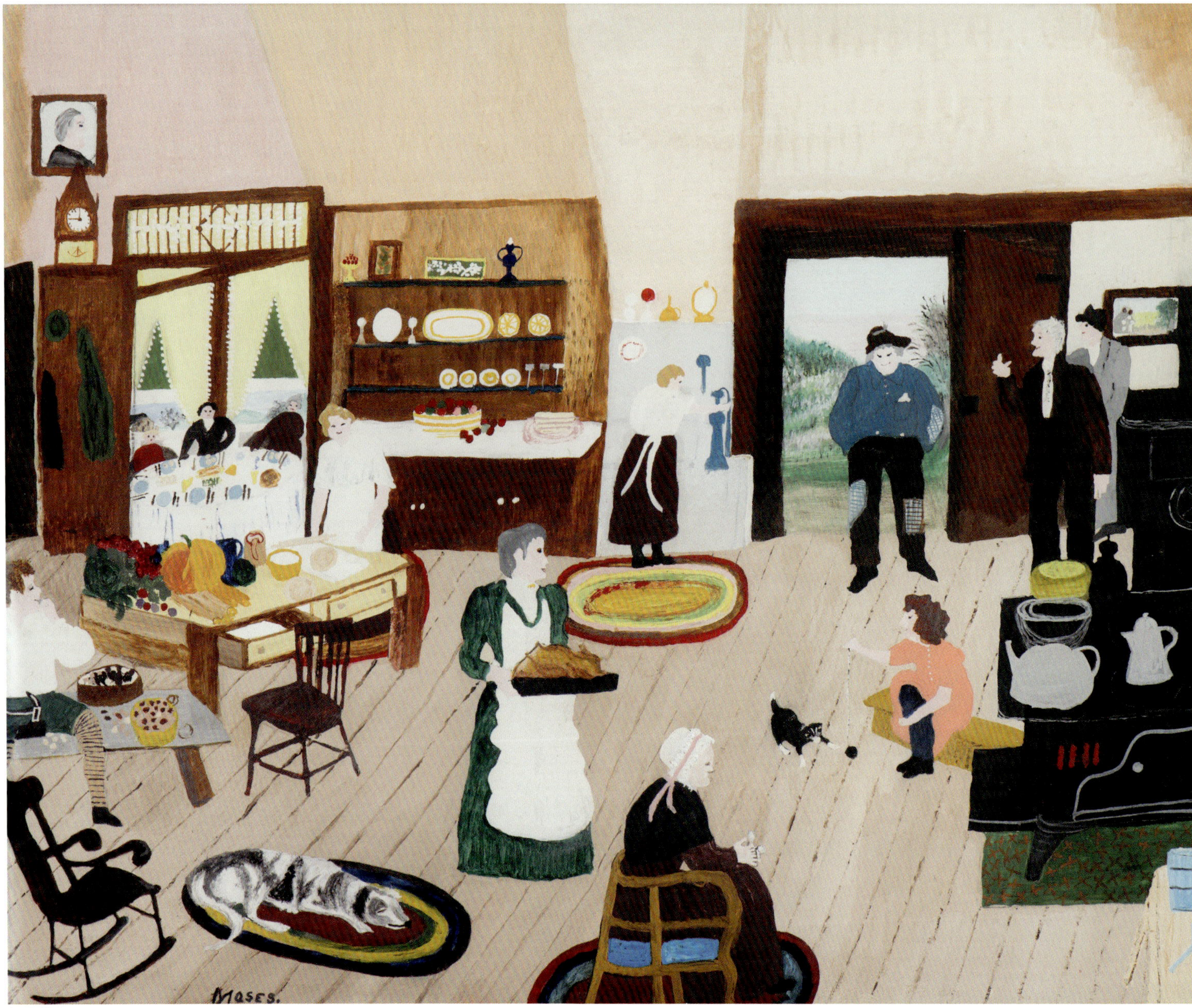

GRANDMA MOSES

•

A Tramp on Christmas Day, 1946
Oil on academy board, 15⅜ × 19⅜ in / 39 × 49.2 cm
Shelburne Museum, Vermont

A Tramp on Christmas Day is an early work by self-taught American artist Anna Mary Robertson, known best as Grandma Moses (1860–1961). This interior scene shows a large family celebrating Christmas. A traditional bird (see p.227) is being carried to the oven for roasting as vegetables are being prepared and the table is being set for dinner. A dog rests on a rug as a young girl keeps the cat entertained with a ball on a string. A man, presumably the aforementioned tramp, dressed in patchwork clothes, stands imposingly in the doorway, bringing a sense of menace to the otherwise tranquil composition. Despite only taking up painting when seventy-eight years old, Moses would produce some two thousand works before her death. Drawing on her vivid imagination, she also found inspiration in the rural landscape surrounding her home in upstate New York, where she resided among her very large nuclear family: five children, nine grandchildren, and over thirty great-grandchildren. Without access to sophisticated materials, she often used cardboard instead of canvas and matchsticks instead of paintbrushes. This gave her works a naive, rudimentary quality, which is highly regarded for its nostalgic charm, capturing a bygone spirit of American country life. Her work quickly rose to prominence and was reproduced as stamps, prints, and, Christmas cards. She is still celebrated today for illustrating the holiday spirit and conveying a form of quaint "Americanness" that speaks to a preindustrial time.

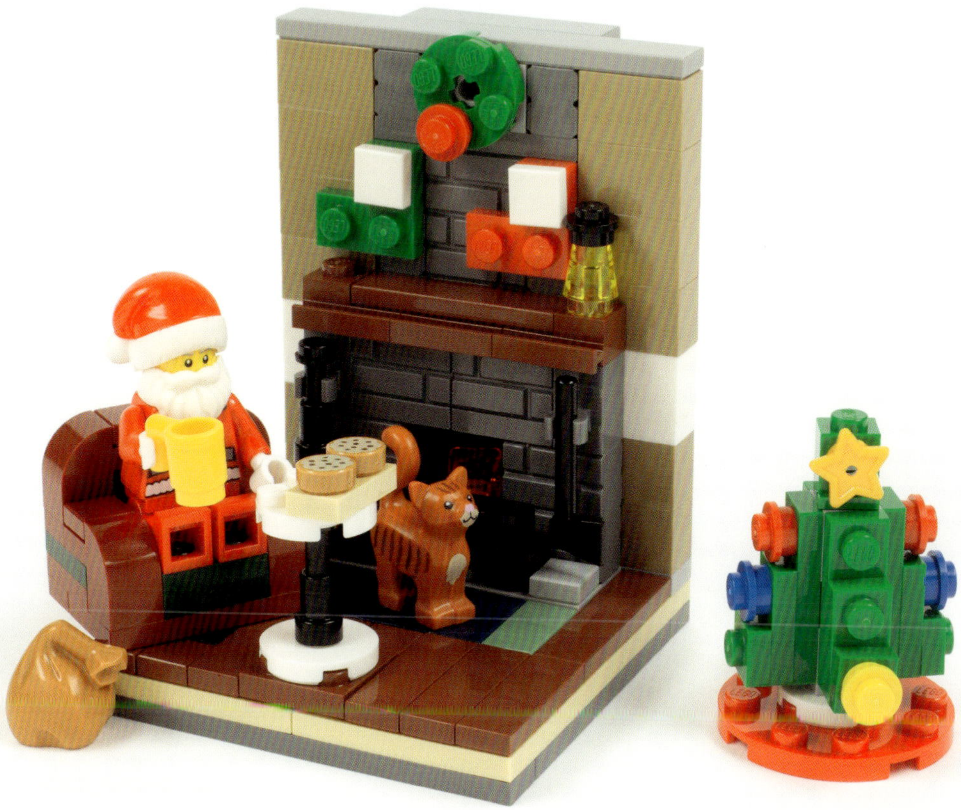

LEGO

•

Santa's Visit, 2015
Plastic, dimensions variable

Santa Claus enjoys a cookie and a mug of milk beside a fireplace hung with colorful stockings in a scene familiar to millions of parents for whose children Lego has become an essential part of Christmas. Since 2009, fans of the Danish plastic bricks have been able to buy special Christmas sets, although the initial launch of the Winter Village Toy Shop (a toy shop with a Christmas tree, festive trimmings, and presents) was rather inconspicuous. The Christmas Lego market has grown in popularity and the release of annual sets to add to the Winter Village is now hotly anticipated each year. In its present form, the standard interlocking Lego brick dates from 1958 and has come a long way from the original wooden toy company founded in 1932 by Danish carpenter Ole Kirk Kristiansen (1891–1958). An abbreviation of the Danish phrase *leg godt* (meaning "play well"), Lego has given millions of children worldwide endless hours of educational play, but the emphasis on Christmas (the sets are complemented by extremely popular Advent calendars) has brought the brand even greater popularity, particularly in the United States. This 2015 set specifically refers to the US tradition of leaving cookies and milk out for Santa Claus, a practice that dates back to the Great Depression of the 1930s. Elsewhere, children leave Santa wine (France), Guinness (Ireland), beer (Australia), sherry (United Kingdom), rice pudding (Denmark), or handwritten letters (Germany).

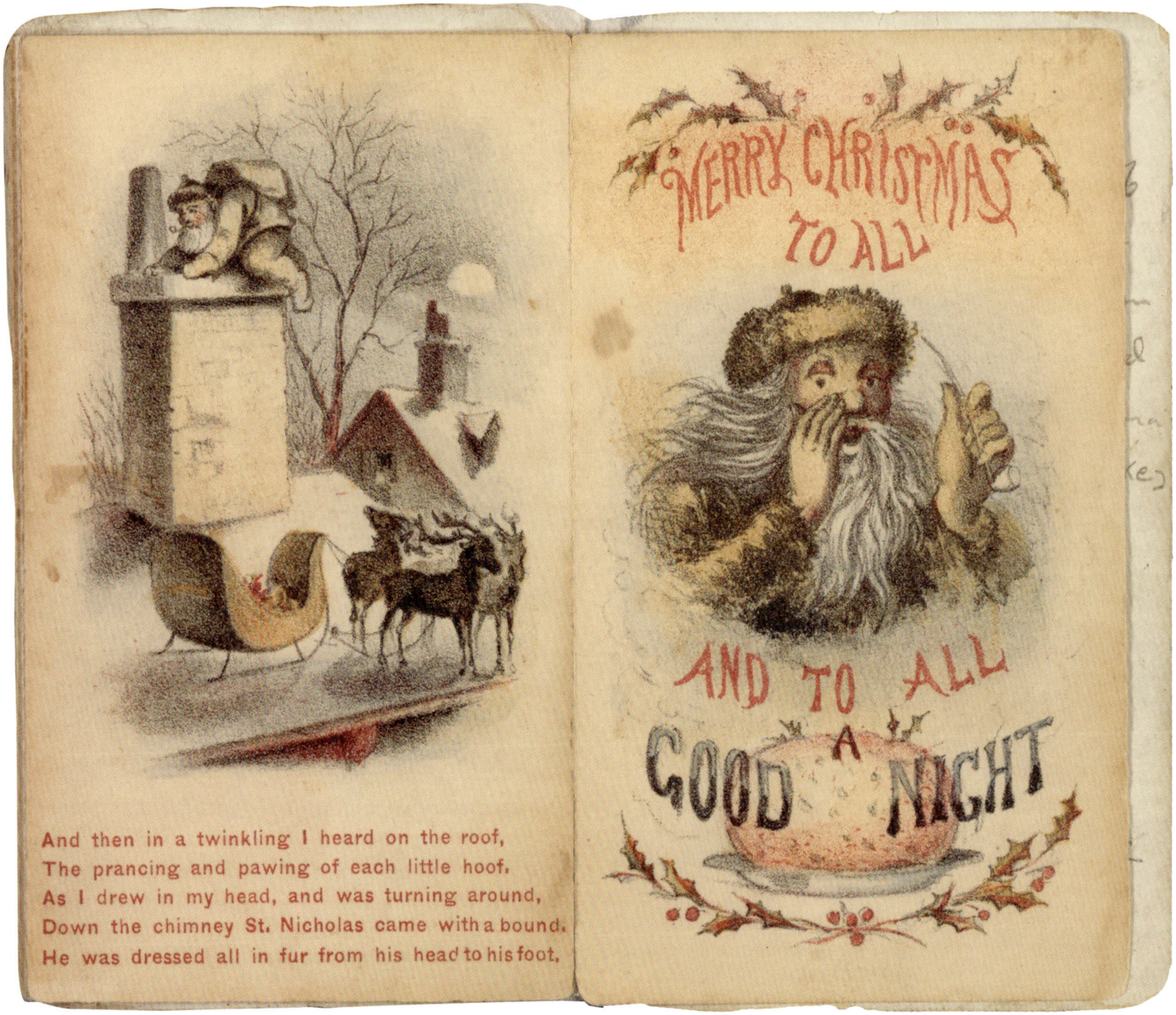

CLEMENT CLARKE MOORE

•

"A Visit from St. Nicholas," 1864
Panoramic, colored lithograph,
4 × 2½ in / 10.5 × 6.5 cm
Published by L. Prang & Co., Boston

Clement Clarke Moore's poem "A Visit from St. Nicholas," now more commonly known by its opening line, "Twas the night before Christmas," is essential Christmas reading, often recited to children on Christmas Eve night before they go to sleep. This delightful panorama, folded accordion-style to create pages, was originally published by Louis Prang (see p.90) as part of a set alongside six other stories. They were presented in a hinged box and known as *The Christmas Stocking Library* due to their small size—perfect for placing in a hanging stocking as a present. Moore's charming poem tells the dramatic story of a man who awakens to find Santa Claus at his home and proceeds to watch Saint Nicholas go about the business of delivering presents. It is a celebration of the magic of Christmas that has captivated the imagination of generations upon generations of children. Theologian Moore (1779–1863), who wrote the poem in 1822 for his children's entertainment, never could have expected it would be his legacy—he didn't even plan for it to be published. Yet it has widely shaped the way that we imagine Santa Claus (see p.115). Since this was published, Santa has given up his pipe and changed the color of his suit, but he's otherwise the same "right jolly old elf" indeed.

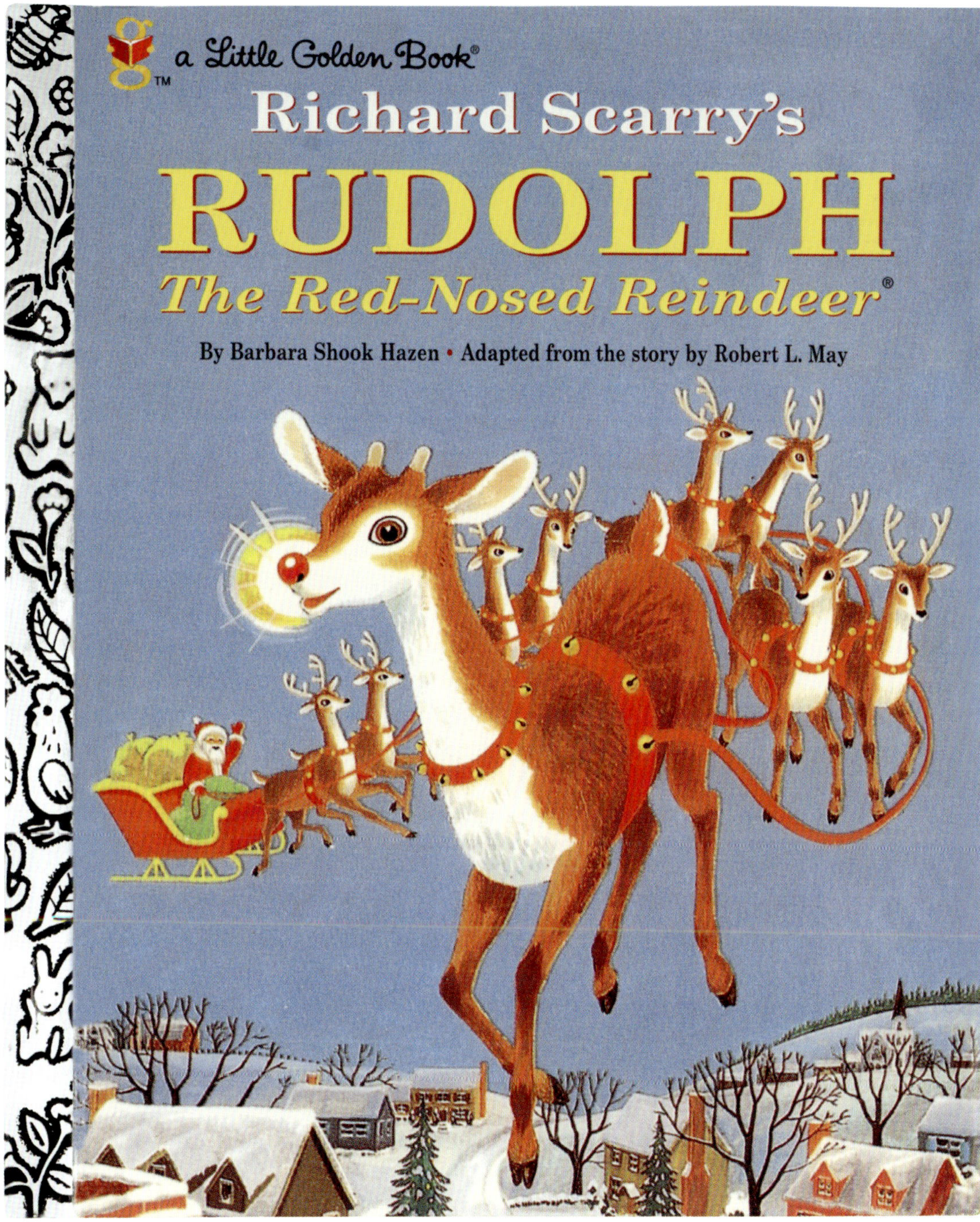

RICHARD SCARRY

•

Front cover of *Rudolph the Red-Nosed Reindeer* by Barbara Shook Hazen, 1958
Printed book, 8¼ × 6¼ in / 21 × 15.9 cm
Published by Western Publishing, Wisconsin

An early eighteenth-century illustration first showed Santa's sleigh being pulled by a solitary, unnamed reindeer. The poem "A Visit From St. Nicholas" by Clement Clarke Moore (1779–1863), published in 1823, introduced the eight reindeer from Dasher to Blitzen, while author L. Frank Baum (1856–1919) later increased the list to ten, none of which featured a glowing red nose. It wasn't until 1939 that *Rudolph the Red-Nosed Reindeer* first debuted, as a free pamphlet, written in rhyme by Robert L. May (1905–1976), an advertising copywriter for the Montgomery Ward Company in Chicago. The original pamphlet was devised by May, at the behest of his boss, as a promotional tool to boost sales over the Christmas holiday in an uncertain economy that was only beginning to recover from the Great Depression. The pamphlet was given out to children who visited the Montgomery Ward department store, and in the first year more than two million copies were distributed. The story quickly became a classic and took on a life of its own. The iconic song followed in 1949, penned by Johnny Marks (1909–1985) but since recorded by countless musicians from almost every genre of music. The story itself was revised, reinterpreted, and repackaged numerous times (see p.68), including the version pictured here illustrated by Richard Scarry, published in 1958 by Western Publishing as part of the Little Golden Books series.

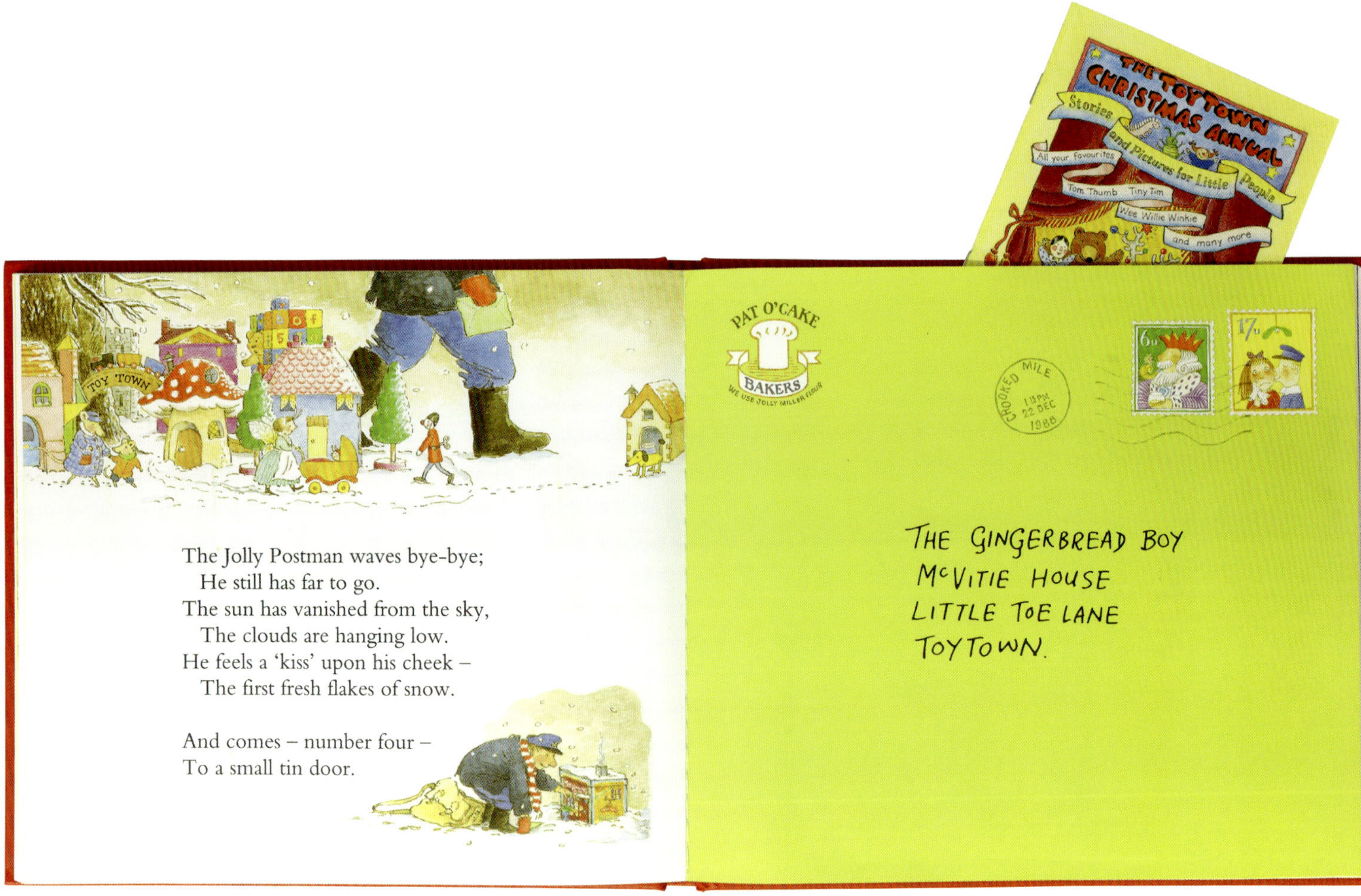

JANET AND ALLAN AHLBERG

•

The Jolly Christmas Postman, 1991
Printed book, 8 × 17⅝ in / 20.2 × 45 cm
Puffin Books, London

The Jolly Christmas Postman, a children's book by British authors and illustrators Janet (1944–1994) and Allan Ahlberg (1938–), first published in 1991 by Heinemann, follows an unnamed mailman as he delivers Christmas cards to many famous fairy-tale characters. The innovative production means that all these Christmas cards exist as physical items in the book, so kids can actually enjoy the hands-on, interactive play of removing them from their envelopes and handling and reading them. Here we see "The Toy Town Christmas Annual," which features puzzles, facts, and even advertisements for the Toy Town health club, being delivered to the Gingerbread Boy of Little Toe Lane. There are also a get-well note and a jigsaw puzzle from the King's Men to Humpty Dumpty, who is recovering from his "big fall" in the hospital, among many others. Splitting the duties between them for the many books they published together, Janet created all of the delightful illustrations seen in books by the Ahlbergs, while Allan wrote the often rhyming text. *The Jolly Christmas Postman* is the sequel to *The Jolly Postman or Other People's Letters* from 1986, which was conceptually the same as the Christmas title. *The Jolly Christmas Postman* has gone on to sell millions of copies and become a children's classic.

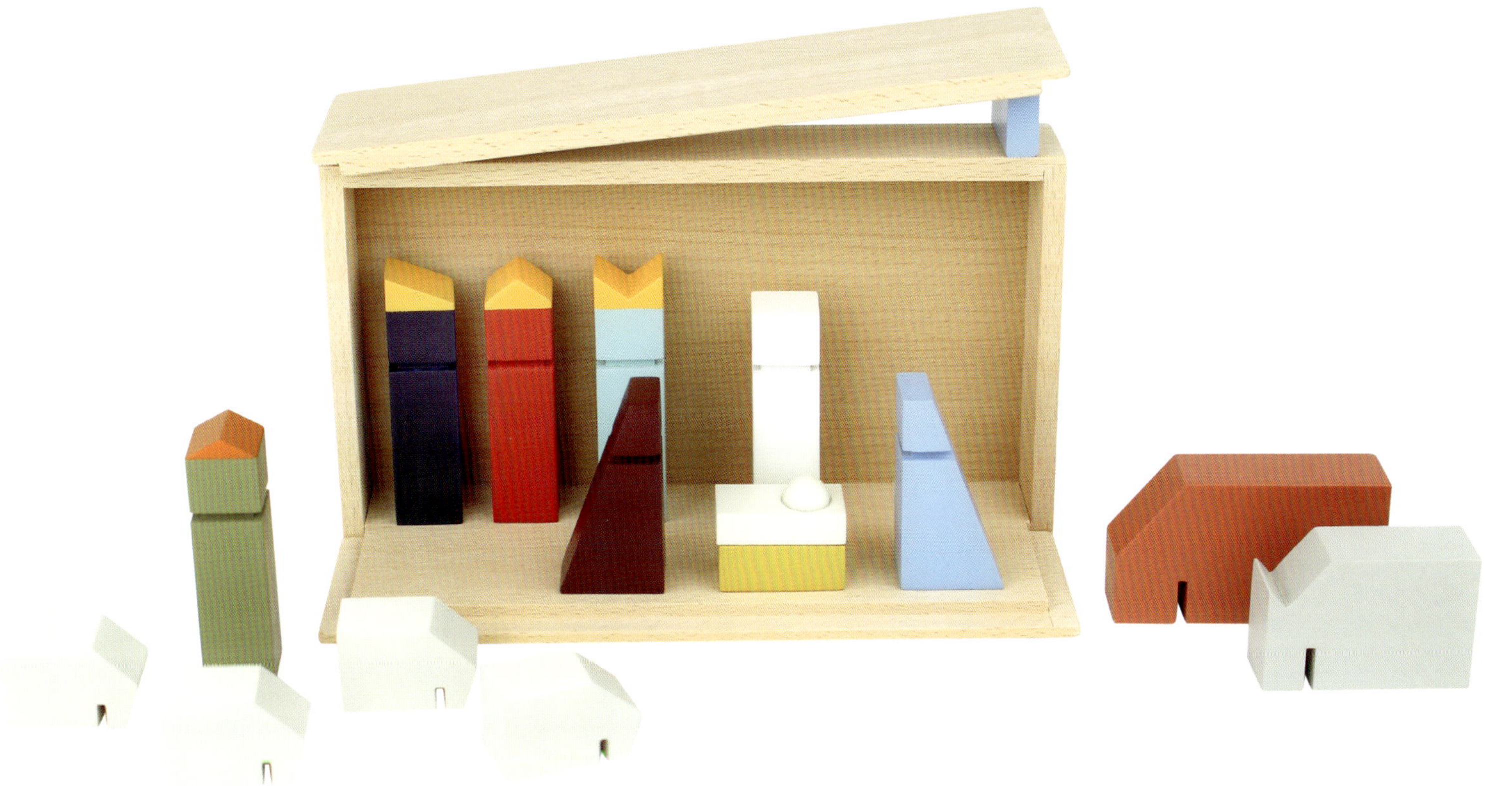

FLORIS HOVERS

•

Nativity Scene, c.2022
Beech wood, 9½ × 5 × 1½ in / 24 × 13 × 4 cm
For Ikonic Toys

For those who find tinsel and some of the more garish Christmas decorations a little over the top, this Nativity scene, the creation of Dutch designer Floris Hovers (1976–), might just be the perfect answer. Hovers' pared-down interpretation of the Nativity scene (see pp.74, 169, 210) includes a set of colorful, minimalistic wooden figures: Joseph, Mary, baby Jesus, the three kings, the angel Gabriel, a shepherd, four sheep, an ox, and a donkey. The wooden barn that houses the Nativity scene is formed by the box that stores the figures, the lid forming the roof. Somewhat surprisingly, perhaps, given the complete absence of detail, each wooden shape is easy to identify. Mary is clearly the blue triangle while Joseph is her brown counterpart, the three kings can be identified by their crowns, the animals by their different sizes, and the angel Gabriel by the fact he is pure white. Stripping back the figures to what is essential and showing an innate understanding of both color and shape, Hovers's Nativity scene is at once instantly recognizable and completely new. Cleverly, he succeeds in making this mass-produced Nativity scene look as though it might be the product of a small artisan workshop. Hovers designed his Nativity set for the Dutch-based company Ikonic Toys, which, since it started in 2015, has set out to sell toys created by leading Dutch designers that are not only fun but that also make people think.

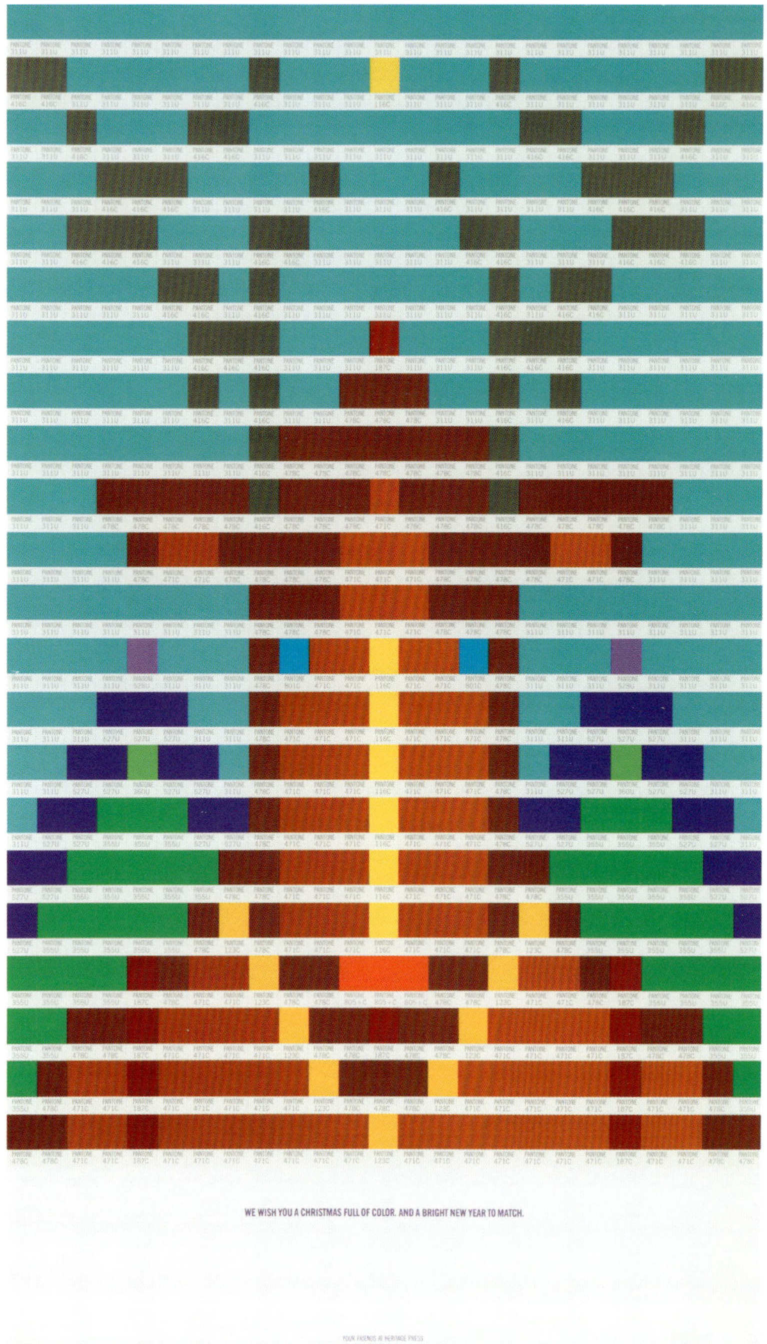

WOODY PIRTLE

•

We Wish You a Christmas Full of Color, and a Bright New Year to Match, c.1980
Offset lithograph with paper perforated support, 24⅜ × 14⅛ in / 61.7 × 35.9 cm
Cooper-Hewitt, Smithsonian Design Museum, New York

This Christmas card, commissioned by New York-based limited-edition book publishers Heritage Press in the early 1980s, is the work of prolific American graphic designer Woody Pirtle (1944–). Offering traditional season's greetings both in words and color, it features a heavily pixelated, red-nosed reindeer (see p.73) against a backdrop of Christmas trees. Look more closely and it becomes clear that the image is continuously interrupted by lines of Pantone color references. In a witty nod to both the significance and the ubiquity of the Pantone color system and to the then popularity of recently introduced computer games, Pirtle created a Christmas greeting that is absolutely of its time. The American company Pantone, best known for inventing its eponymous standardized coloring system in the early 1960s, created a list sorted by shades of more than two thousand colors universally used by industry and the creative world. The pixel—the smallest unit of image data—had recently made the transition to popular culture as video games, such as the phenomenally successful Pac-Man, caught fire (see p.183). Multi-award-winning Pirtle started his eponymous firm in Texas in 1978 and, after this card was created, would go on to join forces for many years with Pentagram, the London-based international design consultancy, before reestablishing his own firm in 2005. As for Heritage Press, which commissioned this modern take on the Christmas card, the company shut its doors in 1982.

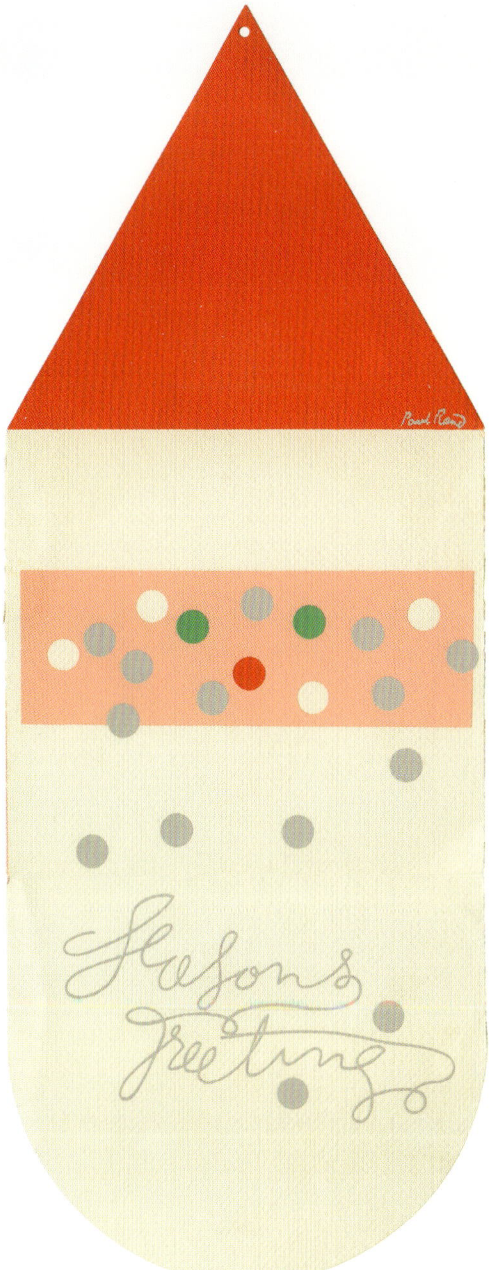

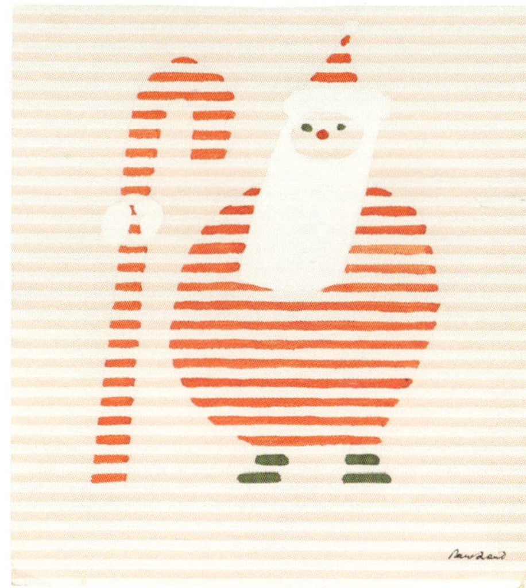

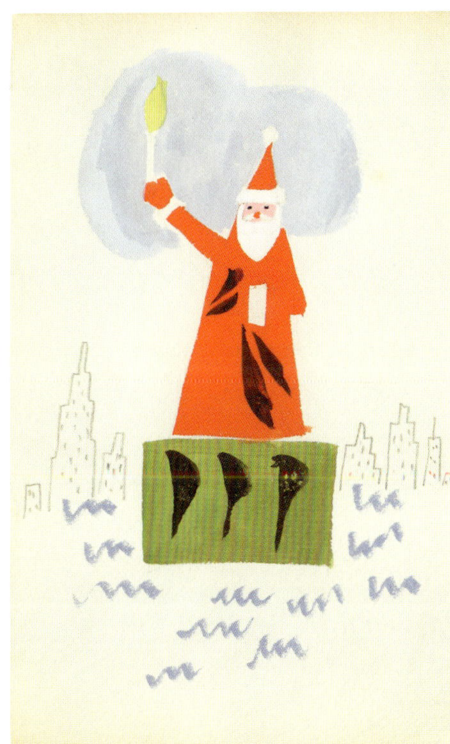

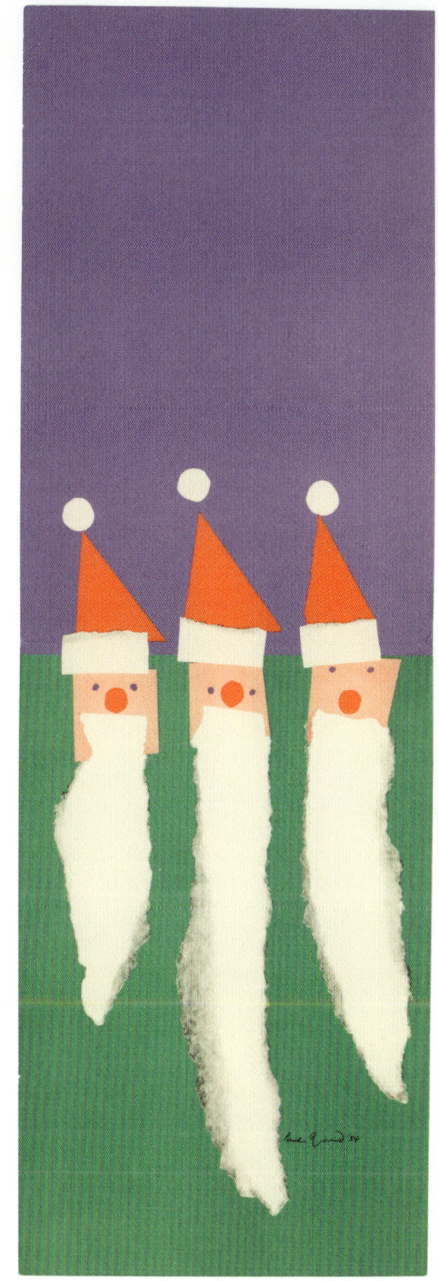

PAUL RAND

•

Collection of Christmas illustrations, c.1955
Acrylic on paper and cardstock with collaged elements, dimensions variable
Letterform Archive, San Francisco

New York-born Paul Rand (1914–1996) is one of the most influential graphic designers of the twentieth century. These meditations on one of Christmas's most recognizable symbols—Santa Claus—were among a collection of twenty-eight small works that were sold at auction in 2018 for more than $16,000. They exemplify Rand's style, conveying the maximum amount of meaning through a minimal amount of form, employing simple geometric shapes and color palettes. Rough collages, such as the trio of bearded Santas (far right), evoke the spirit of Christmas through a child's eyes, the heady anticipation of a visit from Saint Nicholas. Some of them were created on wallpaper samples (such as the figure, top center), where the pattern is incorporated into the overall design. Trained at Brooklyn's Pratt Institute, New York's The New School, and Art Students League of New York, and once a professor at Yale University, Rand was heavily influenced by European modernist design. He became art director of *Esquire* magazine (see p.137) at the age of twenty-three (a position he held from 1936–41) and taught design at several institutions of higher education, but he's best known for his pioneering work in commercial design. He created some of the most iconic corporate logos, including those of IBM, UPS, and the ABC television network. His embrace of simplicity in form and function ushered in a new era of commercial art in the United States, establishing himself as a household name in the process.

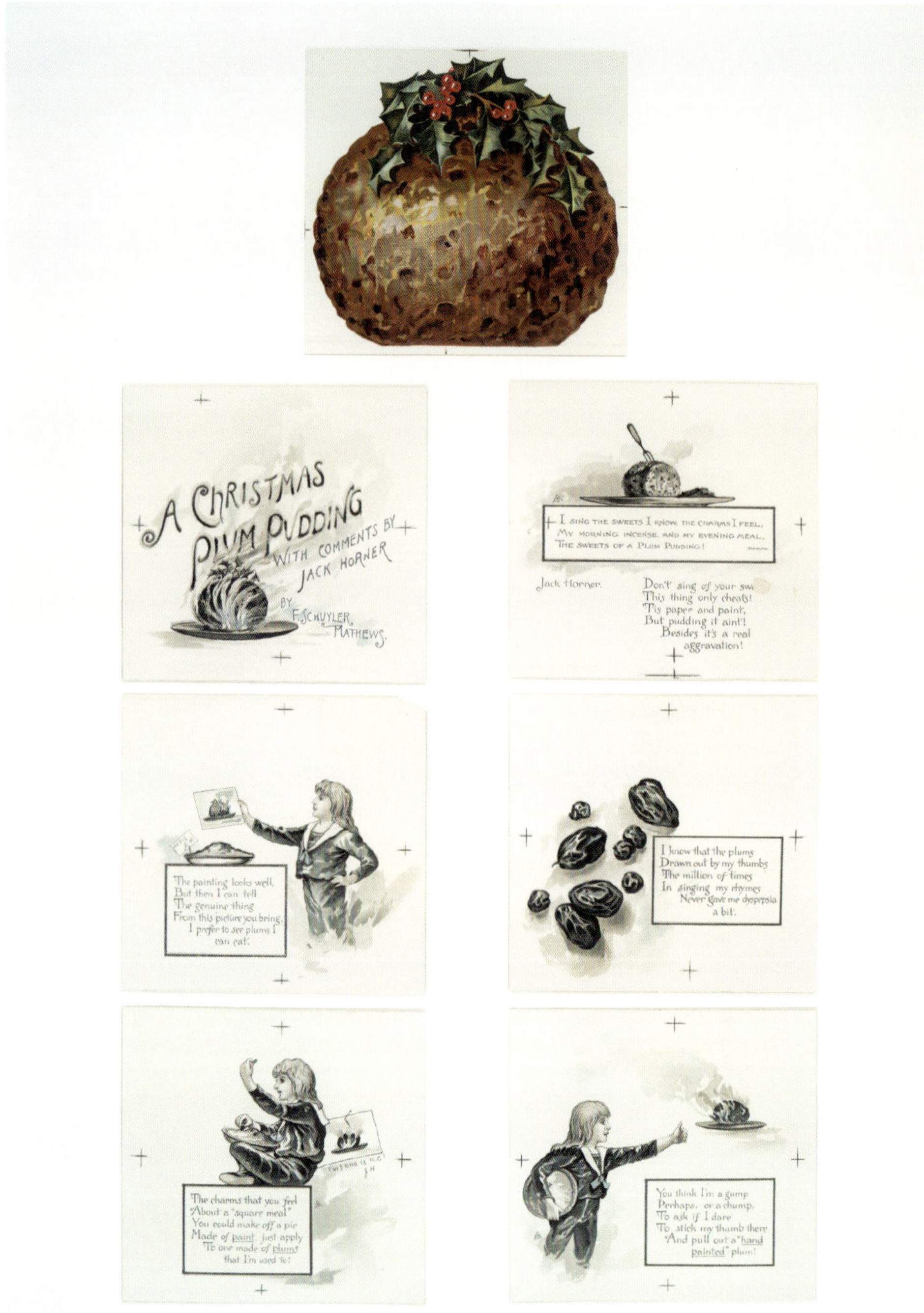

F. SCHUYLER MATHEWS

•

A Christmas Plum Pudding, c.1899
Chromolithographs, dimensions variable

Christmas pudding has long been a favorite festive desert in Great Britain (see p.147). A cannonball-shaped, stodgy dish made with dried fruits that were collectively known as "plums" in medieval times, it is dried out on hooks to deepen its flavor before being cooked in cloth and served with brandy butter or cream. This sheet of proofs for a small book, created by American author and illustrator F. Schuyler Mathews (1854–1938), seems to conflate the traditional Christmas pudding with the story of "Little Jack Horner" from the popular English nursery rhyme, who provides commentary on the action of this short tale. As the lyrics of the original rhyme go, Horner was eating a Christmas pie when he stuck his thumb inside it to pull out a plum. In the story told here, also in rhyme, Horner addresses a painting of a Christmas pudding with mistrust, because it is known as a plum pudding but features no plums. He decides he's better off sticking to the pie he knows, in case the "hand-painted plums" of this illustrated pie gives him stomach problems. Published by Louis Prang, who was known for producing small festive books (see p.84), the pages of this interesting little story would be cut to the shape of a Christmas pudding before being bound by string at the top, allowing it to be read as well as hung on trees as a beautiful pudding-shaped decoration.

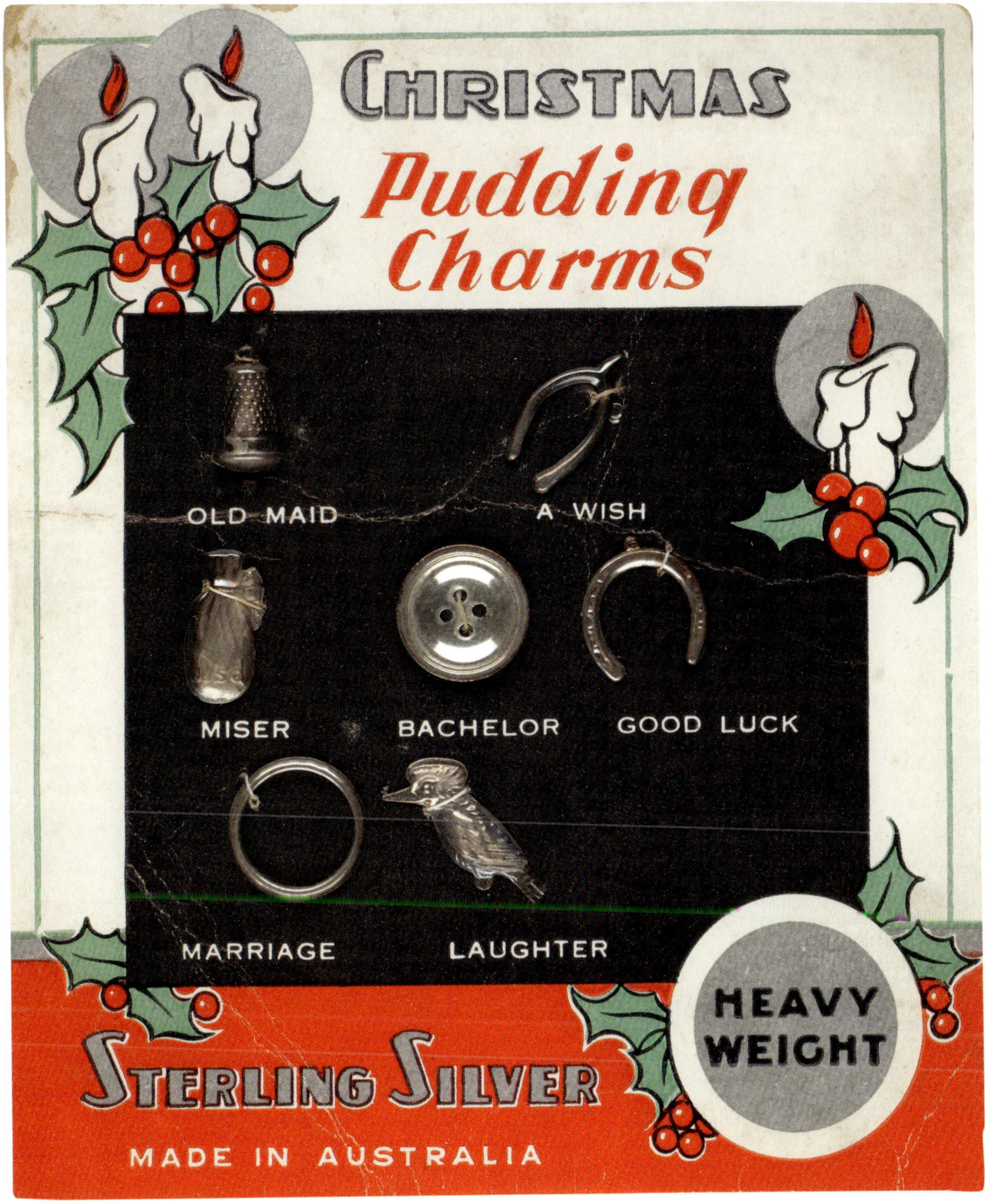

UNKNOWN

•

Christmas Pudding Charms, c.1950
Sterling silver, cardboard mount,
5 × 4⅜ in / 13 × 11 cm
Museums Victoria, Melbourne

Dating from around the middle of the twentieth century, these sterling silver charms were designed to be hidden inside a Christmas pudding; when discovered by diners on Christmas Day, they were seen as playful tokens of their luck to come. Traditionally, a Christmas pudding had thirteen ingredients—one for Jesus Christ and each of the twelve disciples—plus a hidden coin. Whoever found the coin in their slice of pudding would enjoy good luck the following year. In the Middle Ages, this lucky person, regardless of their social status, became "Lord of Misrule" on a day when social norms were reversed. The pudding charms that later replaced the coin each have their own significance: the horseshoe indicates a year of good luck to come, the ring projects that marriage may be on the cards, while the old maid thimble means the opposite. As with many Christmas traditions, coming together to stir the Christmas pudding on Stir-Up Sunday (the last Sunday before Advent) is said to have been introduced to Great Britain by German-born Prince Albert in the nineteenth century (see p.101). Expensive pudding charms like these became very popular, because after the holidays, they were also worn as pieces of jewelery. Albert's wife, Queen Victoria, was a devoted fan of the charm bracelet—a chunky silver bracelet to which individual charms could be added (see p.116), making each bracelet unique to the wearer—thanks to her, the bracelet became an enduringly popular piece of jewelry.

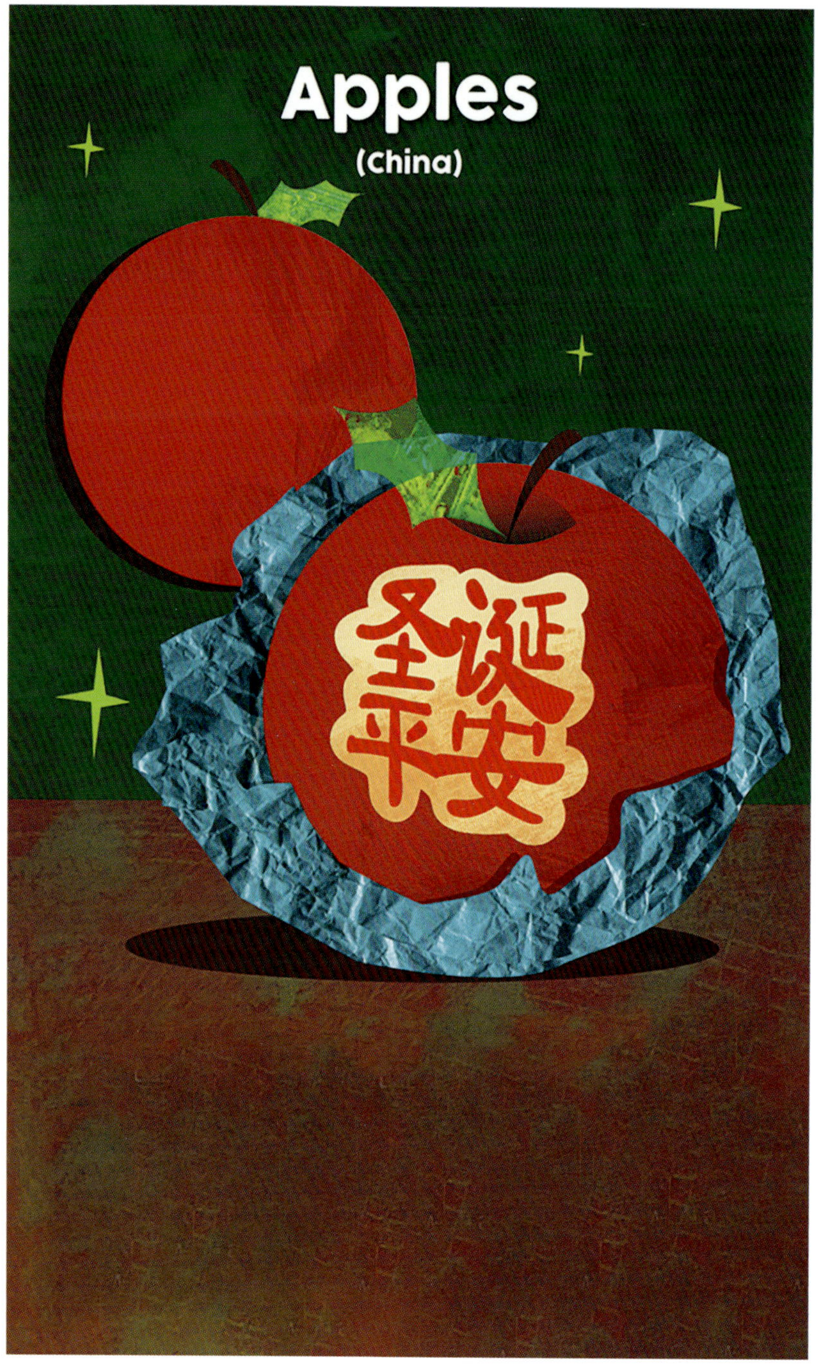

CDA

•

Apples, c.2000
Digital illustration, dimensions variable

As an officially atheist state, historically steeped in Confucianism, Taoism, and Buddhism, the People's Republic of China does not formally recognize Christmas. In this east Asian country, December 25 is a workday like any other, and yet, in urban shopping malls and stores, you will likely hear Christmas music and see Santa hats along with other festive products as retailers capitalize on the growing interest in this Western celebration. In Mandarin, Christmas Eve is translated as *Píng'ān Yè* (平安夜, or "evening of peace"), which derives from the carol "Silent Night." Similar to the Mandarin word for "peace" is the word for "apple," *píng guǒ* (苹果), and so the tradition of eating apples on December 24, it is claimed, will bring you a safe and peaceful new year. This illustration shows how these "peace apples" are typically stenciled with messages of encouragement or decorated with Christmas motifs. Young people are particularly keen on Christmas, which is increasingly seen as a social occasion, in contrast to the family-oriented Chinese New Year observed a few weeks later. Many are finding new and unusual ways to mark the season, and gift these decorative peace apples, wrapped in colored paper or presented in boxes, to each other. The custom has become so popular that retailers now raise the price of the fruit during December.

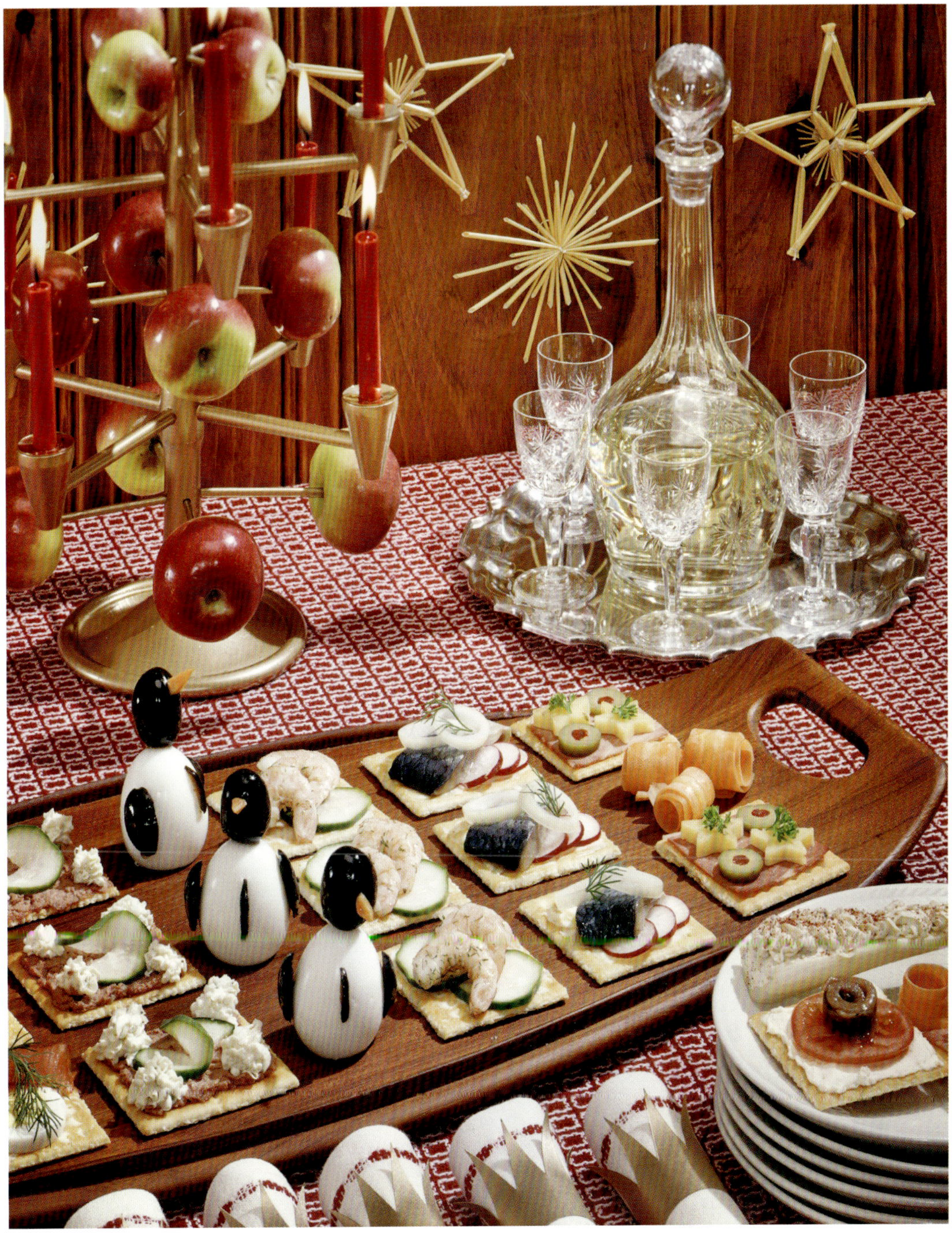

L. FRITZ

•

Smorgasbord, c.1958
Photograph, dimensions variable

Across Scandinavia, Christmas celebrations only truly start when the seasonal smorgasbord—called the *julbord* (Christmas table) in Sweden—is served on December 24. Made up of many, many courses, there are strict rules as to what is eaten, and how. Smorgasbord translates as "a wide variety of everything" and the Christmas feast is precisely that; it sometimes involves so many dishes that the month of December is spent preparing its many components. The smorgasbord traces its roots back to the sixteenth century, when the well-to-do gathered to enjoy elaborate buffets, with herring as their centerpiece. Today, a smorgasbord, or *julbord*, is still unthinkable without the small, pickled fish. Cooks may vary their accompaniments, but dill and radish are faithful companions, as seen in this photograph from the late 1950s of just such a Christmas feast, set on a table also bearing a "tree" with rosy-colored apples and burning red candles. While busy cooks may no longer have the time to dress their boiled eggs to appear as penguins—the creative use of black olives adds to the glamour of the egg—they usually take the time needed to create small bite-size pieces of delicious food, such as the shrimp and cucumber bites. After these cold bites have been eaten, diners feast on cold meats, hot dishes, cheese, and dessert; every item is assembled to look as good as it tastes. Presentation is key: the red apples and candles here complement the red-and-white tablecloth and the Christmas crackers (see p.33) waiting to be pulled.

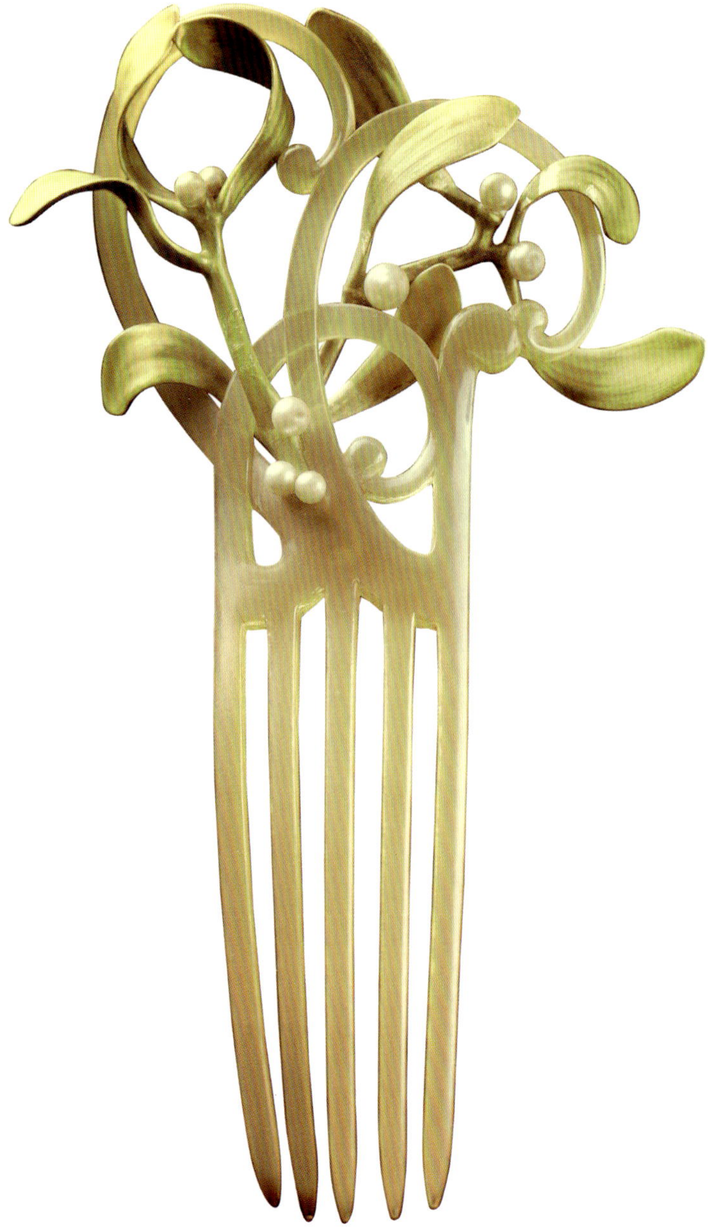

HENRI VEVER

•

Mistletoe comb, 1900
Enamel on chiseled gold and pearls,
$6\frac{5}{8}$ × 4 in / 17 cm × 10 cm,
Musée des Arts Décoratifs, Paris

Kissing under the mistletoe is near the top of the pantheon of ubiquitous Christmas traditions, even if it seems a little more problematic in current times. It is everywhere: represented on television and in film, referenced in worldwide Christmas hits, and even included on the cover of sheet music. This subtle five-pronged comb, designed by French jeweler Henri Vever (1854–1942) at the turn of the twentieth century, sees the twisty green branches of the mistletoe plant winding around the handle and the white, sticky berries of the plant represented by small pearls. A woman wearing this comb as a decoration in her hair would appear to always be standing under the mistletoe, which as the tradition entails would allow a man to steal a kiss from her. This likely started among the working class in England in the eighteenth century, during parties for those that worked downstairs in grand homes, before spreading around the world. Henri Vever, alongside his business-savvy brother Paul (1851–1915), inherited his grandfather's Parisian jewelry company in 1881. He was soon known throughout the world as one of the leading artists and designers of the French Art Nouveau movement, alongside other jewelers, such as René Lalique (see p.144). Designs from this era, which reached its peak in 1900, were characterized by floral designs, asymmetry, and curved lines, all of which are present in this particularly festive piece.

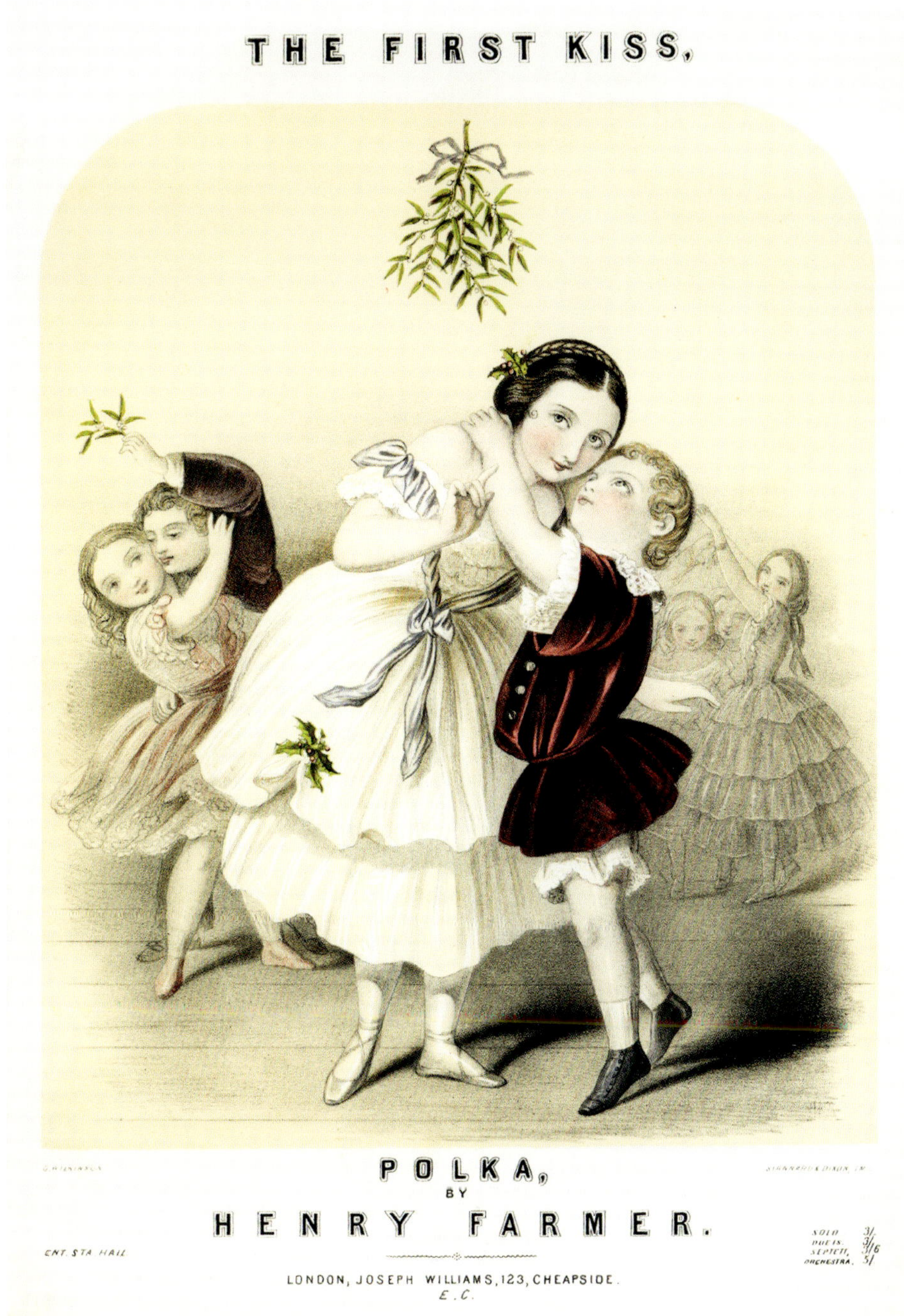

HENRY FARMER

•

The First Kiss, Polka, c.1840
Colored lithograph, 10⅝ × 8⅞ in / 27.2 × 22.5 cm
Published by Joseph Williams, London

Children, dressed in their best clothes for the holiday, dance beneath a sprig of mistletoe as a young boy tries to steal a kiss from an older girl and his companion holds more mistletoe above the head of another. This image from around 1840 appears on the cover of the sheet music for "The First Kiss, polka," by the English composer Henry Farmer. The inclusion of mistletoe links the music to Christmas, because the plant has long been associated with the holiday, although how the association began is not entirely clear. The parasitic plant, which grows on trees, has been considered a symbol of fertility since ancient Greece and was venerated by the early Celts for its ability to flourish in the dead of winter. The practice of kissing beneath the mistletoe was thought to have originated among household servants in England, who hung it up at parties. A man could ask for a kiss from any woman standing beneath the mistletoe. Sheet music became increasingly popular after the invention of an affordable upright piano in 1827 made singing and playing music the principal form of home entertainment. The polka became a dance sensation by the 1840s and was considered particularly shocking since couples whirled frenetically in each other's arms.

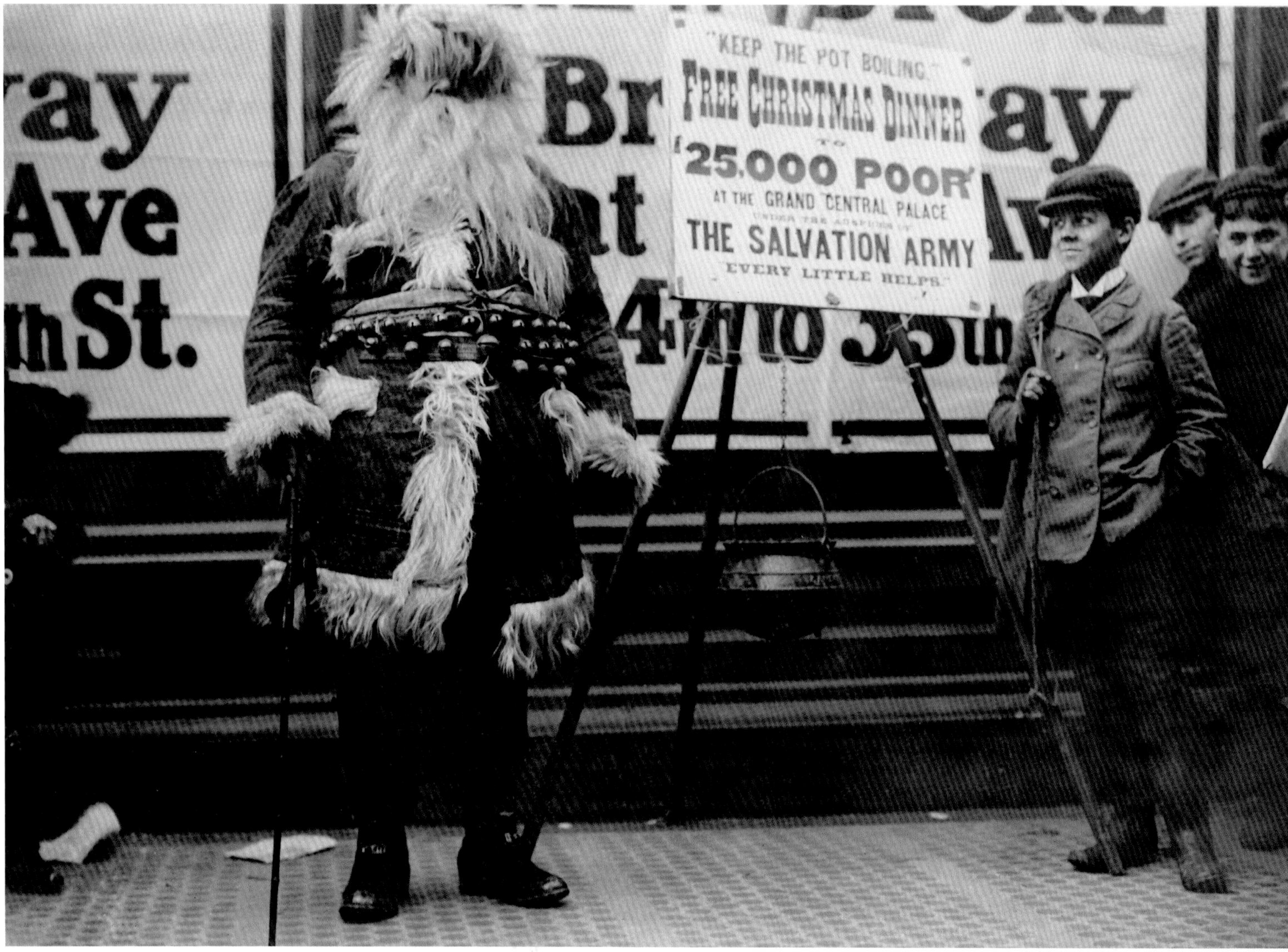

SALVATION ARMY

•

Santa, c.1910
Photograph, dimensions variable

The Salvation Army was founded in 1865 by Englishman William Booth (1829–1912), a street preacher whose objective was to reach the most unfortunate in London's East End, and his wife Catherine. His Christian Mission organization was highly successful, recruiting thousands of converts and newly minted evangelists to spread the gospel. A scant decade later, across the pond in San Francisco, California, Salvation Army captain Joseph McFee bemoaned the poverty in the city. He was bound and determined to find a way to feed the poor—Christmas dinner, at least. But how? He recalled something he'd seen during his sailing days: a kettle known as "Simpson's Pot" that served to collect donations for the needy in Liverpool. Thus inspired, he installed a similar pot at the Oakland Ferry Landing accompanied by a sign reading "KEEP THE POT BOILING," and the Salvation Army red kettle tradition was born. This black-and-white photograph, from the very early twentieth century, is a fine example of this display. Standing outside the Grand Central Palace in New York, a man dressed as Santa Claus, including a belt of bells to make sure he's always heard, mans a presumably red bucket, imploring people to donate so that twenty-five thousand poor may eat a free Christmas dinner. The mission has since spread and has helped more than thirty million people from accross the world. Indeed, the familiar bell ringers and their distinctive red kettles remind us of the true meaning of Christmas.

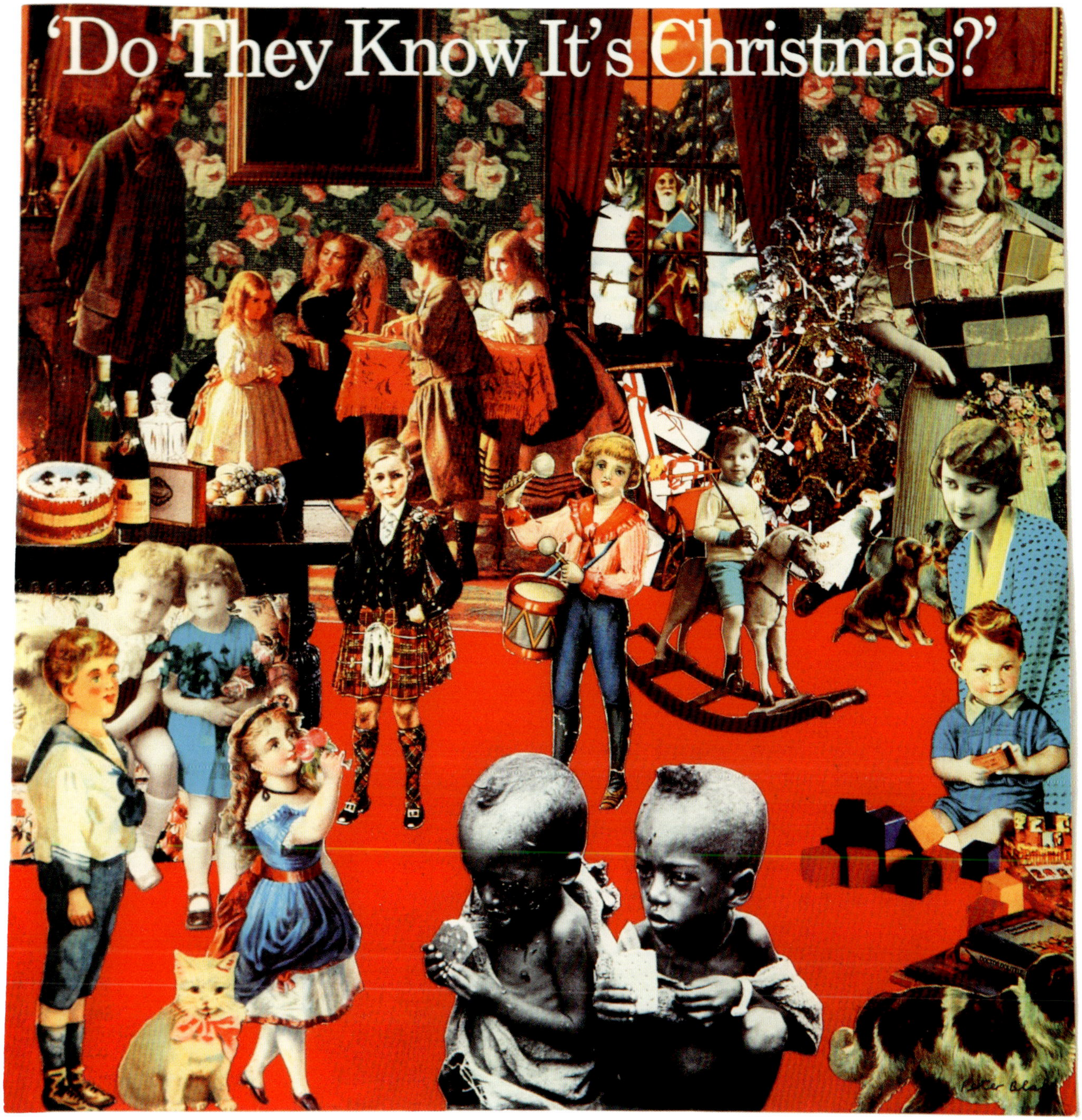

PETER BLAKE

•

"Do They Know it's Christmas?" artwork, 1984
Collage on paper, dimensions variable

Happy children play with newly opened presents while doting parents await with cake and wine. Pets frolic, a father warms himself beside the fire, and, outside, Santa observes the festivities through the window. Interrupting this nostalgic scene of Yuletide abundance is a jarring sight: a black-and-white image of two starving Ethiopian children. The British artist Peter Blake (1932–) designed this collage for the cover of Band Aid's 1984 single "Do They Know it's Christmas?," a charity song written by Bob Geldof and Midge Ure that raised £8 million for relief efforts amid the Ethiopian famine of 1983–85. Just as the shocking BBC news reports of the country's suffering had moved Geldof to action, so Blake sought to create a stirring image that, like the song's lyrics, juxtaposed the decadence of Christmas in the West with the desperate plight of those in need. The song, which was recorded in a single day by high-profile rock and pop acts, mostly from Great Britain and Ireland, urged listeners to "Feed the world, let them know it's Christmas time." It became the fastest-selling single in UK chart history, rocketing to the coveted number one spot where it remained for five weeks. Blake was a natural choice to design the artwork, having famously created the sleeve for The Beatles' *Sgt. Pepper's Lonely Hearts Club Band* (1967). His collage was later released as a limited-edition print, signed by Geldof and the artist, to raise more funds for charity.

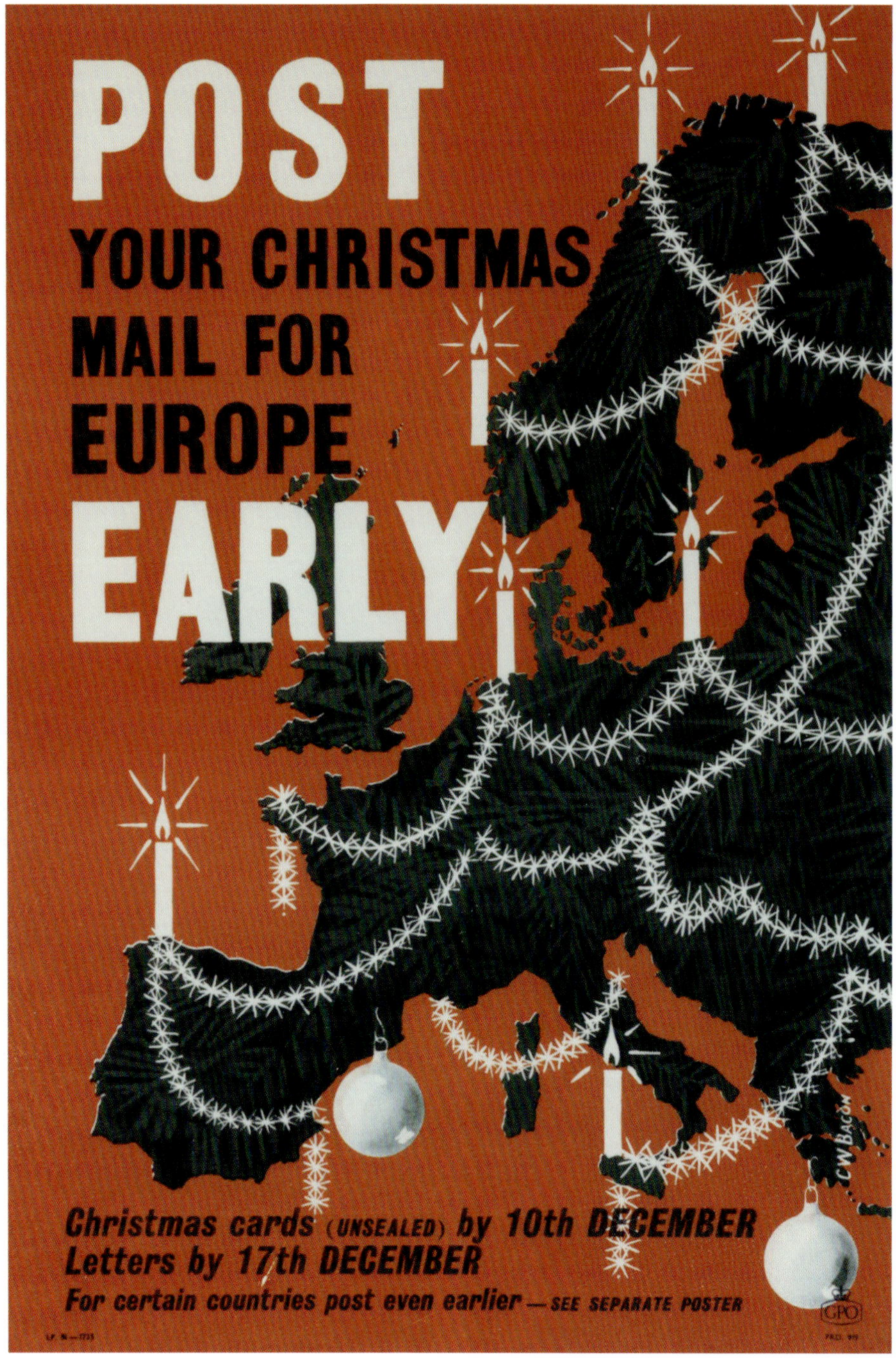

CECIL WALTER BACON

•

Post your Christmas Mail for Europe Early, 1957
Poster paint and collage on board,
40 × 25 in / 101.6 × 63.5 cm
Postal Museum, London

"Post your Christmas Mail for Europe Early," advises this British poster of November 1957, which turns the continent of Europe into the silhouetted branches of a Christmas tree decorated with tinsel and candles (see p.22). Designed by the British artist and illustrator Cecil Walter Bacon (1905–1992), the poster was one of a long-running series of public information posters designed to pass important information to the public. In Great Britain, as elsewhere before the advent of email and social media platforms, Christmas greetings were all sent to loved ones by mail (see p.198) and, as is human nature, people invariably left mailing their cards as late as possible. This led to a huge volume of mail arriving at the same time just before the Christmas holidays, stretching the resources of the postal department. To combat this, the General Post Office PR department commissioned a series of posters to get their message across, starting in 1934, when the department was created, and lasting until the 1960s. Leading illustrators and artists, including Bacon, turned the "Post Early for Christmas" campaign into a huge success. So much so, that in 1969 the message was amended to read "Don't Miss the Christmas post," a subtle tweak to combat people posting too early. Bacon was known for his prolific output for British Railways, the Post Office Savings Bank, and London Transport; he also designed the covers for early Raymond Chandler novels.

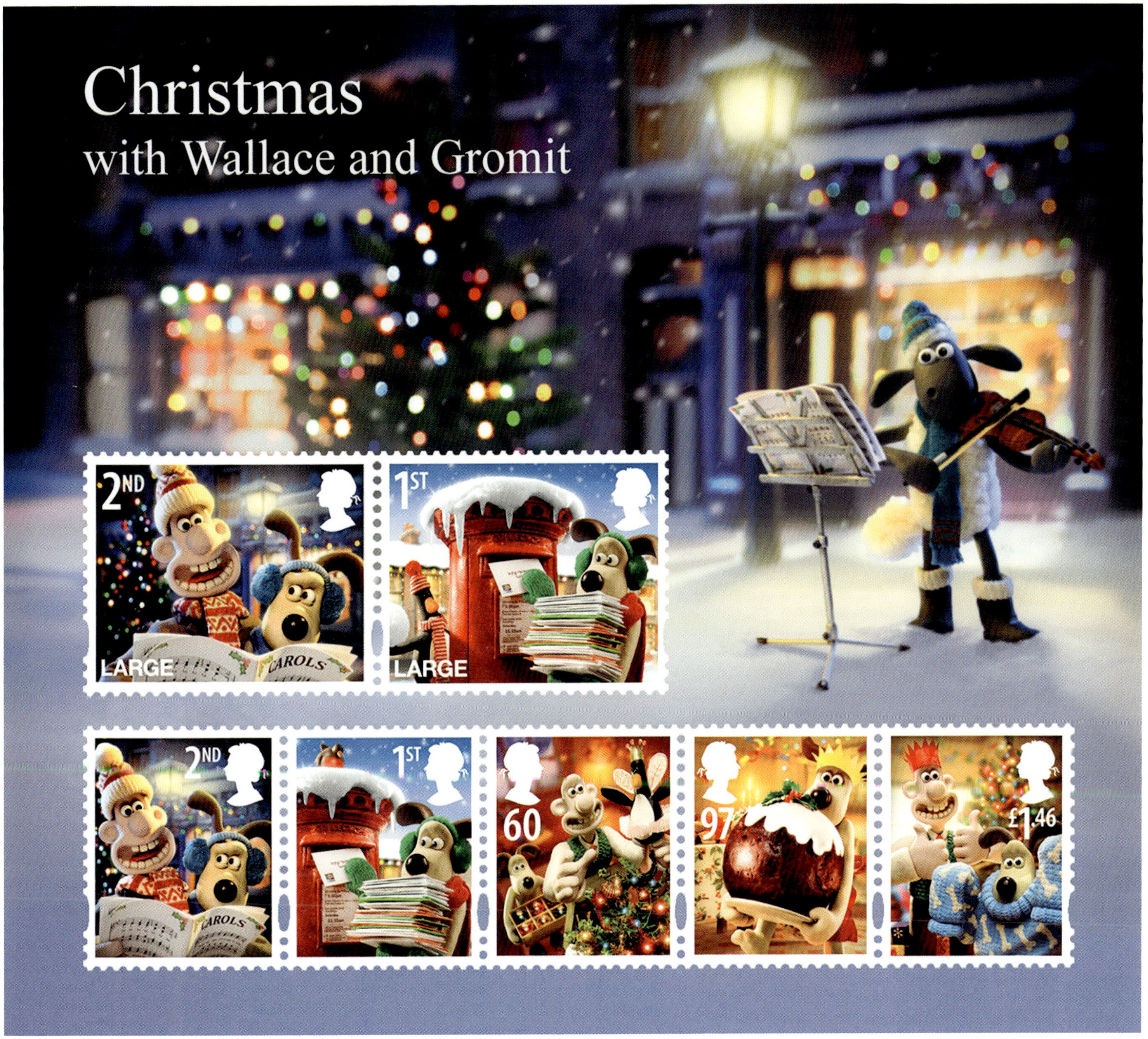

AARDMAN ANIMATIONS AND ROYAL MAIL

•

Christmas with Wallace & Gromit, 2010
Sheet of seven self-adhesive stamps, large: 1 × 1¼ in / 2.4 × 3 cm; standard: 1 × ¾ in / 2.4 × 2 cm

Overflowing with gentle humor and intricate detail, these charming Wallace & Gromit stamps appear like stills from the films that made the animated duo a worldwide phenomenon. Their cracking capers, such as *The Wrong Trousers* (1993) and *A Close Shave* (1995), are a popular Christmas fixture in Great Britain, whether as part of the festive television schedule or emblazoned on gifts, from sweaters to mugs. In 2010, Royal Mail invited the scatterbrained, cheese-loving inventor and his canny canine to star on its Christmas stamps. The brief was simple: to show the pair performing their seasonal traditions. Each stamp began as a sketch by creator Nick Park (1958–) before models, props, and wintery sets were painstakingly constructed by the Aardman team.

On the first-class stamp, Gromit balances a tower of cards while mailing a letter to Santa (see p.136); the wider large letter version shows the same scene, but reveals the villainous penguin Feathers McGraw lurking with a snowball. The arch antagonist is disguised as a Christmas fairy on the 60p stamp, and Gromit is again left to do the heavy lifting on the 97p stamp, staggering under the weight of an enormous Christmas pudding. For his trouble, he is rewarded with a ridiculously oversize bone-themed sweater on the £1.46 stamp. The pair go caroling on the second-class stamp, although Gromit's expression leaves little doubt as to Wallace's abilities. Royal Mail first issued Christmas stamps in 1966.

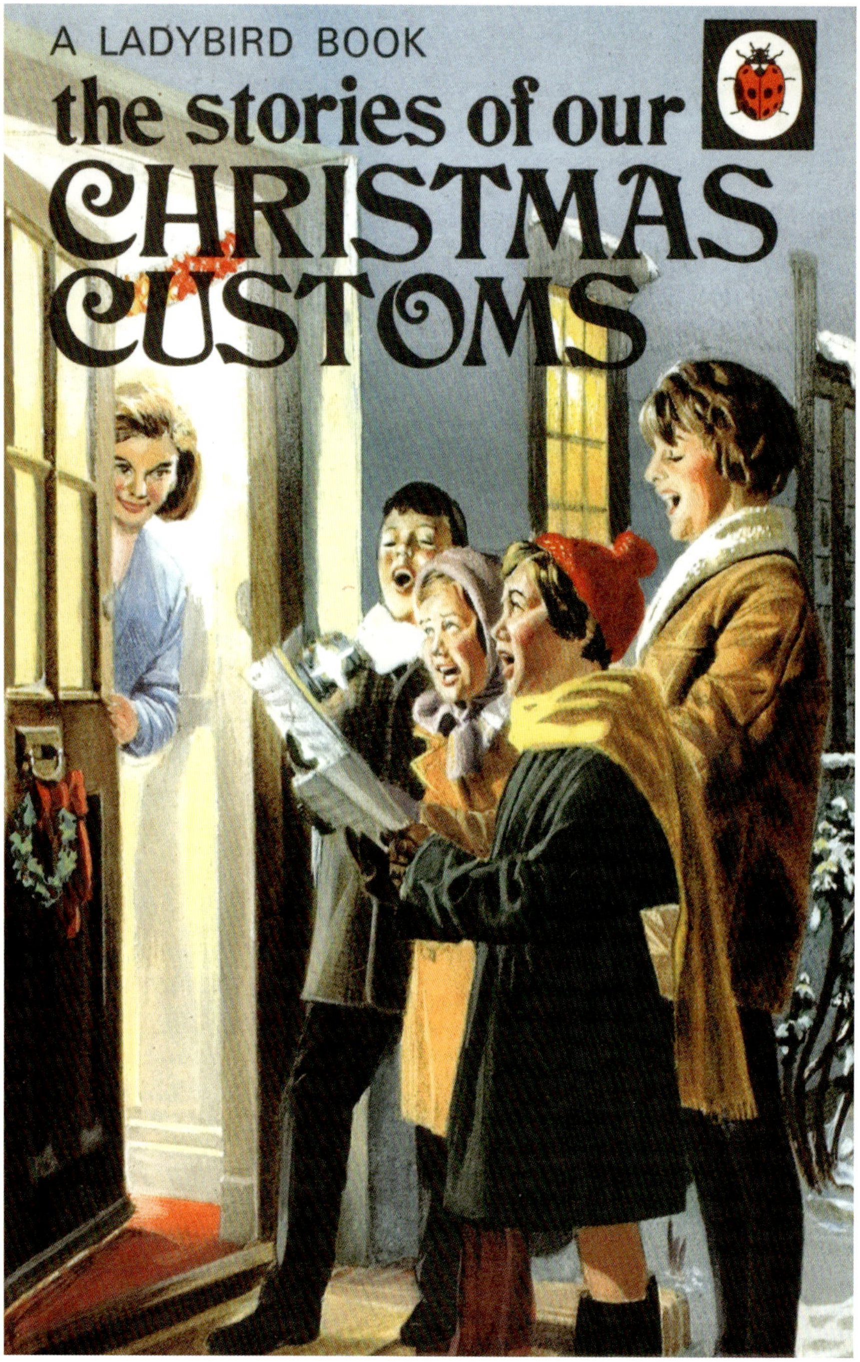

FRANK HAMPSON AND NORAH FLORENCE PEARSON

•

Front cover of *The Stories of Our Christmas Customs*, 1964
Printed book, 7 × 4¾ in / 18 × 12 cm
Published by Ladybird Books, London

A whole generation of British children growing up in the 1960s and 1970s, long before the Internet made information instantly accessible, turned to the pocket-size, hardback Ladybird books as a reliable and informative way of learning. This 1964 book is typical of the format: twenty-five pages of impeccably correct information about Christmas accompanied by twenty-five different illustrations, provided by Frank Hampson (1918–1985), better known as the creator of the extremely popular *Eagle* comic book hero, Dan Dare. After leaving *Eagle* in 1962, Hampson illustrated ten books for Ladybird before ill health forced his retirement; *The Stories of Our Christmas Customs* was his first. The text by Norah Pearson is packed full of information about British Christmas rituals, such as the idiosyncratic Christmas pantomime (see p.118), the pagan origins of Christmas celebrations, why people put up Christmas trees (see p.130), and why they exchange presents. The publishing company Wills & Hepworth, founded in 1867 in Loughborough, England, to publish guidebooks and street directories, introduced the Ladybird brand in August 1914 specifically for children. The book's design would remain unchanged for decades: its unique size, 7 by 4¾ inches (18 by 12 cm), was determined purely by the fact that a book could be made from one large standard piece of paper, which was folded to make the fifty-six pages with no waste: a crucial consideration during the shortages of World War I.

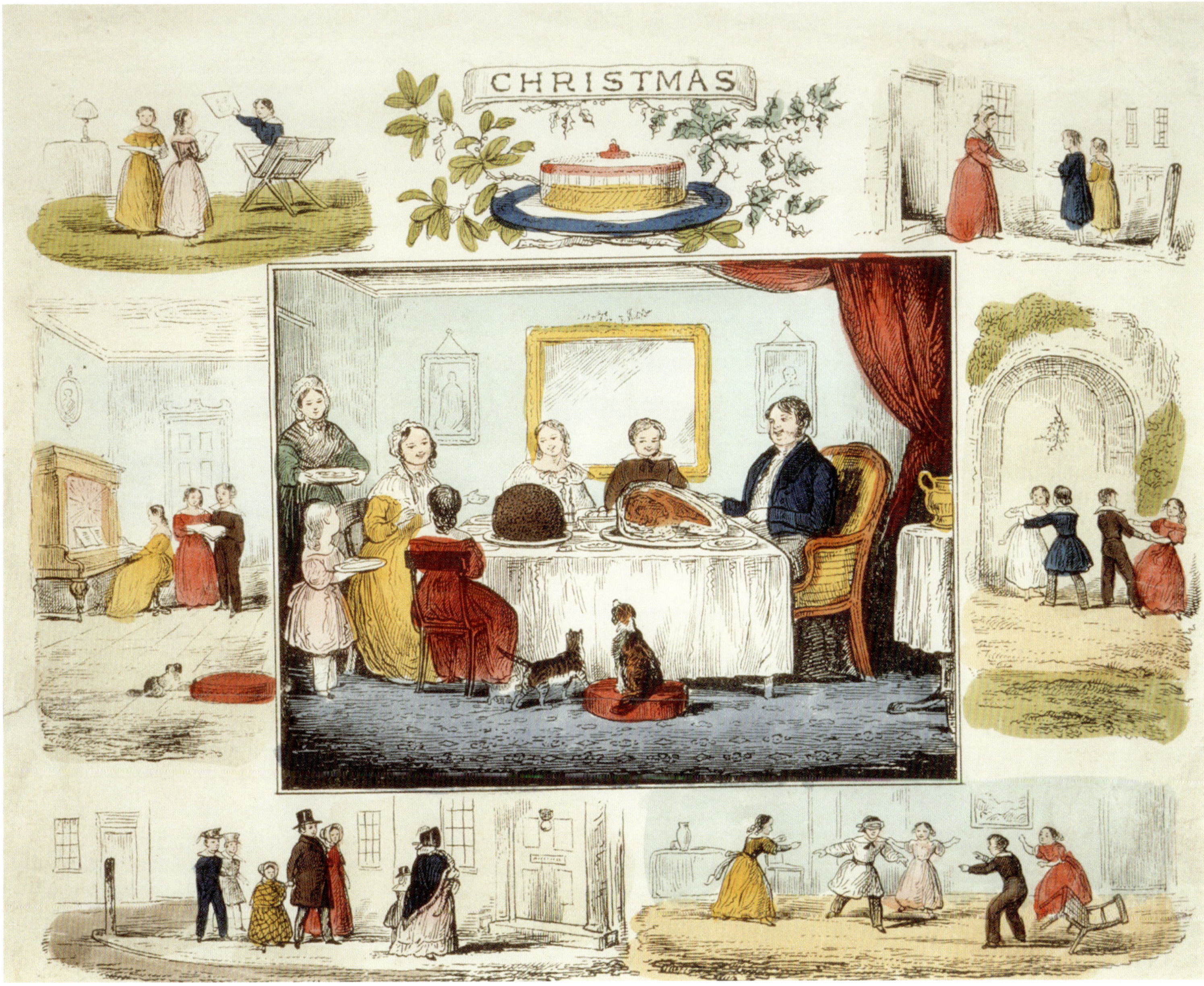

UNKNOWN

•

Christmas broadsheet, c.1840
Hand-colored lithograph, dimensions unknown
Victoria & Albert Museum, London

When Queen Victoria ascended to the throne in 1837, Christmas was little celebrated in Great Britain. That changed during the 1840s, in large part thanks to the influence of Victoria's beloved husband and consort, the German-born Prince Albert, who single-handedly introduced numerous German Christmas customs that became widely adopted. In this hand-colored lithograph from around 1840 by an unknown artist, headed "Christmas," a well-to-do family celebrate in a series of vignettes. At the heart of the page, the happy family gathers around a dining table to enjoy their Christmas meal. The surrounding images depict the family's different Christmas pursuits, from the children playing games to visiting friends, giving Christmas alms to the poor and gathering around the piano. The illustration appeared at the start of the decade, when Christmas began to take shape as a family event. It was Prince Albert who, in 1848, first gathered his family around a bedecked Christmas tree indoors (see p.130), festooned with candles, homemade decorations, small gifts, fruit, and candies, establishing a tradition that continues. Likewise, the practice of exchanging Christmas cards had started in 1843 (see p.198) and the peculiarly British custom of pulling Christmas crackers at the dinner table started in 1847 (see p.227). While the family in the broadsheet had these joys to come, the Victorian emphasis on the family—with the preparation of the meal, the playing of games, and the singing of carols—was already clearly established.

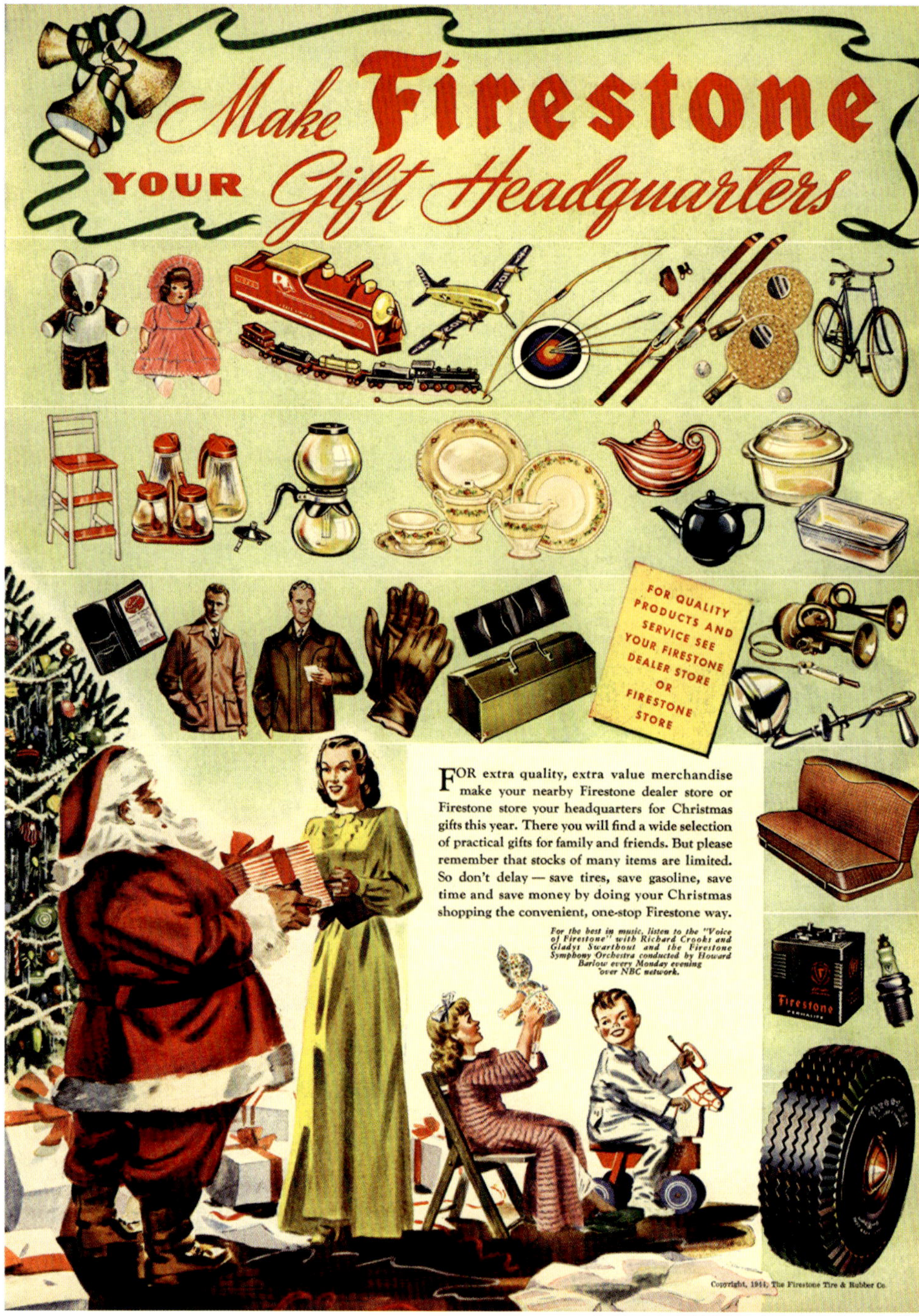

FIRESTONE TIRE AND RUBBER COMPANY

•

Christmas Gift Guide advertisement, 1944
Print, dimensions variable

The wide range of gifts in this 1944 magazine advertisement by the Firestone Tire and Rubber Company might disguise the fact that wartime rationing was in place in the United States, but the accompanying text reminds shoppers that visiting a Firestone store will help them "save tires, save gasoline"—both resources in short supply. In a nod to the rigid gender divisions that operated in 1940s America, the gifts are carefully sorted: a row of children's toys, a coffee maker or a dinner service for mom, and driving clothes and accessories for dad. Founded in 1900 in Akron, Ohio, Firestone had long since ceased to be purely a seller of tires. Its innovations in tire technology—it developed synthetic rubber to deal with wartime rubber shortages—were paralleled by equally creative promotion: it started its own radio program in 1932, its own TV show in 1943, and opened department stores across the country. The myriad of goods in Firestone's advertisements was replicated in their crowded shop windows. While adults visited the store to examine the latest electrical goods or recreational equipment, such as skis and bicycles, the kids enjoyed Toyland, which offered dolls for girls and airplanes for boys. Firestone also offered a "Lay Away" service; a forerunner of the Christmas clubs now used by many retailers. Shoppers chose their gifts, which were removed from sale, but only got to take them home once they had finished paying for them in installments.

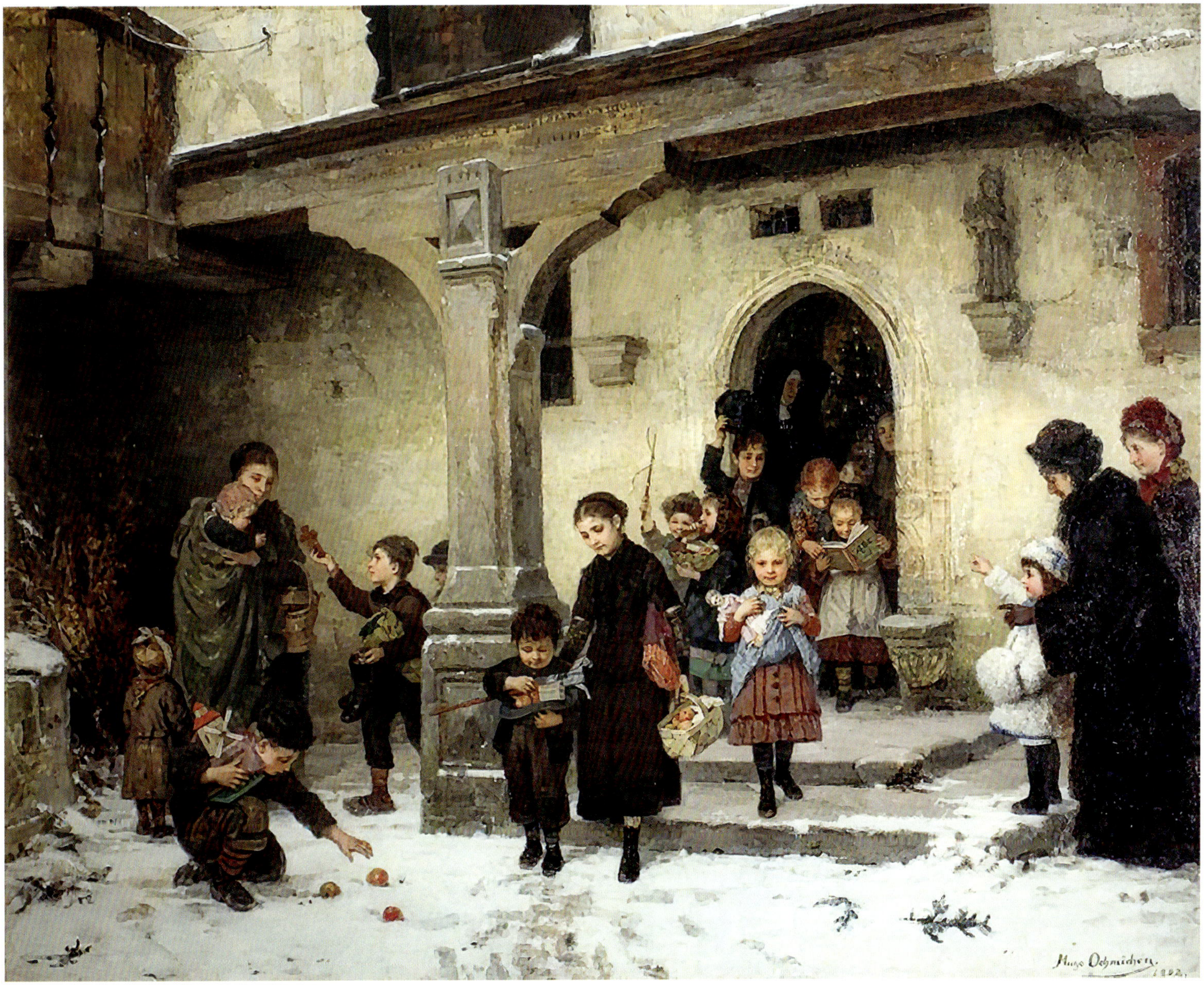

HUGO OEHMICHEN

•

Christmas Presents, 1882
Oil on canvas, 35 × 44½ in / 89 × 113 cm
Young V&A, London

Christmas Presents, by German painter Hugo Oehmichen (1843–1932), depicts a cold, snowy Christmas scene composed of children dressed in winter clothes, holding toys, books, and baskets of fruit. Behind them in a doorway, a nun and a candlelit Christmas tree are visible (see p.22). As the children proceed into the bright and snowy foreground, we see their animated faces engrossed in their gifts, which they clutch or share with one another. We get the sense that the scene is a portrait of charitable Christmas giving from the church to children in need. To the right, two women and a child are standing, dressed in finer clothing replete with bonnets and hand muffs. The child is dressed in white in stark contrast to the children carrying gifts, who wear brown, gray, and green. Oehmichen was known for painting people and portraits. As a German artist, we might assume *Christmas Presents* represents Germany of that time and is a portrayal of Catholic ideology at Christmas. In the 1880s, German Catholics believed that their Christmas presents were bestowed upon them by Jesus as opposed to the Sinterklaas (see p.220) or Saint Nicholas (see p.15). Giving was not simply about bestowing gifts, but about giving back to the community and helping the less fortunate. *Christmas Presents* powerfully imbues the viewer with a charitable mood of Christmas, reminding them of the Christian virtues of the season and one's responsibilities in society.

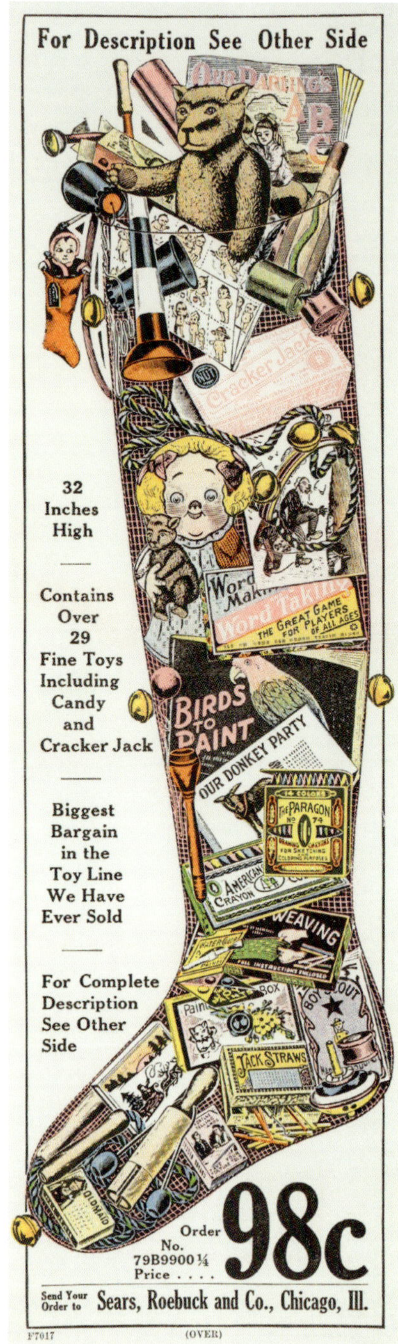

SEARS, ROEBUCK AND COMPANY

•

Prefilled 98¢ stocking advertisement, 1927
Print, 10½ × 3½ in / 26.7 × 8.9 cm
Historic New England, Boston

Every parent knows that assembling a Christmas stocking can be a time-consuming part of shopping for a child, involving the selection and purchase of many small items, such as toys, trinkets, and candy. This advertisement-cum-mail order form shows that in 1927 Sears, Roebuck and Co., based out of Chicago, Illinois—now a large chain of American department stores operating under the name Sears—saw an opportunity to take the work out of it for parents. For 98 cents, one could buy a fully assembled stocking (see pp.110, 166), busting at the seams with more than twenty-nine items—toys, candy, games, crafts, and more—that measured a staggering thirty-two inches (81 cm) tall and weighed four pounds (1.8 kg). This weighty stocking is illustrated as a see-through sock in this advertisement, showing the discerning shopper what is included in the ready-made gift, and features a more detailed list of inclusions on the back. These items were mail order, so one need only send this off to receive a fully packaged, ready-to-hang stocking. Even in 1927, this was incredible value. Such marketing on the part of Sears was nothing new; the Sears, Roebuck and Co. catalog expanded throughout the last half of the 1800s until, by the beginning of the twentieth century, it offered practically everything for sale. It's no surprise the company did a brisk business at Christmastime, having positioned itself as a one-stop shop for gifts.

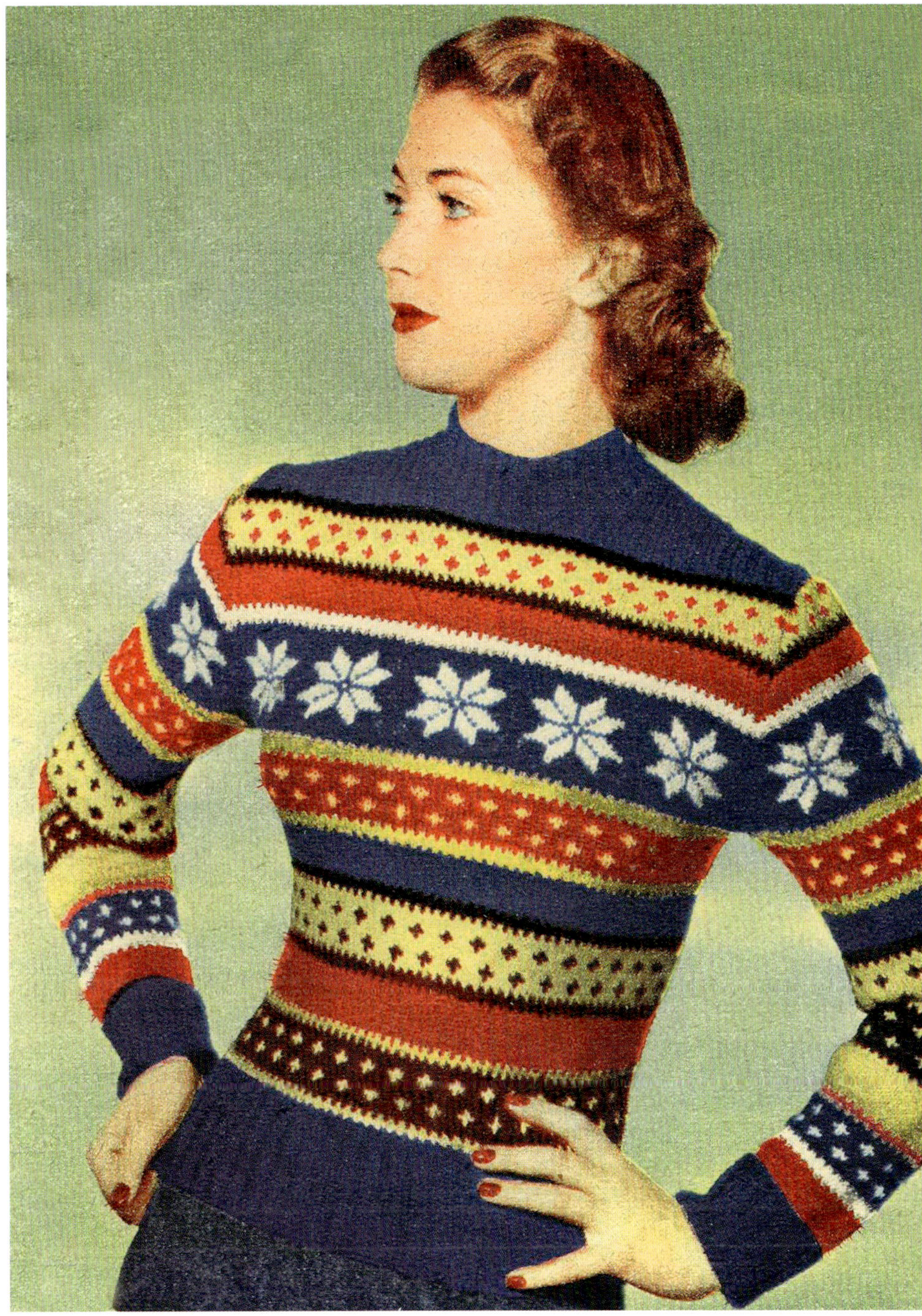

JOHN BULL

•

Christmas sweater, c.1950s
Color lithograph, dimensions variable

Come the start of the festive season in the northern hemisphere, the streets are awash with people coddled in cozy knitwear. This is not a new phenomenon, as is evidenced by the illustration here, from a mid-twentieth-century edition of the British magazine *John Bull*, showing an upstanding young woman sporting a fetching festive knit. In the Nordic regions of Europe, as far back as the fifteenth century, heavily patterned sweaters made from sheep's wool were a necessity due to the plummeting temperatures in the winter. The white "snowflake" pattern on this woman's sweater, now a staple of Christmas winterwear, is of Norwegian origin and is based on an eight-sided rose. As winter sports became more common, the fashion for Nordic knits spread across Europe. In the United States, cardigans sported by mainstream movie stars, such as Rex Harrison in *My Fair Lady* (1964), further popularized the trend for knitwear in general, just as Colin Firth's reindeer sweater in *Bridget Jones's Diary* (2001) later helped inspire a range of kitschier fare. On a day in early December every year in the UK, millions of people in offices and schools put on their most garish garment to celebrate Christmas Jumper Day and raise money for charity. When a sweater isn't enough, matching pajama sets for all the family (see p.117) are also available. The ultra-patriotic *John Bull* magazine was in print sporadically between 1906 and 1960, but it hit its stride after World War II, when this illustration was printed.

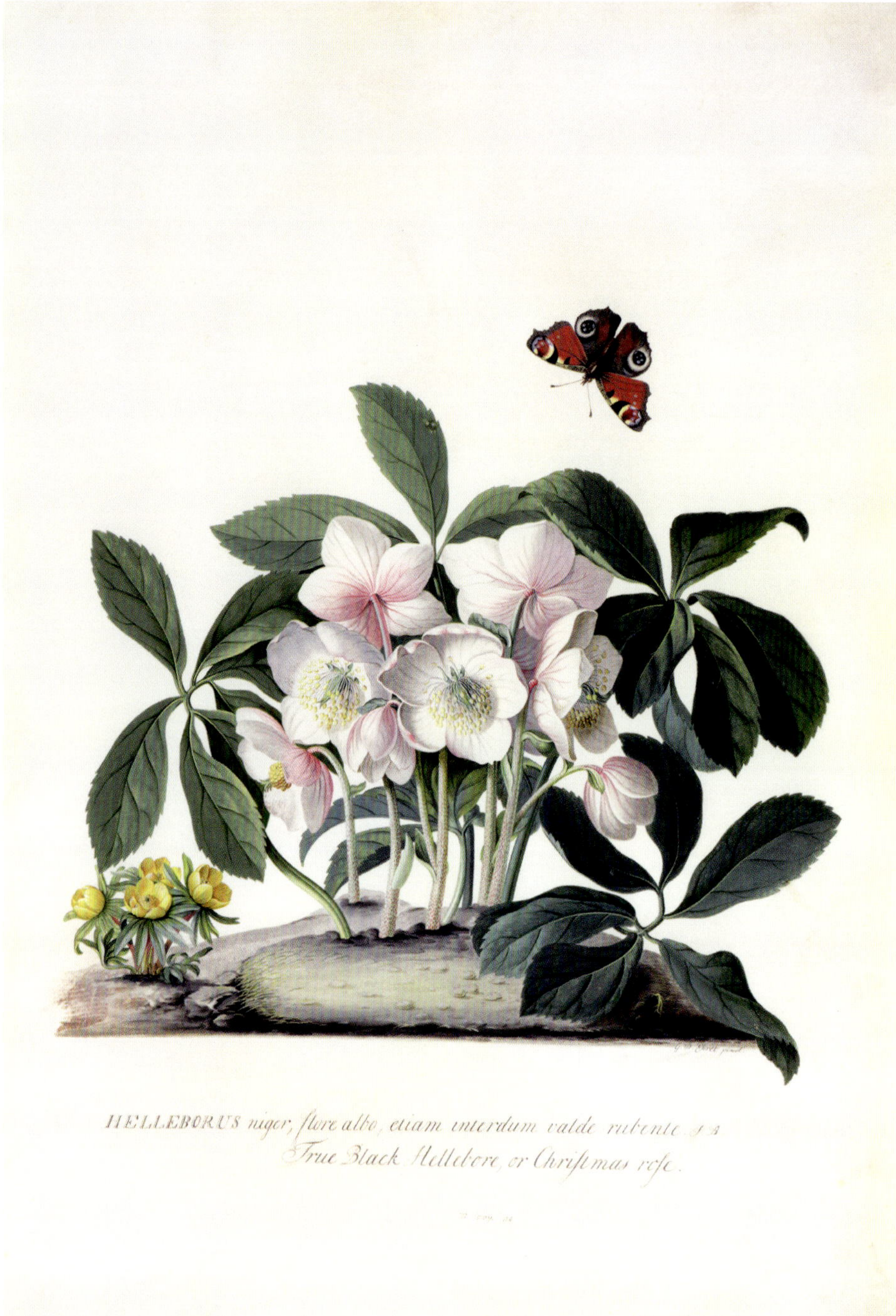

GEORG DIONYSIUS EHRET

•

Christmas Rose, c.1745
Watercolor and bodycolor on vellum,
21 × 14½ in / 53.2 × 37 cm
Victoria & Albert Museum, London

This botanical study of the Christmas rose (not a rose at all but, in fact, a poisonous hellebore, *Helleborus niger*) and winter aconite (*Eranthis hyemalis*), by noted German draftsman and botanist Georg Dionysius Ehret (1708–1770), shows the flowers of both plants at different stages of opening and from various angles. The Christmas rose is common around Christmastime, because it flowers in the winter and is unaffected by snow or ice, and it gets its common name from a Nativity legend. Shepherds watching their flocks by night (Luke 2:8) were visited by an angel who told them of the birth of Jesus (see pp.38, 209). They left their sheep to visit the newborn, taking with them gifts of honey, fruit, and white doves. A young shepherdess called Madelon, who also witnessed the angel, followed the shepherds to the stable where the Christ Child lay swaddled in the manger. Madelon watched as the Magi laid their gifts of gold, myrrh, and frankincense before the baby, and as the shepherds followed with theirs. With nothing to give, she scoured the snowy hills for flowers to offer, but finding nothing began to cry in despair. Seeing her weeping, the angel settled next to her, and where his feet touched the ground, a bush of pink-tipped Christmas roses appeared through the white blanket of snow—the perfect gift for the Prince of Peace.

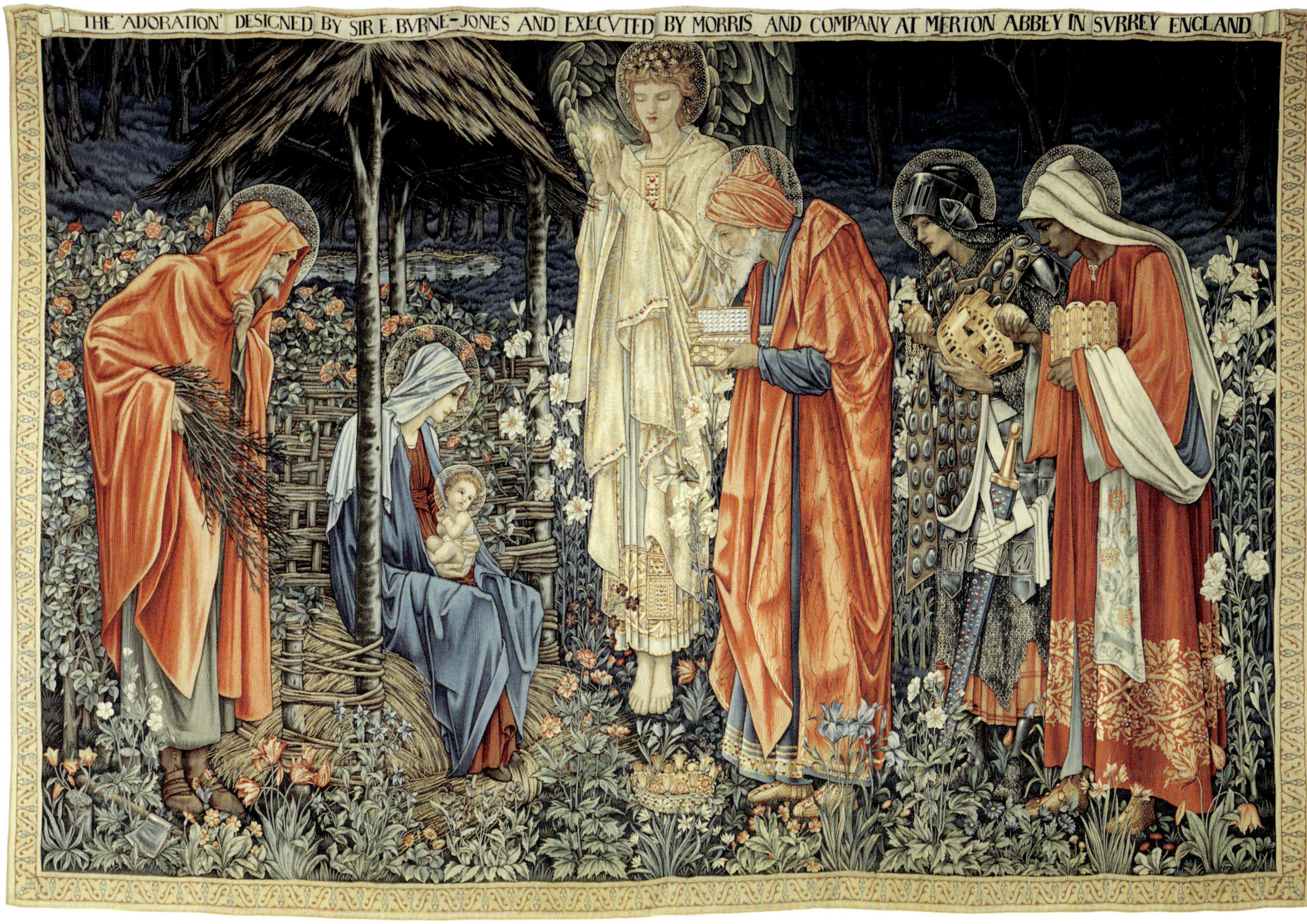

MORRIS & COMPANY

•

The Adoration of the Magi, c.1902
Handwoven tapestry,
8 ft 4 in × 12 ft 2½ in / 2.6 × 3.7 m
Art Gallery of South Australia, Adelaide

The infant Christ, held by the Virgin Mary, turns toward three kingly visitors from the east, who have been led by an angel holding a radiant star. Each king, whether dressed in sumptuous robes or medieval armor, bears a gift of gold, frankincense, or myrrh, presented to Jesus in worship. By removing their crowns, they show deference to the child, alluding to his divine sovereignty. This tapestry, produced by British decorative arts manufacturer Morris & Co., is one of the finest pieces of Victorian religious art. Its subject is the visit of the Magi to Bethlehem recorded in the second chapter of Matthew's Gospel, but its composition draws from a medieval retelling of the story, in which the wise men become three kings named Melchior, Balthazar, and Caspar (see p.26). The composition was designed by Pre-Raphaelite painter Edward Burne-Jones (1833–1898), with William Morris (1834–1896) and his assistant John Henry Dearle adding further detail, color, and ornamentation, including the proliferation of flowering plants. Morris was at the forefront of the late-nineteenth-century English tapestry revival and his company's medieval-inspired textiles and handcrafted objects had a significant influence on the decoration of churches and homes. Taking two years to weave at his Merton Abbey workshop in London, this was his most popular tapestry; a further nine versions were produced, each with a unique border design. The version shown was commissioned for Sir George Brookman (1850–1927), an Australian philanthropist.

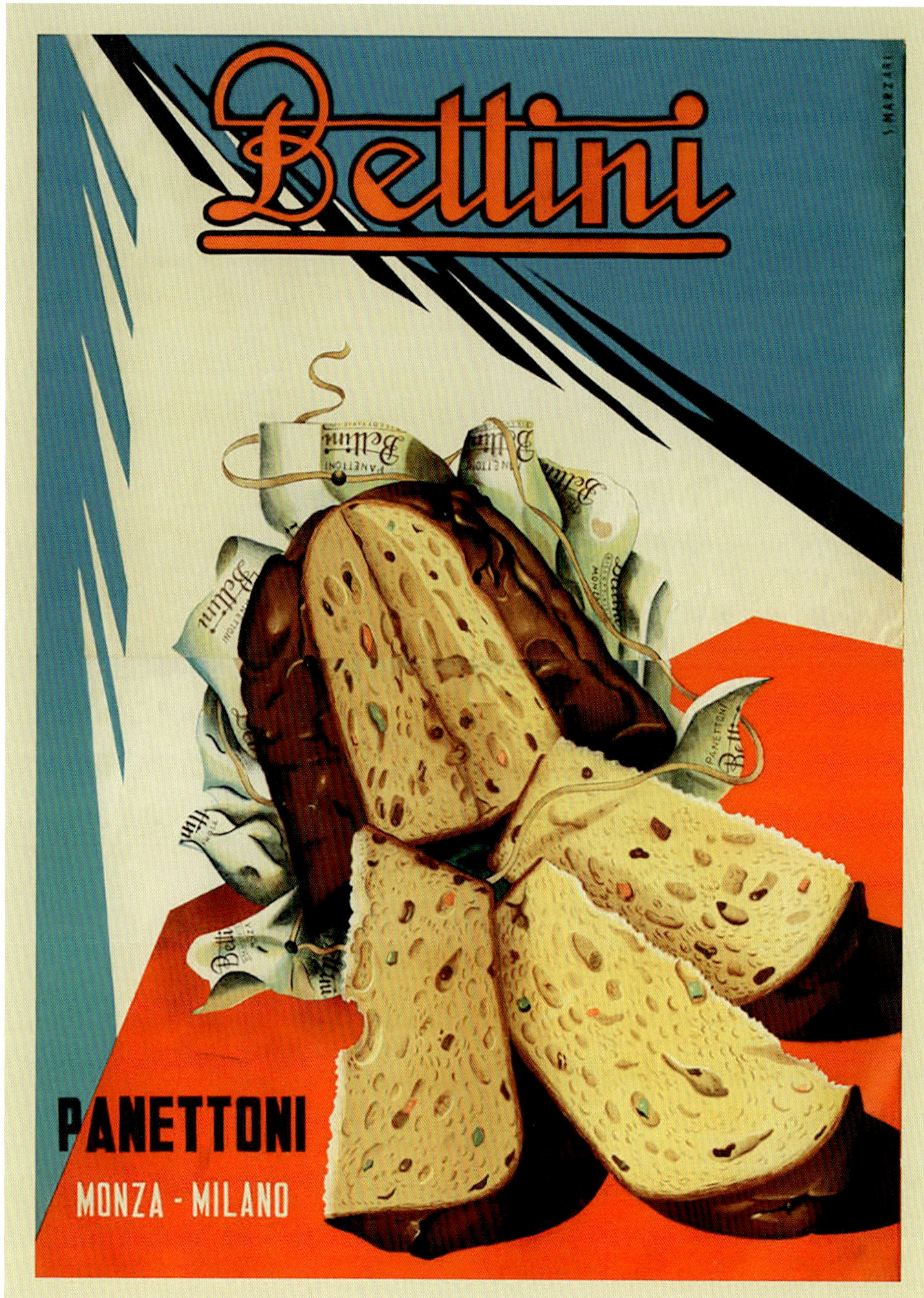

BETTINI

•

Panettone advertisement, 1951
Poster, dimensions variable

In front of a dramatic, black-and-white stylized silhouette of the renowned Duomo cathedral in Milan is a sliced panettone, a type of sweet bread widely eaten in almost every Italian home as an indispensable part of the Christmas meal. For such a ubiquitous dish, the provenance of panettone remain the subject of fierce debate, with the most common claims being that it originated in Milan, although whether that was in the time of the Romans or more recently is not entirely clear. What is indisputable is that panettone is a glorified, sweetened sourdough bread. Its name comes from the Italian word *panetto* (meaning a "small loaf"), but it is more complex than that description suggests. Panettone is made from several sourdoughs that must be left to rise for enough time to produce its light, fluffy texture. An assortment of candied citrus peel and raisins, egg yolks, and butter are then added. Once cooked, the bread is left to cool upside down for up to twelve hours to stabilize and prevent it from collapsing, giving it its characteristic dome shape. The procedure is sufficiently complicated that most people prefer to buy their panettone from firms, such as the Bettini company of Monza in northern Italy, who created this 1951 advertisement. From 1919, the Bettini family's panettone company produced as many as fifty thousand cakes a year, each packaged in a distinctive green-and-white box. The factory eventually closed down in 2019, after one hundred years of service.

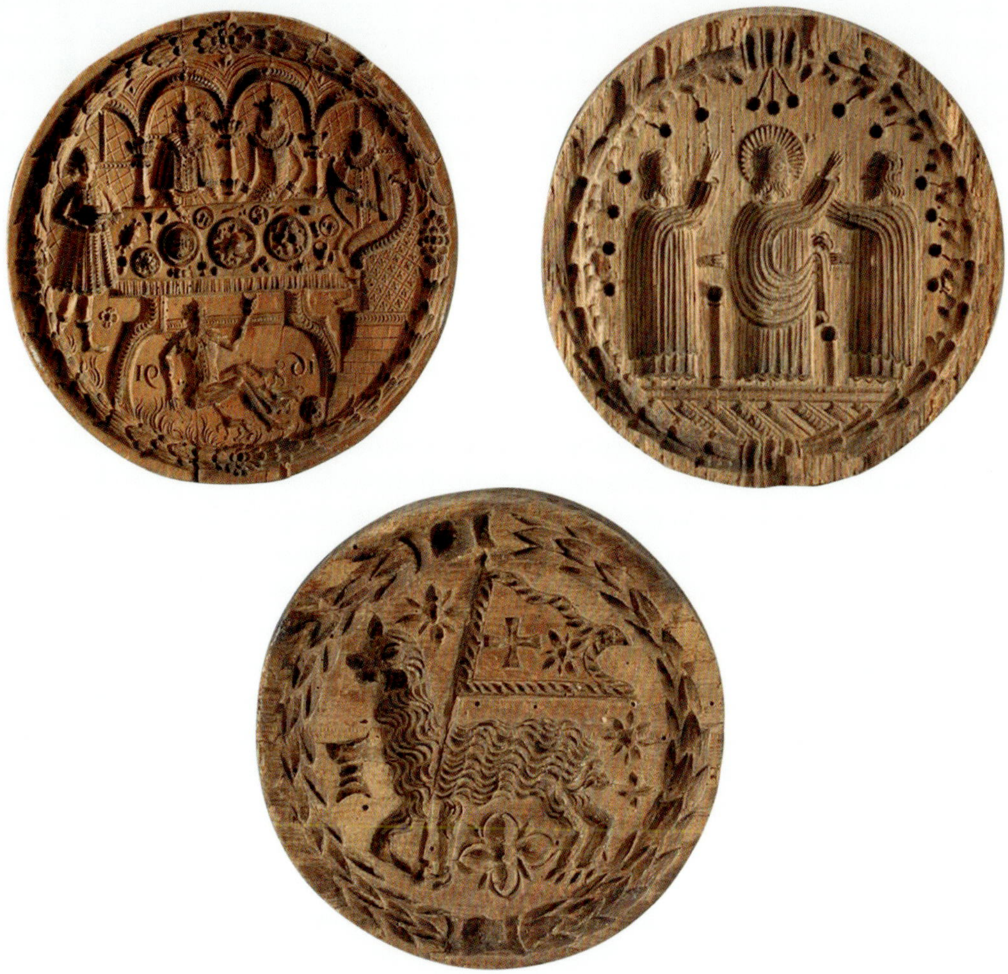

UNKNOWN

•

Christmas bread molds, 1691
Carved wood, D. 12½ in / 31.5 cm
Nordiska Museet, Stockholm

An image of a serving girl carrying a domed dish to add to the plentiful goblets and plates at the table is carved into the most intricate of these three bread molds. The seated revelers, to whom she attends, wear elaborately decorated costumes, including embroidered doublets, lace ruffs, and, on the left-seated figure, a lined cape and a hat perched jauntily atop his head. The abundance of food and drink seen here is matched by the excesses of carved decoration across these three pieces, with barely an inch of surface unadorned by various elements. Three kings and an animal holding a standard complete the set. Bread molds, which impress a design in the top of a loaf prior to baking, are commonly used for ritual Christian practice, both for communion loaves and for ceremonial feasts, including Christmas. These examples entwine the great Swedish traditions of wood carving and the extravagant, festive *julbord* (Christmas table) meal (see p.93), whose multiple courses of pickled and cured fish, breads, meatballs, and a centerpiece of cooked ham known as *julskinka* have changed little since its creation. However, this embodiment of the Swedish prosperity that followed the end of the Scanian War (1675–79) carries a surprising additional warning against avarice. The tormented beggar seen under the table, sores licked by the dogs that surround him, identifies one scene as the parable of the rich man and Lazarus, whose comforts will be reversed starkly in the afterlife.

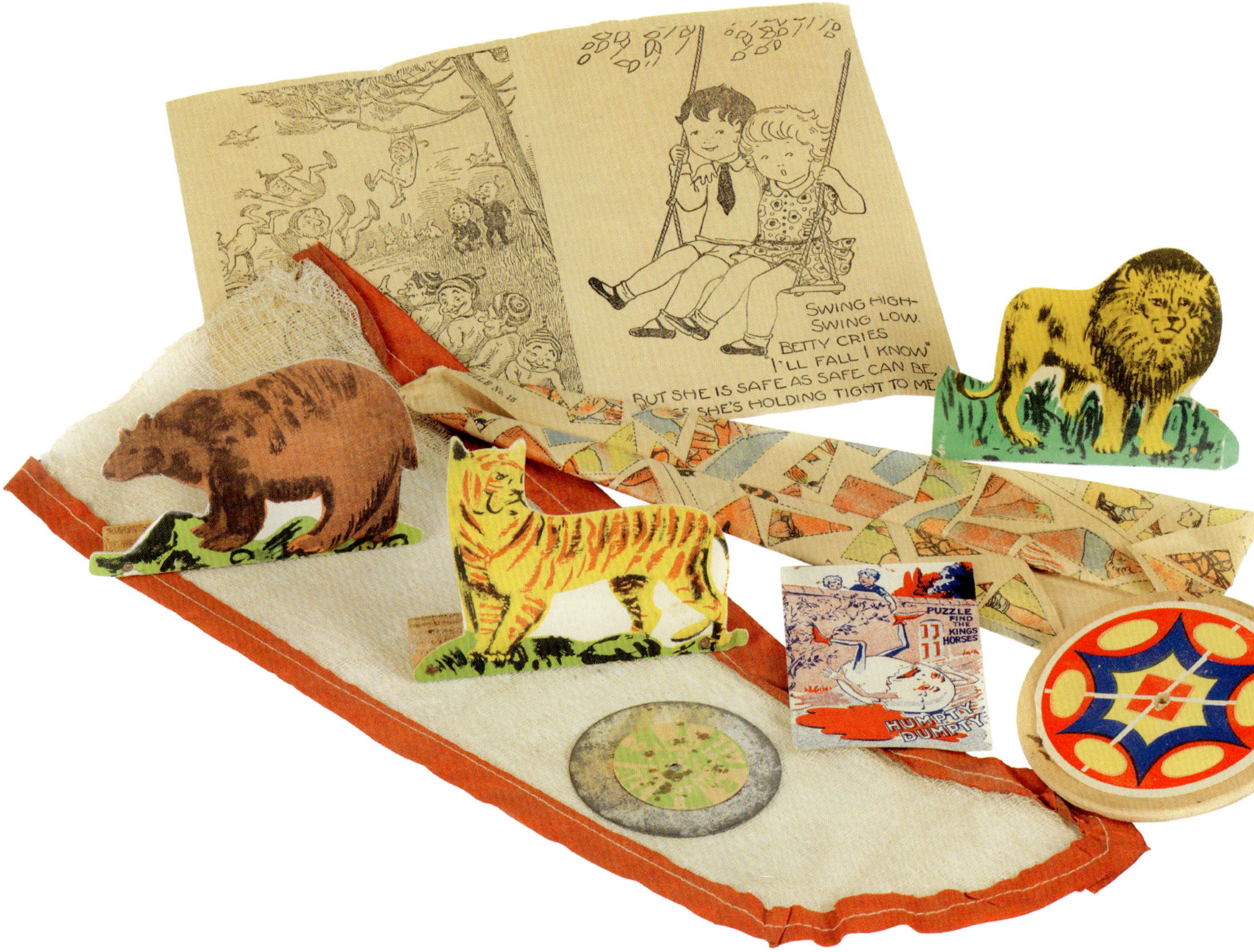

UNKNOWN

•

Christmas stocking with gifts, 1940
Paper, wood, metal, textile, cardboard,
16½ × 6½ in / 41.9 × 16.5 cm
Imperial War Museum, London

There have been many occasions when Christmas celebrations have continued during times of conflict (see p.123) and World War II was no different—although its privations brought great changes to festivities across Europe. This British child's stocking from 1940 neatly encapsulates how people were forced to adapt to the shortages and restrictions of wartime. The stocking's contents were made from low-quality paper—which had become increasingly hard to source as the war continued—but demonstrate the renowned British "wartime spirit" with inventive animals made from cardboard, a carefully chosen story book, and puzzles. From 1941, to save paper, gifts were no longer wrapped up, which meant few surprises on Christmas morning. Presents were often practical: the most popular for Christmas 1940 was soap. With the introduction of food rationing on January 8, 1940, the traditional Christmas dinner tested the cook's ingenuity. Instead of dried fruit, which was hard to find, Christmas cakes (see p.216) and puddings were bulked out with grated carrots and bread crumbs. Home entertainment was based on sing-a-longs around the piano and hours of family board games. The Christmas break itself was shortened; in Great Britain, the Boxing Day holiday on December 26, introduced in 1871, was temporarily suspended as workers returned to shops and factories straight after Christmas Day to boost the war effort. However, many families later look back on their simpler wartime Christmases with affection.

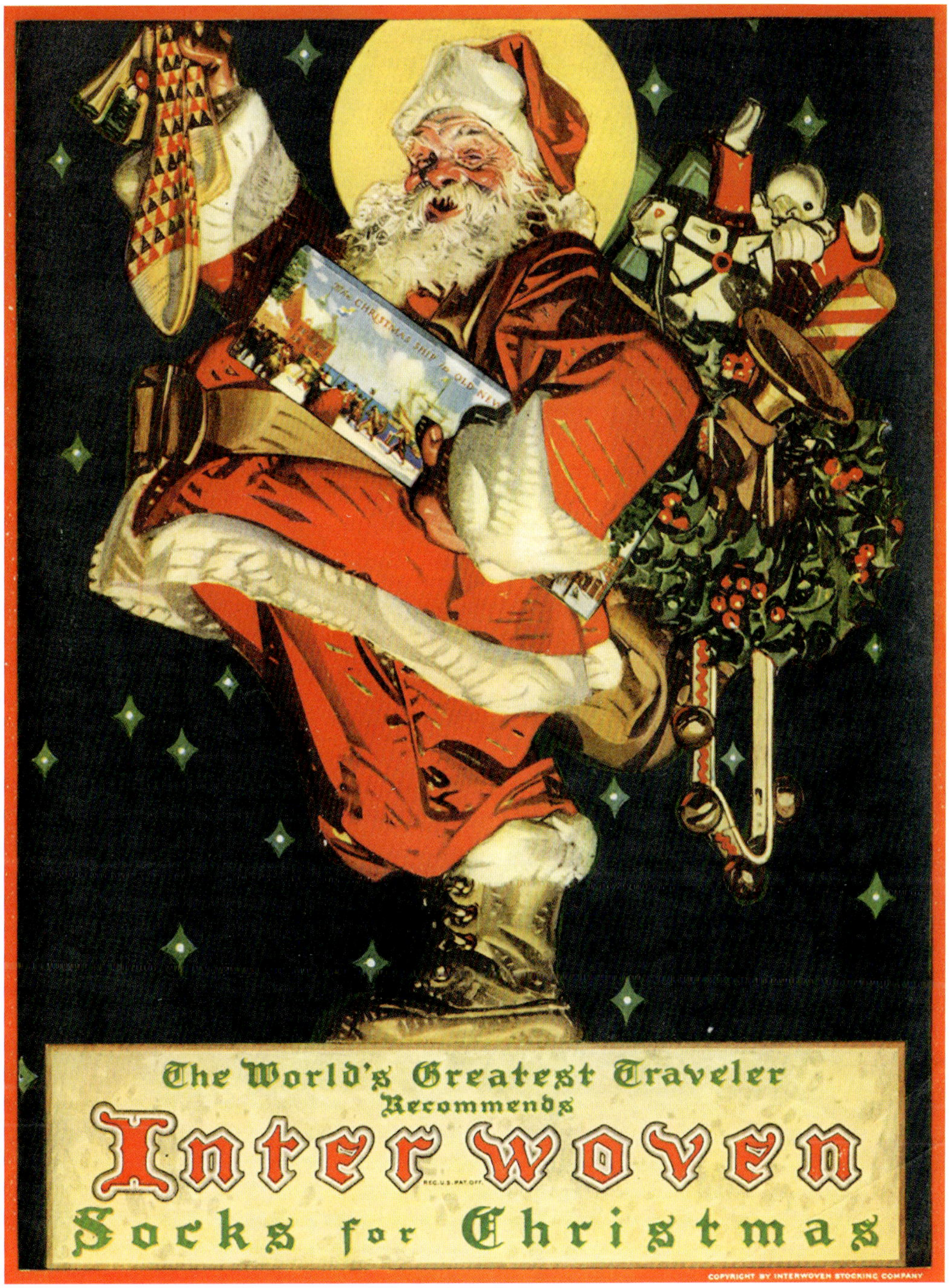

J. C. LEYENDECKER

•

Advertisement for Interwoven Socks, c.1920
Print, dimensions variable

A red-cheeked, gray-bearded, rather chubby Santa Claus holds up a pair of colorful socks in this Christmas advertisement for one-time US hosiery brand leader, Interwoven Socks—and in a moment it helped define the visual representation of an icon. Likely influenced by Thomas Nast's depiction of Santa Claus in *Harper's Weekly*, this advertisement helped ingrain this jolly, overweight, bearded man in a red suit edged with white fur in the common consciousness. It bears a great resemblance to the Haddon Sundblom Santa commissioned by Coca-Cola in 1931 (see p.13), which, perhaps due to the size of the brand the image was for, is more well-known now. The illustration, which appeared on the cover of the December 17 edition of the hugely popular *Saturday Evening Post* was the work of German-born Joseph Christian (J. C.) Leyendecker (1873–1951), one of America's most prolific illustrators. Leyendecker's Santa Claus took time to evolve: his first Santa, which appeared in the *Post* in 1912, was a thin, old man dressed in a dirty red coat inspired by the founder of the red-coated Salvation Army (see p.96), William Booth (1829–1912), who had died earlier that year. Mentor of the more famous Norman Rockwell, Leyendecker illustrated 322 covers for *The Saturday Evening Post* between 1896 and 1950, and drew many more advertisements, including highly influential images for Arrow shirt collars.

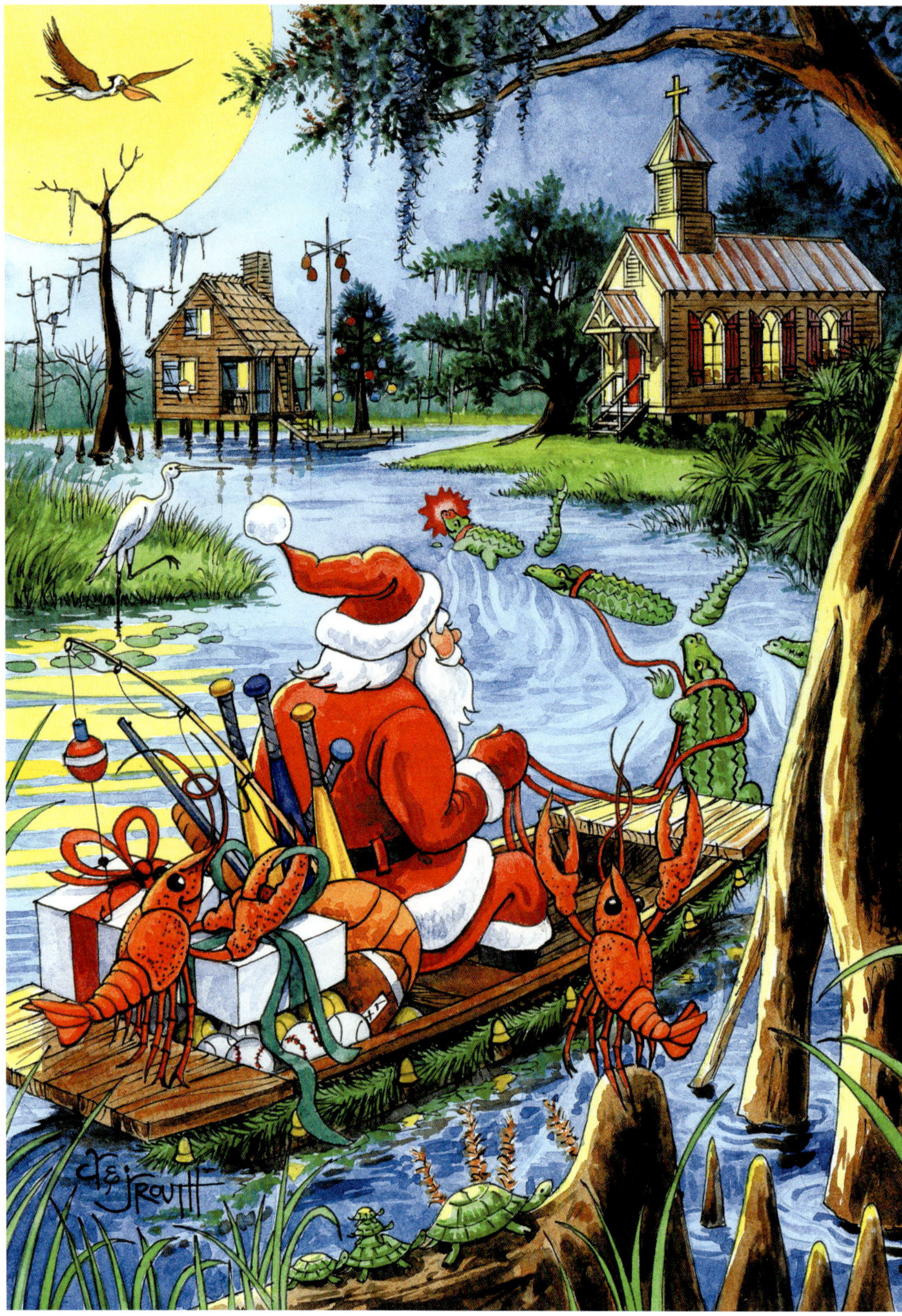

CRAIG AND STAN ROUTH

•

Santa's Bayou Trek, c.2000
Printed cardstock, 7 × 5 in / 17.8 × 12.7 cm
Routh Collection, Louisiana

On the night before Christmas, Santa Claus travels along a bayou in the Louisiana swamp in a pirogue, a flat-bottom canoe, drawn by alligators and helped by crawfish toward a characteristic stilt house and a traditional wooden church. This Christmas card was designed by Louisiana native Craig and his father, Stan Routh, who since 1994 have specialized in creating light-hearted images that celebrate the unique culture of the Southern states bordering the Gulf of Mexico, often featuring distinctive Christmas traditions. The inside of each card features a standard festive greeting, while on the reverse is a recipe, usually created by Craig's wife Leslie, for something delicious—in this case, a crawfish pie, inspired by the creatures on the front. Other recipes also star native ingredients, such as the pecan-crusted catfish and the shrimp and corn soup. The tradition of sending Christmas cards originated in Great Britain in 1843, when civil servant Sir Henry Cole wanted to encourage more people to use the recently established Post Office. Cole worked with his friend, the artist John Horsley, to design the first commercial Christmas cards (see p.198). From 1860 onward, virtually everyone in Great Britain could send Christmas greetings to their friends and family. It took until around 1875 for Christmas cards to become equally affordable in the United States, when a German-born printer, Louis Prang (see p.84, 90), started to mass-produce lithographed designs in Boston, earning himself the title of "the father of the American Christmas card."

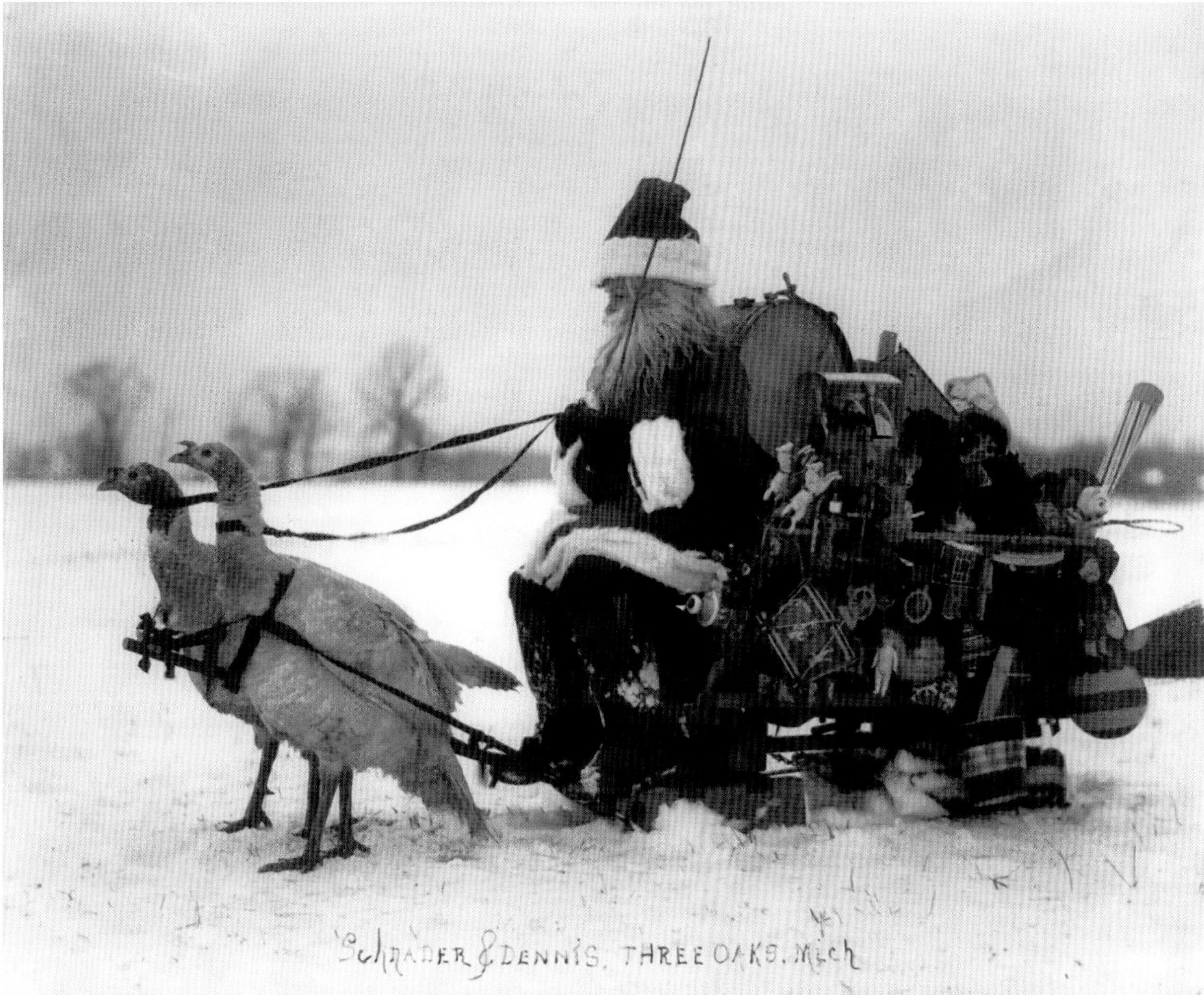

SCHRADER & DENNIS

•

"Santa Claus" with Christmas toys on a sled drawn by white turkeys, c.1909
Photographic print, dimensions variable

This example of a real photo postcard, known as RPPCs to collectors, certainly skews the traditional idea of Santa and his sleigh in a humorous direction. A young child dressed in full Santa regalia, including false beard, sits upon a wooden sled piled high to the sky with presents. Instead of the traditional eight reindeer (nine, counting Rudolph), two snowy white turkeys pull the makeshift sleigh across the snowy ground, making use of a rather sophisticated-looking harness system. Real photo postcards feature a photograph on the recto and a postcard's traditional address lines and blank space for a note on the verso. These essentially exist in two types: those made as one-of-a-kind cards by lay photographers, often featuring pictures of family and personally meaningful places—Kodak began marketing special photo paper with printed postcard backs in 1902 and a special camera that took postcard-size film in 1903—and those mass-produced by various companies and offered for sale. This one appears to be the latter and bears the mark of Schrader & Dennis of Three Oaks, Michigan, a popular manufacturer of RPPCs. Frequently those made for sale featured a humorous bent, sometimes bawdy and sometimes vanilla. This image almost certainly elicited many a chuckle around Christmas more than a hundred years ago.

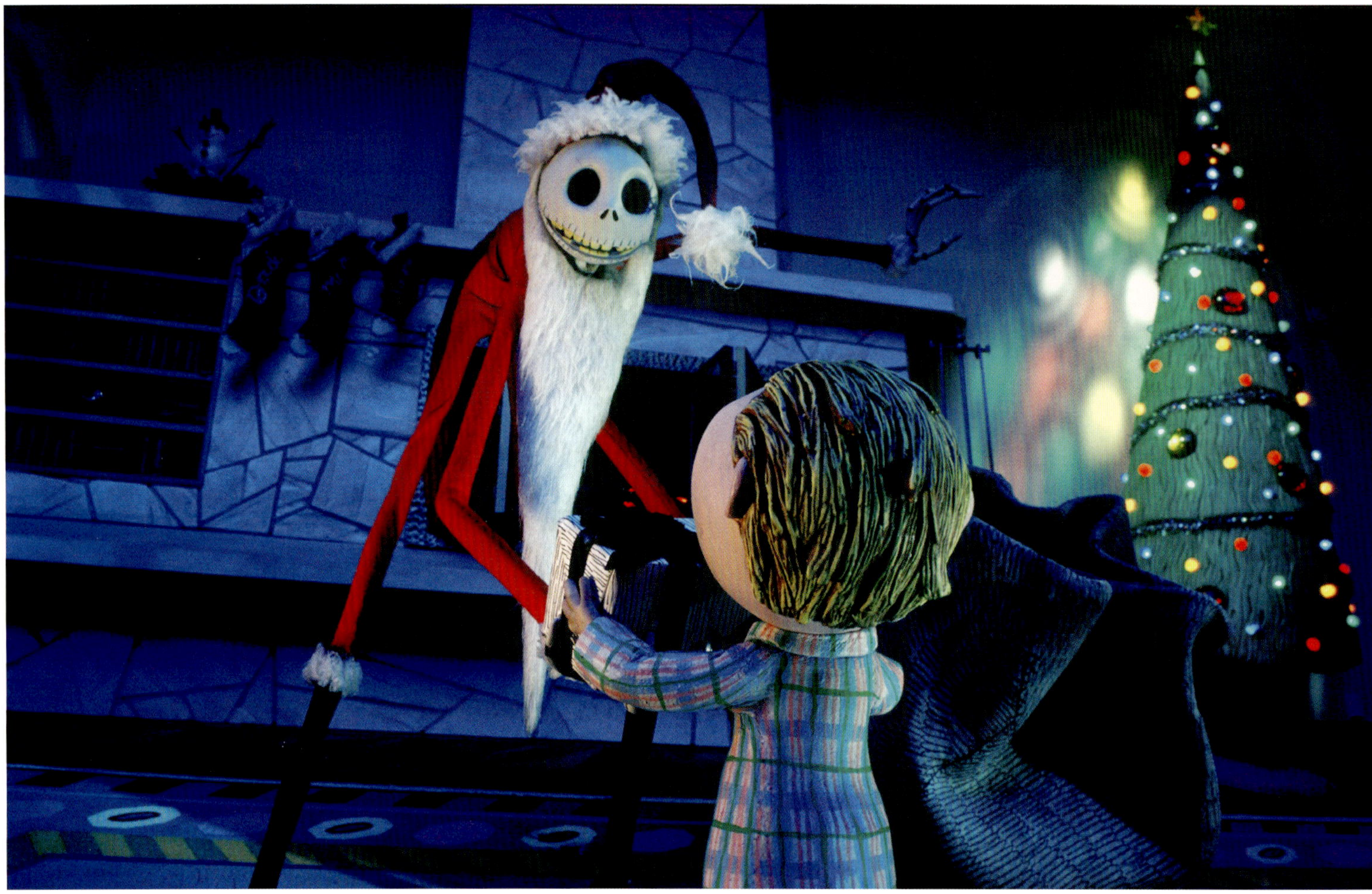

HENRY SELICK

•

Still from *Tim Burton's The Nightmare Before Christmas*, 1993
Animation, dimensions variable
Touchstone Pictures / Tim Burton Productions

In the early 1990s, the Christmas movie genre was ripe for reimagining; the same old plots and tropes had been done to death. Then, in 1993, along came *Tim Burton's The Nightmare Before Christmas*, the musical brainchild of Tim Burton, who had originally conceived of the idea in 1982 as a poem he wrote while working as an animator at Walt Disney Studios. Directed by Henry Selick, known for his stop-motion animation films, it tells the story of Jack Skellington, the king of Halloween Town, who accidentally discovers Christmas Town and subsequently decides he and his Halloween Town cronies should "improve upon" Christmas by applying some of their own dark ideas to the holiday. After orchestrating the kidnapping of the real Santa Claus, Skellington takes flight to deliver his own selection of terrifying, ghoulish gifts in a sleigh pulled by skeletal reindeer, which is eventually shot down by the military. But never fear—Santa is ultimately freed and saves Christmas. The film was made using stop-motion animation (see p.68) and elevated the medium to new heights. Roger Ebert, the famous American film critic, in his initial review, posited that the film's visual effects were as revolutionary as those of *Star Wars*. The movie's songs and music, written by Danny Elfman—former front man of new-wave band Oingo Boingo—were also widely praised. Despite the passage of time, the film continues to be massively popular, ranking highly on movie review aggregator sites and lists of top Christmas films even now.

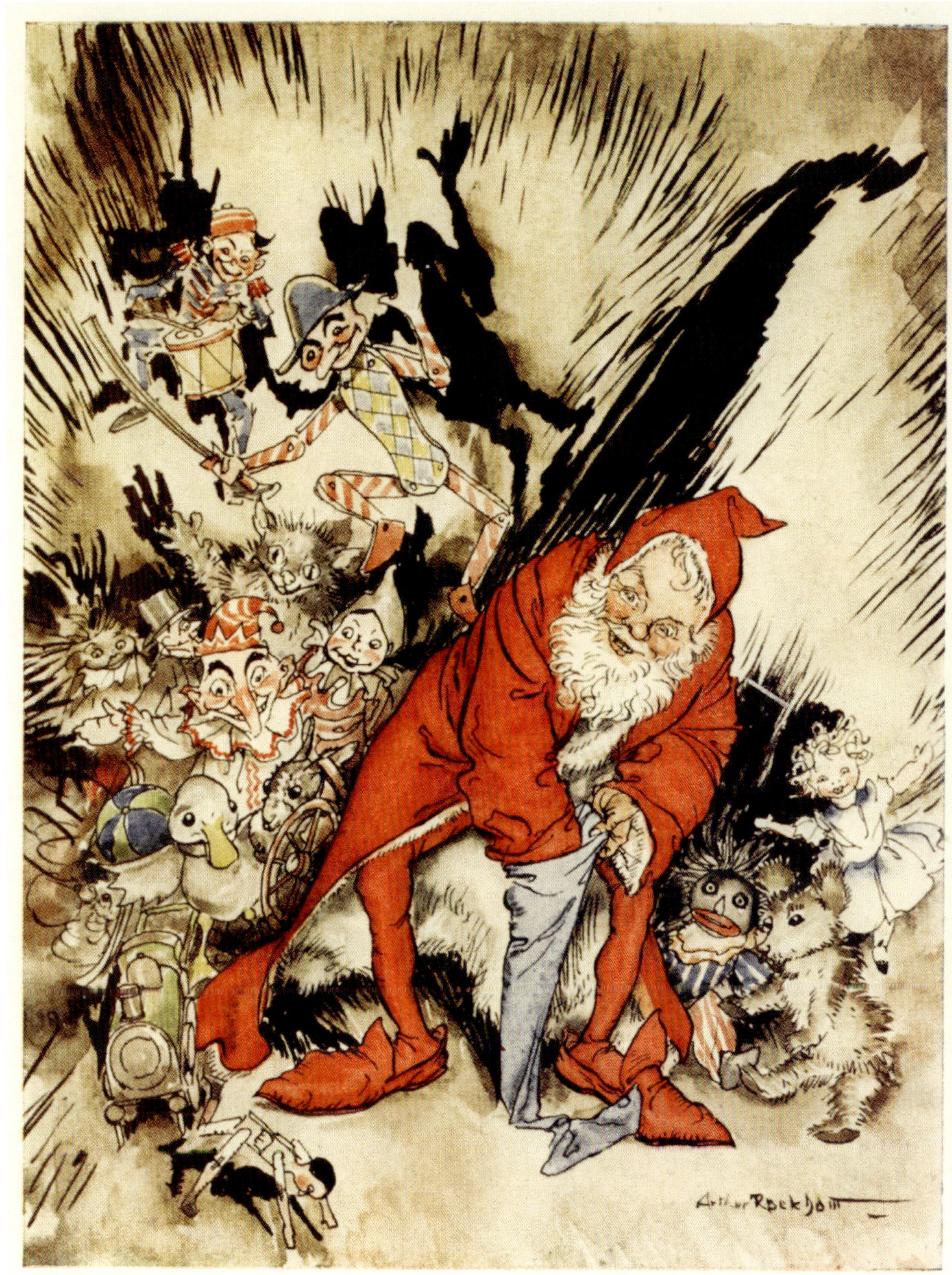

ARTHUR RACKHAM

•

Illustration from "A Visit from St. Nicholas"
by Clement Clarke Moore, 1931
Pen, ink, and watercolor, 8⅞ × 5¾ in / 22.5 × 14.6 cm
British Library, London

Surrounded by toys, Father Christmas stuffs a stocking in this illustration from a 1931 edition of one of the most famous of all American poems, Clement Clarke Moore's "A Visit from St. Nicholas" (see p.84), drawn by one of the most renowned British illustrators of his generation, Arthur Rackham (1867–1939). The poem tells of a sleeping household on Christmas Eve awaiting the arrival of Father Chrsitmas and his eight reindeer. Originally published anonymously in 1823, the poem was later renamed after its famous first words—"Twas the night before Christmas, and all through the house / Not a creature was stirring, not even a mouse"—and first introduced readers to Santa's original eight named reindeer. Moore initially denied authorship, concerned that his children's poem would tarnish his academic reputation; he only admitted in 1837 that he had, indeed, written the classic. London-born Rackham is perhaps better known as the illustrator who brought to life J. M. Barrie's Peter Pan stories, but his depiction of Father Christmas shows his unique style; having trained as a journalistic illustrator, he drew strong pen and ink outlines, then filled them in with watercolors. Rackham's Father Christmas resembles a goblin with his thin legs and long, pointed boots, and is in many ways as frightening as he is reassuring, not helped by the gang of menacing-looking toys gathered around him.

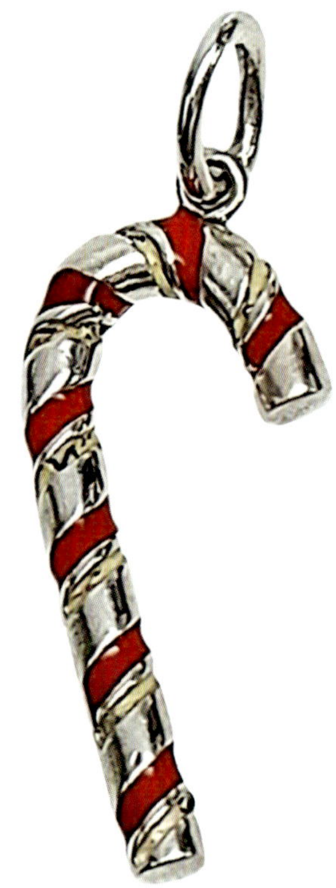

TIFFANY & CO.

•

Candy cane charm, c.20th century
Sterling silver and enamel, 1¼ × ½ in / 2.5 × 1.3 cm
Private collection

World-renowned as a top luxury jeweler, the name Tiffany & Co. is as recognizable as its trademarked blue hue (officially Pantone's 1837 Blue); (see p.88). Tiffany introduced the charm bracelet to their catalog in 1889. It became one of its signature items and created a demand among customers for fine, sterling silver jewelry. This petite candy cane charm, made to look like the traditionally peppermint-flavored stick candy that is so synonymous with the season, can also be worn as a pendant and was likely produced in the mid-twentieth century. It is crafted from sterling silver and enameled with red and gold. This model, which is also made in the iconic Tiffany blue, has since been discontinued and fetches a fair price on the secondary market. The company was founded in 1837 by Charles Lewis Tiffany (1812–1902) in New York City, where it quickly found success as a seller of "fancy goods." It was the first American retailer to hew to the British standard of .925 sterling silver (meaning it is an alloy of at least 92.5 percent silver, combined with other metals, usually copper). It was a benchmark they employed in their jewelry and serving ware alike. Tiffany's offers a wide range of holiday-themed jewelry items, from secular symbols, such as snowmen (see pp.31, 181), to religious symbols, such as crosses—but always and ever remain arbiters of good taste and excellent quality.

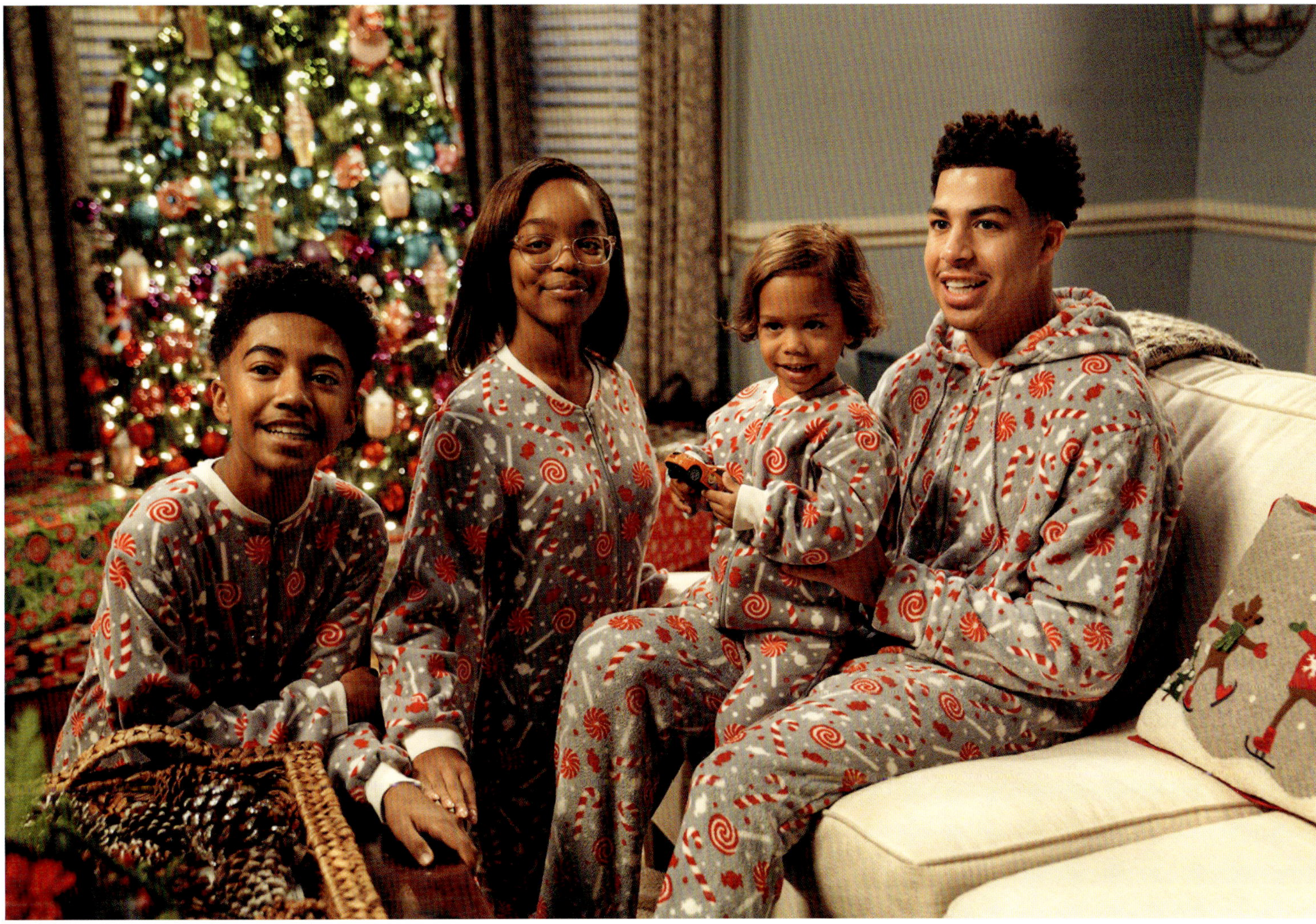

KENYA BARRIS

•

Still from *Black-ish*, 2019
Film, dimensions variable
ABC Television

Coordinating sleepwear sets for the whole family first hit US markets in the 1950s, when Christmas catalogs from retailers, such as Sears, depicted mothers, fathers, and children frolicking in matching holiday getups—everything from robes to sleeping caps to slippers. Pictured here are the children of the fictional Johnson family from the Kenya Barris–penned American sit-com *Black-ish*, played by, from left to right, Miles Brown, Marsai Martin, August and Berlin Gross, and Marcus Scribner, all dressed in matching pajamas. It is fair to say that the trend of dressing in matching festive clothes on Christmas morning has grown massively since the advent of social media. What began as a private family bonding ritual has morphed into a twenty-first-century phenomenon, the fodder for a "best life" depiction of a happy family Yuletide. A-listers, including Reese Witherspoon, Jennifer Lopez, the Kardashian clan, and the diva of Christmas herself, Mariah Carey (see p.154), are among the many famous faces to get in on the act. *Black-ish* is only one of many TV shows to weave matching clothes into their Christmas special story lines. And in a case of life imitating art, the actress who plays the matriarch of the Johnson family, Tracee Ellis Ross, and her famous real-life family—including mother and style icon Diana Ross—have their own Christmas pajama tradition, making for some very festive social media posts, indeed.

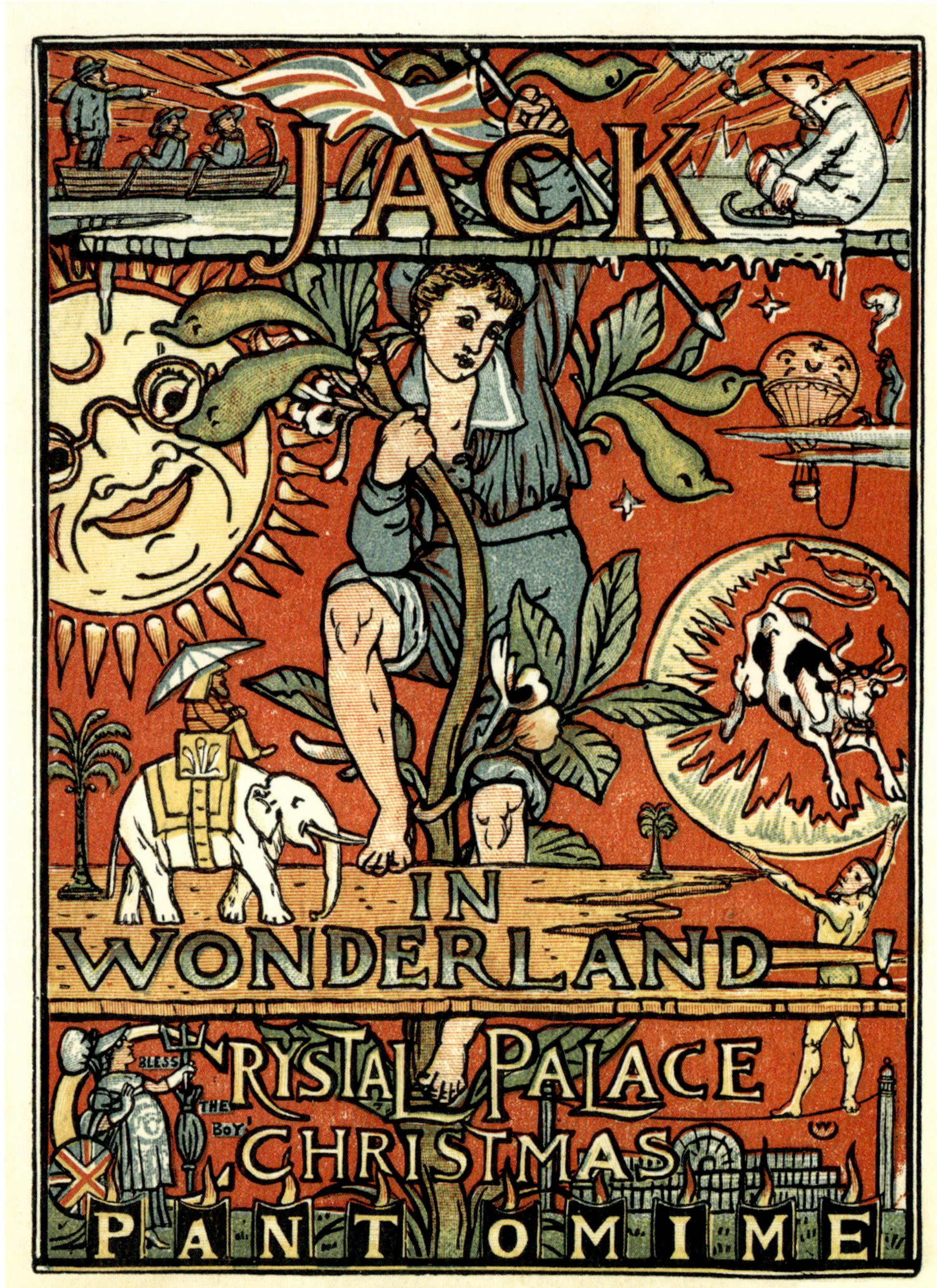

ENGLISH SCHOOL

•

Jack in Wonderland, 1876
Poster, dimensions variable
Private collection

This colorful and busy image—taking its cue from the British Arts and Crafts designer William Morris (1834–1896)—shows a young boy climbing a bean stalk, surrounded by various animals and scenes. It comes from the cover of a program for an 1876 performance of the Christmas pantomime *Jack in Wonderland*. A bowdlerized version of the fairy story *Jack and the Beanstalk*, it was staged at London's Crystal Palace, the glass hall originally built for the 1851 Great Exhibition in Hyde Park. A peculiarly British institution, the Christmas pantomime has its roots in sixteenth-century Italian commedia dell'arte, which combined dance, music, acrobatics, and comedy characters. The pantomime's transformation into to a mainstay of the British Christmas experience—a tradition that continues to this day—was partly due to Prince Albert's efforts to make Christmas celebrations in Great Britain as important as in his native Germany (see p.101). The Victorians began to embrace all things Christmas and the pantomime became one of the season's traditions. Billed as entertainment for the whole family, pantomimes provided a diet of double etendres, gender swapping—the dame is traditionally played by a man and the principal boy by a woman—slapstick humor, audience participation, and contemporary political satire, all incorporated into a relatively small number of central stories. By Christmas 1874, pantomimes were delighting audiences at theaters across the country.

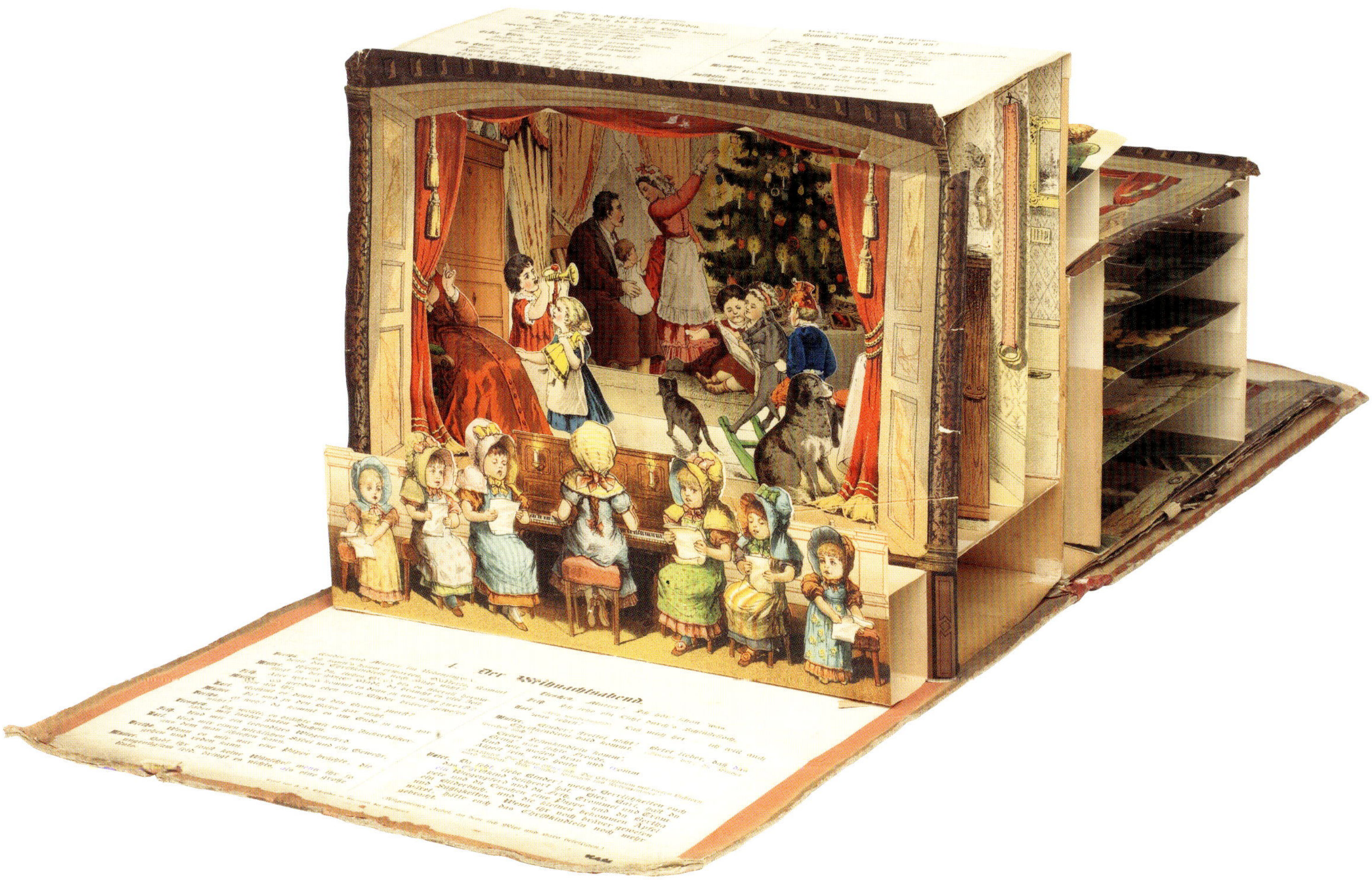

J. F. SCHREIBER

•

Theater Bilderbuch, c.1885
Printed book, 13¼ × 10½ in / 33.6 × 26.5 cm
Victoria & Albert Museum, London

This is Christmas Eve in a traditional German house in the late nineteenth century, as seen through the curtains of a pop-up toy theater book. A mother puts the finishing touches on the immaculately decorated tree—a custom that began in Germany and spread across the world around this time—as the man of the house looks on, taking care of a young baby. Children of various ages play with their new toys—a rocking horse, a doll, a book, and a trumpet—as tradition dictates gifts are opened on Christmas Eve. Sitting quietly, just out of view behind the curtain, a presumably older member of the family relaxes in a chair, away from the chaos surrounding them. Other scenes in this book include *Hansel and Gretel*, *Little Red Riding Hood*, and the *Adoration of the Magi*. They all are set on a three-dimensional stage and accompanied by a piece of dialogue printed in German and a youthful orchestra, such as the one shown here, playing the organ. Toy theaters were popular all over Europe during the second half of the nineteenth century, and German publishing house J. F. Schreiber, founded in 1831, specialized in them. This one is particularly unusual as it features four scenes, two of which are related to Christmas. It was likely this was produced specifically as a gift for the season.

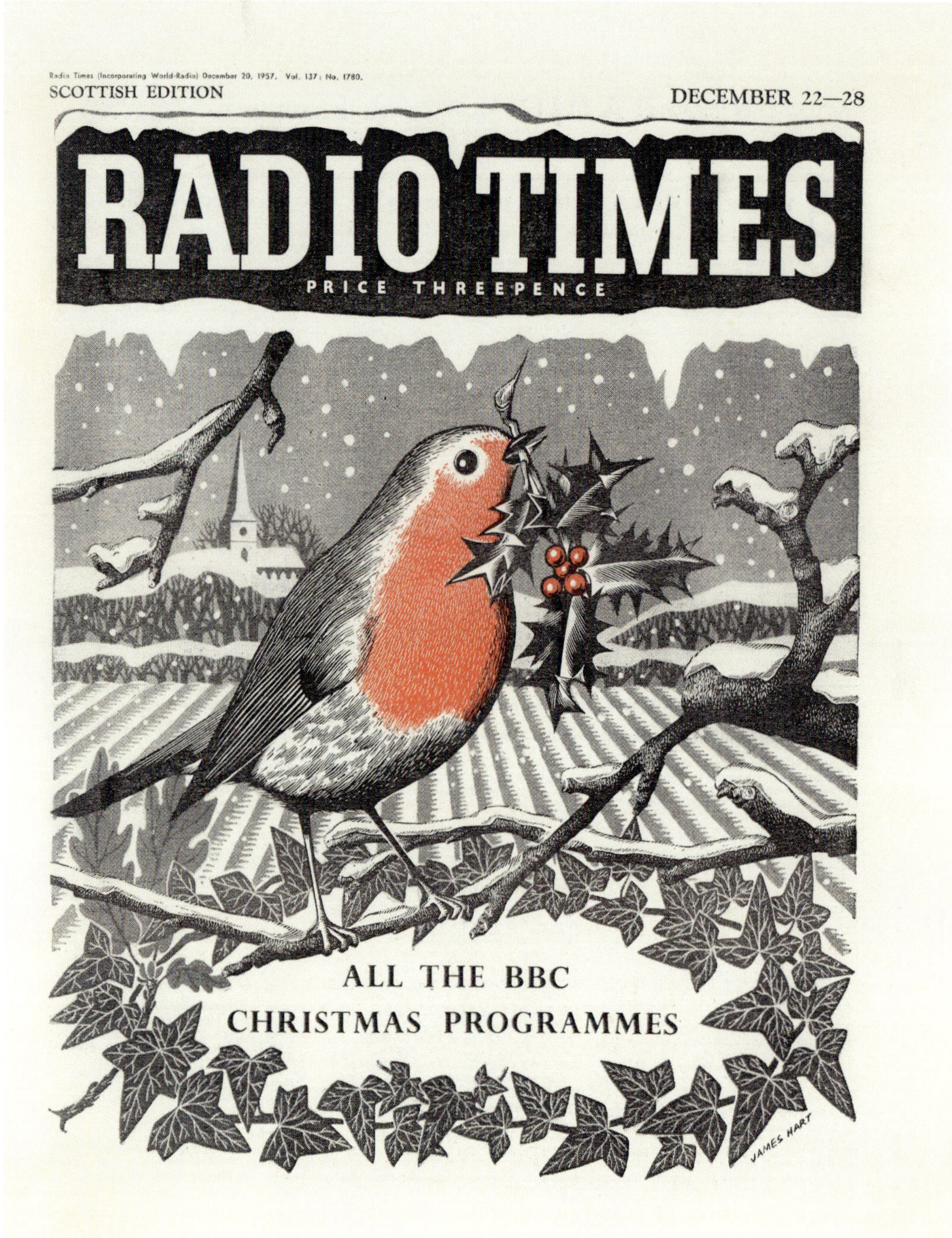

BBC MAGAZINES

•

Front cover of the *Radio Times*, 1957
Colored etching, 11¾ × 8¾ in / 30 × 22.4 cm

A robin, with its bright red breast, dominates an idyllic wintery scene; snow has settled on the trees, hedgerows, and fields, and the church sits proudly in the background. The only splash of color, except for the bird, is the scarlet holly berries the robin holds in its beak (see p.54). The work of an unknown artist, the image appeared on the cover of the 1957 Christmas edition of the *Radio Times*. In Great Britain, the magazine has been a Christmas institution for decades. First appearing in 1923, it was originally a weekly listing of all BBC radio shows in each region of the country—hence its name—with a special festive edition published annually: this one was intended for Scotland. With the arrival of black-and-white television in 1936, the *Radio Times* expanded to include first BBC programming and then eventually all television channels. Over the decades, the Christmas magazine remained the best-selling edition of the year and became as much a part of British tradition as the Christmas address by the reigning monarch and a roast turkey or goose for dinner (see p.227). Such was its popularity from the 1960s to the 1990s, when more than three million magazines were printed every year, that it often sold out. The splash of red on this cover marked the first time color had been used since the end of World War II and anticipated the highly colored covers used since 1963.

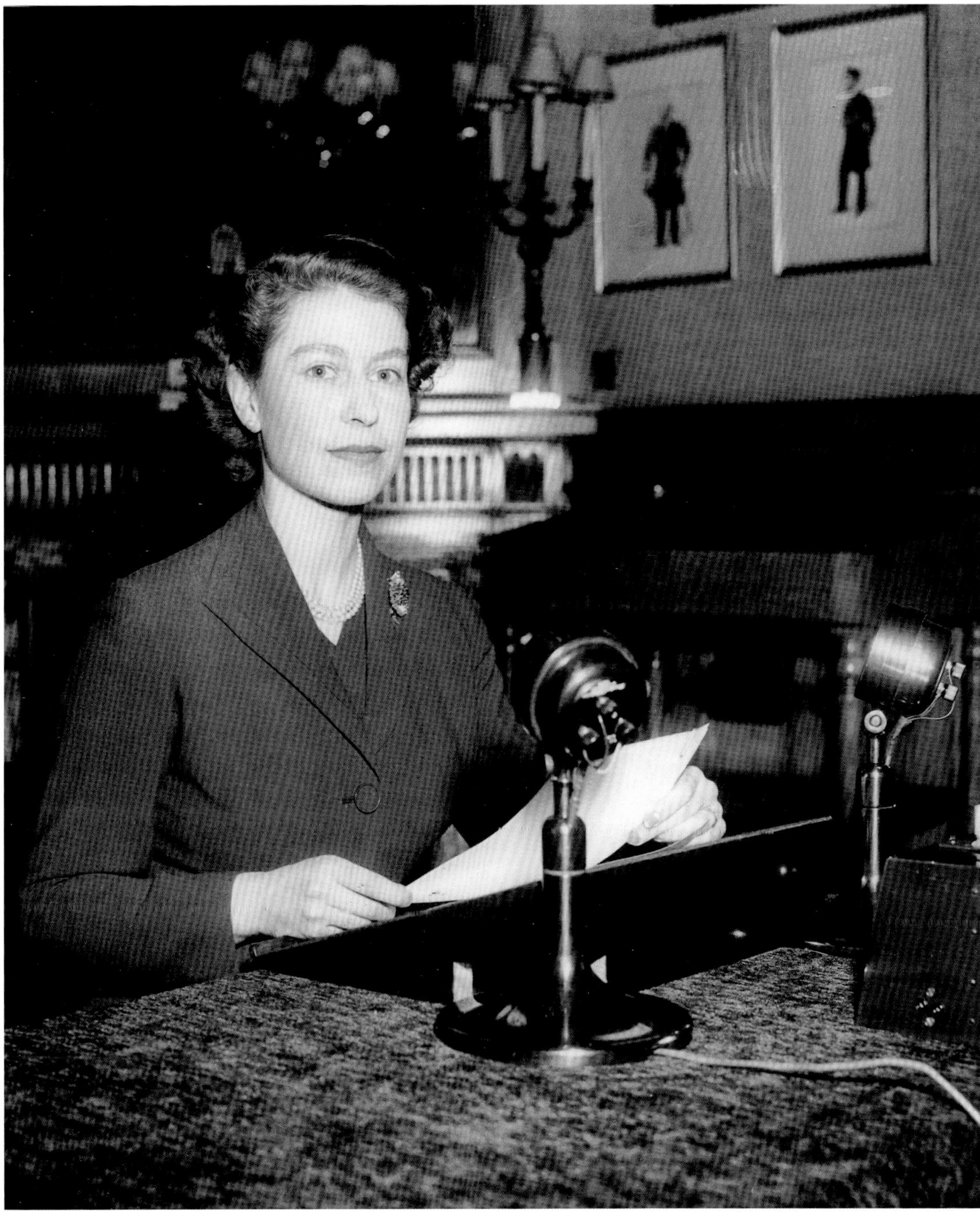

PLANET NEWS LTD.

•

HM Queen Elizabeth II's first Christmas broadcast, 1952
Photograph, 7½ × 6⅝ in / 19.2 × 14.2 cm
Royal Collection Trust, London

In millions of British households, the traditional Christmas dinner is followed by another great festive tradition: watching the Royal Christmas Message on television. Queen Elizabeth II (1926–2022) began televising her messages in 1957, but her very first was for BBC radio in 1952, eleven months after the death of her father, King George VI (1895–1952). Speaking from her study at Sandringham House, the young queen sat at the same desk that her grandfather King George V had used for the first royal Christmas broadcast in 1932. She thanked the nation for its loyalty and affection during the first months of her reign and asked for support ahead of her coronation. Between 1952–2021, Queen Elizabeth II spoke to the nation and Commonwealth every Christmas Day at 3 p.m., with the exception of 1969, when she decided that a fly-on-the-wall BBC documentary, *Royal Family*, had given her and her family enough exposure that year. Usually filmed at Buckingham Palace, the eagerly awaited speeches were largely written by the Queen herself with the aid of her husband, Prince Philip (1921–2021). They typically combined a summary of the year's global, national, and personal events, along with personal reflections. In later years, the monarch's messages became more religious in tone, reflecting her deeply held Christian faith.

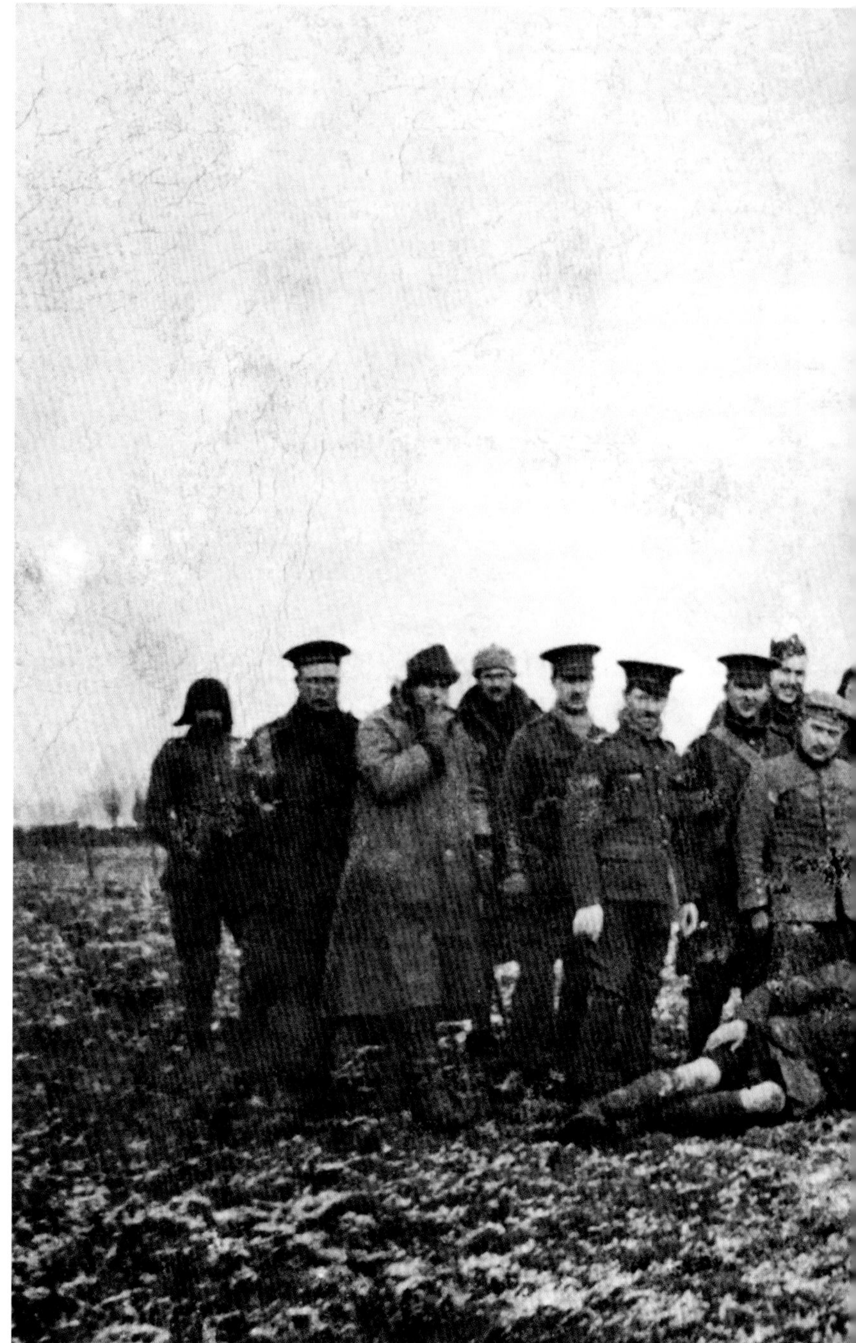

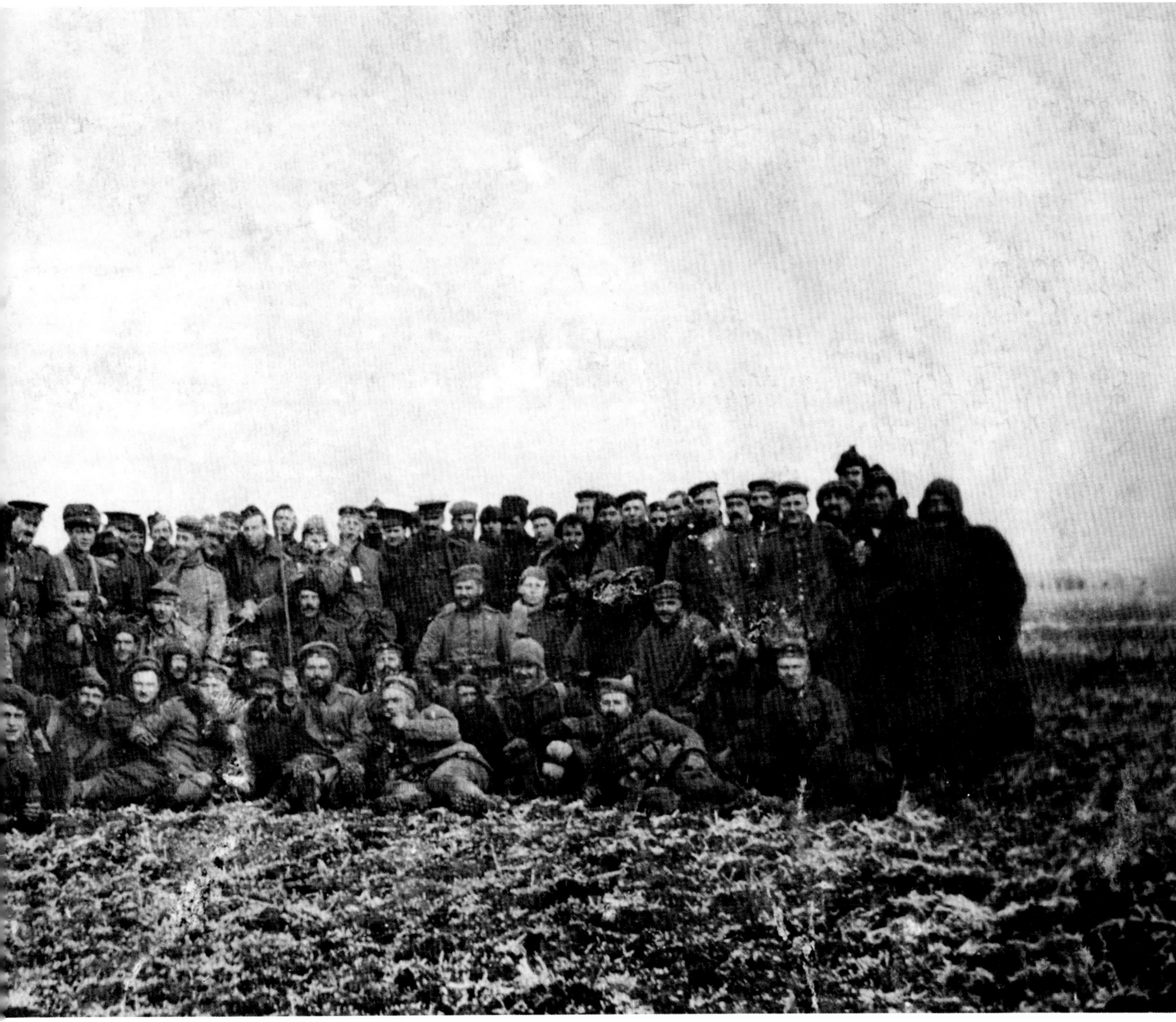

UNKNOWN

•

Christmas Truce, 1914
Photograph, dimensions variable
Imperial War Museum, London

This photograph of a group of soldiers celebrating Christmas on the Western Front in 1914, five months after the start of World War I (1914–1918), would be unremarkable were it not for the fact that it shows British troops, members of the 2nd Battalion, Gordon Highlanders, celebrating with German soldiers. At several locations along the front, British, French, and German soldiers put down their weapons, left their trenches, and crossed no-man's land to meet up on the muddy ground and exchange gifts, sing carols, and show each other photographs of their loved ones, as can be seen here. When the conflict began on July 28, 1914, most people believed it would be over by that Christmas. Instead, by the time of the holiday period, the two sides had dug into lines of trenches that faced each other over hundreds of miles through Belgium and France. As the horror of the high casualty rate of fighting in trenches with artillery and machine guns became clear, the Christmas truce of 1914 acquired a remarkable poignancy. Eventually, up to 100,000 troops took part in the truce across two days. There were even reports that the enemies played a soccer match. Although the truce has become a power symbol of common humanity, mixing with the enemy—known as fraternization—horrified the senior army commanders, who passed harsh rules to prevent it during the remainder of the war.

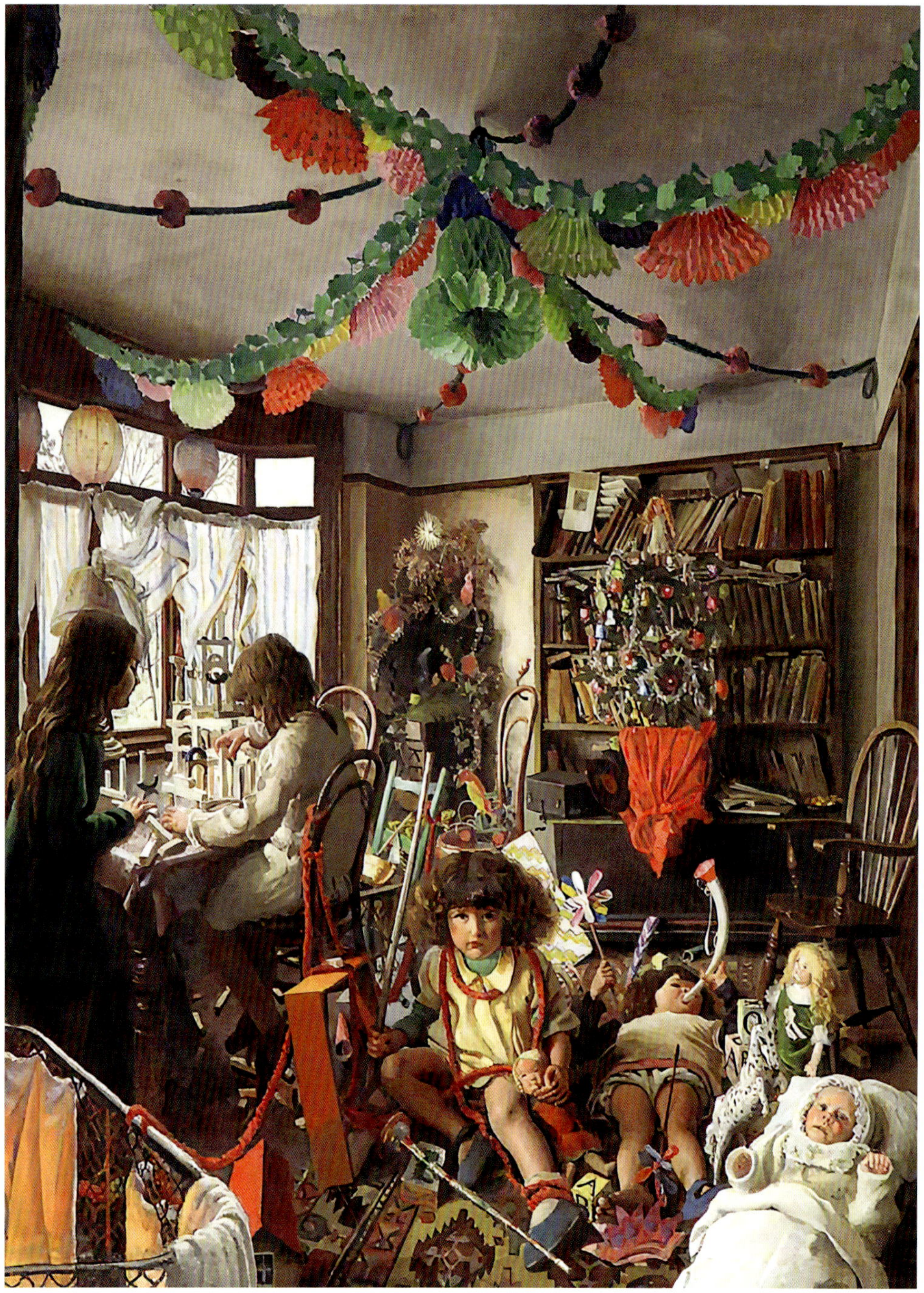

MARK LANCELOT SYMONS

•

The Day After Christmas, c.1931
Oil on canvas on board, 35¾ × 26¾ in / 91 × 68 cm
Bury Art Museum, Greater Manchester

There is a palpable sense of the party being over in this oil painting by English artist Mark Lancelot Symons (1887–1935). Depicting *The Day After Christmas*, Symons shows us the aftermath of the Christmas chaos, when all the presents have been opened, the best trimmings eaten, and the excitement and alcohol has worn off. The paper-chain decorations still hang from the ceiling and the tree still stands in the background, looking a little glum in the cold light of day. The floor is littered with dolls, building blocks, discarded wrapping paper (see p.64), and even a young girl, lying prone on her back and halfheartedly blowing on a party horn. However, December 26 is not merely a meaningless day to be sulked through. In western Europe, it is Saint Stephen's Day, commemorating the first Christian martyr. In Great Britain, it is a holiday known as Boxing Day, when employees and tradespeople traditionally received a "Christmas box" containing a gift or tip from their employers. It now marks the start of a period of deep discounts at shops, similar to Black Friday in the United States following Thanksgiving (see p.203). Symons, born in London to an artistic family, found himself drawn to religion, often delivering sermons on Hyde Park Corner. He filled his later work with religious symbolism, and it's hard not to see this scene as a denouncement of the commercialization of Christmas, when children get bored with even new toys.

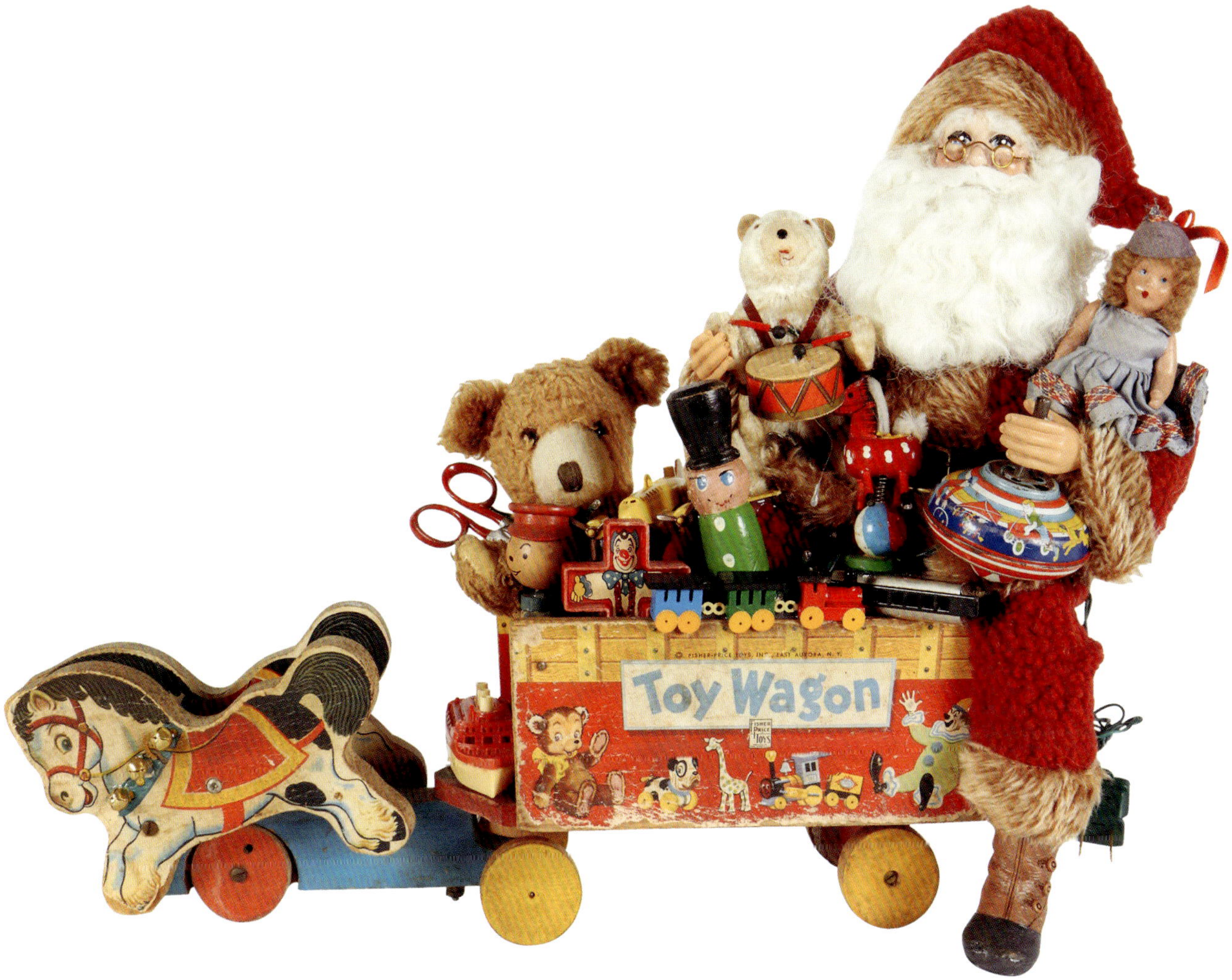

KAREN DIDION

•

Santa on Toy Wagon, 2016
Wood, fiberglass, leather, porcelain, wool, fabrics,
16½ × 17½ × 7½ in / 41.9 × 44.5 × 19 cm
Private collection

A wise old Santa Claus, his gold-rimmed spectacles sliding down his nose, sits proudly atop a wooden toy wagon being pulled by a miniature rocking horse in this piece of contemporary Christmas decor created by American artist Karen Didion. Although signed by the artist herself as being made in 2016, many of the toys featured here, including the wagon itself (produced by Fisher-Price Toys, New York), are reclaimed antique pieces, their popularity spanning decades. From an old spinning top toy to a classic teddy bear and old wooden train set (see pp.13, 200), children throughout the twentieth century would be delighted to wake up to them under the tree. Didion specializes in bringing a vintage charm to contemporary decorations and is most famous for her high-quality Santa Claus figurines. Sold separately or as part of a set, they are all meticulously handcrafted out of fiberglass and feature glass-inset eyes, hand-painted porcelain faces and hands, and real mohair beards. Many of these ornaments come with incidental trinkets, whether those are classic toys, such as here, or more adventurous offerings, such as Italian vespas. What began as an artistic hobby in 1995 is now a family business that produces a new range each year, appealing to those with fond memories of Christmases gone by. They have become very collectible, with the set pictured fetching over $3,000 at auction.

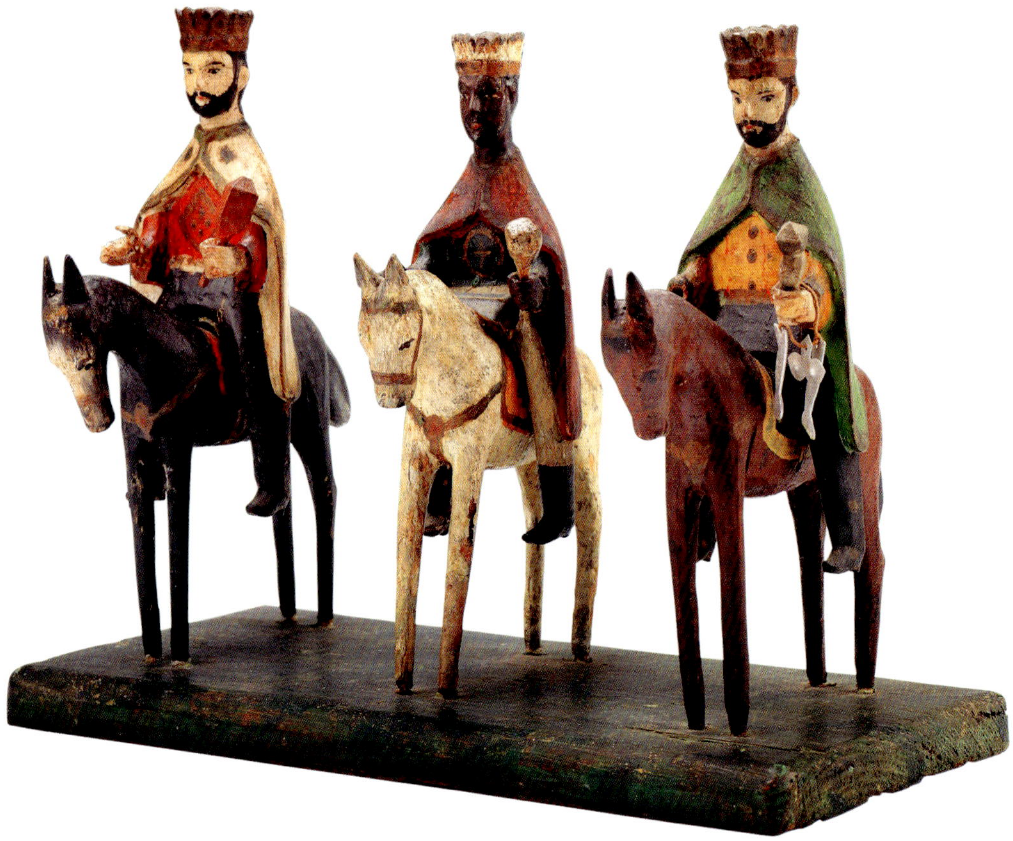

CABAN GROUP

•

Los Reyes Magos, c.1875–1900
Carved and painted wood, metal, and string, 8⅛ × 11⅞ × 6 in / 20.7 × 30.3 × 15.3 cm
Smithsonian American Art Museum, Washington, D.C.

These fine wooden figurines depicting the three kings in their royal finery and bearing gifts of gold, frankincense, and myrrh, were carved and painted by members of the Caban Group, a family of *santeros* (carvers of wooden saints) from the Camuy area of Puerto Rico in the late nineteenth century. Such statues are displayed on dining tables across the Caribbean Island on January 6, when *Día de Los Reyes Magos* (Three Kings Day), otherwise known as Epiphany, is celebrated in commemoration of the Magi's visit to the Christ Child (see p.26). On this day, families get together, eat festive food, and sing songs about *Los Reyes*. The evening before, excited children cut fresh grass, place it in a shoebox under their beds or under the Christmas tree, and wake the next day to find it exchanged for presents left by Gaspar, Melchior, and Balthazar. The Puerto Rican tradition of venerating *Los Reyes Magos* originated in medieval Europe, where the Magi, represented as kings, were a common feature of *presepio* (or crèche) scenes displayed inside and outside of churches. Although the Gospel of Matthew (see pp.14, 80, 150) does not specify the number of Magi, nor their names or ethnicities, various legends sprang up over time and by the Middle Ages their identity as foreign kings from Europe, Asia, and Africa had become widely accepted in Christian tradition. Puerto Rican artists usually depict the Magi riding horses, rather than camels and, as here, the African king Balthazar is almost always shown on a white steed.

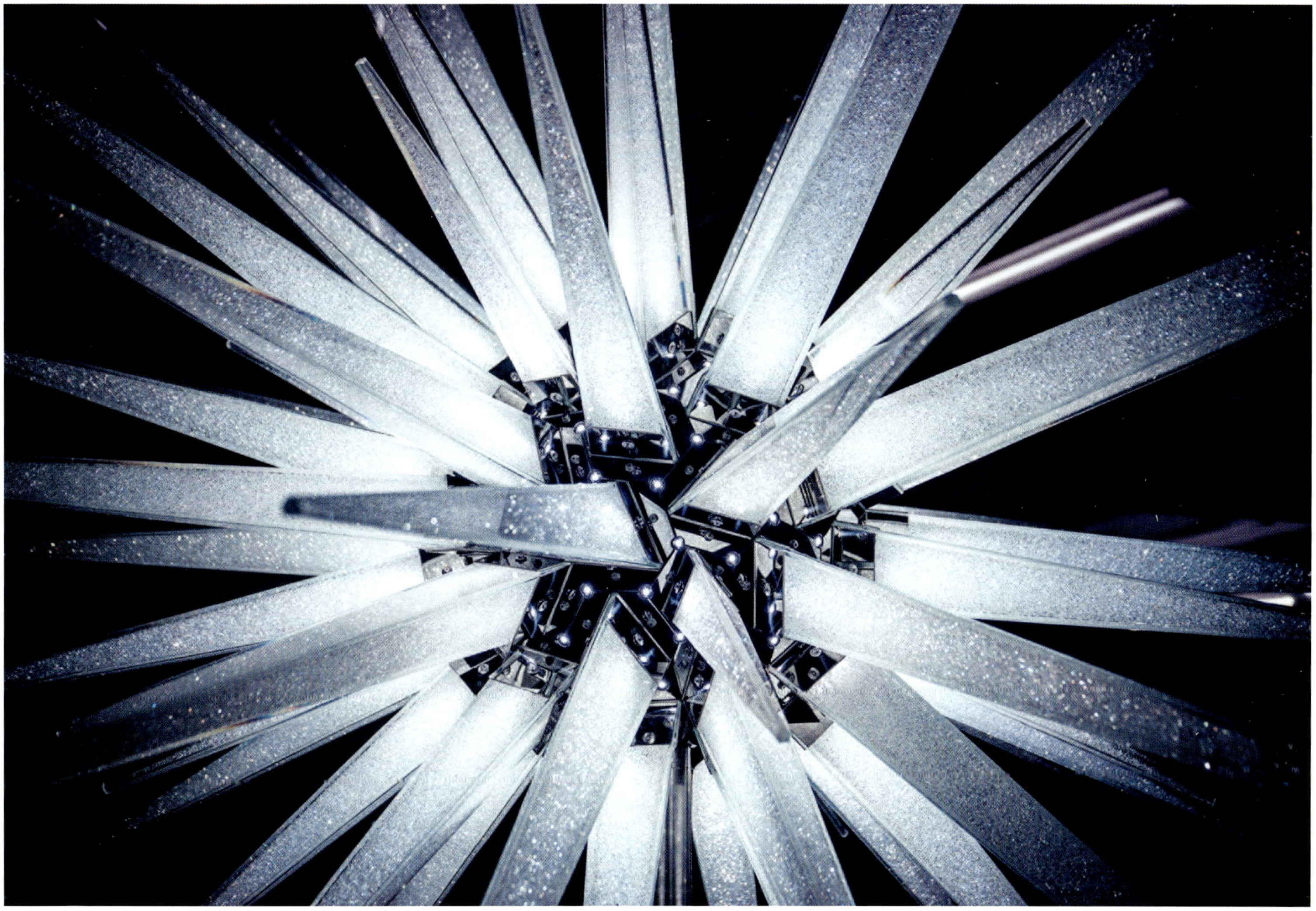

DANIEL LIBESKIND

•

Rockefeller Christmas tree star, 2018
Glass, Swarovski crystals, metal, 9 ft 4 in / 2.85 m
Swarovski

The tradition started during the Great Depression as a twenty-foot (6 m) tree installed by construction workers, a gesture of goodwill to the masses during a dark hour (see p.20). Over the decades, Rockefeller Center's famous Christmas tree has gotten bigger and bigger, and its decorations more elaborate, and its lighting ceremony is now a star-studded event televised nationally in the United States on NBC. The star topper, however, remained a traditional five-pointed flat affair until the 1990s. It has since been upgraded several times to designs as special as the star seen here. Designed by Polish-born architect Daniel Libeskind (1946–), this star, which first topped the tree in 2018, weighs ninety pounds (40.8 kg) and is composed of seventy shatterproof-glass spikes decorated with three million Swarovski crystals. It is specially designed so that it looks the same from any perspective, unlike a typical two-plane star. Glowing with a staggering 106,000 lumens, it is a radiant beacon of light and joy fit for the famous fir. Libeskind is internationally renowned, and perhaps best known for his work designing museums, but he is also well-known to New Yorkers, having designed the Freedom Tower and footprint gardens at Ground Zero, the former World Trade Center site, although ultimately those plans were unrealized.

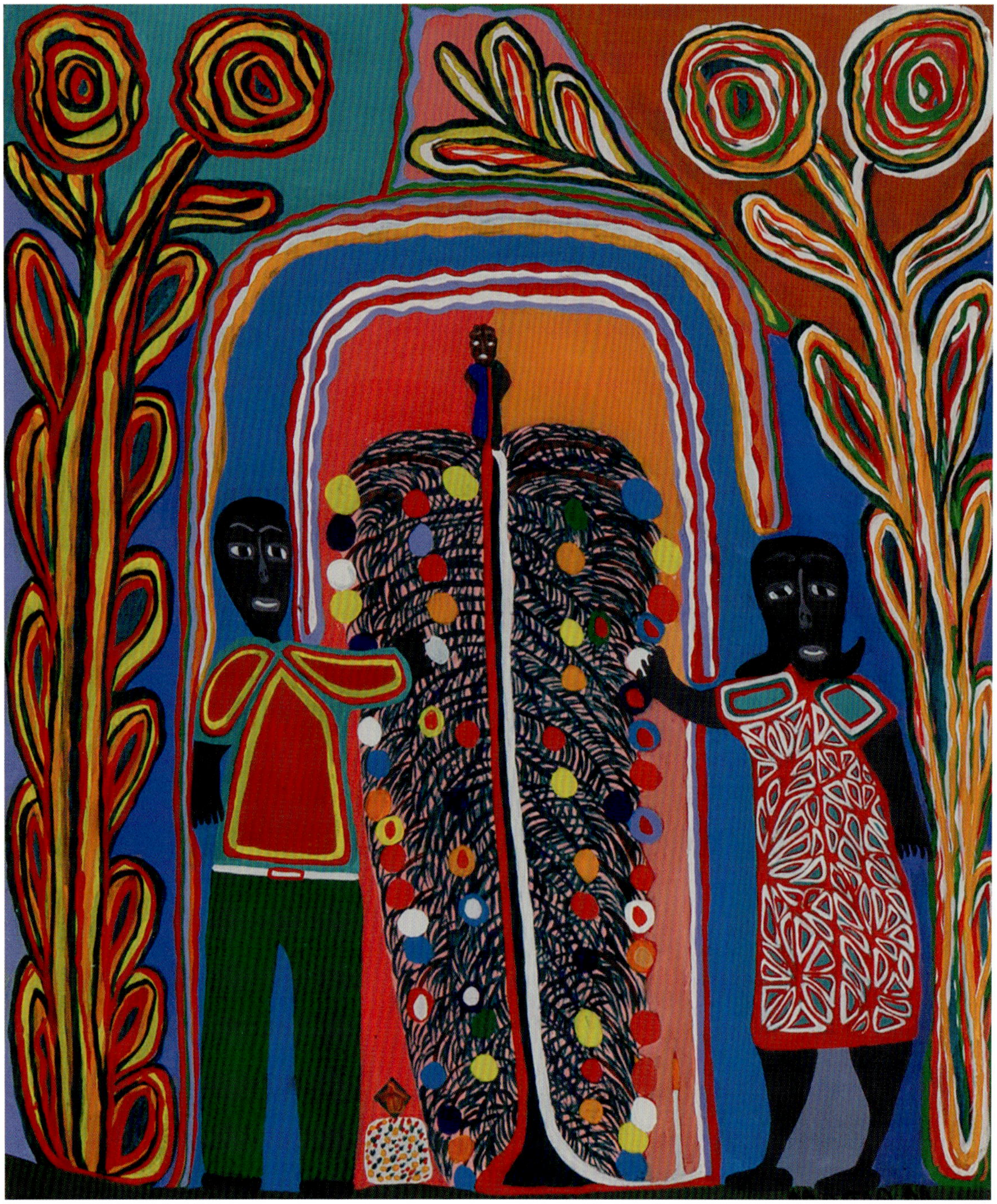

MAGDA MAGLOIRE

•

Christmas Tree, 2006
Acrylic on canvas, 20 × 16 in / 50.8 × 40.6 cm
Private collection

A couple stand either side of a Christmas tree in this painting by the Haitian artist Magda Magloire (1957–2017). They reach their arms outward, hanging the last of a series of brightly colored ornaments on the tree and in turn presenting their handiwork. Around and above them, the stems and flowering heads of plants rise to fill the available space, their forms capturing in a spiraling coalescence, the varied colors of the festive decorations. These plant forms are a hallmark of Magloire's art, a stylized shorthand for her optimistic vision of harmonious nature, and here the contrast of their boldly brushed forms with the finely painted needles of the central tree serves to foreground its importance and power. Magloire's mother, Louisiane Saint Fleurant (1924–2005), was also a celebrated artist, whose focus on abstracted human forms and interest in the symbols of traditional Vodou worship were influential in Magloire's work. Here, just as contemporary Haitian religious practices are formed of a mixture of pagan and Christian beliefs, the tree can be read as both a classic Christmas centerpiece and as the *potomitan* or "central pole" of the Vodou temple from which *loa* spirits descend to inhabit their worshippers. In another of Magloire's works, *Papa Noel* (2009), children enjoy a Christmas Eve *reveillon* meal (a festive evening meal, often including traditional Christmas foods, such as turkey and chestnuts) while Tonton Nwèl (Santa) replaces straw-filled shoes with presents (see p.220).

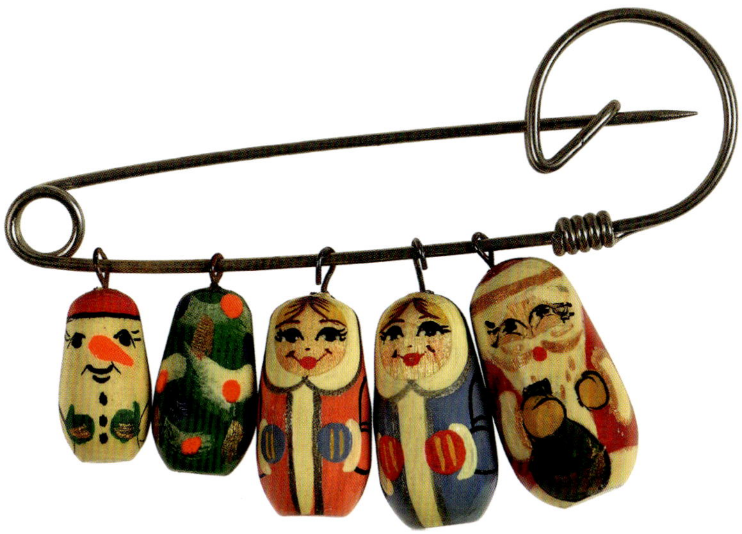

UNKNOWN

•

Antique Russian dolls on a safety pin, c.1900
Hand-painted wood and steel, 2 × 2¾ in / 5 × 7 cm

This antique piece of jewelry is designed to look like Russian nesting dolls, highly decorated miniatures that open to reveal a smaller doll, which reveals another and another of diminishing size. These do not break apart and nest within each other, but they otherwise celebrate the shape, decoration, and thematic harmony of the traditional folk art. This particular specimen probably dates from around the turn of the twentieth century and features a delightful array of Christmas-themed figures: a snowman, a Christmas tree, Santa Claus, and two figures bundled under warm winter layers. Designed to be worn as a brooch, this is a very Russian take on traditional festive costume jewelry (see p.34). Known as *matryoshka* (meaning "little mother") dolls, they may seem like a holdover of a traditional folk art, but they were, in fact, conceived in the 1890s by a Russian toymaker. Less than a decade later, the innovation won honors at the 1900 Paris Exhibition, and the appetite for the diminutive wooden dolls exploded. The production of nesting dolls is a complicated process that begins with lathing the smallest doll, commonly known as the seed doll. The subsequent dolls are traditionally created from the same piece of wood. They are then hand-painted in exacting detail. Initially, these nesting dolls were produced depicting Russian life or religious icons; now, a century later, there are mass-produced sets of every conceivable theme.

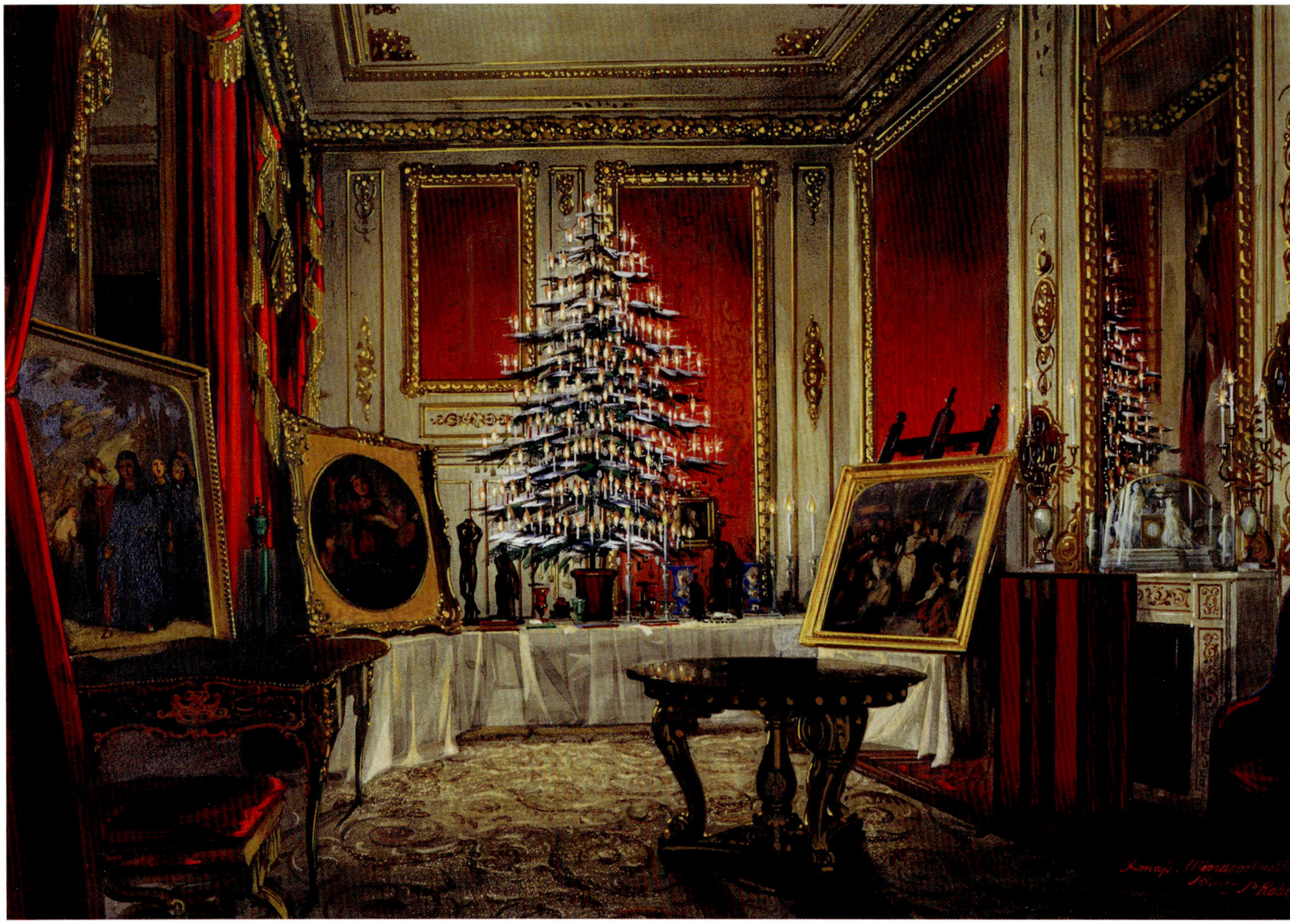

JAMES ROBERTS

•

Queen Victoria's Christmas Tree at Windsor Castle, 1850
Watercolor and bodycolor,
10½ × 15¼ in / 26.5 × 38.6 cm
Royal Collection Trust, London

This watercolor shows a Christmas tree fit for a queen, its candles burning brightly, sitting on a table loaded with presents and three paintings mounted on easels. This was the scene that awaited Queen Victoria in Windsor Castle at Christmas 1850, arranged by her beloved husband, German-born Prince Albert. Having single-handedly introduced many German Christmas traditions to Great Britain, such as decorating Christmas trees and sending cards, the prince ensured that Christmas at the castle was particularly special—much to the delight of the queen. Among the gifts was a bracelet designed by the prince containing a miniature of their aunt Louise, Queen of the Belgians. Victoria commissioned the artist James Roberts (*c.*1800–1867) to paint watercolors of the Christmas rooms as part of a pictorial record of her life with Albert, a common way for the wealthy to create souvenirs of their lives in an era before photography. The queen liked Roberts's watercolor so much that she commissioned a copy in oil by the artist William Corden the following year. The British public followed the royal family's lead in their Christmas celebrations with one exception: while the royal family adopted the European tradition of exchanging gifts on Christmas Eve (see p.119), Britons opened their presents on Christmas Day itself, as remains common today.

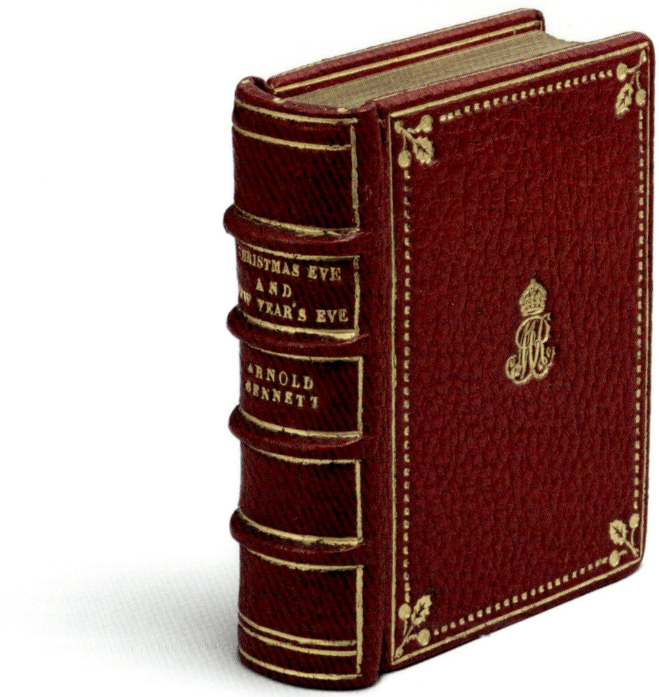

ARNOLD BENNETT

•

Christmas Eve and New Year's Eve, 1922
Manuscript on paper, 1½ × ½ in / 4 × 1.1 cm
Royal Collection Trust, London

This tiny, red morocco leather-bound book stands just 1½ inches (4 cm) tall and includes *Christmas Eve and New Year's Eve,* a special story by English writer Arnold Bennett (1867–1931), for whom the famous omelet dish is named. They were part of a library given to Queen Mary in 1922 for her extraordinary dollhouse, a gift to the queen from the British nation. The dollhouse was conceived by Princess Marie Louise, Queen Victoria's granddaughter, as a showcase of the best of contemporary British arts and crafts in the 1920s, all displayed in a model home at a scale of one inch to one foot (2.5 to 30.5 cm). The library contained diminutive copies of standard works—including the complete works of Shakespeare, four miniature Bibles, and tiny atlases—as well as more than two hundred works by leading contemporary British writers, such as Bennett, Thomas Hardy (1840–1928), Rudyard Kipling (1865–1936), and Joseph Conrad (1857–1924). Princess Marie Louise asked many of the period's leading writers, artists, and designers to contribute, the writers providing either an original piece of work like Bennett or a previously published passage to be turned into a miniature book. Bennett, one of the most financially successful authors of the day, was remarkably prolific, writing more than thirty novels, thirteen plays, seven volumes of short stories, and countless articles for newspapers and journals, as well as millions of words in his daily journal.

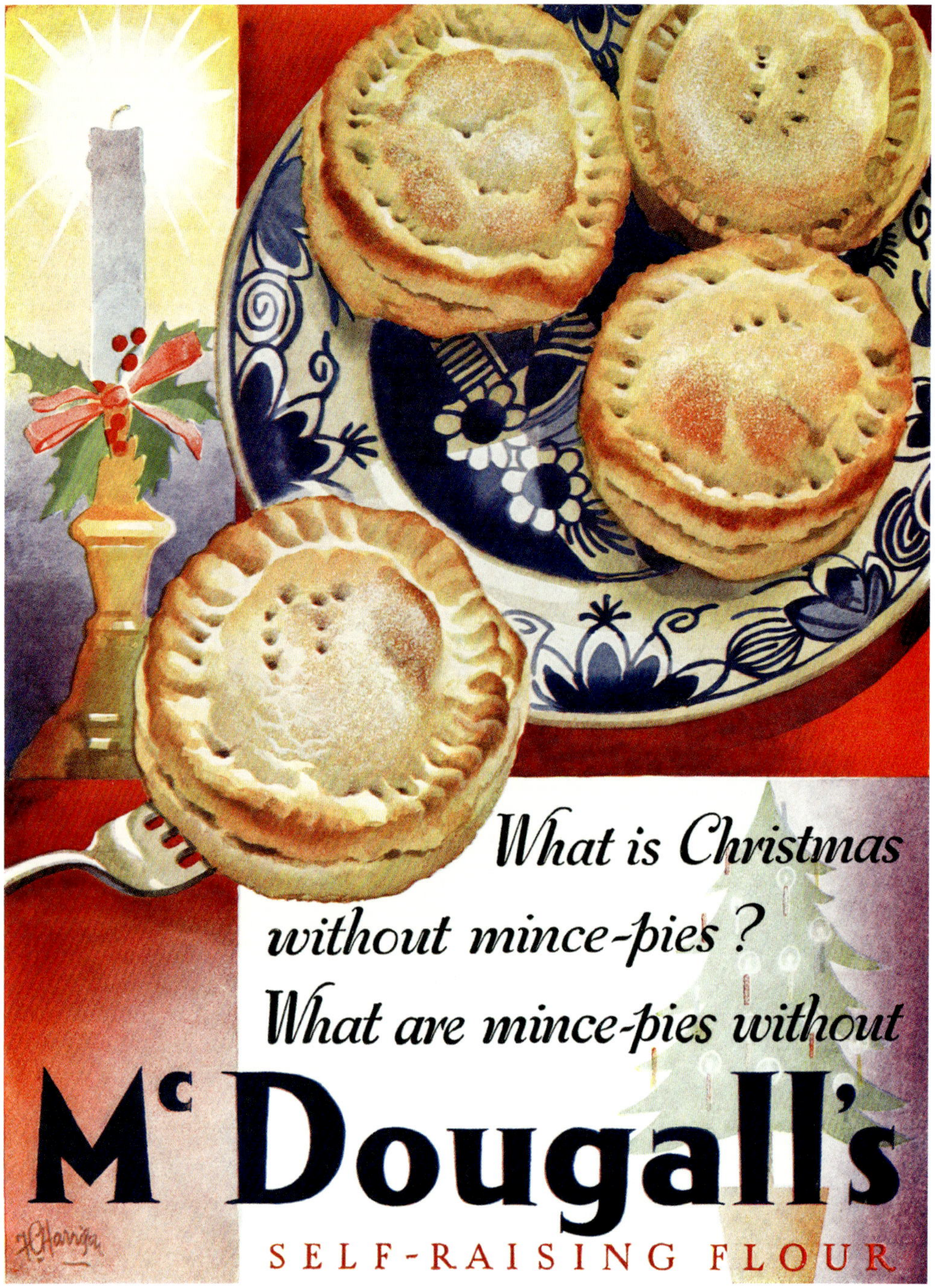

MCDOUGALL'S

•

Flour advertisement, c.1932
Print, dimensions variable

"What is Christmas without mince pies?" asks this colorful advertisement for the British flour company McDougall's. Many Britons would agree—mince pies are as much a part of a British Christmas as the tree and Santa. Every Christmas Eve, children in the UK traditionally leave a mince pie for Father Christmas alongside a glass of sherry, while those in the United States leave a cookie and a glass of milk (see p.83). To advertise McDougall's flour, the illustration features a traditional blue-and-white plate of homemade mince pies, their tops pricked with a fork to let steam escape and their pastry beautifully risen. A holly-adorned candle illuminates the sweet treats. Now often eaten with cream, ice cream, or brandy butter, the original mince pie dating from the Middle Ages was a savoury pastry that contained minced meat, typically mutton but also rabbit, pork, game, or beef. These large medieval pies were filled with a mixture of meat, chopped fruit, and a preserving liquid that prevented the meat from going bad. King Henry V was recorded as serving mincemeat pie at his coronation in 1413. Over the centuries, the fruit content of the pie increased, more spices were added, and, after the arrival of sugar from the West Indies in the 1700s, the pie became sweeter. By the twentieth century, the meat content had all but disappeared and the pies had shrunk to the individual delicacies shown here. A welcome warm treat during the dark winter days.

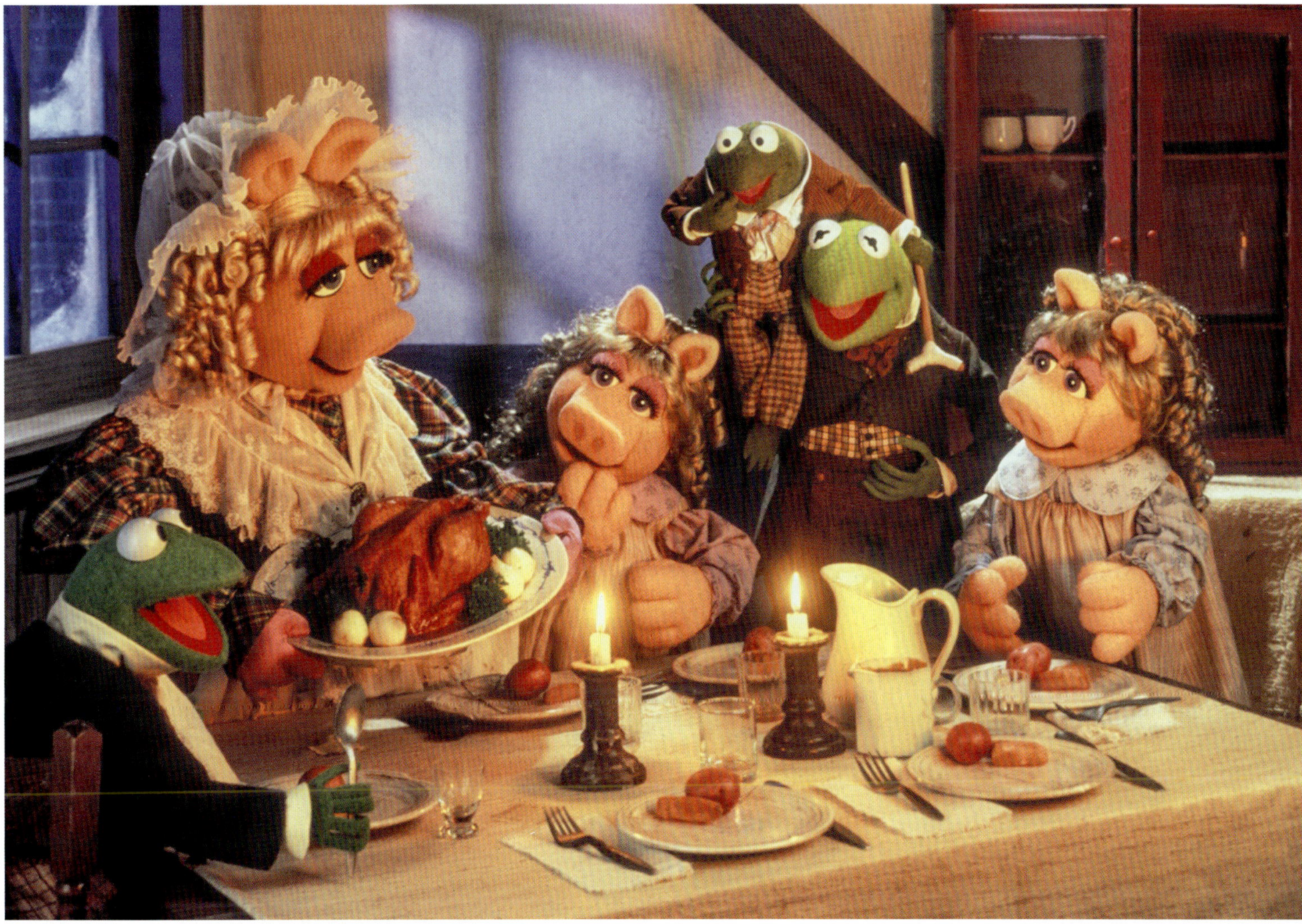

BRIAN HENSON

•

Still from *The Muppet Christmas Carol*, 1992
Film, dimensions variable
Jim Henson Productions / Walt Disney Pictures

Charles Dickens's *A Christmas Carol*, first published in 1843 (see p.79), is perhaps the most famous Christmas novel of all. The story of the miserly Ebenezer Scrooge, who exhibits not even an ounce of mirth until ultimately discovering the true meaning of Christmas, has been adapted countless times on celluloid. The first known movie version, *Scrooge, or, Marley's Ghost* was produced in 1901. Scrooge has been played by esteemed theater actors, including Seymour Hicks (1913, 1935) and Alastair Sim (1950), and comedic titans Bill Murray (1988) and Jim Carrey (2009) alike. The 1992 adaptation of Dickens's classic fittingly features the distinguished British actor Michael Caine in the lead role—but with a rather unusual supporting cast. Muppets Kermit the Frog and Miss Piggy are, respectively, Bob and Emily Cratchit; Robin the Frog is Tiny Tim; and Statler and Waldorf are the ghostly brothers Marley. In this scene, Caine's Scrooge is taken to the Cratchit house on Christmas Day by the Ghost of Christmas Present and shown how appreciative they are of their relatively meager meal of roast goose and chestnuts. The film was director Brian Henson's directorial debut, following the death of his father and Muppets creator Jim Henson in 1990. It includes a veritable Christmas feast of puppeteering wizardry, including, for the first time, the full figure of Kermit the Frog, as he dances down a cobblestone street. Decades on, it remains a beloved classic.

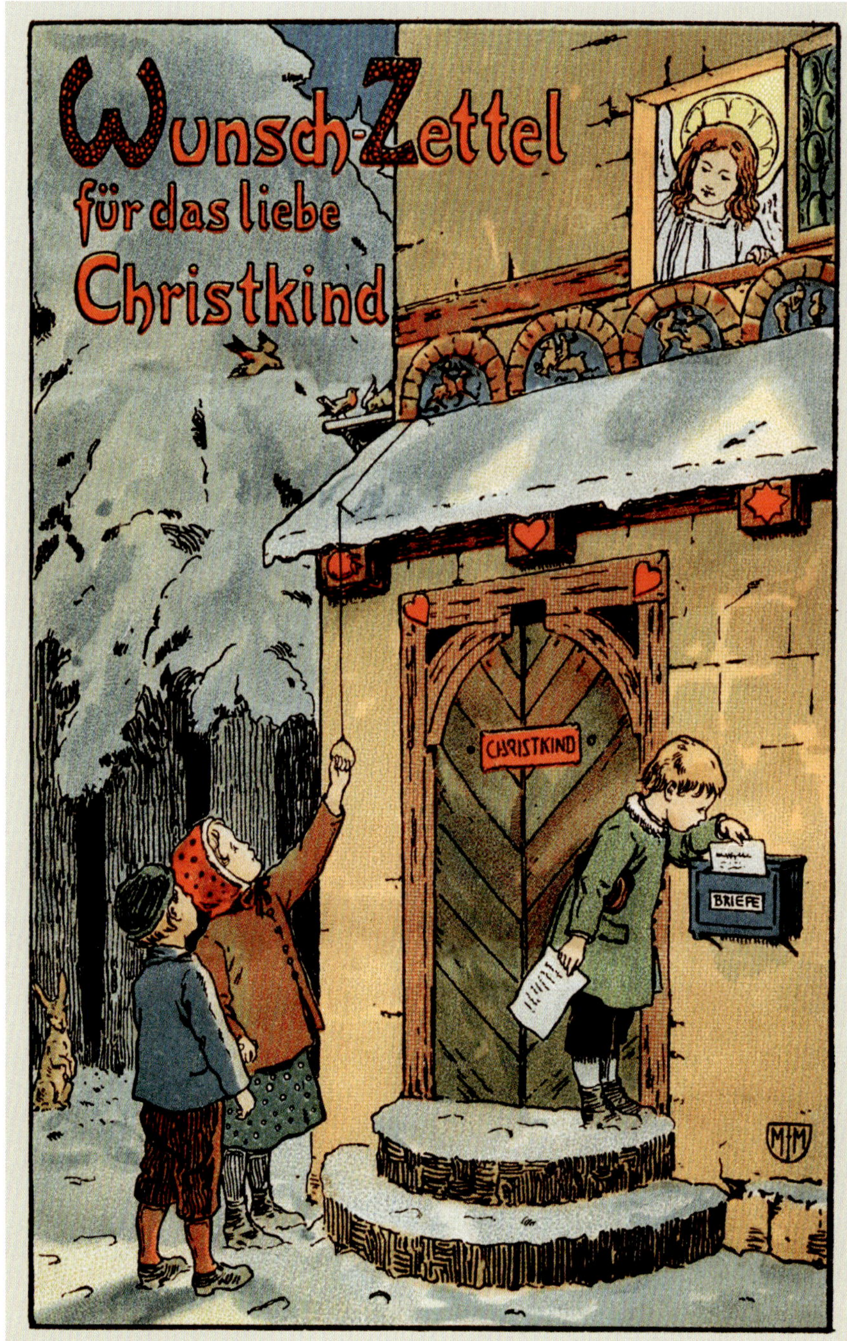

UNKNOWN

•

Wunschzettel für das liebe Christkind (Wish list for the dear Christkind), 1905
Color lithograph, 9½ × 6⅜ in / 24.3 × 16.1 cm
Collection Ursula Kloiber, Salzburg

In many countries that celebrate Christmas, it is not Santa Claus, Father Christmas, nor any version of Saint Nicholas that delivers gifts to good girls and boys, but instead the figure of the Christkind. A spritelike child, usually depicted with blond hair and angelic wings, as the figure at the window in this Austrian poster is portrayed, the Christkind (German for "Christ Child") is intended to represent the incarnation of Jesus as an infant. In this scene, three children approach the house of the Christkind, preparing to deliver their wish lists of presents (see p.136) in the hope they will all be delivered on Christmas Eve, when custom dictates they are opened. As one child drops the letters into the mailbox, another tries to get the angelic figure's attention by playfully pulling on the handle that operates the doorbell. The bell plays a significant role in the tradition of gift giving, as one is rung on Christmas Eve when the presents have been delivered and the Christkind has moved on, a signal that the waiting children are allowed to enter the room and begin to open the presents left for them under the tree. In more recent times, as children have become more readily exposed to advertising featuring *Weihnachtsmann* (Santa Claus), there has been a move by traditionalists to declare that only the tradition of Christkind can truly reflect the real meaning of Christmas.

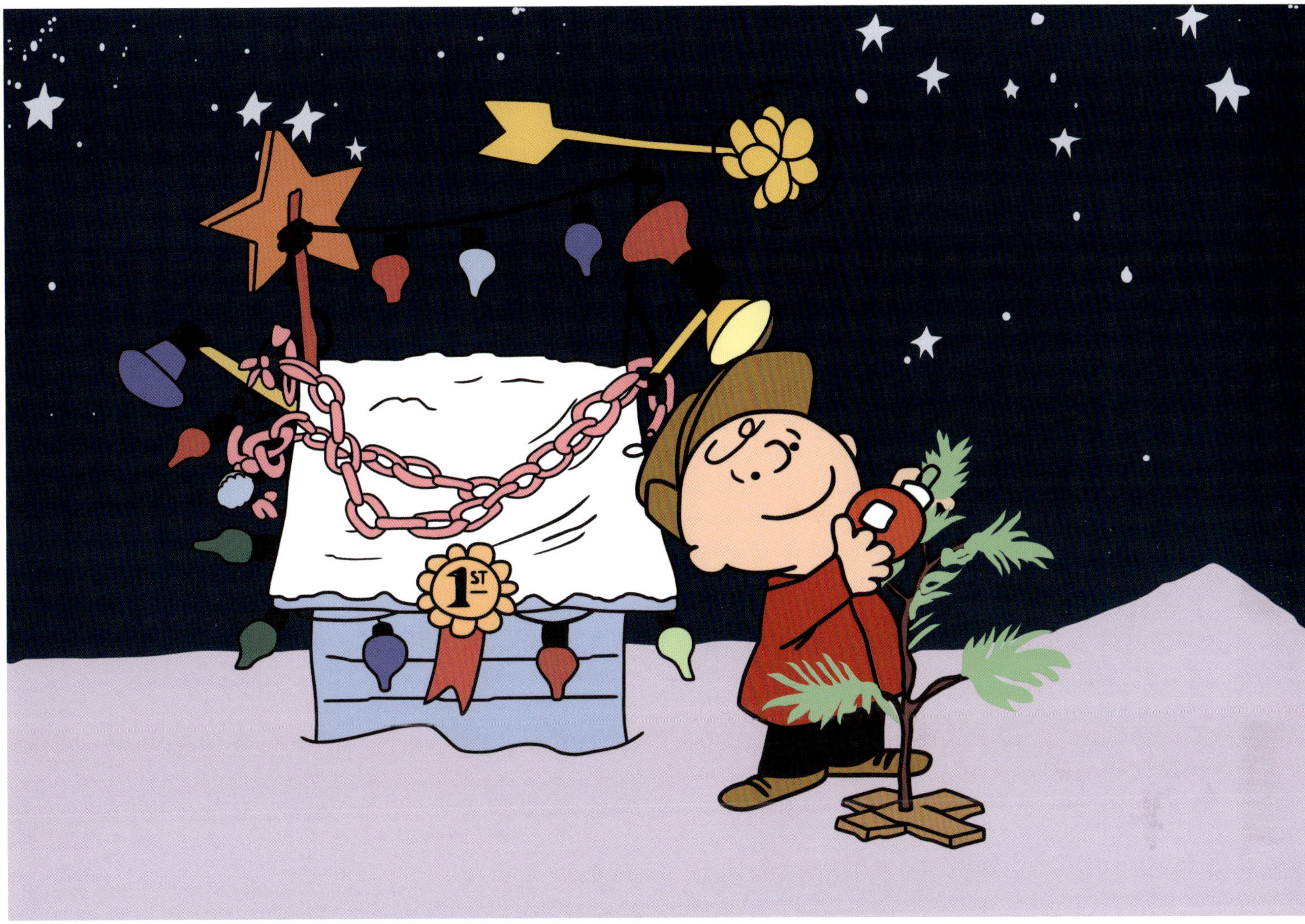

BILL MELENDEZ

•

Still from *A Charlie Brown Christmas*, 1965
Animation, dimensions variable
Lee Mendelson Film Productions /
Bill Melendez Productions / Peanuts Worldwide

A Charlie Brown Christmas was always destined to be a hit, despite being adapted from the source material in a short period of time with a very limited budget. When it aired, 50 percent of American television viewers tuned in to see their beloved Peanuts gang brought to life on the small screen. Charlie Brown, finding himself depressed despite the holiday season approaching, decides to decorate a tree to perk himself up, but he is mocked for choosing a small sapling—a single ornament too heavy for its weedy branches—rather than a large, colorful aluminum tree (see p.164). The others would soon come around, however, to how special a real tree can be. The special became a perennial favorite and is credited with ending the popularity of fake tinsel trees that had been popular in the United States since the late 1950s. Peanuts creator Charles M. Schulz (1922–2000) had total creative control and made a series of unconventional but ultimately brilliant decisions. The first of what would be many Peanuts specials, *A Charlie Brown Christmas* incorporated all the elements that have come to define the iconic cartoons: the unintelligible wah-wah of the adult characters; the swingy jazz score, courtesy of the Vince Guaraldi Trio; and its young characters being voiced by children rather than established voice actors. Year after year, Charlie Brown and the rest of the Peanuts gang—and that scrawny little Christmas tree—reappear to remind us all of the true meaning of the season.

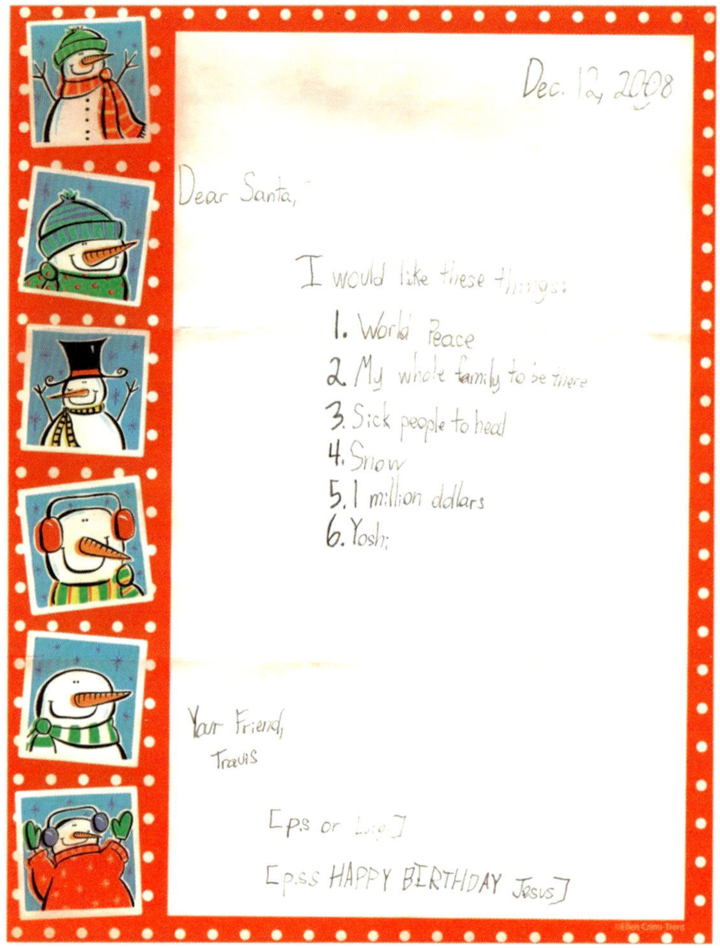

Dec. 12, 2008

Dear Santa,

I would like these things:

1. World Peace
2. My whole family to be there
3. Sick people to heal
4. Snow
5. 1 million dollars
6. Yoshi

Your Friend,
Travis

[p.s or [illegible]]

[p.s.s HAPPY BIRTHDAY Jesus]

TRAVIS

•

Letter to Santa Claus, 2008
Graphite on paper, dimensions unknown

Children have long penned wish lists for Santa Claus. Initially, they burned their letters, believing the ashes (and their requests) would reach their intended recipient. In fact, it wasn't until 1871, when *Harper's Weekly* cartoonist Thomas Nast published an illustration of Santa in his workshop, his desk piled high with letters from good (and bad) little boys and girls, that children began mailing letters to Santa Claus en masse (see p.40). Nast also popularized the notion that Santa lived in the North Pole, establishing an address where real-life missives could be sent. The United States Postal Service (USPS) was so overwhelmed with letters that its Dead Letters Office (DLO) was positively inundated. In an effort to deal with the onslaught, the USPS created Operation Santa in the early twentieth century, ensuring that those Christmas letters would get answered (by local postal staff and volunteers). Letters not intercepted by local postmasters could also end up in Finland, where Santa's Main Post Office, near the Arctic Circle, handles more than two million letters annually. This example, sent by Travis in December 2008, is decorated with images of snowmen in various guises. Travis's quite restrained list is only six items long, but it does feature a call for world peace, the sick to be healed, a request for one million dollars (with which he could no doubt buy many more presents), and a Yoshi, a green dinosaur character from the Mario universe.

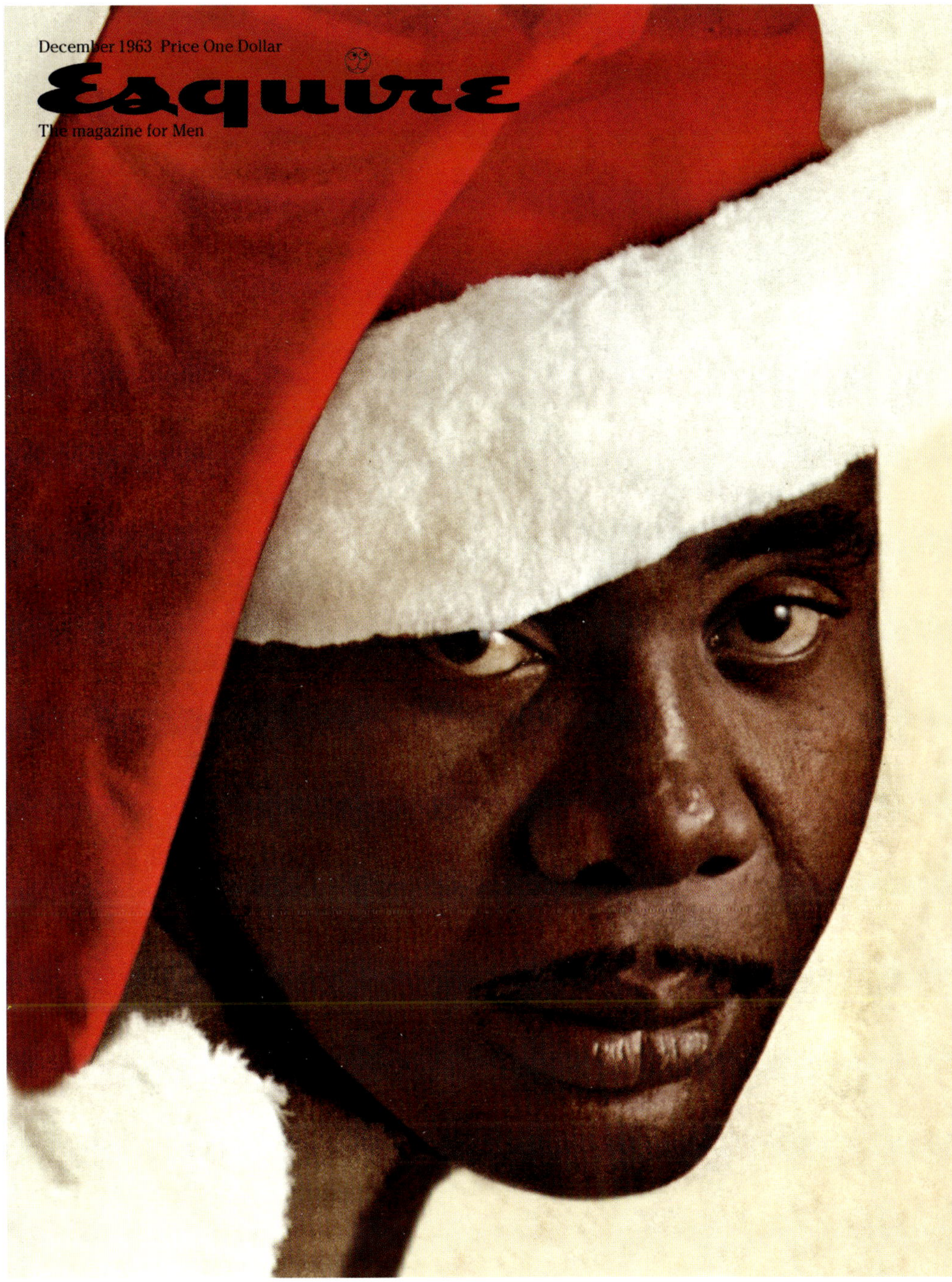

GEORGE LOIS

•

Sonny Liston dressed as Santa Claus, 1963
Printed magazine, dimensions variable
Photograph by Carl Fischer for *Esquire*

This 1963 cover for American magazine *Esquire* depicts the face of the 1962 heavyweight boxing champion, Sonny Liston, wearing a Santa Claus hat. The advent of television, which showed boxing fights live from the 1950s onward, solidified the sport's already huge appeal. Liston was then such a recognizable figure that the magazine, founded in 1933 as a publication for men, ran his image without his name. He was known as a boxer but was notorious for his affiliations with organized crime and his incarceration for armed robbery. In 1963, Black Americans were marginalized and victims of racism through segregation, the enforced practice of separate housing, education, employment, and more. The United States was at war in Vietnam and, when this cover was published, President John F. Kennedy had just been assassinated. Likely the first depiction of a Black Santa that most Americans had ever seen, this cover came at a particularly tumultuous and violent time in America's history. The cover was a potent social and political statement, at once a veneration of Liston but a stark commentary on a country that was racially and culturally divided. So powerful was the provocation, that manny of *Esquire*'s advertisers pulled out, subscribers demanded refunds, and the magazine ultimately lost hundreds of thousands of dollars in revenue. This further demonstrated the tragic fact that, as designer George Lois perhaps intended, "goodwill toward men" carried irony more than sentiment.

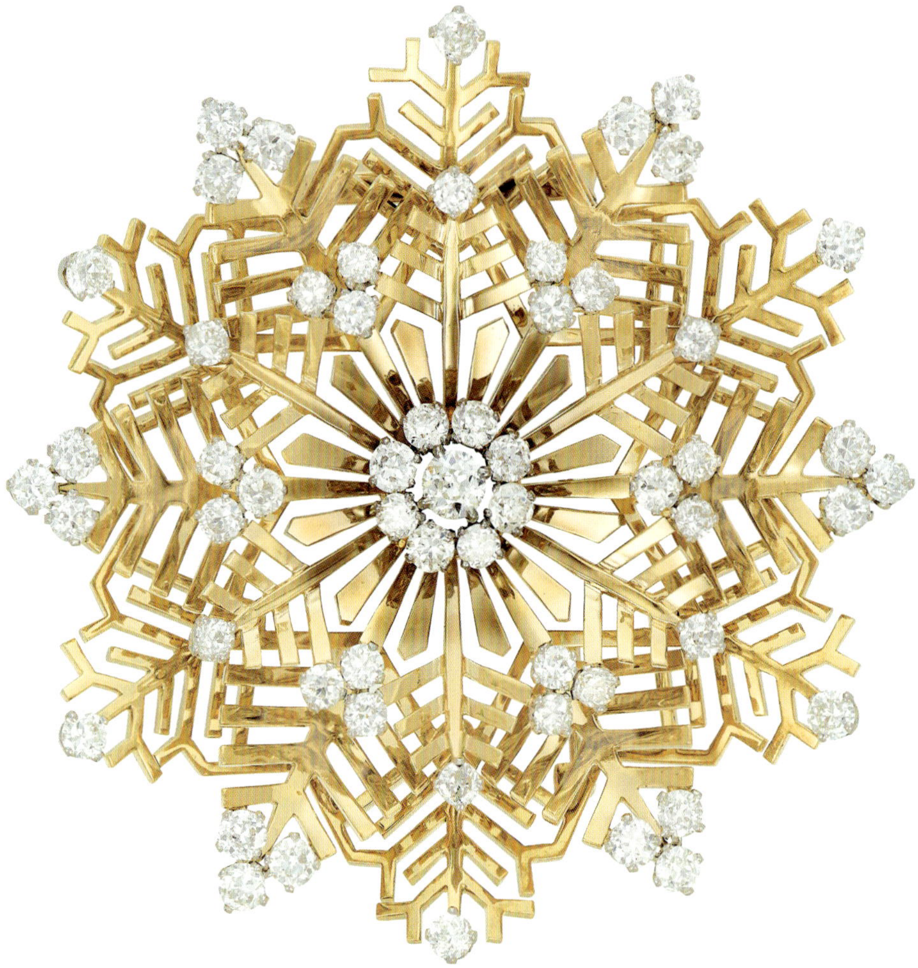

VAN CLEEF & ARPELS

•

Snowflake brooch, 1948
Gold and platinum-set cut diamonds,
approx. 2½ × 2½ in / 6.4 × 6.4 cm
Private collection

In many ways the ultimate Christmas gift, this magnificent gold and diamond brooch created by French jewelry house Van Cleef & Arpels in 1948 captures the unique beauty of a snowflake in solid form. At the center of its twelve interlocking 18-carat yellow-gold branches sits a large cluster of cut diamonds, with a single stone and trios of gems set alternately at the tip and midway on each branch, with a total weight of 5.50 carats. A revolutionary design, the brooch used transitional cut diamonds set in platinum using the 1933-patented Mystery Set, a concealed mounting beneath the diamonds that gave them added brilliance. Designed in-house, the snowflake concept has proved timeless enough to remain in production today. Van Cleef & Arpels is a jewelry house founded on love: the company was set up in 1895, a year after Alfred Van Cleef (1872–1938), son of a Dutch gem cutter, married Estelle Arpels (1877–1960), the daughter of a French precious-stone dealer, and its first boutique opened on Paris's exclusive Place Vendôme ten years later. From the outset, it was known for its imaginative design, technical ability, and craftsmanship. Its mission—to produce fabulous jewelry that said more about the customer's taste than their bank balance—led to a client list that included Wallis Simpson, Jacqueline Onassis, Marlene Dietrich, and Elizabeth Taylor.

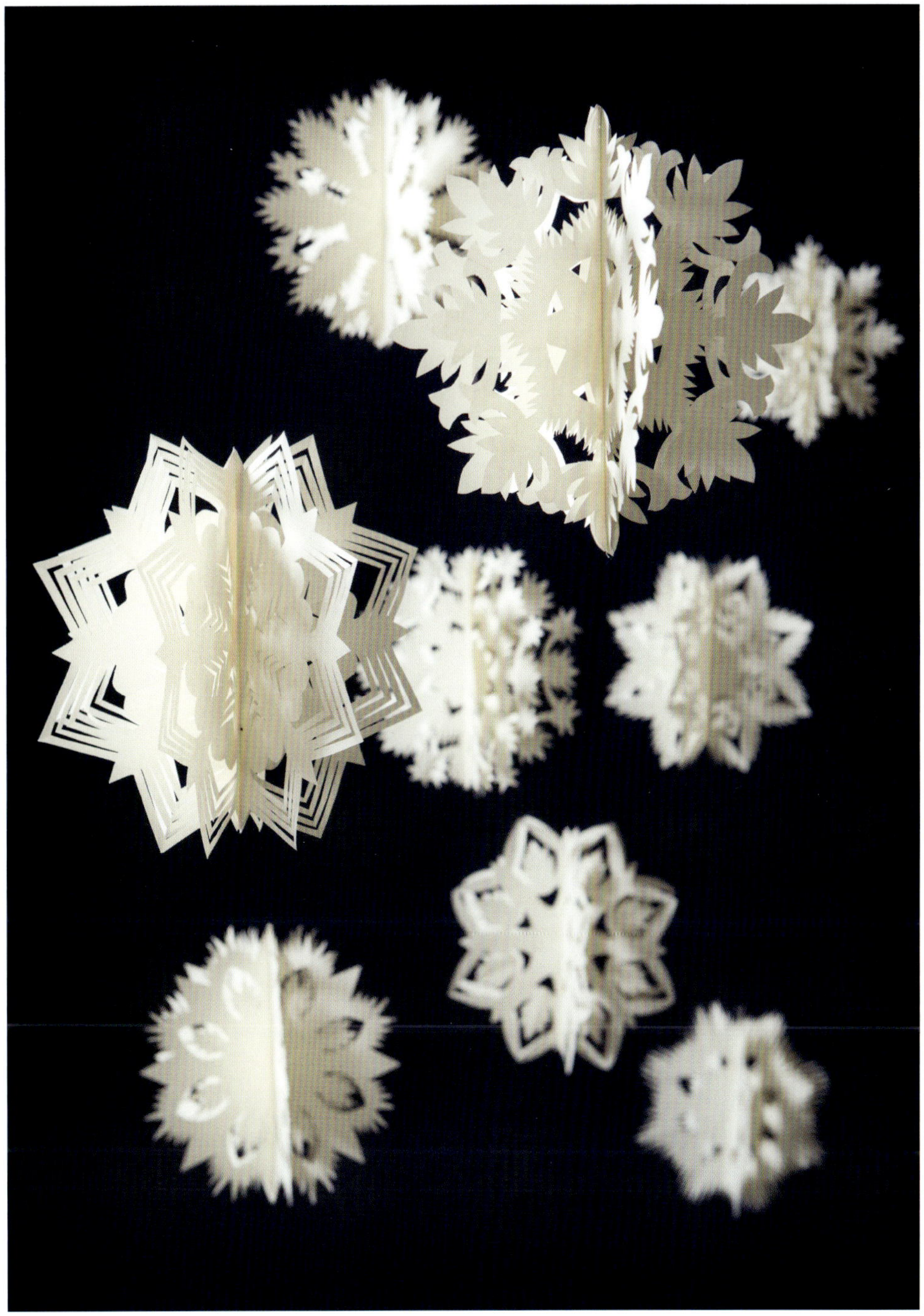

LENA NILSSON

•

Paper snowflake decorations, 2016
Cut paper, dimensions variable
Nordiska Museet, Stockholm

Suspended in midair against a dark blue background, as though falling from a cold winter sky, hang nine folded-paper snowflake decorations created by Lena Nilsson, head of decoration at the Nordiska Museet, Stockholm. Cut from crisp, creamy white paper, they display an impressive array of intricate paper-cutting techniques and a variety of distinct forms, including arrowed chevrons and thistlelike blossoming heads, which seek to convey the accepted wisdom that no two snowflakes are alike. The snow stars pictured represent a fraction of the five hundred handmade paper decorations Nilsson crafted for the museum's renowned annual Christmas tree display. There is a strong tradition of paper folding as an educational activity for children across Germanic and Scandinavian countries, most notably with the eight-point, woven paper-strip Froebel star, originally created by Friedrich Fröbel, the German educationalist and founder of the kindergarten concept. The documentation of the creation of these snow stars is part of the museum's outreach activities for a young audience and chimed with the wider Swedish taste for craft-based education known as *slöjd*. The stars are made by carefully cutting a unique design into a folded sheet of 4¾-inch (12 cm) square paper. When unfurled, the cuts are repeated in perfect symmetry across each of the folds and several of these flat stars can be stitched or glued together like a book to make a three-dimensional sculptural object.

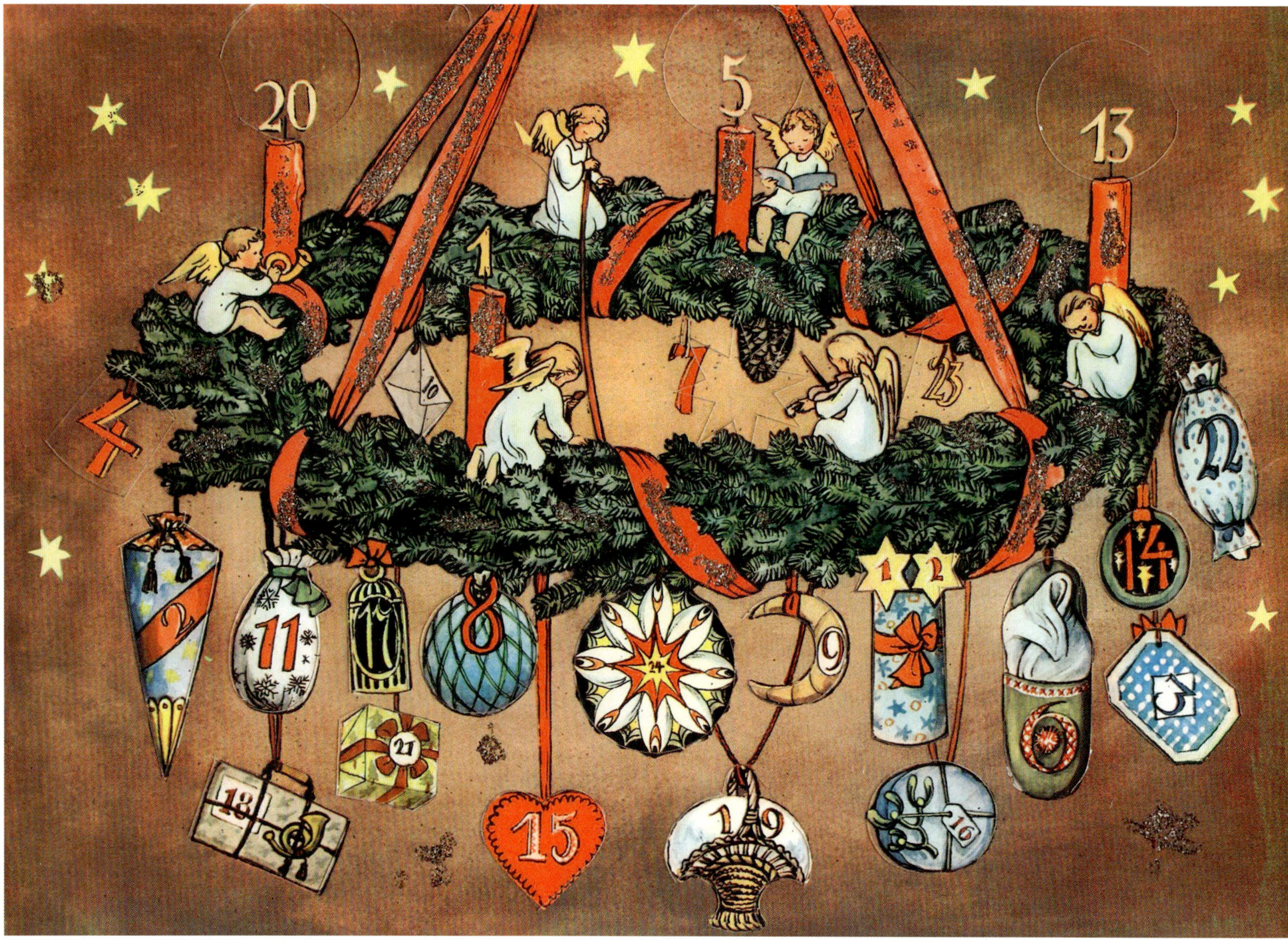

ELISABETH LÖRCHER

•

Advent calendar, 1950
Illustration on cardstock, dimensions unknown
Produced by Richard Sellmer Verlag

As with many of the most popular Christmas traditions, the paper Advent calendar originated in Germany, a direct descendant of calendars first created by early nineteenth-century German Protestants who, to help show the passage of the days leading up to Christmas Day for impatient children, marked the twenty-four days of Advent by chalking each day on a door or wall. The first physical calendar was handmade from wood in 1851; printed paper calendars came later. During the first decade of the twentieth century, Gerhard Lang (1881–1974) created a calendar made from two printed pages: one sheet contained twenty-four images to be cut out and the other a cardboard page with twenty-four poems Lang composed. Each day, a child cut out an image and stuck it onto the corresponding poem. Lang continued to develop his Advent calendars over the decades, adding chocolates and doors to open until, by the 1930s, most German families had one. World War II brought production to a halt, but it was revived in 1945 thanks to Richard Sellmer, whose company produced this calendar designed by Elisabeth Lörcher (1898–1961), who illustrated several of the company's most popular designs. In this calendar, dating from 1950, baubles and decorations hang from a traditional Advent wreath (see p.143). On top of the wreath, angels sit between the candles. The wreath, another German invention, has four candles—one for each Sunday of Advent.

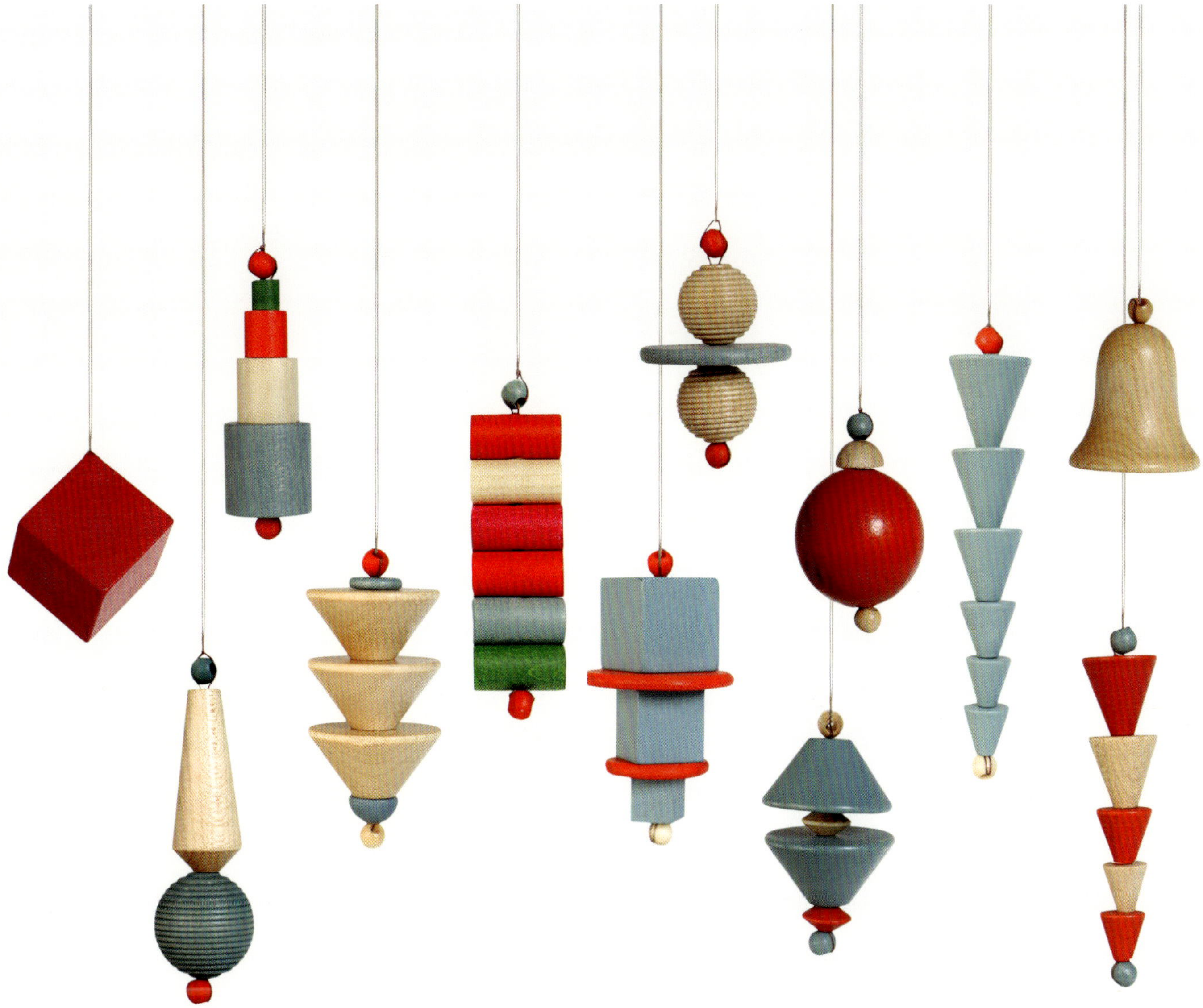

JOHANNES GABRIEL

•

Bauhaus Christmas Ornaments, c.1930
Turned maple wood and string, dimensions variable

With their spare, minimal appearance, this collection of wooden decorations might not appear to share much in common with the gaudier festive Christmas decoration (see p.175), but they are indeed intended to be hung on the tree. Designed by the German architect Johannes Gabriel in around 1930 for his family's use, the ornaments are hand-turned in maple wood and notable for their muted palette. Gabriel chose to keep some of the decorations in their natural wood (the bell) while restricting his color palette to blue, dull red, and pink. The inspiration for Gabriel's little wooden decorations—the geometric forms of the costume designs of Oskar Schlemmer (1888–1943)—reveal their creator's links with the Bauhaus, the influential art and design school founded by German architect Walter Gropius (1883–1969) in Dessau, Germany, in 1919. These wooden decorations are based in particular on the costumes Schlemmer designed for his most famous work, *Triadisches Ballett* (Triadic Ballet), which was widely performed while Schlemmer was at the Bauhaus between 1921 to 1929. In the twelve dances of the ballet, mirrored in the twelve ornaments shown here, the costumes gradually transformed the bodies of the dancers into geometric forms on stage. The original set was found in the estate of an architect from Cologne who was known to have purchased many Bauhaus products directly from the school.

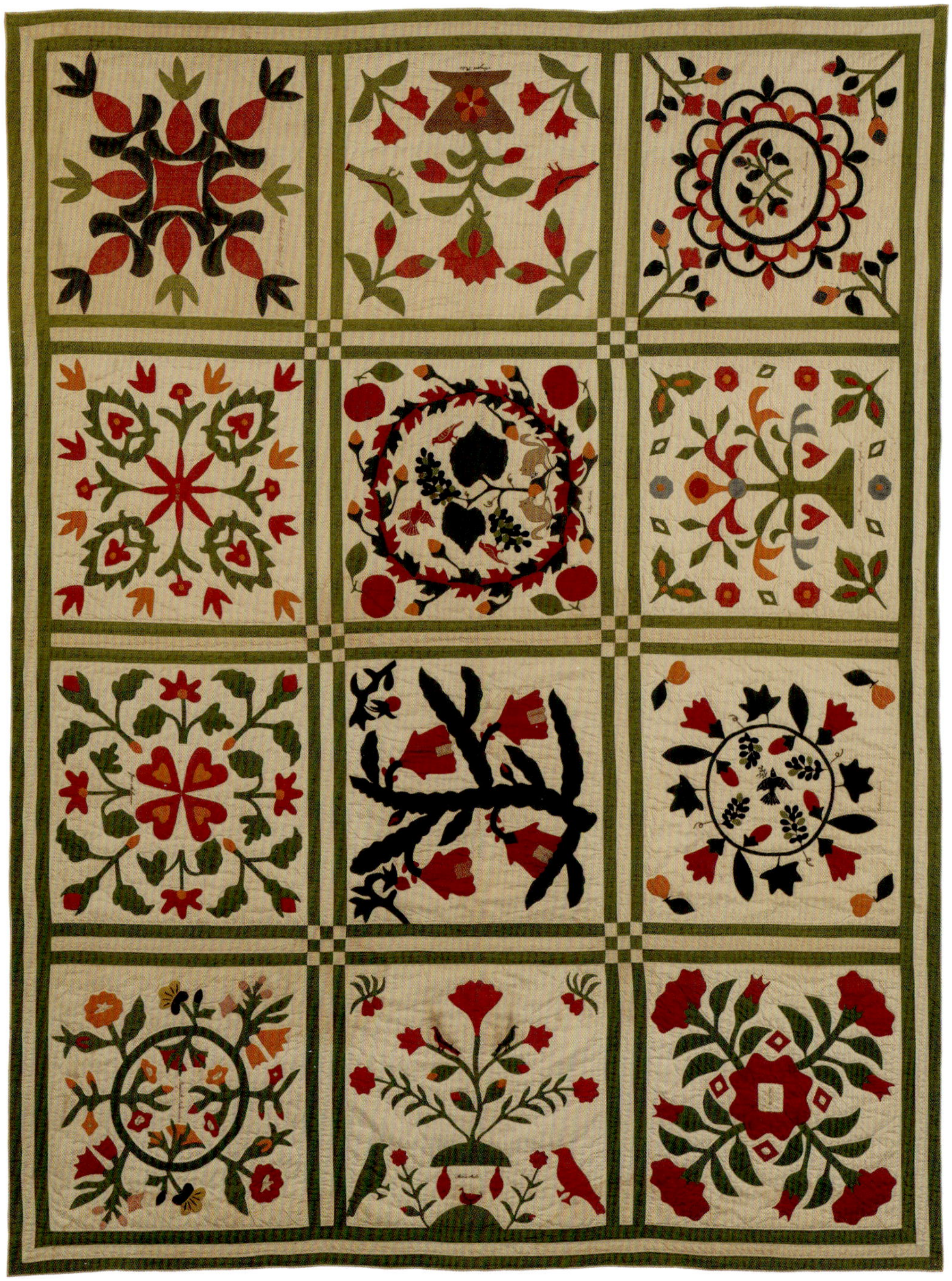

VARIOUS

•

Quilt, c.1859
Cotton plain weave appliquéd and pieced top with cotton, silk, and wool embroidery, 93 × 71½ in / 236.2 × 181.6 cm
Museum of Fine Arts, Boston

Dating from around 1859, this commemorative album quilt was made to celebrate Christmas in New Jersey by ten individual women. It consists of twelve distinctive squares, each contained within a green border with a unique design appliquéd and embroidered onto a cream background. Using a palette predominantly of red, orange, and shades of green, the designs include a Christmas cactus, squirrels, grapevines, and birds. Each individual quilter has inscribed their particular contribution on the back in red or beige silk thread, or in black ink. Quilting as an art form has an illustrious past, dating back to medieval times, when quilts were first made to use as bedcovers. From their earliest creation, quilts have been highly valued, treasured as family heirlooms. Today, quilting is a pastime with twenty-one million participants in the United States alone, and Christmas patterns are among the most popular. During Colonial times, quilting was a common hobby among well-to-do women, who showed off their embroidery and appliqué skills in their work and enjoyed the social dimension of making their individual contributions to communal works, such as this. The poor had neither the time nor the resources to purchase fine cottons, silks, and wool, so they created their own type of quilting—stitching together cloth patches to make quilts. By the time this quilt was produced, commercially printed blockwork and patches of fabric had been available since around 1840, highlighting the exclusiveness of this handwork quilt.

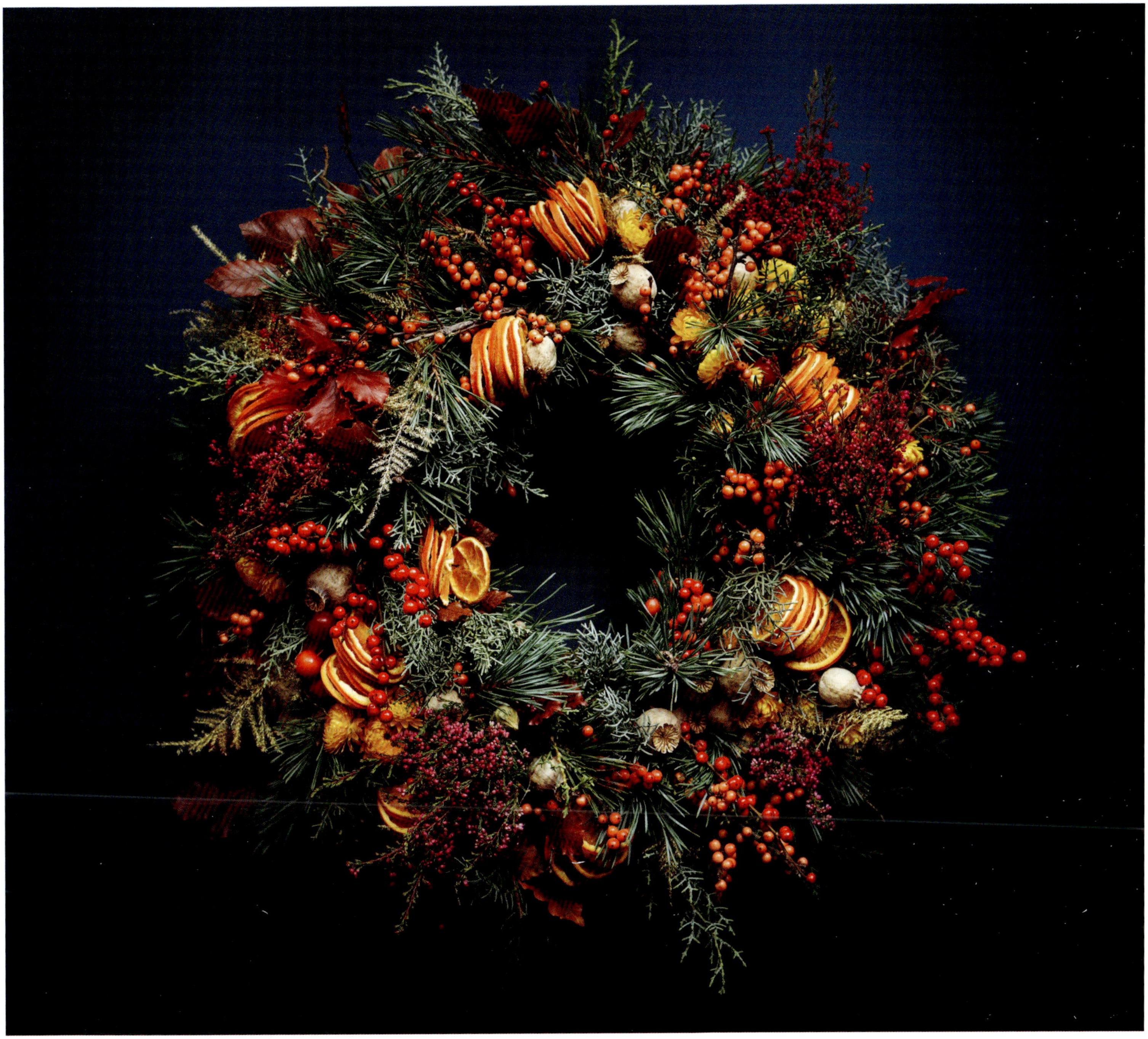

SCARLET & VIOLET

•

Elterwater Wreath, 2018
Assorted leaves and fruits, dimensions variable

Hanging a wreath on the front door, the wall, or the mantel has become an essential Christmastime decoration. Photographed against a striking black background, this unique, warm-toned wreath from Vic Brotherson of London florists Scarlet & Violet is full of imagery closely associated with the time of year, from prominently showcasing slices of oranges that one would find in a stocking (see p.166) to the small red berries associated with holly (see p.31), all set on a background of festive foliage. Scarlet & Violet was set up in 2006 and has become the go-to florist for lavishly loose and natural bouquets and arrangements, including their annual Christmas wreaths. The origins of the custom are closely related to that of the Christmas tree, and likely began in sixteenth-century Europe. Large evergreens were pruned to both make them a more manageable size for bringing indoors but also to ensure they stood in the shape of a triangle to represent the trinity—the Father, the Son, and the Holy Ghost. Trimmings were bundled together to avoid waste, and so the first wreaths were born. German Lutheran pastor Johann Hinrich Wichern (1808–1881) is credited with turning the wreath into a symbol of the Advent (see p.140), originally using a wooden cartwheel to mount twenty-four red and white candles, one lit each day in the countdown to Christmas. Over the years, these two customs converged and, thanks to prominent displays in more recent literature and television, the Christmas wreath is now a Yuletide staple.

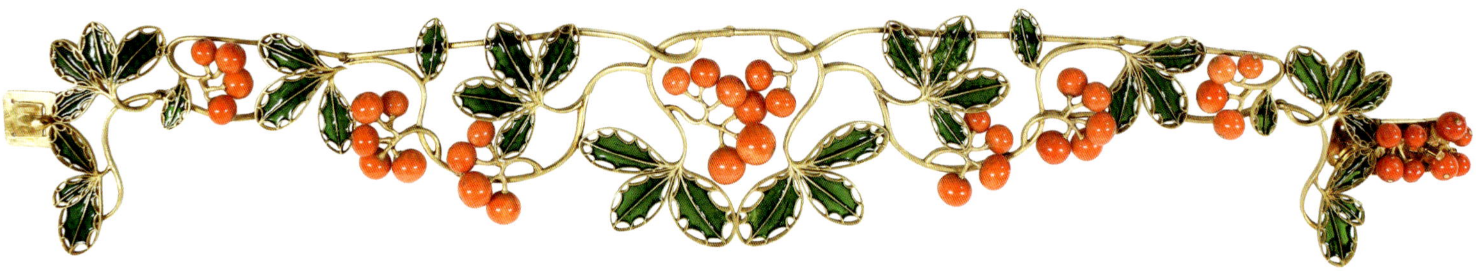

RENÉ LALIQUE

•

Holly choker, c.1897–1900
Gold, enamel, and coral,
2 × 14⅜ in / 5.3 × 36.4 cm
Musée Lalique, Wingen-sur-Moder, France

Clusters of red berries, made of carved and polished coral, sit at the ends of twisting golden tendrils and between glassy green leaves fanned in pleasingly symmetrical groups on this choker necklace by French jeweler and glass artist René Lalique (1860–1945). The year 1900 was incredibly important for Lalique: his theatrical display stand and outlandish creations for the *Exposition Universelle* in Paris were rapturously received by critics and the public alike, and his works played a vital role in defining the aesthetic of the burgeoning Art Nouveau movement. By this point, the vitreous enamel *plique-à-jour* technique used to create the holly leaves had been developed to unrivaled levels of mastery by Lalique—a trademark inclusion in each of his jewels that anticipated his later career success as a sculptor and designer in the medium of glass. The natural world was a principal source of inspiration for Lalique, both for its symbolic, ritual, and historic meaning as well as for the physical characteristics and structures of flora and fauna in which he delighted in discerning a stylized sense of pattern and rhythm. Here, the evergreen holly plant, symbol both of ancient Celtic winter solstice and Jesus's Crucifixion in Christian theology (see p.218), is depicted as less a wild bush than a carefully selected and arranged wreath, with its prickly, spiked leaves softened by their encasement in a surrounding lattice of gold to fit Lalique's controlled vision of nature.

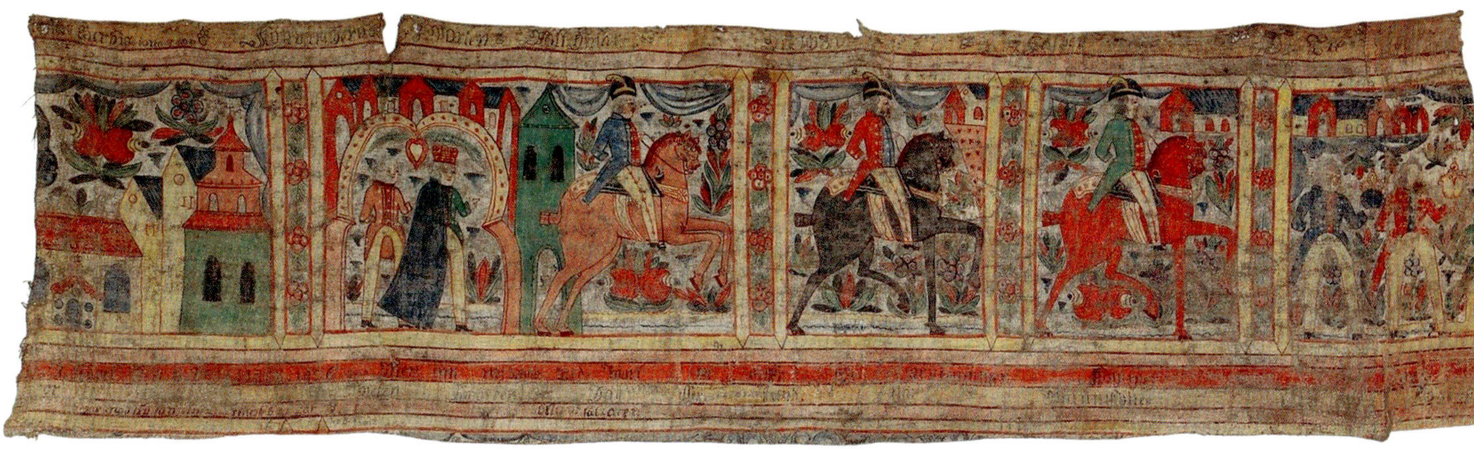

UNKNOWN

•

Swedish folk art mural, 1826
Linen, 32 × 105 in / 81.3 × 266.7 cm

This decorative linen mural, known in Swedish as a *kurbits*, depicts figures from the Bible separated in bounded frames akin to a comic strip. Dressed in contemporary Swedish clothing, King Herod stands with an advisor on the left-hand side and the three wise men process in dressage unison as cavalry men toward the right. Around them in vibrant egg tempera tones, dulled by age and regular use as a festive decoration at Christmas time, are the spires and facades of a simply rendered urban environment. In the borders of these scenes and interspersed in every available space between buildings and people are plant forms with leaves that alternate in decorative symmetry between red, green, and blue. Most noticeable among this verdant display are those with strange red eyes or breastlike bulges at their centers—the *kurbits* plant with hanging gourds that lends its name to the style of folk art. The ever-present poles of Swedish folk art depictions from this period are nature and Christian religion. For the lives of simple farming peoples—for whom such a crafted textile would be a conspicuous display of wealth—scripture was made manifest and comprehensible in the trappings of daily life and surrounding nature was tamed as an increasingly abstracted pattern that could be repeated and passed from artisan to artisan. Also known as a *bonad*, or wall hanging, these religious murals were often hung on walls to brighten up dark farmhouses during Christmas celebrations in Sweden during the eighteenth and nineteenth centuries.

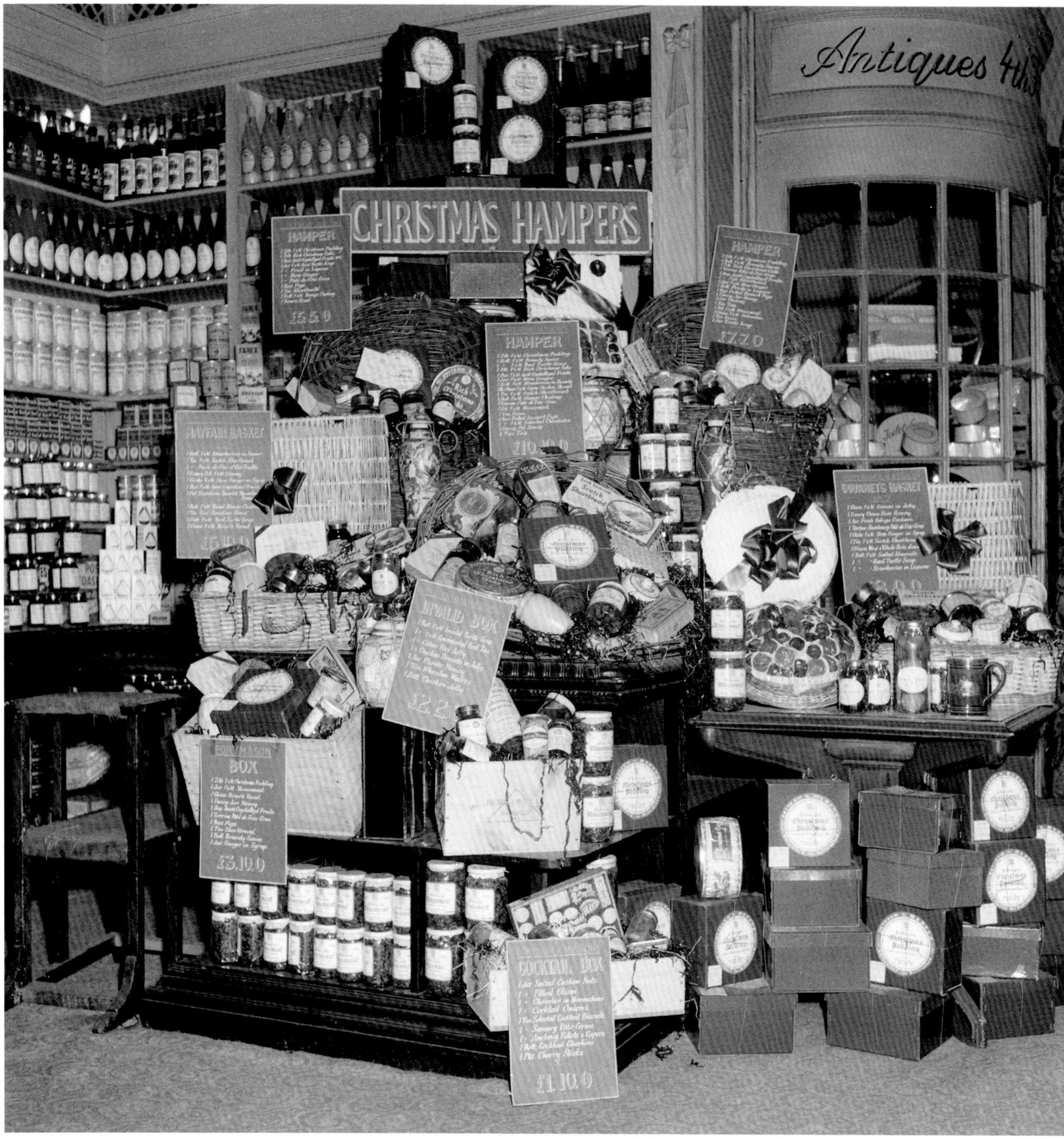

HENRY GRANT

•

Fortnum & Mason Christmas hamper display, 1953
Cellulose acetate negative, 2⅜ × 2⅜ in / 6 × 6 cm
Museum of London

A wicker Christmas hamper from the luxury London food emporium Fortnum & Mason remains as desirable a gift today as it was when this image was taken by British social photographer Henry Grant (1907–2004) in 1953, showing a pile of different hampers with blackboards detailing the various food and drink each contains. Fortnum & Mason claim to have come up with the idea of the hampers in the 1730s at the request of upper-class travelers, who were leaving London by stagecoach to travel to their country estates and needed a picnic for the journey. Over the centuries, the hampers became inextricably linked with the British Empire as families dispatched them to send a taste of home to relations around the world. Founded as a grocery store in 1707, Fortnum & Mason has built a reputation not just for the high quality of its products but for its iconic mint-green packaging, and particularly for its Christmas hampers. Grant's image of the hamper stand captured an opulence few Britons could have imagined after the rationing and privations of World War II, and the Piccadilly store still comes into its own every Christmas. Crowds flock to see its renowned Christmas window displays (see pp.204, 227) and to buy Christmas treats, the pinnacle of which remains the wicker hamper stamped with the instantly recognizable F&M logo.

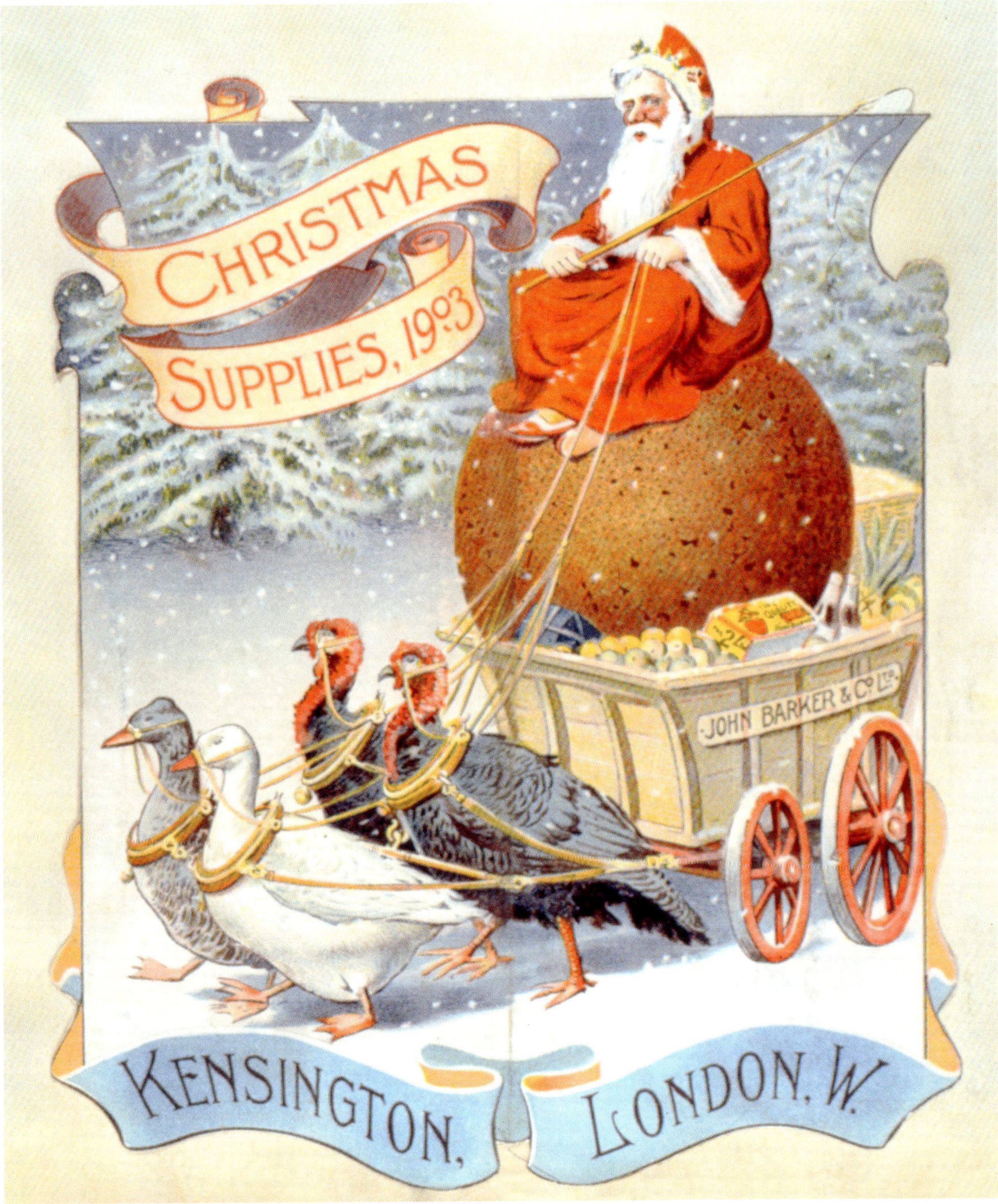

JOHN BARKER & COMPANY

•

Christmas Supplies advertisement, 1903
Poster, dimensions variable

This 1903 advertisement for the West London department store John Barker & Co. shows Father Christmas sitting atop a Christmas pudding as he delivers festive food supplies in a cart pulled by geese and turkeys. The advertisement also originally included a border featuring an array of gifts that could be found inside the store. At the start of the twentieth century, department stores—a one-stop destination for the shopper—were growing rapidly in popularity. They allowed the busy housewife (at the time it was invariably women who shopped) to purchase everything she needed under one roof. Gone were the days of making their way up and down the main street. John Barker & Co.—later renamed Barkers of Kensington—was one of many contemporary London department stores vying for business, including the perhaps more well-known Selfridges, Harvey Nichols, Liberty, and Harrods (see pp.62, 227). Although there had been adepartment store in London as early as 1796, the first actual department store was Le Bon Marché in Paris, which had started in the early nineteenth century as a small shop but by 1865 had grown into a far larger establishment. Before the advent of supermarkets, John Barker & Co. and other stores stocked a wide variety of provisions, including everything needed for the Christmas celebrations.

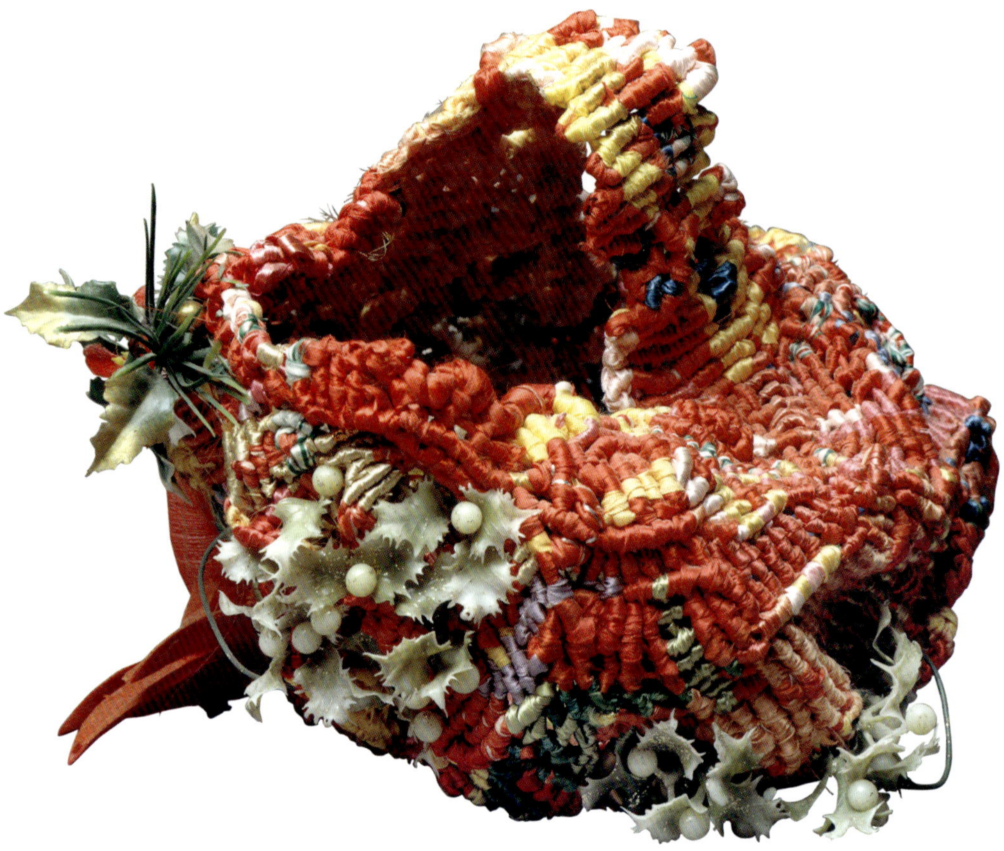

ED ROSSBACH

•

Christmas Basket, 1968
Synthetic ribbon and plastic found objects, 7⅜ × 12 × 9⅜ in / 18.7 × 30.5 × 23.8 cm
Smithsonian American Art Museum, Washington, D.C.

Considered the doyen of contemporary American textiles, Chicago-born Charles Edward "Ed" Rossbach (1914–2002) spent decades as a professor at the University of California, Berkeley, where he influenced generations of fiber artists. He originally studied painting and design, but while stationed in the Aleutian Islands of Alaska during World War II, he discovered traditional fiber arts and started weaving his own baskets out of tundra grasses. Aside from his teaching duties, Rossbach was a prolific creator and a major figure in the Bay Area fiber arts movement of the 1960s and 1970s, which also included his wife, Katherine Westphal, Pat Hickman, and Lillian Elliot. *Christmas Basket* utilizes pieces of gift-wrap ribbon, plastic holly leaves, and stray poinsettia petals made of fabric to create a cohesive form out of what could otherwise be considered the detritus of the holiday. Its predominantly red and orange color palette could see its weave mistaken for the plumage of the Christmas turkey. Rossbach is known for using traditional weaving techniques from cultures around the world, and for incorporating untraditional materials in his work—newspaper, foil, twigs, film, staples, rice paper, and fabric, just to name a few. He was a pioneer who challenged audiences to see the beauty in lowly materials and even trash.

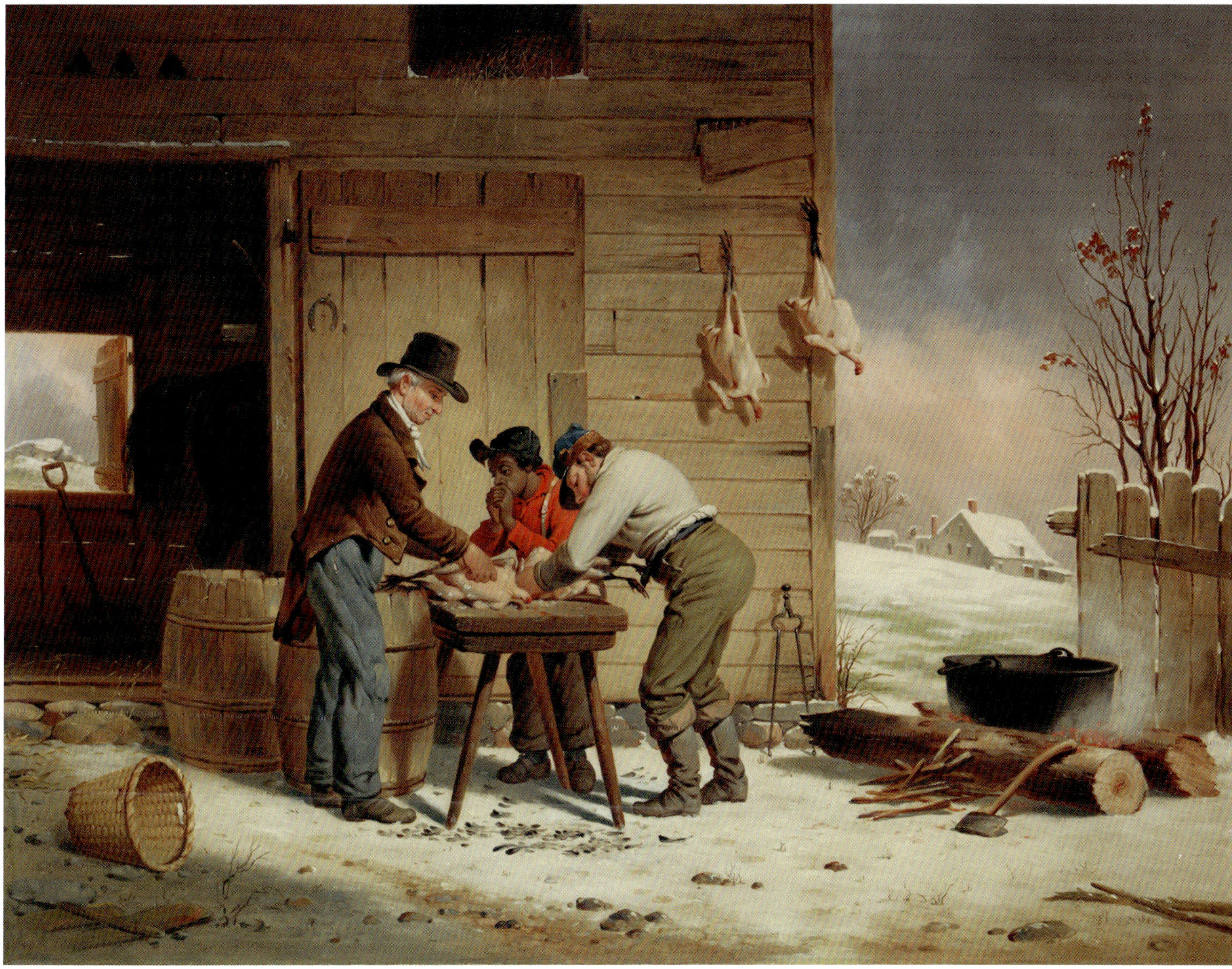

FRANCIS WILLIAM EDMONDS

•

Preparing for Christmas (Plucking Turkeys), 1851
Oil on canvas, 23 × 33 in / 58.4 × 83.8 cm
Metropolitan Museum of Art, New York

Although he took his inspiration from seventeenth-century Dutch genre paintings, New-York-born Francis William Edmonds (1806–1863) captured a contemporary US debate in his 1851 painting, *Preparing for Christmas (Plucking Turkeys)*. Two older white men pluck turkeys on an outside table in a farmyard in preparation for the traditional Christmas meal of roast bird (see pp.133, 156), seemingly impervious to the December chill. Two already featherless turkeys hang behind the men, while a large pan heats up by an open fire. A younger black man blows into his hands to warm them. Has he already taken his turn and is simply having a break from the chore, or he has been excluded from this important work? Edmonds and other contemporary New York artists often placed African-Americans in their paintings, sometimes as figures of fun, but sometimes depicted with great sensitivity. In the decade leading up to the Civil War (1861–65), the question of slavery and its expansion westward dominated every facet of American life. As a child, Edmonds had attended a Quaker school, where he was taught the moral obligation to end slavery. As an adult, he successfully pursued a business career alongside his painting, which led to him becoming an influential figure in New York City.

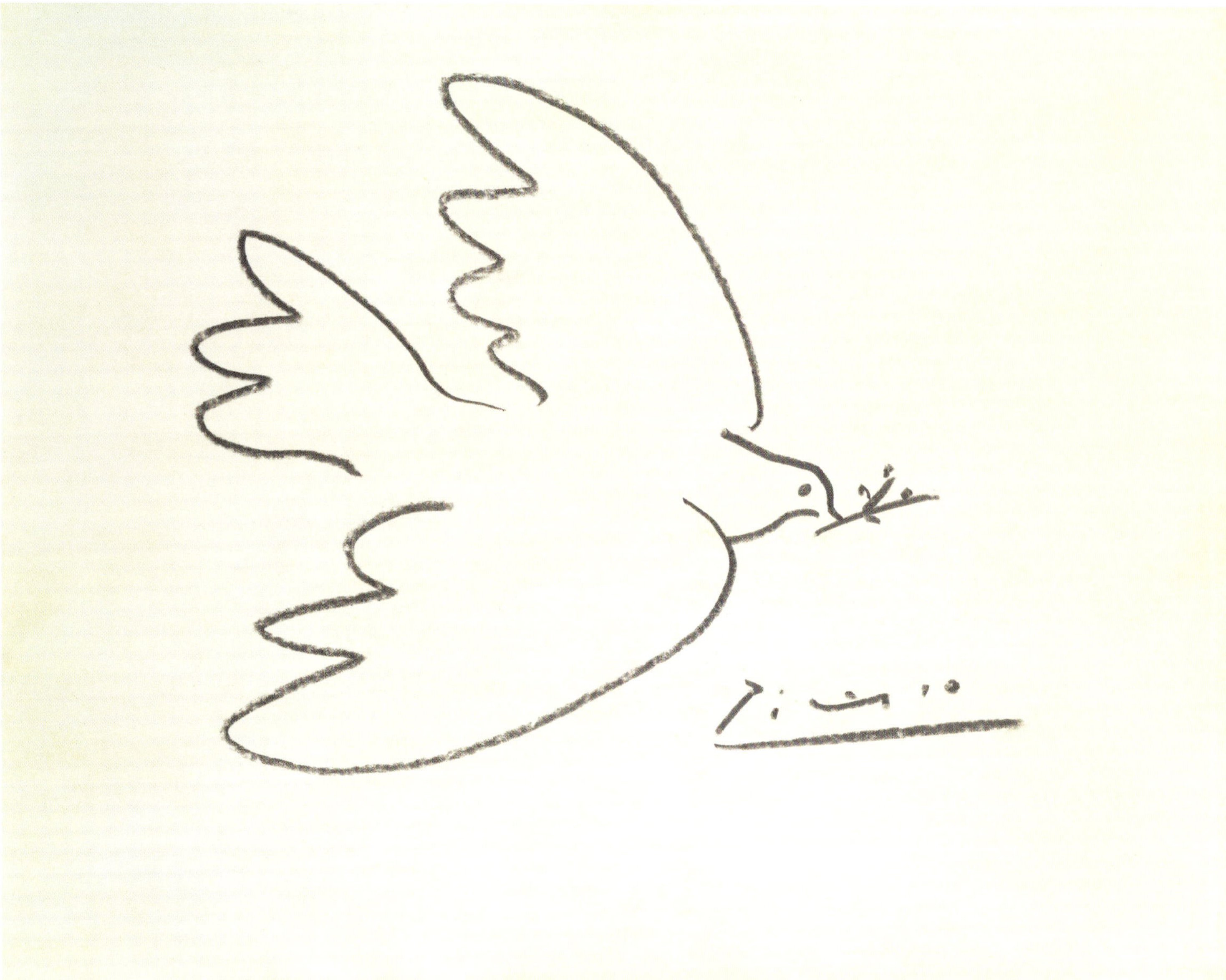

PABLO PICASSO

•

Dove of Peace, c.1950
Pastel on paper, 22⅜ × 30 in / 56.7 × 76.2 cm
Musée National Picasso, Paris

Though commodified in modern times and emblazoned on Christmas ornaments, mugs, shirts, and myriad other items, Pablo Picasso's Dove of Peace originally had nothing to do with Christmas at all. In fact, there really is no one singular Dove of Peace. After painting his political masterpiece *Guernica* in 1937, Picasso (1881–1973) quickly became a symbol of antifascism and antiwar sentiment in general. He was later asked to create an artwork that specifically represented peace, and in 1949 he created *La Colombe* (*Dove*), a realistic depiction of a Milanese pigeon (not a dove at all, but similar in appearance) based on a photograph given to him by his friend and artistic rival Henri Matisse (see p.27). The dove was a very personal symbol for Picasso, acting as a reminder of his father, a painter, who had regularly drawn the doves they kept at their family home in Málaga, Spain. Picasso began rendering his doves as line drawings, generally with an olive branch, another symbol of peace, clutched in its beak, as here. These sparer doves became an enduring sign of the peace movement of the second half of the twentieth century. It makes sense that the dove became so closely associated with Christmas, a time of year that embodies "peace on Earth and goodwill toward men." However, connections go back farther, with the dove also being compared to the Holy Spirit during the baptism of Jesus in Matthew 3:16 and Luke 3:22.

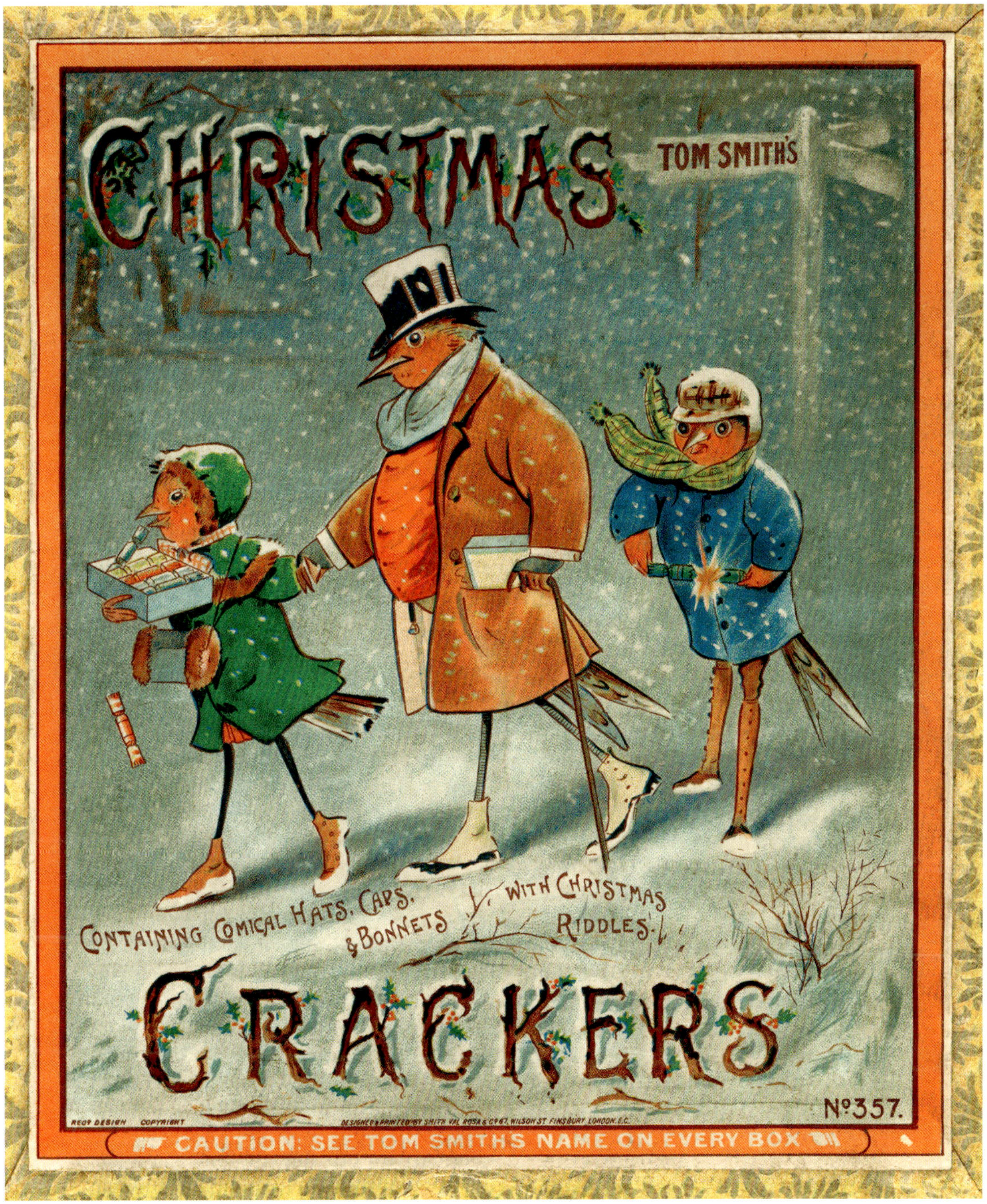

TOM SMITH'S

•

Christmas crackers, c.1870–90
Printed cardstock, dimensions unknown

A cheery trio of red robins, warmly wrapped up against the cold, adorn the printed lid of a box of Victorian Christmas crackers. The birds—in their overcoats, scarves, and hats—are themselves carrying crackers made by London firm Tom Smith's. As well as the crackers, the box, we are told, contains comical hats, caps, and bonnets, together with Christmas riddles. The invention of Christmas crackers (see p.33), now an established part of many a British Christmas meal, are often credited to Tom Smith (1823–1869), a confectioner and baker in London's Clerkenwell district. While on a trip to Paris, Smith discovered the "bon-bon," a sugared almond wrapped in a colorful twist of tissue paper, and found them hugely popular at Christmas. To boost sales, Smith added first a love message, then small trinkets, and finally a device to make a popping sound, inspired by the crackling of his log fire (see p.183). In 1847, he patented his first explosive cracker device, although he only perfected it during the 1860s. It comprised two narrow strips of paper—one coated in silver fulminate and one with an abrasive surface—which, when pulled, created friction and a small explosion. The novelty was instantly popular. Smith's son Walter (1854–1923) took the cracker farther, adding fancy paper hats, and novelties and gifts from around the world. Both father and son tried their best to make the cracker a year-round treat—but it became most closely linked with Christmas, and remains so today.

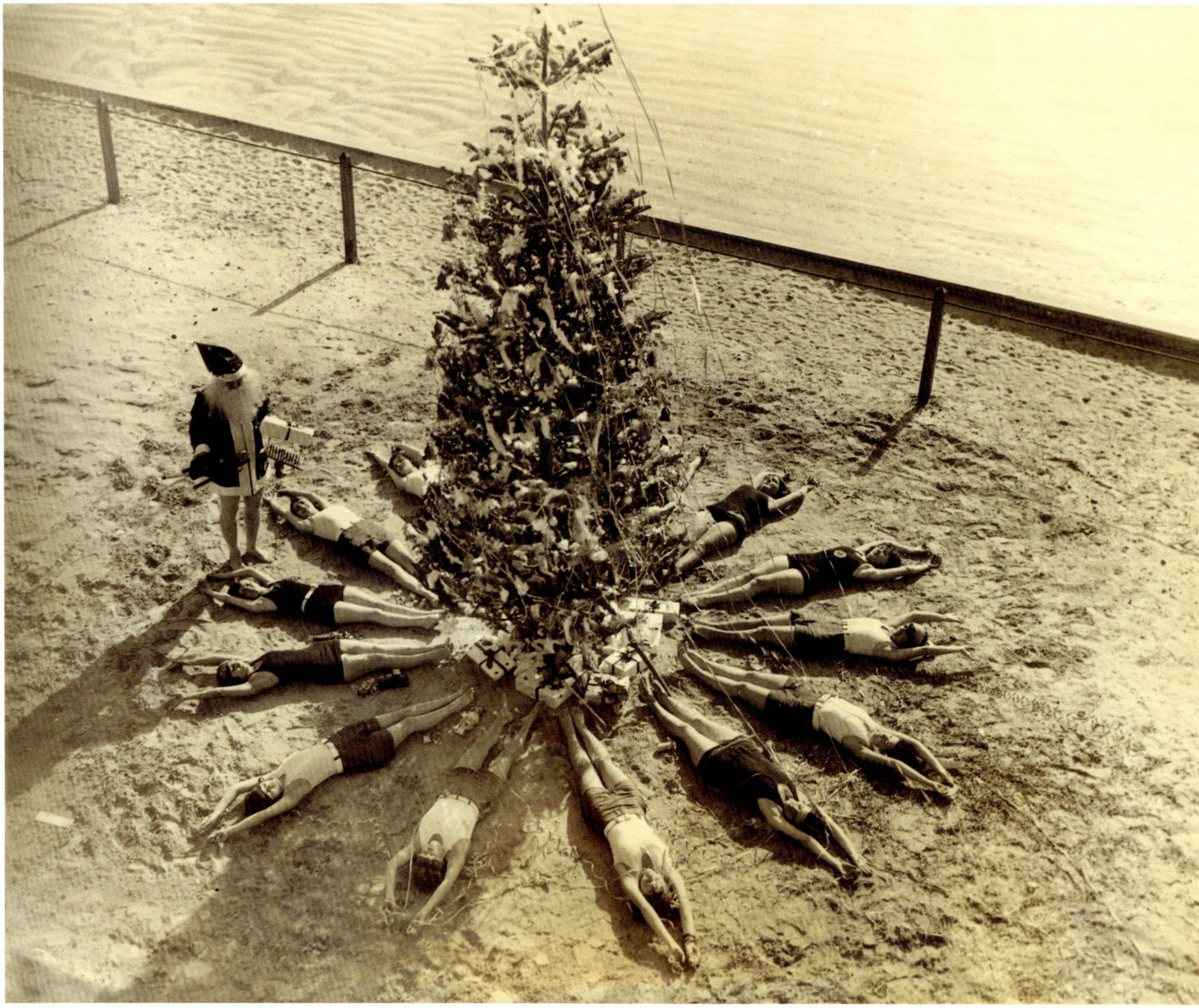

GEORGE RINHART

•

Christmas Scene on California Beach,
Gelatin silver print, dimensions variable

Christmas books, movies, music, and iconography almost always feature snowfall, and because of that, activities such as sledding, snowball fights, and building snowmen have become inextricably linked with the holiday (see p.179). But what about in places where it doesn't snow, or very rarely snows, in the winter? California is just such a place, and as you can tell from this photograph taken by prolific American photographer George Rinhart, the lack of winter precipitation doesn't dampen their festivities. Here, we see a group of sunbathers basking in the hot sun around a decorated Christmas tree, complete with wrapped presents underneath (see p.128). Standing over them is a Santa Claus figure, wearing an appropriately abbreviated and cooler costume. Where the weather is warm in December, atypical Christmas traditions have developed, including surfing Santas (see p.71), the building of "sand snowmen"—replete with sunglasses, of course, to protect their coal eyes from the harsh rays—seashell tree decorations, and much more. In Caracas, Venezuela, where temperatures rarely deviate throughout the year, the city closes its streets to vehicles so that residents can roller-skate to early-morning Mass on Christmas. Rinhart, born in 1944, amassed one of the largest private collections of American photography.

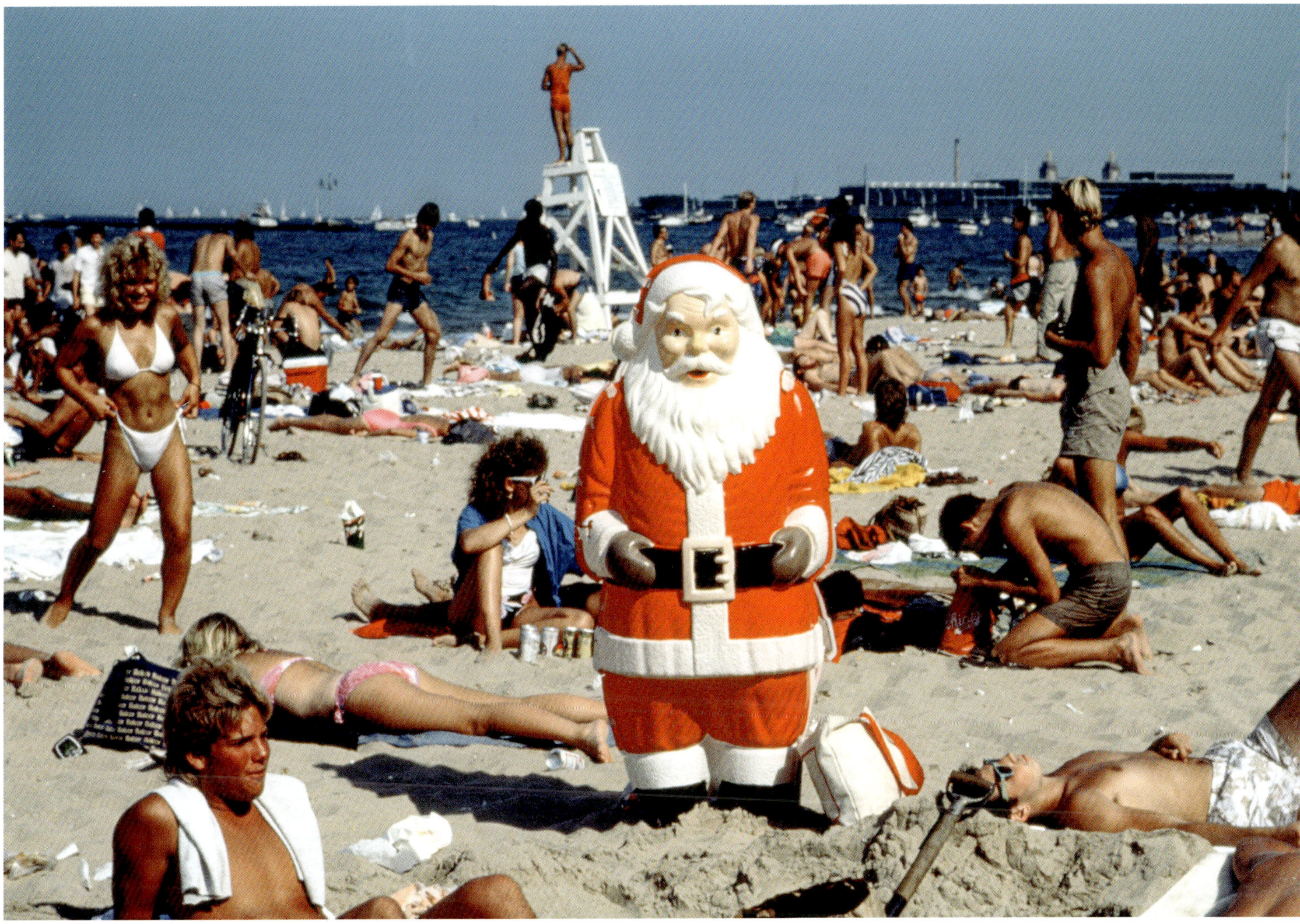

THOMAS HOEPKER

•

Santa Claus on a City Beach in July, 1986
Photograph, dimensions variable

It is the height of summer in Chicago and the beach is packed with sunbathers and swimmers who all seem oblivious to the large inflatable Santa Claus in their midst. The incongruous sight caught the eye of German photographer Thomas Hoepker (1936–), who is known for his stylish color features and reportage all over the world. While Santa's presence on the sand may have been a playful prank, the celebrating of Christmas in July, known sometimes as "half Christmas," is an intriguing phenomenon. The first recorded occurrence took place in 1933, when a girls' camp in North Carolina dedicated two days to celebrating Christmas in July, complete with carols, a Christmas tree, Santa, presents, and fake snow. American retailers first introduced Christmas in July discounts in the 1950s as a novel way to increase sales. Some shoppers took the concept a step farther, choosing to celebrate Christmas in July themselves by organizing themed social gatherings at home or on the beach. In the southern hemisphere, December 25 is the peak of summer and it is not unusual to see surfing Santas on Australian beaches (see p.71). Barbecued shrimp are a popular dish Down Under, where, instead of wearing ugly sweaters the trend is for Christmas-themed Hawaiian shirts. In South Africa, people often spend December 26 picnicking on beaches, while in many Latin American countries families spend Christmas Day by the sea, eating the leftovers from their Christmas Eve feasts.

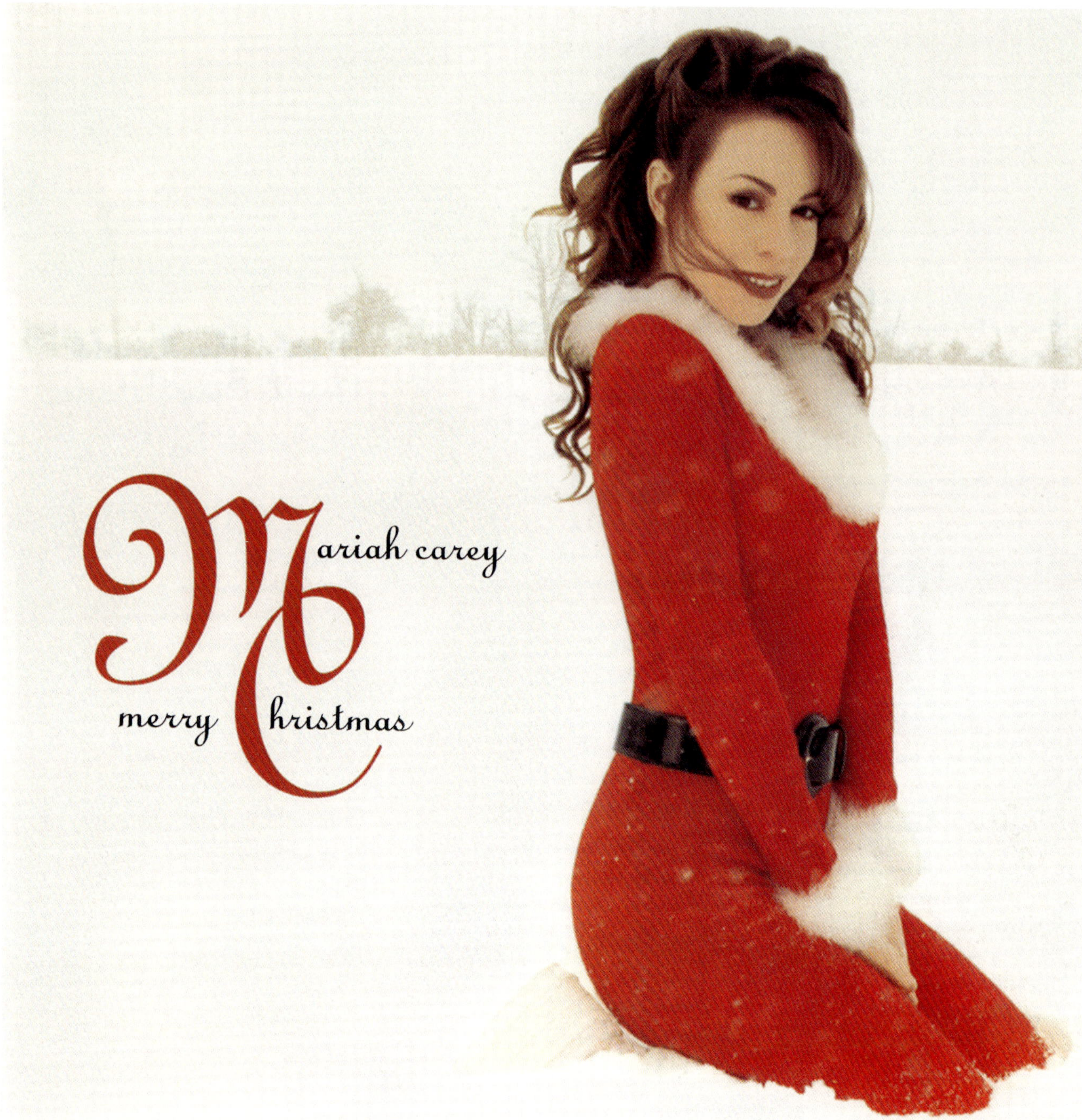

MARIAH CAREY

•

Merry Christmas CD cover, 1994
Printed paper, 4⅝ × 4⅝ in / 12 × 12 cm
Released by Columbia Records, New York

In many households, it's not officially the Christmas season until Mariah Carey (1969–) hits the high note in "All I Want for Christmas Is You." Released in 1994 as the lead single from the singer's *Merry Christmas* album—the iconic cover of which can be seen here, showing Carey kneeling in the snow, wearing a fur-trimmed red bodysuit and a black belt so associated with Santa Claus—the song became an instant classic. The single has been a perennial charter on the Billboard Hot 100 in the United States, particularly since the advent of streaming, but it first reached the top of the Billboard charts in 2019—before repeating the feat again in 2020, 2021, and 2022—making it the song with the longest span between its first and last weeks in the top spot, as well as the single with the longest journey to number one. Put simply, it's a Yuletide juggernaut. It has inspired a children's book, an animated movie, an Amazon Music documentary, and has been featured in many beloved holiday films, including in the crucial Christmas pageant scene in *Love Actually* (2003). Inspired by the jangly, feel-good sounds featured on offerings from Phil Spector's 1963 musical masterpiece *A Christmas Gift for You*, "All I Want for Christmas Is You" is the gift that keeps on giving, year after year after year.

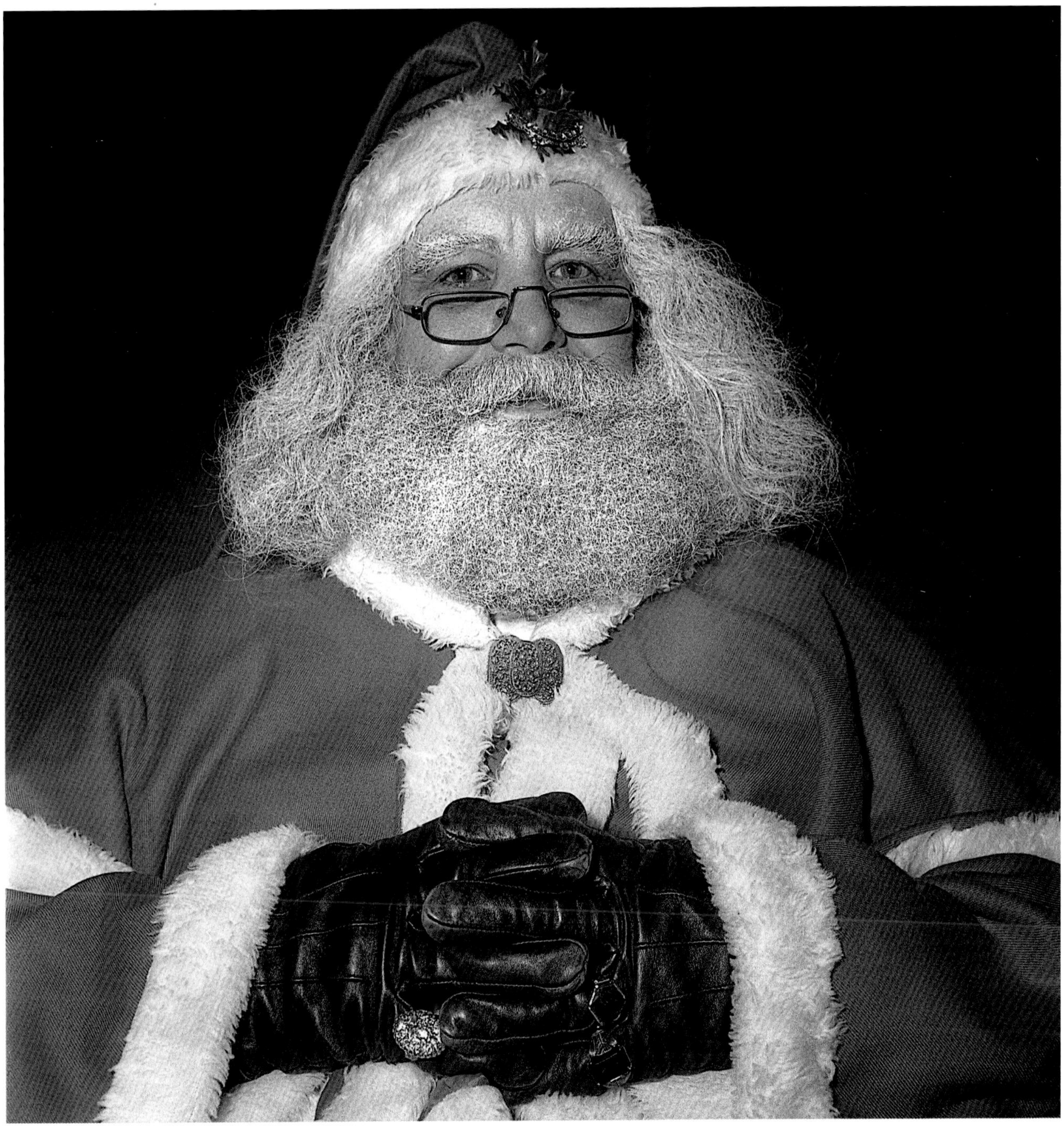

WALTER WAYGOOD

•

Black Gloved Gothic Santa, 2004
Photograph, dimensions variable
Private collection

For many children, Christmas would not be complete without a visit to Santa in his grotto. Walter Waygood (1956–) has fond memories of the tradition, so much so that he turned it into a forty-year photographic project, documenting the different faces of this legendary character. The Welsh photographer began shooting department store Santas in 1980 as part of a larger project documenting life in various retail establishments in South Wales. The black-and-white series, known as *Family of Santa Claus*, now features a large archival and contemporary collection of Santas across the UK, and while their costumes are all virtually identical, as would be expected, each one is a distinct personality. This leather-gloved Santa, looking thoughtfully over his spectacles, exudes a regal air; his bushy white beard and hair seemingly the genuine article. Conversely, other beards appear comically false, reducing Santa to a pair of eyes peeking out from behind a mass of white curls. Waygood's head-and-shoulder portraits display a gentle humor and visual directness that evokes the work of photographers, such as August Sander (1876–1964) and Diane Arbus (1923–1971), while channeling the illustrations of Thomas Nast and Haddon Sundblom (see p.13), who defined the modern image of Santa Claus in the nineteenth and twentieth centuries. With department store closures, grottos have increasingly relocated to garden centers and heritage railways, but Waygood contends that the magic of visiting Santa will never disappear.

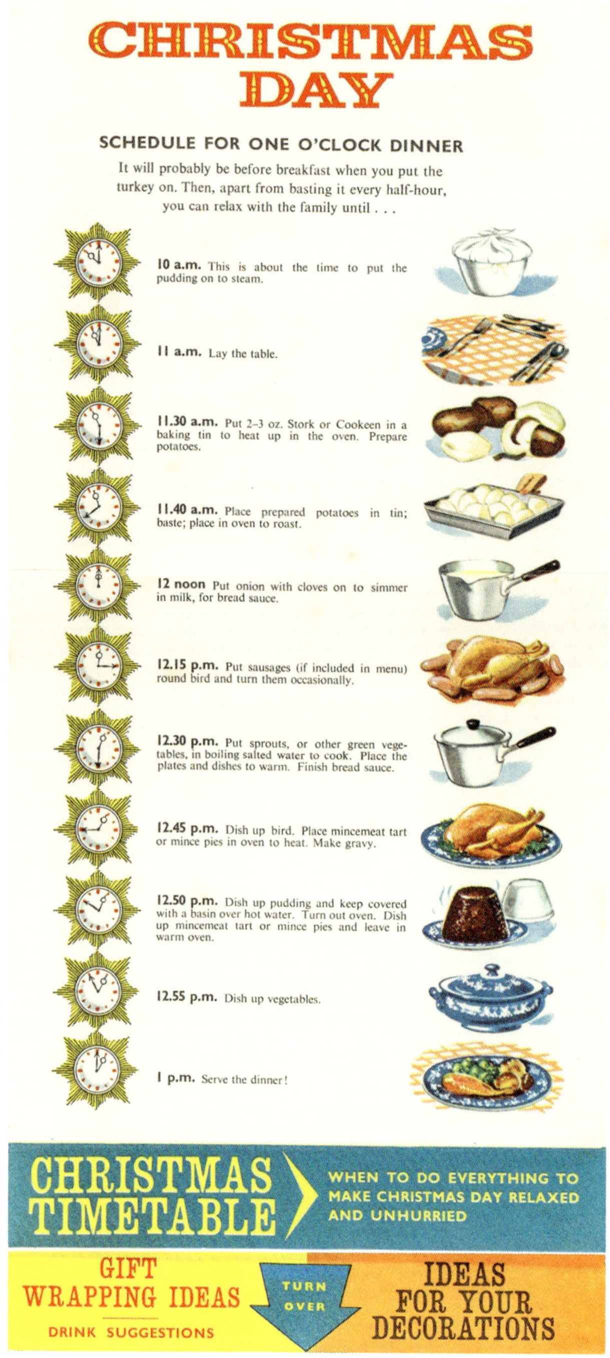

STORK

•

Christmas Day schedule from
"Enjoy Christmas with Stork," 1956
Illustrated leaflet, H. 8¾ in / 22 cm
Wellcome Collection, London

The Christmas lunch is a challenge for virtually any cook, so this colorful Christmas meal planner would have been welcome in many households when it appeared in 1956. Its calm series of steps and timings belie the sheer effort involved—although it does acknowledge, "It will probably be before breakfast when you put the turkey on"—especially given that this meal includes both Christmas pudding (see p.90) and mince pies (see p.132). The meal planner was created by the British producers of Stork margarine, a butter substitute, in the same year it launched the Stork Wives Club to provide advice and support for home cooks, who were at the time almost certainly women. Postwar rationing had only ended in July 1954 and, as food became more readily available, cooks faced pressure to make every mealtime special—particularly at Christmas. Launched in 1920, Stork built up a loyal following of devotees who agreed that it produced lighter, fluffier cakes and better cookies compared to butter. By the time this Christmas planner appeared, the Stork Wives Club had 191,000 women members, eager for cooking advice and new recipes. This double-sided leaflet, folded to create fourteen pages of Christmas dinner timings, advice on how to wrap presents, tips on table decorations, and more, had a cover featuring a cheery stork dressed as Santa carrying the real Santa in his sack. The upbeat mood continues with the simple, if relentless, instructions to have the full Christmas lunch ready to serve at precisely 1 p.m.

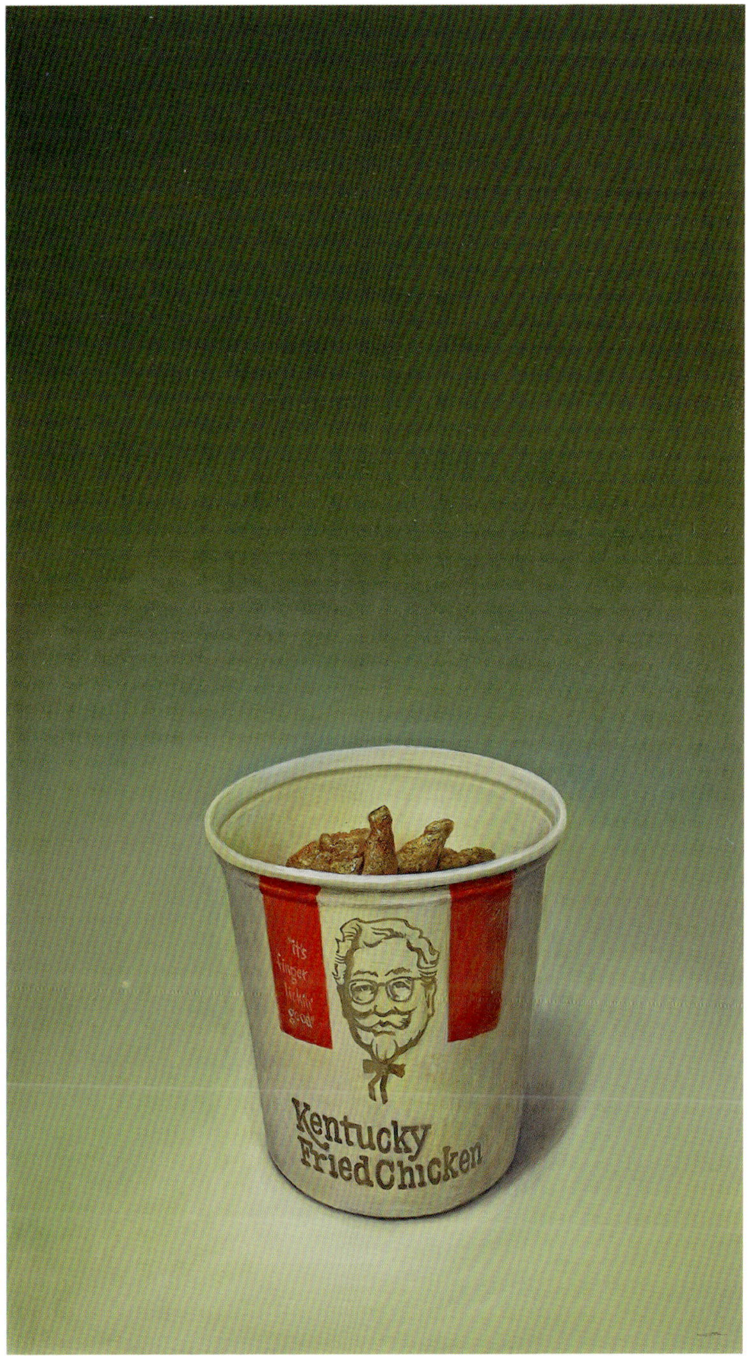

KEIKI YAMADA

•

A Joyful Christmas Party, 2020
Oil and tempera on wood, 35¾ × 20⅛ in / 91 × 51 cm
Shihodo Gallery, Tokyo

It's believed that the Japanese tradition of eating chicken at Christmastime was born from American expats. Unable to procure turkey for the holidays, they turned to chicken instead. Of course, the Japanese have their own fried chicken dish—chicken *karaage*—but it was Kentucky Fried Chicken that was able to capitalize on those home-for-the-holidays feelings and turn them into big business. KFC franchises exploded in Japan during the 1970s, when the country's appetite for all things Western, including Christmas itself, was insatiable. The restaurant's "Kentucky for Christmas" campaign began in 1974 at its Japanese franchises and became immediately popular; each December, Colonel Sanders statues are now dressed as Santa Claus. In fact, Christmas Eve is the busiest day of the calendar year for the chain in Japan, when sales jump to ten times the average. It is when a highly anticipated Christmas meal, featuring a rotating assortment of sides—always with fried chicken as the centerpiece—goes on sale. Japanese painter Keiki Yamada (1978–) captures the essence of Christmas in Japan with *A Joyful Christmas Party*. His artwork often features solitary, everyday objects—often food—in still life: a package of candies, a piece of fruit, a bowl of noodles. Starkly evocative, this piece explores the intense connection between food and memory. Indeed, those sentimental feelings of Christmas conjure up the sweet smell of baking cookies, the spice of mulled wine, and for many, the satisfying aroma of freshly fried chicken.

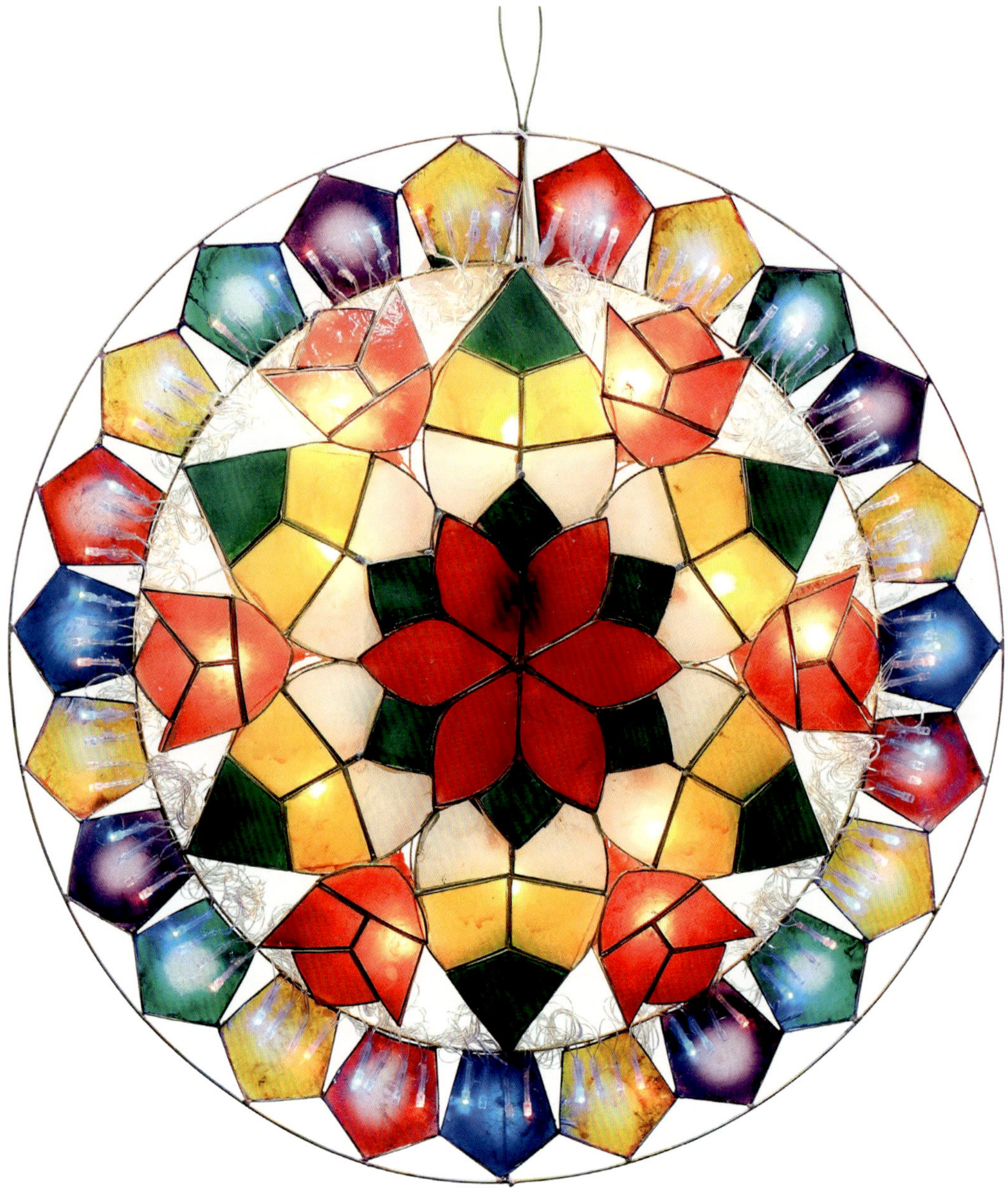

PAROLS OF AMERICA

•

Tulip Capiz Parol, 2020
Capiz shells, brass, and Christmas lights,
D. 25 in / 63.5 cm

Nobody in the world does Christmas quite like the Filipinos. In fact, 92 percent of Filipinos are Christian, making Christmas a high holiday indeed (see p.37). The sights and sounds of the holiday season reign supreme throughout the so-called "Ber" months—September, October, November, and December—then into January for good measure, making it the country that celebrates Christmas for the longest of any worldwide. One of the most popular and long-standing Christmas traditions in the Philippines is the star-shaped *parol*, as seen here, which symbolizes the Star of Bethlehem. These colorful lanterns are often handmade and typically constructed of either paper and bamboo or shell and wire. This modern example is made of Capiz shells, named after the province in the Philippines where they are particularly abundant, and illuminated using Christmas lights. Dating back to the Spanish colonial era in the country, from around 1565, original lanterns were made of sheets of white paper formed into a rectangular or oblong shape with a small candle inside. Similar lanterns can be seen in other Spanish-speaking countries and the southern United States. Colorful *parols* are hung in windows or outdoors, creating a breathtaking illuminated display. The city of San Fernando, Pampagna, goes one better. For more than a century, it has hosted the Giant Lantern Festival, a kaleidoscopic parade of giant *parols* and lanterns boasting a carnival-like atmosphere—a Christmas festival like no other.

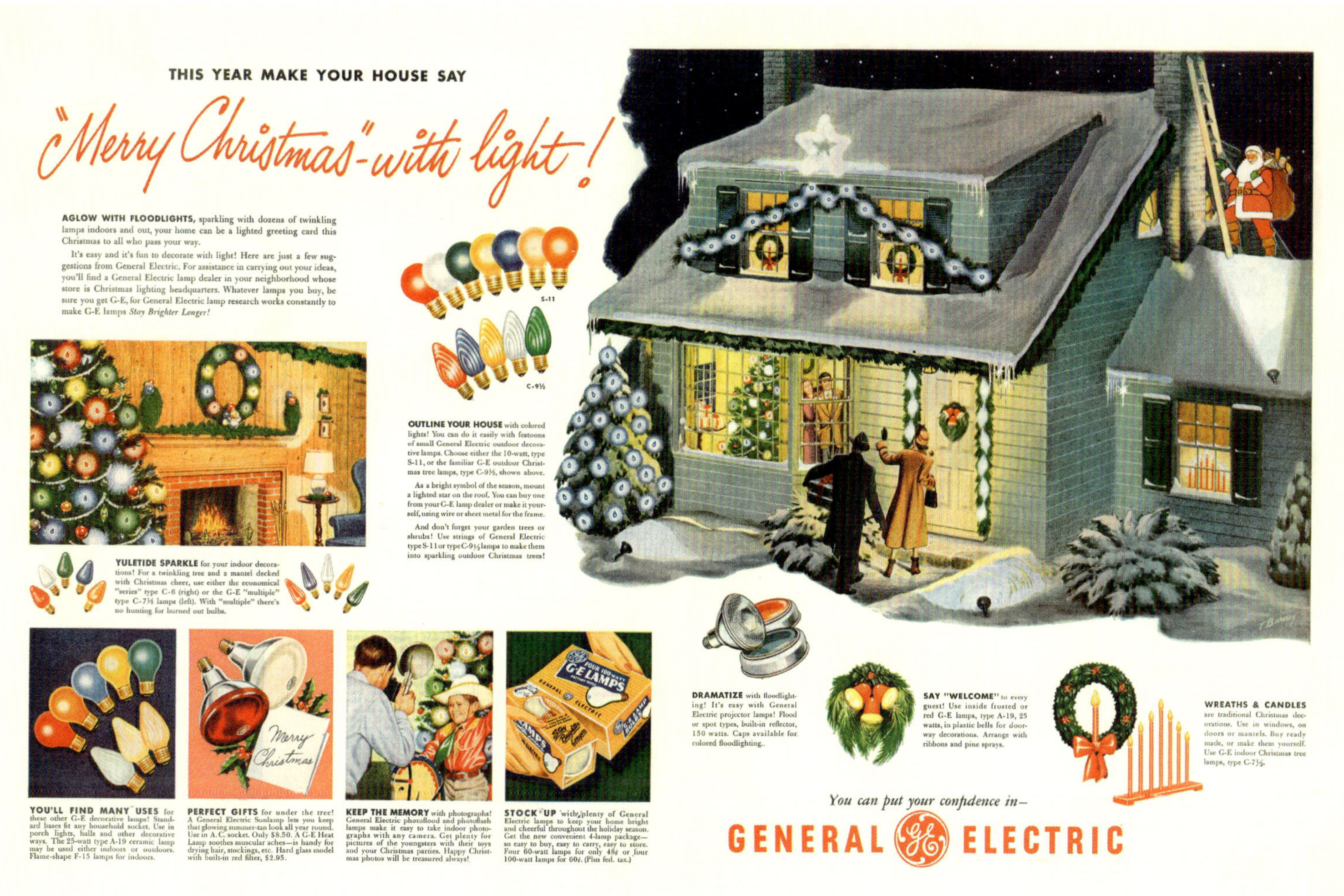

GENERAL ELECTRIC

•

"Merry Christmas—with light!" advertisement, 1949
Print, dimensions variable
Published in the *Saturday Evening Post*

This 1949 advertisement featured in the *Saturday Evening Post* shows the various styles of indoor and outdoor Christmas lights sold by General Electric at the time and portrays them as a staple of mid-century middle-class life, adorning both the outside and the inside of the typical American family home. The use of Christmas lights on indoor trees dates to the seventeenth century in Germany, when people would affix lit candles to their trees with pins or melted wax (see p.22). Although unsafe, this tradition spread throughout Europe and eventually to North America through migration. In 1880, Thomas Edison (1847–1931) created the first outdoor Christmas lights display on his laboratory using electric lights, having patented the electric lightbulb earlier that year. This was the first Christmas light display separate from the tree indoors. Two years later, in 1882, an inventor associate of Edison's, Edward Johnson, made the first string of indoor Christmas lights to light his tree. The trend did not begin to catch on, however, until the early 1900s, approximately a decade after Edison and others founded General Electric in 1892. The initial lights—both indoor and outdoor—were very expensive, costing hundreds of dollars (thousands in today's money) just to light a tree, never mind the house (see p.207). General Electric began selling light kits in 1903, but because they were still too expensive for many households, a trend developed and continued into the 1930s whereby families could rent their lights from various department stores.

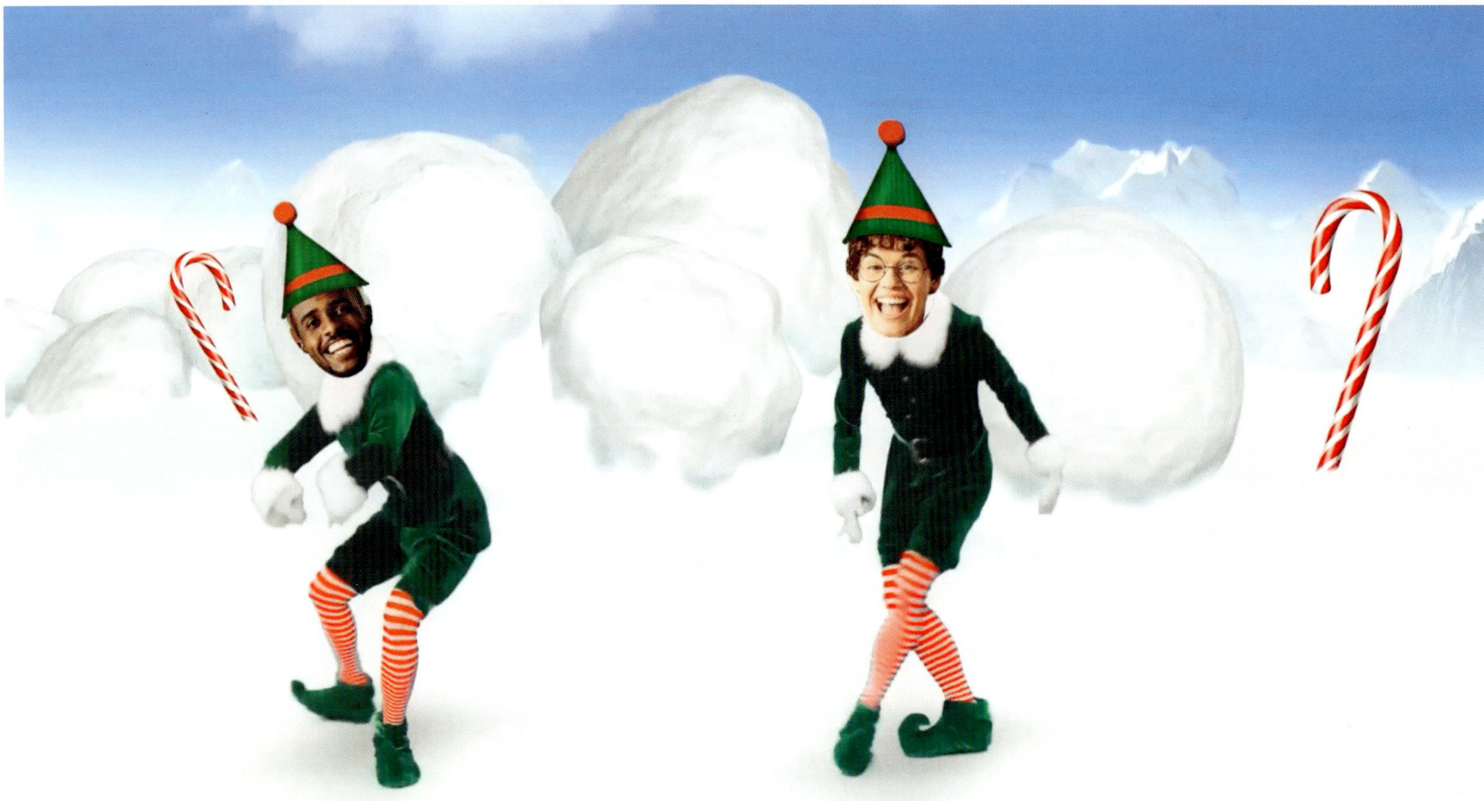

ELF YOURSELF

•

Classic Scene, 2022
Digital image, dimensions variable
Created by Evolution Bureau

Elf Yourself is a free interactive website (and app) where, come December every year, visitors can upload images of their faces to be superimposed onto the androgynous bodies of Christmas elves. These elves, wearing green outfits with red and white striped tights, are animated into short videos that contain exuberant synchronized dancing to festive music. Users can choose and customize where exactly their animation unfolds: a party, the office, Santa's workshop, or the streets of Los Angeles or New York, before sharing their creations with friends and family via email and messenger services. Launched as a Christmas campaign in 2006 by Evolution Bureau, a US advertising agency, and just prior to the advent of the iPhone, Elf Yourself has elicited more than 193 million visitors and turned 123 million people into dancing elves. When released, Elf Yourself instantly went viral, rapidly assimilating into popular culture. Its success has since been propagated by social media platforms, such as Facebook and Instagram, and it revolutionized the idea of personal Christmas greetings and cards with personalized messaging options. Despite it speaking to a more twentieth-century mode of guerrilla marketing, there is a certain innocence to this cultural artifact. As a shareable form of visual media, it shares similarities with, but undoubtedly predates, the cultural complexity and divisiveness of memes today.

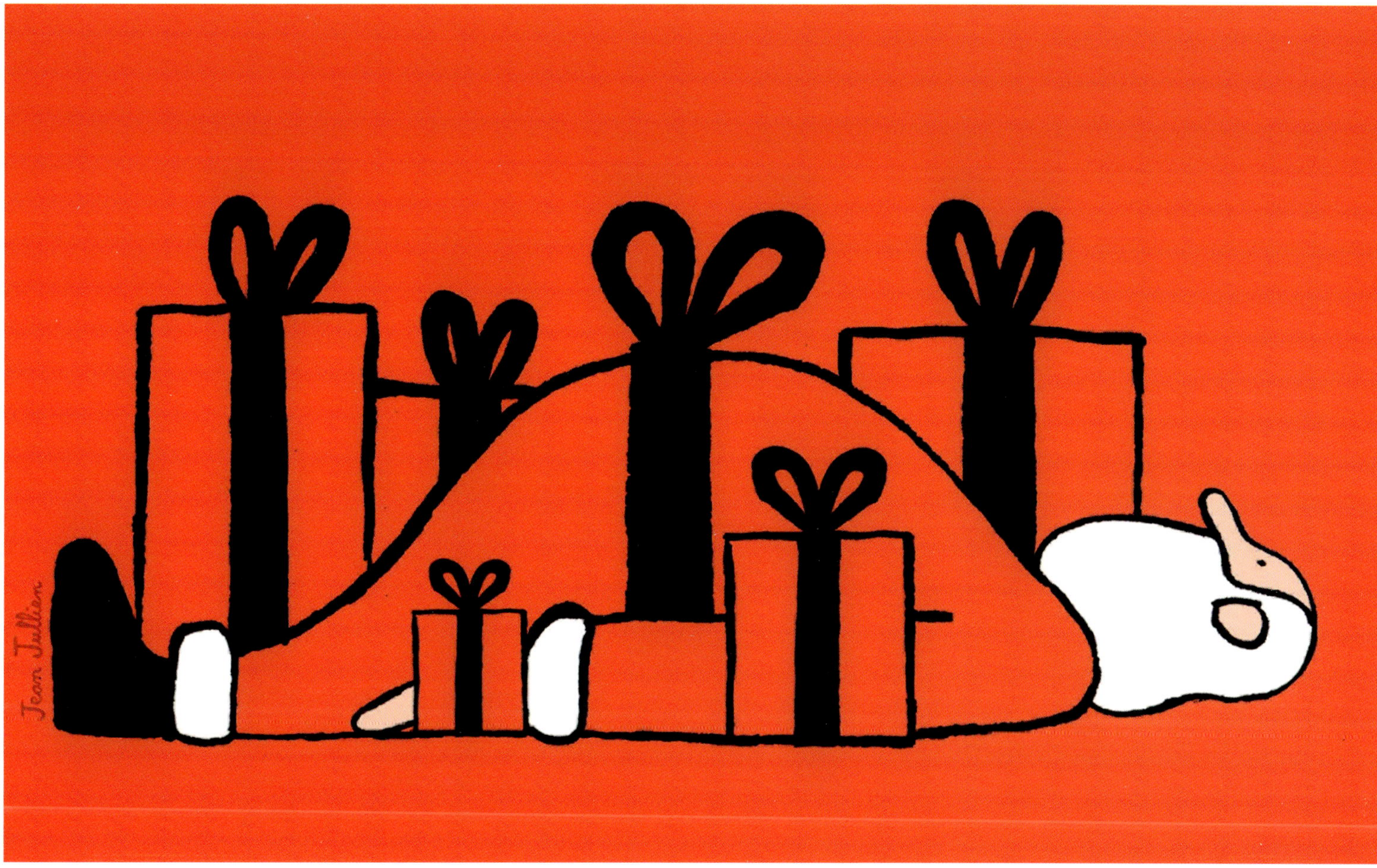

JEAN JULLIEN

•

An Extra Special Gift, 2015
Digital illustration, dimensions variable
For *The Guardian*

The work of French graphic designer and illustrator Jean Jullien (1983–) is often called childlike, a descriptor that Jullien appreciates, because he sees a link between his work and his overwhelmingly happy childhood. Here, in a drawing created for the "12 cartoons of Christmas" series, that appeared in *The Guardian* newspaper in 2015, Santa is seen lying on his back, perhaps nodding off as a long night of delivering presents nears its end, his iconic black belt tied in a neat bow, his figure blending in with the gifts wrapped in red and black lying around him. Jullien attributes his style largely to an early obsession with comic books (see p.174)and also to his father's love of pop culture, which fascinated him and fueled his imagination. Born in Cholet, France, before moving to London in his twenties for art school, Julien attended Central Saint Martins and the Royal College of Art. As a child, he drew constantly in sketchbooks that he carried everywhere he went. His drawings are unpretentious and inclusive; they have the rare ability to feel accessible to all who view them, uniting people under the banner of understanding and shared experience. Astute observations and witty depictions of things that are so familiar to us all—such as Santa—are shown in a new light, and act as a humorous and sometimes cutting visual commentary on life.

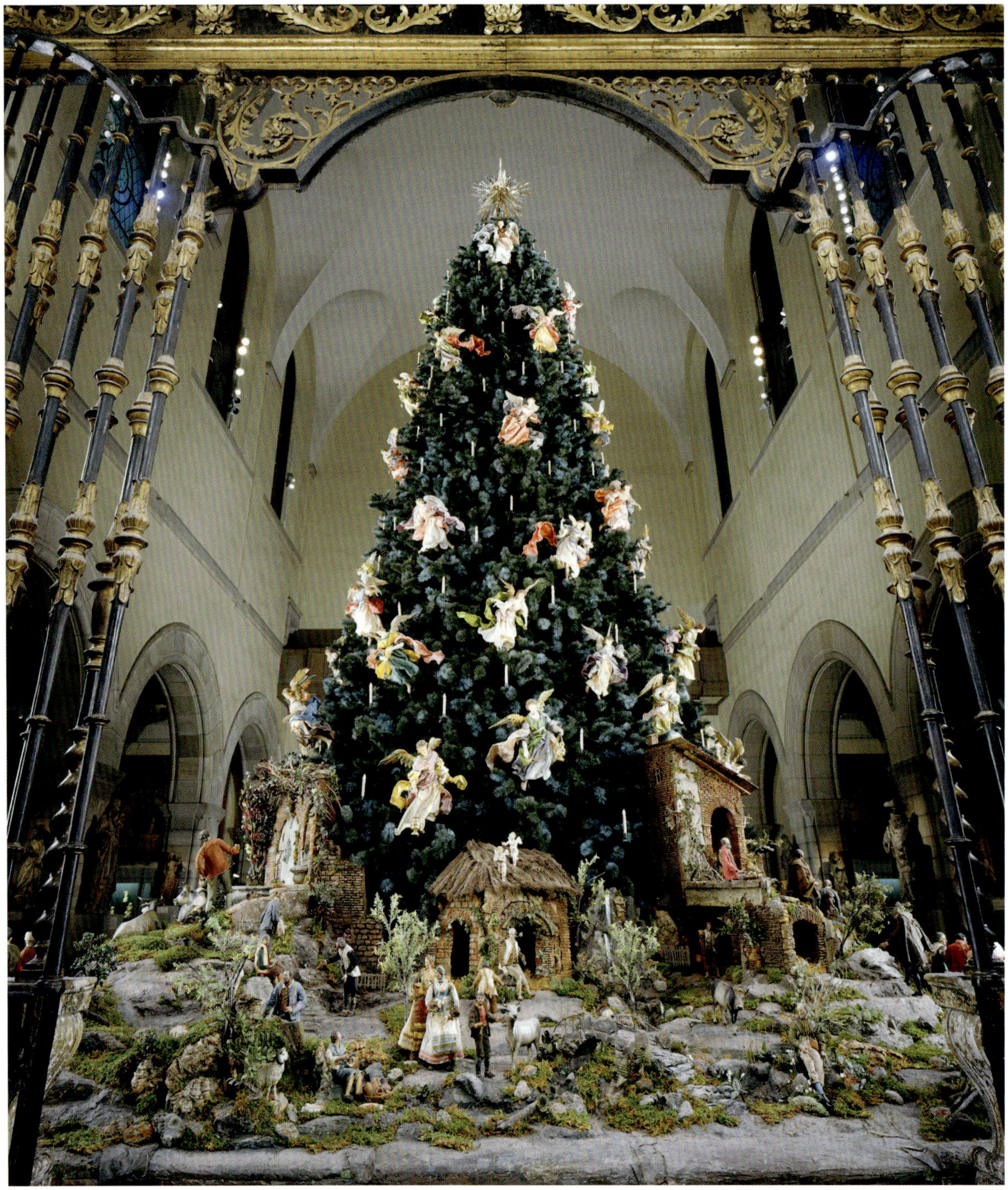

LORETTA HINES HOWARD

•

Angel Tree with Neapolitan crèche, c.18th–19th century
Blue spruce, H. 20 ft / 6 m
Metropolitan Museum of Art, New York

The tradition common to many of the great museums of the world of erecting a magnificently decorated Christmas tree for the festive season has been enthusiastically embraced by New York City's Metropolitan Museum of Art for over fifty years. In a city known for its lavish Christmas decorations and famous trees (see p.20), the Met's tree stands out. Standing in the Medieval Sculpture Hall, the large twenty-foot (6 m) spruce tree is decorated with twenty cherubs and sixty angels (see p.75)—angels are God's messengers, while cherubs remain in his presence, singing his praises—and sits in front of a choir screen, originally from the Cathedral of Valladolid in Spain. Around the base of the tree is the Met's collection of carved créche figures, collected by American artist Loretta Hines Howard (1904–1982), who started the tradition of using them to decorate the tree in 1957 before donating her entire collection to the museum in the early 1960s. The Nativity scene around the base of the tree, with houses, a fountain, fifty animals, and more than seventy figures, reflects the traditions of Naples, where the ceramic figures were created by Baroque artists in the 1700s. The tree brings together two strands of Christianity: the Roman Catholic tradition of creating Nativity scenes and the Protestant tradition of decorating the tree. As well as its Christmas tree, the Met also transforms its Cloisters for Christmas with displays of ivy, shining lady apples, holly laden with red berries, pinecones, and hazelnuts.

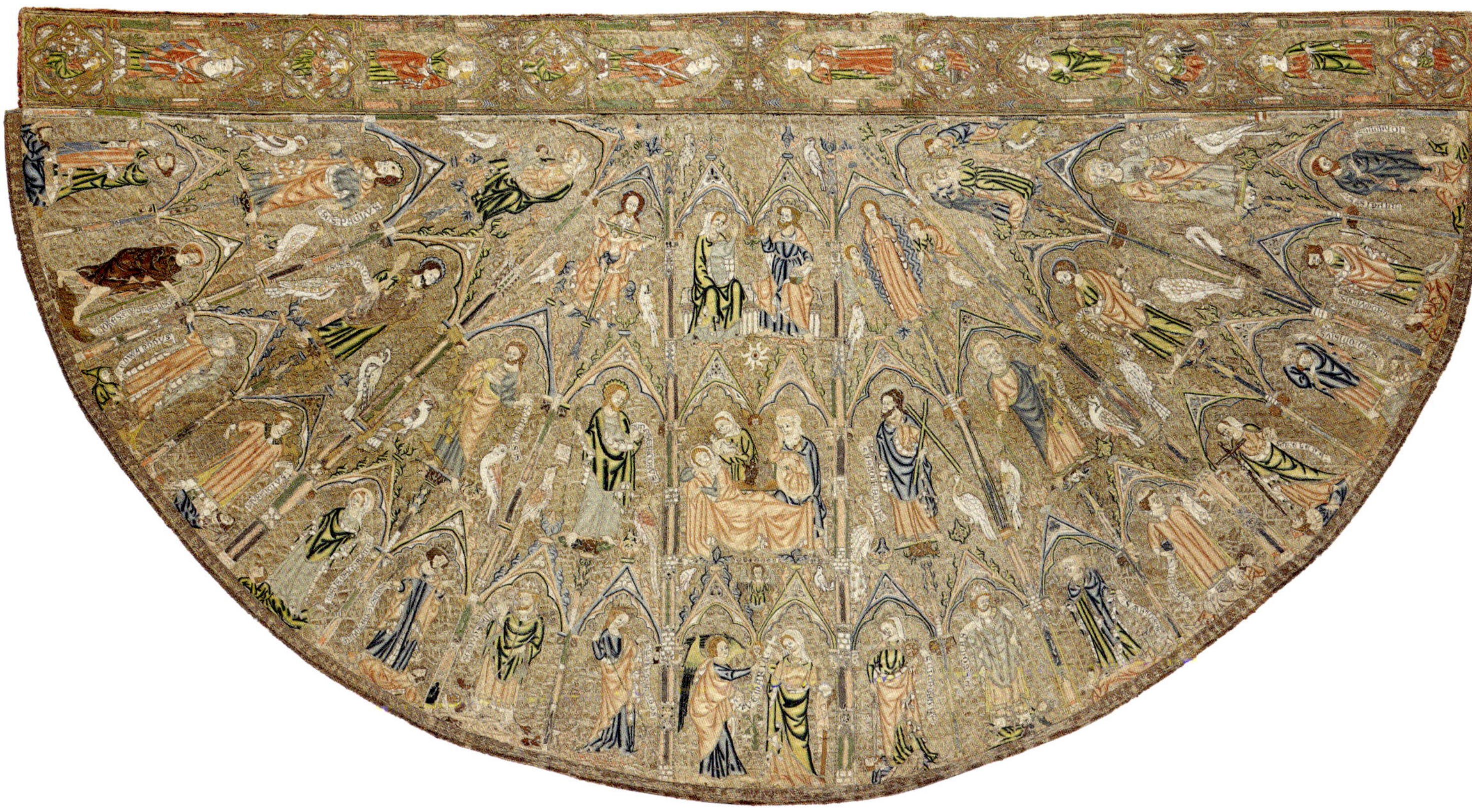

UNKNOWN

•

Toledo Cope, c.1320
Embroidered linen, silver-gilt thread and silk,
66½ × 126¾ in / 169 × 322 cm
Catedral Primada de Santa María, Spain

At the center of this intricately embroidered English cope—a semicircular cloak worn by senior priests during ceremonies—is the Christmas Nativity scene, the miraculous story of the Virgin birth. Mary reclines on a bed, gazing at her newborn baby, while Joseph is seen dozing, and an ox and donkey peer at Jesus over their manger. Above blazes the star that guided the three wise men to the stable. The back of the fourteenth-century Toledo Cope—so named because it was housed in the Catedral Primada de Santa María in Toledo, Spain, soon after it had been embroidered in England—would have been visible to the congregation throughout most of a church service. While the priest faced the altar, the cope illustrated the biblical story for the largely illiterate audience and underlined the wealth and power of the Roman Catholic Church. This form of embroidery was known as *opus anglicanum*, or English work, and the handful of copes known each required about fifty thousand hours of work—or around five or six years of work for a team of four embroiderers. This cope was worn for the extended Christmas celebrations that in medieval Europe lasted from Christmas Eve to Twelfth Night and displays remarkable craftsmanship; its rich embroidery, using silk, gold, and silver thread, re-creates foliage, birds, masks, and numerous saints—some of which are seen trampling their tormentors—framed by a lavish backdrop of Gothic arches.

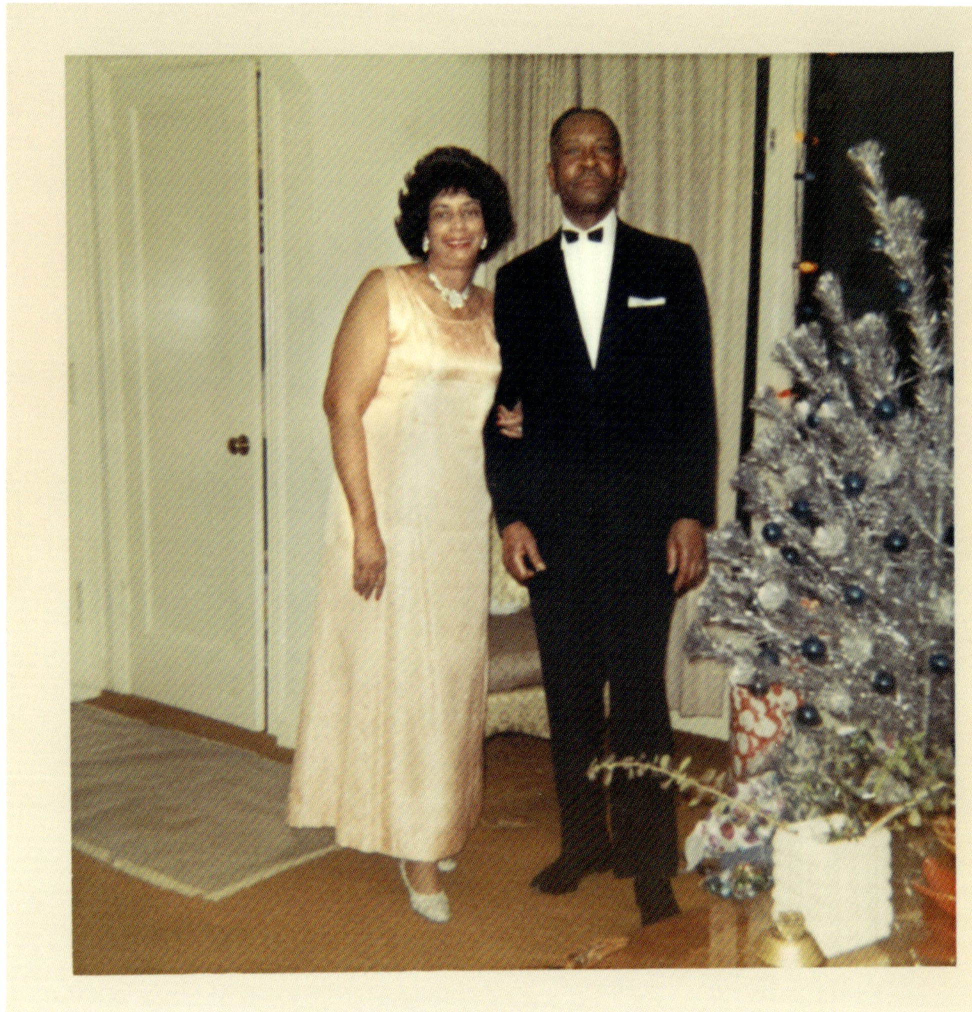

UNKNOWN

•

Untitled, 1969
Chromogenic print, 3½ × 3½ in / 8.9 × 8.9 cm
Portland Art Museum, Portland, Oregon

This striking instant film photograph, taken during the holiday season in the late 1960s, is formally untitled. It features an African-American couple, dressed in formal wear, standing by a silver foil Christmas tree—a telltale sign of the era, but perhaps one that was coming to an end for that style of decoration (see p.135). Vernacular photography is different from fine-art photography in many ways. Generally, these images were not created by trained photographers, and they were not intended to be exhibited beyond perhaps being shown to friends and family. These are the photographs one finds at estate sales, at thrift stores, and at auctions, and it has only been in the last couple decades that they have begun to be examined with a critical eye. Once meant to document private moments, these photographs now find themselves thrust into a new context altogether. Because of their unposed nature, showing real people doing real things, they provide an unparalleled look at the way people lived. Often they provide more questions than they answer and hint at narratives they are incapable of fully exploring. The open door in this instance is perhaps a sign that this couple was rushing to a glamorous, festive engagement but stopped to take a quick picture as they left. This photograph was given as a gift to the Portland Art Museum in 2017 and was featured in the exhibition *Representing: Vernacular Photographs of, by, and for African Americans,* curated by Julia Dolan.

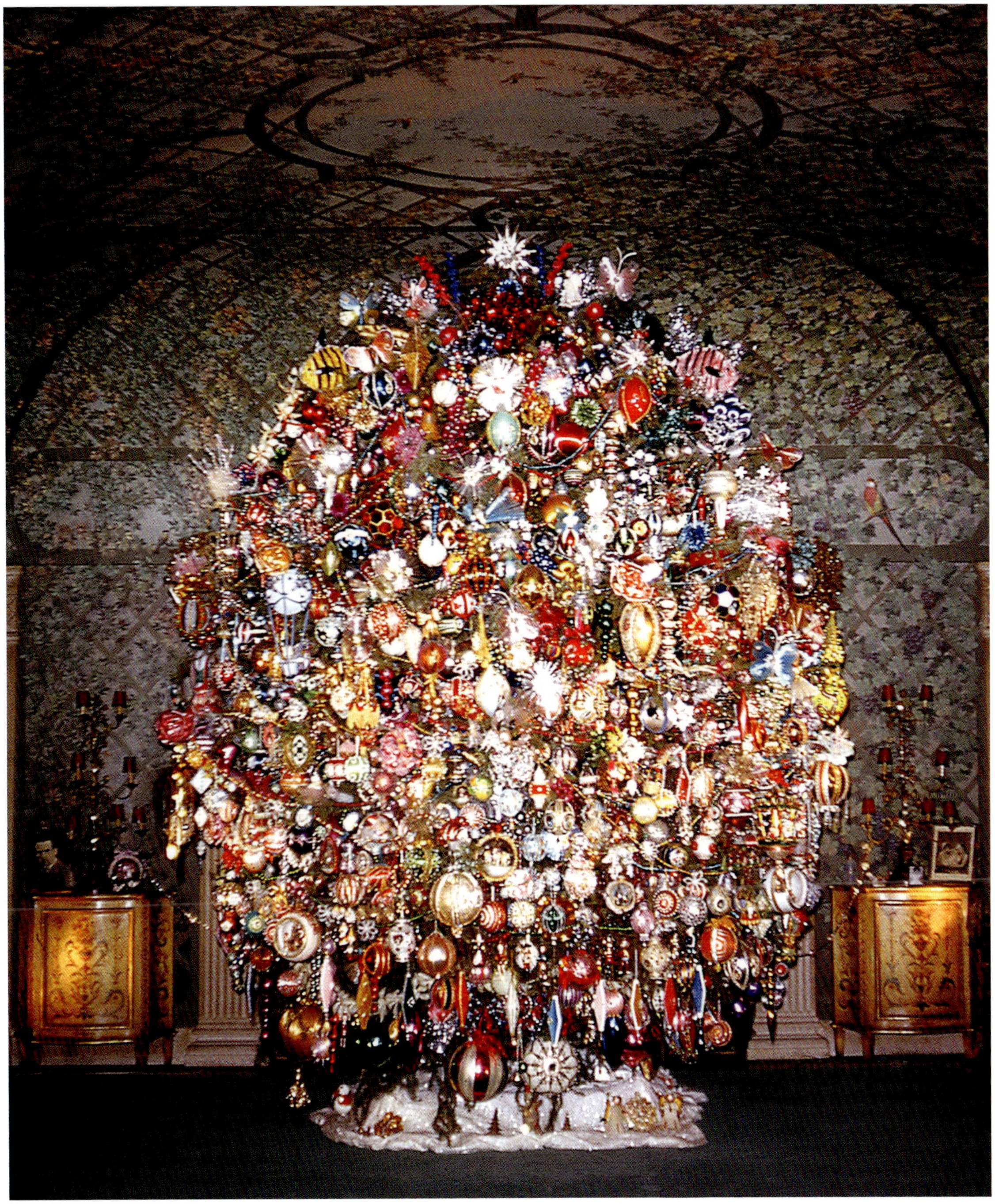

HAROLD LLOYD

•

Christmas Tree at Greenacres, c.1950s
Douglas fir, 20 × 9 ft; D. 30 ft / 6.1 × 2.7 m; D. 9.1 m

There can't have been too many private, indoor Christmas trees in the world that were grander and more heavily decorated than that of American silent movie star Harold Lloyd (1893–1971). Standing at the foot of his family orangery on his fifteen-acre California estate Greenacres (that also once housed the state's largest swimming pool), this glittering behemoth is actually three Douglas firs lashed together and stands at 20 feet (6 m) high, 9 feet (2.7 m) wide and measures 30 feet (9.1 m) around. It would take Lloyd and his family from Thanksgiving until Christmas to fully decorate the tree in the early years, but it soon became too time-consuming, and he eventually had the evergreen fireproofed so that it could remain standing all year round.

The branches can barely be seen through all of the ornaments that adorn them; at the time this photograph was taken in the 1950s, the tree held over five thousand of them. Many were rare and expensive, purchased from luxury retailers, such as Saks Fifth Avenue in New York (see p.204), but others were handmade and personal, gifted to him by friends. Lloyd was one of the most influential comedy actors of the silent movie era, starring in more than two hundred films over the course of his career. In the 1990s, in recognition of his love of Christmas, world-renowned ornament designer Christopher Radko (see p.175) re-created two baubles from this famous tree, including one gifted to Lloyd by fellow silent film star Charlie Chaplin.

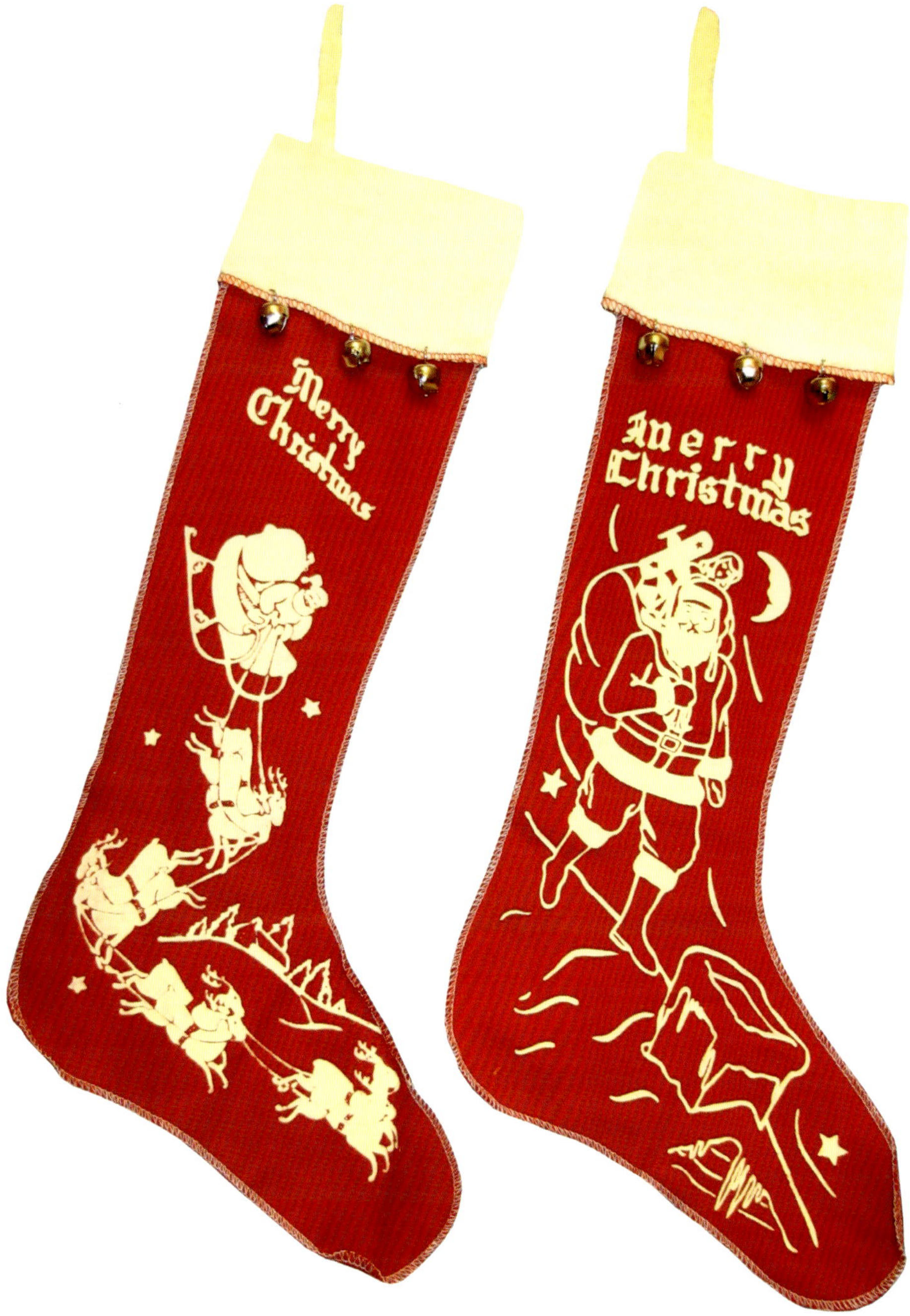

PRIMITIVES BY KATHY

•

Stocking Set—Large Bell, c.21st century
Felt and metal, 18 × 8½ in / 45.7 × 21.6 cm

In Santa's traditional red and white, with bells attached to the fabric turn ups, these felt Christmas stockings from the twenty-first century feature scenes of Santa Claus flying his reindeer-drawn sleigh through the sky and preparing to descend down a chimney. Hanging up the Christmas stocking is one of the most widespread traditions of Christmas Eve; most commonly, children awake in the morning to find it full of little gifts and treats, frequently including an orange pushed down into the toes. The ritual has barely changed over the years, although there are variations in where stockings are hung; on the mantelpiece or at the foot of the bed; and whether they are special stockings, a father's sock, or even purchased complete with gifts from a store (see p.104). There are also different explanations of how the tradition began. One popular tale tells the story of a recently widowed man who worried that his three daughters would never marry, because he was too poor to afford a dowry. Saint Nicholas (see p.15), knowing the family were too proud to accept charity, slid down the family's chimney one night while they were asleep and, finding the girls' stockings drying by the fire, filled them with gold coins. The influence of this story, and the many like it, can still be seen today with the frequent inclusion of gold coins—made of chocolate rather than precious metal—and the symbolic "golden" orange in modern stockings.

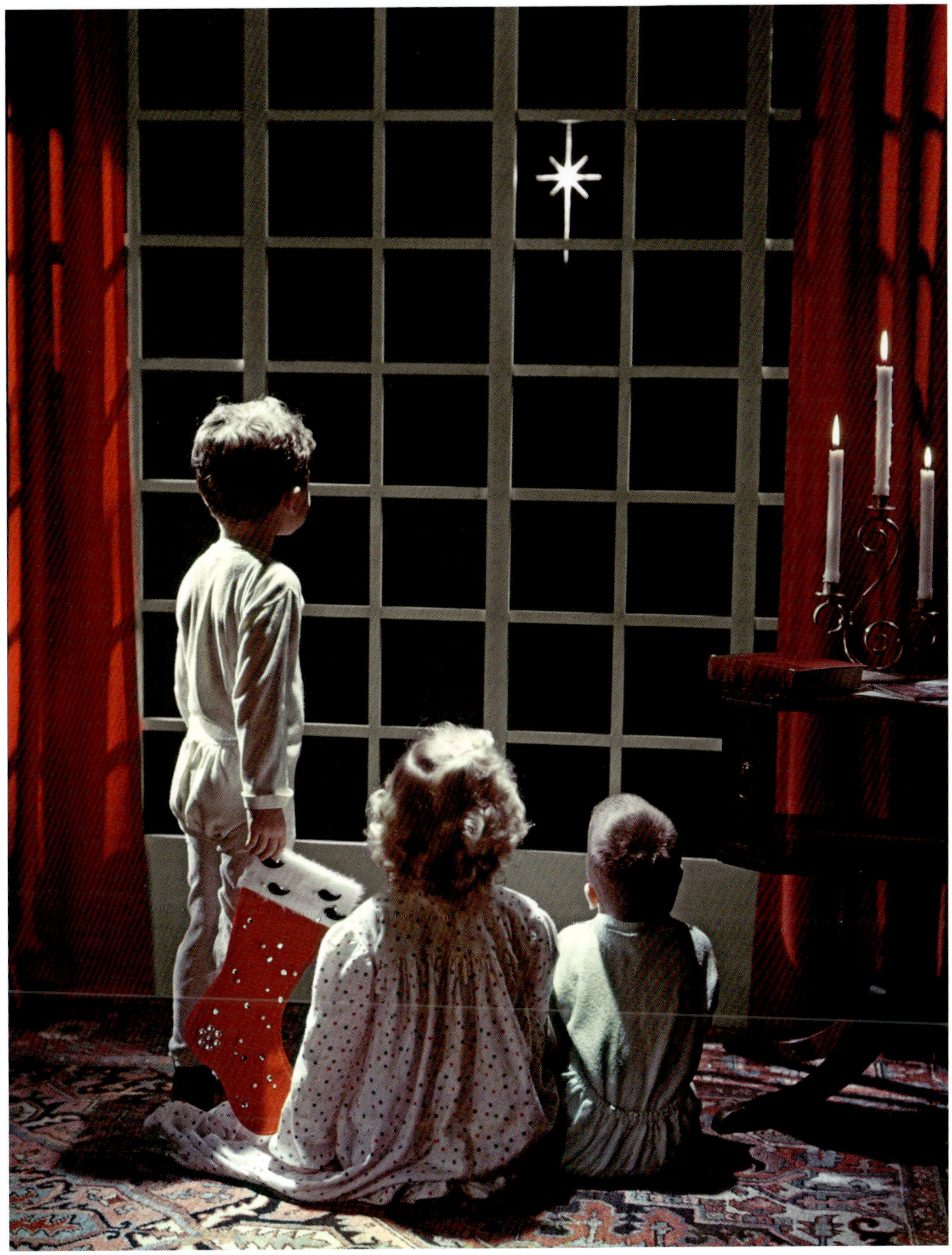

H. ARMSTRONG ROBERTS

•

Christmas Star, c.1950s
Photograph, dimensions variable

This untitled shot from prolific American photographer H. Armstrong Roberts squeezes in as many references to Christmas traditions as possible in what is a relatively serene and peaceful composition. This color photograph shows three young children—two boys and a girl—gazing out French doors at the brightest star in the sky. Each are dressed in their nightclothes, patiently awaiting the arrival of Santa Claus. One is seen holding a traditional fur-trimmed stocking tightly in his hand. The star is a ubiquitous Christmas symbol—one that the three wise men followed to witness the birth of Jesus (see p.26) and that now sits atop a the majority of Christmas trees in people's homes (see p.53), as well as adorning a large variety of Christmas cards and decorations (see p.29). The book on the table to the side could be a traditional Christmas tale often read to children on Christmas eve, such as Clement Clarke Moore's "A Visit from St. Nicholas" (see p.84), or even a copy of the Bible, featuring the origins of the Nativity story (see p.10). H. Armstrong Roberts was one of the pioneers of stock photography, a practice that stretches back to the early twentieth century, where images from a catalog can be sold for certain uses. Stock photography allowed newspapers and magazines to save money by not keeping a photographer on staff. This example from the 1950s exudes a sense of Christmas anticipation.

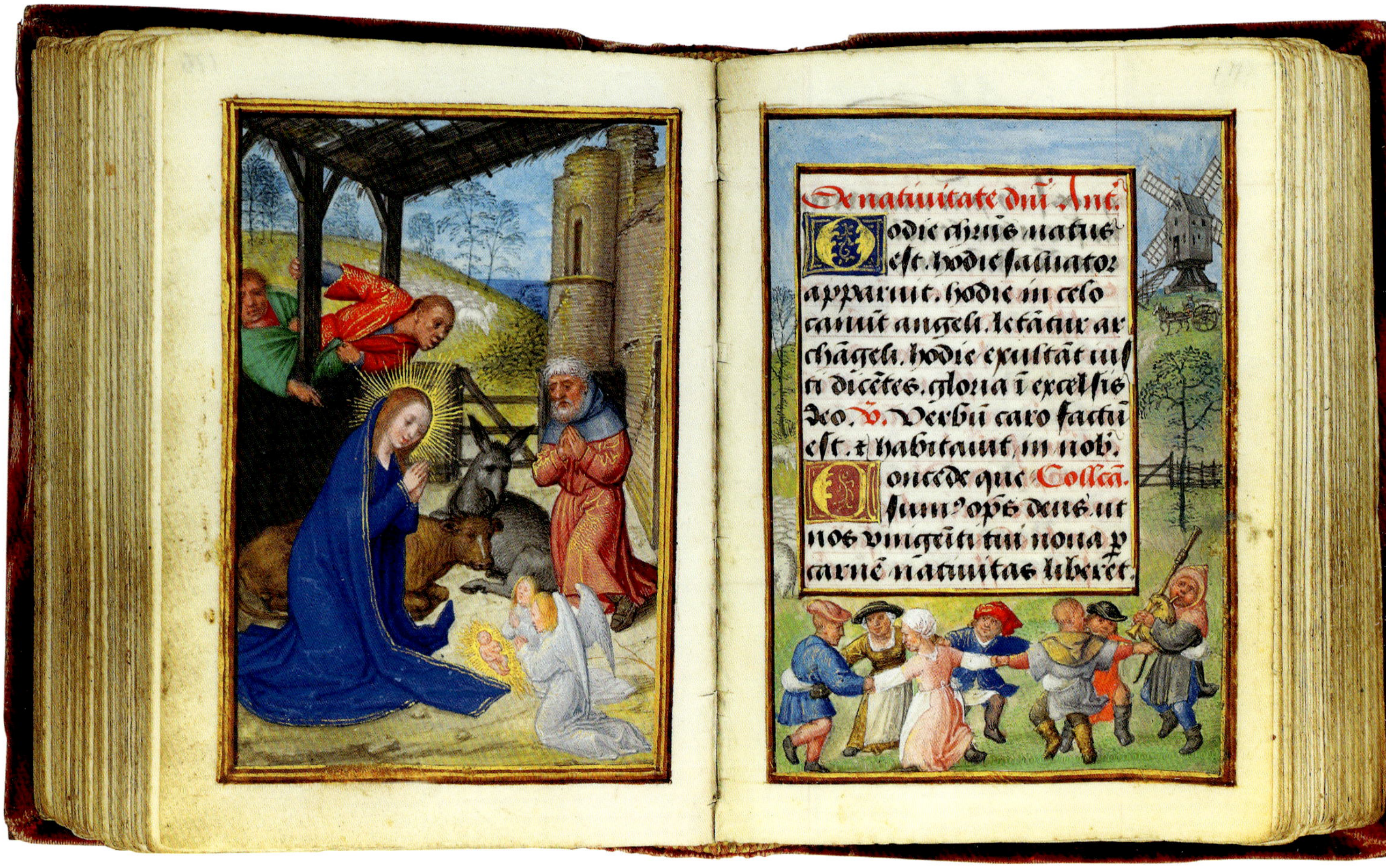

SIMON BENING

•

Pages 176–177 of *The Imhof Prayer Book*, 1511
Illuminated manuscript on vellum,
3½ × 2½ in / 9 × 6.2 cm
Private collection

The Virgin Mary, Joseph, and two kneeling angels clasp their hands in prayer as they bow their heads and gaze at the child of Christ lying before them in a heap of hay (see p.225). Two shepherds crane their necks and reach over the stable wall to try to get a better look at the baby Jesus, while nearby a group of townsfolk celebrate by dancing and playing music in a field. The unusual sight of a windmill in the background of this otherwise traditional Nativity scene perhaps gives a clue to its origins. Illustrated by renowned Belgian illuminator Simon Bening (*c.*1483–1561), *The Imhof Prayer Book* was likely written for a merchant banker, Hans Imhof, in Antwerp in 1511 and features text in Latin and Dutch and eleven full-page miniatures. Among the scenes illustrated include many with a particular focus on Christ, including his arrest and betrayal, the Crucifixion, and his subsequent Resurrection. Like many books of hours, this was likely a functional prayer book and the text would have been recited in church or at home. The text on the recto here opens with a prayer to Christmas, perhaps spoken allowed on Christmas Eve or on Christmas Day. Personal prayer books small enough to be carried in a pocket and kept close by their owners were once very popular and seem to have been Bening's specialty. During his lifetime, he was known as one of the finest illuminators of manuscripts in Europe, and *The Imhof Prayer Book*, his earliest dated work, is seen as one of his most accomplished.

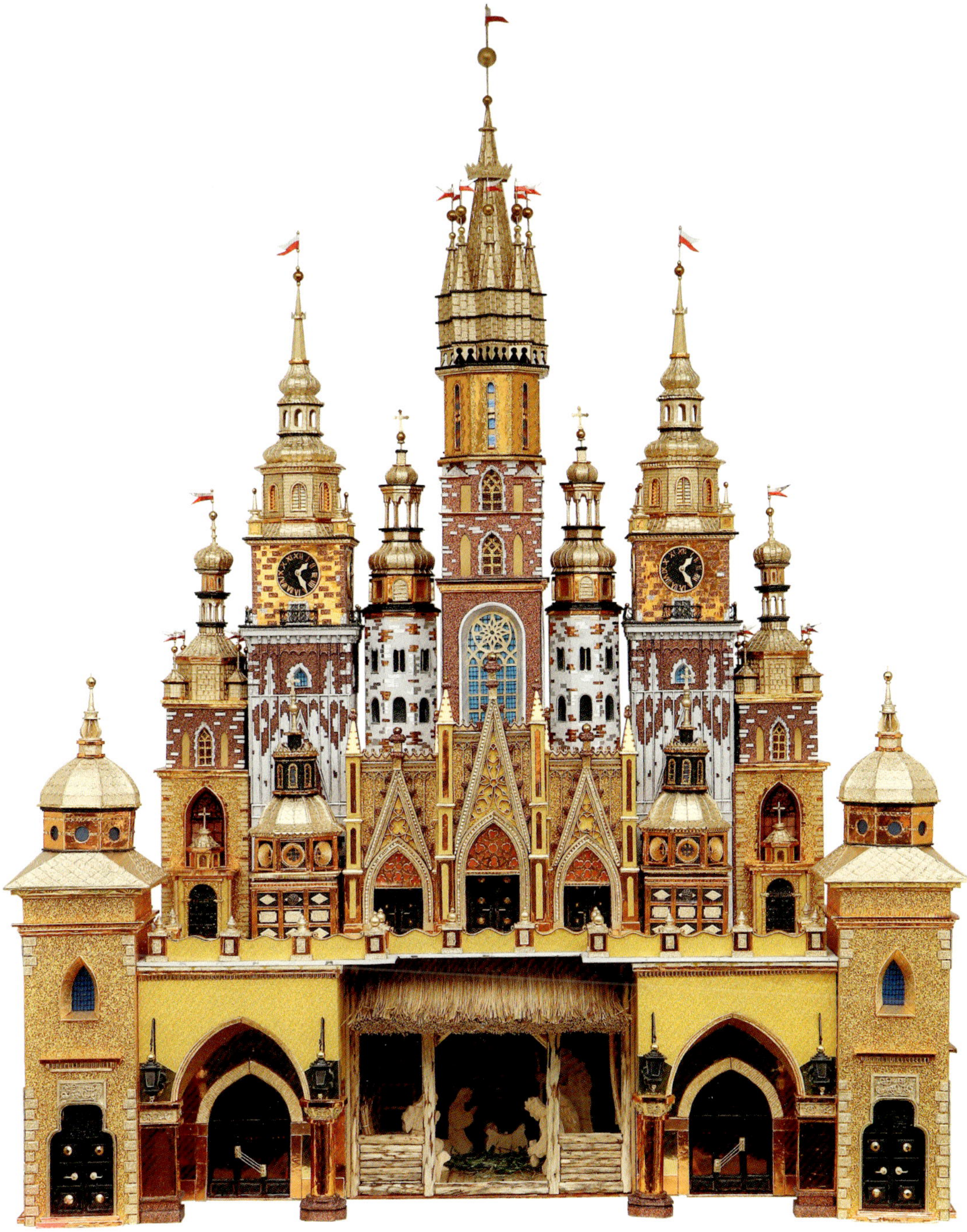

VARIOUS

•

Kraków *Szopka*, 2018
Materials and dimensions variable

Since Christmas 1937, the Polish city of Kraków has mounted an extravagant and unique event every year: a display of hundreds of handmade *szopki* or Nativity scenes (see pp.10, 39, 74). On the first Thursday in December, crowds of Cracovians gather in the city's beautiful main square to study the year's offerings at the foot of the statue of Adam Mickiewicz (1798–1855), the Polish Romantic poet. There are no hard and fast rules about what constitutes *szopki,* which come in materials, from colored aluminum foil to steel and wood, and use a wide range of hues—often the brighter, the better. The convention is, however, that each *szopka* is effectively a miniature representation of Kraków itself. Since the tradition first started in the nineteenth century, when carpenters and bricklayers sought to occupy themselves in the dead of winter, the citizens of Kraków have made the tradition their own with the annual display of flamboyant structures that appear part castle, part Nativity scene, and part marionette theater, ranging from a few inches to several feet tall. A typical *szopka* will contain one or many of Kraków's easily recognizable landmarks, such as Saint Mary's Basilica, Wawel Castle, the trade hall, and Barbican. Some display figurines representing characters—both past and present—from the city. In this example, on the ground floor is a manger scene, a nod to Poland's Catholic heritage. Although the competition is open to everyone, seasoned *szopka* makers will spend most of the year crafting their entries to try to win the first prize.

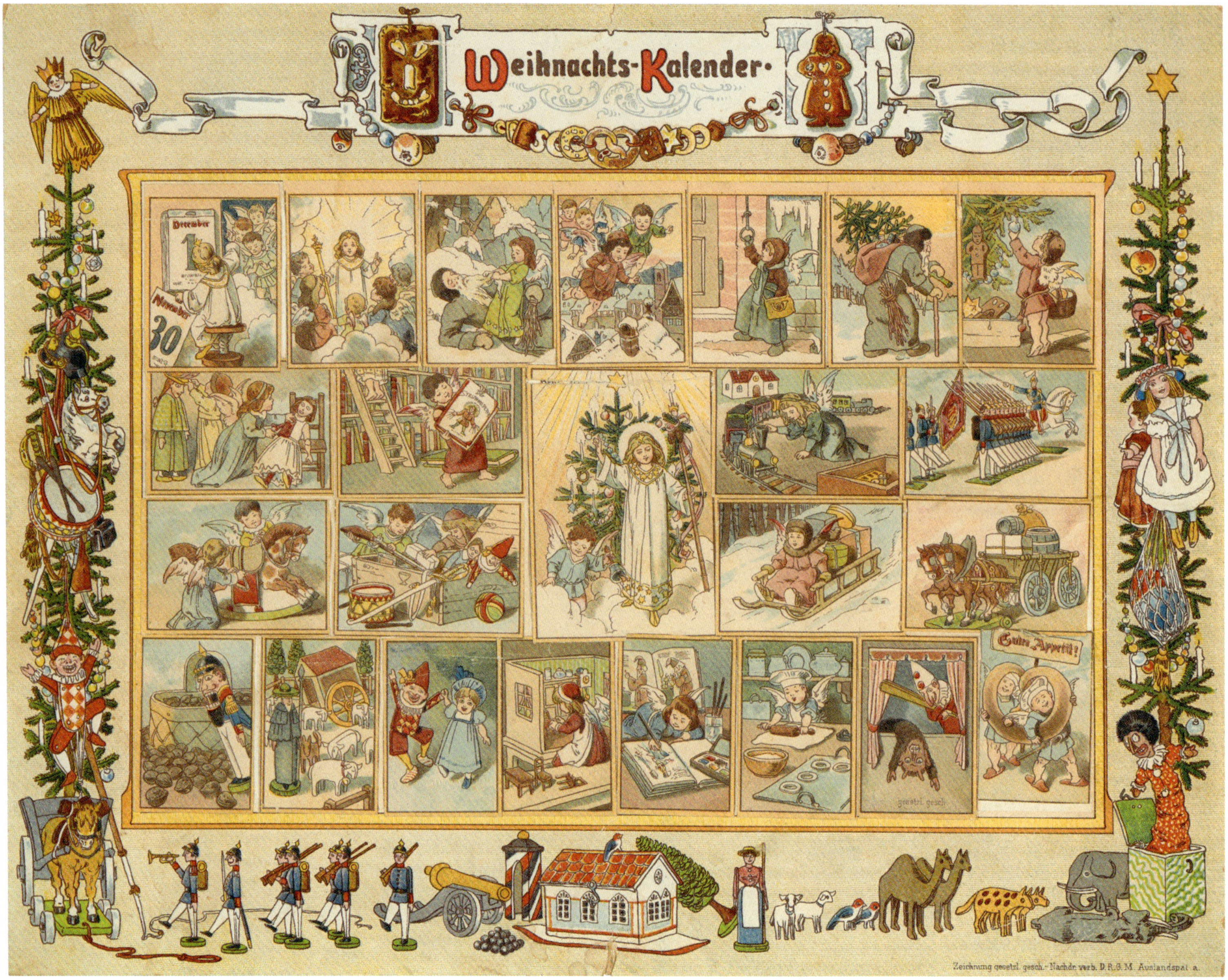

RICHARD ERNST KEPLER

•

In the Land of the Christ Child, c.1910
Illustrated cardstock, dimensions unknown
Produced by Reichhold & Lang, Munich

Scenes of Christmas the Christ Child preparing for Christmas fill this Advent calendar, made in Germany in the early 1900s. Illustrated by German Richard Ernst Kepler (1851–1927), this example of a traditional calendar asks children to cut and paste the twenty-four images seen here onto a seperate piece of cardstock featuing religious script. For many children today, the opening of the first door of an advent calendar on December 1 remains the start of the countdown to Christmas Day. Behind each door, one might typically find a picture, a chocolate, a small gift or toy, or—in Advent calendars for grown-ups—possibly a beauty product, a piece of jewelry, or even an alcoholic drink. The idea of marking the lead-up to Christmas—the word "Advent" comes from the Latin *adventus,* meaning "coming toward"—by chalking marks on the door or lighting candles was already an established German tradition when Gerhard Lang (1881–1974) is said to have conceived of producing paper calendars for his printing firm, Reichhold & Lang. Recalling the childhood thrill when his mother attached twenty-four cookies in separate bags to a piece of cardboard and allowed him to eat one a day during the countdown to Christmas Day, Lang began to devise his own Advent calendars from 1903. Sales were initially slow but took off in the 1920s. Around sixteen million Advent calendars are sold annually in Great Britain alone.

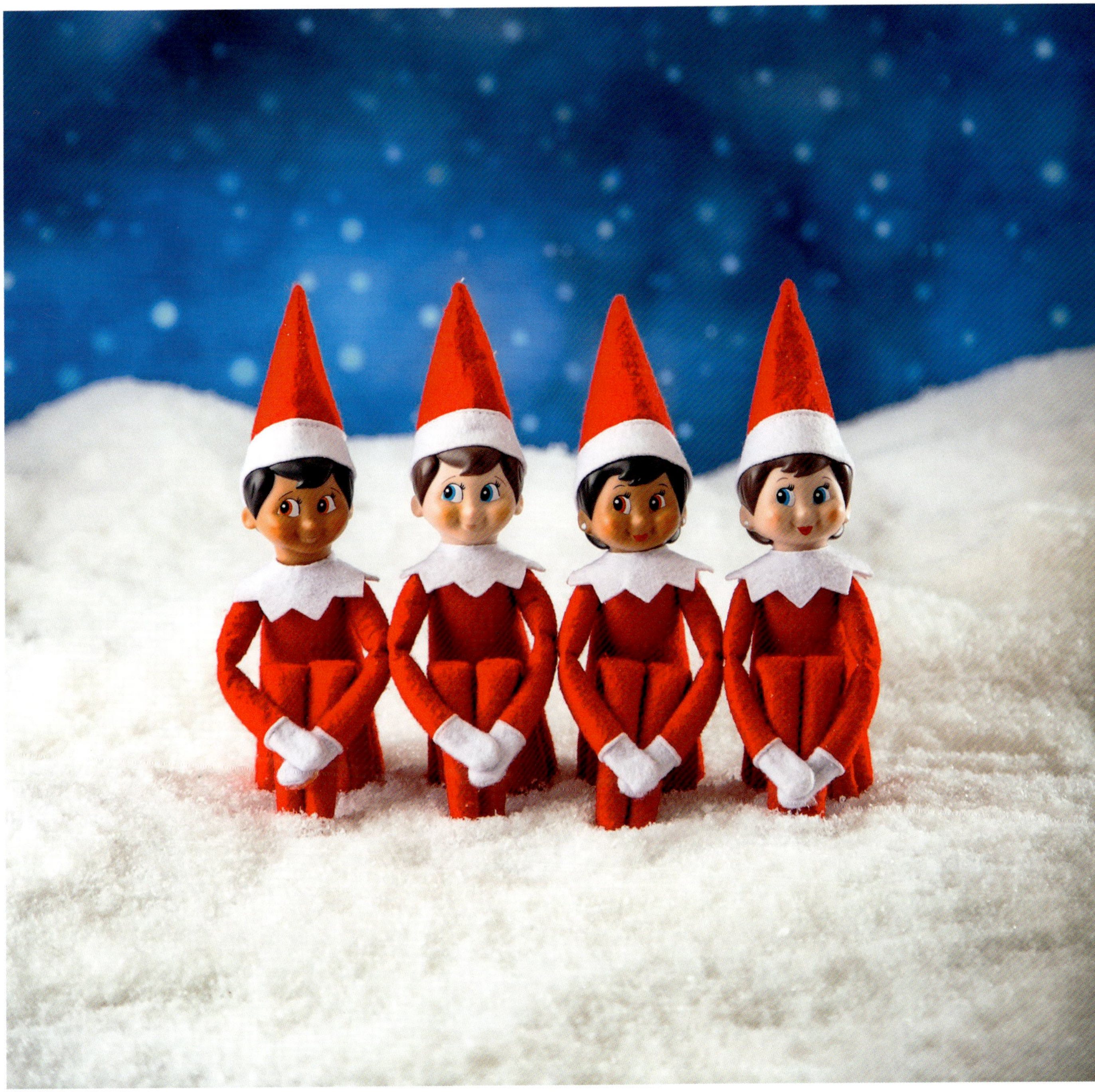

CAROL AEBERSOLD AND CHANDA BELL

•

Scout Elf, 2005
Plastic and felt, 14¼ × 2⅜ in / 36 × 6 cm
The Lumistella Company

When Carol Aebersold (1948–) and her daughter Chanda Bell (1974–) wrote their charming story about an elf who hid in a family's home as Santa's eyes and ears, they never could have known it would become a worldwide phenomenon. They self-published *The Elf on a Shelf: A Christmas Tradition* in 2005, hand-selling it to customers at trade shows and bookstores. With a little luck, word of mouth, and the help of an early celebrity devotee or two, the book took off. A companion doll soon followed, modeled after the kitschy Japanese knee-hugger elves of the 1950s and 1960s, wearing a red suit and a pointy red hat. The Scout Elf is meant to appear on Thanksgiving Day and remain until Christmas, reporting to Santa Claus on whether children have been naughty or nice, and communicating Christmas wishes while changing position within the home daily. But the book states one important caveat: children must not touch the elf, otherwise it may lose its magic and not be able to report back to Santa, leaving the child without any toys on Christmas Day. To date, 17.5 million Scout Elves and counting have been adopted globally. They're also one of Christmastime's most viral objects, photographed in innumerable precarious, unlikely, and hilarious situations. Now an iconic symbol in Christmas celebrations, the Elf on the Shelf tradition helps families create joyful memories and merry moments that last throughout generations.

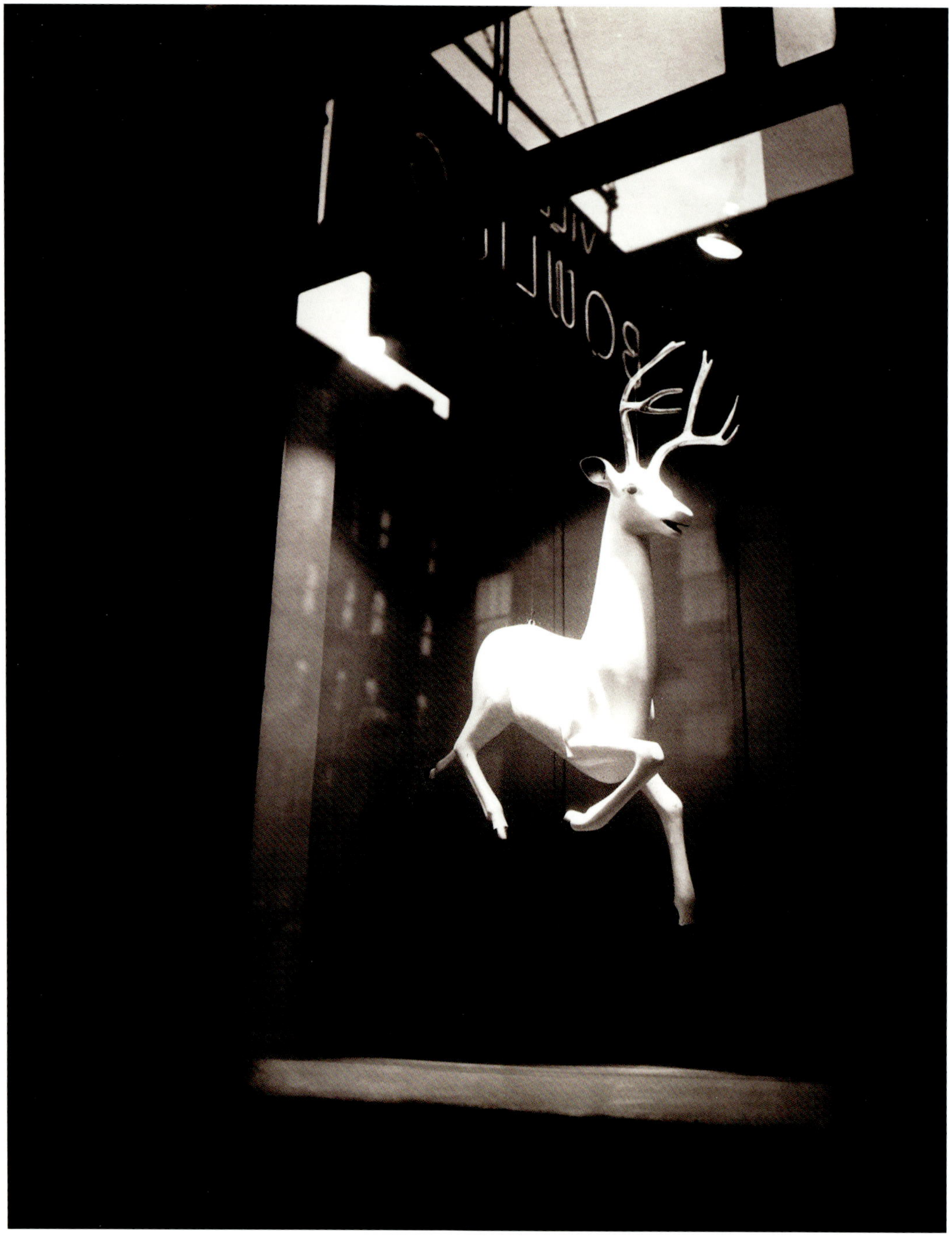

BERENICE ABBOTT

•

Designer's Window, Bleecker Street, 1947
Gelatin silver print, 23 × 18⅞ in / 58.4 × 47.9 cm

The angular composition of this Christmas-themed photograph from 1947 reflects the trademark style of American photographer Berenice Abbott (1898–1991), who typically documented urban life with sophisticated originality. At the center of the composition, a white reindeer is suspended gracefully in a window display on New York's Bleecker Street, which runs between Greenwich Village and the East Village. In the background, strong diagonals allude to the impressive verticality and scale of Manhattan's high-rise buildings. The city is known for celebratory window displays around Christmastime, from Saks Fifth Avenue's famous light show (see p.204) to Bergdorf Goodman's elaborate scenes. This example is the antithesis of these—a simple, elegant reindeer, but with no less festive spirit. Abbott's photography embraced honesty and precise composition, characterized by strong contrasts and shadows as seen in this work. In 1929, a feeling of nostalgia propelled her to return to New York, a city she loved for its endless dynamism and dramatic panorama of skyscrapers and bridges. But rather than focusing on its inhabitants, she turned her lens to the idiosyncratic architecture and urban transformation during the era of the Great Depression. In 1935, Abbott embarked on a photobook titled *Changing New York*—a colossal undertaking that represented a turning point in her career and a milestone in the history of early twentieth-century photography when it was completed in 1940.

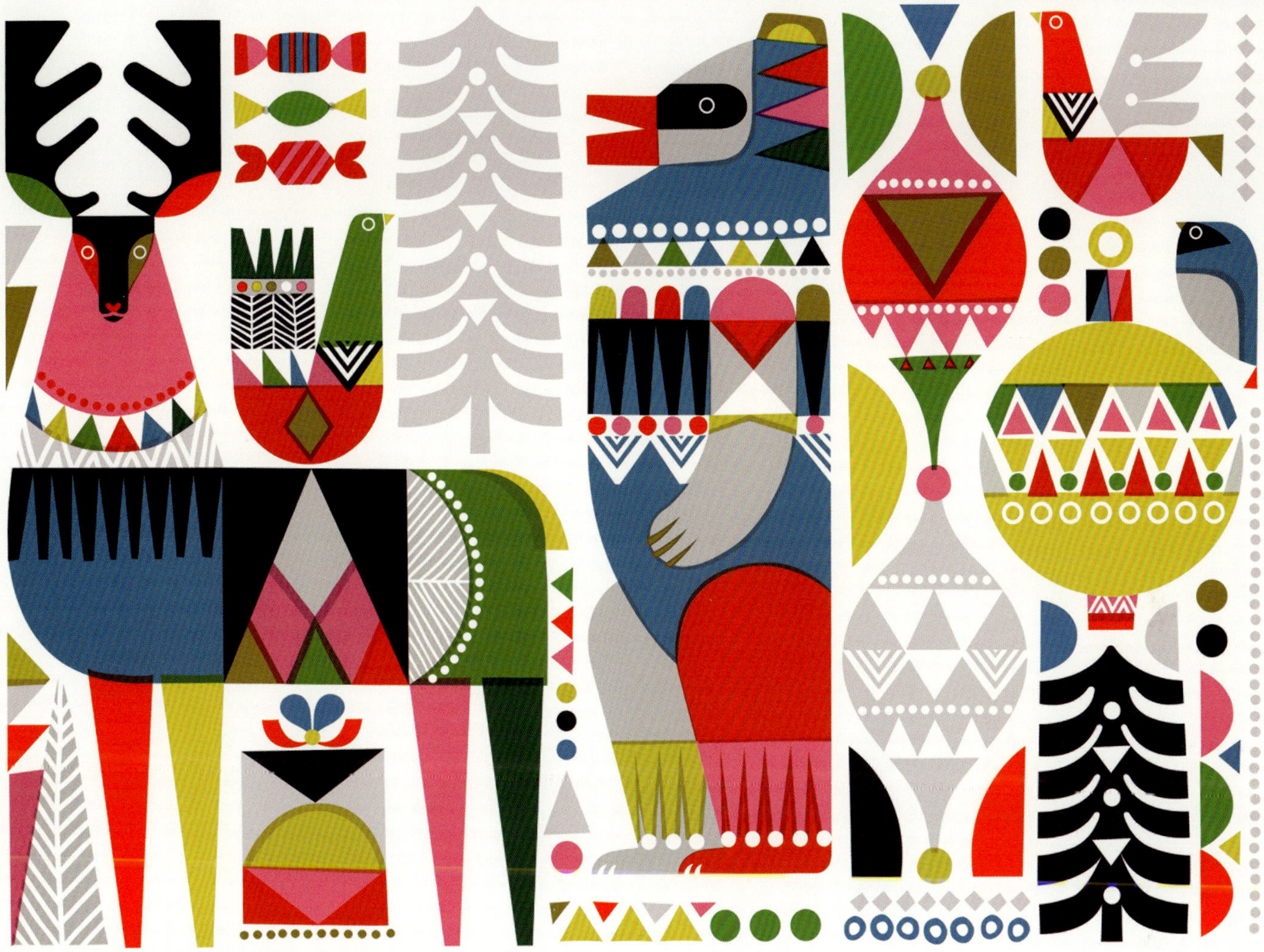

SANNA ANNUKKA

•

Festive branding, 2015
Digital illustration, dimensions variable
For Nordstrom

Department stores around the world celebrate Christmas in a wide variety of ways. From advertisements that have become must-watch short films every year to elaborate multimedia shows and increasingly elaborate window displays that illuminate their storefronts (see pp.204, 227), the festive season, with its massive incentive to spend money, is an important time of year for huge retailers. Nordstrom, the American luxury department store chain, commissioned British-Finnish artist Sanna Annukka to design their festive branding in 2015. The motif seen here shows her exploring symbolic forms closely associated with Christmastime, all rendered in bold, colorful geometric patterns. A reindeer is surrounded by candy and a wrapped present topped with a bow, while monochrome trees, decorated ornaments, and festive birds slide neatly into place alongside each other on the canvas. Nordstrom has strong links to Scandinavia, being founded in 1901 in Seattle, Washington, by Swedish-American businessman John W. Nordstrom, and that shines through in these designs. Annukka attended Brighton University in the UK, where she discovered a passion for printmaking, painting, and illustration. Inspired by her Scandinavian roots, her designs for Nordstrom were applied to everything in store and online, including Christmas cards, decorations, coffee cups, and checkouts, and they also provided the illustrations for their annual Christmas catalog.

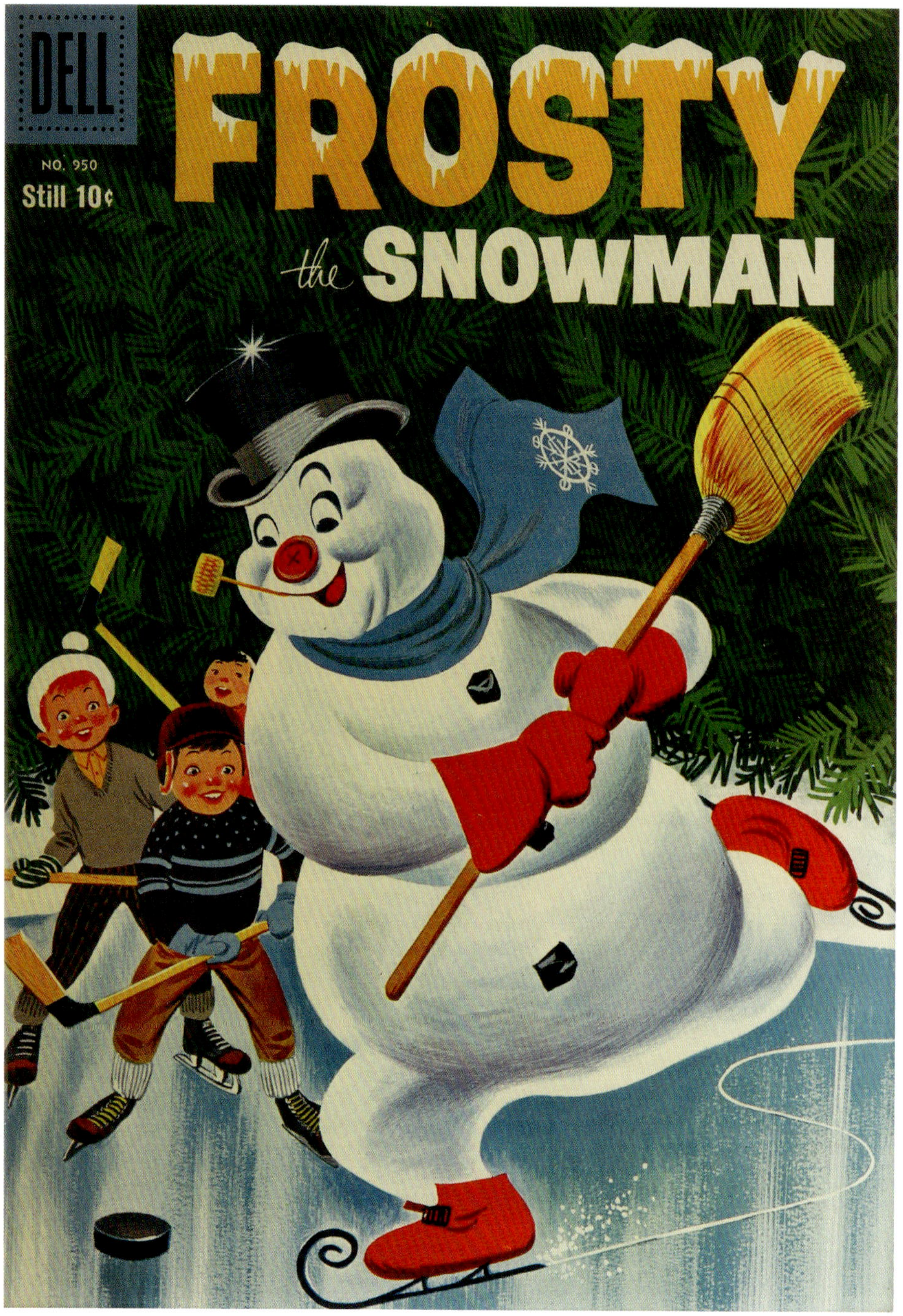

DELL PUBLISHING

•

Frosty The Snowman, 1958
Colored pen and inks, 10½ × 7½ in / 26.7 × 18 cm

Frosty the Snowman is a ubiquitous sight at Christmastime. Originally the title character of a popular seasonal hit song, quick-thinking capitalists seized upon his marketability and spawned a bounty of branded merchandise almost immediately. Comic books were one of the more popular ways to get a Frosty fix. This is issue number 950, published by Dell, and it features six festive stories starring the titular snowman. In one, an owl steals his magic hat, leaving it for Frosty to find on a weathervane high atop a farmer's barn. In another, Frosty begins to melt during an unseasonably warm winter, but one of the local children ingeniously secures him a job in a local ice cream factory, allowing him to stay cool during the warmer days. The song came about after Gene Autry's rendition of Johnny Marks's "Rudolph the Red-Nosed Reindeer" (see p.85) reached number one on the US charts during the week of Christmas in 1949. On the heels of that success, songwriters Walter "Jack" Rollins and Steve Nelson approached Autry in 1950 about recording their new song, "Frosty the Snowman." True to the lyrics of the song, Frosty is often seen wielding his broom—as on the cover of this comic where it stands in for an ice hockey stick—wearing his iconic magic black top hat, with his signature corncob pipe hanging from his mouth. Dell published comics from 1929 until 1974 featuring many well-known characters, such as Pinocchio and Tom and Jerry.

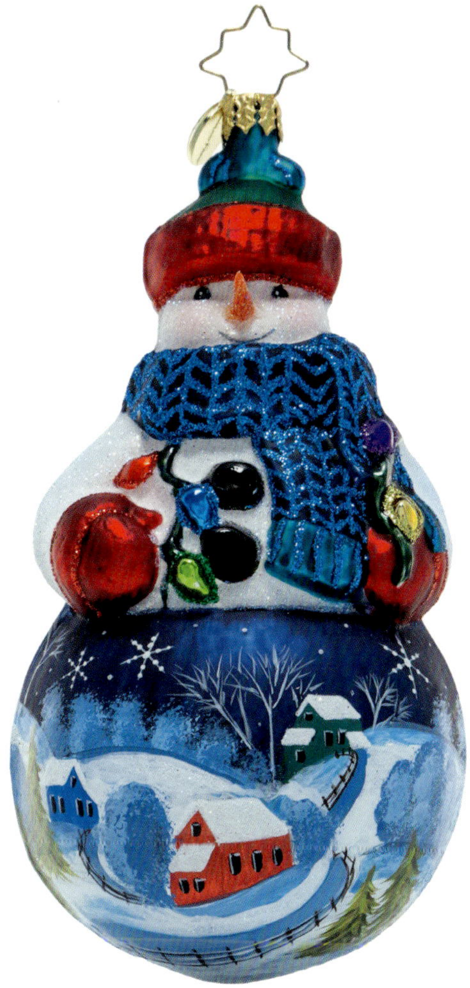

CHRISTOPHER RADKO

•

Winter's Snowy Scene, 2022
Hand-blown European glass,
6 × 3 × 3 in / 15.2 × 7.6 × 7.6 cm

In many American homes, including those of Oprah Winfrey and Dolly Parton, the Christmas tree is only truly ready when that year's Christopher Radko glass bauble has been added to its laden boughs. This example from 2022 shows a snowman bundled up in scarf and hat, a snowy landscape sketched across his bulbous body. Each year, around five hundred new glass Christmas and holiday ornaments are launched by the man the *New York Times* called the "Czar of the Christmas Present." Designed in the United States, the glass decorations are created in a process that takes seven days and guarantees that no two baubles are alike. Each bauble is hand-blown (see p.28) before the cooled glass undergoes a silvering process to give the decoration its luminosity. After painting, the baubles are further embellished by hand, and the essential glitter added. These different processes ensure the unique quality of each decoration. Over the years, Christopher Radko ornaments have become highly desirable collector's items, not least because 40 percent of each year's designs are instantly retired. Their exclusivity is all the more remarkable given that Radko started his company following the collapse of his family's Christmas tree stand in 1984, which shattered many of the one thousand European, glass-blown ornaments collected by four generations of the family. Unable to find like-for-like replacements, Radko started his own ornaments company and had them lovingly remade by hand in Poland.

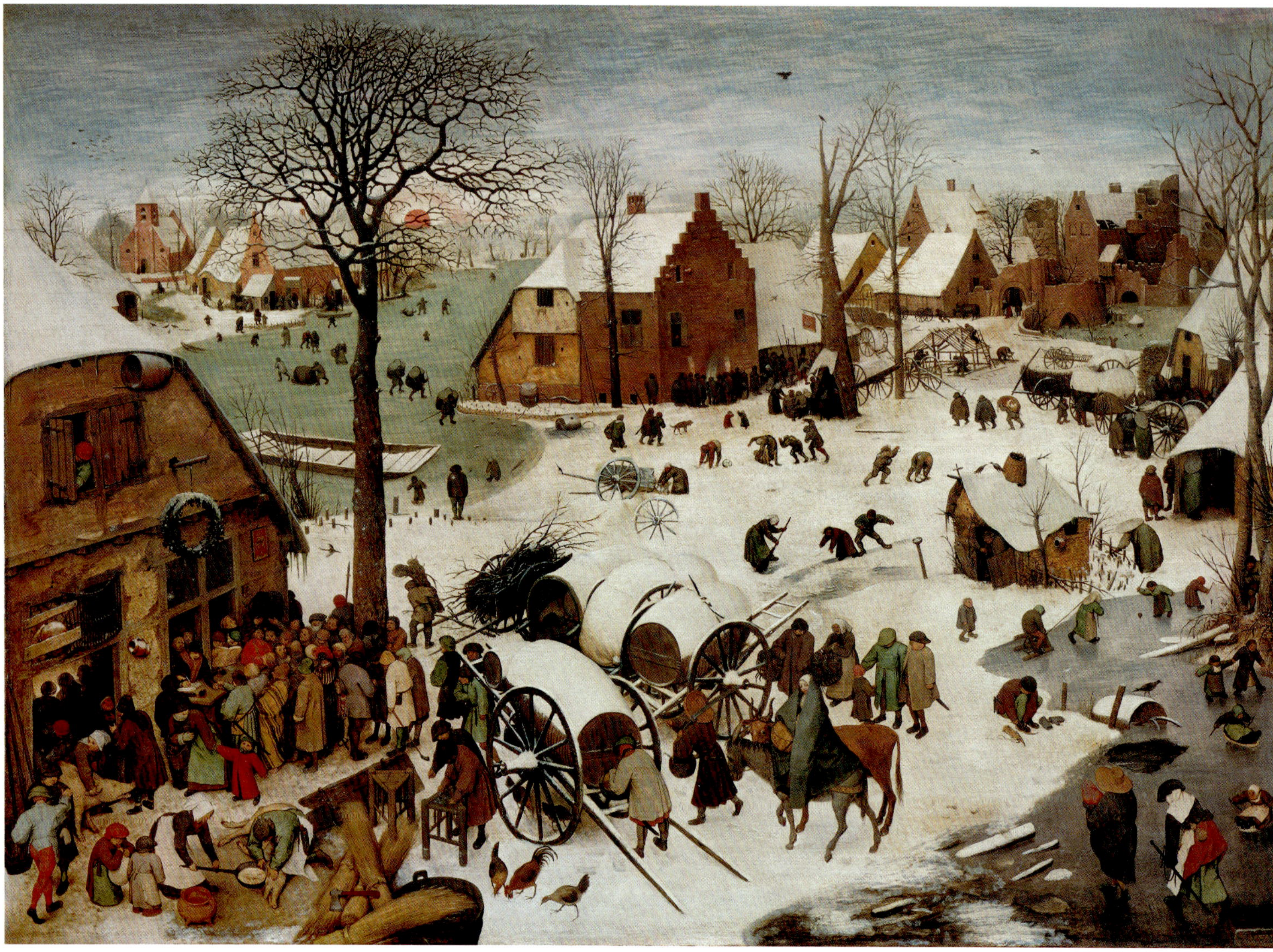

PIETER BRUEGEL THE ELDER

•

The Census at Bethlehem, 1566
Oil on panel, 46 × 64.8 in / 116 × 164.5 cm
Royal Museums of Fine Arts of Belgium, Brussels

As the sun sets beyond the snowy rooftops, this wintry Flemish village is teeming with activity. Men and women trudge across the frozen river, carrying out their chores, while others stop to enjoy a drink; children play games in the snow and skate on makeshift toboggans (see p.70). In the foreground, a crowd gather at a tavern to pay their taxes, while a pregnant woman riding on a donkey is led by her betrothed husband. Were it not for the title, it would be easy to overlook this painting's biblical theme, taken from the second chapter of Luke's Gospel (see pp.10, 14, 106), in which Mary and Joseph leave their home in Nazareth and travel to Bethlehem to register in a census for tax purposes. In choosing to transpose the story from first-century Judea to sixteenth-century northern Europe, Pieter Bruegel the Elder (*c.*1525–1569) treats this prologue to the birth of Christ as a contemporary event, providing an intimate glimpse into everyday Flemish life. Despite playing a significant role in the Nativity story, this was the first painting to tackle the episode. The inclusion of a small red-and-yellow sign on the tavern wall bearing the Habsburg imperial two-headed eagle references the unjust taxes forced upon the Flemish by Philip II of Spain (1527–1598). It is balanced by the Virgin dressed in blue, whose presence points to the hope of the coming Christ, the redeemer and liberator of the poor and oppressed.

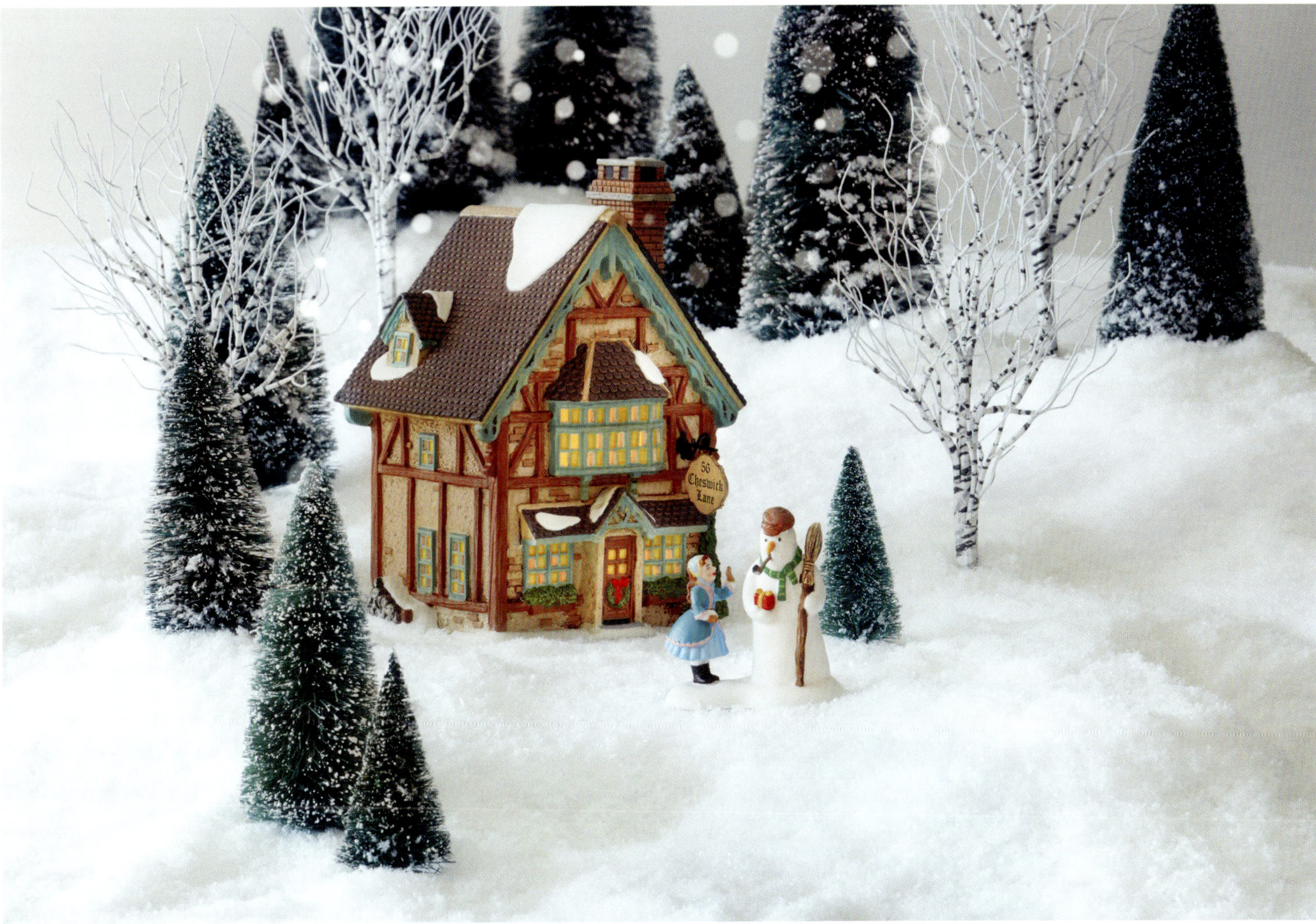

DEPARTMENT 56

•

56 Cheswick Lane scene, c.2010
Hand-painted porcelain, dimensions variable

Lights shine from the windows of this hand-painted ceramic model building, a wreath hanging from its door (see p.143), as a young girl puts the finishing touches to her snowman, evoking a powerful nostalgia for Christmases past. This Victorian festive scene is part of the Dickens' Village series, produced by Department 56. The US company was founded one Christmas in the early 1970s, when a group of employees from an upmarket Minneapolis florist, Bachman's, drove out of town for dinner at a country inn. As they turned a corner, ahead of them lay a small village, the houses glowing against the glistening snow. At dinner, they reminisced about Christmases past and had the idea of creating a miniature lighted village. In 1976, Department 56—the number of the department for which they had worked at Bachmans—produced its first series of six hand-painted ceramic buildings, named the Original Snow Village. In 1984, they launched the Dickens' Village series, the work of father and daughter Neilan and Barbara Lund, which consisted of seven shops and a church. The popularity of the Dickens' Village ensured that the set was added to and is still updated every year with new models. Meanwhile, Department 56's series of highly collectible miniature scenes has expanded to include a Harry Potter village and an alpine village among many others, and setting up a village at home has become a Christmas tradition in many American families.

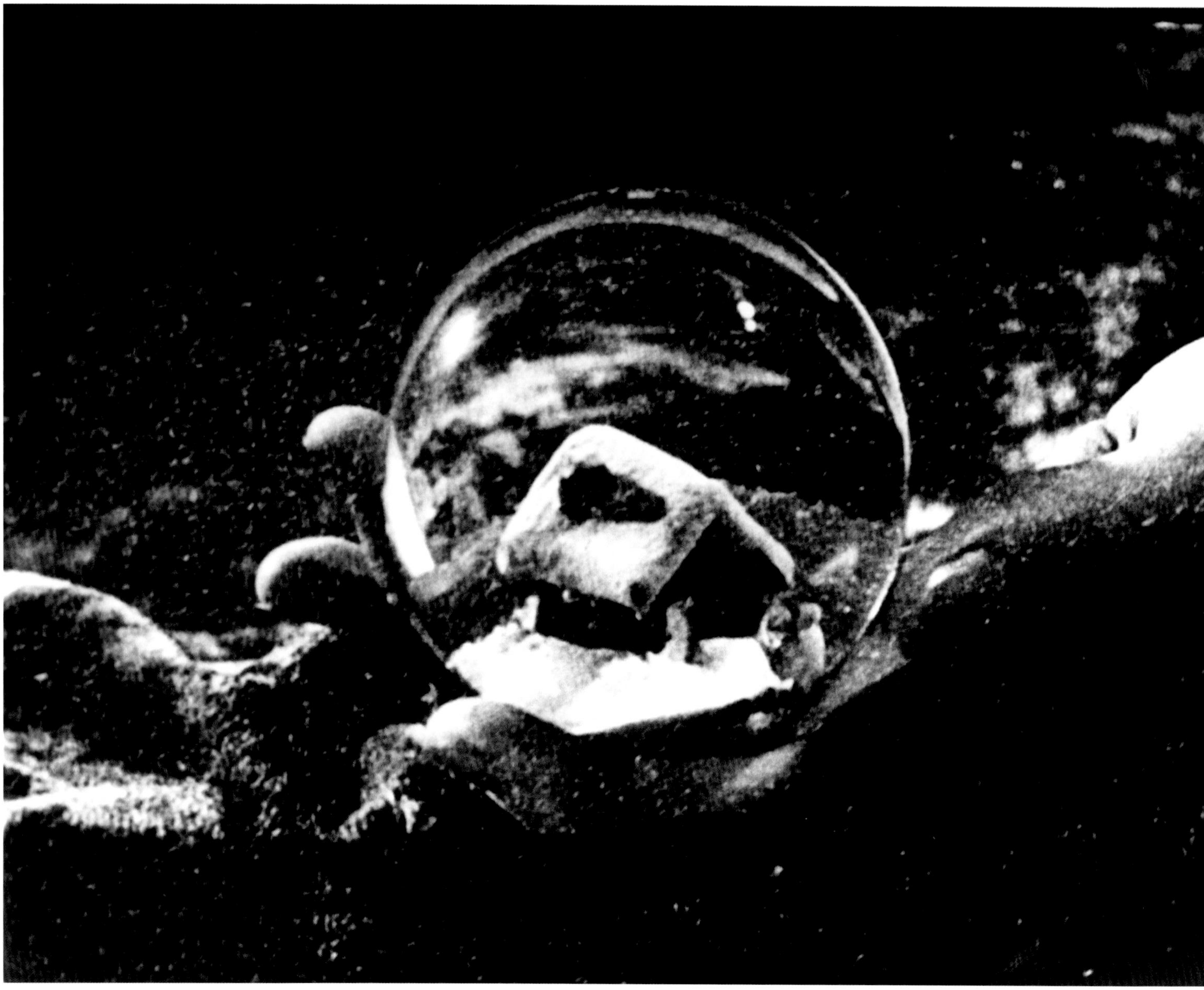

ORSON WELLES

•

Still from *Citizen Kane*, 1941
Film, dimensions variable
RKO Radio Pictures / Mercury Productions

There is something magical about a snow globe. A world inside a glass bubble, perfect and calm, it encapsulates an idealized moment in time. It also affords the owner the power to create a white Christmas, no matter where in the world they live. That kind of control isn't easy to come by; perhaps that's why this holiday decoration remains so popular and nostalgic. This still from the 1941 classic film *Citizen Kane* by Orson Welles (1915–1985), shows a very famous example of the snow globe. In the movie, the title character, Charles Foster Kane, an incredibly wealthy newspaper publisher and magnate, connects to his childhood through the snow globe. It represents a safe, happy moment before he became rich and powerful, and the metaphor continues to play out over the course of the film. No matter how much wealth or power Kane amasses, he can't buy the one thing that would bring him comfort—the chance to travel back in time to the moment he recalls when holding the snow globe. The original prop used in the film was made by Austrian Erwin Perzy (1876–1960), who is credited with creating the first ever snow globe in the early twentieth century. The same Viennese family business that made that most famous of globes continues to create these magic orbs, harnessing the family know-how and craftsmanship of more than a century. Many people dream of a white Christmas (see p.58) and the snow globe, unlike anything else in the world of holiday decor, helps them make that dream come true.

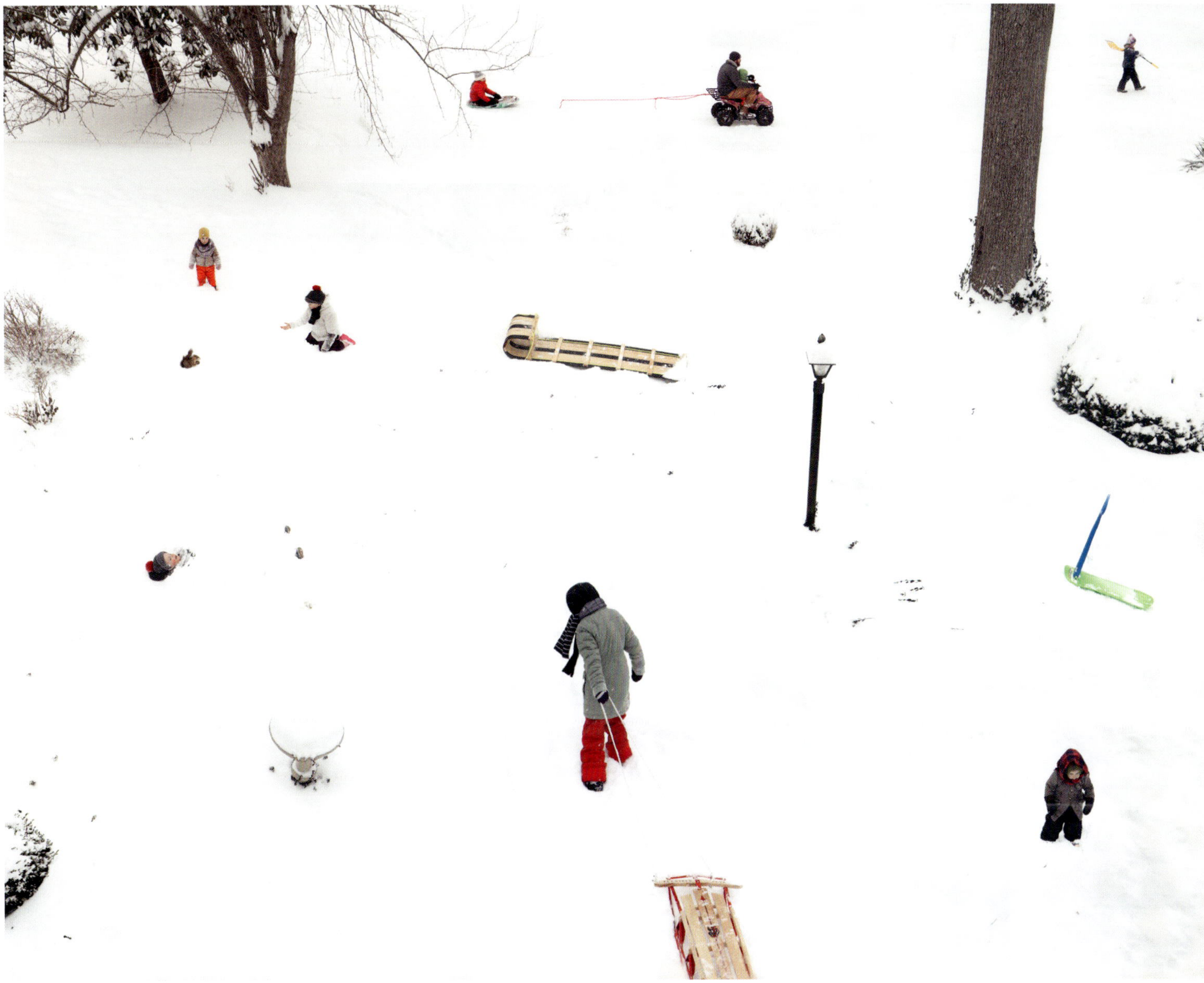

JULIE BLACKMON

•

Snow Days, 2021
Archival pigment print, dimensions variable

On a cold winter's day, a group of children appear to be playing in the snow in this photograph by the Springfield, Missouri, native Julie Blackmon (1966–). However, look more closely and it becomes apparent that there is more to the deceptively simple image. Shot from above, Blackmon's photograph shows a group of young kids taking advantage of a snow day when the schools are closed, every child's dream when they are growing up—spending a day making snow angels and sledding down a large hill. Each child is engaged in his or her own activity, separated by an abundance of snow. On closer examination, they seem to become more of a tableau and their activities, although all traditional wintery games and fun, take on a surreal quality: while one child near the center of the image pulls a toboggan (see p.70), another has been buried lying down in the snow, with only their head and feet visible, as one might do on the beach. Another kneels in the snow playing with a squirrel, while the figures in the background and a buried streetlight suggest a distortion of scale. Blackmon is inspired by her roles as a mother and as a lifetime resident of Springfield to photograph everyday life with her own distinctive approach. Her image is both calm but verging on the bizarre, both domestic and yet epic in scale. Blackmon lays out an unspecified narrative from which the viewer can construct their own story.

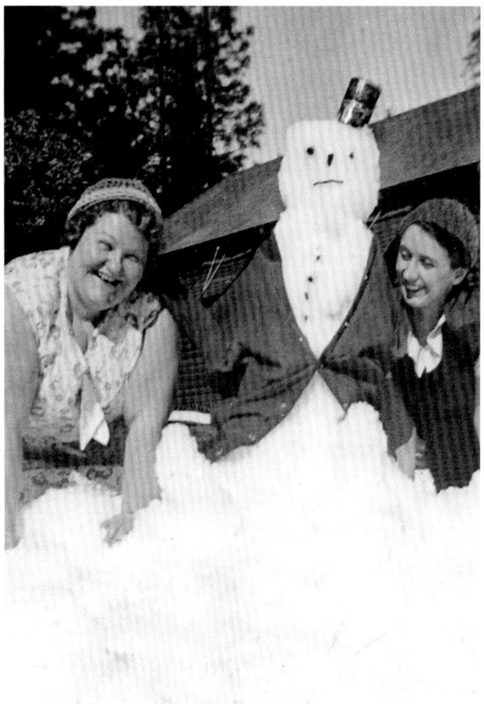
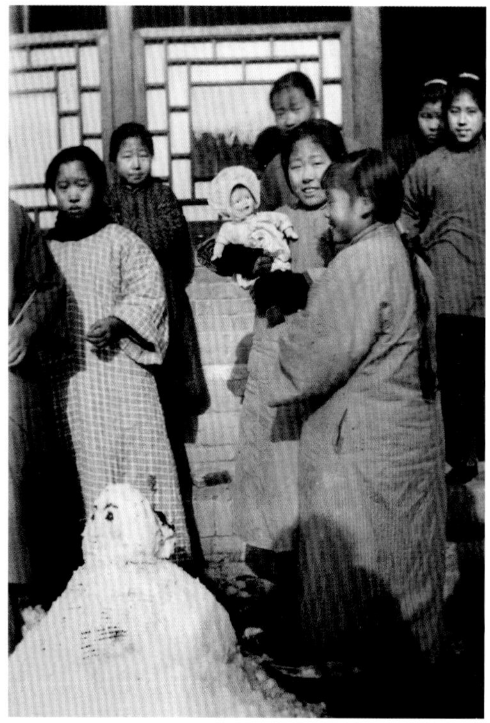
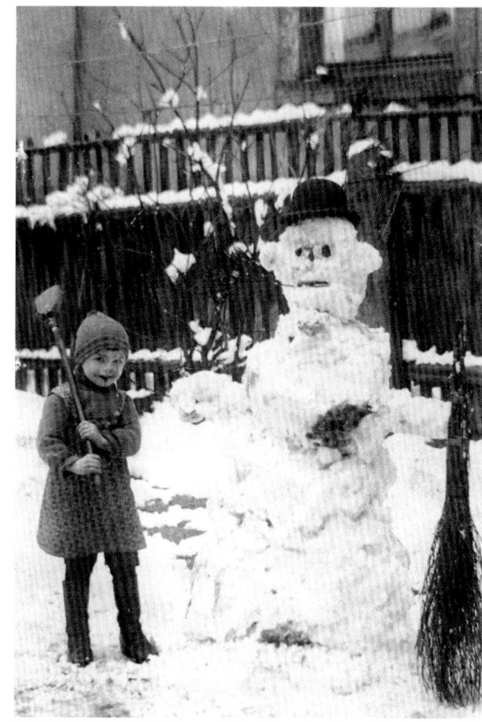

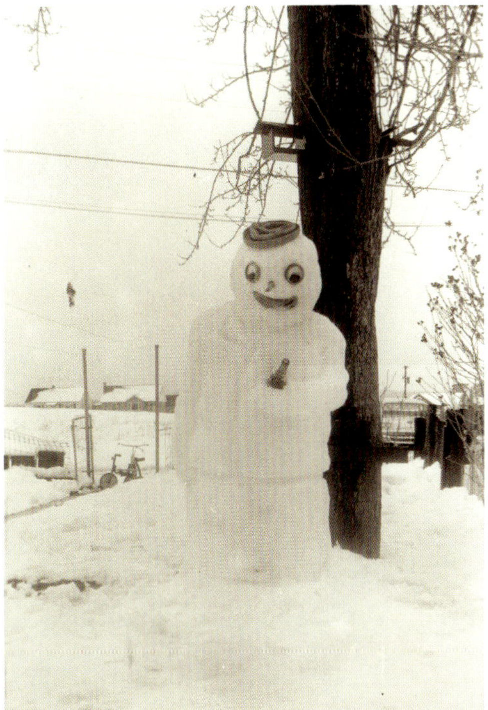

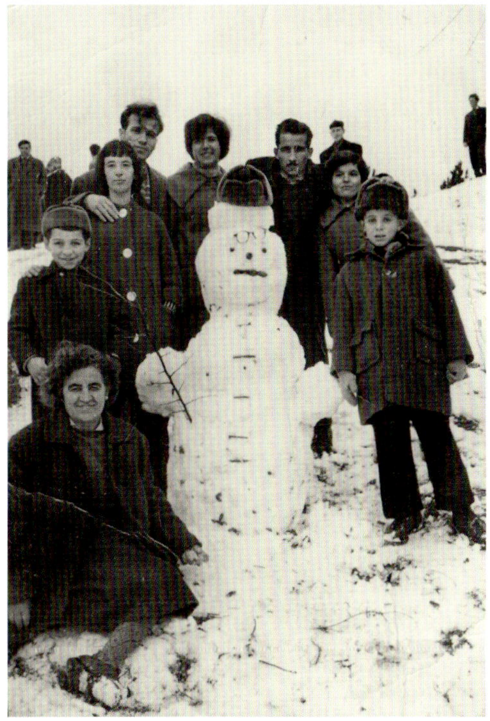

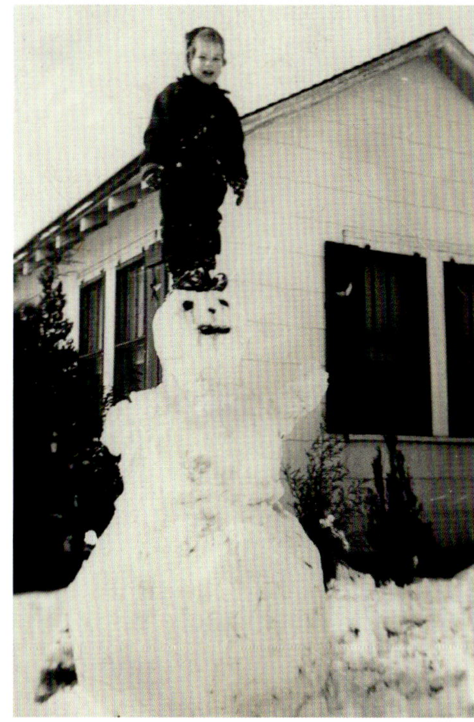

ERIC OGLANDER

•

Snowman photograph collection, c.19th century
Vernacular photographs, dimensions variable

A photograph of a snowman is perhaps the ultimate irony, permanently capturing the most ephemeral part of a cold, wintry Christmas. Snow melts and no snowman lasts forever—but the image lives on. American artist Eric Oglander (1987–) has long been captivated by the transience of snowmen and the enthusiasm with which all kinds of people build them. His obsession dates back to finding a snowman photo on eBay. Oglander recalls, "After I saw one, I started buying every snowman I found compelling." The result is a collection of hundreds of black-and-white photographs dating back to the late 1800s, not just of snowmen but also of the people who built them. The snowmen builders largely come from middle- and upper-middle-class families from both North America and Europe, but also from as far away as China. The photographs radiate happiness, humor, and playfulness; the snowmen are dressed up and one is even cradling a bottle. Each image is unique and yet they are all linked by the central snowy figure. They are also precious, reflecting a time when each image was valuable because of its cost and the finite number of images in a roll of film, unlike today's limitless picture taking. For Oglander, creator of the viral Instagram account "Craigslist Mirrors," the snowmen images are vernacular photography (see p.164) at its best, or what he calls "melting folk art"—a record of lifestyles as transient as the snowmen (see p.57) themselves.

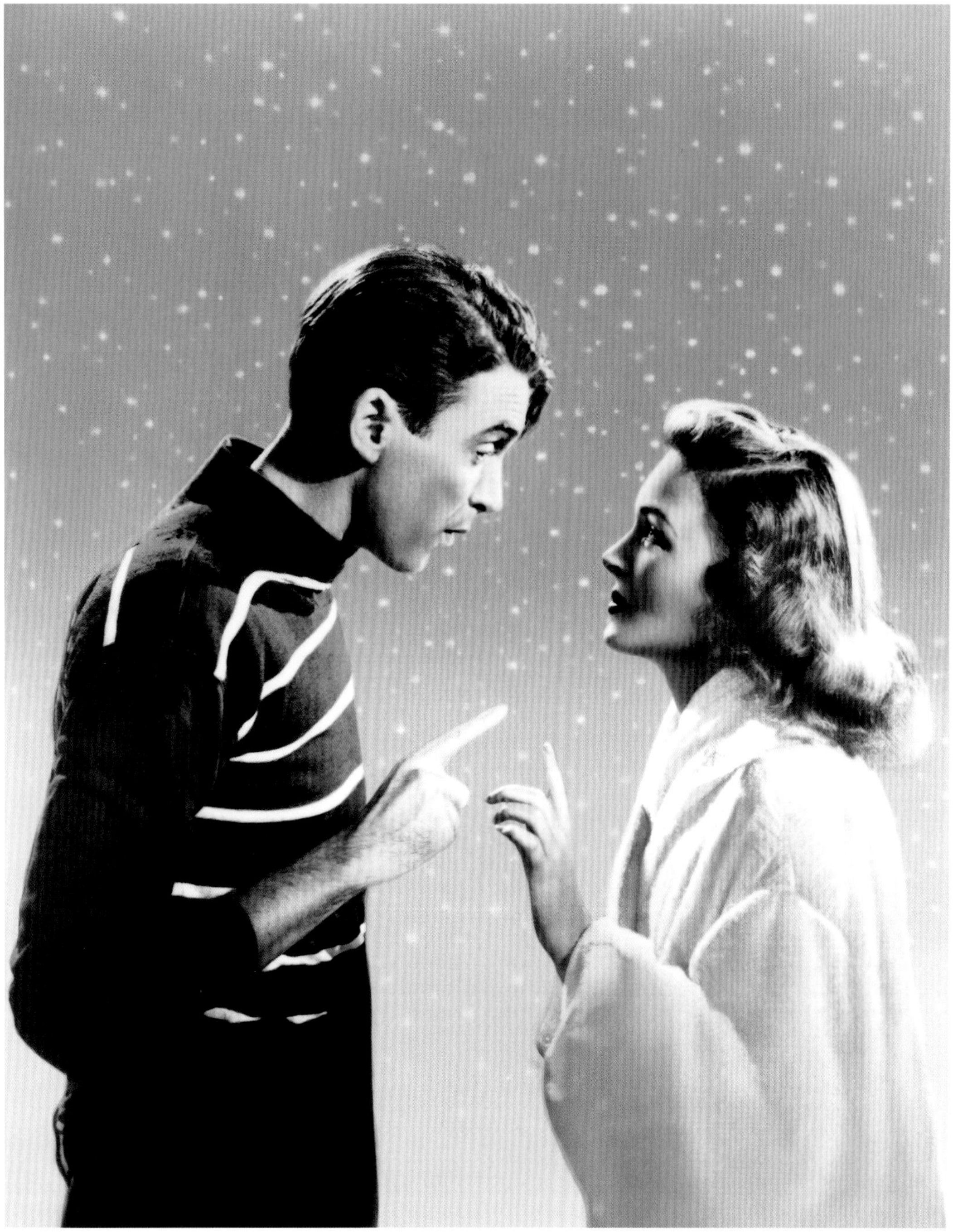

FRANK CAPRA

•

Still from *It's a Wonderful Life*, 1946
Film, dimensions variable
Liberty Film

Against falling snow, young George Bailey, played by James Stewart, talks with his future wife, Mary Hatch, played by Donna Reed, in the 1946 classic *It's a Wonderful Life*. For a favorite that is now watched as an annual celebration of the Christmas spirit in many households, the movie had a difficult creation. Based on a short story by US author Philip Van Doren Stern—itself based loosely on *A Christmas Carol* by Charles Dickens (see p.79)—the story was rejected by Cary Grant, for whom it was originally intended. After the screenplay was repeatedly rewritten, including by the celebrated wit Dorothy Parker, the film was released to little immediate success, despite the presence of Stewart and Reed and the direction of Frank Capra (1897–1991). The film tells the story of George, who has foregone a glittering career to run his family's loan business in the small town of Bedford Falls, achieving limited success. Convinced that his life is a failure, he attempts suicide one Christmas Eve. An "angel second class" named Clarence intervenes and shows George the positive impact he's had by revealing how Bedford Falls would have changed for the worse if George had not lived. Realizing the value of family and friends, George concludes that it is, indeed, a wonderful life. In the final scene, a bell rings on the Christmas tree, signifying that Clarence has earned his angel wings. The film's importance in American cultural history saw it added to the Library of Congress's Film Registry in 1990.

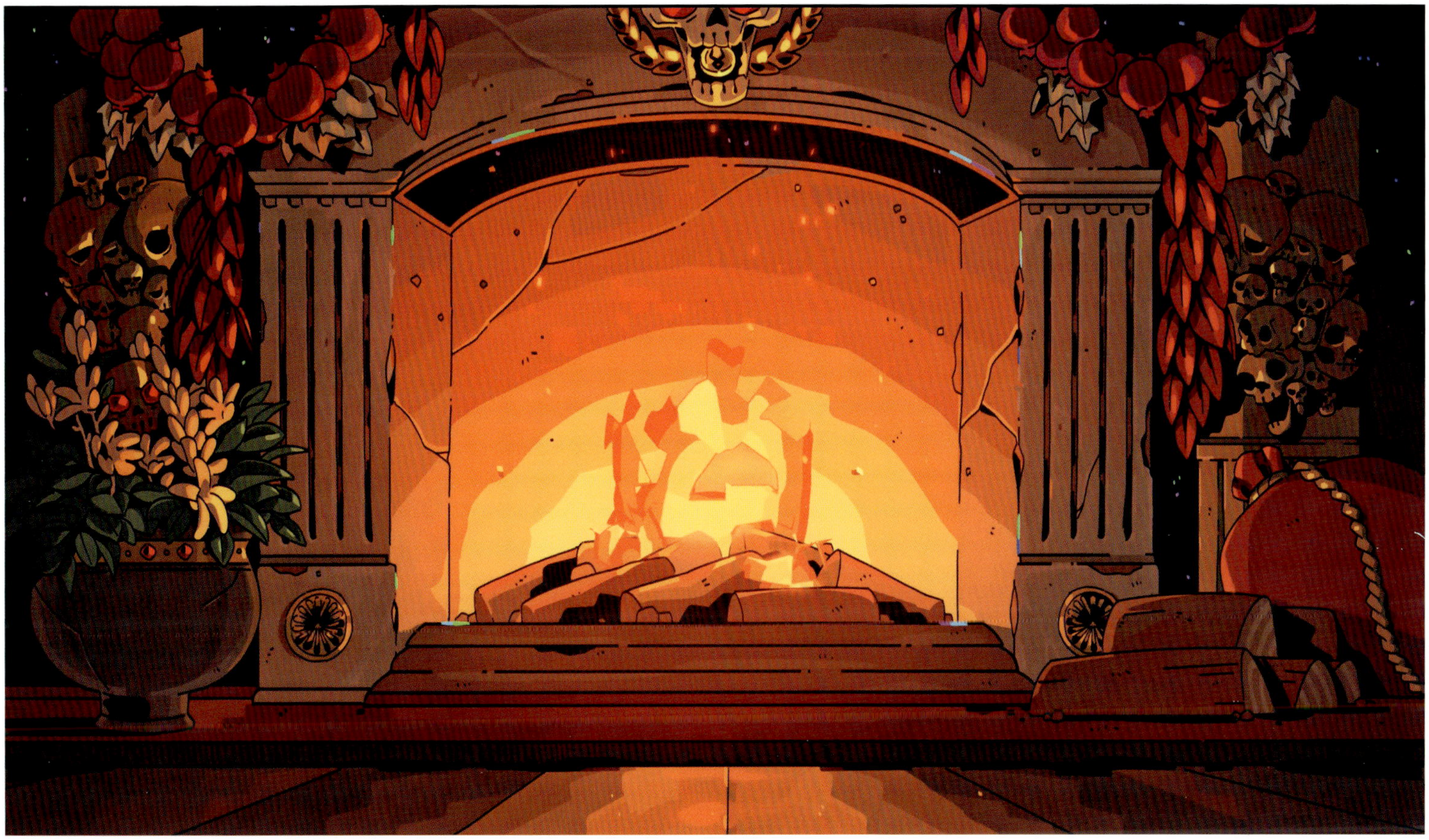

SUPERGIANT GAMES

•

Still of House of Hades Yule log, 2020
Digital animation, dimensions variable

The tradition of the Yule log, where a specially selected log is burned on a hearth on Christmas Eve, is an ancient practice, taking place long before Christmas as it is now celebrated existed. Early celebrants burned the log during *jól*, a Norse festival that commemorated the winter solstice and welcomed the return of longer days. Over the centuries, the pagan tradition intermingled with Christian rituals, and ultimately the terms Christmastime and Yuletide became conflated. A traditional Christmas Yule log, often a large tree, was meant to burn throughout the twelve days of Christmas (see p.17), spanning from Christmas Day to the Epiphany. Today, though, for many, the idea of the Yule log is a more secular concept that conjures the sentimental feelings of cozying up to the fireplace with loved ones on a snowy Christmas Day. "The Yule Log," first aired in 1966, was the brainchild of Fred Thrower, station manager at WPIX-TV in New York; instead of running dead air on Christmas, the station ran footage of a roaring fire, allowing those in homes without to enjoy the tradition. The entire package was a seventeen-second affair, run in a continuous loop. The choice of onscreen fire today is much more varied. Streaming and video services, such as Netflix and YouTube, offer various options in high definition, some running for twenty-four hours. This example is from the video game Hades, developed by Supergiant Games.

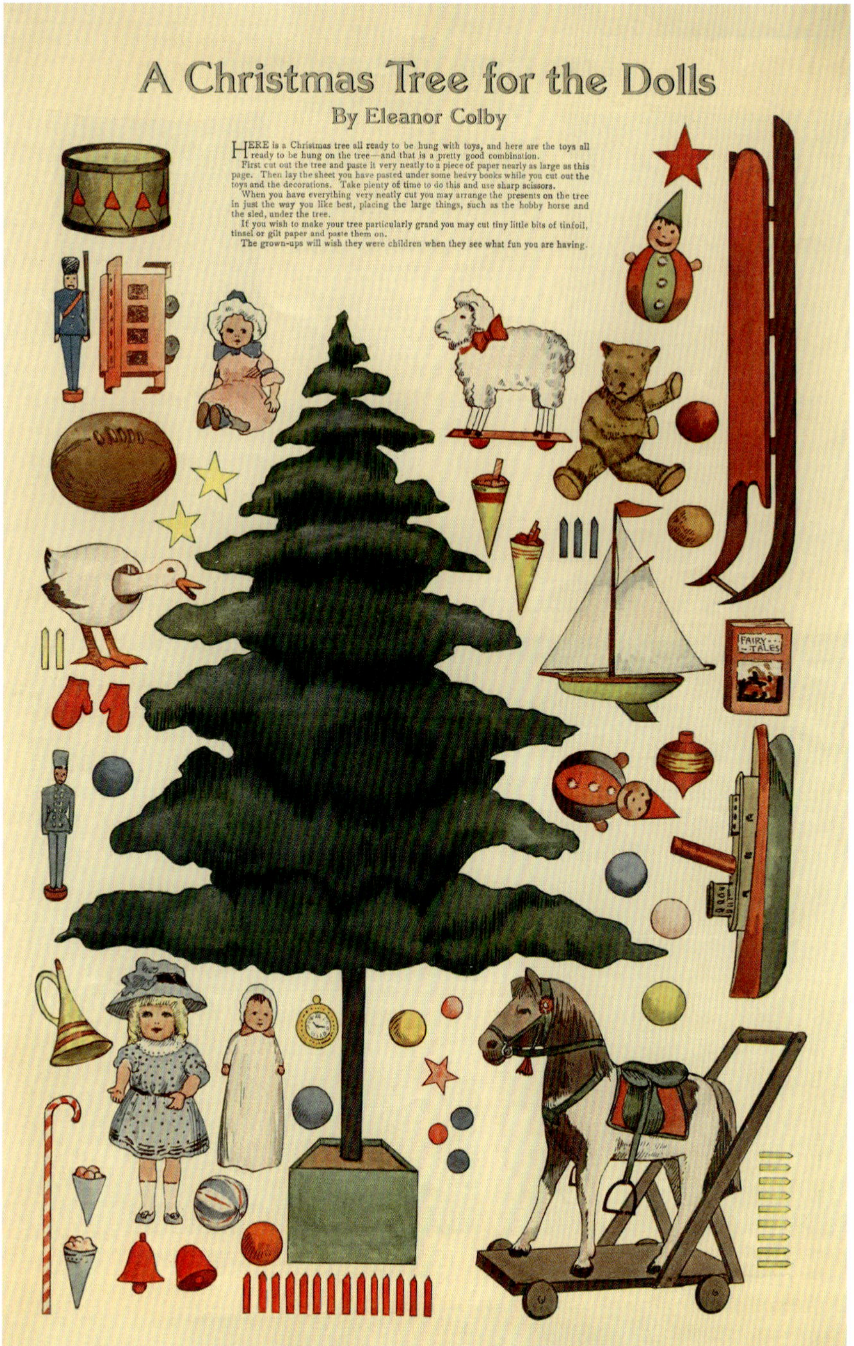

LOU ELEANOR COLBY

•

A Christmas Tree for the Dolls, 1911
Printed paper, dimensions variable
The Strong National Museum of Play, New York

A slightly bossy set of instructions appears at the top of the page of this 1911 cutout-and-make paper Christmas tree for a doll's house (see p.131). The work of pioneering American art teacher Lucy (Lou) Eleanor Colby (1870–1956), the paper toy was intended to be both fun and educational. Colby's instructions tell the children how to first cut out the tree, making sure the scissors are sharp, and then the many other toys and Christmas decorations of various sizes, including a sled, a nutcracker, a candy cane, and baubles for the tree. The flat paper cutouts were then intended to be glued onto a firmer base before they were ready for playing with. Colby's day job was as assistant supervisor of drawing for schools in St. Louis, Missouri. In 1909, she published *Talks on Drawing, Painting, Making, Decorating, For Primary Teachers,* which she intended as a helpful companion for art teachers. The book was ahead of its time. Colby argued that there was no set way of teaching a child to draw, paint, or make things: what mattered was that they were taught *how* to hold a paintbrush or, as was needed here, to cut properly using sharp scissors. Paper toys were not new; the Japanese had perfected the art of making toys with origami (which means "to fold paper") but the popularity of paper toys took off in the nineteenth century as the costs of printing and paper fell, making this the ideal gift for Christmas.

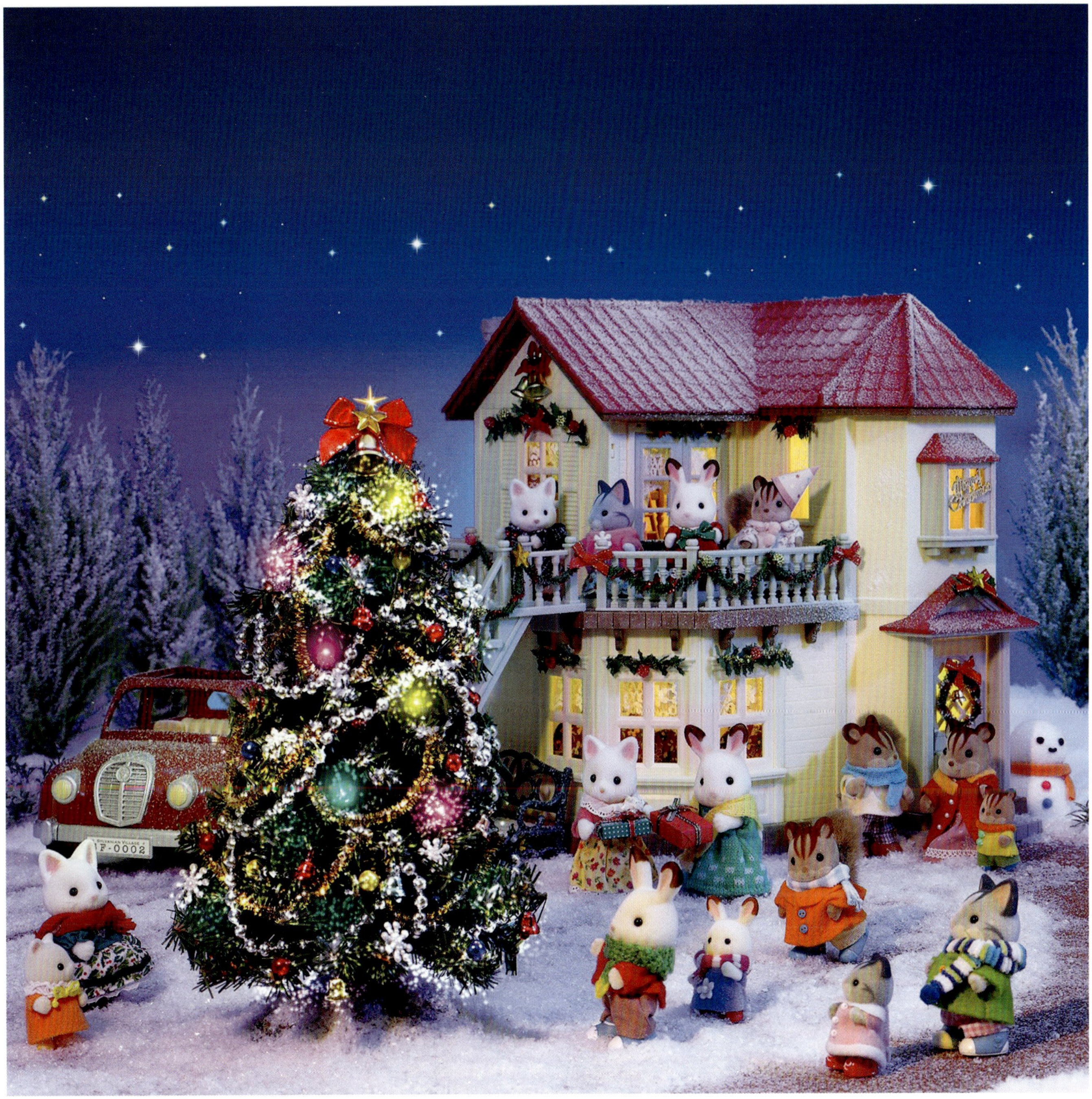

SYLVANIAN FAMILIES

•

Sylvanian Families Christmas, 2015
Flocked plastic, dimensions variable

In the snow-covered driveway and looking down from the balcony of a townhouse garlanded at every opening with festive wreaths and bells, four families of anthropomorphic toy animals are gathered to admire a richly decorated Christmas tree. It is a scene of almost impossibly wholesome, romantic perfection, entirely fitting with the stated brand values of the Sylvanian Families toy line from which they come: nature, love, and family. Using the prefix sylvan—meaning "of the forest"—for their name, the toys were conceived as a woodland twist on the traditional dollhouse by Japanese toy company Epoch in 1985 and branded as Calico Critters by distributor Tomy for the US market. They quickly achieved huge success internationally, selling more than one hundred million units to date, with tie-ins including an animated television series and theme park. The scene pictured features several standard "family" sets, including Chocolate Rabbits, Walnut Squirrels, Gray Cats, and Silk Cats, each with their own official names and character traits. In style, their clothes, just like their cars and houses, hark back to a nostalgically reimagined mid-century past lacking any modern distractions—all the better for encouraging the kind of imaginative, interactive play for which they are designed. Sylvanian Families do produce limited-edition Christmas-themed toys, such as a gingerbread house (see p.214) and a sled driven by a Santa Claus Lion in which he carries intricately rendered gifts for children.

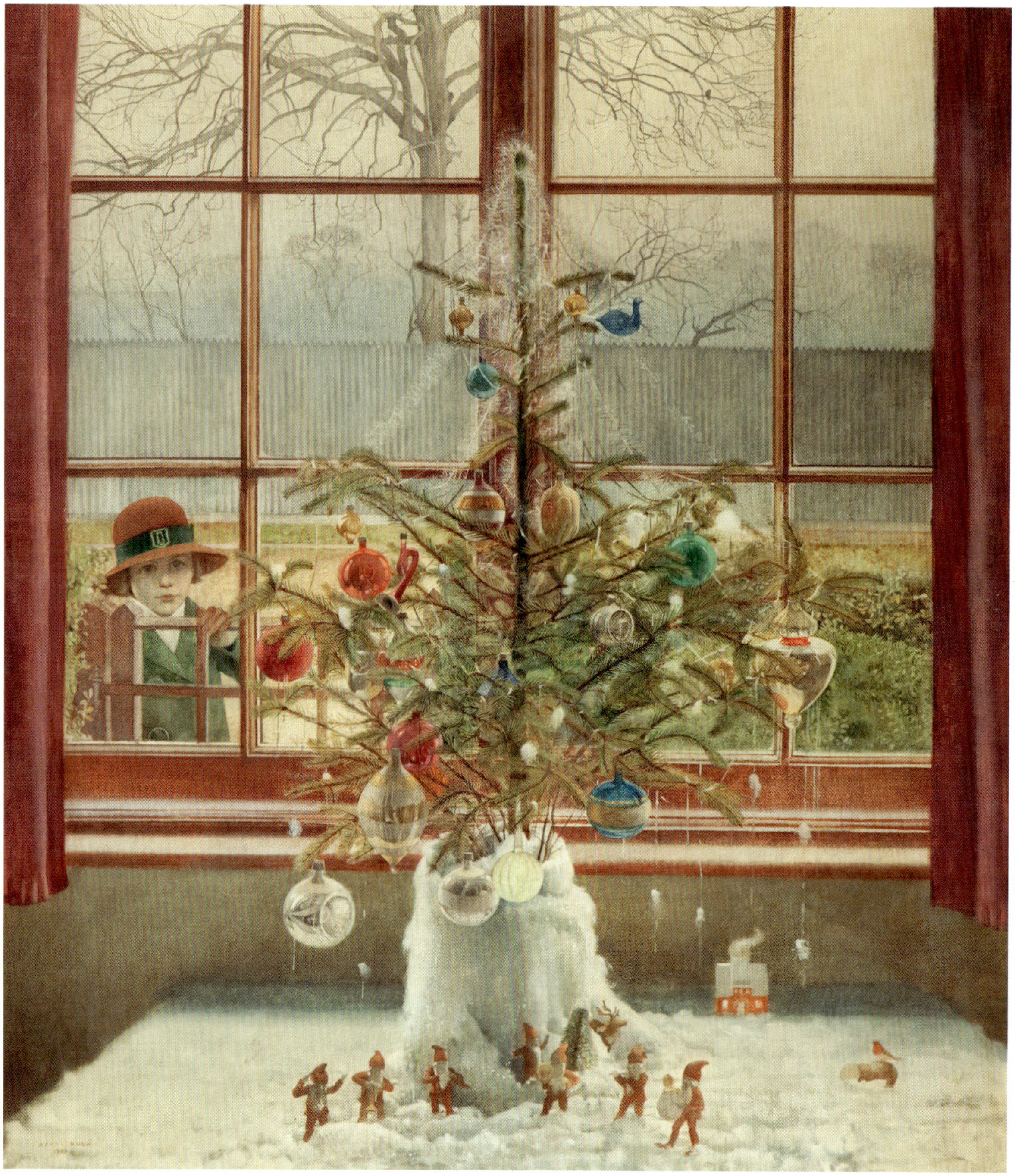

HARRY BUSH

•

The Christmas Tree, 1933
Oil on canvas, 41⅜ × 37½ in / 105 × 95 cm
Grundy Art Gallery, Blackpool, UK

What could be more inviting than a Christmas tree in a window? This artwork by British painter Harry Bush (1883–1957) depicts a rather humble evergreen tree placed on a table in front of a window overlooking a gated garden, as an intrigued child peers longingly inside, mesmerized by the scene. Bush was known for painting landscapes, townscapes, and figures, and this work indulges in each. While small in scale, the tree is joyfully decorated with blown-glass ornaments of varying sizes, each one a different shape and all brightly colored. Some even seem too large for such a little tree, but the asymmetrical placement helps the arrangement feel whimsical and celebratory. Strands of tinsel catch the light and it appears there are miniature orbs, giving the effect of snowflakes, dancing around each branch. Wrapped in cotton batting to resemble freshly fallen snow, underneath the tree there is a merry band of elves and a small house off in the distance. These little figures were typically made of porcelain or papier-mâché and commonly placed under trees, on table settings, and even on cakes to create a magical festive scene (see p.177). Truly a world of its own, this tiny, decorated tree and underlying snowscape conjure up a bit of magic and wonder. Perhaps the youngster looking in represents all of us, wrapped up in the spirit of Christmas and allowed to express childlike awe at the decorations and celebrations at this most wonderful time of the year.

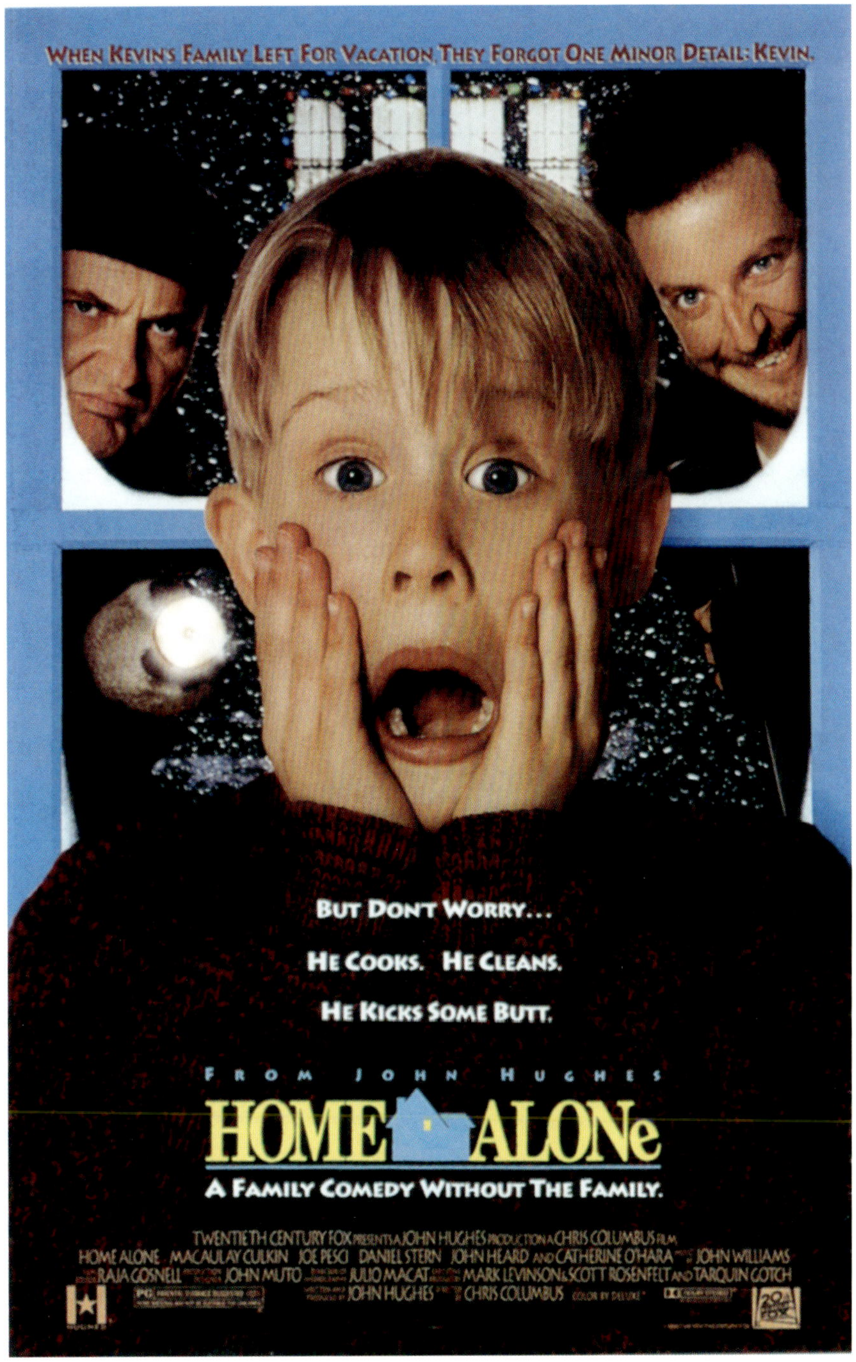

CHRIS COLUMBUS

•

Poster from *Home Alone*, 1990
Poster, dimensions variable
20th Century Fox / The Walt Disney Company

Packing for his holiday, writer and film producer John Hughes (1950–2009) imagined what would happen if he forgot his kids. From that parental nightmare was born one of the most popular of all Christmas movies, *Home Alone*, directed by Chris Columbus. Starring Macaulay Culkin (1980–) as eight-year-old Kevin McCallister, the youngest of five children who, having been accidentally left behind as his chaotic family heads to Paris, France for the Christmas vacation, fights off a series of raids by a pair of hapless burglars (played by Joe Pesci and Daniel Stern) who target his family's suburban Chicago home, with increasingly entertaining—and grimace-inducing—booby traps. Premiering in Chicago in November 1990, the movie went straight to the top of the US box office listings and remained there for twelve weeks, making a huge star of its child lead. The movie is a barely disguised morality tale: being initially thrilled to find himself "home alone," because he can finally do just what he pleases, Kevin increasingly misses his family, warts and all. With its easy-listening soundtrack filled with classic Christmas tunes, slapstick violence, quotable lines, and backdrop of the trappings of Christmas, the film outgrew its seasonal origins to become an all-round favorite: by the time its run in theaters ended, it was the third-highest grossing movie of all time. Such huge success fostered a franchise that saw further *Home Alone* films produced.

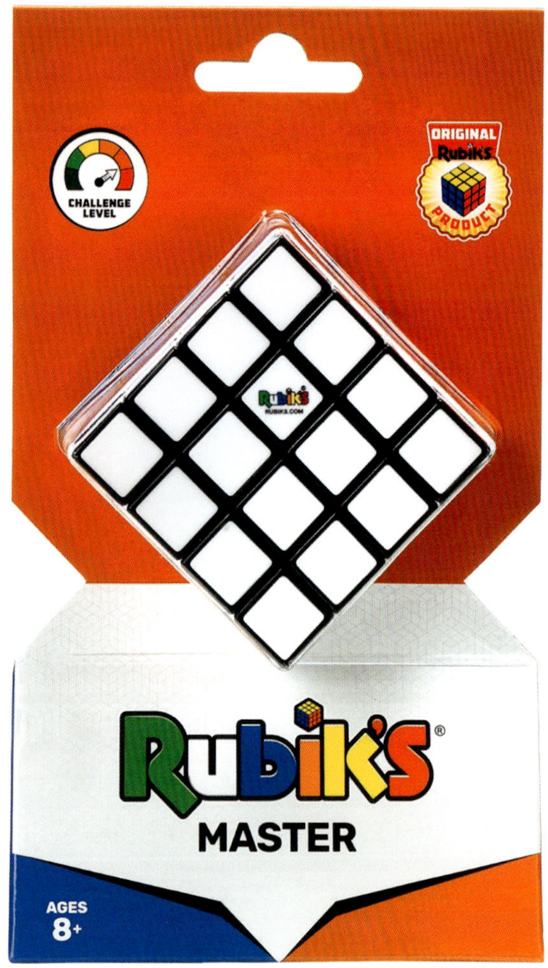

SPIN MASTER

•

Rubik's Cube, 2020
Plastic, 3⅞ × 3⅞ × 3⅞ in / 10 × 10 × 10 cm

If the thought of finding everything on your child's Christmas list sends a wintry chill down your spine, it's likely because the "it" toys of the season have always so quickly disappeared from shelves. The Rubik's Cube became a worldwide sensation in the early 1980s. Invented by Hungarian architect Ernő Rubik in 1974 and originally known as the Magic Cube, this deceptively simple, colorful puzzle box features nine different colored squares on each face, with the goal being to twist the cube so that each side displays a uniform color. It became an instant hit, selling over one hundred million units between 1980 and 1982, and even became the star of an animated series in 1983 called *Rubik, the Amazing Cube*. This wasn't, however, the first hard-to-get toy. In the 1950s, it was the accessories of Mr. Potato Head (originally made for an actual tuber), and the Hula-Hoop, which sold a staggering twenty-five million units in its first four months. Cabbage Patch Kids were all the rage in the 1980s. Tickle Me Elmo was so difficult to find that it inspired real-life brawls between aspiring shoppers and fetched upward of one thousand dollars on the black market. The phenomenon of retail mayhem is so absurd that it even inspired the movie *Jingle All the Way* (1996), in which a father played by Arnold Schwarzenegger goes to incredible lengths to find the season's most sought-after toy for his child.

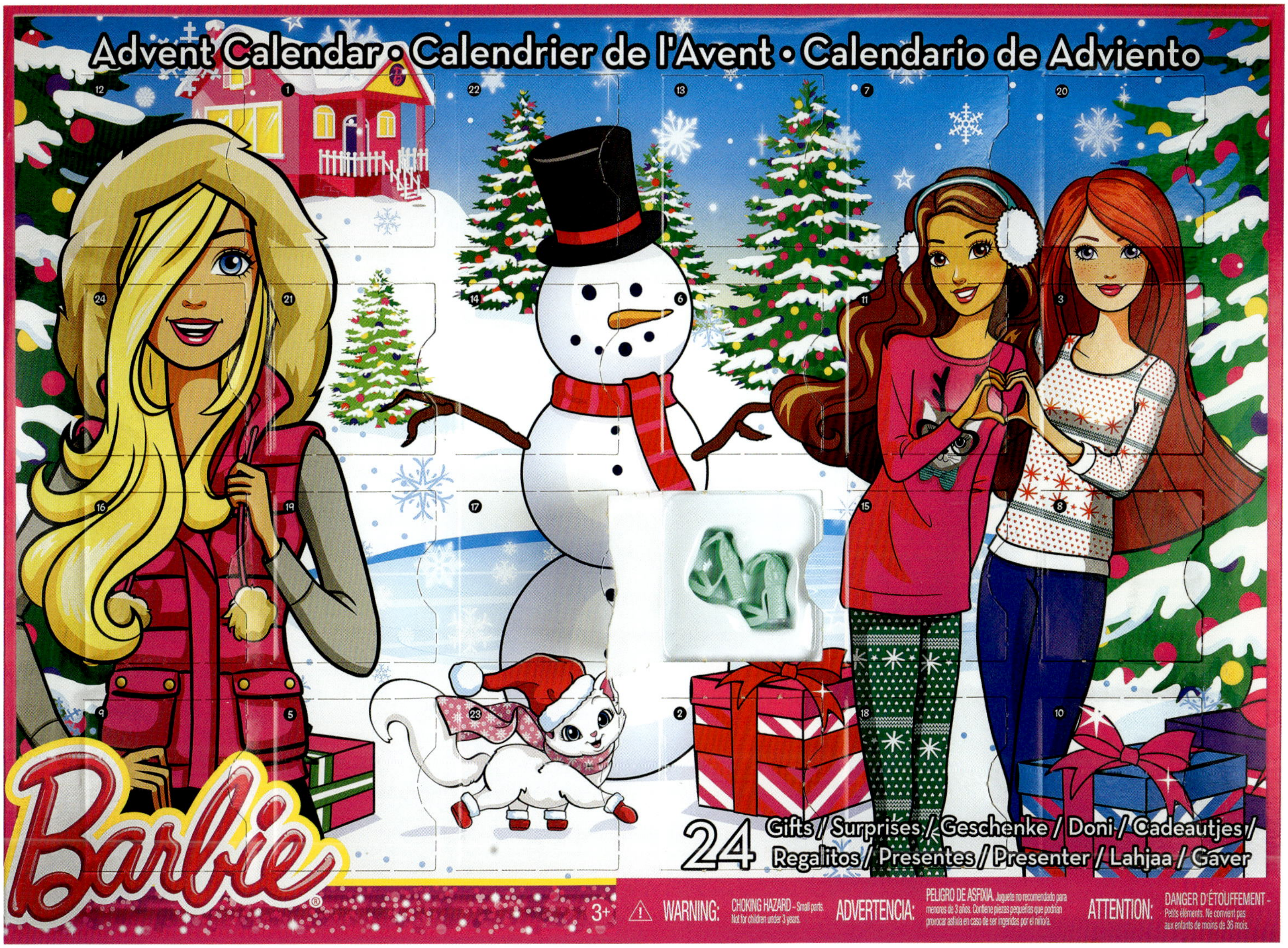

MATTEL

•

Barbie Advent calendar, 2017
Card and plastic,
18 × 12¾ × 2 in / 45.7 × 32.4 × 5.1 cm

This 2017 calendar by Mattel features twenty-four doors, and behind each one is hidden an accessory for a Barbie, the iconic fashion doll created by Ruth Handler and launched in 1959. These include earrings, high heels, purses, and hats, all of which help Barbie look a bit more festive. Like many Christmas traditions, the Advent calendar began in Germany (see pp.140, 170). Practitioners would leave chalk marks on their doors or light candles each day in observance. The first paper Advent calendars were printed by German Gerhard Lang (see p.170) in the early 1900s. Inspired by his own family's tradition, Lang pioneered the little paper doors and their reveals that are hallmarks of modern-day Advent calendars. Meant to be opened one day at a time until Christmas, the doors traditionally uncovered a small treat, trinket, or Bible verse. Today, Advent calendars have been secularized and can be found in every conceivable theme, for adults and children alike. There are calendars that deliver twenty-four cheeses or beers to your door to try a new one each day. Seemingly every animated character and toy has its own companion calendar, lest any child's favorite be left out of the mix. But Advent calendars aren't all fun and games; sometimes they can be extravagant. Consider Tiffany & Co.'s 2021 edition, adorned with artwork from Basquiat and chock-full of jewelry (see p.116) and other merchandise from the luxury retailer, which was priced at $150,000.

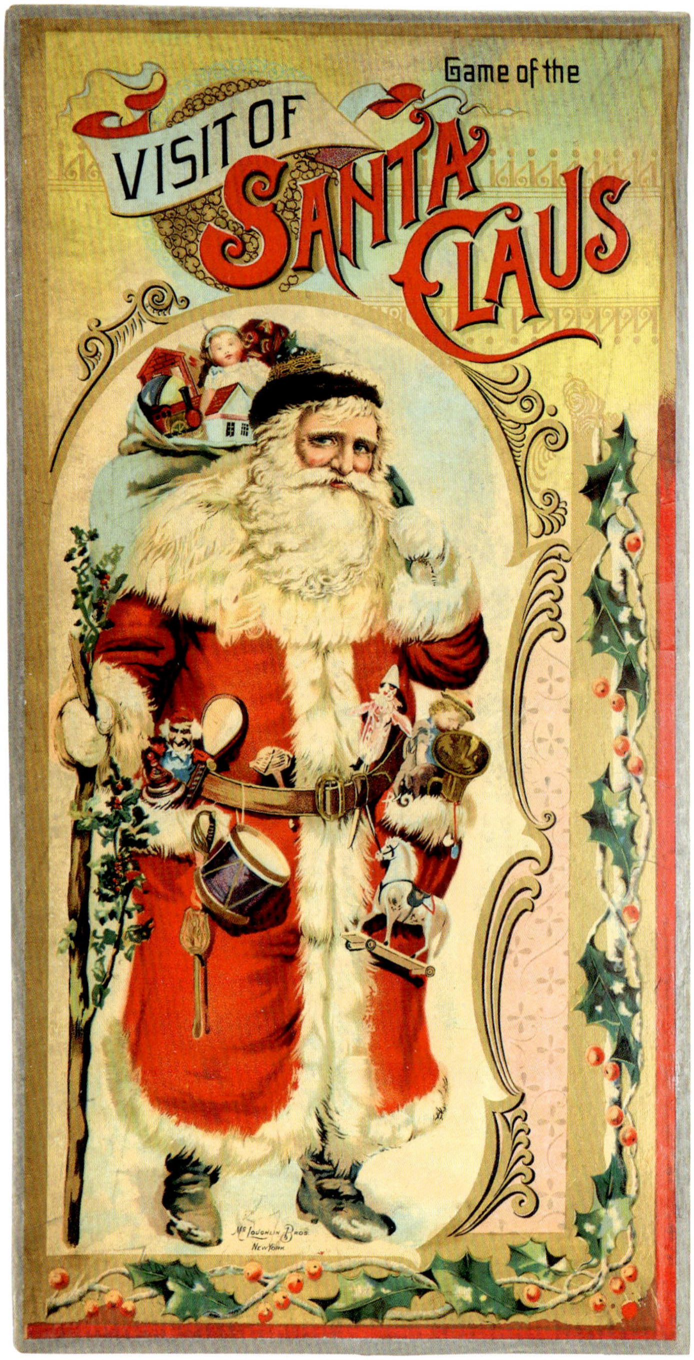

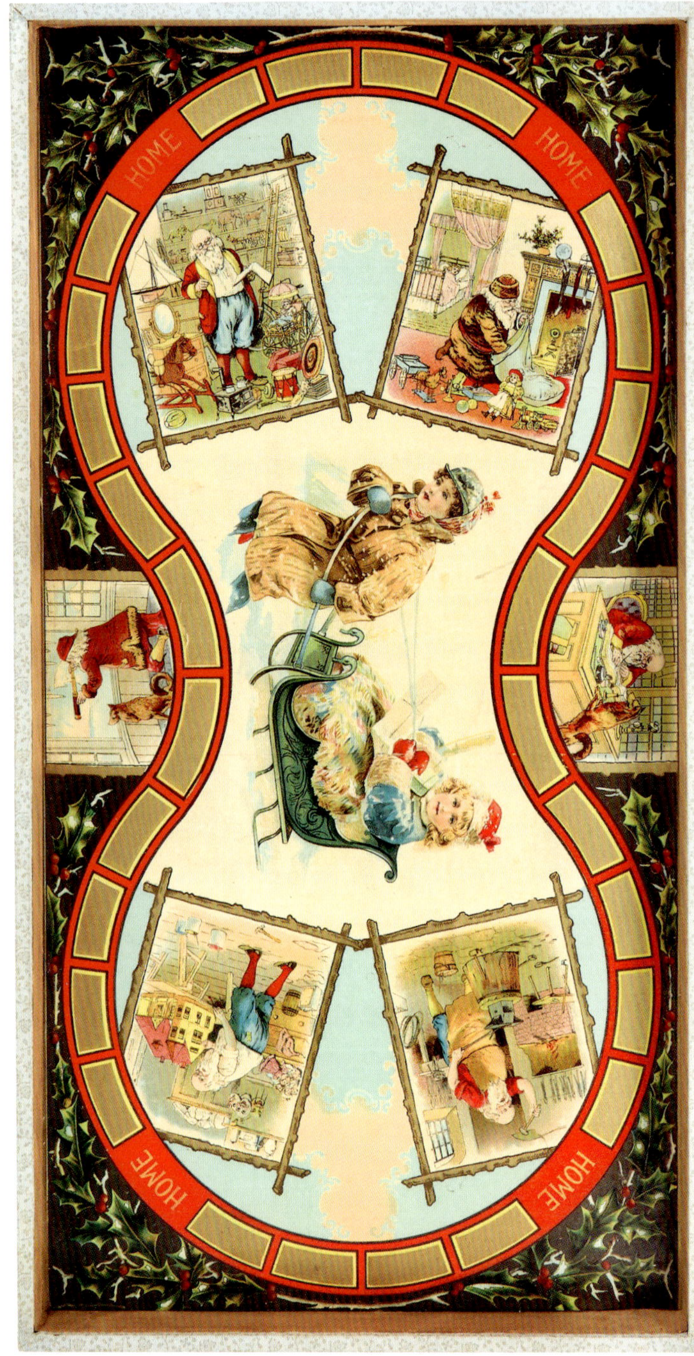

MCLOUGHLIN BROTHERS

•

Game of the Visit of Santa Claus, c.1890
Printed paper and cardstock,
20 × 10½ in / 50.8 × 26.7 cm

The outer case of this board game, created by the McLoughlin Brothers company, depicts a cherubic, benevolently smiling Santa Claus with an overflowing cornucopia of gifts slung over his shoulder. So numerous are they that additional prizes, including a wooden horse, spinning top, Mr. Punch puppet, and toy drum, have had to be fastened to his belt. He supports himself on a holly-branch walking stick, while around him exaggerated scrolls and curlicues reminiscent of late nineteenth-century commercial advertisements are arranged. Founded in 1858 in New York, McLoughlin Brothers pioneered color printing for children's books and eventually repurposed the technology to create a vast array of brightly colored puzzles and board games. It had particular success with such seasonal "holiday" games designed for an increasingly commercialized gift-giving market and grew to be the most successful US games company at the turn of the twentieth century. This game is designed for up to four players, who each spin an "indicator" to move the figure of Santa around the board, attempting to direct him to their home, where he will deliver presents represented by "gift cards." The aim of the game is to try to collect the most cards by stopping Santa from visiting the other players' homes. The central image hints at the proverbial fates of naughty and nice children—one child in the toboggan (see p.70) has all the gifts, while the other is destined to pull her friend, sporting a wistful look of regret.

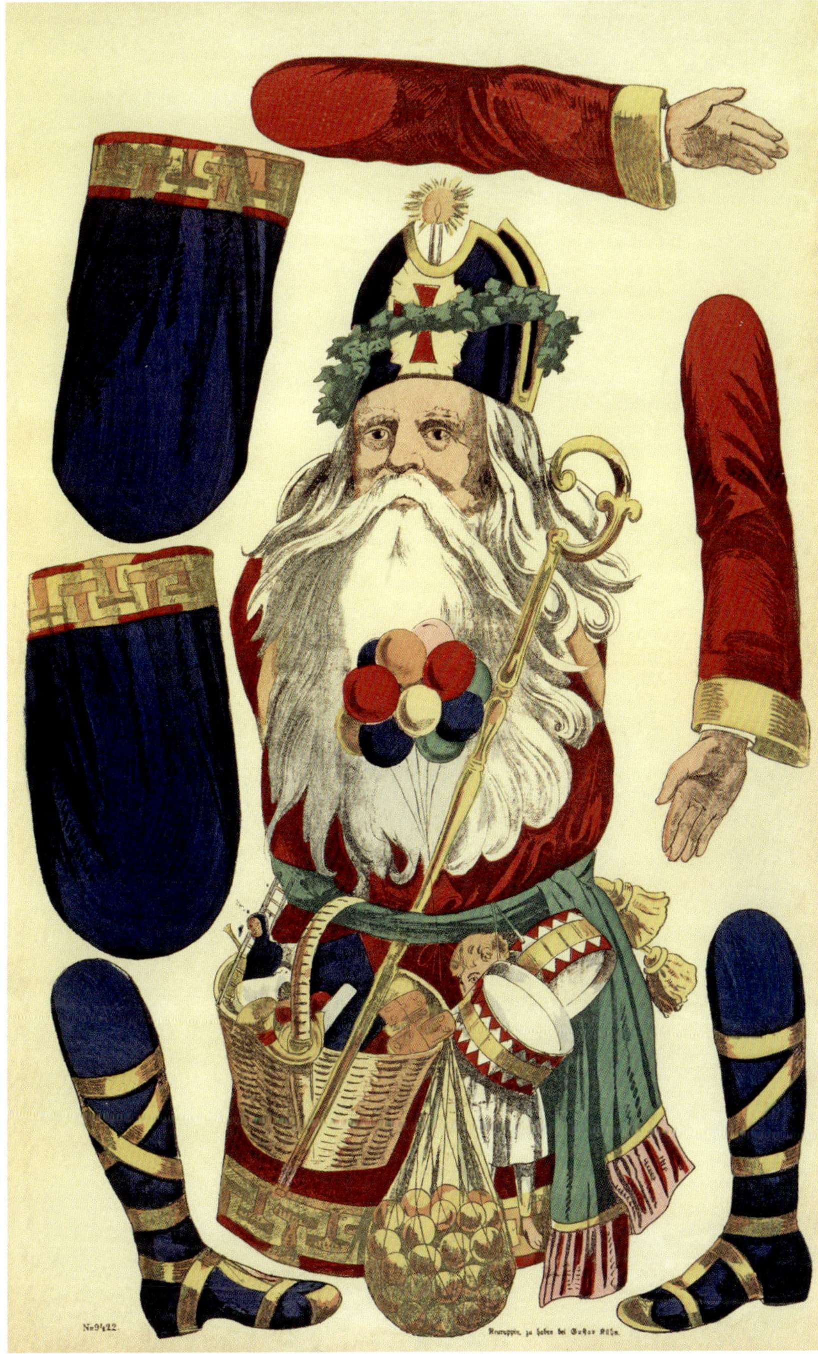

UNKNOWN

•

Cutout picture: Saint Nicholas, c.1860
Color lithograph, 16½ × 10¼ in / 42 × 26 cm
Private collection

Germany has a reputation for precise and detailed craftsmanship, and this illustration of Saint Nicholas, presented in many pieces, is no different. Designed to be cut out and woven together to create a paper decoration or toy (see p.184), this work was produced in the mid-eighteenth century and shows the classic image of Saint Nicholas as wise and slender, dressed in red-and-blue robes and carrying a scepter. This representation is based on the Bishop of Myra (see p.15), patron saint of children, and the inspiration for festive gift givers from many cultures, such as the Dutch Sinterklaas, the British Father Christmas, and the more American Santa Claus. In this beautifully illustrated lithograph, he can be seen with presents—including a doll, some drums, a sack of oranges, and a basket that includes musical instruments and other goodies—hanging from his sash rather than in a sack over his shoulder. This sheet is marked in the bottom corner as number 9422 and was likely part of a larger set of cutout figures and scenes, collectively known as *bilderbogen*, or illustrated broadsheets. These were often based around a particular theme—Christmas, for example—and aimed at a general audience. They were sometimes used to disseminate ideas or political agendas, but they also provided general amusement and merriment, and the cutout sheets could be used as decorations or toys for children once assembled.

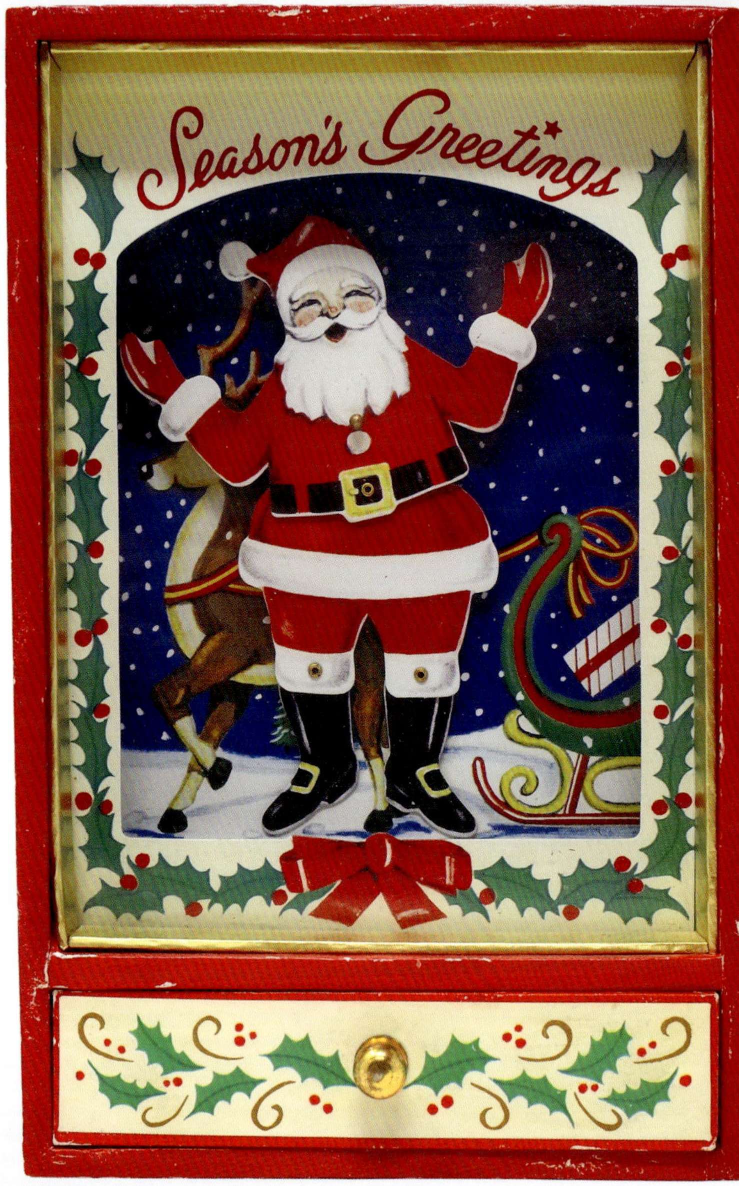

OTAGIRI MERCANTILE COMPANY

•

Dancing Santa Music Box, 1979
Wood, glass, paper, 8¼ × 5¼ in / 21 × 13.3 cm

The San Francisco Music Box Company, a once-popular chain store often found in malls but now only operating online, is known for its high-quality music boxes. Many, like the one pictured here, featured scenes made of heavy paper with hinged parts that actually moved. This piece was manufactured in 1979 and features a small trinket drawer at the bottom. When the box is wound, opening the drawer releases a trigger that causes "Jingle Bells" to play and Santa Claus to do a jolly dance. The Otagiri Mercantile Company was the third-party manufacturer of these boxes. Established around 1947 by husband and wife Goro and Chiyoko Otagiri, it started as a stoneware company whose wares were hand-painted and glazed by a small cadre of artists in Japan and then exported to America for sale. The pieces were so singular that the term "Otagiri" now refers to both the brand and its specific style of stoneware, which was copied by numerous other manufacturers. Other similar Otagiri music boxes feature clowns (variously dancing, juggling, riding a horse, or walking a trapeze), hot-air balloons moving through the air, a dancing snowman, a Ferris wheel that turns, a cowboy on horseback, a pumping oil well, and so on. But the dancing Santa, now discontinued, is no doubt one of the most popular and sought-after designs, and it provides a wonderful air of cheerful whimsy at Christmastime.

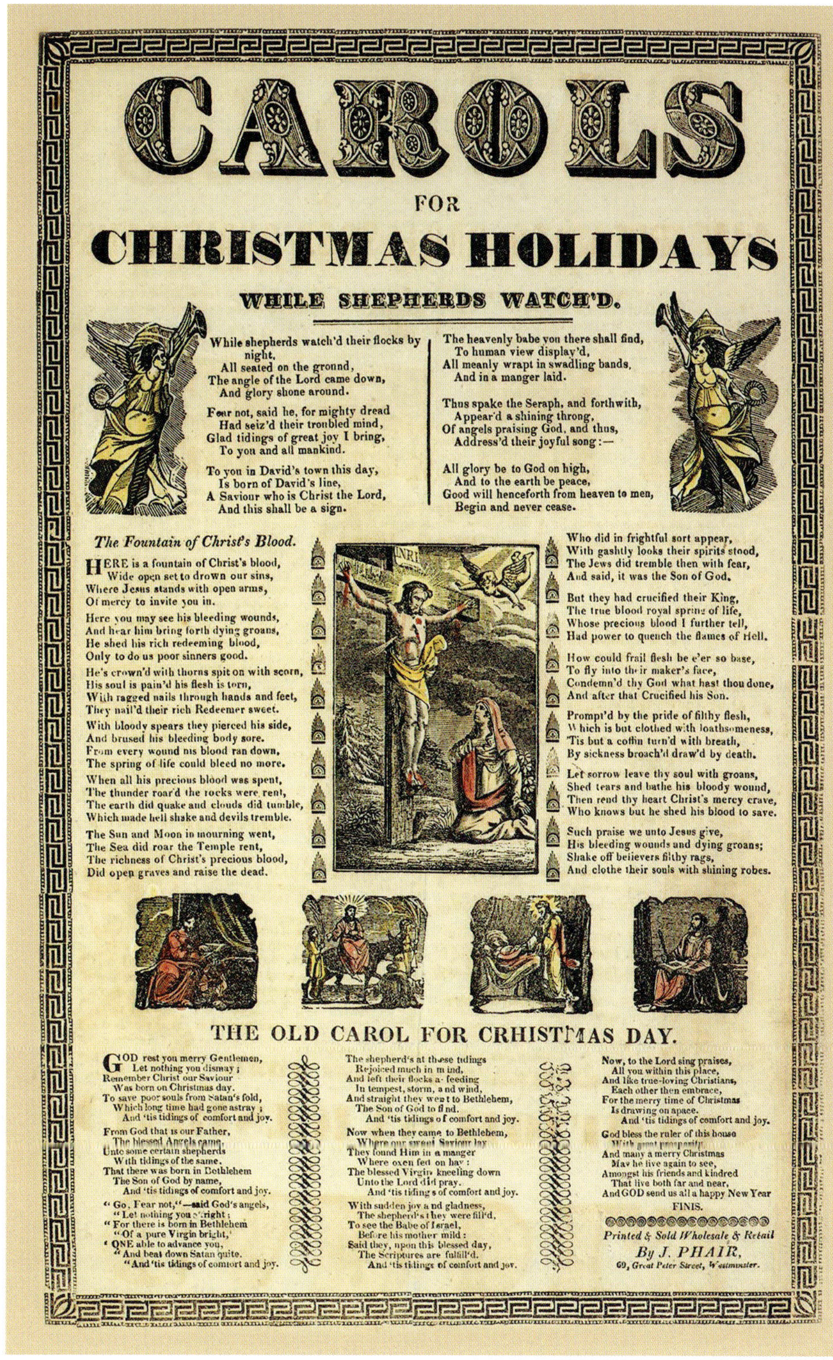

CAROLS
FOR
CHRISTMAS HOLIDAYS

WHILE SHEPHERDS WATCH'D.

While shepherds watch'd their flocks by night,
All seated on the ground,
The angle of the Lord came down,
And glory shone around.

Fear not, said he, for mighty dread
Had seiz'd their troubled mind,
Glad tidings of great joy I bring,
To you and all mankind.

To you in David's town this day,
Is born of David's line,
A Saviour who is Christ the Lord,
And this shall be a sign.

The heavenly babe you there shall find,
To human view display'd,
All meanly wrapt in swadling bands,
And in a manger laid.

Thus spake the Seraph, and forthwith,
Appear'd a shining throng,
Of angels praising God, and thus,
Address'd their joyful song:—

All glory be to God on high,
And to the earth be peace,
Good will henceforth from heaven to men,
Begin and never cease.

The Fountain of Christ's Blood.

HERE is a fountain of Christ's blood,
Wide open set to drown our sins,
Where Jesus stands with open arms,
Of mercy to invite you in.

Here you may see his bleeding wounds,
And hear him bring forth dying groans,
He shed his rich redeeming blood,
Only to do us poor sinners good.

He's crown'd with thorns spit on with scorn,
His soul is pain'd his flesh is torn,
With ragged nails through hands and feet,
They nail'd their rich Redeemer sweet.

With bloody spears they pierced his side,
And brused his bleeding body sore.
From every wound his blood ran down,
The spring of life could bleed no more.

When all his precious blood was spent,
The thunder roar'd the rocks were rent,
The earth did quake and clouds did tumble,
Which made hell shake and devils tremble.

The Sun and Moon in mourning went,
The Sea did roar the Temple rent,
The richness of Christ's precious blood,
Did open graves and raise the dead.

Who did in frightful sort appear,
With gashtly looks their spirits stood,
The Jews did tremble then with fear,
And said, it was the Son of God.

But they had crucified their King,
The true blood royal spring of life,
Whose precious blood I further tell,
Had power to quench the flames of Hell.

How could frail flesh be e'er so base,
To fly into their maker's face,
Condemn'd thy God what hast thou done,
And after that Crucified his Son.

Prompt'd by the pride of filthy flesh,
Which is but clothed with loathsomeness,
'Tis but a coffin turn'd with breath,
By sickness broach'd draw'd by death.

Let sorrow leave thy soul with groans,
Shed tears and bathe his bloody wound,
Then rend thy heart Christ's mercy crave,
Who knows but he shed his blood to save.

Such praise we unto Jesus give,
His bleeding wounds and dying groans;
Shake off believers filthy rags,
And clothe their souls with shining robes.

THE OLD CAROL FOR CRHISTMAS DAY.

GOD rest you merry Gentlemen,
Let nothing you dismay;
Remember Christ our Saviour
Was born on Christmas day.
To save poor souls from Satan's fold,
Which long time had gone astray;
And 'tis tidings of comfort and joy.

From God that is our Father,
The blessed Angels came,
Unto some certain shepherds
With tidings of the same.
That there was born in Bethlehem
The Son of God by name,
And 'tis tidings of comfort and joy.

"Go, Fear not,"—said God's angels,
"Let nothing you affright;
"For there is born in Bethlehem
"Of a pure Virgin bright,
"ONE able to advance you,
"And beat down Satan quite.
"And 'tis tidings of comfort and joy.

The shepherd's at these tidings
Rejoiced much in mind,
And left their flocks a-feeding
In tempest, storm, and wind,
And straight they went to Bethlehem,
The Son of God to find.
And 'tis tidings of comfort and joy.

Now when they came to Bethlehem,
Where our sweet Saviour lay
They found Him in a manger
Where oxen fed on hay:
The blessed Virgin kneeling down
Unto the Lord did pray.
And 'tis tidings of comfort and joy.

With sudden joy and gladness,
The shepherd's they were fill'd,
To see the Babe of Israel,
Before his mother mild:
Said they, upon this blessed day,
The Scriptures are fulfill'd.
And 'tis tidings of comfort and joy.

Now, to the Lord sing praises,
All you within this place,
And like true-loving Christians,
Each other then embrace,
For the merry time of Christmas
Is drawing on apace.
And 'tis tidings of comfort and joy.

God bless the ruler of this house
With great prosperity
And many a merry Christmas
May he live again to see,
Amongst his friends and kindred
That live both far and near,
And GOD send us all a happy New Year

FINIS.

Printed & Sold Wholesale & Retail
By J. PHAIR,
69, Great Peter Street, Westminster.

J. PHAIR

•

"Carols for Christmas Holidays," c.1830
Print, dimensions variable
British Library, London

During the 1830s and 1840s, Christmas celebrations in Great Britain changed significantly under the influence of Queen Victoria's German-born husband, Prince Albert. Christmas now centered on the family and featured many German traditions introduced by the prince consort, including the singing of Christmas carols. The popularity of these new songs was boosted by the publication of books of sheet music, but those who could not afford to buy a whole book could buy a Christmas carol broadside: a single large sheet printed with three Christmas carols. J. Phair Printers of London published this example around 1830, tapping into the growing popularity of singing Christmas carols at home, and it includes an early appearance of now well-known carol "God rest ye merry gentlemen." Also printed on the sheet was "The Old Carol for Crhistmas" (sic), the spelling mistake suggesting that speed was of the essence and proofreading an expensive luxury when the broadside was published. Broadsides were produced cheaply and originally used to publish royal proclamations and official statements, but they came to be used by printers to publish material about all kinds of topics, including seasonal songs for Valentine's Day and Christmas Day. While frequent typos and spelling mistakes litter the text, the lavish drawings that accompany the carols, showing scenes from Christ's life, may well have compensated for the hurried typesetting for the intended audience.

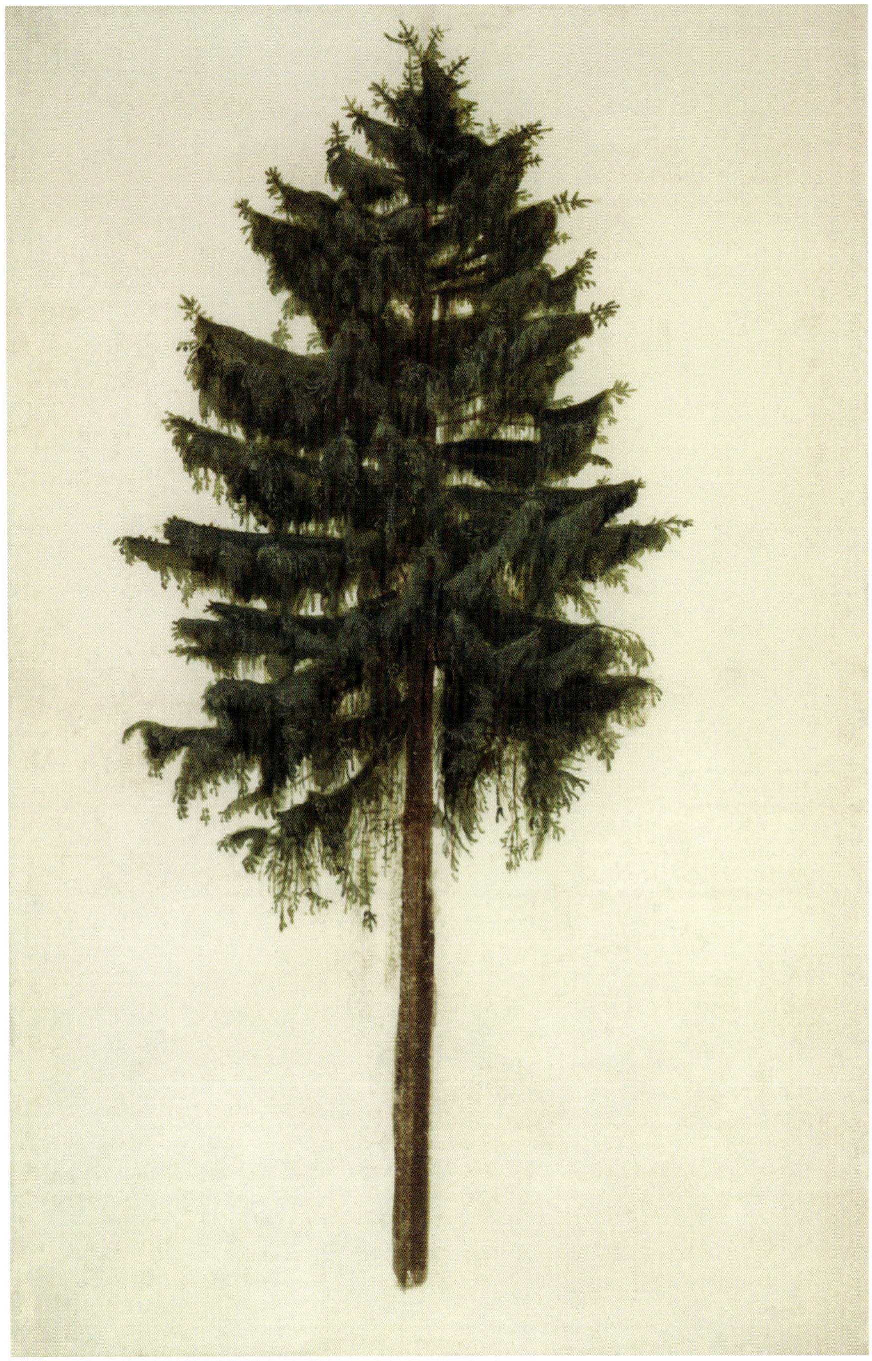

ALBRECHT DÜRER

•

Spruce tree (Picea abies), c.1497
Watercolor on paper, 11½ × 7⅝ in / 29.3 × 19.4 cm
British Museum, London

This careful watercolor study of a spruce tree, with its tall, thin trunk and dense branches placed against a blank page, underlines the talent of the greatest painter of the Northern Renaissance, Albrecht Dürer (1471–1528). For the German-born painter, such studies were a key part in preparing to paint his larger pictures in oils and part of his endeavor to represent nature as accurately as possible. This image may well have been painted on Dürer's return to his native Nuremberg after the first of two trips he made to Italy between 1494 and 1495. His practice of painting detailed studies from nature and his use of landscape in his larger works helped establish landscape as a subject worthy of painting in its own right rather than simply as a background to religious scenes or portraits. The spruce tree (see pp.20, 162, 165) was held in special affection in northern Europe. An evergreen, it was a reminder in the depths of dark winters of the promised return of warmer days. Its role in celebrating Christmas can be traced back a thousand years. While the Romans used fir trees to celebrate the New Year, it was in northern Europe that the spruce was adopted as a symbol of Christmas. Trees were traditionally kept outdoors; the Protestant reformer Martin Luther (1483–1546), a close friend of Dürer, was said to have first brought the tree indoors and to have added candles to its branches to recapture the brilliance of the night stars inside.

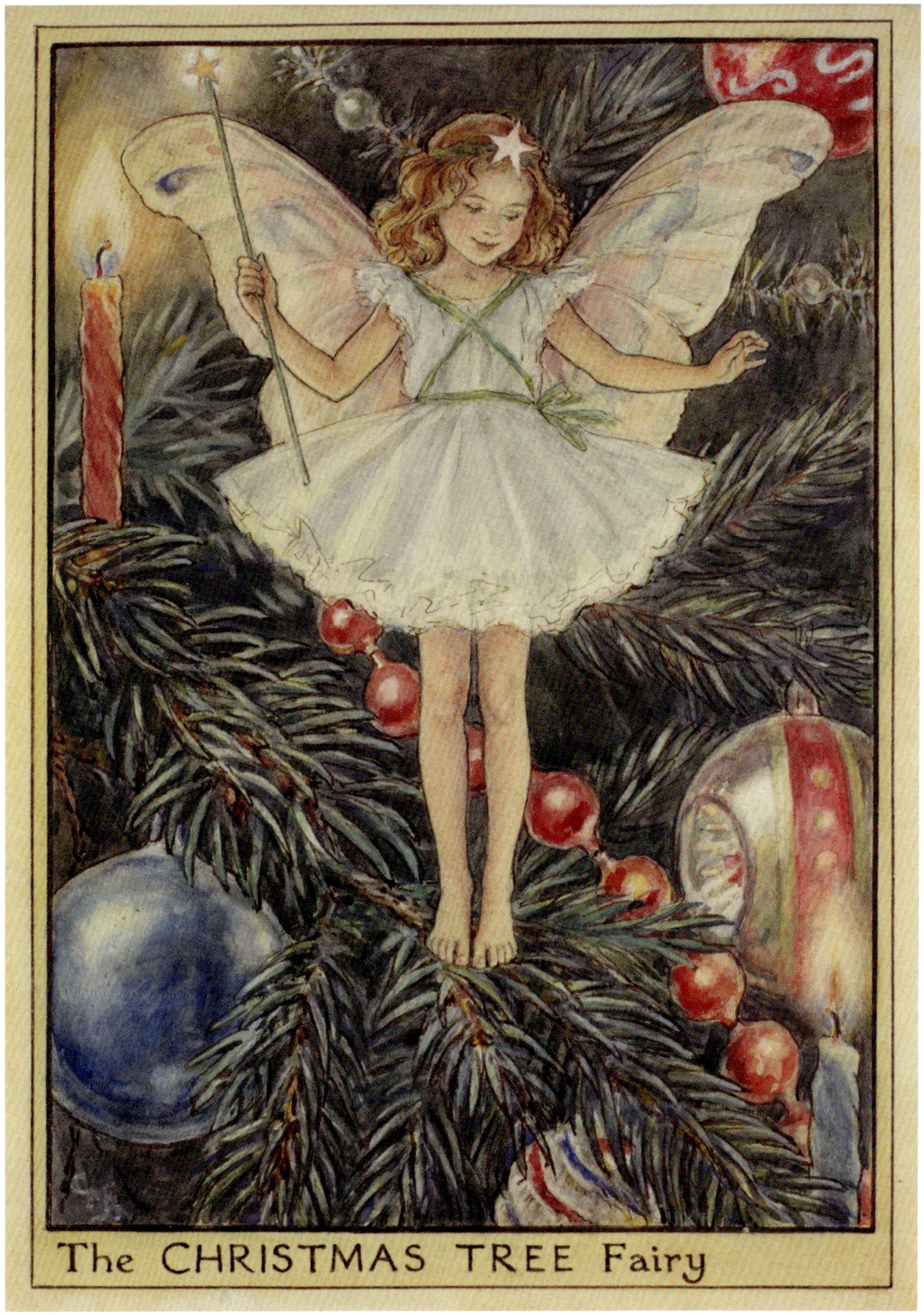

CICELY MARY BARKER

•

"The Christmas Tree Fairy"
from *Flower Fairies of the Trees*, 1940
Watercolor, 5½ × 4¼ in / 14 × 10.8 cm
Published by Blackie & Son, London & Glasgow

Standing amid the candles and baubles on the branch of a Christmas tree is "The Christmas Tree Fairy," a pixielike angelic fairy (see p.222) painted by the British illustrator Cicely Mary Barker (1895–1973). Since her first book, *Flower Fairies of the Spring* was published in 1923, Barker's beautiful drawings of the tiny flower fairies—the biggest is just eight inches (20 cm) tall—have garnered a devoted following. Each fairy is unique and appears alongside a botanically accurate illustration of a British plant, accompanied by a poem about both the plant and the fairy. Barker was one of many artists who benefited from the great surge in the popularity of fairies after World War I ended in 1918, as people sought to escape its horrors and the misery of postwar life (see p.123).

Basing the fairies on real children at her sister's nursery school, Barker began each illustration as a loose sketch that she then worked up into more detailed watercolors. Over the decades, Barker went on to produce farther volumes of fairy illustrations that eventually covered the four seasons: "The Christmas Tree Fairy" was first published in her collection of *Flower Fairies of the Trees* in 1940, but also featured in her posthumous collection *Flower Fairies of the Winter* (1985). Like Barker's other fairies, the Christmas Fairy was not merely decorative: they were all responsible for taking care of their particular plant. As the plant grew, Barker explained, so did the fairy.

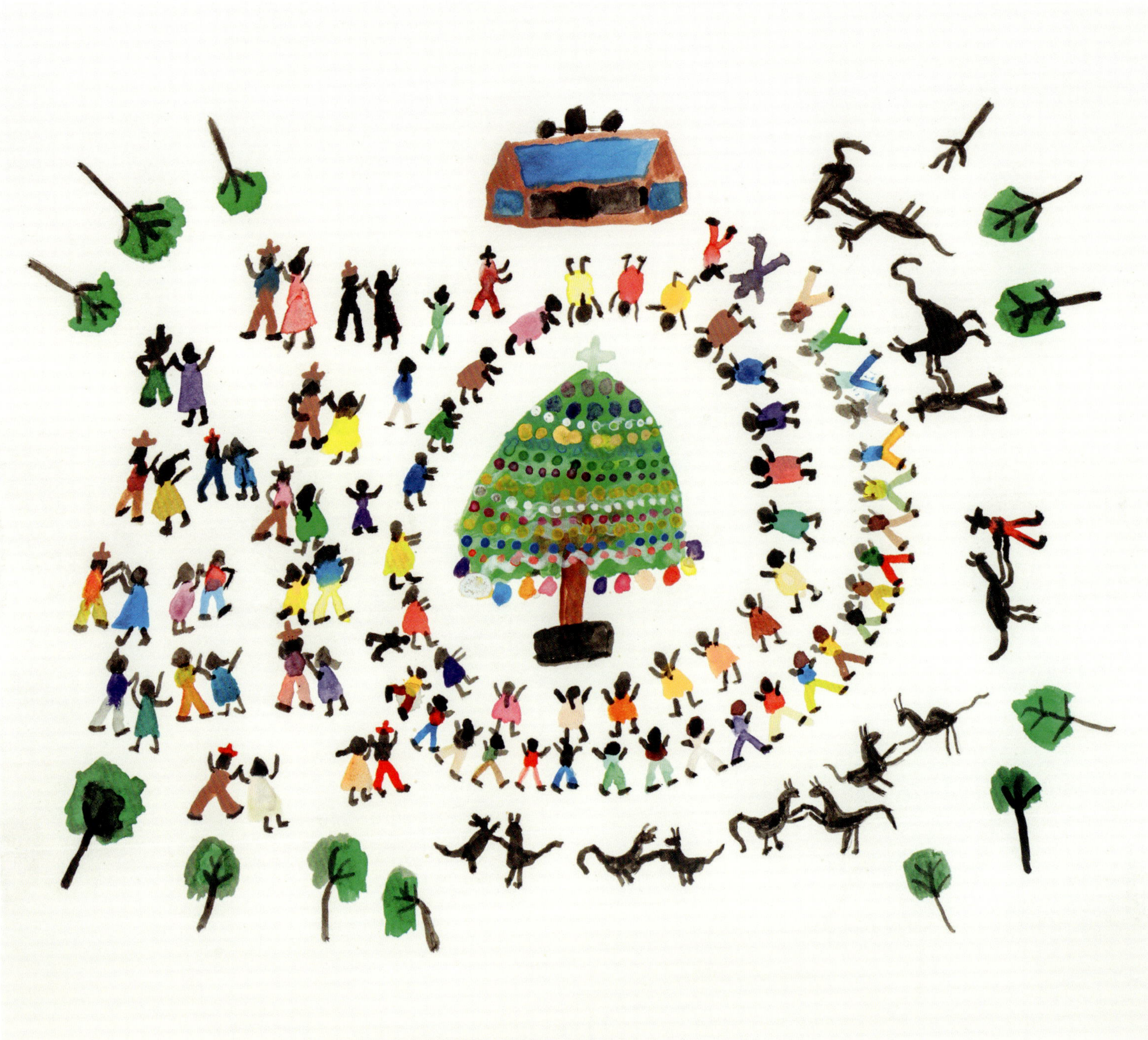

GRACE KEMARRE ROBINYA

•

Christmas Dancing, Laramba, 2019,
Watercolor on paper, 11 × 14 in / 28.3 × 37.8 cm
Art Gallery of South Australia

A large, meticulously decorated Christmas tree stands tall in the center of this celebratory watercolor by award-winning Aboriginal painter Grace Kemarre Robinya (1942–). Spiraling outward from the towering evergreen, residents of Laramba, a small town in the Northern Territory of Australia (with a population of 189 as of the 2021 census), dance with each other, in pairs and holding hands, with the only building for miles the station house in the background. Not content with letting the human population of Laramba have all the fun, native animals, too, partner up and celebrate Christmas with dance. Robinya has lived in remote Aboriginal communities of Australia throughout her life, and in recent years has dedicated her time to documenting the important moments, memories, and places of her life. Napperby Station, where she and her husband worked as a domestic and ringer, respectively, while raising their growing family, is the only building visible in this piece. Her work has helped draw attention to the plights of rural communities. *Raining at Laramba*, for which Robinya won the 2021 Vincent Lingiari Art Award, captures the dramatic vistas of rain falling in desert country, where the fight for water rights is an important issue. Despite being so remote, the traditional rituals of Christmas help bring the town together.

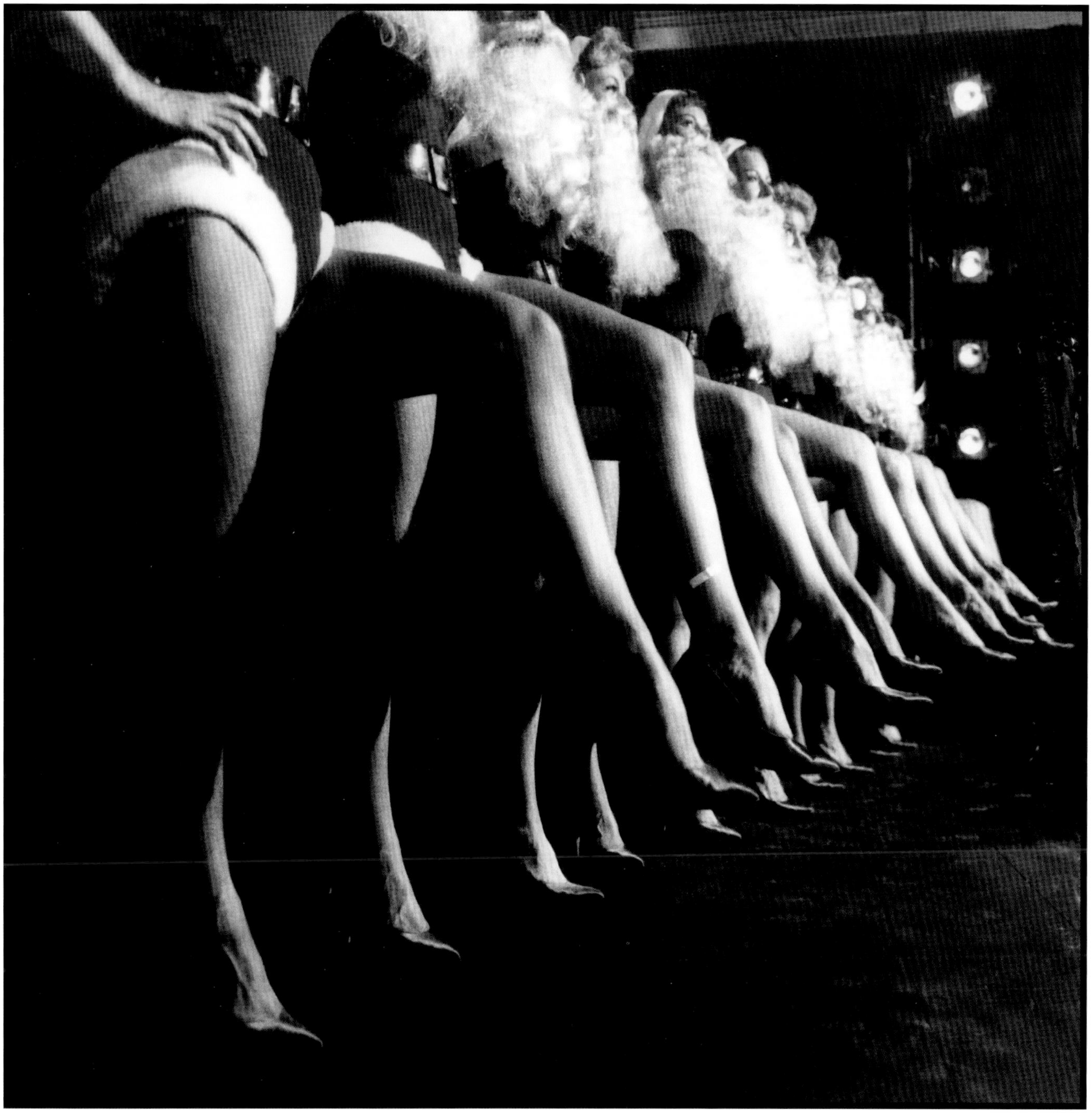

DENNIS STOCK

•

The legs of dancers at Radio City Music Hall, NYC, 1959
Photograph, dimensions variable

It is no surprise that this scene of dancing women dressed up as Santa Claus—beard, belt, and all—shot by American journalist and photographer Dennis Stock (1928–2010) takes place at Radio City Music Hall in New York. The iconic venue is closely associated with dancing and the holidays, being the home of the Rockettes dance company and the host of the *Radio City Christmas Spectacular*, an annual musical stage show featuring the troupe since 1932. Inspired by the Tiller Girls, a British precision-dance group that found fame stateside with the Ziegfeld Follies, the Missouri Rockets were founded by choreographer Russell Markert in 1925. They made their Broadway debut that year and were discovered by American promoter Samuel "Roxy" Rothafel (1882–1936), who expanded the group, redubbed them "the Roxyettes," and brought them to New York. Renamed the Rockettes in 1934, the group is known for their crisp choreography and uniformity. The dancers perform several sequences, their shoes fitted with microphones so that the taps can be heard throughout the auditorium. The famous "Parade of the Wooden Soldiers," in which the dancers are dressed like toy soldiers and move in perfect synchrony, has been an institution since the beginning. There are few more iconic performers in New York than the Rockettes. Dennis Stock was known for his memorable portraits of Hollywood stars, as well as his energy-filled portraits of jazz musicians.

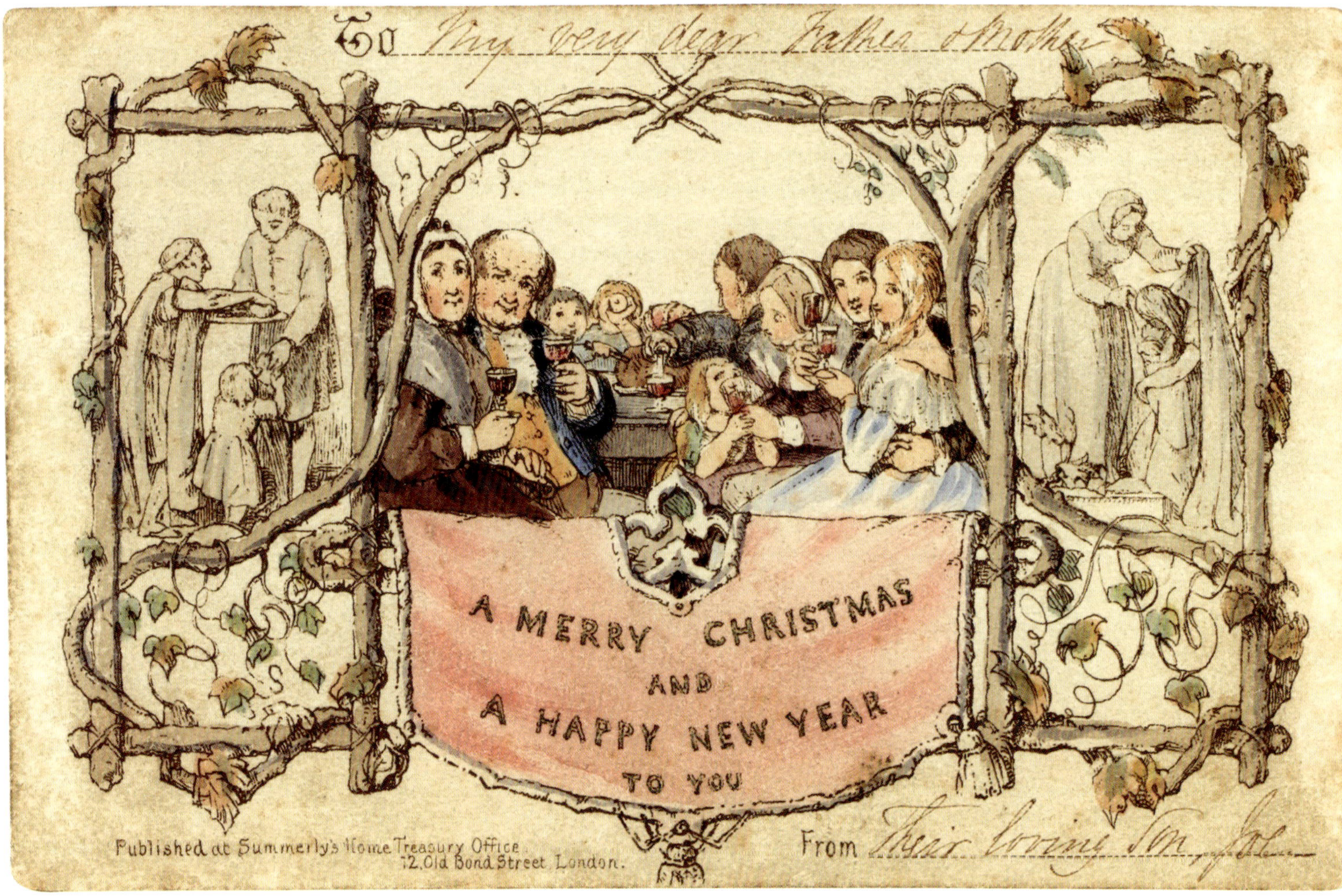

JOHN CALLCOTT HORSLEY

•

The first Christmas card, 1843,
Color process engraving, 4½ × 5⅝ in / 11.4 × 14.6 cm

A Victorian family are gathered around the dinner table, toasting the festive season. Framed by vine-wrapped boughs, they are flanked by scenes of people caring for the poor and needy. Conveying a sense of celebration and charity, this convivial illustration was designed for the world's first Christmas card, created by the British civil servant and inventor Sir Henry Cole. With unanswered letters piling up at his home and little time for Christmas missives, he invited his friend, the artist John Callcott Horsley (1817–1903), to help him produce a time-saving solution. Horsley's illustration was printed on cardstock in an edition of one thousand, but at the considerable price of one shilling (24 cents), few copies of the hand-colored card were sold. Although Cole's Christmas card was a commercial failure, he was ahead of his time; the concept later caught on and by the 1860s, prompted by technical advances in printing and the growing commercialization of Christmas, Victorians were exchanging and displaying seasonal cards in great numbers. The enthusiasm for card sending was encouraged by the Penny Post, which Cole had helped to introduce in 1840, allowing cards to be sent anywhere in Great Britain at a uniform rate. Lithographer Louis Prang (see p.90) introduced the Christmas card to the American market in 1875 and they were an immediate hit; within five years he was reportedly printing five million cards a year. Today, despite the prevalence of email, the tradition is a multimillion-dollar industry.

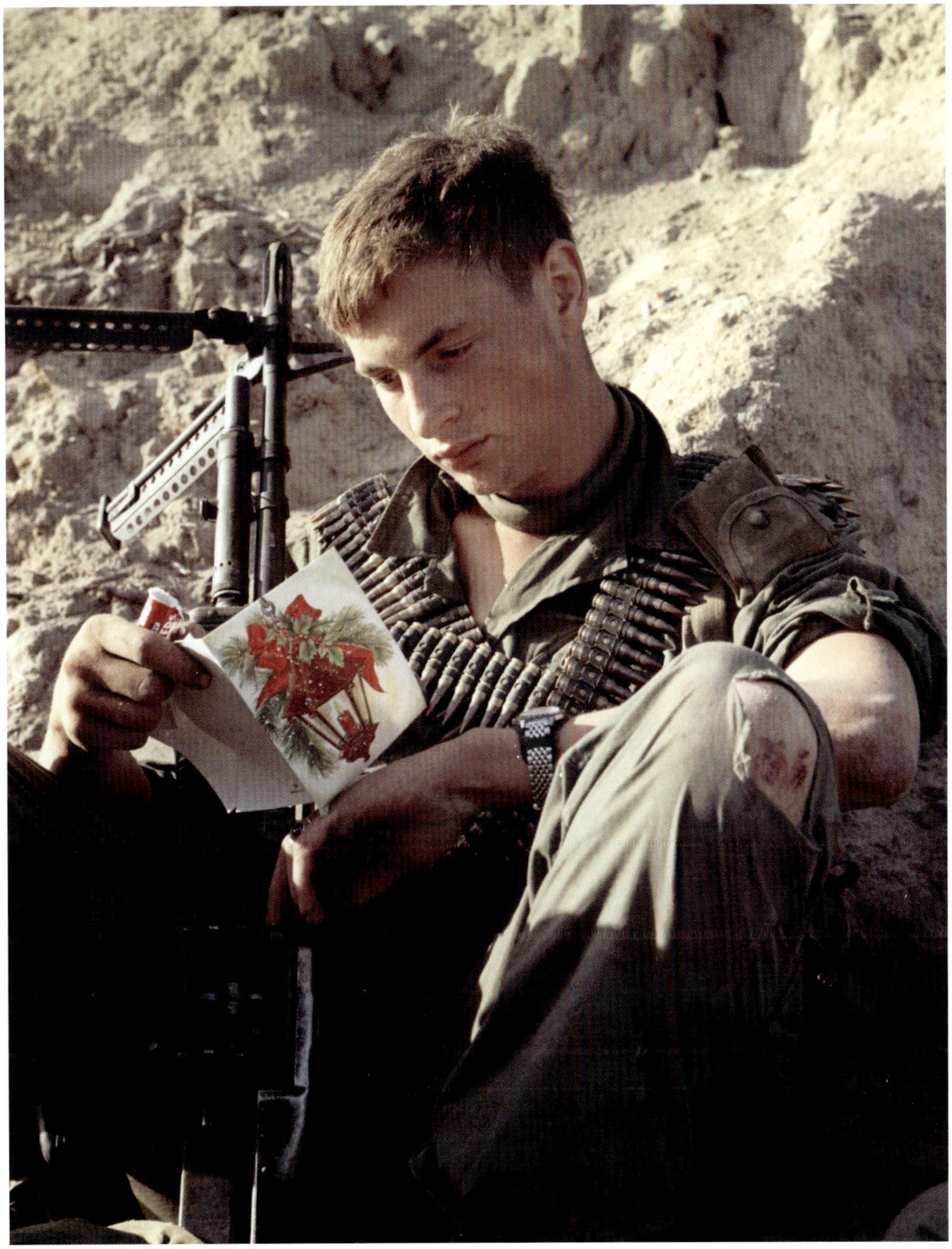

UNKNOWN

•

US soldier reading a Christmas card in Vietnam, 1967
Photograph, dimensions variable

Christmas is a time for mirth and merriment, but it's also a time for bittersweet reflection—thinking about those we've loved and lost, and those we can't be with during the holidays. Indeed, some of Christmas's most iconic ballads center around the poignancy of separation, such as "White Christmas," "I'll Be Home for Christmas," and "Have Yourself a Merry Little Christmas" (see p.30). It probably comes as little surprise, then, that all three of those songs were written during World War II, a time when millions of families were torn apart by the global conflict. President Franklin D. Roosevelt spearheaded the creation of the United Service Organizations during the war in an effort to bolster troop morale, transporting Hollywood stars to entertain soldiers deployed overseas, particularly around the holidays. But such efforts could only accomplish so much. Christmas on the front lines was, and remains, a brutally lonely place for G.I.s thousands of miles away from their families. It makes the mail call, their opportunity to get a little piece of home, an incredibly precious gift. In this photograph, P. F. C. Wayne Baldwin of Groveland, Massachusetts, reads a Christmas card from home while serving in Vietnam. The symbolism of the Life Savers also included in his care package was surely not lost on him either.

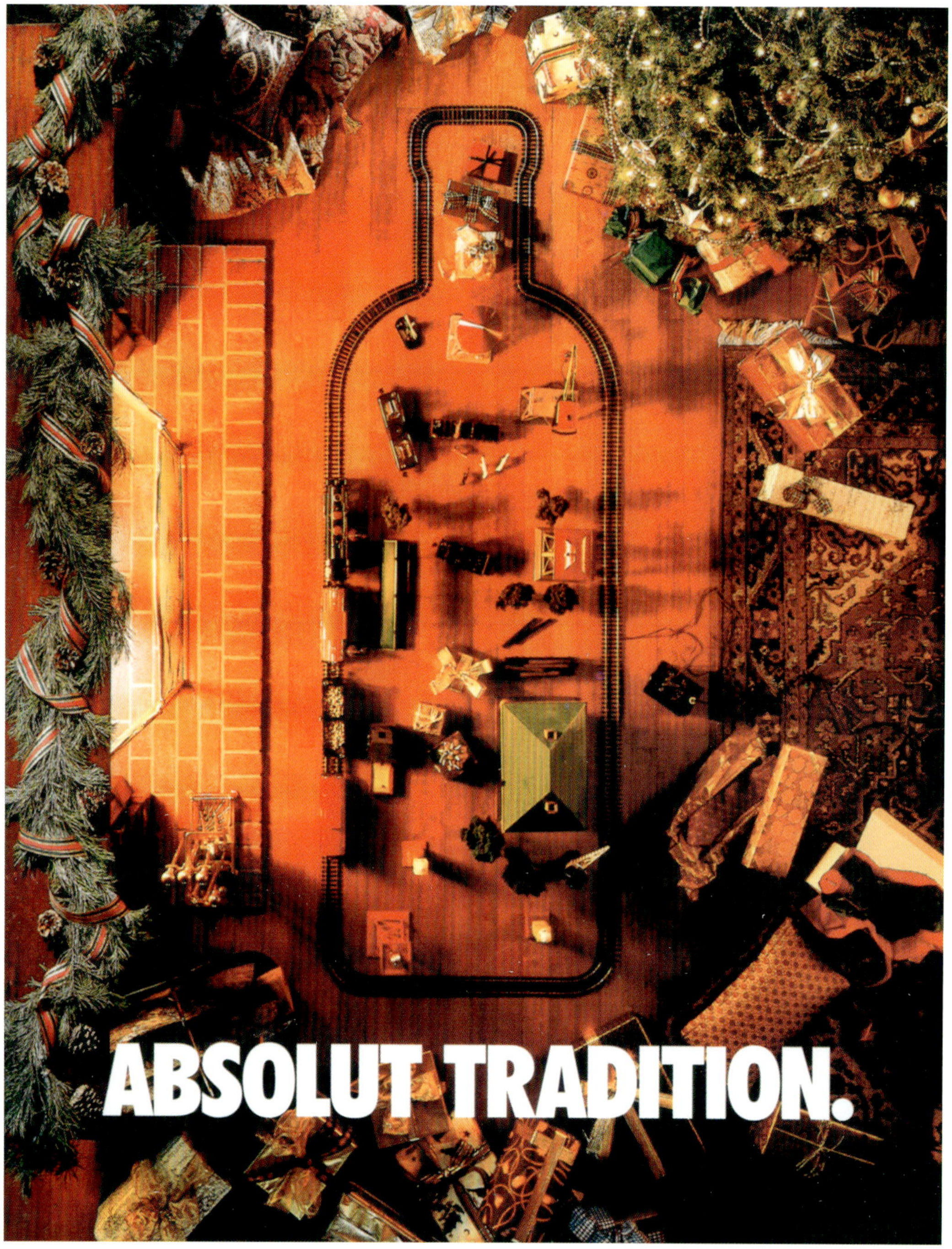

ABSOLUT VODKA

•

"Absolut Tradition" advertisement, 1995
Print, dimensions variable

When Swedish entrepreneur and iconoclast Lars Olsson Smith introduced his vodka to consumers in Stockholm, it was to subvert the city's liquor monopoly. He offered customers free boat rides to the distillery, which was located outside the city limits, and undercut prices considerably. But it was the recipe—made from local ingredients and using a then cutting-edge distillation process—that made Absolut Rent Brännvin (literally translated "absolute pure vodka") a success. The brand floundered after its creator's death in 1913 and throughout the twentieth century, until it was relaunched on its centenary. Trademark issues in the United States necessitated its name change to simply Absolut, and the now-iconic bottle was commissioned based on a centuries-old apothecary bottle found in a Stockholm antique store. The advertising campaign showcasing the brand's distinctive bottle silhouette was launched in 1981, featuring the tag line "Absolut Perfect," and made Absolut vodka an instant worldwide success. More than 1,500 variations on the theme have followed since, including contributions from famous artists, such as Andy Warhol, Keith Haring, and Ralph Steadman, among others. Its annual Christmas advertisements are its most anticipated, and often the most ambitious. In 1988, the company featured a functional glittering snow globe (see p.178) in magazine inserts ("Absolut Wonderland"). In 1994, fashion designer Donna Karan produced a pair of gloves for its "Absolut Warmth" campaign.

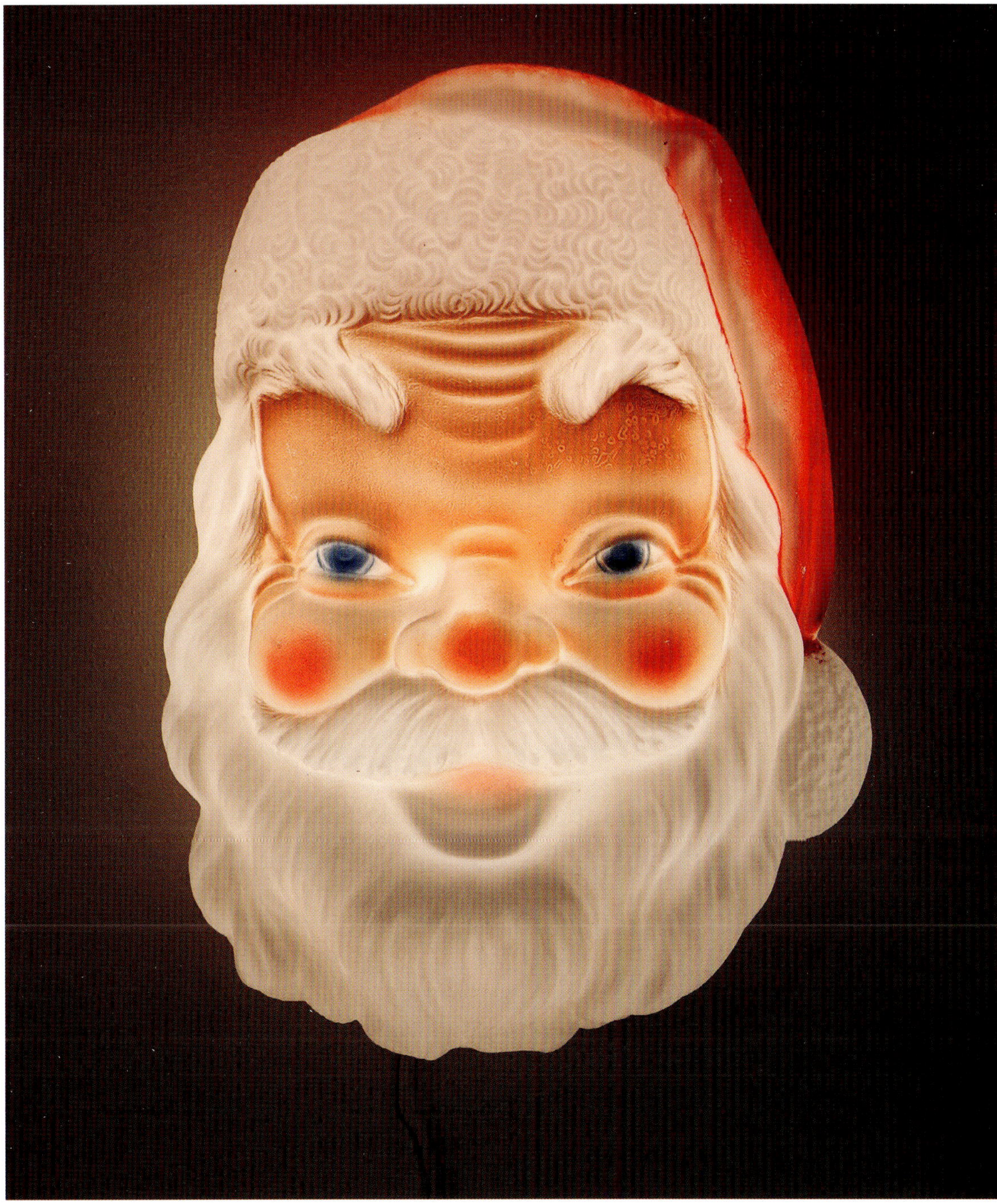

EMPIRE PLASTIC CORP

•

Santa Claus decoration, 1968
Blow-mold plastic, 16 × 13 × 7 in / 40.6 × 33 × 18 cm

This Santa Claus decoration, produced in 1968, is one of hundreds of Christmas-themed offerings produced by American company Empire Plastic Corp, one of the leading manufacturers in this niche of Christmas kitsch. Beco was the first company to introduce blow-molded Christmas decorations; its wares appeared in the 1962 Sears Christmas catalog. Such items quickly became a sensation, and several companies jumped into the fray, including Empire Plastics, Heller, Artistic, and Mold Craft. The manufacturing process for blow molding, modeled after blowing glass, was first patented in the United States in 1881. A hollow tube called a parison was filled with melted plastic, then placed in a metal mold and inflated with air, forcing the plastic to the edges. After cooling, the finished product was removed. It was an ideal method for making glass bottles, but the available materials for blow molding plastic (cellulose nitrate, and later cellulose acetate) had their drawbacks: brittleness and a tendency to shrink or distort, for starters. It wasn't until the 1940s, when innovations in plastic led to low-density polyethylene, that the process revolutionized packaging in industries across the board. American artist Don Featherstone invented the first blow-molded decoration of note, the pink flamingo, in 1957. It was a veritable overnight craze, and the slim avian forms graced lawns everywhere. These blow molds (also known as light-ups) are more collectible now than ever, particularly the Christmas related items.

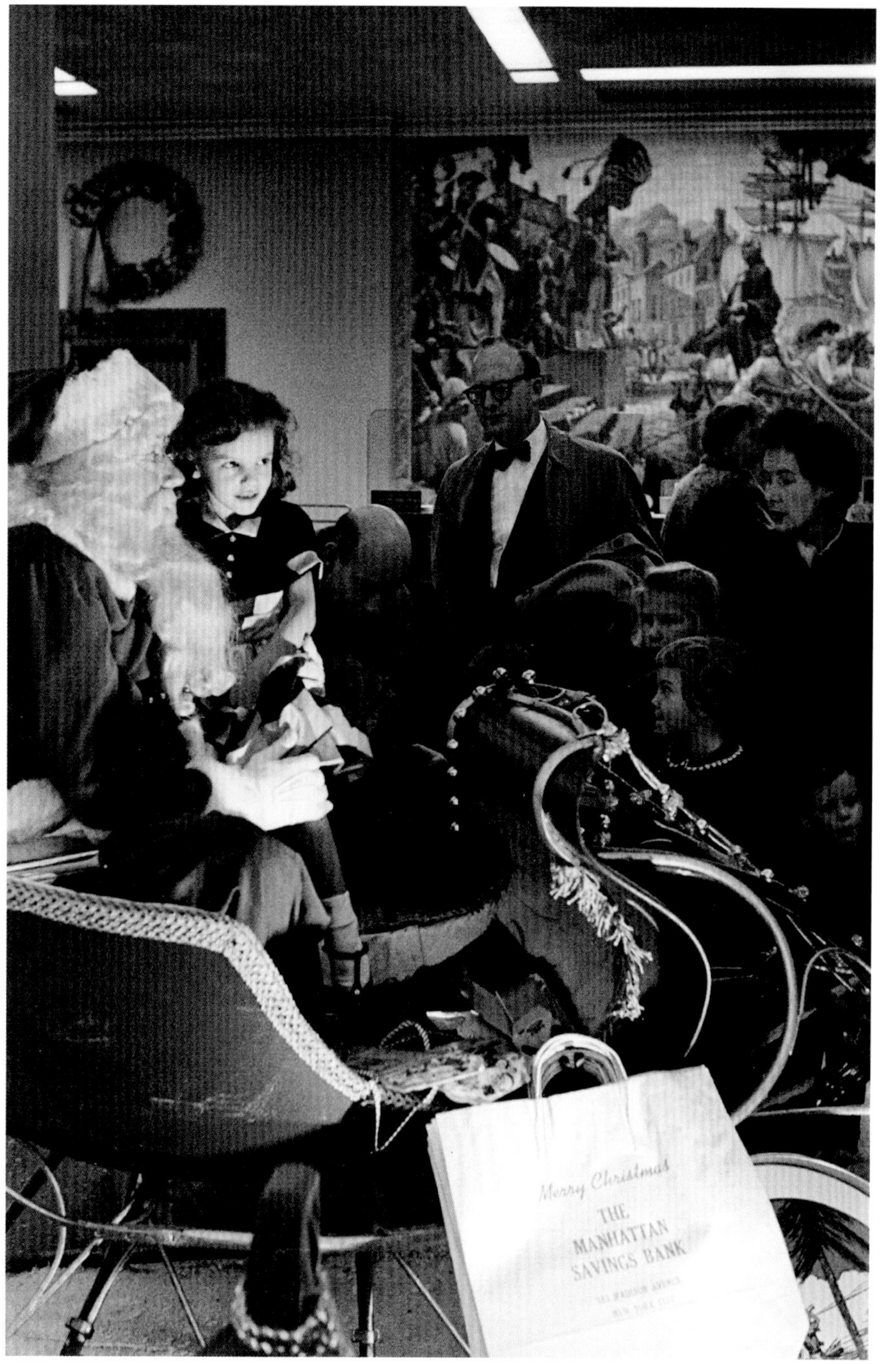

INGE MORATH

•

New York, Santa Claus at the Manhattan Savings Bank on Madison Avenue, 1958
Photograph, dimensions variable

A talented linguist, journalist, and prolific photographer, Austrian-born Inge Morath (1923–2002) had already made a name for herself as a photographer before capturing *New York, Santa Claus at the Manhattan Savings Bank on Madison Avenue* in 1958. This photograph reveals a young girl sitting on the lap of Santa, while other children, accompanied by their parents, line up in anticipation. In the background, a mural showing the arrival of European colonists draws connections between the religious and imperial roots of the Christmas tradition in America. Born in Austria but raised in Berlin during World War II, her ability to speak several languages opened many doors for her as a photographer after the conflict, and, after working for the photojournalist Ernst Haas and upon the invitation of Robert Capa, she joined Magnum Photos in Paris in 1955, becoming the first European female member. As a foreigner in the United States and a shrewd observer of people, Morath turned her camera to the rise of consumerism during the postwar boom of the 1950s, often capturing people partaking in activities, such as window-shopping, and visiting department store Santas like this one (see p.155).

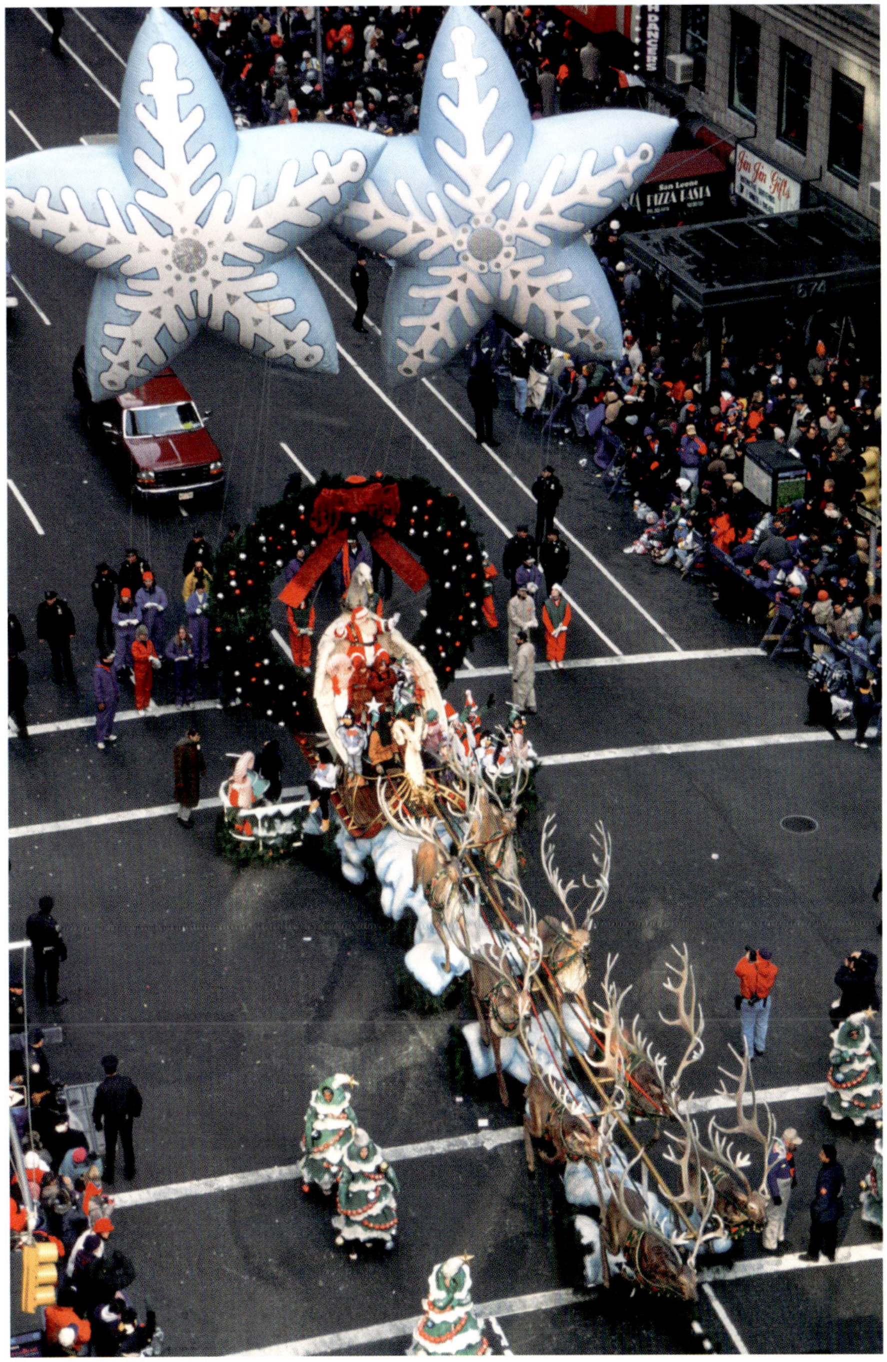

MACY'S

•

Thanksgiving Day Parade, New York City, 1996
Photograph, dimensions variable

The Macy's Thanksgiving Day Parade has been a New York tradition for nearly a century and marks the start of the Christmas season in the United States. The parade is a massive production involving the work of thousands of people and includes balloons as high as four-story buildings, but the main attraction is always Santa Claus and his reindeer on the final float. This overhead photograph shows the 1996 iteration, Santa's sleigh flanked by a huge wreath, with human Christmas trees parading alongside (see p.48). The first-ever parade was held in 1924 to celebrate the opening of the store's expanded flagship location in Herald Square, Manhattan. Macy's was touted as the "world's largest store," boasting one million square feet of shopping space and spanning an entire city block. The parade was billed as a "marathon of mirth," and it was a marathon indeed. The route stretched more than six miles (9 km), circuitously winding its way from 145th Street in Harlem to Macy's 34th Street headquarters. The circuslike festivities included a procession of musicians, employees dressed in festive costumes, and a menagerie of live animals on loan from the Central Park Zoo. The giant helium balloons that have become the hallmark of the parade were introduced in 1927. Since 1953, the event has been televised by NBC, allowing generations upon generations of saucer-eyed children to watch in wonder and anticipation as Santa Claus makes his triumphant return to the city.

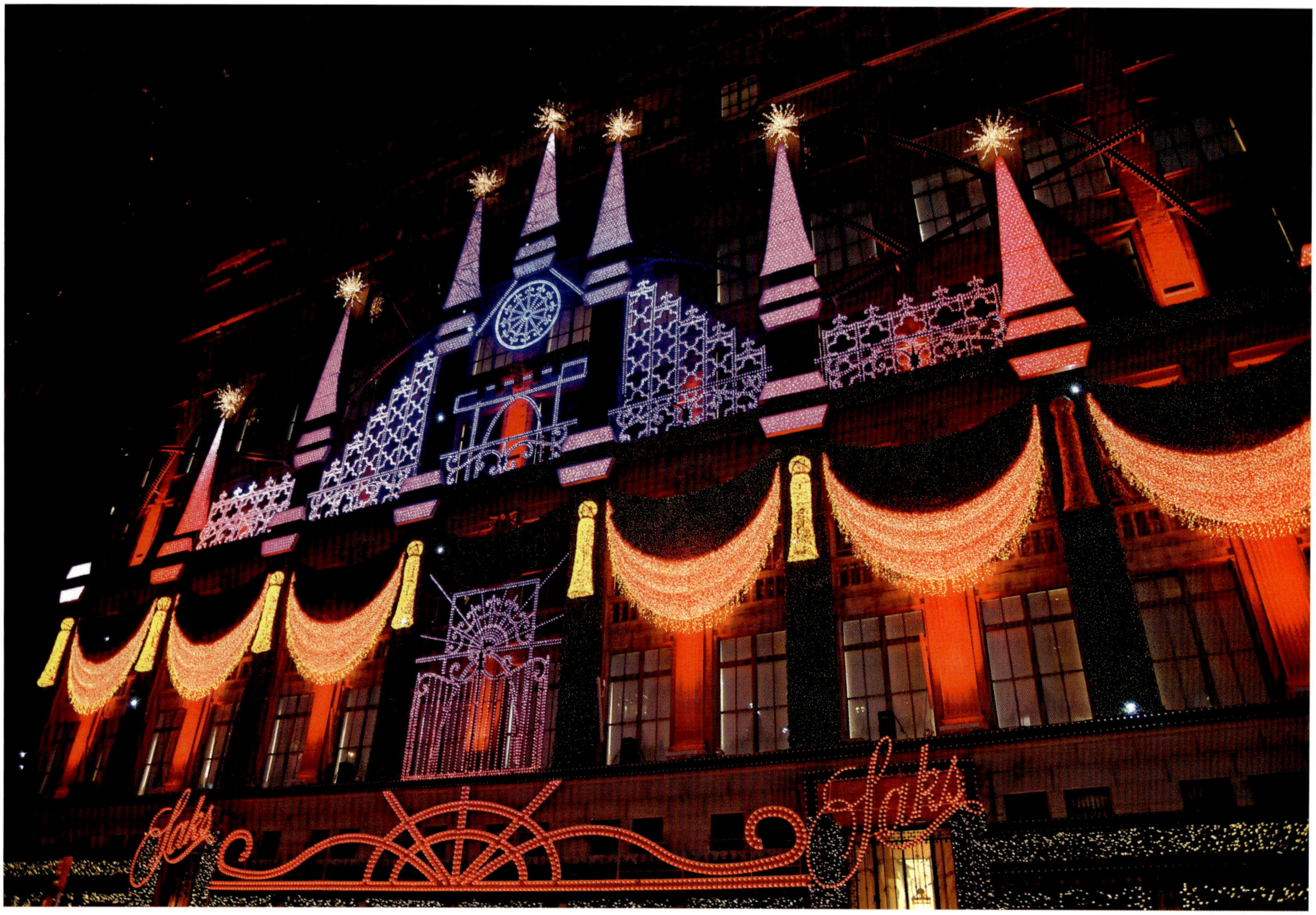

SAKS FIFTH AVENUE

•

Theater of Dreams, 2018
Light installation, dimensions variable

Every Christmas since 2004, the iconic New York City department store Saks Fifth Avenue turns its ten-story-high and a whole city block-wide-facade into a spectacular holiday light show. This 2018 display, "Theater of Dreams," continued the tradition with an ode to Broadway and its theatrical shows. The light show plays every evening from Thanksgiving week in late November—the same day on which Saks reveals its Christmas window displays—until early January. The four-minute light-and-music show plays every ten minutes, creating a total of more than two thousand shows that are watched by more than six million spectators. The 2018 show was set to John Williams's musical arrangement of "There's No Business Like Show Business." The large sweeping arcs paid homage to the nearby music halls, with their distinctive Art Deco details, while gorgeous red curtains replicated those seen inside the city's theaters. The light show was premiered in a live-streamed broadcast of 120 dancers on Fifth Avenue and a spectacular firework display in the sky above Manhattan. The result of months of planning, the light show takes shape in a series of detailed storyboards before it is finally tuned in a series of animations that consider the placement of every individual light before construction starts in late September. Fifth Avenue is a very festive place at Christmas, being that right across the street from Saks is the iconic Rockefeller Christmas tree (see p.20).

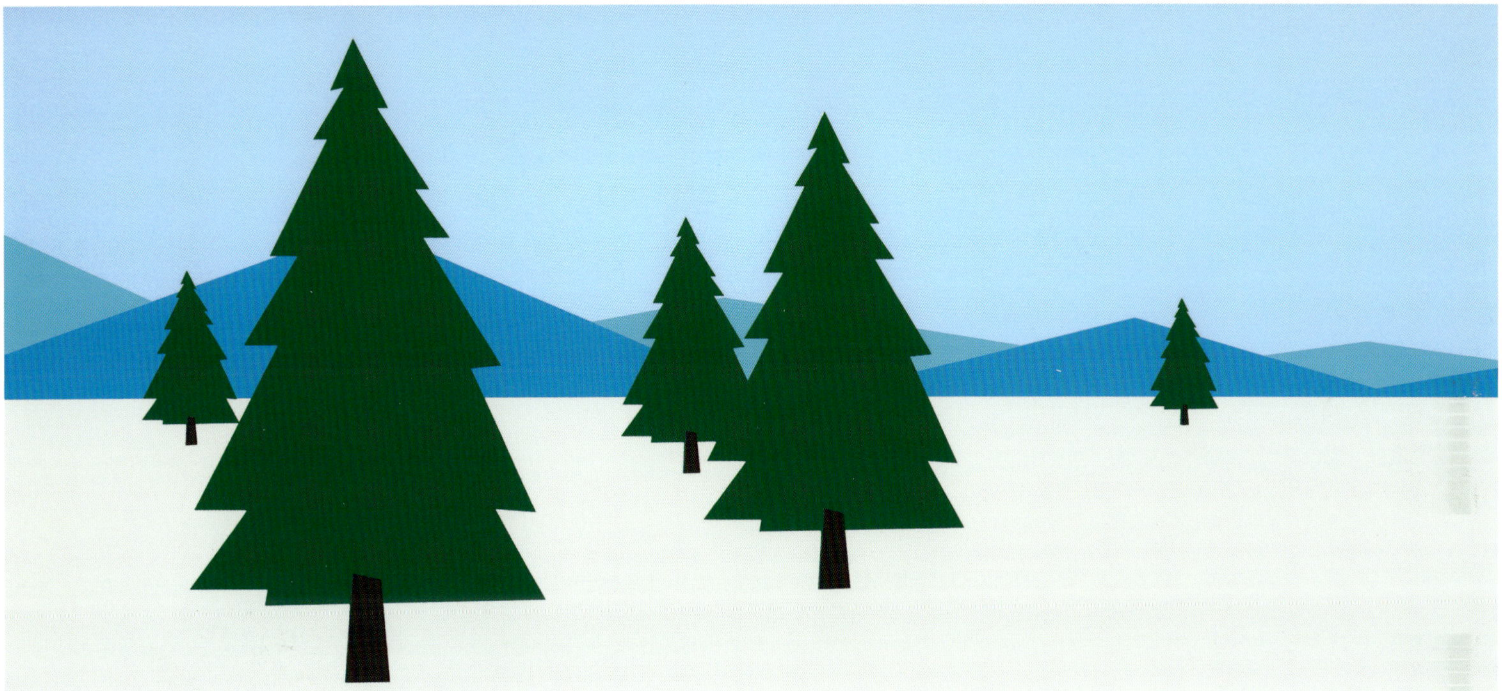

JULIAN OPIE

•

Winter Landscape, 2003
Silk-screen print on paper, 11¾ × 26 in / 30 × 66 cm
British Museum, London

Five green fir trees rise out of the snow-covered ground as the frigid blue hills loom in the background beneath an icy winter sky in this landscape by leading British contemporary artist Julian Opie (1958–). The image began life as a Christmas card but was later reproduced as a limited-edition silk-screen print on paper, numbered on the back out of fifty. Opie's intention was, he said, "to introduce something of the cold emptiness of northern hemispheres." To that end, the perspective for Opie's image came from a train journey, and the way your peripheral vision renders landscapes as they stream by the window. Opie's body of work has moved from his early steel sculptures via installations, video, and pop covers—including the thickly outlined portraits of the four members of Blur—to designs, such as this, that appear simpler but whose simplicity is, in fact, grounded in centuries of artistic tradition. Opie is particularly fascinated by nineteenth-century landscape paintings that use the composition of "a view" to capture the sublime. This particular piece no doubt conjures the memories for many that have experienced a cold, snowy winter, and even tried to capture that one perfect shot to immortalize it forever.

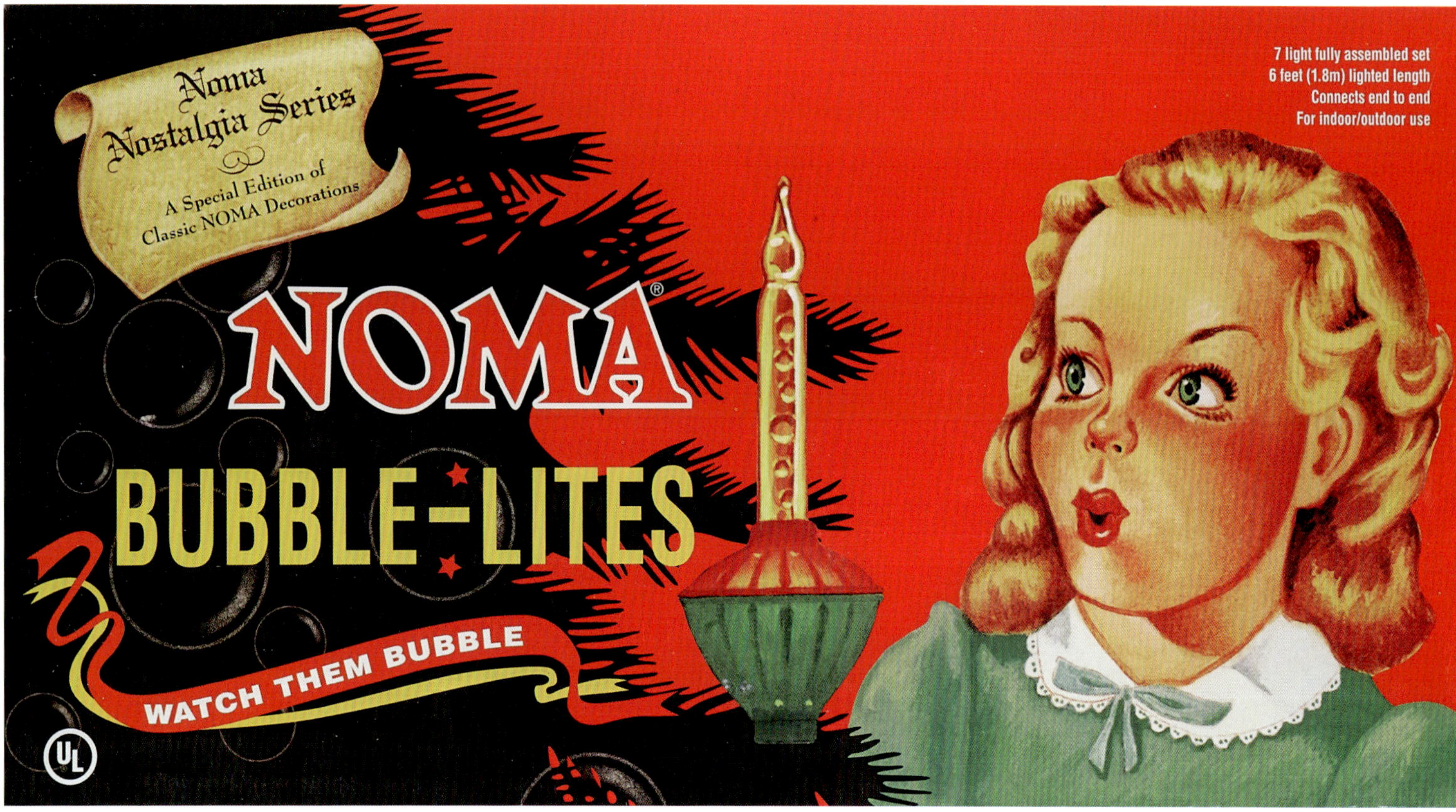

NOMA

•

Bubble-Lites packaging, c.1946
Cardstock, 7⅜ × 13⅞ in / 18.5 × 35.3 cm

The practice of lighting Christmas trees dates to seventeenth-century Germany, when celebrants placed candles among the branches. Popularity of the practice didn't take hold in England until 1848, when an illustration of the royal family gathered around a candlelit Christmas tree created a veritable craze (see p.130). Three decades later Edward Hibberd Johnson first conceived the idea of using electric lights to illuminate a Christmas tree (see p.159). By 1903, Christmas string lights were on the market—though they were strictly the province of the wealthy. Post–World War II prosperity, in addition to improved mass-production methods, brought electric Christmas lights into the mainstream—and they haven't gone anywhere since. NOMA (National Outfit Manufacturer's Association) was a leading retailer in the market and responsible for many innovations in holiday lighting, including parallel wiring, all-rubber cords, and Bubble-Lites. Today considered a paragon of Christmas kitsch, the Bubble-Lite is comprised of a plastic tube containing methylene chloride, a liquid with a low boiling point, which is illuminated and bubbles when heated by a small light in the casing below. Each light clips on to the tree branch, and then the whole top-heavy apparatus inevitably tips over, as aficionados know all too well. Nowadays, LED technology has made Christmas lighting more affordable and safer than ever, guaranteeing multitudes of modern-day buyers who appreciate these bubbling wonders.

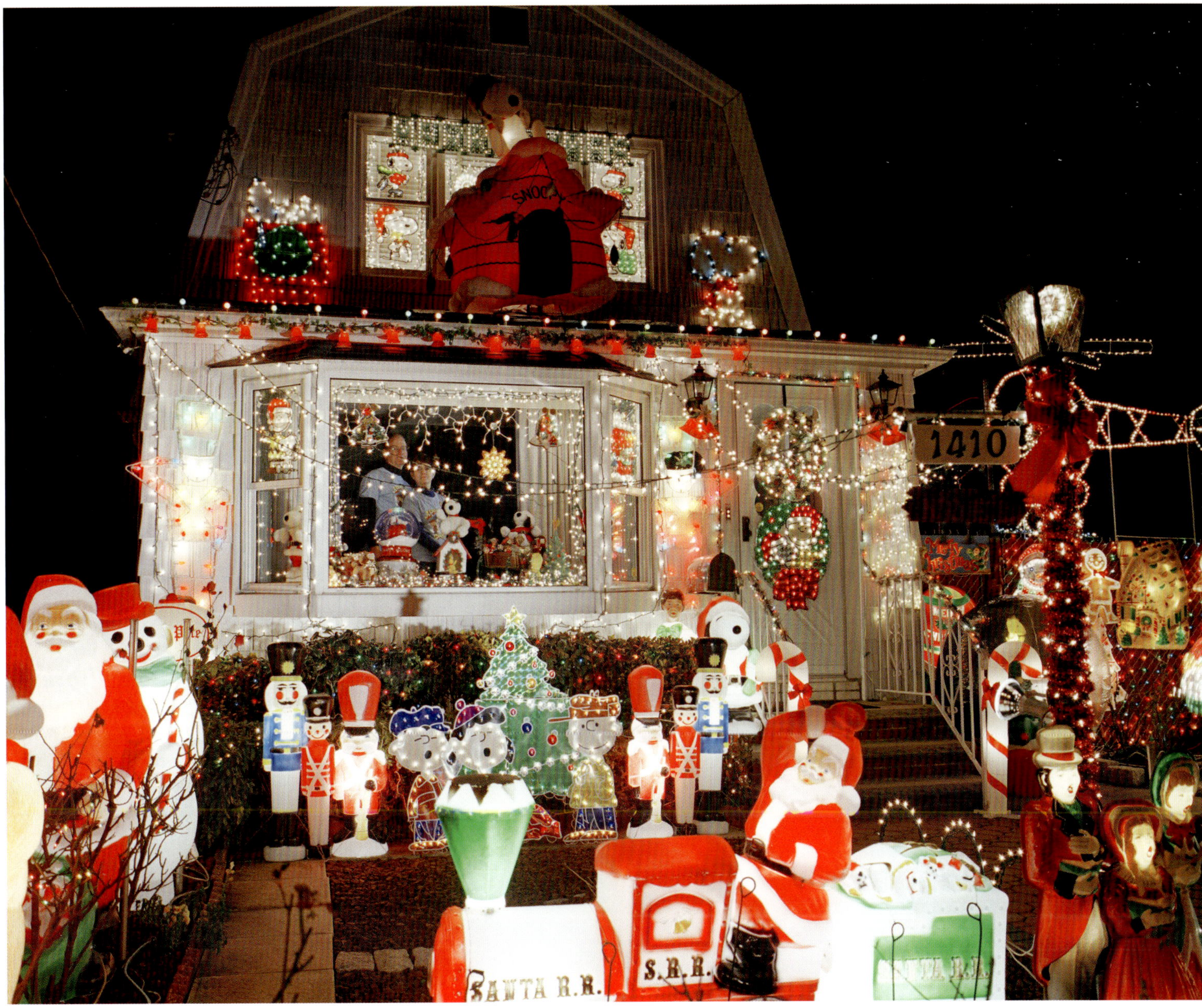

DANELLE MANTHEY

•

Lucy and Lou, Brooklyn, NY, 2009
Photograph, dimensions variable

This Brooklyn home is radiant with colored lights and glowing decorations, from Santas and snowmen to soldiers, carol singers, and *Peanuts* characters. A proud couple in matching Christmas sweaters (see pp.105, 117, 135) stand at the window, framed by strings of fairy lights. The image is one of more than forty photographs from *American Christmas*, a decade-long project and book by photographer Danelle Manthey, who traveled across twelve states, from New York to California, documenting the most ostentatious light displays she could find. Manthey's childhood memories of driving around her neighborhood admiring the colorful light shows that brightened the long winter nights at Christmastime inspired the series, which began in 2003 in her hometown of Sioux Falls, South Dakota. As the project progressed, she discovered an entire online community of Christmas light enthusiasts, who frequent forums and publish blogs on the subject. Many spend months working on their displays, which contain thousands of lights and ornaments, and some even design and build their own decorations. Manthey's passion to seek out the country's best suburban light-show designers led her to the conclusion that their activities constitute a distinct form of American folk art, even though most don't consider themselves to be creative. Manthey always made a point of spending time with her subjects, learning about their craft before respectfully composing her shot to capture the individuality, dedication, and joy of each display.

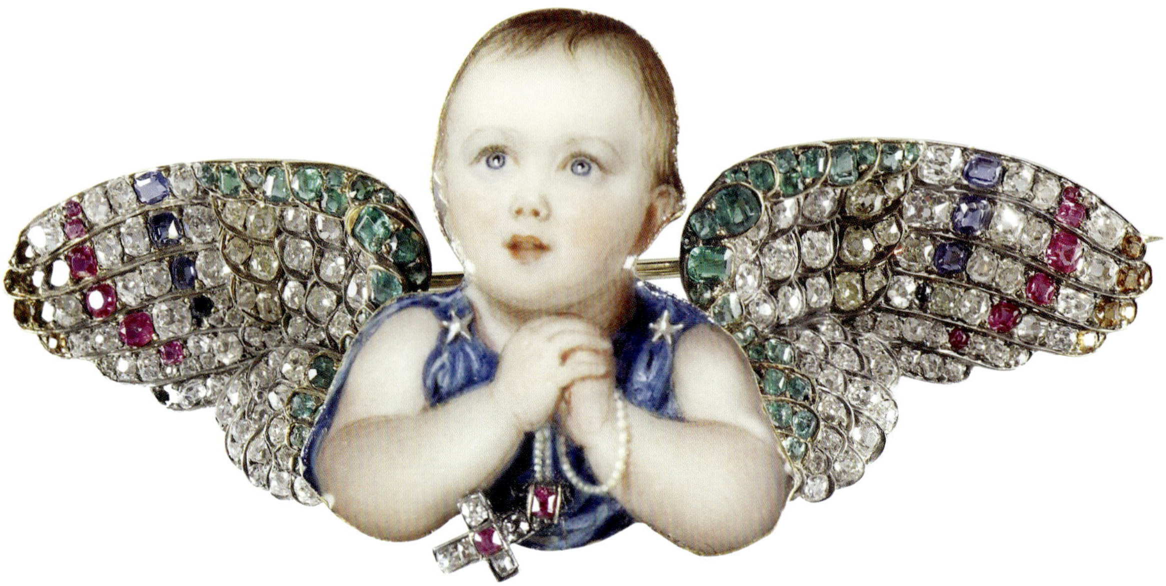

WILLIAM ESSEX

•

Brooch of Victoria, Princess Royal, 1842
Enamel, gold, sapphires, rubies, emeralds, diamonds, and topazes, 1⅜ × 2⅝ in / 3.5 × 6.8 cm
Royal Collection, London

This exquisite enamel, gold, and jeweled brooch depicts a real child—Princess Victoria, the first child of Great Britain's Queen Victoria—and was a Christmas present from the baby's father, Prince Albert, to his beloved wife and sovereign in 1842, gifted two years after the princess's birth. The brooch held a special significance, because it was designed by Albert himself, inspired by a cherub painted by the great Italian Renaissance painter Raphael (1483–1520) in the 1500s. For her part, Queen Victoria was thrilled with her present, noting in particular the quality of the workmanship, and how pleased her husband was that she appreciated his very thoughtful gift. The brooch shows an angelic-looking princess royal clasping a string of pearls from which hangs a crucifix fashioned from diamonds and rubies. Mounted in gold, the cutout enamel miniature was copied by the artist William Essex (1784–1869), who had worked for the queen before becoming the prince's enamel painter, from a circular miniature originally painted by Sir William Ross (1794–1860). Sir William's picture, showing the princess against a cloudy sky, proved so popular it was copied many times. To Essex's portrait of his daughter, Prince Albert added wings made of numerous diamonds with a sprinkling of emeralds, rubies, and sapphires. Albert is widely credited with having introduced many Christmas institutions to Great Britain, but as was usual in his native Germany, the couple exchanged their gifts on Christmas Eve.

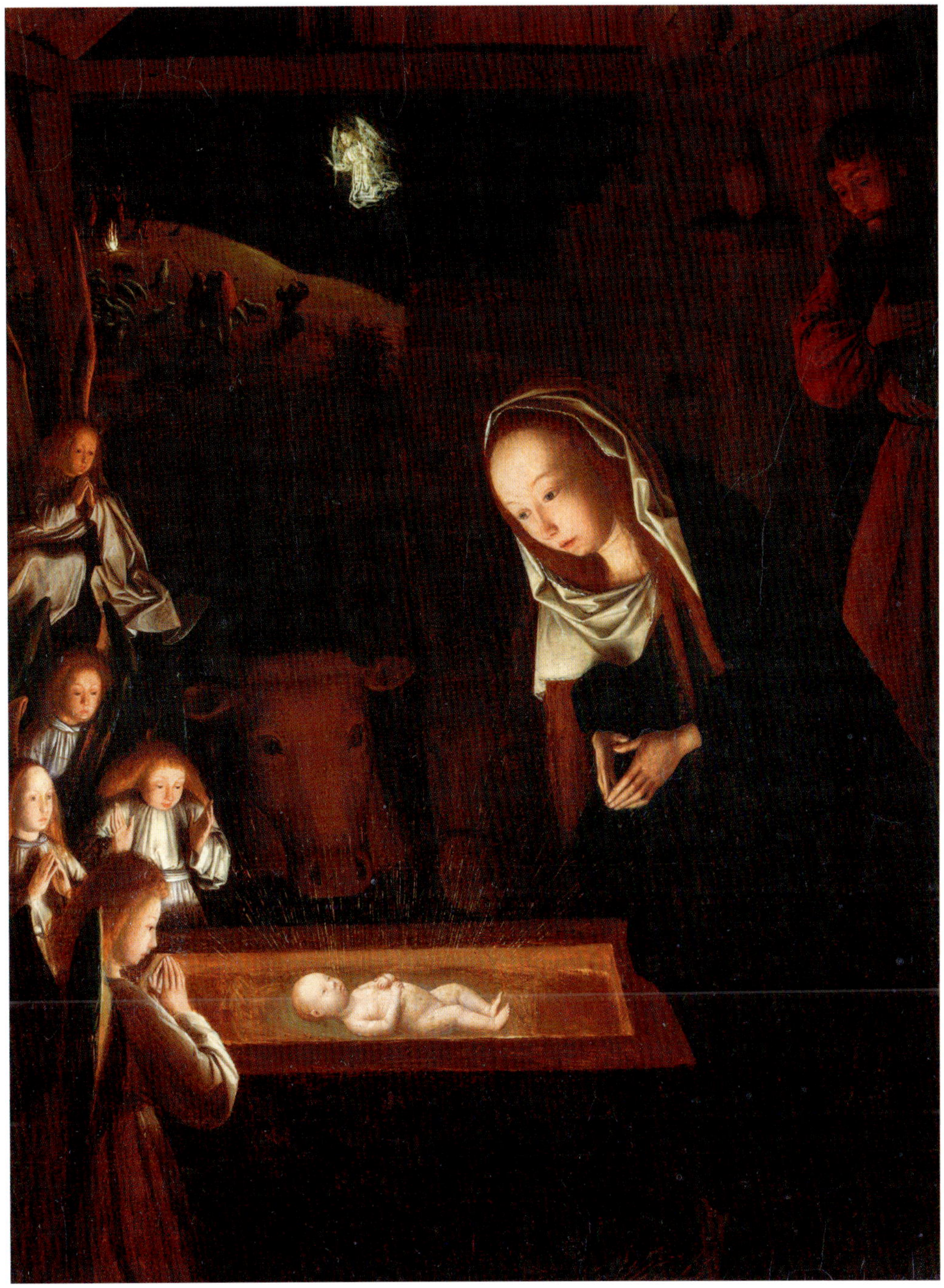

GEERTGEN TOT SINT JANS

•

The Nativity at Night, c.1490
Oil on oak, 13⅜ × 10 in / 34 × 25.3 cm
National Gallery, London

A divine light emanating from the infant Christ illuminates his mother, Mary, and a group of adoring angels, who gaze in amazement at the child in the manger. An ox and donkey also peer at the baby, but the golden glow, seeming to emanate from the child himself, does not light their heads as it does the soft skin of Mary's devout face (see p.11). While some of the angels are praying, one stands with his hands raised in rapture at the sight of God born as a human. On the right of the picture, almost hidden by the gloom, is Joseph, who looks on from the shadows, separated from Mary, his espoused. Outside, on the hill, shepherds tending to their sheep encounter an angel hovering in the night sky, who has appeared to announce the savior's birth; one shepherd has fallen to his knees in astonishment, while another shields his eyes from the angelic herald's radiance. Painted by the Early Netherlandish artist Geertgen tot Sint Jans (*c*.1465–1495), this small scene tells the traditional Christmas story as recorded in the second chapter of Luke's Gospel, in which the baby Jesus is born in a stable, "because there was no room for them in the inn." This painting was one of the earliest to depict the Nativity at night and was probably made for private devotional use. It conveys the wonderment of Christ's birth while alluding to his self-description as "the light of the world" in the eighth chapter of John's Gospel.

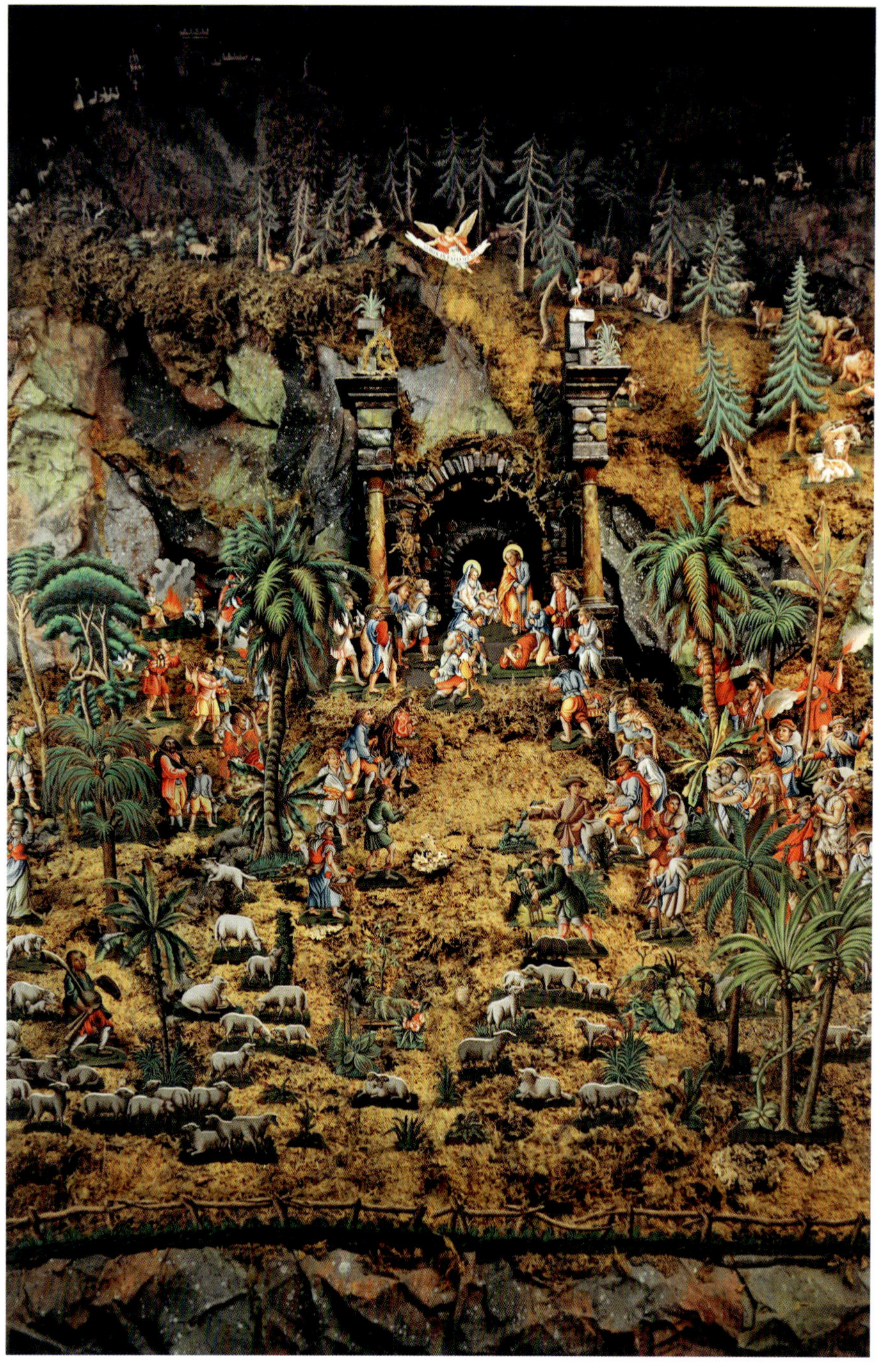

WENZEL FIEGER

•

Paper Nativity Scene, c.1890
Gouache on cardstock,
H. 1¼–5½ in / 3–14 cm (figures)
Bayerisches National Museum, Munich

This Nativity scene could only come from one place. The central European region of Moravia—the eastern part of the former Czechoslovakia, now part of Czechia—has developed its own Nativity tradition, using steep backdrops and two-dimensional figures in complicated designs made entirely from paper. This scene, which dates from around 1890, shows the shepherds visiting the baby Jesus, surrounded by their flocks. The detail is part of a much larger scene pieced together from more than one thousand individual pieces, like a highly complicated puzzle. The choice of material dates back to the imposition of a ban on Nativity scenes in European churches in the second half of the eighteenth century, when people started to make their own Nativities at home from easily sourced materials, such as clay, bread dough, and paper, which were much cheaper and easier to shape than wood. Created by Moravian artist Wenzel Fieger (1860–1924), the Nativity reflects the region's distinctive Christmas aesthetic. It was intended to teach children about the birth of Jesus, and Fieger included numerous minor characters to attract their interest, plus two cows relieving themselves, and set the story against a backdrop of steep forests that would have been familiar to them. While this Nativity is hand painted, as the scenes grew more popular they were sold printed, ready to be cut out and assembled against a homemade backdrop of twigs and moss.

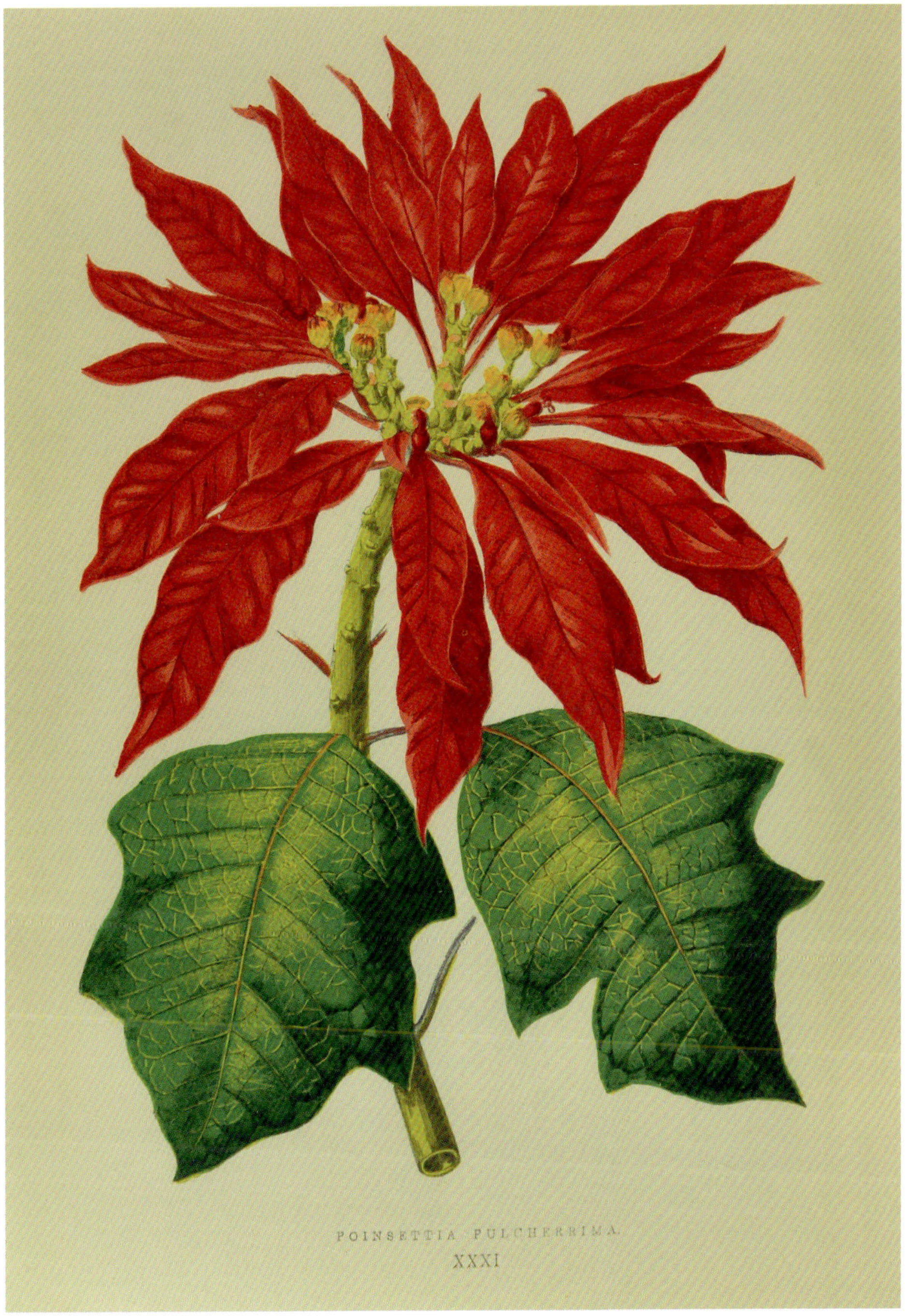

EDWARD JOSEPH LOWE

•

Plate XXXI from *Beautiful Leaved Plants*, 1872
Colored wood engraving, H. 10⅛ in / 25.7 cm
Published by Bell and Daldy, London

The startling red of the poinsettia makes it a familiar Christmas plant, adorning homes with its cheerfully colored leaves. This detailed botanical illustration of a *Euphorbia pulcherrima* (poinsettia) appears in a book of colored wood engravings entitled *Beautiful Leaved Plants: Being a Description of the Most Beautiful Leaved Plants in Cultivation in This Country,* compiled by the English polymath Edward Joseph Lowe (1825–1900). The poinsettia is native to southern Mexico, where it flowers during the winter, and was said to have been used by the Aztecs to make a purple dye and to cure fever. Its cultivation beyond Central America was the result of the horticultural enthusiasm of the first US ambassador to Mexico, Joel Roberts Poinsett, who in 1928 sent some specimens to friends in the United States and after whom it was later named. Its association with Christmas is underlined by a traditional Mexican tale in which a poor young girl could not afford to buy a gift for the baby Jesus. When she instead placed a bunch of weeds on the Nativity scene at church, they were miraculously turned into bright red flowers. Poinsettias became a popular part of Christmas in Mexico, where it is known as *flores de Noche Buena* (flowers of Holy Night) before spreading to the United States, where today millions of the plants are sold every Christmas.

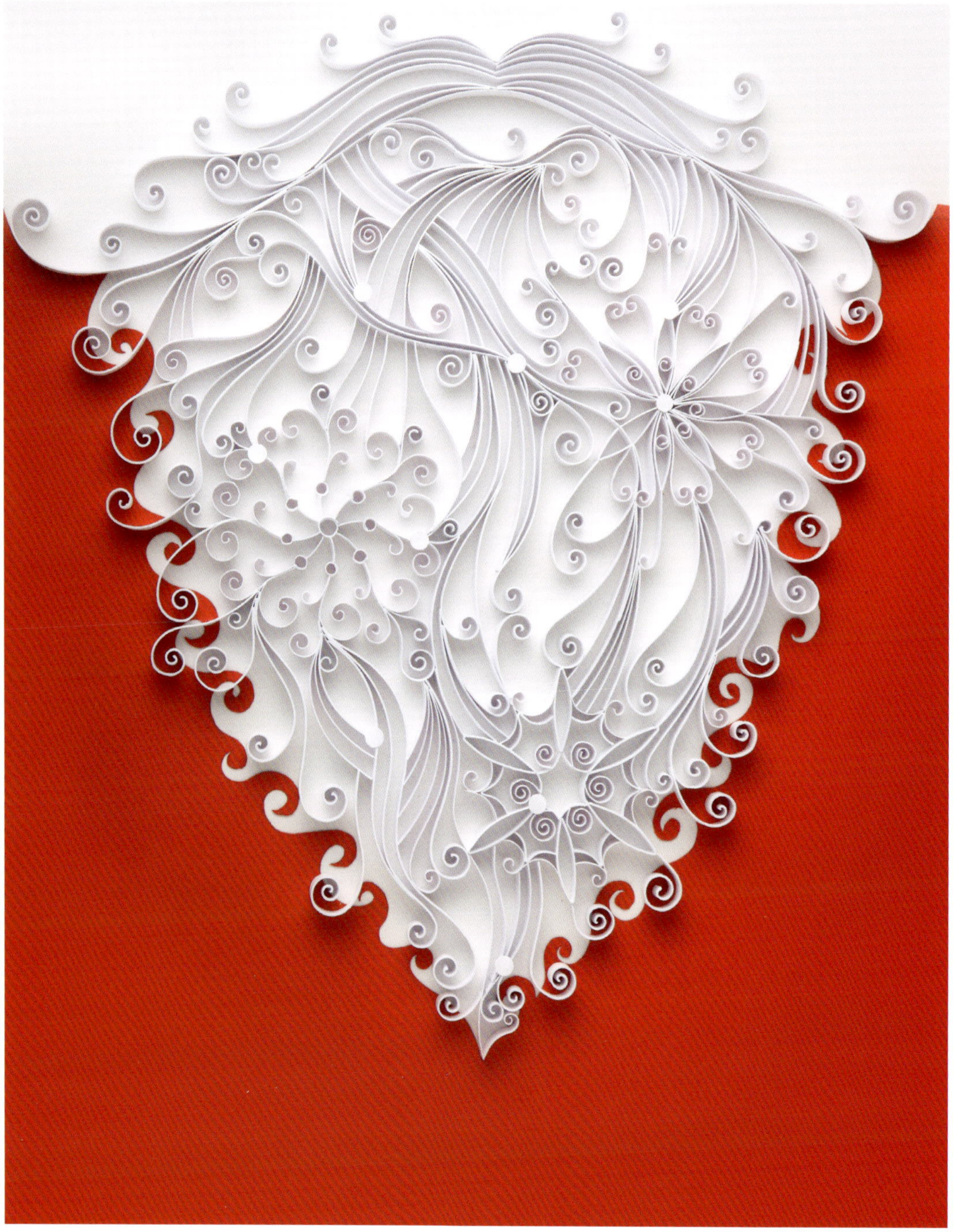

YULIA BRODSKAYA

•

Original artwork for *The Christmas Book*, 2009
White and colored paper, dimensions unknown
For Neiman Marcus

The Neiman Marcus *Christmas Book* is the American luxury retailer's annual Christmas catalog (see pp.28, 62, 173). Pictured here is the original artwork for the 2009 edition of the catalog, featuring the work of renowned Russian paper artist Yulia Brodskaya. What might first appear as digital vector art is, in fact, a 3D paper sculpture. Brodskaya creates "paper illustrations" mostly using an old technique called quilling, in which strips of paper are arranged to create intricate designs and images. Here, we see Santa's iconic white beard, featuring a grand array of patterns and designs, set against a flat red background. There are no overt references to Santa Claus or Christmas here, but it is unmistakable who is being portrayed. Neiman Marcus is renowned for *The Christmas Book*, published annually since 1939. Among the general items one would expect to find—clothes, fragrances, home goods—Neiman Marcus also offers a selection of "Fantasy Gifts." These are often one-of-a-kind gifts not available to buy in store, with prices starting at tens of thousands of dollars and going up into the millions. The 2022 edition offered, for example, a $3.2 million Cartier diamond tiara from 1935; a $330,000 all-pink Barbie Maserati Grecale Trofeo SUV (of which only three exist); and a $295,000 polo trip to Aspen, Colorado, including luxury accommodations, exclusive seating at a polo match, professional polo lessons, and more.

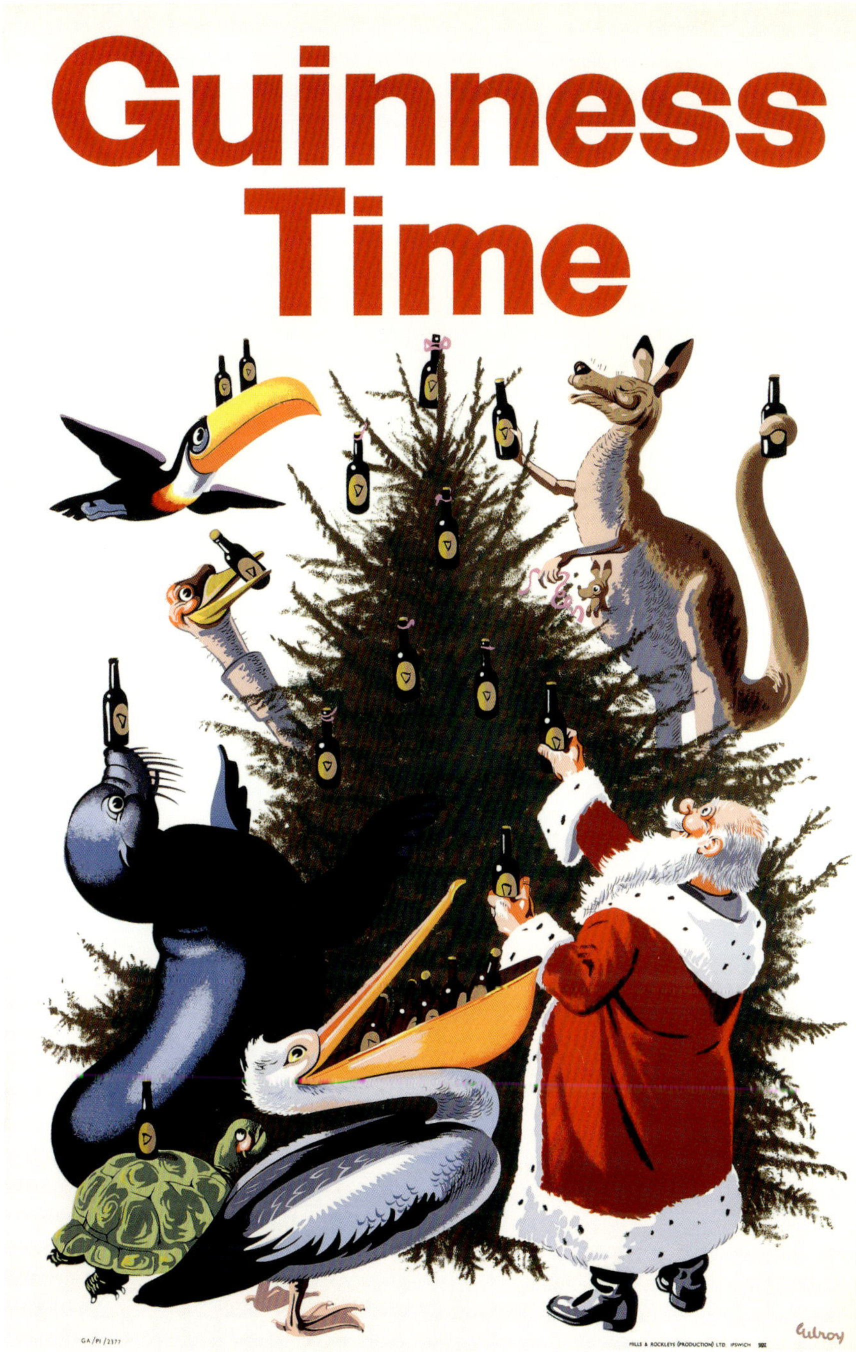

JOHN GILROY

•

Guinness Time, 1958
Color lithograph, 30 × 20 in / 76 × 51 cm
Guinness Archives, Dublin

Santa Claus, without his iconic fur-trimmed red hat (see p.111), decorates a large Christmas tree with bottles of stout, with a helping paw, flipper, and beak provided by his animal friends. The animals are all closely associated in the UK with Guinness, the famous Irish brewery for which this advertising poster was created by the English artist John Gilroy (1898–1985). Originating from the brewery of Arthur Guinness (1725–1803) in Dublin in 1759, for more than 150 years Guinness didn't advertise to the public, instead relying on word of mouth to sell its beer. In 1929, after the first advertisement appeared insisting "Guinness is Good for You," a steady stream of iconic posters followed, with over fifty created by former newspaper cartoonist Gilroy. Inspired by a sea lion he saw at the circus balancing a ball on its nose, he replaced the ball with a pint of stout, spawning an entire series in which zookeepers had their beer stolen by an ever-growing menagerie of characters, including a turtle, an ostrich, a crocodile, a kangaroo, and the most well-known of all, the toucan, all of which appear in this festive poster that matter-of-factly states that Christmas is "Guinness Time." Guinness often produced Christmas-themed advertisements, including one in which Santa carries a tree in one hand with the tag line "Guinness for Strength," and another where a man gleefully wakes up on Christmas morning to a bottle of stout in his stocking (see pp.104, 166).

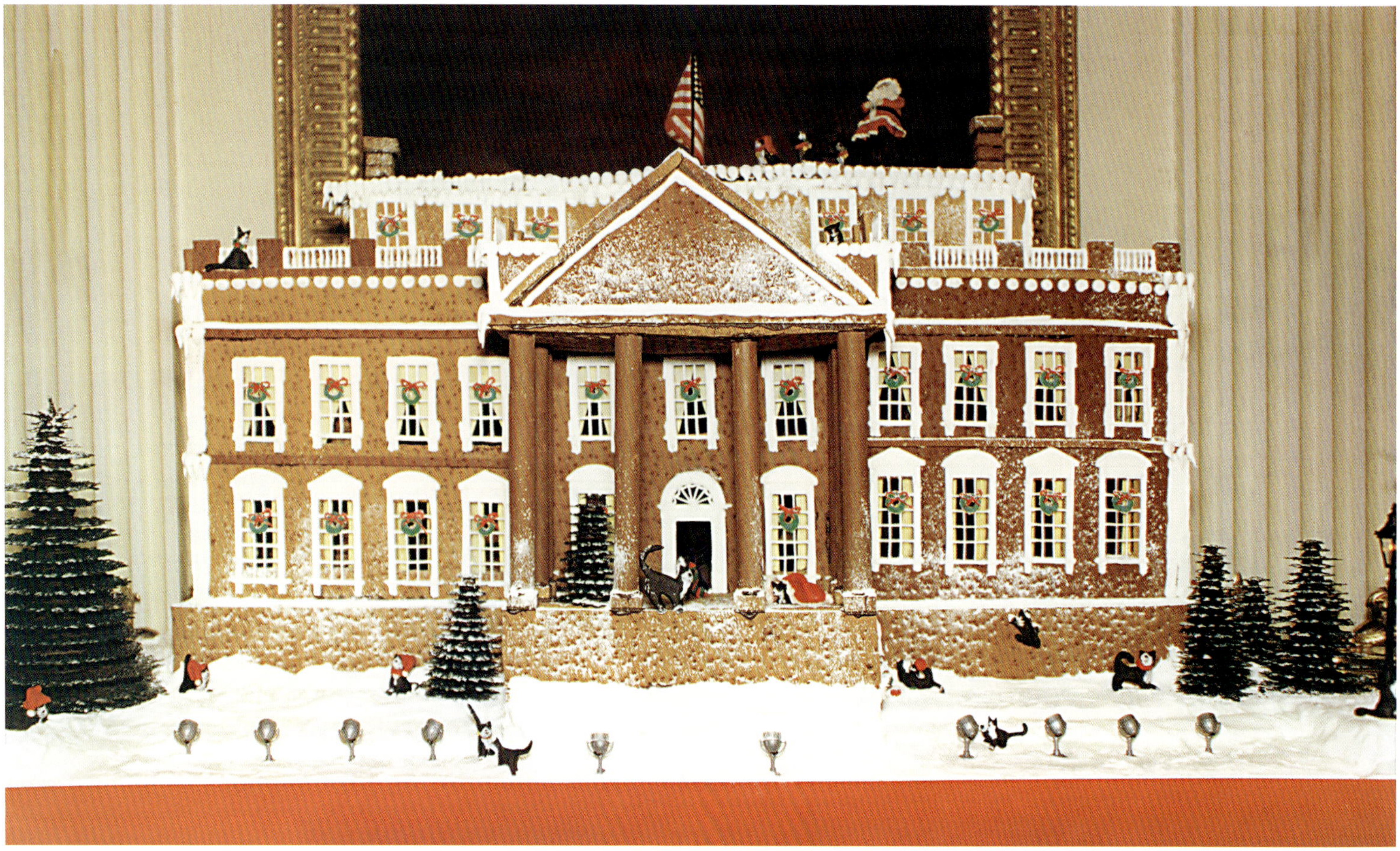

ROLAND MESNIER

•

House of Socks gingerbread house
for the White House, 1993
Gingerbread and marzipan, dimensions unknown

Gingerbread is an ancient recipe, and its ability to hold its shape when baked makes it an ideal architectural dough. Gingerbread houses originated in the sixteenth century in Germany, and many believe that they became popular after the publication of the Brothers Grimm's *Hansel and Gretel*, which features a temptingly delicious gingerbread cottage at its center. This one, in the shape of the White House by American pastry chef Roland Mesnier (1944–2022), is named after the Clinton family's pet cat Socks and features twenty-two marzipan sculptures of the First Feline cavorting around the White House exterior. Gingerbread has had a place at the American president's table since the beginning (First Lady Martha Washington had a recipe), but it wasn't until 1968 that the White House gingerbread house became an annual tradition. President Lyndon B. Johnson (1908–1973) was given an A-frame gingerbread cottage as a Christmas gift and put it on display in front of a gilded mirror in the White House's State Dining Room, where the details could be viewed from all angles. The next year, incoming president Richard Nixon (1913–1994) tasked White House chef Hans Raffert with installing another confectionary cottage. As the years passed, the houses became bigger and more elaborate, reflecting the details and tastes of the First Family across several administrations. The tradition continues annually and is a hallmark of Christmas at the White House.

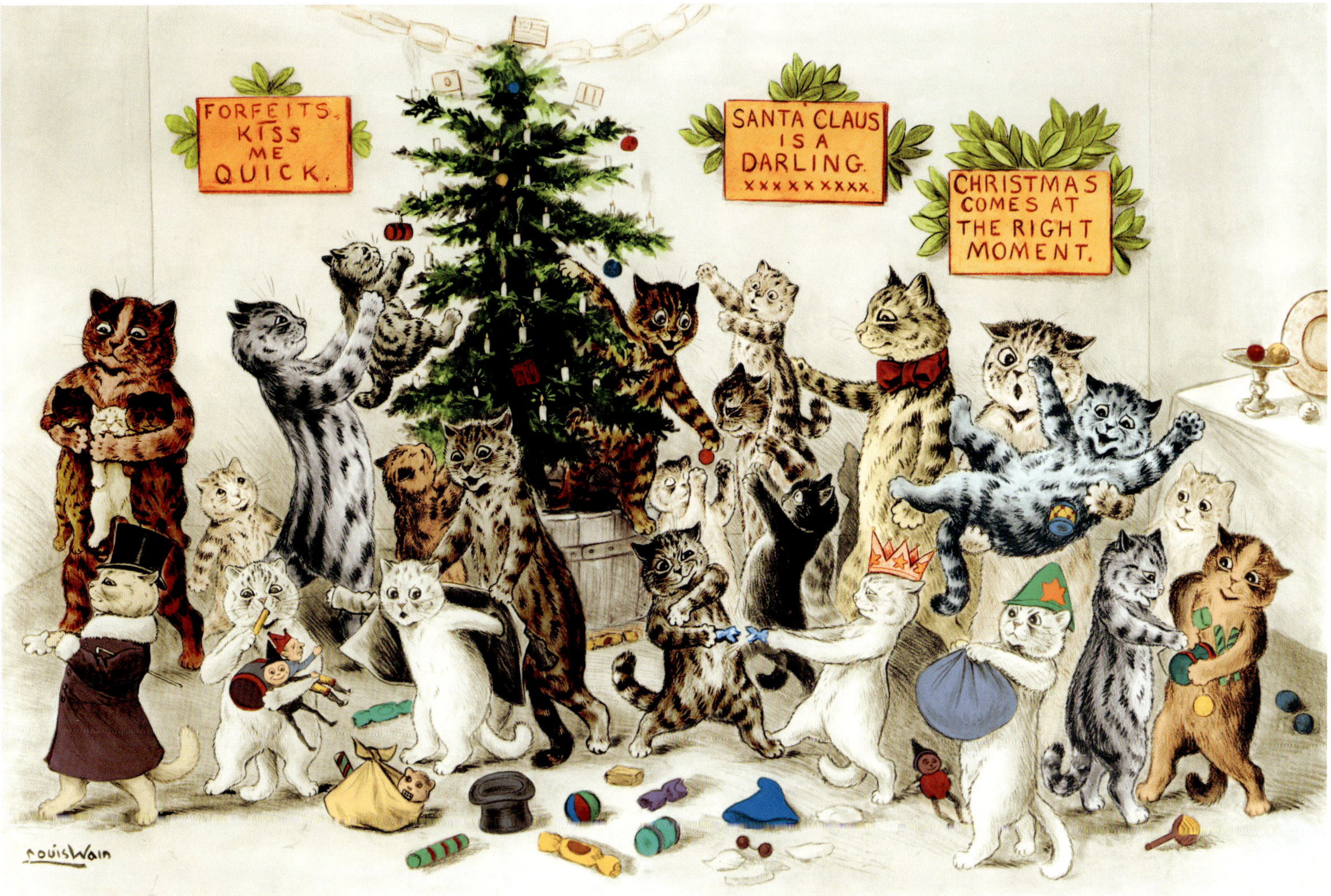

LOUIS WAIN

•

Cats Decorating Christmas Tree, 1906
Pen drawing, 8 × 10 in / 20.3 × 25.4 cm
Library of Congress, Washington, D.C.

English artist Louis Wain (1860–1939) was one of the most notable artists of his era and had risen to prominence after drawing *A Kitten's Christmas Party* in 1886, which comically merged the subject of anthropomorphized cats with the theme of Christmas. *Cats Decorating Christmas Tree*, completed in 1906, continued this trend. In this drawing, a large family of cats come together in what could be a domestic living room to celebrate Christmas. Younger cats play with toys, pull crackers, and make mischief, while the elder cats help them hang ornaments on the carefully decorated traditional Christmas tree. These illustrations became hugely popular as the subject of postcards, greetings, and Christmas cards. In the late nineteenth century, cats were not regarded as lovable pets; they were considered to be disease-spreading pests and they were permitted indoors solely for the purpose of catching rats. Wain, as an eccentric individual with undiagnosed mental health problems, identified with the maligned creatures, regarding them as misunderstood and poorly treated by society. He served as chairman of the National Cat Club and joined several animal charities, including the Society for the Protection of Cats and the Anti-Vivisection Society. As an illustrator, he worked primarily for *The Illustrated London News*, and his charming scenes of cats behaving likes humans became a vehicle to parody the social norms and customs of nineteenth- and early-twentieth-century society.

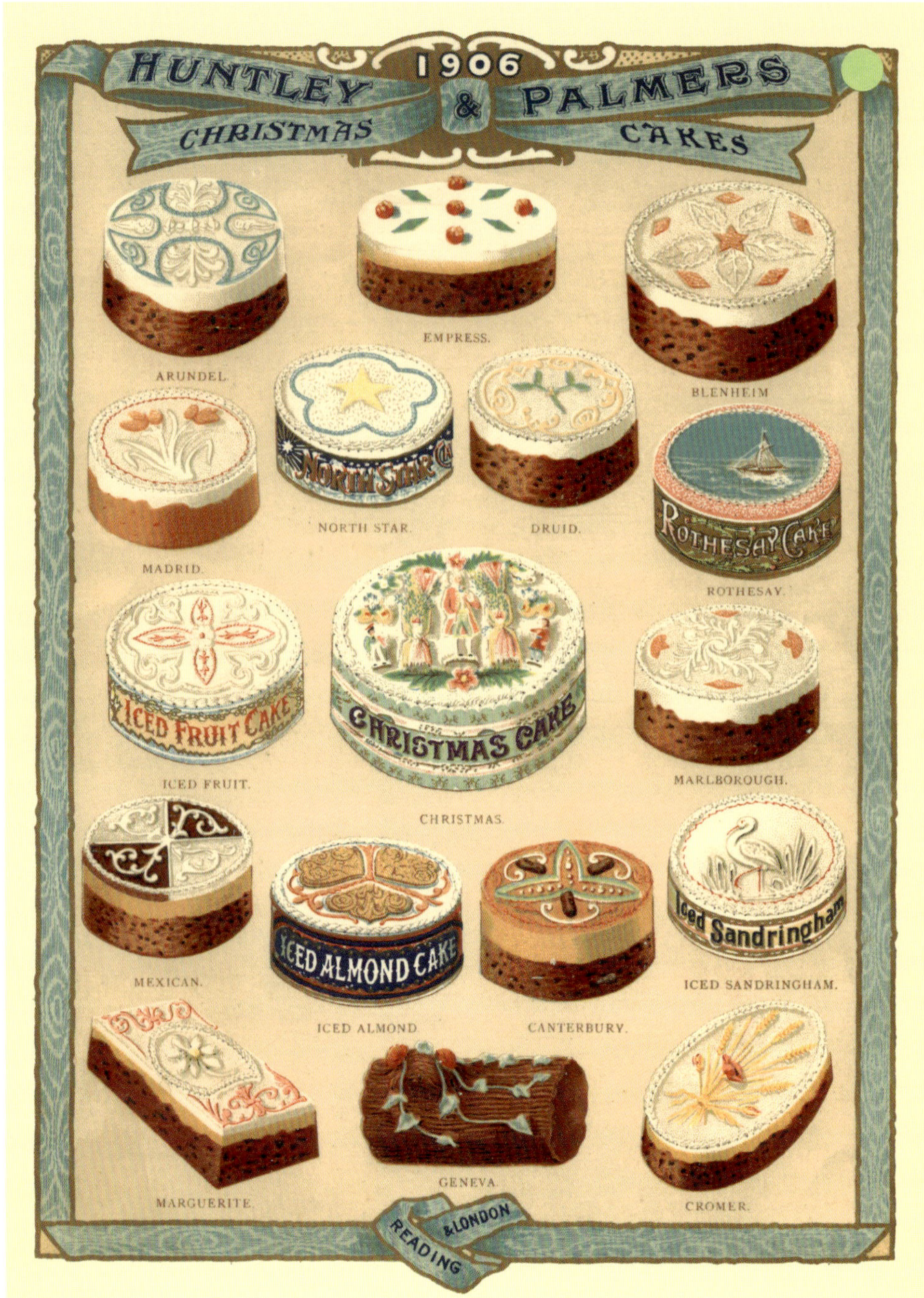

HUNTLEY & PALMERS

•

Christmas Cakes advertisement, c.1906
Print, dimensions variable

The names of the various Christmas cakes on this early twentieth-century advertisement for the British biscuit or cookie makers Huntley & Palmers include repeated nods to the British royal family and castles and palaces around the country: Sandringham was the residence of King Edward VII in eastern England; the Empress cake refers to his queen, Alexandra, Empress of India; Arundel is a medieval castle owned by the Duke of Norfolk; and Blenheim Palace is one of England's largest houses. Christmas cakes made with dried fruit are a long-standing British tradition that can be traced back centuries to a plum porridge people ate to fortify themselves for fasting over the Christmas period. Around the sixteenth century, people started to use richer ingredients in the porridge, replacing the oats with flour and eggs, until the pudding thickened to resemble more familiar modern fruitcakes (see p.108). Spices, such as cinnamon, were later added to the cake, an acknowledgment of the exotic Asian origins of the three wise men, as were layers of marzipan and icing. Founded in 1822, Huntley & Palmers became one of the most renowned global food companies over the following 150 years, noted for its attractive packaging and its innovative advertising. The Victorians enjoyed a wide range of Christmas cakes, many decorated with wintry scenes, and Huntley & Palmers successfully tapped into the growing market for store-bought decorated cakes.

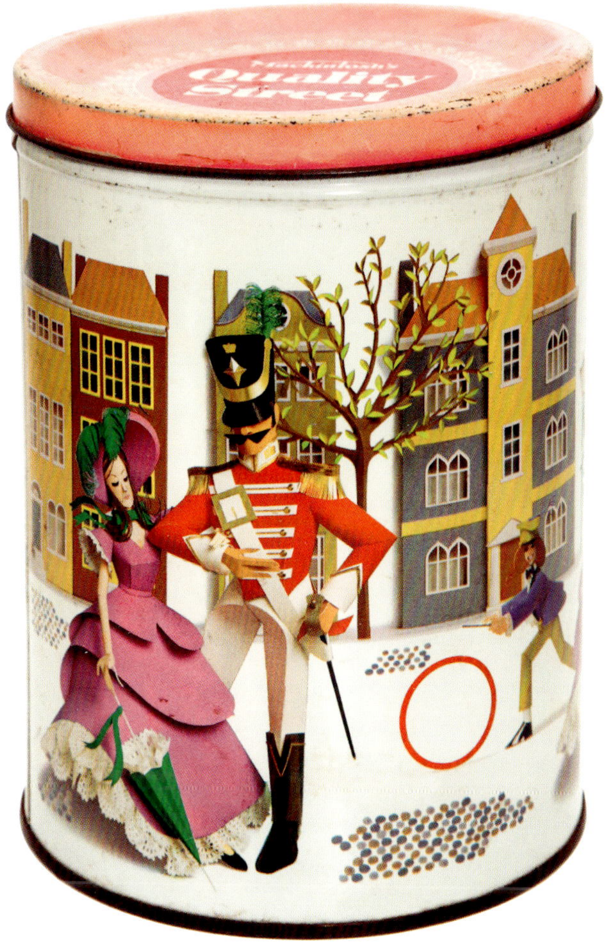

MACKINTOSH'S

•

Quality Street tin, c.20th century
Tin, dimensions unknown

Angular takes on the brand's Regency-era mascots, Miss Sweetly and Major Quality, feature on this seasonal tin of Quality Street. The popular candies, with their colorful jewel-like wrappers, were launched by Harold Mackintosh (1891–1964) in 1936 and became a festive favorite among British families, thanks to packaging and advertising campaigns making them synonymous with Christmas. Recognizing a gap in the market for affordable selection boxes, the enterprising confectioner developed a range of eighteen individually wrapped candies—eleven chocolates and seven toffees—at his factory in Halifax, where Quality Street are still made today by Nestlé. Named after J. M. Barrie's 1901 play and presented in attractive packaging, the new product was aimed at the working class but found a broad market. Generations of families have scrambled to find their favorite and argued over whether the chewy toffee penny, smooth caramel swirl, or praline-filled green triangle is the best. Today, there are eleven varieties, with "The Purple One" (previously hazel in caramel) a perennial favorite. This candy first contained a Brazil nut, which was replaced in the 1940s because of wartime shortages; but despite its hazelnut center, it is still shaped like a Brazil nut. In the 1990s, Nestlé changed the historical round tins to an octagonal design and soon after removed its Regency-era characters in an attempt to position Quality Street as a younger, fresher brand. Today, the candies remain one of the most popular Christmas chocolate choices.

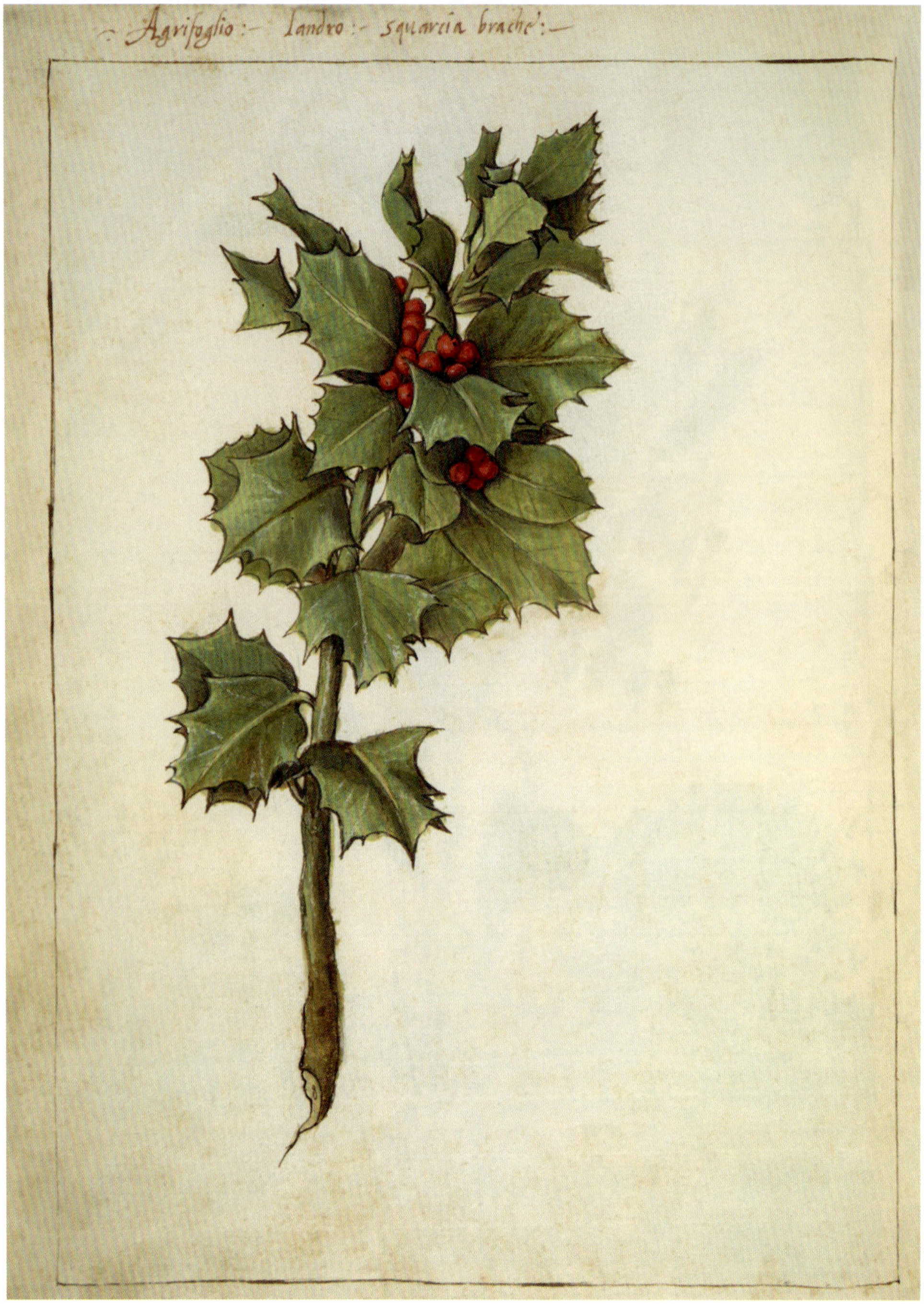

GHERARDO CIBO

•

Ilex aquifolium from *Paintings of Flora of the Roman States*, c.1564–84
Pigments on paper, 13½ × 9 in / 34 × 22.5 cm
British Library, London

This painting of a sprig of holly comes from a sixteenth-century herbarium, the *Discorsi*, which provides an Italian commentary on the *De Materia Medica* ("On Medical Materials") of the Greek physician and botanist Dioscorides (d. *c.*AD 90). The original Italian manuscript was assembled and illustrated by Gherardo Cibo (1512–1600), an artist, herbalist, and grandson of Giovanni Battista Cibo, better known as Pope Innocent VIII. Holly has long been a symbol for many wintery religious festivals, before Christmas even existed. In Celtic mythology, the Holly King ruled during the six "dark" months between midsummer and midwinter, with the Oak King ruling during the rest of the year. Just before the winter solstice, ancient Romans celebrated Saturnalia, a festival dedicated to Saturn, the god of agriculture. Social norms were relaxed, slaves were free to disrespect their masters, and work was suspended. Holly, as an evergreen, represented immortality and renewal; it was often given as a gift for good fortune. Early Christians adopted the holly during Saturnalia but changed its symbolism secretly; for them, the spiny leaves represented the crown of thorns, and the red berries denoted Christ's blood (see pp.54, 144). The pagan holiday eventually became the Christian one when December 25 was officially designated as the birthday of Jesus, and now holly leaves can be seen on Christmas cards, decorations, and has been mentioned in a number of classic Christmas songs (see p.30).

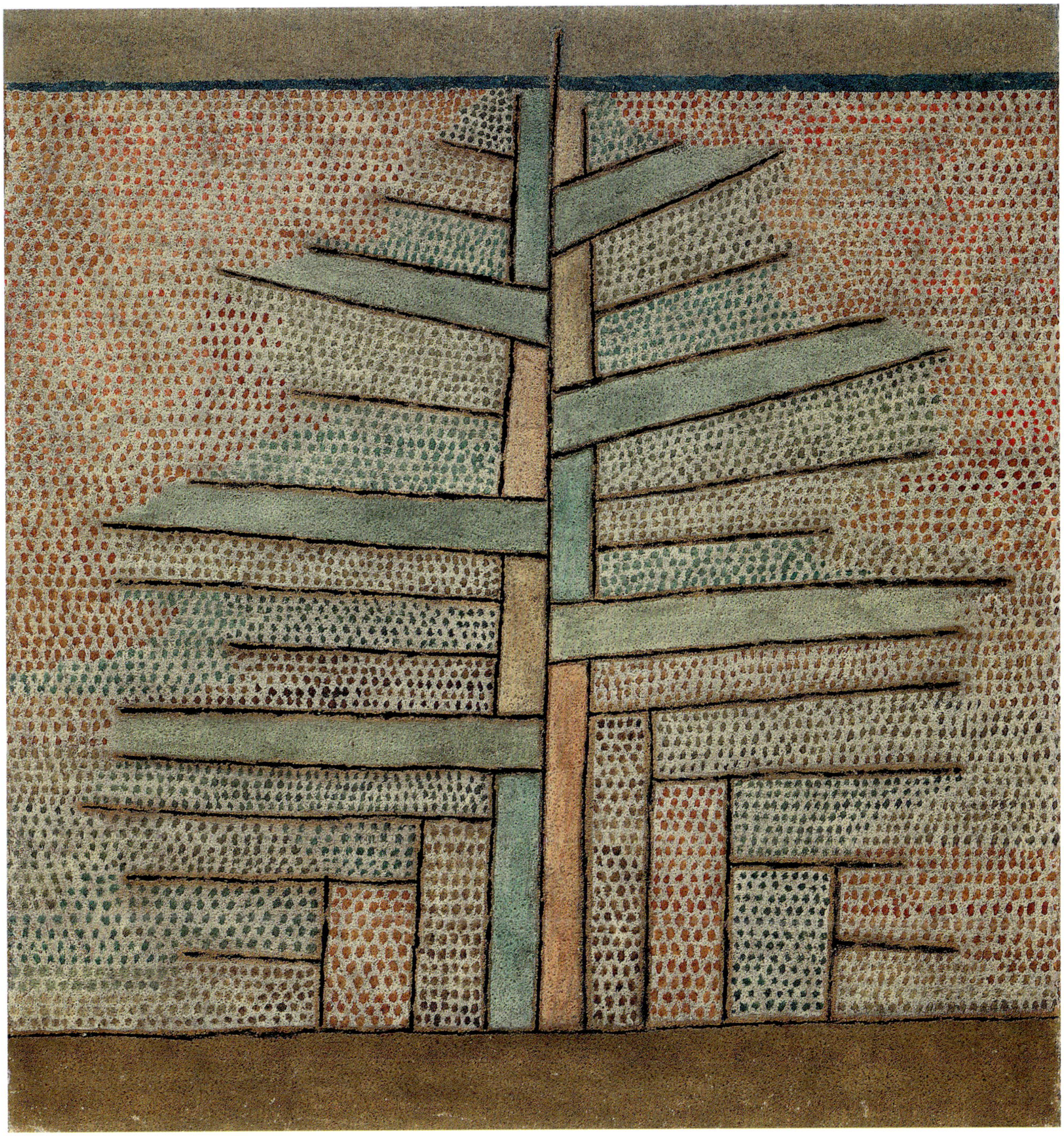

PAUL KLEE

•

Pine Tree, 1932
Oil on canvas, 20¾ × 20 in / 52.7 × 50.8 cm
Private collection

Although it makes no attempt to be realistic, this is recognizably a Christmas tree—or more accurately, a fir tree (see p.205). Fir trees are a favorite option for many when choosing a real Christmas tree for their homes. They hold their needles and, as can be clearly seen in this work, they have a wide base, all the better for accommodating many presents. These trees played a significant role, not just in the paintings of the Swiss-born German artist Paul Klee (1879–1940), but also in his philosophy. He painted them partly because, he explained, the artist resembled a tree: its trunk the individual; its crown, their ideas; and its roots, life's meandering ways. Over a lifetime blighted by illness, Klee painted not just single trees but also forests and landscapes filled with trees. Primarily a draftsman, he often asked his students to observe and then draw the branches of trees. When he painted *Kiefer* in 1932, Klee was teaching at the Dusseldorf Academy in Germany, following ten years teaching at the Bauhaus in Berlin, then Dessau, before he was fired by the Nazis, who later branded his art "degenerate." This fir tree, with its subdued palette of forest greens and browns, employs the pointillist style Klee started to use around 1930. His highly individualistic, almost childlike aesthetic, although influenced by movements such as Expressionism, Cubism, and Surrealism, was so unique that the tree remains today immediately recognizable as a "Klee."

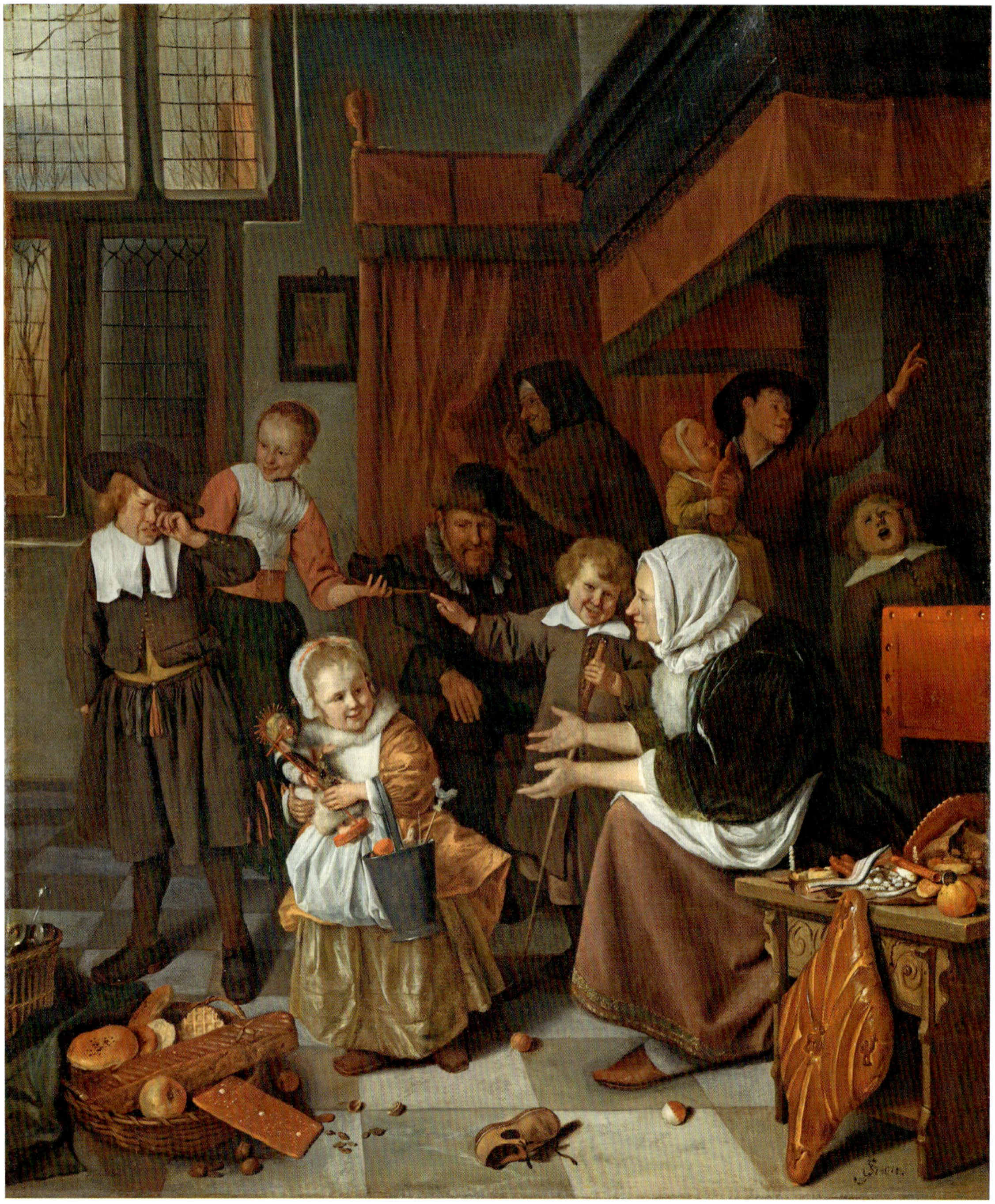

JAN STEEN

•

The Feast of Saint Nicholas, c.1665–68
Oil on canvas, 32⅜ × 27¾ in. / 82 × 70.5 cm
Rijksmuseum, Amsterdam

Saint Nicholas Day, also known as the Feast of Saint Nicholas, is celebrated each year on December 5 or 6 in western Europe, during the season of Advent, in remembrance of Saint Nicholas of Myra (see p.15) (Sinterklaas in Dutch), the notoriously generous patron saint of children and the inspiration for the modern-day Santa Claus (see p.13). This oil painting by Dutch Golden Age painter Jan Steen (1626–1679) tells the story of how the feast day would play out in the Netherlands, including all the traditions adhered to. Children lay out shoes in the days leading up to the celebration, often filled with hay and carrots for Sinterklaas's horse (see p.128), in the hope that they will be filled with goodies if they have been well behaved. The smiling young girl at the front of the painting can be seen, clog gleefully discarded in front of her, with a bucket full of treats. In contrast, the wailing boy behind her has just discovered his shoe—being passed around by the smirking pair beside him—is full of twigs, the customary "gift" for those children who have been naughty. Traditional food, including fruit stuffed with coins, surrounds the group. Jan Steen was one of the leading genre painters of the seventeenth century, portraying, as many were, the inside of Dutch homes at that time. His customary sense of humor and wonderful storytelling are both evident in this festive piece.

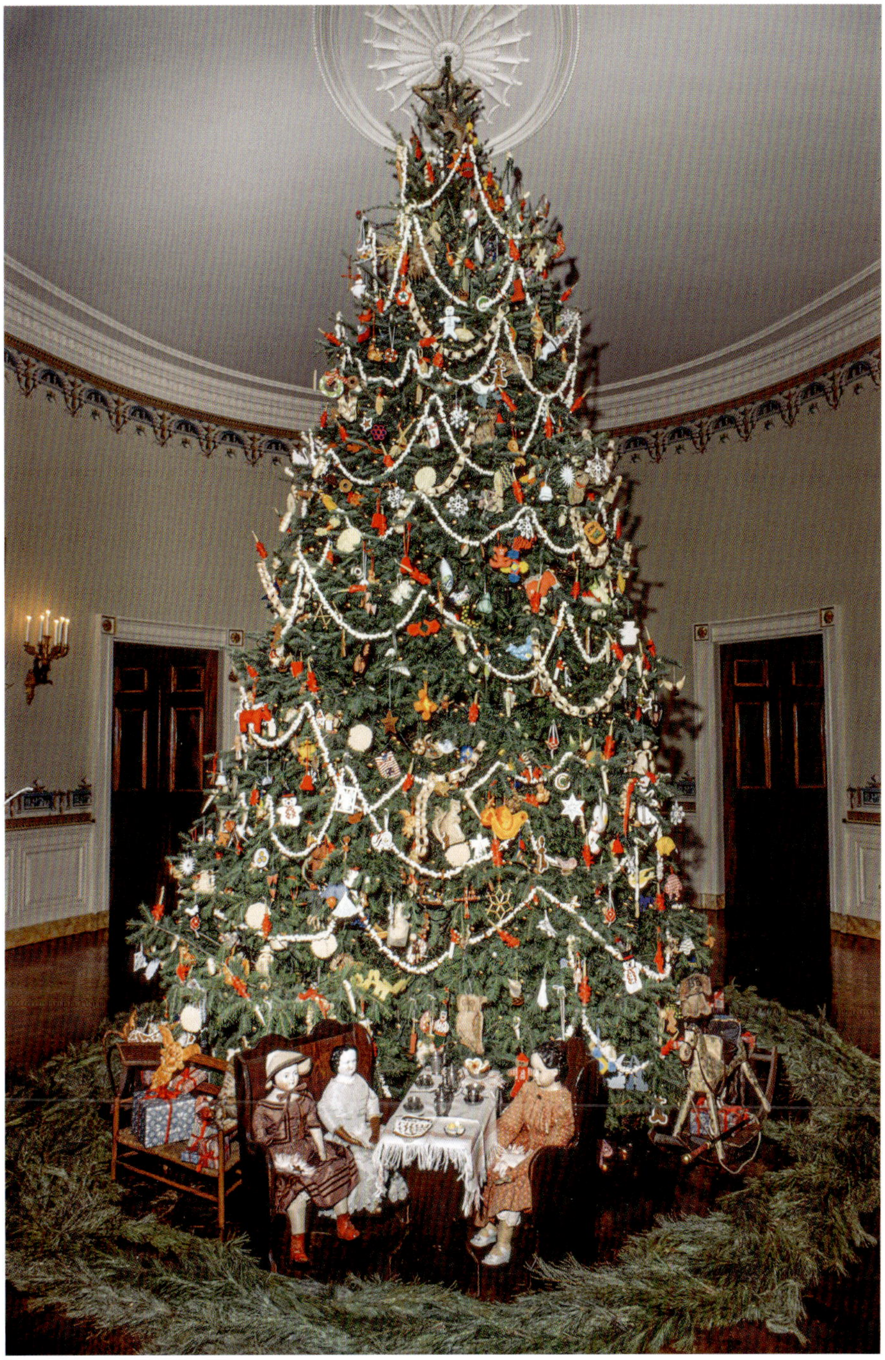

JOSEPH H. BAILEY

•

Blue Room Christmas Tree, 1975
Color photograph, dimensions variable
The White House Historical Association,
Washington, D.C.

For Christmas 1975, First Lady Betty Ford chose the theme of "A Children's Christmas" for the decorations of the White House: almost three thousand ornaments, including some made by volunteers from Colonial Williamsburg, the living history museum and foundation based in Virginia. Dried flowers, fruit, acorns, pinecones, straw, and yarn adorn the famous Blue Room's Christmas tree in this photograph, and the Museum of American Folk Art lent the White House an assortment of old toys, dolls, cradles, a train, rocking horse, and a wagon to place around the base of the tree. The idea of a themed White House Christmas tree was comparatively new: First Lady Jackie Kennedy introduced the idea in 1961, when she chose a theme based on the Russian composer Pyotr Tchaikovsky's ballet, *The Nutcracker Suite* (see p.43), for which the ornaments were made by disabled veterans and senior citizen craftspeople across the United States. Today, there are no fewer than seventy-seven Christmas trees dotted around the White House, although the official White House Christmas tree still resides in the Blue Room, where First Lady Mamie Eisenhower established the tradition of always erecting a tree back in 1953. It was not a given that the White House Christmas tree would become such a public celebration: many of the earlier presidents and their families chose to keep their Christmas celebrations private or, as in the case of President Theodore Roosevelt in 1901, to not put up a tree at all.

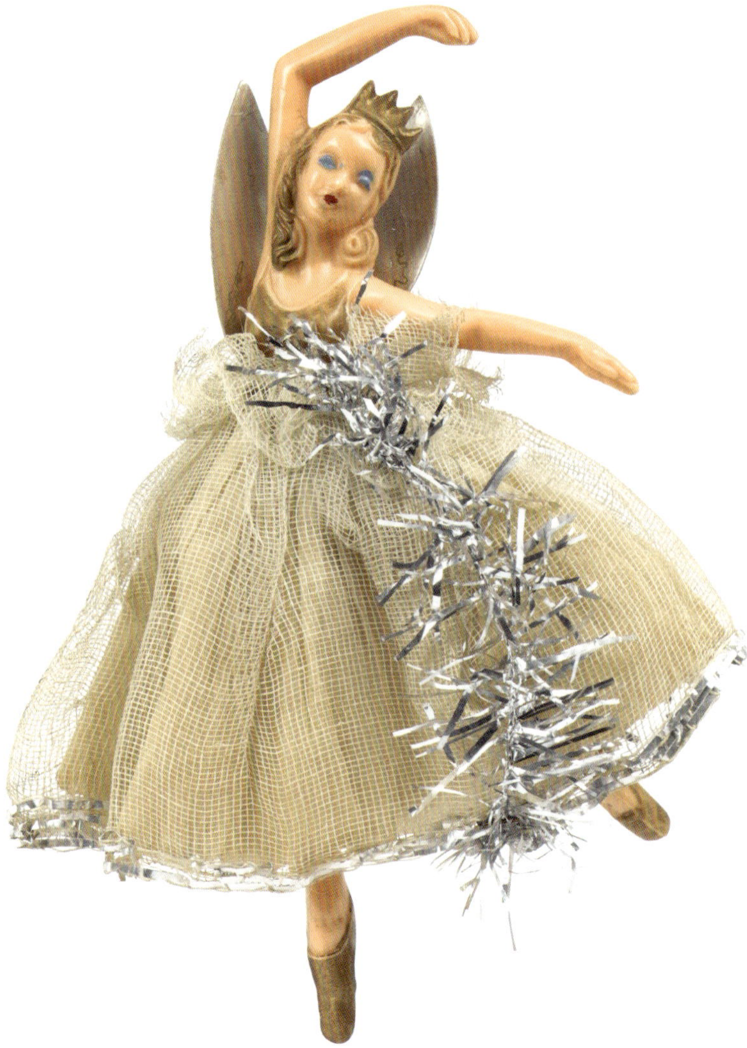

ENGLISH SCHOOL

•

Christmas fairy decoration, c.1930–60
Molded painted plastic, cardboard, paper, and netting, 5⅜ × 2⅜ in / 13.7 × 6 cm
Museum of the Home, London

Precisely when fairy dolls became an integral part of the British Christmas tradition is unclear—earlier trees were topped by stars or angel figures (see p.75)—but, for much of the twentieth century, a Christmas tree was only truly decorated when the fairy was placed at the very top. Made of yellow plastic sometime between 1930 and 1960, this fairy comes complete with silver cardboard wings, gold shoes, and a ballerina skirt of woven cotton net with silver edges and tinsel. On top of her golden hair sits a golden crown, and her arms are raised in a most ballerina-like pose. In the 1950s, fairy dolls were mass-produced by a number of manufacturers, including Palitoy and Rosebud, and mainly sold undressed because, in an era of home sewing, their costumes could be made at home and changed over time. Scraps of fabric, tinsel, gold, and glitter being all that was needed to transform the fairy into a tree topper. The only requirement was that the figure not be too heavy for the tree to support. Fairy dolls have long been part of British culture. In the 1920s, Cicely Mary Barker illustrated a series of fairy books, which including her "Christmas Tree Fairy" (see p.195), the popularity of which may have played a part in the fairy replacing the angel at the top of the Christmas tree.

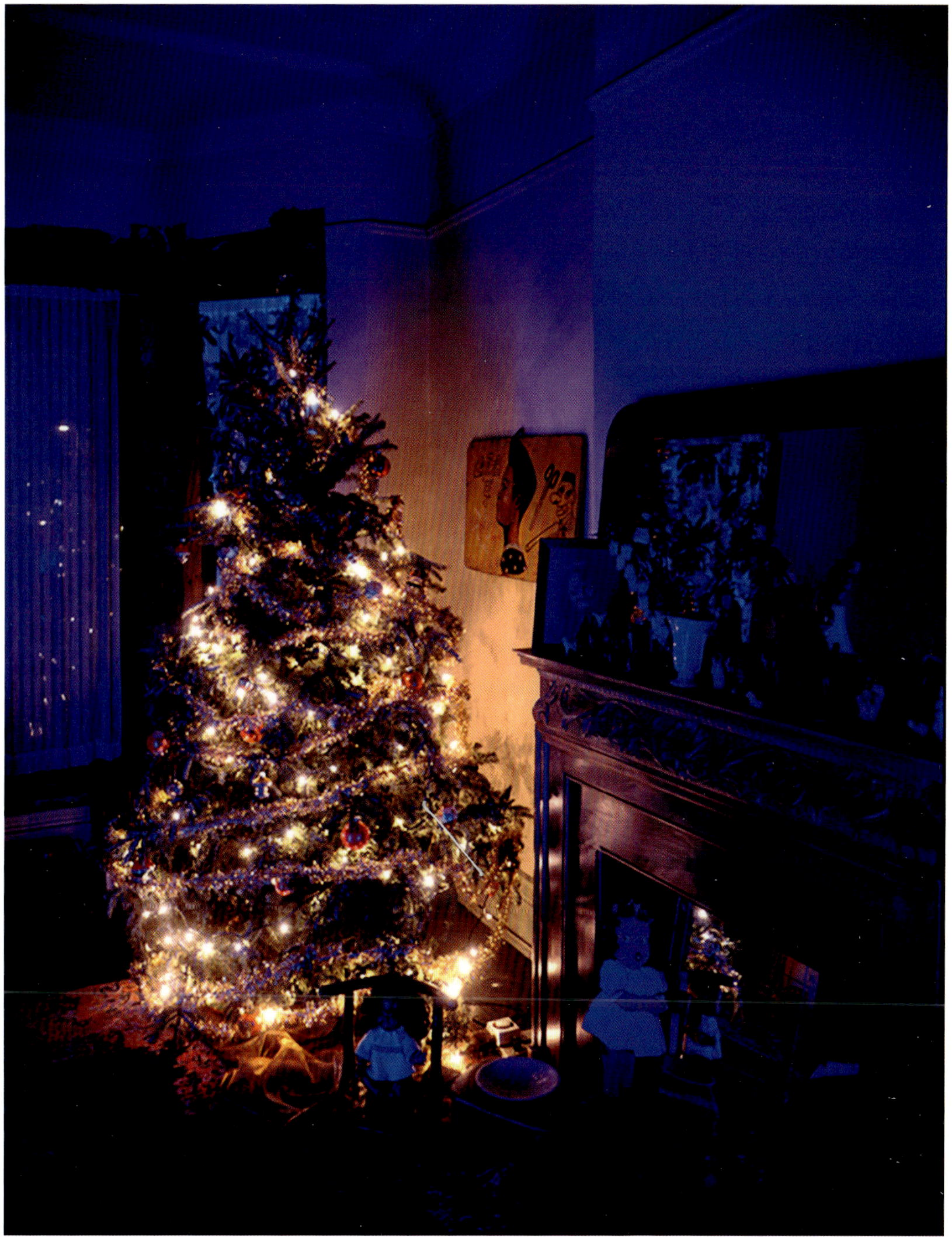

KERRY JAMES MARSHALL

•

Black Xmas, 2002
Ink-jet print on paper,
58 × 46 in / 147.3 × 116.8 cm

Black Xmas was created in 2012 by influential contemporary artist Kerry James Marshall (1955–), who is appreciated today for drawing attention to the absence and perceived "otherness" of the Black identity in art history and popular culture more broadly. In this work, toys designed in the 1950s specifically for Black children are laid out beneath a decorated Christmas tree, which shines brightly in a dimly lit room. In the same interior, pictures of Black models and landscapes are illuminated with black light, also known as ultraviolet light, giving the quiet room an iridescent and magical glow. Born in Birmingham, Alabama, but raised in Los Angeles from 1963, Marshall witnessed an era of race riots and the emergence of the Black Power movement, as well as the Black Arts movement from which he takes aesthetic inspiration. As demonstrated in *Black Xmas*, he doesn't solely intend to politicize the Black or African-American identity, but seeks to emphasize the normal, everyday lived experiences of the Black community in the United States. Although devoid of human figures, this ambiguous work could be interpreted as a symbolic commentary upon racial segregation—the artist indicates that even the consumer culture surrounding Christmas has historically been racialized. Alternatively, Marshall contrasts the historical "whiteness" of the Puritan Christmas tradition with the absence of a Black subjectivity in relation to the festive holiday.

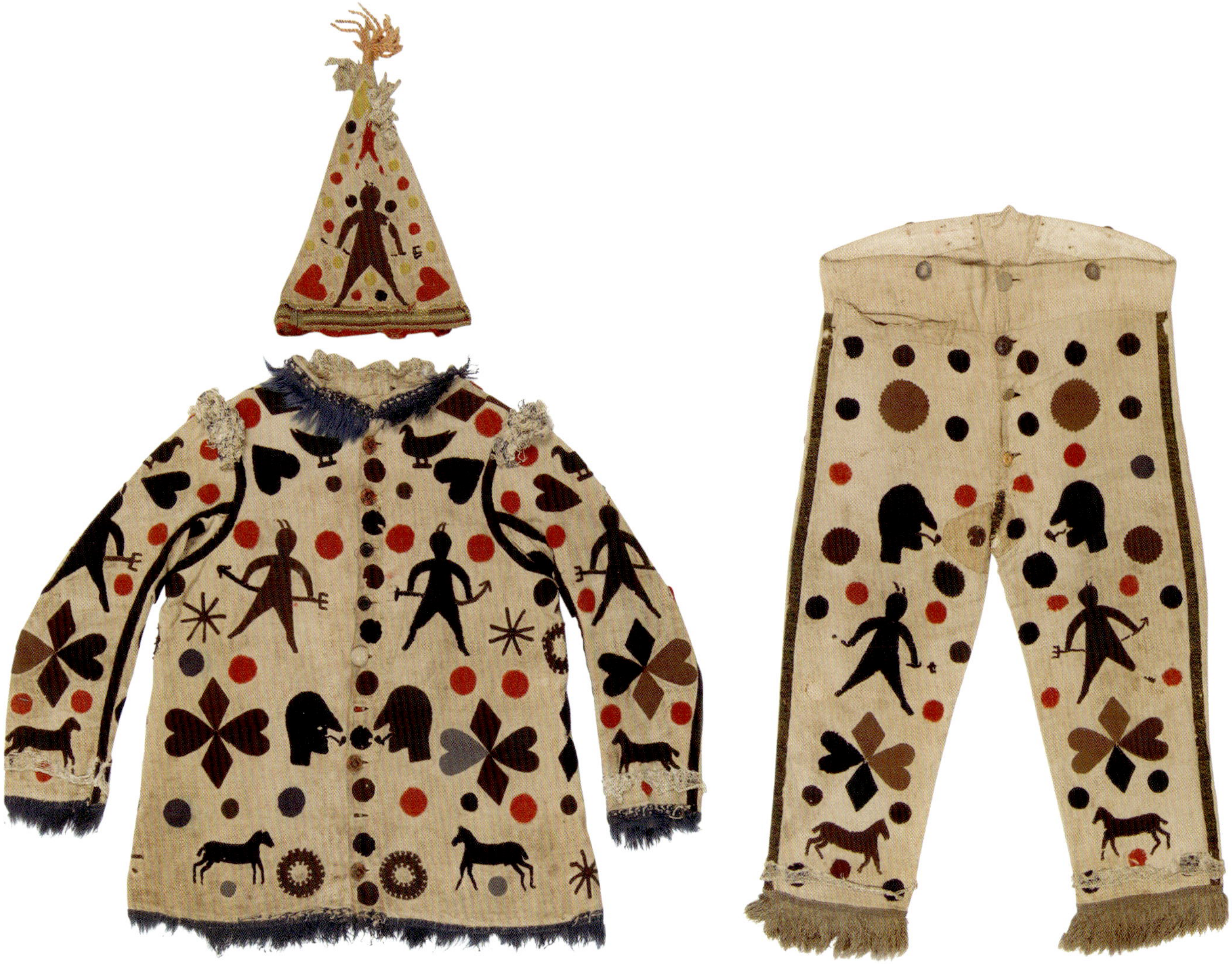

UNKNOWN

•

Mummers Costume: jacket, pants, and hat, 1829
Appliquéd natural linen, jacket:
H. 31 in / 78.7 cm; pants: H. 41½ in / 105.4 cm;
hat: H. 9½ in / 24.1 cm
Philadelphia Museum of Art

This linen costume, consisting of jacket, hat, and pants, with its playful appliqués of devils carrying pitchforks, hearts and diamonds, and wool fringes, was a familiar part of the British Christmas in the late eighteenth and nineteenth centuries, when it would have been worn by a mummer (an amateur actor who appeared in folk plays). British mummers donned costumes and masks to perform plays and dances at many festivals, but were particularly visible around the Christmas season. The mummers, who were exclusively male, would gather in small groups to parade from house-to-house through the streets, performing a short play in which the hero was killed in a fight and then brought back to life by a doctor, in an echo of the Christian Resurrection story. The idea probably originated in medieval Europe, when masked performers visited houses during festivals, such as the winter solstice. Adopted with gusto in Great Britain, the action coalesced around the story of England's patron saint, Saint George. A fool in cap and bells—who may have worn this costume, because the back of the hat includes the initials T. F., which probably stand for Tom Fool—was often present to add levity, alongside a cast of characters, including Father Christmas and "the doctor." These humorous plays are considered early versions of the pantomime, performed enthusiastically every Christmas in Great Britain (see p.118).

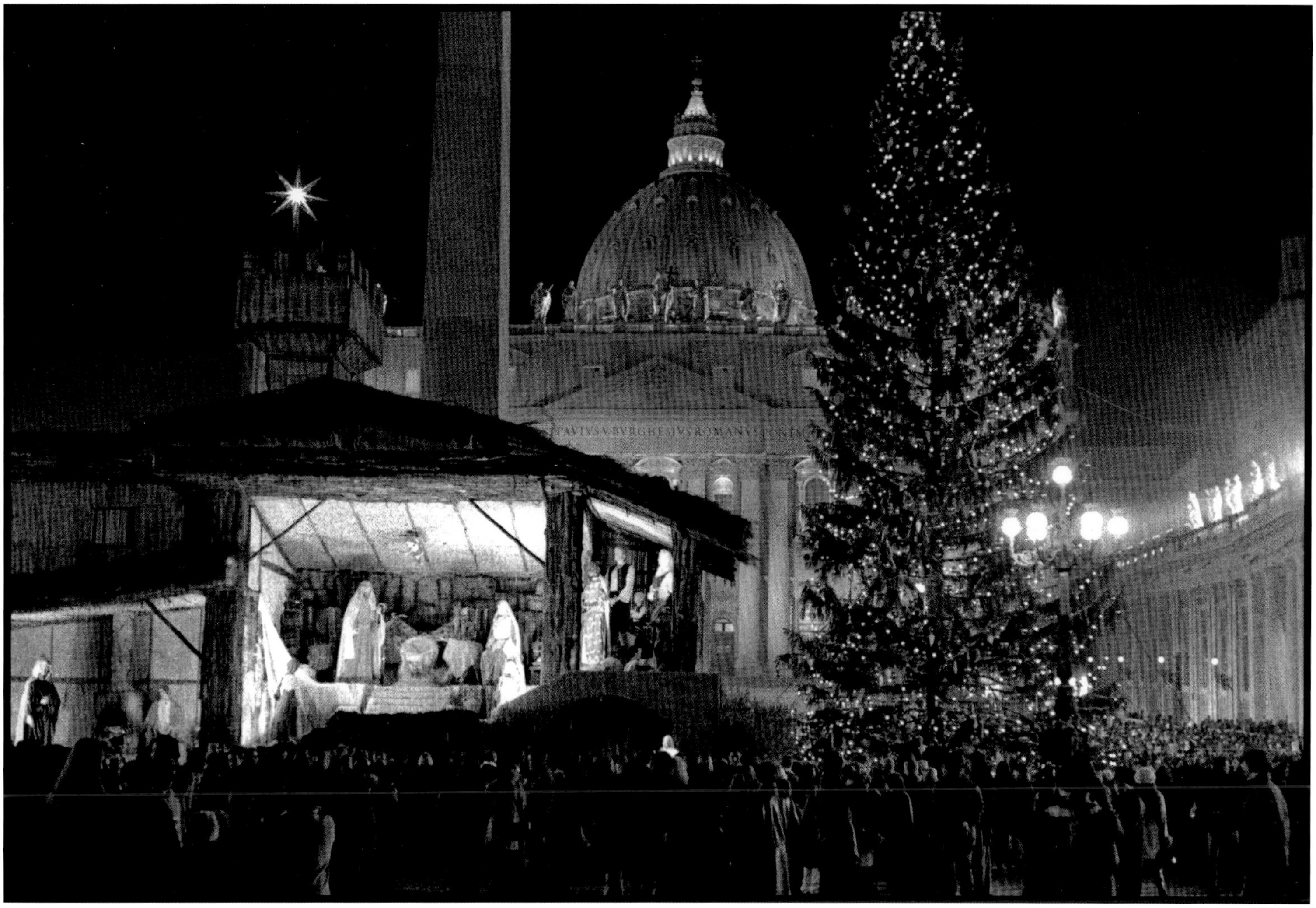

LEONARD FREED

•

Rome, St. Peter's Square, 1999
Photograph, dimensions variable
Magnum Photos

Brooklyn native Leonard Freed (1929–1996) was working as a freelance photographer when Edward Steichen, curator of photography at the Museum of Modern Art in New York, acquired a few of his pieces for the museum. Steichen was an early admirer of Freed's work and advised him to steer clear of commercial photography, profoundly altering the trajectory of Freed's career. Freed was long enchanted with Europe and traveled there numerous times, especially to Italy. His images of the country, taken over the span of almost fifty years, capture the beauty and exuberance of Italian life in moments small and large. This photograph documenting Christmas at the Vatican, with the dome of Saint Peter's Basilica in the background, is depicted in black and white—as all of Freed's work was—lending a layer of reverence and austerity to the festive tableau. The tradition of placing a Christmas tree as well as the life-size Nativity scene (see pp.39, 168) in Saint Peter's Square started in 1982 during the pontificate of Pope John Paul II. Every year the Vatican Christmas tree is donated from a different European country—in 1999 that was the Czech Republic (known as Czechia). Freed remained a leading member of the Magnum Photos cooperative and he is best known for his pioneering documentary work on the American civil rights movement and the Black experience in New York City, as documented in his seminal works *Black in White America* and *Police Work*, among others.

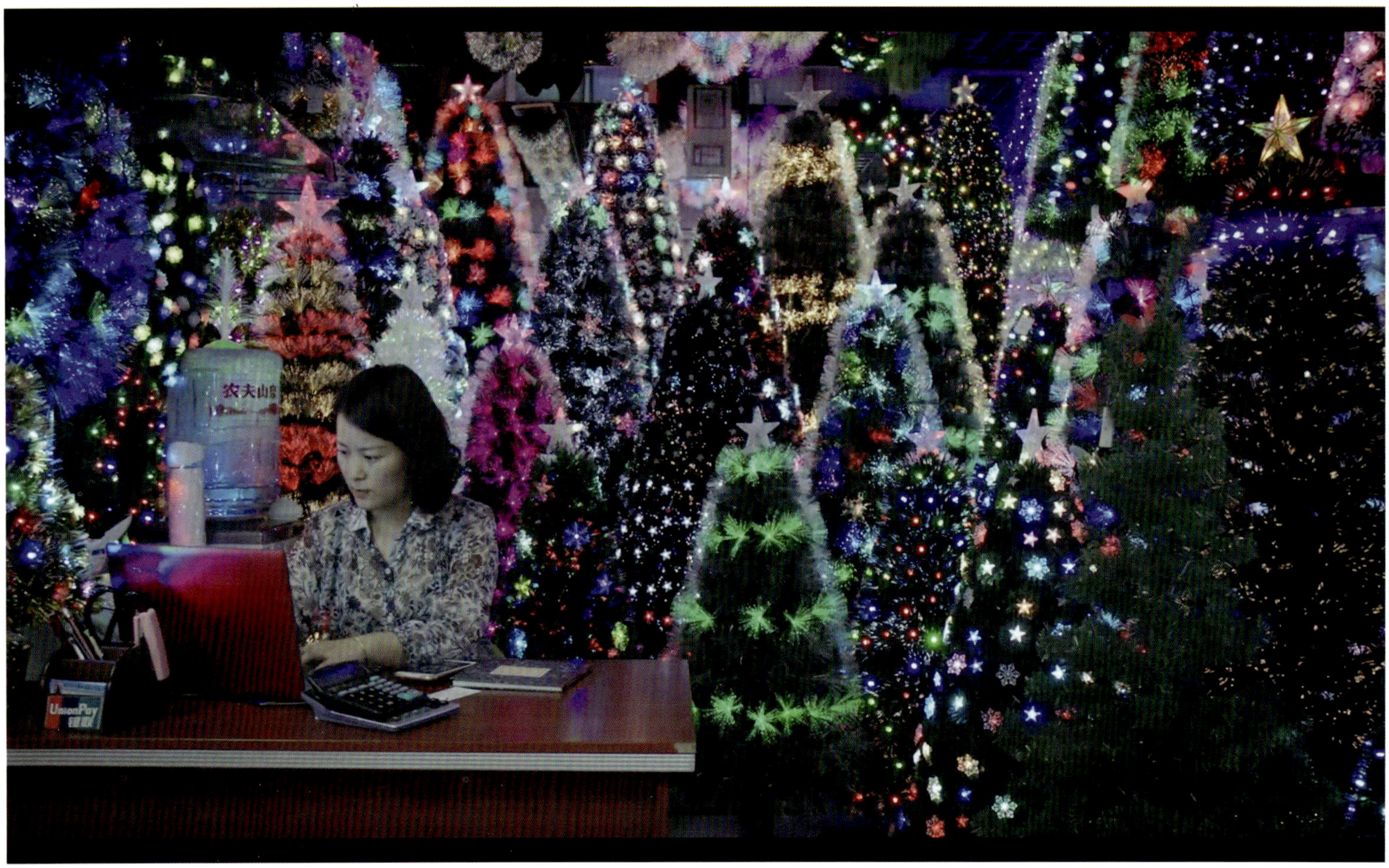

MIKA ROTTENBERG

•

Cosmic Generator (Tunnel Variant), 2017
Single-channel video installation (sound, color), dimensions variable

The film *Cosmic Generator* (2017) by the New York-based artist Mika Rottenberg (1976–) explores a kaleidoscopic world in which the United States, China, and Mexico are linked by an imaginary secret system of trade tunnels. This video still—in which a solitary woman works on a laptop, next to a water cooler and a forest of fake trees (see pp.164, 231)—articulates the inherent alienation of a globalized, capitalist economy. Filmed in the Chinese market city of Yiwu, also known as Trade City, the female workers in *Cosmic Generator* sit alone among countless plastic decorations: shimmering threads of tinsel and artificial, illuminated Christmas trees. By paying close attention to excessive commerce, the film reveals the surprising yet banal inner workings of capitalism. Like much of Rottenberg's video installations, which convey a sense of wonder, claustrophobia, and discomfort, we are also presented with an ironic analogy between migration issues and the large-scale circulation of goods. The artist proposes we rethink the consumerist tradition of Christmas by looking more closely at the systems and networks of rampant production and labor behind the annual holiday, all of which tap into gendered and racial dynamics. Taking on surreal and absurdist elements, Rottenberg's work has often been ascribed to the genre of magical realism though her films maintain a connection with documentary practice.

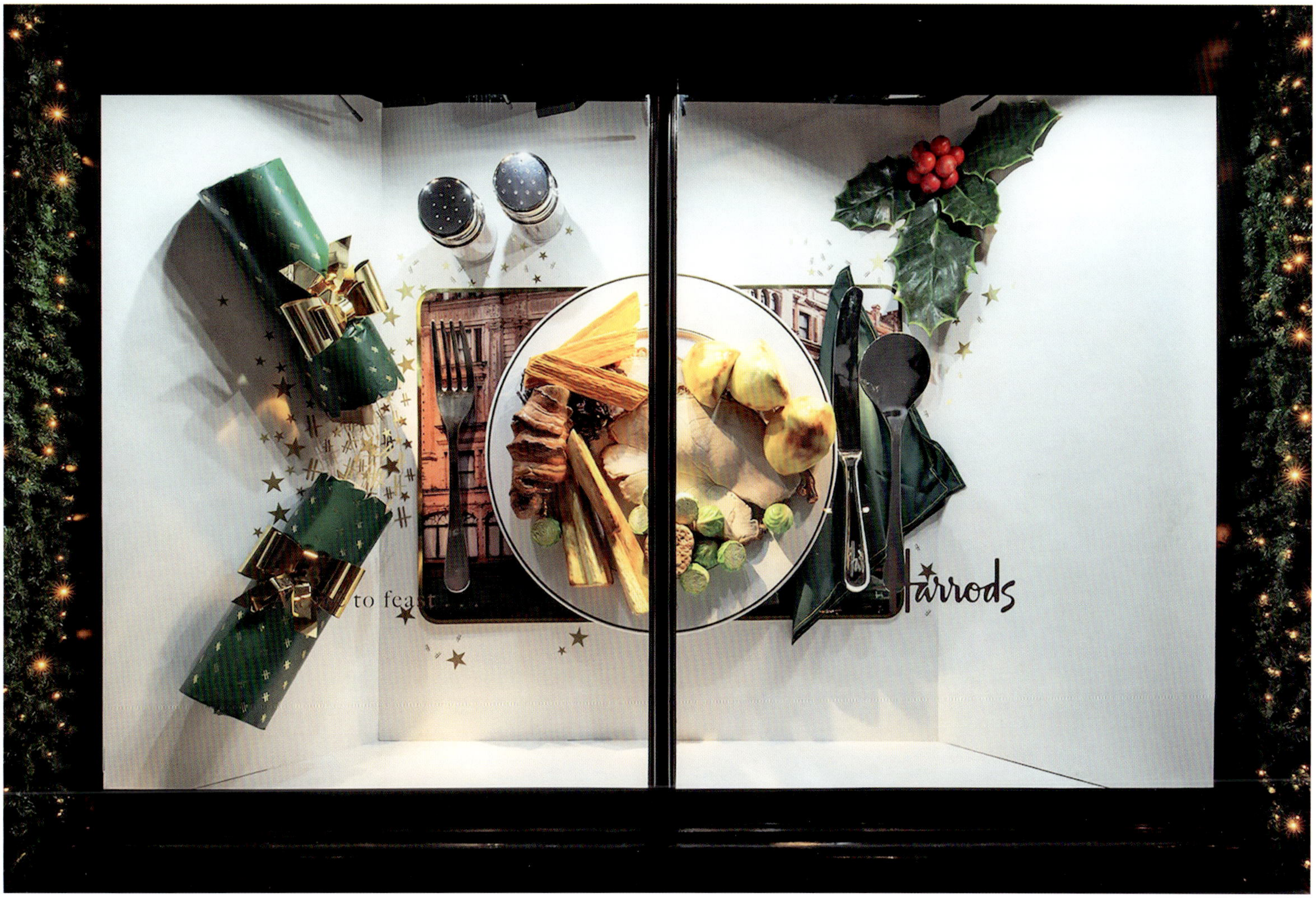

HARRODS

•

A Harrods Feast, 2018
Fiberglass and painted wood, dimensions variable

Each Christmas, the London department store Harrods—its visual merchandisers working often with external fabricators—creates a dazzling display in its fifty-two windows. Here, in one of the largest street-level windows, an enormous plate, on a Harrods photographic placemat, is filled with a realistic Christmas dinner fashioned from airbrushed fiberglass. Sliced turkey and a traditional British pig-in-blanket sausage wrapped in bacon sit next to roast potatoes larger than most of their intended onlookers' heads, while a cracker in Harrods racing green snaps forth branded gold confetti. The whole tableau is enlivened by the implausibly angled suspension, with these giant objects floating at ninety degrees to the floor. Complex and often mechanical moving Christmas window displays, originally pioneered in the nineteenth century at London's Fortnum & Mason, are a staple of large department stores the world over, usually unveiled long before the beginning of December to signify the beginning of the Christmas gift-buying period. They are often designed to appeal first and foremost as an "experience" to children and at times only obliquely as a retail advertisement, as for example Harrods' 2012 series of ten windows in which leading Disney characters appeared dressed in couture by Versace and Missoni among others. While most Christmas window displays envision fantastical worlds, with this realistic dinner plate Harrods brought a very real-life Christmas tradition to the display case.

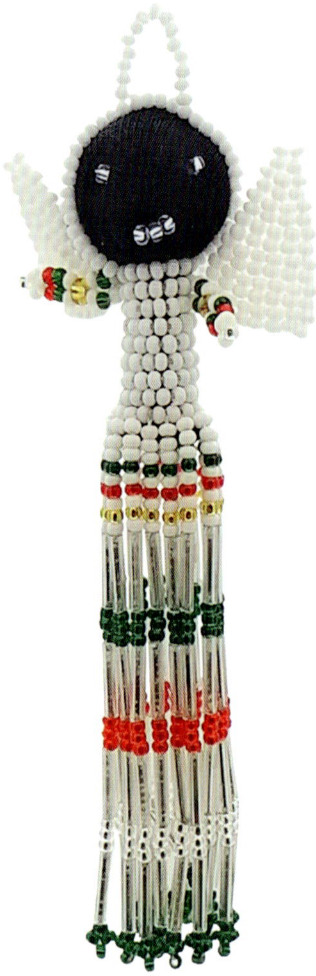

BONGISIWE

•

Bongisiwe's Angel, c.21st century
Colored beads and felt, H. 4 in / 10.5 cm
For Woza Moya

Angels have traditionally been placed atop Christmas trees to represent Gabriel (see pp.14, 87), the archangel of revelation, who informs the Virgin Mary that she will be the mother of Jesus. This example of an angel decoration was handcrafted using gold, white, red, and silver beads by a woman named Bongisiwe, in South Africa, and sold by Woza Moya, a social enterprise that was established in 2002 and whose primary objective is the reduction of poverty through craft. A project started by the Hillcrest AIDS Center Trust, Woza Moya assists those in desperate need to acquire a skill and earn an income through the sale of their craft. This puts income back into vulnerable communities at the heart of the pandemic. A predominantly Christian country with strong historical links to Great Britain and the Netherlands, Christmas is a popular holiday in South Africa, and they indulge in many of the same traditions and customs as western Europe. Angels are a popular choice of decoration, but also available are Christmas puddings, robins, reindeer, and snowmen, all made primarily from colorful beads. Glass beads have been incorporated seamlessly into indigenous artistic traditions in southern Africa over the past century and serve as ideal material for adornment and dress. In South Africa, in particular as the twentieth century progressed, beadwork became increasingly associated with the expression of "traditional" precolonial African identity.

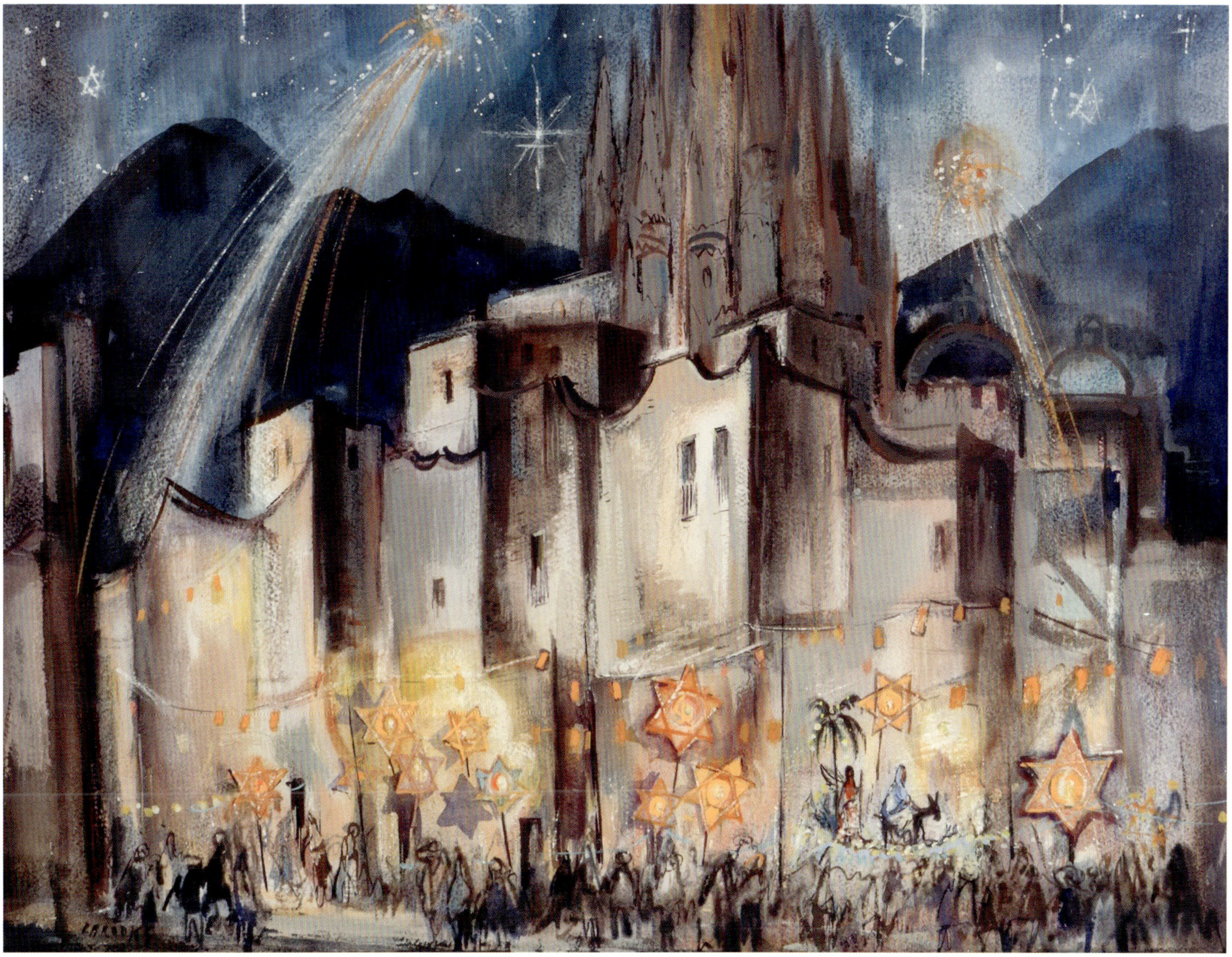

LEONARD BROOKS

•

Christmas Posada, San Miguel de Allende, Mexico, c.1953
Watercolor and gouache on paper,
18¼ × 23¾ in / 46.3 × 60.3 cm
Smithsonian American Art Museum,
Washington, D.C.

Every evening for the nine nights before Christmas, the beautiful colonial Mexican town of San Miguel de Allende, a long-time favorite of artists, writers, and expatriates, stages a *posada*, the excitement and liveliness of which is captured in this watercolor and gouache painting from the 1950s by London-born Canadian artist Leonard Brooks (1911–2011). *Posada*, which means "hostel" or "inn" in Spanish, is the name given to a festival that takes place in towns and villages across Mexico in which inhabitants reenact the Christmas story of Mary and Joseph's search for an inn in Bethlehem. Candlelit processions make their way slowly through different neighborhoods on each of the nights. A girl dressed as Mary sits on a donkey while a boy, dressed as Joseph, leads her through the streets accompanied by musicians, locals, and tourists carrying candles and lanterns (see p.158). They knock on doors and sing a song entitled "Pidiendo Posada," in which they ask for lodging but are turned away by an answering song from within. On the last night, Christmas Eve, the couple are finally given a room at the inn, an event celebrated by fireworks and live music. Here, Brooks captures the crowds and the magical quality of the *posada* as Mary, dressed in blue, and Joseph search for a place to stay. Brooks moved to San Miguel de Allende after World War II and lived there until his death, at the age of one hundred.

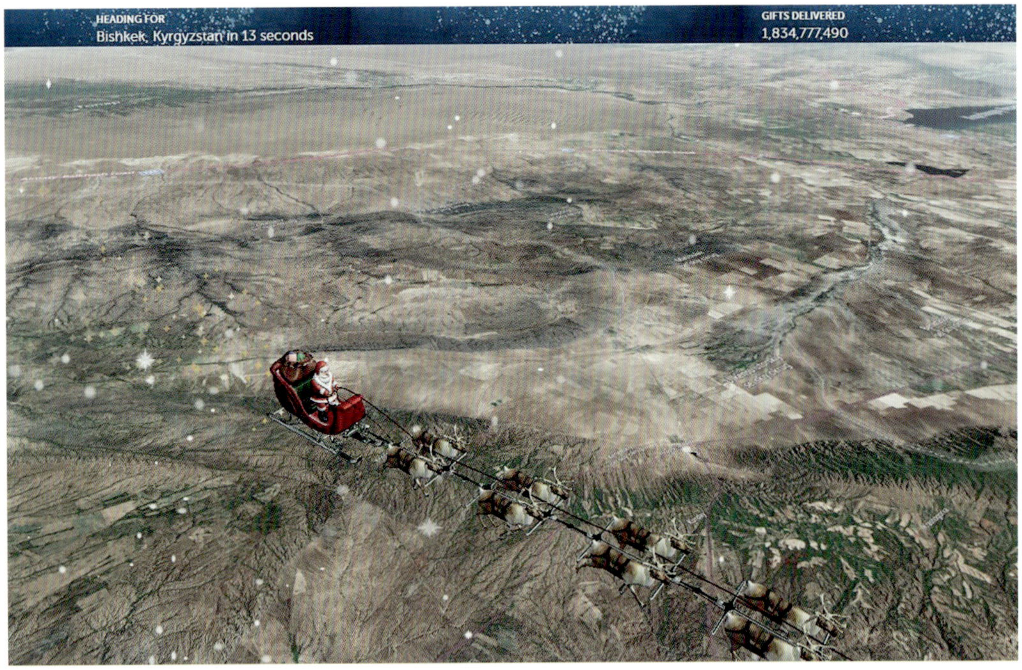
HEADING FOR
Bishkek, Kyrgyzstan in 13 seconds
GIFTS DELIVERED
1,834,777,490

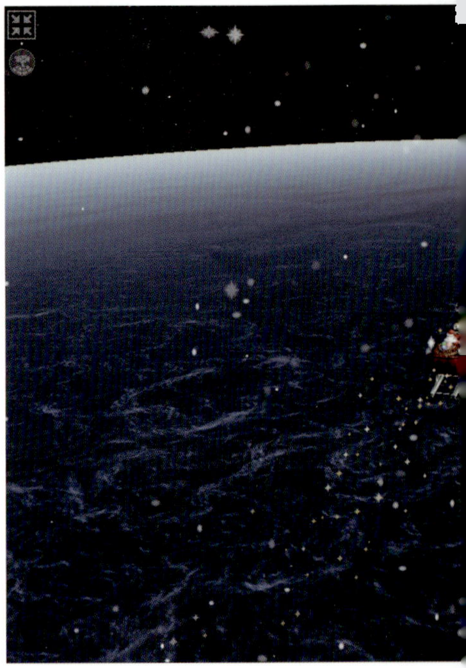

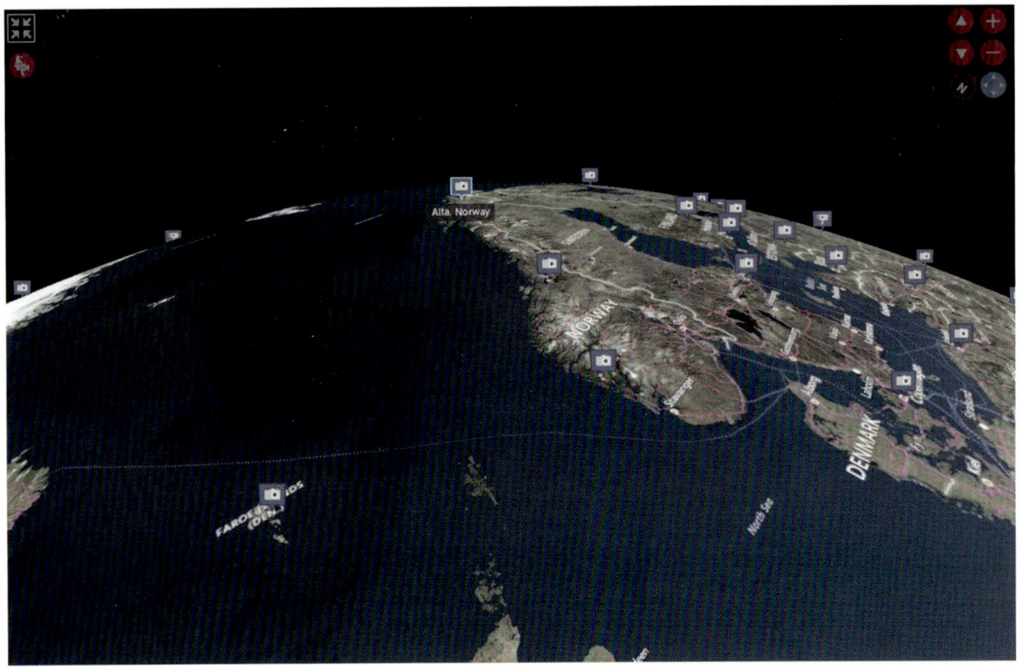
Alta, Norway
NORWAY
DENMARK
North Sea

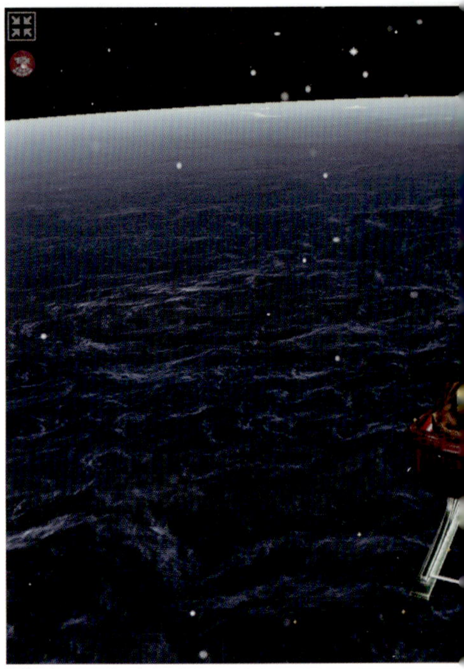

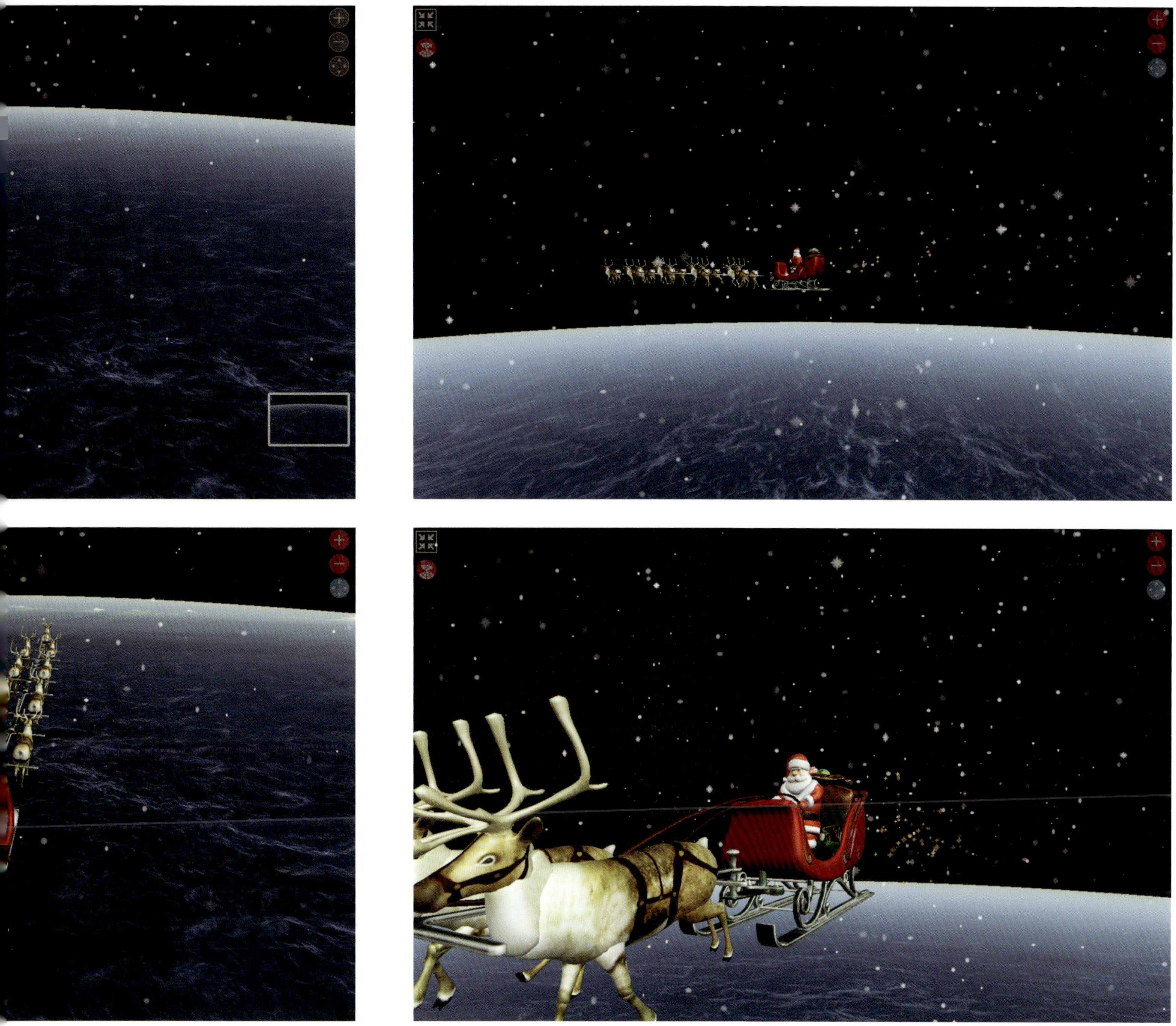

NORAD

•

Santa Tracker, 2022
Phone line, website, and app

Every December 24, starting at 6 a.m. EST, NORAD (North American Aerospace Defense Command) undertakes a special mission: tracking Santa Claus across the world's skies as he makes his deliveries. What makes this unusual is that NORAD's day job is defending North America's airspace against hostile attack. Their duty to track Santa Claus came about by accident. In 1955, Sears department store (see p.104) placed an advertisement in a newspaper urging children to call Santa at a phone number they gave—but it inadvertently provided a number belonging to the Continental Air Defense Command (CONAD) in Colorado Springs. Colonel Harry Shoup (1917–2009) was the commander on duty the night the first young child called the misprinted number asking for Santa. Quick to realize what had happened, Colonel Shoup told the child he was, indeed, Santa. As more and more children called, a duty officer was assigned to answer "Santa's line" and a new tradition was born. After the formation of NORAD in 1958, the ad hoc service was formalized and, since then, NORAD has reported every year on Santa's location to millions of children, not just in North America but across the world. Now, a web page and app track his every move, making it possible to follow Santa's progress from any location. The popularity of the service is evident in the number of users: several million visitors from across the globe track Santa each December 24 and volunteers answer more than 130,000 calls.

INDEX

Page numbers in *italics* refer to illustrations

FURTHER READING

Barnaby, Hannah and Fazenda, João. *It's Christmas Everywhere: Celebrations from Around the World*. London: Phaidon Press, 2022.

Byrd, Byron Keith. *O Christmas Tree*. New York: Rizzoli, 1989.

Byrd, Byron Keith and D'Agostino, Carla Torsilieri. *The Christmas Tree at Rockefeller Center*. New York: Lickle, 1997.

Gotelli, Dolph. *Wonder and Delight: A Dolph Gotelli Christmas*. Naperville: Sourcebooks, 2013.

Richter, Bob. *A Very Vintage Christmas: Holiday Collecting, Decorating and Celebrating*. Lanham: Rowman & Littlefield, 2016.

Connelly, Mark. *Christmas: A History*. London: I.B. Tauris, 2012.

Flanders, Judith. *Christmas: A Biography*. London: Pan Macmillan, 2017.

Forsyth, Mark. *A Christmas Cornucopia: The Hidden Stories Behind Our Yuletide Traditions*. New York: Viking, 2016.

The Metropolitan Museum of Art. *Christmas is Coming!*. New York: Abrams, 2019

Muhlberger, Richard. *The Christmas Story: Told Through Paintings*. New York: The Metropolitan Museum of Art, 1990.

Palmer, Alex. *The Atlas of Christmas: The Merriest, Tastiest, Quirkiest Holiday Traditions from Around the World*. Philadelphia: Running Press, 2020.

Rockwell, Norman. *Norman Rockwell's Christmas Book*. New York: Abrams, 2009.

Struthers, Jane. *The Book of Christmas: Everything We Once Knew and Loved About Christmastime*. London: Ebury, 2012.

Voger, Mark. *Holly Jolly: Celebrating Christmas Past in Pop Culture*: Raleigh: Two Morrows, 2020

Weir, Alison. *A Tudor Christmas*. London: Jonathan Cape, 2018.

Williams, Jane. *The Art of Christmas: The Nativity through the Eyes of Great Painters*. London: SPCK, 2021.

Winn, Christopher. *The Book of Christmas*. London: Hardie Grant, 2018.

CREDITS

New York Public Library: The Miriam and Ira D. Wallach Division of Art, Prints and Photographs, Print Collection: 90; NOMA: 206; Noma Bar/Dutch Uncle: 31; Nordiska Museet: 109, Karolina Kristensson 139; Courtesy Nordstrom and Sanna Annukka: 173; North American Aerospace Defense Command: 230–231; © Office Depot, Inc.: 160; ParolsofAmerica.com: 158; Penguin Random House: Rudolph The Red-Nosed Reindeer by Richard Scarry. © 1958. Used by permission of Penguin Random House LLC. All rights reserved 85, 86; Pook & Pook: 190; Portland Art Museum, Portland, Oregon/Gift of Peter J. Cohen (2017.26.8): 164; Courtesy Primitives by Kathy: 166; © Radio Times/Intermediate Media Co.: 120; Courtesy of Raffaella & Tobia Fletcher: 21; Regts – Delft Tiles: 26; Rijksmuseum, Amsterdam: 220; Christmas Tree, 1987 © Robert Mapplethorpe Foundation. Used by permission: 44; Collection of Roland Mesnier: 214; Royal Collection Trust/© His Majesty King Charles III, 2022: 131; Royal Mail, stamp designs by Aardman Animations Ltd and Royal Mail. © and TM Aardman Animations Limited/Wallace & Gromit Limited 2010. All rights reserved. 'Wallace & Gromit' (word marks) and the characters 'Wallace' and 'Gromit' are trade marks used under licence from Aardman Animations Limited/Wallace & Gromit Limited: 99; © The Saul Steinberg Foundation/Artists Rights Society (ARS), NY/DACS, London: 51; Scala, Florence: © 2022 176, Austrian Archives 69, © 2022, bpk, Bildagentur fuer Kunst, Kultur und Geschichte. Photographer Christian Krug 38, Christie's Images, London 58, 172, 213, The British Library Board 218, © 2022, Cooper-Hewitt, Smithsonian Design Museum/Art Resource, NY. Gift of Diane and Sandy Besser, Santa Fe, New Mexico (1997.95.2) 148, © 2022, Cooper-Hewitt, Smithsonian Design Museum/Art Resource, NY. Gift of Unknown Donor (2000-26-66) 61, © 2022, Cooper-Hewitt, Smithsonian Design Museum/Art Resource, NY. Photographer Matt Flynn. Design Woody Pirtle Studio 88, © 2022. Photo Josse 94, The Metropolitan Museum of Art/Art Resource 162, © 2022. Museum of Fine Arts, Boston. All rights reserved. Gift of John Henry and Susan Steele Guswa in memory of the Jacob Henry Steele family 142, Photo: 2022, digital image, The Museum of Modern Art, New York. Gift of Time Inc. 421.1953.1.5. © Succession H. Matisse/DACS 27, © 2022, The Philadelphia Museum of Art/Art Resource. Purchased with funds contributed by various donors in memory of Anne d'Harnoncourt 224, Smithsonian American Art Museum/Art Resource. Gift of the artist, 1970.193. Used by permission of Thomas Watson, c/o The Permissions Company, LLC. All rights reserved 67, Smithsonian American Art Museum. Gift of the Ford Motor Company. Photo /Art Resource 229; SenseiAlan (CC by 2.0) via Flickr. © Coca-Cola: 13; Shutterstock: Photo: Guy Bell/© Shirazeh Houshiary 46, Unknown/Condé Nast 35; SIK-ISEA, Zürich: 23; Smithsonian American Art Museum: 126; © Snowman Enterprises Ltd, 1978: 57; © Spin Master 188; Photograph courtesy of Sotheby's, Inc.: © Jeff Koons 73, Printed by permission of the Norman Rockwell Family Agency. Copyright ©1947 the Norman Rockwell Family Entities 63; Courtesy of The Strong, Rochester, New York: 184; Supergiantgames LLC.: 183; Swarovski: 127; Tasha Tudor and Family: 77; Te Papa (CA000670/001/0001): 71; © TfL from the London Transport Museum collection: 60; Copyright of The University of Manchester: 14; © Van Cleef and Arpels: 138; © Victoria and Albert Museum, London: 10, 32–33, 119; © Walter Waygood: 155; Warner Bros. Entertainment Inc. All Rights Reserved: 12 Wellcome Collection: 156, 211; The White House Historical Association: 221; Courtesy Woza Moya: 228; Paper art by Yulia Brodskaya created for Neiman Marcus Christmas book: 212.

PUBLISHER'S ACKNOWLEDGEMENTS

A project of this size requires the commitment, advice, and expertise of many people. Special thanks are due to the following for their knowledge, passion, and advice in the selection of the works for inclusion, as well as to Sam Bilton, Dolph Gotelli and David Trigg for writing the thematic essays that open the book:

Sam Bilton
Food historian, writer, and cook, with a particular focus on historical recipes.

Byron Keith Byrd
Contemporary American artist and creator of bespoke Christmas trees for private and corporate clients.

Dolph Gotelli
International expert and lecturer on Christmas, holiday rituals, and Santa Claus. Professor Emeritus of Design at University of California, Davis.

Bob Richter
American Vintage Lifestyle Expert, author, and TV personality. Author of *A Very Vintage Christmas* (2016), Vintage Living (2019) and *A Very Vintage Holiday* (2023).

David Trigg
Writer, critic, art historian and regular contributor to books on art.

We are particularly grateful to Rosie Pickles, Laine Morreau and Katy Sprinkel Morreau for researching and compiling the longlist of entries for inclusion. Additional thanks are due to Jen Veall for her picture research, and to Caitlin Arnell Argles, Theresa Bebbington, Vanessa Bird, Nina Chang-Smith, Tim Cooke, Rebecca Morrill, João Mota, Frankie Moutafis, Michele Robecchi, Matilda Southern-Wilkins, and Rachel Ward for their invaluable assistance.

Finally, we would like to thank all the artists, illustrators, photographers, collectors, libraries, institutions, and museums who have given us permission to include their images.

TEXT CREDITS

The publisher is grateful to the following writers for the individual entry texts:

Tim Cooke: 11, 12, 19, 21, 28, 33, 39, 41, 42, 46, 50, 51, 52, 56, 57, 59, 60, 62, 65, 74, 79, 80, 83, 87, 88, 91, 93, 95, 98, 100, 101, 102, 108, 110, 111, 112, 115, 118, 120, 123, 130, 131, 132, 138, 140, 141, 142, 146, 147, 149, 151, 156, 162, 163, 166, 169, 170, 175, 177, 179, 181, 182, 184, 187, 193, 194, 195, 204, 205, 208, 210, 211, 213, 216, 219, 221, 222, 224, 229, 231; **Lydia Figes**: 18, 44, 55, 82, 172, 179, 202, 215, 223, 226; **Diane Fortenberry**: 14, 36, 106, 218; **Tom Furness**: 63, 71, 75, 77, 109, 128, 134, 139, 144, 145, 185, 190, 227; **Laine Morreau**: 25, 30, 34, 40, 45, 47, 48, 53, 66, 68, 78, 85, 86, 104, 113, 114, 150, 152, 159, 161, 164, 174, 192, 212; **Katy Sprinkel Morreau**: 17, 26, 27, 31, 35, 38, 43, 49, 58, 61, 67, 70, 84, 89, 96, 116, 117, 127, 129, 133, 135, 136, 148, 154, 157, 158, 171, 183, 188, 189, 197, 199, 200, 201, 203, 206, 214, 225; **Rebecca Morrill**: 23; **Bob Richter**: 13, 20, 22, 64, 178, 186; **Michele Robecchi**: 73; **Hanna Noorali and Lynton Talbot**: 15, 24, 103, 137, 160; **David Trigg**: 10, 29, 37, 69, 76, 81, 92, 97, 99, 107, 121, 126, 153, 155, 176, 198, 207, 209, 217.

Phaidon Press Limited
2 Cooperage Yard
London E15 2QR

Phaidon Press Inc.
111 Broadway
New York, NY 10006

phaidon.com

First published 2023
Reprinted 2024

ISBN 978 1 83866 596 8
ISBN 978 1 8386 6933 1 (T. Ed.)

A CIP catalogue record for this book is available from the British Library and the Library of Congress.

Commissioning Editor: Victoria Clarke
Project Editor: David Tibbs
Production Controller: Lily Rodgers
Cover Design: Julia Hasting
Layout Design: João Mota
Typesetting: Cantina

Printed in China